MALT
WHISKY
YEARBOOK
2014

www.maltwhiskyyearbook.com

First published in Great Britain in 2013 by
MagDig Media Limited

ISBN 978-0-9576553-0-0

MagDig Media Limited
1 Brassey Road
Old Potts Way, Shrewsbury
Shropshire SY3 7FA
ENGLAND

E-mail: info@maltwhiskyyearbook.com
www.maltwhiskyyearbook.com

Previous editions

Contents

Introduction

Part of the preparation for this, the 9th edition of Malt Whisky Yearbook, has been travels around Scotland to numerous distilleries. Everywhere we went, we saw evidence of an irrepressible optimism in the industry. New distilleries being built and existing ones being upgraded to increase production. The demand for, in particular, Scotch whisky is very much on the up but this also goes for Irish whiskey and Bourbon. But their is also turbulence in the whisky world. Flavoured whiskies, created to meet the competition from other spirits, is a hot topic (not least in Scotland) and will, no doubt, continue to be soo for years to come. With this, and much more, going on – it is a challenge and a joy to once again publish a new edition of the Malt Whisky Yearbook!

My excellent team of whisky writers have excelled themselves again this year and contribute with some fascinating articles;

In Malt Whisky Yearbook 2007, *Gavin D Smith* highlighted the hottest emerging whisky markets at the time. Seven years later he goes back to see if the predictions were right and how succesful the producers have been.

First England, the the Empire, then the World! *Charles Maclean* tells the story about how Scotch began to conquer the world.

At the moment there are more mergers and acquisitions in the world of whisky than ever before. *Ian Buxton* wants to know how this will affect the future of whisky.

Today, wood finished whiskies have become commonplace but how did it all start? *Jonny McCormick* takes you back to the beginning of finishing.

New distillers around the world have thrown away the rule book and want to create whisky their way. *Dominic Roskrow* has met with some of the trailblazers.

There is one good reason why you should drink whisky in the company of others - you have more fun, as evidenced by *Neil Ridley´s* visits to some great whisky gatherings.

Few people are so widely travelled in Scotland as *Hans Offringa*. Follow him on the whisky road as he visits some of his favourite places.

Japanese whisky is becoming more and more available in other parts of the world. *Nicholas Coldicott* explains why and what we can expect in the future.

In Malt Whisky Yearbook 2014 you will also find the unique, detailed and much appreciated section on Scottish malt whisky distilleries. It has been thoroughly revised and updated, not just in text, but also including numerous, new pictures and tasting notes for all the core brands. The chapter on Japanese whisky is completely revised and the presentation of distilleries from the rest of the world is larger than ever. You will also find a list of more than 150 of the best whisky shops in the world with their full details and suggestions where to find more information on the internet and through books and magazines. The summary of The Whisky Year That Was has been expanded again this year, in order to reflect on the exciting times. Meet whisky aficionados from all over the world explaining why whisky has become popular in their country and how it is enjoyed. Learn about some of the world´s biggest blended whiskies and the malts that contribute to their success. Finally, the very latest statistics gives you all the answers to your questions on production and consumption.

Thank you for buying Malt Whisky Yearbook 2014. I hope that you will have many enjoyable moments reading it and I can assure you that I will be back with a new, 10th anniversary edition in 2015.

Great care has been taken to ensure the accuracy of the information presented in this book. MagDig Media Ltd can, however, not be held liable for inaccuracies.

**Malt Whisky Yearbook 2015 will be published in October 2014.
To make sure you will be able to order it directly, please register at
www.maltwhiskyyearbook.com.**

**If you need any of the previous eight volumes of Malt Whisky Yearbook,
some of them are available for purchase (in limited numbers) from the website
www.maltwhiskyyearbook.com**

Acknowledgments

First of all I wish to thank the writers who have shared their great specialist knowledge on the subject in a brilliant and entertaining way – Ian Buxton, Nicholas Coldicott, Charles MacLean, Jonny McCormick, Hans Offringa, Neil Ridley, Dominic Roskrow and Gavin D. Smith.

A special thanks goes to Gavin and Dominic who put in a lot of effort nosing, tasting and writing notes for more than 100 different whiskies. Thanks also to Gavin for the tasting notes for independent bottlings and to Nicholas for the Japanese notes.

The following persons have also made important photographic or editorial contributions and I am grateful to all of them:

Mitch Abate, Iain Allan, Tommy Andersen, Alasdair Anderson, Bobby Anderson, Russel Anderson, David Baker, Nick Ballard, Keith Batt, Jan Beckers, Barry Bernstein, Monica Berry, Cornelia Bohn, Etienne Bouillon, Stephen Bremner, Andrew Brown, Graham Brown, Alex Bruce, Gordon Bruce, Alexander Buchholz, Simon Buley, Sarah Burgess, Stephen Burnett, Marie Byrne, Pär Caldenby, John Campbell, Peter Campbell, Alexandre Campos, Bert Cason, Karen Chaloner, Ian Chang, Kirsty Chant, Ian Chapman, Yuseff Cherney, Ashok Chokalingam, Stewart Christine, Gordon Clark, Margaret Mary Clarke, Douglas Clement, Willie Cochrane, Francis Conlon, Graham Coull, Sandy Coutts, Jason Craig, Georgie Crawford, Andrew Crook, Gloria Cummins, Francis Cuthbert, Kirsty Dagnan, Tiffany Daugherty, Susie Davidson, Stephen Davies, David Doig, Jean Donnay, Anna Drummond, Ludo Ducrocq, Alicia Eason, Jonas Ebensperger, Lenny Eckstein, Graham Eunson, Joe Fenten, Tim Ferris, Hannah Fisher, Thomas Fleischmann, Robert Fleming, Tim Forbes, Sean Foushee, Simon Fried, Robert Fullarton, Jesse Gallagher, Rosemary Gallagher, Ewan George, Gillian Gibson, John Glass, Kenny Grant, Andrew Gray, Katia Guidolin, Jasmin Haider, Wendy Harries Jones, Axel Hartwig, Joanne Haruta, Steve Hawley, Ralph Haynes, Mickey Heads, Holger Henrich, Emma Hibbert, Paul Hooper, Robbie Hughes, Bernhard Höning, Jill Inglis, Rick Jagdale, Mika Jansson, Pat Jones, Philippe Juge, Jens-Erik Jörgensen, Marko Karakasevic, Jenny Karlsson, Raphael Käser, Andrew Laing, David Lang, Bill Lark, Mark Lochhead, Alistair Longwell, Eddie Ludlow, Horst Lüning, Eddie McAffer, Iain MacAllister, Christine McCafferty, Des McCagherty, John McCarthy, Alan McConnochie, Alistair McDonald, Andy Macdonald, John MacDonald, Polly MacDonald, Lynne McEwan, William McHenry, Sandy Macintyre, Doug McIvor, Alistair Mackenzie, Bruce Mackenzie, Ewen Mackintosh, Ian MacMillan, Grant MacPherson, Patrick Maguire, Dennis Malcolm, Graham Manson, Martin Markvardsen, Stephen Marshall, Chris Maybin, Kwanele Mdluli, Lee Medoff, Jennifer Meehan, Roger Melander, Alicia Messina, Chris Middleton, Leah Miller, Andrew Millsopp, Euan Mitchell, Pritesh Mody, Henric Molin, Rune Molvik, Ryan Montgomery, Carol More, Nick Morgan, Alex Höjrup Munch, Andrew Nairn, Andrew Nelstrop, Johanna Ngoh, Hasse Nilsson, Alexey Ostrovskyy, Casey Overeem, Daniel Palmer, Mahesh Patel, Sean Phillips, Don Poffenroth, Allan Poulsen, Michael Poulsen, Keshav Prakash, Anssi Pyysing, Robert Ransom, Alec Reid, Mark Renner, Bryan Ricard, Nicol van Rijbroek, Patrick Roberts, Jackie Robertson, James Robertson, Stuart Robertson, Liz Robson, Colin Ross, David Roussier, Ronnie Routledge, Hans Rubens, Steve Rush, Joseph Sammons, Kelly Sanders, Alexey Savchenko, Ernst Scheiner, Birgit Scheithauer, Daric Schlesselman, Jacqui Seargeant, Andrew Shand, Nicholas Sikorski, Sam Simmons, Severin Simon, Daniel Smith, Gigha Smith, Cat Spencer, Alison Spowart, Vicky Stevens, Karen Stewart, Pamela Stewart, Billy Stitchell, Katy Stollery, Morgan Svensson, Jim Swan, Chip Tate, Jack Teeling, Marcel Telser, Davide Terziotti, David Thomson, Roselyn Thomson, Jarrett Tomal, Joanie Tseng, Michael Urquhart, Laura Vernon, Clare Vickers, Ranald Watson, Mark Watt, Andy Watts, Stuart Watts, Iain Weir, James Whelan, Nick White, Ronald Whiteford, Robert Whitehead, Anthony Wills, Alan Winchester, Helen Windle, Ellie Winters, Gordon Winton, Alan Wolstenholme, Stephen Woodcock, Ho-cheng Yao, Patrick van Zuidam.

Finally, to my wife Pernilla and our daughter Alice, thank you for your patience and your love and to Vilda, the lab, my faithful companion during long working hours.

Ingvar Ronde
Editor
Malt Whisky Yearbook

Emerging Markets Revisited

We call them emerging whisky markets – countries where consumers just recently have started to take an interest in the most popular spirit in the world. Every producer in the Scotch whisky industry is struggling to get their piece of the pie but how succesful have they been and what happens next? To give you the picture, Gavin D Smith has met with some of them.

The 2007 edition of the Malt Whisky Yearbook contained a feature of mine titled 'Scotch Whisky Conquers New Markets,' which explored key emerging export territories for Scotch. Eight editions on, it seems high time to catch up with how matters have panned out for Scotch whisky abroad. Did everything proceed as predicted, or have there been disappointments and pleasant surprises?

Back in 2006, when the article in question was being researched, Richard Burrows, then Chairman of the Scotch Whisky Association (SWA), declared that "The geographic diversity of growth is notable. We believe Asia, Eastern Europe and the Americas all offer further strong opportunities for the Scotch whisky industry to build on the worldwide growth in bottled in Scotland malt and blended Scotch whisky brands."

By common consent there were then three major 'emerging markets', namely Russia, China and India, but the SWA also suggested that the names of Brazil and Turkey should also be added to the list, and commentators spoke about the 'BRIC' nations – namely Brazil, Russia, India and China. All these countries had a number of factors in common: comparative economic stability, a growing aspirational middle class with significant disposable income and an established taste for spirits of one kind or another. As in most export markets, the bulk of trade was dominated by a handful of large companies with Scotch whisky interests, due principally to the necessity of investing large sums.

To discover how Scotch has fared in export markets it makes sense to begin with some headline figures. According to the Scotch Whisky Association (SWA), the value of Scotch whisky exports hit a record level of £4,3 billion in 2012 – the eighth consecutive annual increase.

The SWA's Rosemary Gallagher explains that "Scotch delivered £135 a second in exports, and the equivalent of 1,19 bottles was shipped worldwide last year. In the last

Introduction party for Chivas´ The Night Magnum

Rosemary Gallagher, SWA's Communications Manager

ten years the value of Scotch whisky exports has risen by 87%. Demand is increasing from both mature and emerging markets. Single malt exports have risen over the last ten years by 190% from £268 million to £778m."

Given these statistics, it is clear that the optimism expressed by so many distillers' representatives in 2006/7 was justified, and one reason why the Scotch whisky industry appears to have a relatively stable and positive future is the sheer global diversity of markets in which Scotch now sells.

During the mid-1990s, the economic situation in Europe was relatively stable and positive. The great economic crises and recessions that currently dog so much of the continent had yet to strike. Yet Scotch whisky exports have survived and thrived because there is no longer such a reliance on European markets and the USA as was the case half a century ago, though the USA and France continue to occupy the two leading spots in the Scotch whisky export 'top 10.' France, however, recorded a 19% fall in the value of Scotch whisky imports during 2012, and a 25% drop in volume. Despite its economic woes, triggered by the outbreak of the subprime mortgage crisis and financial

crisis of 2007–08, the USA has weathered the storm in terms Scotch whisky consumption.

According to Rosemary Gallagher of the SWA, "The USA remains the top market by value for Scotch whisky with exports breaking through the £700 million barrier for the first time to reach £758 million in 2012. Demand from the USA is expected to increase as consumer confidence grows and many people trade up to premium brands."

Paul Scanlon, International Commercial Director for Chivas Brothers makes the valuable point that "Because Scotch is such widely sold product, if there is decline in one market there is always growth in another. For example, Spain is down 10%, but China, India, Vietnam and Africa are doing well."

The financial crisis has largely affected the USA and Europe, and has not had a significant impact on most 'developing' countries. This is partly because Asian economies are less integrated into the global market and previous experience of recession led them to be better prepared for what has occurred in the past five years or so. Similarly, Latin America boasts very stringent banking regulations as a result of having to cope with previous economic turbulence.

Paul Scanlon, International Commercial Director for Chivas Brothers

How important is China?

To give some sense of the confidence behind the global reach of Scotch whisky and the 'strength in depth' and clear potential of many markets, while China is invariably seen as a crucial and very valuable emerging territory, a representative of one of the most significant Scotch whisky companies privately expressed the view recently that if the Chinese market for Scotch disappeared overnight, it would barely cause a ripple in the company's share price.

However, despite signs that the momentum of growth in China's economy is slowing down, the country has fulfilled most of its potential, as expressed by the representatives of Scotch whisky companies back in 2006.

The SWA's Rosemary Gallagher notes that 'Asia continues to grow in significance with exports to the distribution hub of Singapore up 7% to £339 million last year. Exports to Taiwan increased 7% to £165 million, and direct shipments to China experienced growth of 8% to £72 million. In total, the Chinese market for Scotch is estimated to be worth more than £100 million."

With regard to the six month period to 31st December 2012, a Diageo company spokesperson reports that "In China, brands grew 59% as super-premium Scotch continued to gain share, driven by Johnnie Walker Blue and the innovations Johnnie Walker Gold Label Reserve and John Walker & Sons Odyssey."

"In the faster growing markets of Asia, we continued to deliver strong double-digit top line growth, driven in part by the 28% net sales growth of super-premium scotch. In South East Asia, Johnnie Walker posted 27% net sales growth and gained further share. This was driven by the successful Johnnie Walker Double Black and Johnnie Walker Platinum label launches, price increases and the halo benefit from the Johnnie Walker 'Voyager' marketing programme."

One notably successful venture undertaken by Diageo in China has been the creation of luxurious 'embassies, which operate under the name of the 'Johnnie Walker House,' firstly in Shanghai during 2011. Since the opening of the Shanghai 'House,' sales of Johnnie Walker whisky in China have increased by 64% year-on-year to 2013, with the prestigious Johnnie Walker Blue Label growing by 45% over the same period.

Diageo's Head of Whisky Outreach Dr Nick Morgan adds that "Building on our insight that luxury consumers want to connect with our brands in physical spaces, we opened a second Johnnie Walker House in Beijing, now the world's largest 'embassy' for luxury Scotch whisky. In the same vein, the John Walker & Sons 'Voyager' set sail on the seas of South East Asia docking at nine ports on a journey inspired by the original trade routes of Johnnie Walker whisky."

Paul Scanlon of Chivas Brothers says that "To an extent, China is up and down. The shift has moved a bit from China as the rising star, with a wider spread of markets now. Chivas Regal is the leading blended Scotch in China, and we have seen reasonable growth in malts, which now account for around 50,000 cases per year. However, the whole international spirits market has slowed down in China, with less entertainment and gifting."

This has come about principally as a result of government measures introduced to combat corruption and focused on banning lavish banquets and spending on luxury products using public funds. However, despite this development, Paul Scanlon declares

Chivas Regal is the leading blended Scotch in China

that "We see this as probably a temporary blip, with short term impact on high-ends products. Consumers are going straight to malts in many cases, instead of via blends as is customary. The picture for single malts in China is looking even rosier than expected. The Glenlivet has been the fastest-growing single malt in the past few years."

The dramatic overseas growth in single malts sales during the past few years has already been noted, and one malt brand which has enjoyed exceptional success in export arenas during that period is The Macallan.

The Edrington Group's Director of Malts Ken Grier declares that "In the last five years our identified markets for growth have not disappointed. Regions we identified at the time as key emerging markets have become established, and the results have been pleasing. While some remain far from mature, opportunities are not diminishing. The Macallan is reinforcing its position as the number one single malt brand in some of the most important global markets."

"In 2007, The Macallan was nurturing identified emerging markets in China and Russia; both of these have experienced strong relative growth in terms of percentage: up 285% and 320% respectively in the

last five years, the strongest growth for any one brand in these markets."

Along with China, Russia was the most highly anticipated market for major growth back in 2006, and the SWA's Rosemary Gallagher notes that "The growth of Scotch whisky exports to Russia, a market estimated to be worth in the region of £200 million, boosted shipments via Latvia and Estonia in 2012. Direct exports to Latvia were up 48% to £79 million and to Estonia they were up 28% to £69 million."

A Diageo spokesperson says in relation to the six months period to 31st December 2012, "In Russia and Eastern Europe, Diageo maintained its leadership position in the Scotch category and leveraged innovation to insulate Diageo from competitors, resulting in double-digit net sales growth in Scotch."

Paul Scanlon makes the point that "In Russia the value is great. With both blends and single malts we are achieving two to three times what we make in other countries."

Research commissioned by VinExpo – the Bordeaux-based wine and spirits exhibition operator – suggests that Scotch whisky consumption in Russia is likely to rise to 4,7 million cases in 2013, and will grow up to 6,5 million cases by 2016, overtaking sales in the UK which are expected to reach 5,6 million cases.

Great potential in India but high import tariffs remain an issue

When it comes to India – fifth in the 'top 10' table of export markets by volume in 2012 – the SWA's Rosemary Gallagher notes that "India has great potential, but the 150% import tariff remains a significant barrier. The tariff, combined with local state taxes, places Scotch at a considerable disadvantage and penalises Scotch whisky drinkers in India. Nevertheless, exports to India increased by 17% to £62 million last year. We are hopeful that a European Union/India Free Trade Agreement will lead to a gradual reduction in the tariff and open up the market."

Chivas Brothers' Paul Scanlon declares that "The best of the 'BRIC' countries for malts is India, which is way ahead of predictions. It now accounts for around 100,000 cases of malts. Historically, it is a blend market, but in both domestic and duty free arenas we're seeing huge success with malts. Duty-free in particular is growing strongly and airports such as Delhi have put in a lot of work rejuvenating retail areas and promoting single malts."

The on-going importance of India to the Scotch whisky industry has been reflected by the fact that Diageo plc took effective control of United Spirits in July 2013. United Spirits produces Bagpiper, one of India's best-selling domestic whiskies, and in terms of Scotch, the firm owns the Whyte & Mackay portfolio, which includes The Dalmore and Jura single malts.

Clearly, there are significant advantages for Diageo in controlling an existing major Indian drinks company, with a distribution and sales infrastructure already in place.

"Through this acquisition we have transformed Diageo's position in India," noted Diageo Chief Executive Officer Ivan Menezes when the takeover deal was completed.

"We will now begin the work to identify and capture the significant growth opportunities within this attractive market."

However, Diageo has already worked hard to establish and grow sales to India, and referring to the six months' trading period to the end of 2012, a spokesperson notes that "In India Johnnie Walker Black Label and Red Label depletions grew 41% and 33% respectively, on the back of Formula 1 activations and through the 'High Ball' signature serve programme."

Meanwhile, the fourth 'BRIC' nation, Brazil, has seen strong overall Scotch whisky growth as the economy – the world's sixth-largest – has prospered in recent times. In 2011, for example, Scotch whisky exports

Taking control of United Spirits has given Diageo an advantage in the potentially huge Indian market

rose by 48% to £99m in value, making Brazil the industry's 9th biggest market. 2012 saw a slight hiccup, however, as values fell by 16%, although volumes held up well, and analysts predict that during the next three years they may rise from its current level of less than four million cases to 5,5 million cases. Paul Scanlon of Chivas Brothers considers that "Brazil is doing very well, particularly with locally-bottled Scotches like Passport, Teachers and Bells."

Within South America it is not just Brazil that has demonstrated impressive growth for Scotch whisky sales during the last few years, with Paul Scanlon of Chivas noting that "Chile and Peru were not really on our radar six or seven years ago but are now doing well."

Rosemary Gallagher says that "In South America, Scotch whisky is one of the UK's fastest growing exports to Mexico, increasing by 14% to £92 million in 2012. The expanding markets of Colombia and Peru have been given a further boost as a result of the Free Trade Agreements ratified by the European Parliament last December. Once ratified, the Association Agreement with Central America will benefit Scotch whisky exports to that region."

A Diageo spokesperson reports that for the six months period to 31st December 2012, "Growth across Latin America was primarily driven by Scotch, where Johnnie Walker, Buchanan's and Old Parr extended their leadership positions. Performance in Brazil was driven by the continued growth of Scotch, in which Diageo extended its category leadership and gained share.

"The very strong top-line performance in the Andean market (Venezuela and Colombia) was driven by 39% net sales growth across the Scotch portfolio. Strong growth in Mexico was driven by Scotch with Johnnie Walker increasing net sales 28% and Buchanan's 19%, after sustained investment in the 'Keep Walking Mexico' and 'Share Yourself' campaigns."

Africa becoming more important

One continent in which major growth potential was not widely anticipated back in 2006/7 is Africa. The SWA's Rosemary Gallagher declares that "African markets are becoming increasingly important for Scotch whisky producers. This growth is expected to continue as the population becomes wealthier and more urbanised."

"Exports of Scotch whisky to Africa were £239m last year, up 7% from £224 million the previous year. South Africa has been an important market for Scotch whisky for several years, but now other parts of Africa are experiencing rapid growth. For example exports of Scotch whisky to Angola were up 84% to £19 million last year and to Nigeria they increased 87% to £19 million."

She adds that "Alongside Asia, Africa is one of the fastest growing developing markets for Scotch whisky. Economic growth is occurring and individual disposable incomes are increasing for many. There is a growing middle class in many cities across Africa who see Scotch whisky as an aspirational drink. We expect this to continue as the economy strengthens across the continent."

Paul Scanlon of Chivas Brothers declares that "Markets like Angola and Nigeria are 'second tier' markets which compensate for falling sales in some European countries. Angola now recovering from a brutal civil war, and the success of oil drives the affluence in these African countries. We have opened new offices in Angola and Nigeria during the last year. This is a blends market at the moment, with consumers not yet being into malts. South Africa is now seeing an explosion in single malts, after growth in sales of premium blends like Chivas Regal and Johnnie Walker Black Label. The Glenlivet is performing very well there."

Unsurprisingly, Diageo's sales in Africa have also been thriving, with a spokesperson noting for the six months to 31st December 2012 that "In Africa, we have focused on 13 key cities in 10 countries to drive Johnnie Walker. As a result, approximately 10 million new consumers have been introduced to the brand which posted excellent growth with net sales up 38% and volume up 32%, leading the performance of international spirits in the region. In Nigeria, Johnnie Walker doubled net sales supported by the launch of the Johnnie Walker 'Giants' campaign, sponsorship and sampling events, and in East Africa, Johnnie Walker grew net sales 38%."

If Africa has proved a pleasant surprise for the major Scotch whisky players, then various other countries around the world have also provided somewhat unexpected bonuses in terms of Scotch whisky sales. Paul Scanlon nominates Vietnam and Cambodia as other 'second tier' markets in the same vein as Angola and Nigeria, noting that

"Vietnam has a very young population with very affluent consumers who love international brands, entertaining and going out."

He adds that "Turkey is a great market for us. There is a clash between an essentially Muslim country and an affluent and more secular population, and Scotch is doing well."

Within Europe, Rosemary Gallagher of the SWA notes that "Exports to Poland have also been growing, with direct shipments worth £43,3 million in 2012, up from £42,1 million the previous year. This was on the back of considerable growth in exports to Poland in 2011.

"Scotch whisky is seen as an international and aspirational drink with young affluent consumers switching to Scotch whisky from other drinks, particularly vodka. Whisky now accounts for 10% of the value of spirit sales in Poland. As consumers become more knowledgeable about Scotch they are trading up to premium blends. The removal of the import tariff, which was as high as 75% when Poland joined the European Union in 2004, has made Scotch whisky more accessible for Polish consumers in recent years."

Growth is the result of many factors working together

To give a snapshot of how the global picture has changed in terms of Scotch whisky exports, Edrington's Ken Grier points out that in terms of single malts, "The Macallan has added 18 new markets to its portfolio – from 59 in 2007 to 77 in 2012 – and is currently the number one single malt brand in nine markets, namely Taiwan, Japan, China, Russia, South Korea, Singapore, Hong Kong, Indonesia and Kazakhstan. In addition, it is the number two malt Scotch brand in the USA, Spain, Malaysia, Vietnam, Mexico, Saudi Arabia, Israel and Cambodia."

Rosemary Gallagher says that "Scotch whisky continues to lead the way for UK food and drink exports. Growth is a result a number of factors, including successful trade negotiations, excellent marketing by producers, growing demand from mature markets, particularly the USA, and the growing middle class in emerging economies."

Given that the Scotch whisky industry involves a great deal of forward planning and even crystal ball-gazing due to the time lag between production and consumption – an absolute minimum of three years – it is not surprising to find most companies in the industry increasing production on a relatively dramatic scale, by adding capacity to existing distilleries, re-commissioning 'silent' distilleries and even building new ones.

Following its £40 million spend on the creation of its highly productive, state-of-the-art malt distillery at Roseisle, Diageo plans to build another plant on a similar scale alongside Teaninich, at Alness in the Highlands, while Chivas Brothers is to develop a new and capacious malt distillery close to the River Spey at Carron, near Aberlour.

These are just the highest-profile ventures currently in the pipeline, and behind growth in capacity lies major investment in the infrastructure of maturing, blending, bottling and distributing the actual product.

"There is confidence in the future of the industry," declares Rosemary Gallagher, "illustrated by the £2 billion capital investment that Scotch whisky producers have committed over the next three to four years."

Thanks to an increasing ability to keep its eggs in so many baskets, it seems highly unlikely that the Scotch whisky industry will suffer the sort of dramatic 'bust' that has historically followed boom' in the near future, and the scale and scope of investment taking place across Scotland suggests that whisky makers are optimistic the good times will last for many years to come.

Gavin D Smith is one of Scotland's leading whisky writers and Contributing Editor to www.whisky-pages.com and www.forwhiskeylovers.com. He regularly undertakes writing commissions for leading drinks companies and produces feature material for a wide range of publications, including Whisky Magazine, Whisky Advocate, Whiskeria, Drinks International and Whisky Etc. He is the author of more than 20 books, including The Whisky Men, Ardbeg: A Peaty Provenance, Discovering Scotland's Distilleries and Goodness Nose (with Richard Paterson). He collaborated with Dominic Roskrow to produce a new edition of the Michael Jackson's Malt Whisky Companion in 2010 and was also a major contributor to the 2012 publication 1001 Whiskies You Must Try Before You Die. His latest books are The Whisky Opus, co-written with Dominic Roskrow and Let Me Tell You About Whisky, co-written with Neil Ridley.

How Scotch Began to Conquer The World

First England, then the Empire, then the World! During the last 150 years, Scotch whisky has, like no other spirit, performed a victory march around the globe. What strategy made Scotch the world's favourite tipple? Charles Maclean has followed in the foot steps of the early pioneers.

Until the late 19th Century, England was considered to be an 'export' market by whisky distillers and blenders, so one can agree with Ross Wilson that: "From its very inception, Scotch whisky was an export"[1].

Throughout most of the 19th Century, Irish whiskey commanded the home market – even within Scotland where spirits merchants sold around three times as much Irish as Scotch. In England, the ratio was even higher. Several Lowland distilleries made 'Irish' in pot stills from mashes of wheat, un-malted and malted barley; others sent their spirit to Ireland to be blended with Irish whiskey.

Indeed, until the 1860s the amount of Scotch sent to England was negligible. Winston Churchill famously remarked: "My father would never have tasted Scotch, except on a grouse moor or some other damp and dreary place"[2].

In the 1860s, whisky – both Irish and Scotch – was a working class drink. Professor Michael Moss maintains that the quantities of 'Irish' made in Scotland "almost certainly took place to cater for demand from the

great many Irish immigrants into Scotland during the 1860s"[3]. This may be so; other commentators maintained that the appeal of Irish (and lack of it with Scotch) was down to flavour and consistency. William Ross, managing director of the Distillers Company Ltd., told the Royal Commission on Whiskey in 1908 that popularity of Irish was "chiefly because of its uniformity of style", while Scotch malt whiskies varied enormously and were also heavier in style.

The solution to the problem was to blend several malt and grain whiskies together in order to create products whose flavour was 'designed' to appeal to a broad market, and which did not vary from batch to batch. Furthermore, having a consistent product made possible its branding, trade marking and promotion. In regard to the latter, the task facing the whisky producers was to take Scotch out of the shebeen and low tavern and make it 'respectable'.

The first branded Scotch was Usher's Old Vatted Glenlivet (1853), originally a blend of malts, but after the Spirit Act of 1860 allowed the blending of malt and grain whiskies under bond, a true blended Scotch

BRITANNIA COMES TO TOWN.

Usher's grandson told the Royal Commission 1908 that before 1860 very little whisky was sent for sale in England, but after that year "the trade in Scotch whisky increased in leaps and bounds".

Blenders were conscious that the English palate was somewhat less robust that that of the Scots. The same Royal Commission asked Samuel Greenlees, of Greenlees Brothers, Campbeltown and Glasgow, (whose Lorne Whisky was the first to be registered as a trade mark, and the most popular whisky in London during the 1870s):

"How did you decide what kind of blend you were going to make and export to England?"

"By what we considered was the blend of whisky to suit the palate of the public at the time. The Irish whiskey, having less flavour than Scotch, we reduced the flavour and made it more palatable than an individual whisky".

His words were echoed by James Buchanan, the creator (later) of Black & White:

"What I made up my mind to do was to find a blend sufficiently light and old to please the palate of the user".

Note his comment about age in an era when there was no legal age requirement

James Buchanan - one of the greatest entrepreneurs in the Scotch whisky industry of the 1800s

and when much was sold with minimal aging.

Buchanan went to London in 1879 as Charles Mackinlay & Co.'s agent, but set up on his own account five years later. He was not the first to open an office in London. This accolade goes to Arthur Bell, who appointed a London agent in 1862. The latter reported that Bell's whiskies were too 'heavy' and not sufficiently alcoholic, to which Bell pointed out that, since he aged his whiskies for a couple of years, the strength reduced, "...but if your friends value the strength more than the quality, we must just send them new whisky"[4]. The agent did not last long, and Bell withdrew from the London market in 1871, returning only in 1889.

Lorne Whisky - the first to be registered as a trade mark

During the 1880s all the major whisky firms, and many smaller ones, opened offices in London and other major English cities, and from these platforms began to look for markets beyond the United Kingdom.

Scotch in the colonies

Scottish businesses played a central part in colonial expansion during this period, establishing networks of communication that stretched from Hong Kong (e.g. Jardine, Matheson & Co.) and Australia, to the Americas and southern Africa. By the 1880s the British Empire was the single largest trading unit the world had ever seen.

Emigration, Imperial and military service were significant factors in the development of the colonial trade, as ex-patriots continued to seek what was familiar from the

A sales card for John Walker's Old Highland Whisky from 1877

home market. Scots played key roles in colonial administration and mercantile development, and formed tight-knit communities, which kept in close touch with families at home. Many whisky companies used these contacts to great advantage.

For example, as early as 1856 Thomas H. Slater, a grocer, tea blender and spirits dealer in Glasgow since 1834, was sending whisky, wine, bottled ale and various provisions to ex-pat contacts in Australia, India, South Africa, South America, the West Indies, Canada and the United States. Slater was joined by George Smeaton Rodger in 1865; the firm became Slater, Rodger & Co in 1873 and a limited company in 1885. By the following year they had established a Continental agency to look after their European markets and were shipping to forty-five countries; by 1888 they were active in seventy different markets. In 1911 the company became a wholly owned subsidiary of John Walker & Sons.

Alexander Walker, who had joined his father in the business in the 1850s, exploited contacts among wool merchants visiting Kilmarnock's carpet and weaving industry, to begin participating in a consignment trade with Australia, whereby parcels of whisky were shipped with other goods, sold by the ship's master or the owner's agent at the port of destination, then paid for less an agreed percentage. In this way Australia became the first large export market for Johnnie Walker.

By the 1880s Alexander was a partner in Mason Brothers, an import-export house with branches in London and Sydney. But a series of unsuccessful adventures in the consignment trade convinced Alexander to change the method of marketing whisky in

THE POPULAR
SCOTCH
IS
"BLACK & WHITE"

JAMES BUCHANAN & CO.
SCOTCH WHISKY DISTILLERS.
By Appointment to
H.M. THE QUEEN
AND H.R.H.
THE PRINCE OF WALES.

An ad for Buchanan's Black & White Scotch from circa 1900.

Alexander Walker, the son of John Walker, paved the way for the brand in Australia

The first reference to Walkers trading in America and India is in 1883. In 1885 agents were appointed in Penang and Singapore, and in 1896 in New Zealand. Alexander also opened a shop in Paris, but an absence of orders raised suspicions and sent an envoy to investigate: he could find no trace of the manager or the shop. Walker's then used agents with exclusive rights for the whole of Europe, but the arrangement wasn't too successful, and, in 1911, they were replaced by separate agents for each European country.

The second of the 'Big Three' firms, James Buchanan & Co, has an impressive list of 59 'Foreign and Colonial Agencies' on its 1887 letter-head, which gives a good idea of the global spread of agencies by this time. Most markets had

Australia and take direct control of sales. In 1887 he sent his second son, Jack, to take charge of Mason's business in Sydney, with the aim of establishing a separate branch of Walker's, dealing exclusively with whisky. Jack re-organised the business and established a branch office with a network of travellers to solicit orders. Within two years Walker's Kilmarnock Whisky was the leading brand in Sydney.

The firm was also active in South Africa, which was covered by three agents in 1887. This arrangement proved troublesome, so in June that year Rolfes Nebel & Co. were given exclusive rights and by 1889 they were selling 25-30,000 cases. South Africa soon took over from Australia as Walker's largest export market, and Rolfes Nebel continued as agents until October 1914 when anti-German feeling and a boycott of goods supplied by German firms, forced Walkers to cancel the agency.

more than one agent, and some had up to eight: Australia, New Zealand, India, Burma, Ceylon, the Far East, Samoa, South Africa, the Caribbean, the U.S.A., Canada, South Africa, North Africa, the Levant and Europe. The latter were in Paris, Boulogne, Calais, Nice, Hamburg, Gibraltar and Malta, which, as the company's historian observed, "suggests that the Continental trade was limited to British tourists, expatriates and ships' stores: a qualification that probably applied to many other territories"[5].

It might justifiably be claimed that John Dewar & Sons' entry into export markets was prompted by an order from the great Scottish philanthropist, Andrew Carnegie, to be delivered to the President of the United States, Benjamin Harrison, in September 1891, since it prompted Tommy Dewar to undertake a two-year long world tour.

Kingussie,
N.B.

Cluny Castle, September 21, 1891.

Messrs John Dewar & Sons,
    Merchants,
       Perth.

Gentlemen:

      Can you get a small keg,—say nine or ten gallons,—of the best Scotch Whisky you can find, and ship it addressed as follows:

        To the PRESIDENT,

          The Honorable Benjamin Harrison,

            Executive Mansion,

              Washington, D. C.,

                U. S. A.

Send bill to me.

      Yours very truly,

      Andrew Carnegie

The letter that started Dewar's business in the USA

Aged 28 in 1892, Tommy had been sent to London by his older brother seven years earlier. On the first of his 'Rambles Round the Globe'[6], he visited 26 countries – beginning in the U.S.A. and Canada, proceeding through the South Pacific to the Antipodes, then returning via S.E. Asia, Aden, Egypt and France – and appointed 32 agents.

In a promotional booklet published in 1898, Dewar's manager for the North of England was asked:

"Do you do much export trade?"

"An enormous one, many thousands of cases going away every month – in fact, I might say almost every week. We have always on hand at least 10,000 cases ready for shipment to various parts of the world, literally from China to Peru. For this foreign trade we keep a big staff of bottlers and packers who don't touch a drop for home consumption".

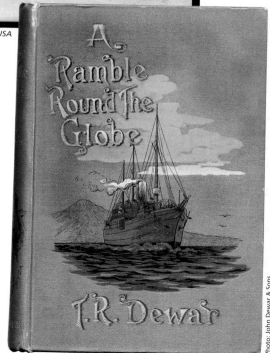

*Tommy Dewar compiled his travel experiences in the book
A Ramle Round The Globe*

Photo: John Dewar & Sons

& Baxter], but don't get their Special as it is far too Islay.

"I think the first plan is best, viz. blend a quarter cask of the 9/- blend with an octave of 7 or 8 year old Glen Grant, then bottle that off...For the 'get up' I would simply label it "Special Highland Liqueur. A. Bell, Perth, N.B. [i.e. 'North Britain', as Scotland was referred to at this time]".

"Don't make the colour strong, as a light coloured whisky is liked better out here. Sample the Glen Grant well before blending as also the 9/- blend as all future business in Launceston depends upon this shipment."

He went on: "[Mr. Wilmot, the agent] thinks he will do mostly in bulk as the Tasmanians like jars better than cases".

In another letter, from Melbourne, he notes:

"The money that is spent here in advertising must be something enormous and they all say nothing can be done without it."

Photo: Diageo Archives

Arthur Bell, the first of the big whisky producers to open an office in London

The smaller firms followed

Smaller firms followed the example set by the larger players. In the 1890s, Arthur Bell's preoccupation was export markets, particularly Australia. The same year that Tommy Dewar made his first world tour, he sent his younger son, Robin (aged twenty), and his sister Louie to the southern hemisphere to visit far-flung relations, explore markets and appoint agents in Ceylon, Australia, Tasmania and New Zealand.

Robin wrote from Launceston, Tasmania, in September 1892, where he appointed a "safe & old-established firm" as agent for the northern part of the island:

"You will remember before I left that some old Glen Grant or Highland Park blended with the 9/- blend [the firm's most expensive one] would do very well, or another proposal was to get it from R&B [Robertson

Indeed, by the 1890s fierce competition and the cost of advertising, particularly in Australia, had become a problem. When the Distillers Company appointed its first traveller 'in the colonies and elsewhere to open up connections abroad' in 1886, a budget of £250 for 'showcards, advertisements and maps' was allocated. The traveller appointed agents in Egypt, Greece, Turkey, Australia and India, but by 1889 he was devoting too much time to other business interests and his contract was terminated. He was replaced by John Stuart Smith as 'Foreign and Colonial Traveller', and now (1892) the advertising budget in Australia alone was £1,250. A second traveller was appointed in 1893 and by 1897 the company had a branch office in Melbourne.

pirits were accumulated for the export market 'with some emphasis …on the more ighly flavoured Highland and Islay malts'. he company built its first malt distillery, nockdhu, in 1894 largely owing to the rowth in exports.

Greenlees Brothers' is reputed to be the rst firm to sell its whiskies in Japan, where heir Old Parr brand was particularly popular ind remains so). Andrew Usher & Co. "was ble through its sales overseas…to give dinburgh its Usher Hall"[7].

J. & G. Stewart, Edinburgh, who "had een shipping their blend to Spain since arly in the last [19th] century… began the xtension of the firm's business around the /orld [in the 1880s]. So successful were they nat by the 1890s the name of Stewart be- ame a household word in Sweden"[8].

John Begg Ltd., owners of Royal Lochna- ar Distillery and of the popular John Begg lue Label brand, established warehouses ear the port of Aberdeen for ease of ex- ort.

Mackie & Co., whose leading brand was Vhite Horse, were exporting cased goods .e. whisky in bottles, rather than in casks r stone jars], at least by 1883, and in 1896 ne of the company's directors toured most f the overseas markets appointing agents. nd so on…

hus were the foundations of the global xport trade in Scotch whisky laid. Even by 1900, the volumes were still relatively small, however, at 5,3 million proof gallons (13,75 million litres). The big impetus to export came after 1900, and particularly after 1909, when Lloyd George's 'People's Budget' in- creased the duty on spirits sold in the home market by a third – the highest rise in duty since 1860. The expansion of the export mar- ket until it dwarfed the home market will be explored in a subsequent article.

However, by 1900 the foundations of the export market for Scotch whisky had been soundly laid – based upon the skill of the blenders, who made whiskies with broad appeal; the personalities who, in the early days, used the Scots diaspora and appointed agents all over the world, and the compa- nies which supported those agents with (sometimes substantial) promotional bud- gets.

As one Leith spirits merchant, Archibald Cowan, told the 1908 Royal Commission:

"We could never get a whisky into Austra- lia or India until we began to blend".

1 Wilson, Ross, Scotch: The Formative Years (London, 1970) p.147
2 Quoted by Cooper, Derek, A Taste of Scotch (London, 1989) p.81
3 Moss, Michael, The Making of Scotch Whisky (Edinburgh, 1981) p.103
4 House, Jack, Pride of Perth (London 1976) p.14
5 Spiller, Brian, The Chameleon's Eye (London, 1984) p.23
6 Ever an ardent self-publicist, Tommy Dewar published an amusing account of this tour, A Ramble Round the Globe, in 1894
7 Wilson, Ross, op.cit p.153
The Usher Hall, which opening in 1914, is Edinburgh's leading concert hall
8 Wilson, Ross, ibid. p.152

Lloyd George's People's Budget increased the whisky export

Charles MacLean has spent the past twenty-five years researching and writing about Scotch whisky and is one of the leading authorities.
He spends his time sharing his knowledge around the world, in articles and publications, lectures and tastings, and on TV and radio.
His first book (Scotch Whisky) was published in 1993 and since then he has published nine books on the subject, his most recent being Charles MacLean's Whiskypedia, published in 2009. He was elected a Keeper of the Quaich in 1992, in 1997 Malt Whisky won the Glenfiddich Award and in 2003 A Liquid History won 'Best Drinks Book' in the James Beard Awards. In 2012 he also starred in Ken Loach's film The Angel's Share.

The Fight
for a piece of the
Whisky Pie

Mergers and acquisitions in the whisky industry seem to come in waves and during the last year, business has been rife with negotiations and offers. Will these activities affect the future of Scotch whisky and what are the implications for the consumers? Ian Buxton is searching for answers.

Here's an interesting thing: the whisky industry's PR machine is normally happy enough to provide information to support publications like this but on this occasion quite a few of them came over all coy.

"It's not something we comment or speculate on," said Chivas Brothers. And William Grant & Sons were no more forthcoming. "Thank you, but we don't wish to comment on this," was their reply.

At least they did reply. The more usual response was simply to ignore my questions – which of course only made me more interested.

So what was the explosive and controversial issue that I had raised? Well, let me quote the brief from your Editor. He wanted a report on how recent take-overs had affected the industry and a look at what effect this might have on both on single distilleries and brands and the industry in general.

Immediately what comes to mind is Bruichladdich/Remy; Glenglassaugh/BenRiach; Burn Stewart/Distell and of course Diageo buying into United Spirits and what effect that might have on Whyte & Mackay. One could also speculate on a possible acquisition of Beam.

He asked me to get "comments from different kinds of people within the whisky industry and community" but as you can see that started to prove a little challenging, particularly when people were asked to comment on the record. Some did but, as we shall see, their remarks tended to the predictable or safe; nothing in fact which the intelligent observer of the industry (that's you, dear reader) probably hadn't already worked out for themselves.

For example, the leading independent stock market analyst on the whisky industry, Alan Gray of Sutherlands simply replied;

"The acquisitions of Bruichladdich and Burn Stewart by Remy Cointreau and Distell respectively confirm the considerable interest in Scotch Whisky at the present time and the desire of major drinks companies to build up their Scotch Whisky portfolios."

"Moreover, in the case of South Africa's Distell, its £160m purchase of Burn Stewart suggests that the industry's view of Africa as potentially an exciting market is not misplaced."

Bunnahabhain distillery - part of the deal
when Distell Group took over Burn Stewart Distillers

Fraser Thornton, Burn Stewart's MD, raises a glass to a successful future with Distell Group

"As for Diageo's purchase of a major stake in United Spirits this is clearly not only a strategic move to give it a significant presence in a huge Indian whisky market but also holds considerable opportunities for expanding sales of Scotch, especially if tariff barriers can be reduced ."

Now – no offence to Alan who is an old friend and who did at least take the time to respond – but this is hardly earth-shattering stuff. So let's begin by summarising what's been happening since the last issue of the Malt Whisky Yearbook.

• In July 2012, Remy Cointreau of France purchased the Bruichladdich Distillery Company for £58m, including debt. Commentators referred to this as Remy's 'entry' into the Scotch whisky business, neglecting (or not knowing) that between 1981 and 1990 they owned Glenturret. Welcome back!

• In March 2013, in an unexpected and surprisingly low-key manner, the owners of the re-opened Glenglassaugh distillery sold it to the South African backed BenRiach Distillery Company Ltd. The owners were described as Lumiere Holdings, reputedly a group of Eastern-European private investors. Quite what happened to the Scaent Group, who originally purchased and re-opened Glenglassaugh has never been satisfactorily explained, though I understand that at

least some of the people behind Lumiere were also involved in Scaent. Quite why there wasn't an open sale with multiple possible buyers is a mystery; I understand that at least one other approach was made and rebuffed. Could the price (undisclosed naturally) have been higher? Presumably the owners had their reasons but it is a puzzle.

• And then in April, another South African buyer, the Distell Group swooped on Burn Stewart, paying £160m for the Tobermory, Deanston and Bunnahabhain distilleries, the Scottish Leader brand and maturing stocks. The two companies had been in a joint venture arrangement in Africa since 2007.

• Finally, in July, Diageo completed arrangements to purchase just over 25% of the shares in Indian distilling giant United Spirits and, in a complex arrangement, gain effective management control of United. Though India was the focus of the deal, United Spirits also happened to own Whyte & Mackay, which it had bought in May 2007 in a highly-leveraged £595m takeover. At the time of writing, Diageo (which controls some 35,5% of global Scotch whisky sales) is seeking formal approval from the UK's Office of Fair Trading (OFT) in respect of the Whyte & Mackay element (accounting for around 1,2% of sales).

What is more, persistent rumours surround
Loch Lomond Distillers and the associated
companies. A private equity consortium was
widely reported to be buying the privately-
held group back in March and April but
there has been no subsequent development
at the time of writing.

Big companies are getting bigger

Now one could perfectly well see this as the
continuance of a long-term trend to consolidation: after all, back in 1969 there were
13 publicly quoted (i.e. you could buy a
share in them) Scotch whisky companies.
Today there are now no 'pure' Scotch whisky
companies on the world's stock markets, and
just 5 quoted drinks companies of any scale,
all with widely spread interests (Diageo,
Pernod-Ricard, Beam, Brown-Forman and
Campari). Leaving aside newly started boutique distillers the ranks of privately-owned
independents have been severely reduced as
well, so this merger and acquisition activity
is nothing new.

But it is unusual for so much to happen in
such a short period of time and, thankfully,
some of those involved were willing to comment on the background to the changes.

For example, John Alden, Head of Marketing at Burn Stewart, said:

"The global whisky market has been one
of the fastest growing drinks segments and
whisky is the world's largest spirit category by volume after vodka. We expect
both emerging and developed markets to
continue to grow in particular in terms of
value despite the ongoing global economic
challenges."

"Distell's acquisition of Burn Stewart sup-
ports this global growth, with a long term
aim to enhance our Scotch malt portfolio's
international footprint. The last few years
have shown double digit increases, both in
volume and value, for malt brands in general and we're cautiously optimistic that this
will continue. Burn Stewart hopes to achieve
greater growth through strengthening our
route to market partnerships in our core
markets such as Taiwan, South Africa and
the Baltics, as well as strong brand growth
in markets such as Russia, USA and France.
Distell's strong presence in Sub-Saharan
Africa also opens opportunities in emerging
African markets."

"Here on home soil, whisky tourism
presents an opportunity – for instance, we
recently invested £600,000 to develop the
Deanston Visitors' Centre in Doune, near
Stirling, which after one year of being open
to the public is showing strong growth numbers in terms of visitors."

Only five years after the ressurection of Glenglassaugh, the distillery changed hands again

That all sounds positive. My enquiries to the parent company came to nothing but, on a recent visit to Deanston I was able to quiz Burn Stewart's Master Blender Ian Mac-Millan who seemed very relaxed about the changes. Indeed he welcomed the fact that the distilleries are now owned by distilling people instead of, as recently, a finance company and the Trinidadian government.

Deanston was looking very impressive; the new visitor centre was a welcome invest-ment and the distillery shop now has some rare single cask expressions representing the fruit of many years' experiments by Ian. On or off the record Ian had only good things to say about the changes.

Much the same story came from Billy Walker of BenRiach who was happy to talk to me at some length about his plans for Glenglas-saugh. He sounded excited and I'm pleased to report that there as well the news all seems to be good.

First of all the distillery is already increa-sing production – up from around 300,000 litres last year to a target of 700,000 litres this year. That will improve efficiency and create a 'buzz' round the place. Most of this extra production will be reserved for Glenglassaugh's own use, which will encou-rage the growing number of fans.

Next, the maintenance programme is be-ing stepped up. It can't be denied that there was a forlorn air to some of the buildings at Glenglassaugh but Billy expects that over the next six months visitors will see some dramatic changes.

Most noticeable of all, the roof on the number 1 warehouse at the centre of the distillery is finally being repaired and to make room for the increased production the old malting building, which was in a pretty dilapidated state internally, is being conver-ted to a dunnage-style warehouse with two floors. Happily for lovers of whisky heritage, the old stone steeps will remain in place as a nod to the building's history. The Octave private casks will go on the top floor with the distillery's own barrels living at ground level.

Talking of the private cask programme it will continue – but prices have been increased. According to Walker they were under-priced previously. If you did buy one, you may have got a bargain!

"But there will be no radical change to strategy," he told me. "Glenglassaugh will continue to be aimed at the premium end of the market, reflecting the quality of the spirit."

"We have managed to buy back a further supply of 1978 casks and every old cask in storage is to be reviewed and tasted again. The programme of vintage releases will continue but some casks may be held back to create really old expressions in a number of years' time."

In other improvements, a small bottling line is to be installed in the old Cooperage building to handle bottling of the small cask and vintage expressions and the whole of the distillery interior is being repainted.

There is more good news: Revival and Evolution will continue and the price of Evolution may be reduced; a peated expres-sion will follow very soon and plans are in hand to launch a blended whisky based on Glenglassaugh. So, just in case this was all PR fluff, I asked outgoing MD Stuart Nickerson for his view.

"It's a huge wrench and I am very sorry to go," he told me about his departure from Glenglassaugh "but it's the best thing for the business."

Not every departing Managing Director can afford to be so philosophical but I expect that Nickerson can look forward to resuming his previous, highly successful consultancy work with no shortage of new clients. But on or off the record Stuart was hugely positive about the change, which suggests it was well managed and repre-sents a genuine move forward.

The distillers enter the scene

And, just like Burn Stewart, here's the key difference: the company is now owned by distilling people, not financiers! Much the same could be said of Remy Cointreau and their return to Scotch whisky where Douglas Taylor, Global Brand Director, Bruichladdich Brands described the changes as follows.

"The acquisition of Bruichladdich by the Remy Cointreau group is an extremely positive step, bringing financial stability, improved route to market and crucially, be-cause of the Remy Cointreau de-centralised structure, preservation of our independent spirit. Our aim is to create the most thought provoking whisky possible, therefore we will continue to challenge convention and bring Bruichladdich brands to a broader network of global progressive consumers."

nce again, production has been increased
nd investment in the distillery bodes well
r the future. But, just like Glenglassaugh, I
anted to check this out with someone who
uld be expected to give a straight answer
Mark Reynier. Bruichladdich's old MD was
ways known for his controversial views
nd openly resisted the takeover. Surely he
ad something bad to say. Not so, it seems.

"There is no doubt that Bruichladdich
ill become a much bigger brand than we
uld ever have achieved ourselves," he was
appy to tell me. But he went on to sound a
arning.

"I am still surprised that some existing
otential single malt brands and unmar-
eted distilleries are not given the proper
tention they deserve – there is a rampant
mplacency – perhaps that will change
hen the new distillation capacity increases
me on line."

"The second and third tiers of the industry
e where the potential for some important
ngle malt brands lie – if they get their act
gether," he added. "Which I doubt. And
ere's plenty of room for budding minnows,
ut they'll have to compete with the world-
ide explosion of mini distilleries. Most
mpanies, with very few exceptions, follow

the old industry game of stock, stock, stock
– and do little to develop their brands (a
costly, timely business requiring imagination and skill) instead they're happy to rely
on the traditional, easy buck of bulk stock
values. It's too easy – hence the lack of dyna-
mism that has afflicted this industry."

I'm not entirely sure that's fair. It's my personal observation that the whisky industry
has improved its innovation and speed of response to the market out of all recognition
in the past decade but, frankly, Bruichladdich, Burn Stewart and Glenglassaugh are

After year's of negotiations between Diageo's Paul Walsh and United Spirits' Vijay Mallya, Diageo now has the upper hand in India

pretty small beer in the context of a global market, and that is what the Diageo deal makes clear. The cost so far is in the region of £575m – and that's for around half the shares that Diageo originally wanted to buy. Discussing the 25,02% stake in United Spirits Limited, Ivan Menezes, Chief Executive of Diageo, said:

"USL's strong market-leading position combined with Diageo's strength and capabilities opens an exciting and important new chapter for Diageo in the attractive Indian spirits market. Through this acquisition we have transformed Diageo's position in India, a market which is one of the biggest growth opportunities in our industry. India will become one of Diageo's largest markets and with its increasing number of middle class consumers looking for premium and prestige local spirits brands as income levels rise it will also become a major contributor to our growth ambitions."

India, then is the key to this deal with Whyte & Mackay something of a side issue. In fact, talking to senior Diageo people off the record it's apparent that they are unworried by the eventual OFT decision, whichever way it goes.

Frankly, Jura and Dalmore apart, there's little or nothing in Whyte & Mackay that Diageo wants or needs and they could very well live quite happily without the two single malt distilleries. But the presence they have now established in India – though it

may take some years to become fully effective – is potentially transformational and could underpin Diageo's growth for the next decade or more.

And that, of course, is what their huge expansion of Scotch whisky production is all about. Currently, around 60m bottles of Scotch get past India's high tariff barriers. That may sound a lot but compared to France's 154m in 2012 (a decline of 25% due to tax changes and the economic crisis there it's disappointing.

But bear in mind that Indian-made 'whiskies' account for some 150m cases so the potential if Scotch can grab just a few percentage points is enormous. And that's why in a market where local contacts and feet on the ground are of enormous importance getting control of the major local player is critical for Diageo.

Thus, in 2012, Diageo unveiled plans to invest over £1 billion in Scotch whisky production and maturation over the next five years to meet growing global demand for it brands. The investment will bring:

• A major new malt distillery – another Roseisle, to be built at Teaninich, producing around 13m litres annually, as well as expansion at Teaninich itself.

• A programme of major expansion at a number of Diageo's existing distilleries at Linkwood, Mannochmore, Glendullan, Dailaine, Benrinnes, Inchgower, Cragganmore, Glen Elgin and Glen Ord.

Detailed plans will also be developed for a second new distillery (i.e. Roseisle III) which will be built if global demand for Scotch is sustained at expected levels. My guess is that it's more than likely to happen.

And let's just briefly mention the expansion put in place by their rivals at Chivas Brothers – doubling capacity at The Glenlivet; expanding and re-opening Glen Keith; boosting production at Glenallachie, Glentauchers, Longmorn and Tormore distilleries and building a new super-distillery at Carron on Speyside (the old Imperial site). It's impressive stuff. I'm actually starting to begin to believe the talk of a 'golden age'!

Will there be more?

So now for some speculation (what follows is an entirely personal view). Where will this lead?

The remaining independents will come under pressure. Glenfarclas, for example, are repeatedly approached by larger companies offering the Grant family a huge cheque. But I don't see any change there as George Grant has just joined the Board of Directors. I see this move as a hugely significant and publicly visible symbol of family continuity and commitment to independence. With the distillery in great shape, sales and profits growing and the next generation being groomed to take control, predators will have to look elsewhere.

We've noted the interest in Loch Lomond Distillers. Owner Sandy Bulloch is now 87 and the group's Glen Catrine Bonded Warehouse business has just seen a 21% drop in profits. The company concentrates on the value end of the whisky and vodka business where margins are tight – a new owner would gain significant capacity and the opportunity to take the company up-market in new areas where they could build from scratch.

Over in the USA, Beam Inc has to be considered a take-over target for the likes of Diageo (who could really use the Jim Beam, Maker's Mark and Sauza tequila brands) or Pernod Ricard or possibly even Bacardi. It's a while since they snapped up Dewar's and the Beam brands would fit the Bacardi portfolio really well. Any large purchaser

of Beam would likely shed the low-end vodkas and rums to recoup some cash and concentrate on Beam's attractive premium portfolio.

Likewise, Whyte & Mackay. Personally I can't see that it offers Diageo very much and my understanding is that capital investment in the distilleries (particularly the Invergordon grain plant) wouldn't go amiss. If the OFT rule that a disposal is in order, expect Diageo to cherry-pick the best bits they can and happily collect a cheque for the rest.

Of the medium sized companies, both Highland Distillers and William Grant & Sons are very secure due to their ownership structure. Someone might be attracted by Ian MacLeod Distillers now that they have a second distillery in Tamdhu. Watch this space to see if the necessary investment in building stock and marketing begin to stretch them – willing suitors could gather quickly.

Finally, not all the hugely enthusiastic start-up boutique distillers are going to last the course. There undoubtedly will be casualties among the micro distilling scene, despite the optimism that currently prevails.

Some dreams are going to turn to nightmares as naïve owners discover that, in a fire sale, they have little to fall back on but some second-hand plant.

And out of that personal disaster, new hope will emerge. Which is another story, for another time.

Keeper of the Quaich and Liveryman of the Worshipful Company of Distillers, Ian Buxton is well-placed to write or talk about whisky, not least because he lives on the site of a former distillery!
Ian began work in the Scotch Whisky industry in 1987 and, since 1991, has run his own strategic marketing consultancy business. In addition, he gives lectures, presentations and tastings and writes regular columns for Whisky Magazine, WhiskyEtc, The Tasting Panel, Malt Advocate and various other titles. His most recent books are the two bestsellers; 101 Whiskies To Try Before You Die and 101 World Whiskies To Try Before You Die.

The Beginning of Finishing

Finished malts have become a familiar part of today's whisky offerings. When they first turned up though, they caused both curiosity and dismay. What was the problem and how did it all start? Here is Jonny McCormick looking back at the early days of finishing.

Let us consider an epoch in the whisky timeline which marked a paradigm shift in the approach to whisky maturation. Like the first trickling grains of snow triggering an avalanche, this innovation spurned a prolific movement of bold experimentation in the craft of whisky making. Although a quarter of a century has passed, what perspective has time brought the main protagonists? What has been the legacy for the new generation of whisky drinkers who have picked up a glass in their wake? That moment was the beginning of finishing.

When a maturing whisky is transferred from its original vessel into a second cask with different qualities with the explicit intention of developing additional aromas and flavours, it is said to have undergone finishing. Double Matured, Extra Matured or Additional Cask Enhancement: C'est la même chose. The concept became a catalyst for choice but piqued an emotional response. Was a separate category of Scotch whisky emerging? Some questioned if these were truly whiskies or just novelty products with a delinquent streak. A burst of articles relating to finishing were published in newspapers and magazines conveying the qualms around the topic: a palpable sense of angst, histrionics and suspicion which would elicit little more than an insignificant shrug to the new generation of imbibers.

Finished whiskies have ingratiated themselves into product line-ups and are no longer perceived as the alien invaders of the drinks cabinet. How times have changed.

Genesis of the idea

Yet, some unfinished business remains. There is more than one contender laying claim to the original idea of cask finishing. Who was Scott and who was Amundsen gripping their company's flag above that virgin polar ice?

"It began with us with The Balvenie Classic which we released in the 1980s," asserts David Stewart, The Balvenie Malt Master recalling the non-aged Balvenie, 12 and 18 year old range released in the distinctive bocksbeutel shape.

"Prior to that we only had The Balvenie Founder's Reserve at 8 and 10 years old. The Balvenie Classic were all matured in American oak barrels and then transferred into European oak sherry casks for a period of time. That's why I think we take credit for

Balvenie Classic - W Grants first attempt at a finished whisky

The Balvenie Malt Master David Stewart in 1979

Bill Lumsden, Head of Distilling and Whisky Creation at Glenmorangie C...

being the first to get into finishing. I think it was me who thought 'What would happen if we moved this whisky into here?' We were doing this in the Eighties when that word 'finish' hadn't actually been used. So we say we started it."

How did it feel to watch over those experimental sherry casks? Like the nervous anticipation of an expectant father? No, David Stewart is not a man to get over-excited.

"Well, I suppose it did feel a bit different," he acknowledges calmly. Impatience is not in his character. "I was probably checking these casks every month. We were delighted with what happened. Surprised, in how it added that richness and spiciness to the vanilla and honey from the American oak. We got this lovely balance of both."

The Balvenie Classic had a small production run of approximately 10,000 cases. Smaller still was the 18 year old which came from only 5 or 6 butts and ran to around 1,000 cases. The finishing periods were quite variable meaning some whisky had been in

sherry wood for 9 r... months. What does... the reaction from s...

"We're going ba... now. Consumers we... educated about sin... nowadays. There w... to show how we cre... someone asked dur... have told them."

Next, The Balveni... revealed in 1993, a s... bottle shape that is ...

"It was really Balv... but there was more... volumes growing, w... notes David. "At the... wood, Glenmorangi... sherry finish single m... afterwards."

At this point we mus... angie version of ever... slightly different stor...

of Distilling, Whisky Creation and Whisky Stocks, Dr. Bill Lumsden tell us?

"The origins of the first commercial bottlings of whisky finishes predate me in the company. I know I am sometimes erroneously credited with inventing it, but I didn't. I took a fledgling programme and turned it into something more commercial and experimental," he admits.

Although he was working for the Distillers Company Ltd at the time, Bill can still pinpoint where his fateful journey into finishing began in 1994.

"My first sight of finishing was in an article in GQ magazine which I still buy to this day. I read this fascinating article about a product which Glenmorangie had just launched called Port Wood Finish. It intrigued me. This GQ article came out just at that same time as the job of Glenmorangie distillery manager was advertised."

Bill applied and subsequently was appointed as Glenmorangie Distillery Manager that year.

"At the same time, the company had just bottled two very obscure limited finishes that had been lain down by Neil McKerrow, the former Managing Director. He had casks from Château Mouton Rothschild and some Madeira drums."

Strictly speaking, these were not the earliest finished Glenmorangie whiskies. The company had released a vintage product called Glenmorangie 1963 which went on sale in 1987. Bill explains,

"It was transferred from the classic bourbon barrel into sherry casks for the final 18 months. It was very deliberately switched to try and give it a little

Glenmorangie's first finished whisky

bit more depth and intensity. Although it wasn't actually labelled as such, that was the first of our commercial finishes. But it is, as far as we know, the first deliberate attempt at finishing. Now I know our friends at William Grants, if not disputing the fact that we were first, are challenging it."

I think we'll conclude this in a gentlemanly fashion with honours shared by both companies. We may never precisely untangle who is the Neil Armstrong and who is the Buzz Aldrin of whisky finishing. But we do know they both walked on the moon. Suffice to say, William Grant & Sons and The Glenmorangie Company were independently experimenting with similar concepts around the same time and both led the field.

The experiments begin

Once the idea had worked, they began to run with it. The Balvenie Portwood first appeared on our shelves in 1995 and is one of the longest running finished whiskies. They still bring in around 100 port pipes a year.

"We knew this fortified wine was sweet and would add some richness," comments David. "We get those nice raisins, sultanas, sweetness and winey notes. It's won a huge number of awards in competitions over the years and it's often peoples' favourite Balvenie."

Unlike any other finish which will be in seasoned fresh wood, each port pipe could be 40 years old so the influence of the wood extractives has gone. Brian Kinsman, Master Blender for William Grant & Sons remarks,

"I would strongly advocate that all of the flavour we get in Scotch whisky is wood-derived rather than from previous spirit contents. Port pipes are one of the exceptions. When you open up a port pipe, it's full of debris. It's not liquid; it's just like grape tannin. You can scrape your nails down the cask and you'll see the organic matter," he mimes. "So port probably swings towards the influence of the previous contents but it's probably the only one."

For all other finishes, the casks are brought to the distillery except with rum.

"Rum was a surprise. It just seems to give it that sweetness and tropical spices," notes David.

The Balvenie brought a tanker of rum to the distillery to season their barrels for 6 months before finishing their whisky in these casks for another 6 months.

Not all the experiments were successful, David admits honestly.

"I was given a budget on top of the finance for sherry and bourbon wood that we need for our fillings. We have tried brandy, cognac and Armagnac and they really haven't worked for us. They just seem to fight with each other and don't really improve the whisky. We have tried some red and white wines, and they've not really worked either. We may not have used a white wine that was sweet enough. Red wine seems to make the whisky drier and dominates it quite quickly." Brian Kinsman agrees,

"With cognac, I think it's the French Oak thing, isn't it? French Oak and our spirits don't necessarily work. We've always ended up with a dry note. Some finishes work but it just doesn't fit our taste profile for Balvenie or Glenfiddich."

David concurs, "If we don't think it's worked, it's not approved."

The fruits of their many successful finishes were showcased in their recently concluded limited edition range which began with the infamous Balvenie Islay Cask in 2000.

"We were experimenting in the late 1990s and thought why don't we do a peated Balvenie? The only way I could see to try this was to put some Balvenie into casks which have held an Islay malt. Of course, we use Islay malts for our blends so we accumulated the empty casks and sent them up to Duff-town. We put 17 year old Balvenie in them for 4-6 months and quite quickly, you could see it pick up this smoky, peaty note from what was ingrained in the wood. People always wanted to know what the Islay distillery was but we could not and did not want to say," rebuffs David.

"We use two or three Islay malts in our blends but we used only one particular brand for Islay Cask. You cannot actually call it Islay Cask any longer, but you could then."

This certainly provoked opinions.

"I'm not sure that people on Islay were pleased. I remember speaking to Jim McEwan and he wasn't overly enthusiastic because we were stepping on his toes a little bit, moving into his kind of territory. Now, a lot of people do peated whiskies on Speyside but back then this was something different."

The Glenmorangie Company's early experiments took place at their old Leith headquarters during Lumsden's tenure as distillery

The Balvenie Malt Master David Stewart

manager rather than in Tain. By now, the Wood Finishes were established as part of the core range. Once he moved into whisky making, Bill's instinctive urge to experiment meant things would never be the same again.

"It was entirely about trying to make great flavours. My wish list included casks from Château D'Yquem, Romanée-Conti and different types of oak species from around the world. I was much less senior than I am now, so I had to write things up and seek permission. The first commercial results I produced were the original Glenmorangie 1981 Sauternes wood finish 21 year old and the Glenmorangie 1975 Cote de Nuits finish. I suppose I'm due the credit for expanding finishing into all the different wine and wood types."

"One or two people were quite negative about it," expresses Bill. "I guess the most negative was John Grant of Glenfarclas. Each time he sees me, he says in his view, the finishes aren't real whisky. I just smile. It's up to him and he can hold that view if he wants. I cannot help thinking that in situations where there are negative views then it's driven by "I wish we'd done that". We really blazed a trail. It was the first real inno

Euan Mitchell, managing director at Isle of Arran Distillers

"Arran is a light to medium bodied spirit so there was a feeling that it would adapt quite well to the influence of the new wood at a younger age. I think the market was less receptive to younger whiskies than it is now. It became quite difficult to extend the range and keep that level of interest going. Finishing was one way of looking at that. We definitely won a lot of friends at that time who are still fans of the brand now."

"Bruichladdich took things a stage further with their Premier Cru Collection" say Euan.

"We had a release in Chateau Margaux casks and it's amazing the level of pull a name like that has. It makes you think. Are people really judging it on its merits or is it because of the association? To this day, particularly in Asia, I'm asked 'Could you do a finish like that again?' You can tell that they just want the name on the label."

Arran buy casks direct from the producers and have built up a number of useful relationships.

"You have to know where the casks have come from and you have to be assured that the previous contents have been of good quality. Often, their wines are more expensive than our whiskies!"

Arran malts now carry an age statement and the core range finishes are limited to Amarone, Sauternes and Port. Euan is circumspect about what they have learnt from finishing,

"It seemed to split the market: you had arch-traditionalists who wouldn't touch them with a bargepole and others who were more open-minded and keen to see where it took the flavour profiles. There are people who still come back to us asking for a bottle of the Champagne cask finish. Others say 'I really didn't like that whisky' so they tended to polarise opinion. Looking back, accepting some of the ones we did, there were a few examples that I don't think worked brilliantly well. When I took over the company in 2008, I felt that it had run its course. Arran was becoming too synonymous with wine cask finishes. "

ation for a long time and I'm not trying to ound big headed or egotistical here but the only other thing I've seen which has been quite innovative was Signet and the Quarter Cask idea from Laphroaig. Most people [in the industry] were pretty magnanimous and the best response I could say was the number of people that have tried to follow suit. I mean everyone; Benromach, Edradour, they're all doing it using things that myself or David Stewart did."

Widespread expansion

Revolution spread like wildfire. Finished whiskies were in the ascendancy with substantial numbers reaching the market from various distillers and independent bottlers. The Isle of Arran Distillers were one such company who arrived on the scene at the perfect time to take advantage of the vogue for finished whiskies. Euan Mitchell, Managing Director, joined the company in 2003 when the oldest stock was around 8 years old. The company had committed to not putting an age statement on the label until it was 10 years old. As they developed new flavours, he freely admits there were also commercial reasons behind their extensive programme of finished releases.

The Spirit of the Law

The Scotch Whisky Association's (S.W.A.) Senior Counsel issued advice to distillers in 2010 regarding innovative practices including finishing. Spirit production that differed from traditional production was prohibited especially if it affected the colour, aroma

or
taste
beyond what is
recognised as Scotch whisky. Bill
Lumsden praises them for being proactive,

"The S.W.A. worked very closely with the industry and William Grants and us in particular. As long as we could show evidence that the use of various cask types had been used traditionally in the industry, then they were prepared to accept that. I think they did a great job there."

Bill submitted company documents that helped shape the official S.W.A. guidance on what is and isn't acceptable.

All casks must be completely emptied of their former contents so that any characteristics taken on by the new incumbent is derived from the wood alone. Any residual contents would act as flavouring which would be illegal (though whether independent inspections enforce this is another matter).

Given the vital global role the S.W.A. play in defending the term 'Scotch Whisky', for parity, it's important they did not permit marketeers to play fast and loose with protected wine and spirit terms. Labelling rules were tightened up restricting the use of

A selection of finished whiskies from Isle of Arran Distillers

protected wine names solely for consumer information on the finishing cask but never to market the whisky or mislead consumers into believing they were buying a flavoured whisky. The names and labels of the whiskies produced during the heyday of finishing could no longer be released or replicated today, making them popular with whisky collectors.

Like anyone pushing the boundaries, Bill's techniques have fallen under scrutiny,

"I had one which they said 'You are not going to call that Scotch whisky,' but I was finishing using wood other than oak. It has to be matured in Scotland in oak for a minimum of three years. My whisky was in Scotland, in oak, for 10 years" he emphasises, "but then it was my business if I wanted to change that into barrels made from Brazilian cherry wood. But the S.W.A. said no. Whilst the scientist in me is occasionally frustrated, the realist, the brand ambassador, the Scotsman, and the whisky lover in me understands it is all for good reasons."

Euan Mitchell reports a similar experience,

Port pipes in warehouse 10 at Glenmorangie distillery

Photo: Jonny McCormick

"We had one or two interesting chats with the S.W.A., for sure. The first finished release we put out was the Calvados cask finish."

This, unfortunately, did not appear on the approved list of traditional casks.

"To this day, I think that attitude is slightly wrong. I know they're just trying to protect the integrity of the product. When does tradition begin and end? They opened it up to all still wines so you could have Zinfandel casks from California but we couldn't use Calvados casks from Normandy? I think it's unlikely that no Calvados casks ever made it into the whisky industry. In their opinion, it had to stay off the approved list but it worked very well with Arran!"

Finished whiskies have come a long way but it's not the end. Whisky makers continue to fine tune their blending skills utilising this secondary maturation and commissioning further experimentation. Whiskies are marketed with greater sophistication, elevated beyond a moniker based on the cask's former liquid contents. Think of finished whiskies like a double rainbow. The appearance of a double rainbow against slate grey skies is rather special and the damper parts of Scotland are natural places to see them (that's not an oxymoron; it doesn't rain in Scotland all the time). These occur as an optical phenomenon due to the double

reflection of light through raindrops, creating a slightly fainter rainbow with inverted colour bands.

The analogy is that mature whisky (the light) is reflected for a second time through the raindrop (the finishing vessel). The emergence of a secondary rainbow is the resulting whisky: distillery character parallel and intact though sometimes not shining through as brightly. The second vessel has re-ordered your perception of the flavours. They may hit your senses in a different order but there is still gold at the end of the rainbow.

Whisky writer & photographer Jonny McCormick (@TheWhiskyGuru) specialises in the scientific and technical facets of whisky production, branding, packaging and articulating aspects of the secondary whisky market. He is the creator of the Whisky Magazine Index and the Whisky Advocate Auction Index, a World Whisky Awards judge and his work has appeared in a range of publications including Whisky Advocate and Whisky Magazine. He presided over the legendary opening seminar of WhiskyFest New York 2012 where a ballroom of guests consumed $100,000 of rare whiskies in just 45 minutes.

And I Did It My Way!

Hundreds of new whisky distilleries are springing up across the world. And they're not only making quality whisky, they're throwing away the rule book, experimenting with new flavours and effectively creating a new New World category of whisky. Dominic Roskrow reports.

The world of whisky is changing. Nobody is suggesting that Scotch won't continue to be at the top of the whisky tree and that great single malt whisky doesn't come out of Scotland, but in the future it can't expect to have it all its own way. The number of distilleries around the world far outnumbers the number in Scotland."

"Not only that, but there are an increasing number of whiskies which demand to be taken seriously as world class products and can't be ignored. And at the same time, Scotch producers are putting out some very ordinary, unaged and over-priced whiskies which are doing them no favours and people are noticing."

"As far as I'm concerned the more un-aged whisky from Scotland the better it is for me because having told the world that whisky has to be 10 or 12 years old to be good they've changed the story and it chimes better with what many world distillers are doing."

"Now the world has to stop being so Scottish-centric. Even a company like Compass Box, which isn't in Scotland, has fallen in to the trap. Look at all that business with The Last Vatted Malt. That wasn't the last vatted malt at all, it was the last Scottish vatted malt. If other countries want to sell a vatted malt, they will do."

The speaker, who will remain nameless, is the owner of one of the bigger distilleries in what we might term the New World of

Alex Chasko - whiskey creator at Teeling Whiskey Company

Photo: Teeling Whiskey Company

whisky. And as if to prove the point a month later a sample of whisky from Australian independent bottler Heartwood arrives on my desk with the name Vat Out of Hell. Along with releases called Release The Beast, Velvet Hammer, and Convict.

And the whisky maker quoted above makes points that become increasingly evident as each year passes. Where once Scotland contributed about 100 of the world's 150 significant world distilleries and the other four established whisky producing nations – Ireland, Canada, Japan and The United States – paid due deference, there are quite probably three times as many distilleries elsewhere in the world now that are producing whisky that will eventually be marketed beyond their national borders.

What at the moment is still a trickle of 'new world' whisky will soon become a flood as scores of new distilleries from all sorts of unexpected places start to bottle their maturing spirit.

And it's not just the quantity of new whisky that should unsettle the old order. It's the way that an increasingly confident number of new distillers are bringing innovation to the market and experimenting within the rules so that whiskies with little in common with Scotch but plenty to recommend them are effectively taking whisky on a totally new journey.

Taking their lead from craft brewing, the new distillers are experimenting with malts and grains never used for distillation before; they're using different methods of drying their malts; they're maturing their spirit in unusual casks and in different woods; they are combining different styles of spirit in new and exciting ways, and forming alliances with other small distilleries locally or in other countries. Digger & Ditch contains two malts, for instance, one from Australia and one from New Zealand.

And in the process they're starting to market whiskies that operate within the rules but which are breaking new ground. What would you call an English whisky made of a grist containing wheat, barley and oats? English single pot still whisky? Or what about a New Zealand whisky made from one malt and one grain whisky from the same distillery? A New Zealand single blend perhaps?

As our man at the top of the feature rightly said, nobody's doubting Scotland's place in the whisky world order. But as the French found to their cost in the field of wine, there is no room for complacency and you ignore this sort of new thinking at your peril. At some point down the line – please don't shoot the messenger – Scotland's whisky industry must face up to the new wave of whisky and decide whether to ignore it and not try to fix what's not broken – or to respond to it as the traditional producers in Kentucky have done – and meet the challenge head on on the premise that you must innovate or die.

What the Scottish industry can't do is dismiss the new producers as irrelevant amateurs. Even now, you only have to speak to some of these folk to realise they're clever, fearless, irreverent, and very ambitious. Fancy meeting a few?

Alex Chasko – Teeling Whiskey Company, Ireland

Alex Chasko is an American who cut his teeth on Irish whiskey, working first with Cooley to broaden consumer perceptions of what Irish whiskey might be, and more recently forming The Teeling Whiskey Company with Jack Teeling, one of the family at the core of Cooley. The company was formed specifically to fill a gap in the market for unusual and unique Irish whiskey.

So far the company has released an 'authentic' poitin with an alcoholic strength of 61,5%, The Teeling Small Batch Irish Whiskey, which is a blended whiskey married in used rum casks and unchill-filtered, and a 21 year Old Silver Reserve, which has been matured in ex-Sauternes casks. And it released a whiskey under the name Hybrid which mixed Irish whiskey with Scottish single malt.

There will be further innovations to come. Alex has already introduced this writer to three other 'works in progress' – all of them very good indeed, even unfinished.

"We are offering people a high quality alternative to the standard range of Irish whiskey," he says. "If you are familiar with the better known brands we can provide you with some new and exciting whiskeys. We want to give consumers a little bit more flavour and aroma presented in a way that is unique and easily accessible."

Alex sees the need to innovate as essential to the growth of the whisky market because

oday's customer demand it, but argues that
nything new must be of sufficient quality
r it won't survive.

"If you don't have a quality product you
re dead," he says. "But if you bring quality
o it then new and exciting products are
ery important for the growth of the indu-
try. Our world is becoming a smaller place
nd I think it is only natural for consumers
o seek 'new' and 'special' products. In a
onsumer driven market with information
t people's finger tips, innovative products
re part of the way consumers interact
vith a brand. For me innovation has always
een about revival and rediscovery. I think
revival of forgotten styles will eventually
ecome part of the standard range of
roducts."

Vith scores of new distilleries springing up
cross the world Alex says that there are
nly two ways for the new producers to
o: to explore new directions and produce
omething different; or to emulate what has
one before. For him it's a no brainer.

"Most people approach us with an open
nind," he says. "They understand what
ve are talking about. As long as you have
genuine product that is of high quality
onsumers will respond well. But the sooner
mall distilleries stop trying to copy and start
nnovating the quicker results will follow."

"I think that the future is open for innova-
ive companies who capture the consumer's
nterest and imagination. I don't feel that
he rules are set out in any way for anyone.
eople want new things but they want them
o be authentic and real. I don't see why you
ouldn't have a Scottish version of bourbon
or instance."

Watch this space!

ohn McCarthy – Copper House/
dnams, England

onathan Adnams has a very straightforward
ttitude when it comes to making alcoholic
lrinks. He wants to be able to control every
tage of the production process, from grain
o glass; and he wants his drinks to get a
eaction. He doesn't mind what reaction,
lthough of course he'd prefer it to be
jood. But no reaction at all is his enemy
ecause it implies indifference, and that
n turn means his drink is inoffensive and
otentially bland.

So when the chairman of one of England's

John McCarthy - Head Distiller at Adnams

most loved breweries decided to build a
distillery on site and Adnams charged John
McCarthy with running it, it was clear from
the off that this would be no 'me too'
operation.

And so it has proved. In late 2013 Adnams
released its first two whiskies.One is a single
malt made with local barley and matured
for three years in virgin French oak casks;
the other is a three grain whisky made with
a mash of malted wheat, barley and oats
and aged in new American oak. Next up will
be a 100% rye whisky.

And the innovation doesn't stop with
whisky. The distillery produces distinct and
characterful gins and vodka, has its own
versions of absinthe, and stepped out from
the confines of whisky to produce an eau de
vie made from one of its beers, Broadside.

"We intend to offer small batch, hand
crafted spirits which are interesting to our
consumers," says John. "More than 130
years brewing experience has given us great
confidence. Our knowledge of how diffe-

The Copper House still room at Adnams

rent grains and other raw materials react and influence flavours has been invaluable in producing spirits with complex flavour profiles."

"It was Jonathan Adnams' vision and desire to produce small batch distilled products. As distiller I have been given free rein to innovate and experiment, with little restriction. The possibilities are endless."

"Innovation inspires people to push the boundaries and new ideas, within the definition of whisky, will emerge. As long as we remain within those parameters, or clearly explain when we step outside them, then I think the customer will follow."

"We launched our eau de vie de biere, Spirit of Broadside in 2011. Although this category is well established in pockets around the world, there are few producers in the United Kingdom."

"Many of our customers were already aware of Broadside beer and that gave them the assurance that they would enjoy the spirit. We know many of our customers enjoy discovering new products. Innovation is what we do."

The Ebensperger family – Puni Distillery, Italy

At first glance Italy would seem to be an odd place for whisky making. That's until you take a closer look at the mountainous terrain in the North of the country, and the abundance of cool water in the region.

This is South Tyrol, a region annexed by Italy after the first world war almost 100 years ago and it's home to the Ebensperger family, whose interest in making whisky grew a few years back. Jonas Ebensperger takes up the story.

"I guess one of the starting points was in the early 1990s when my father completed three sommelier courses. In these courses the main focus is put on wines and wine tasting but there were also lessons dealing with distillates.

"He developed an interest in whisky and continued to learn about it after the course and before long the whole family shared his passion. But we did not limit ourselves to just tasting different whiskies and learning about the ways they are made. We started to test the properties of different types of malt during distillation as well."

The plan was to look to create a new style of whisky – one which would satisfy the Italian thirst for younger spirits. The key to the new distillate came courtesy of a local rye, which for generations had been supplied from the region to Austria.

"Our ambition was always to create a new type of whisky, one that can be enjoyed as a new make spirit or very young. This is the Italian way. In Italy, where the climate is rather hot for most parts of the year, people tend to go for refreshing and light."

"We felt that our new whisky should have more passion and finesse than most other malt spirits. That is why, for more than two years, we spent every spare hour and many sleepless nights beside a tiny still like alchemists in search of the perfect mixture."

"Of course like alchemists we failed to reach total and utter perfection but because my father eventually agreed on a recipe we came pretty close. We added malted wheat and malted rye to malted barley and have created a remarkable spirit. It is sweeter and somewhat fresher than other clearac but tastes mellow and gentle even at high gradation. And it provides a distinguished taste of malt and is rich in spiciness because of the rye malt."

The family has made technical adjustments to the distillation process too, and most of the maturation is carried out in casks previously containing Marsala and sweet Italian wine.

Puni Distillery is yet to bottle a whisky but it has two products available, Puni Pure, which is new make spirit, and Puni Alba, matured for more than one but less than three years old. It's a remarkable drink, spicy and sweet, with a smooth honeyed taste, and some nutty and herbal notes. It stands up as an aperitif spirit in its own right.

"Alba means dawn or sunrise in Italian and in a way it marks a new whisky culture in Italy," says Jonas. "And it is the Gaelic word for Scotland. This underlines the great esteem with which we hold Scotland in whisky making."

Darek Bell – Corsair Artisan, USA

Darek Bell doesn't mince his words when he talks about how he got in to craft distilling and set about creating new and exciting whiskey.

With a background in craft brewing, and an ability to distil biodiesel for an old Mercedes he owned, he was logically drawn to

Jonas Ebensperger - one of the founders and owners of Puni, the first malt whisky distillery in Italy

making spirit and eventually building the stills for what would become Corsair Distillery.

And was he ever going to make conventional bourbon? Hell no!

"The explosion in creativity in the craft brewing industry was incredibly exciting," he says. "Extremists in the craft beer world were taking beer to places it had never been before."

"Whiskey, however, seemed stuck in the middle ages. The spirits were all similar and stodgy. There was zero creativity in taste, packaging, or branding. Everything just looked old, farty, stale, tired and corporate. It seemed like a few huge monopolies owned most of the distilleries and were putting zero effort in to new products. Basically it was where beer was in the 1980s."

"The more I got in to whiskey and became a whiskey geek the more I hungered for something new and exciting. I didn't want what my dad drank – I wanted something new. I wanted energy and excitement. If the mega distillers didn't have the vision and balls to make that then hell, we would do it ourselves."

Corsair prides itself on fearless experimentation. More than most there seems to be few limits to the experimentation at the distillery. It makes smoked whiskeys using a library of different flavours created by many different wood fuels to dry the grain.The distillery makes whiskeys that use mash bills foreign to mainstream distilleries utilising grains that are well known in brewing but not distilling, such as chocolate rye malt, biscuit malt or caramel 120. There are spirits made with hops in the mix. There is even whisky made with alternative grains such as Quinoa, which has come out of the health food and green movements.

Darek argues that for the next generation such whiskies make more sense than the traditional ones which put so much store on age.

"This sort of discussion about age can be a turn off to younger consumers," he says.

"I don't think it's a matter of us taking our consumers with us as much as them pulling us to them. Sustainability is not a buzzword for the younger generation. We do not have to explain the back story of a whiskey made with quinoa to the young consumers who walk through the door. They just get it. And they expect us to care about these kind of issues and make them integral to our products."

Patrick Zuidam – Zuidam Distillers, Holland

Aiming to be the best whisky distiller in the world might sound like a lofty ambition. But if you take a look at Zuidam distillery in Holland, its lengthy history making top quality spirits and its huge range of highly respected alcoholic drinks, the aim doesn't seem so silly after all. And then try the range of whiskies on offer. Zuidam is very serious about distilling indeed.

The distillery was set up by Fred Zuidam some 40 years ago and from the off set out to make fine spirits using the very best products. There are no short cuts at the distillery. And so when son and current managing director Patrick decided to try his hand at whisky – a small and logical step for a distillery producing fantastic aged genevers and eaux de vie – it was clear that he would do it properly.

Darek Bell - owner of Corsair Artisan Spirits

Patrick Zuidam and his highly awarded Millstone 100 Rye

The result is Millstone, top quality single malt, and in true Zuidam style, Patrick experimented further.

"I set out to make a rye whiskey and I persuaded my father to let me buy the expensive ingredients," says Patrick. "When I went back to it after a while it was dreadful, and I had to decide whether to tell my father I had wasted his money or leave it and forget about it. A couple of years on and it had turned in to a fantastic spirit. It is my pride and joy."

In addition to the 100% rye whisky, the distillery produces a richly sherried malt, and is working on a three grain whisky containing rye, corn and malted barley and a five grain whisky containing wheat, rye, corn, spelt and malted barley.

Patrick says that quality is everything and it doesn't matter how big or how small a distillery is, it won't survive if it makes bad whisky.

Roger Melander, distillery manager for BOX Distillery in Sweden

"If craft distillers want to have any type of future they will have to distill products that are great," he says.

"If they don't produce whiskies that are better than what the major players are doing they have no business calling themselves a distillery and should go back to selling cars or whatever they were doing before. But I think the good innovative companies could bring new flavours to the consumer. The possibilities are endless."

Roger Melander – Box Distillery, Sweden

Box Distillery is going back for the future as it seeks to make new whisky in the North of Sweden.

Box is some months from bottling its first whisky but I travelled with this book's Editor to the distillery having been highly impressed with a 99 day old spirit, and it's fair to say that every cask of every style maturing away at the wood mill converted in to a

distillery, is of the same stunning quality.

Sweden is, along with Australia, shaping up to be the most important whisky territory in the world. But while the Aussies take a loud, colourful and brash approach to whisky making, the Swedes pay due deference to Scotland while setting out to make vintage Rolls Royce whiskies by seeking out quality over quantity from the ingredients they use, irrespective of the cost.

Box is a classic case in point. On one level it's a traditional distillery making traditional single malt whisky. But on another level, there's an attention to detail at every stage of production which is highly impressive. Roger Melander explains:

"We are not trying to invent the wheel but we are seeking perfection," he says. "We have picked the good things from the Scottish and Japanese production and have also developed new methods with a focus on quality."

"The aim of the continuous improvement requires some creativity and the courage to

Still room at BOX distillery

Photo: BOX Distillery

ry new ideas. In some cases it might be better to go back to the methods. For instance, we don't believe in the use of anti foam, chill filtration and caramel colouring."

Box isn't alone here, but with the attention to detail takes it in to another realm. The emphasis on water temperature, rarely used and long abandoned low yield and high quality grain, and the use of highly responsive Hungarian oak – hence the impressive 99 day spirit from one of the coldest and therefore theoretically slowest maturing distilleries in the world. For Box, innovation comes from going back and improving on what's gone before.

"I am convinced that the number of small scale producers with focus on quality rather on efficiency and yield will result in a new approach to young whisky in the future," says Roger.

"Drinkers are interested in innovation and new flavours, but there is a big difference between new exciting flavours and extreme flavours. I always try to produce what I enjoy myself. Hopefully, it works for our customers as well."

With standards this high it can't fail.

Dominic Roskrow is a freelance whisky writer. He edits Whiskeria and Whiskeria on line as well as his his own online magazines World Whisky Review and Still Crazy. He is a regular writer and reviewer for Whisky Advocate, spcialising in World Whisky. He is the business development director for The Whisky Shop chain and recently set up the Craft Distillers' Alliance, for which he is a director. He has been writing about drinks for 20 years and has just completed his sixth book, The Whisky Opus, published in September 2012. He lives in Norfolk, home of England's first malt whisky distillery, and is married with three children and is one of the few people in the world to be both a Keeper of the Quaich and a Kentucky Colonel.

Whisky
The Most Social of Lubricants

Whisky is so much more than just another drink. Enjoying your dram with other people means not only sharing the whisky experience but also great moments of friendship. Whisky gatherings of all sorts are more popular than ever and Neil Ridley has been to a few of them to see what is going on.

Good times at Maltstock in The Netherlands

'We've heard that a million monkeys at a million keyboards could produce the complete works of Shakespeare; now, thanks to the Internet, we know that is not true.' Robert Wilensky

Ardbeg Distillery Manager Mickey Heads, has a steady hand

When the late Robert Wilensky, renowned professor of computer science at Berkeley College issued his artful observation of the internet before the dawn of the new millennium, little did we know just how profound his remarks would become. Fast forward to 2013 and the combined pincer movement of Twitter and Facebook has, rightly or wrongly, turned everyone with a computer and a Wi-Fi connection into a roving commentator; a story teller; a critic.

The world of whisky has of course succumbed to this way of thinking too and, tracing my own career as a whisky writer, I am as guilty as the next monkey/man when it comes to using the web to voice my thoughts, passions and predictions. On one hand, geographically speaking, social media has enabled whisky lovers across the globe to connect with spirits often far removed from their palates. But on the other, the fast paced consumption of information, often generated by ill-informed opinion formers has left some brands and critics with a bad taste in the mouth when it comes to social media enabling consumers to explore flavours from their keyboards.

But let's not get too hung up on our apparent impending technological implosion. Fortunately the word social doesn't necessarily limit itself to being permanently coupled to its tech savvy sibling, media. Meeting up for a dram with friends is the very foundation on which many of us increase our enthusiasm and knowledge for whisky and fortunately, whisky events, social gatherings and meet ups are also widely acknowledged and supported by the industry.

The good news is that gatherings are more popular than ever, with organisers filling halls all over the globe with like-minded whisky fans. And for the uninitiated, they are not just the domains of the serial whisky nerd, using the opportunity to brag just how many peaty notches on the back bar they have enjoyed.

To many whisky lovers the annual Feis Ile on the island of Islay has become a spirited pilgrimage to one of the most identifiable whisky locations on the planet. Now approaching its thirteenth year, the week long festival attracts visitors from as far afield as Japan, Australia and the USA and for those who have witnessed the events laid on at the distilleries, each year seems to become a more immersive experience for whisky fans.

Jon Beach, owner of the Drumnadrochit Fiddlers whisky bar and confirmed Port Ellen fanatic has for the past three years assembled a spirited group of like-minded fans for a charity tasting of several rare vintages of the closed distillery. 'International Port Ellen Day' culminates in a final dram at the old (now long defunct) filling store and the sense of occasion, coupled with the group's enthusiasm for this hallowed single malt makes for a very unique social drinking experience.

"I.P.E.D. is a chance for me to share the joy of opening these often-seen but seldom drunk bottles in the proper environment with fellow Port Ellen lovers and discuss the different bottles' relative merits," explains Beach. "To drink Port Ellen at the old distillery building should be on everybody's Whisky Bucket List and for me, to help people achieve that goal, is a privilege!"

"You can see that the [Feis Ile] events seem to get bigger, better and wackier every year," explains Bryony MacIntyre, part of Ardbeg's whisky creation team.

"It's a fantastic experience and everyone has a great time, with people often booking their places for the year after before they leave. People are making life long friends from the events too, which is great."

For Eugene Van der Meer, a veteran visitor to the Feis Ile, the camaraderie and sense of community keeps him returning year-on-year.

"It's always absolutely brilliant. The atmosphere, the people and our returning friends make it a wonderful time to visit Islay."

Van der Meer thinks the highlight is the Ardbeg open day, which each year plans its events around specific themes (from 2011's Flamenco costumes to celebrate a Pedro Ximenez-influenced bottling to this year's giant peat bog, in homage to the 'Ardbog' release.)

"They do things differently – from the tours to the games, everything is so well themed and thought out."

Whisky drinkers of Sweden, unite!

But whisky fans don't necessarily need to travel as far afield as Islay to experience the social togetherness that whisky does so well – better, it must be said than any other global spirit. Now in its tenth year, the Swedish Whisky Federation represents Europe's most comprehensive example of how the idea of a whisky club can truly traverse a nation.

"We started in 2003 with seven clubs. Ten years later we have nearly 200 clubs, with over 7,700 members, right across the country," explains Douglas Christianson, president of the federation, "with numbers ranging from five to 404 members in the largest."

The federation coordinates an active social calendar for its members, including organising around eight visiting speakers a year from the world of whisky, from distillers to master blenders, as well as special bottlings (a limited edition Benromach was recently bottled to celebrate its tenth anniversary.) But what's intriguing is the emphasis the federation places on helping to educate members and make what is a very knowledge-heavy subject accessible for anyone who wants to take part.

"Two years ago, some of us on the board wrote all the material needed for a comprehensive whisky education programme," explains Christianson.

"We have three levels: firstly by beginning to educate one or two from each club, we have educated around 70 'teachers'. It is then their role to educate the members in their home club."

For those who really want to immerse

themselves further, the federation then organises a further three days education at Box distillery in Sweden and the ultimate experience in whisky education: five days learning the ropes at the Springbank distillery.

I ask Douglas how important social media is in growing and supporting the membership.

"Well, a computer is not something that makes life easier for me," he laughs, "but the federation is planning to start up some online tastings from distilleries. However the ethos for many of our members is to enjoy whisky in a social situation as well as meet people from distilleries in the flesh and our goal is to continue to bring tasting leaders over to Sweden from Scotland, Ireland and Japan."

To highlight this, Christianson and his team have planned a very special event to help mark their tenth anniversary bringing over the managers from Lagavulin, Talisker and Royal Lochnagar distilleries to host a huge seminar for around 270 of the federation's members.

So given the formidable size and reputation of the federation within the whisky business, does Christianson think it has the potential to influence the style of whisky making aimed at the Swedish palates and perhaps beyond?

"No, I don't think so," he explains. "Yes, distilleries know the type of whiskies we like here in Sweden and there are occasionally

Whisky celebrities like Michael Urquhart and Frank McHardy are frequent guests to the whisky clubs in Sweden

Uisge – the first whisky show in Finland aimed at consumers

pecial bottlings for the market, but it isn't
ur goal to influence where this goes."

)ver in neighbouring Finland, the drive
owards bringing a social whisky event to
he masses has not been an easy one,
lespite enthusiasm from fans and brands
like. Mika Jansson is one of the founders
)ehind Uisge Finland, the country's first
onsumer-facing whisky fair now in its third
ear and Finnish authorities are still keeping
 close eye on the proceedings, due to the
igid legislation when it comes to promoting
lcohol in the country.

"The Finnish laws are, as a Scottish friend
)f mine once said, "draconian" when it
omes to alcohol," explains Jansson. "But
he law is what it is, and we took painsta-
{ing efforts to make absolutely sure that
every-thing we did was fully compliant."

According to Jansson, Finnish law forbids
my advertising and information sharing to
do with alcohol above 22% so "we cannot
even use the word "Whisky" in connection
vith the festival in public – thus the name
Uisge' was born!"

Despite not even having the permission
:o have an official website, word of mouth

quickly spread about the event ('a few newspapers were brave enough to mention the
festival, one cleverly headlining their article
as 'The event you should not hear about'',
laughs Jansson) and in its inaugural year in
2011, Uisge easily outgrew the confines of
an 800 capacity pub, now attracting upwards of 2,000 to its new home, the capacious old student faculty house Vanha Ylioppi-
lastalo right in the centre of Helsinki.

Whisky camping in Holland

From one undoubted success story of commitment to the whisky cause to another.

Every so often, an event so unique, yet
so simple in its construct comes along and
Maltstock, held yearly in the leafy outskirts
of Nijmegen in The Netherlands exemplifies
how the concept of a whisky gathering is
not founded on elitism, nerdery and getting annihilated on rare, unpronounceable
whiskies.

My first visit to Maltstock was back in 2011
and, if I'm honest, as someone who dislikes
the cliquey nature often associated with
malt whisky, I expected to feel a little at
odds with such a gathering of thirsty uber-

enthusiasts. What I found when I arrived at the event's summer camp-style home was the complete opposite.

For the uninitiated, the core of the Maltstock weekend revolves around a passionate sharing of knowledge as well as liquid. The central meeting place at the venue has a number of large tables, groaning under the sheer weight of whiskies, almost all of which are provided by the attendees. Rare Japanese single cask bottlings sit alongside obscure blends from the 1970s and thankfully, more readily available palate-friendly supermarket whiskies – with the ethos to expand your whisky experience at your leisure.

With so many free drams on offer, it's surprising that the place doesn't descend into chaos after a few hours, but herein lies the fundamental principle firmly laid down by its founders, Teun van Wel and Bob Wenting.

"Bob and I have been visiting many whisky festivals for many years," points out van Wel, "and we love them. But there are always several sessions. So you only have a few hours to try some whiskies as well as talk to people. What this equates to is 'too many whiskies, too little time'. It got us thinking: why not bring together enthusiasts for a whole weekend. No rush. Plenty of time to talk and share and enjoy a few drams. In our university days there was a lot of interaction

Sharing whiskies at Maltstock

between all the student clubs. For some reason, it seems that there is hardly any interaction between whisky clubs, so we wanted to try and bring clubs together for a weekend and interact."

The duo neatly highlights this by bringing up the age-old question. "In the end it is all about the people, not the whisky. When we're asked what our favourite whiskies are we always say that it's all about the one's we've shared in good company. Whisky is a very social drink."

The guys have a point here. Whilst some of the more traditional whisky fairs can feel like a conveyor belt, where the emphasis is to pack in as many whiskies as your tokens allow - usually within an afternoon, by having plenty of time to reflect on the several hundred whiskies on offer, you are actually more selective and informed with your drinking. Whether the concept would work outside of the relatively liberal confines of The Netherlands is another matter, but a number of brands including The Balvenie, (brand ambassador Dr Sam Simmons ran a superbly revealing deconstruction tasting of the Tun 1401 release), Tomatin and Nikka, as well as a host of independent whisky bottlers have all run unique tasting events at Maltstock.

The art of getting people relaxed and involved

Similarly, The Whisky Lounge, first started in the city of York in the north of England take a much more relaxed strategy to the traditional whisky event.

"The concept came from wanting to explore whisky myself," explains founder Eddie Ludlow, "but I don't do many things well alone – and drinking is one of those things," he jokes.

"Whisky is one of those drinks that just engenders conviviality and the idea of sharing; ultimately it tastes better when people are talking about it and smiling with a glass in their hand and hopefully this approach still exists in every event we run today."

The Whisky Lounge is not like the archetypal whisky gathering in that it attracts brand new drinkers to each gathering (now up and running in 15 cities across the UK) rather than aiming to appeal to the existing enthusiast.

"We all have to start somewhere," continues Ludlow, "and whilst it's great to drink whisky with other 'whisky people', it's even

Eddie Ludlow (top right) and his wife Amanda, owners of The Whisky Lounge, arrange whisky shows all around the UK

etter to engage with people who don't ave the experience and who are discove-ing whisky for the first time."

The Whisky Lounge is also probably one f the only whisky-orientated events com-anies to successfully integrate a musical lement into the proceedings. Their recent am & Dram event in London focused on lemystifying blended whisky using different nusicians to help highlight the unique per-onalities and characteristics within a blend,

lighting up the Twittersphere as a result and more events are now planned around the UK.

Also keen to keep the 'social' angle close to heart, despite very much embracing the age of social media, are London's Whisky Squad. Started by a group of friends, spearheaded by enthusiast Jason Standing, their approach, as Standing puts it was "to try whisky without having to shell out for a whole bottle at a time. Our first meeting in

The team from the first ever Dramboree with organiser Jason Standing comfortably stretched out on the floor

a local pub brought 12 of us together and before we knew it, we had a whisky club!" Three years down the line and The Whisky Squad hosts two regular tastings a month and has a mailing list of over 300.

Standing thinks the club's success comes naturally, in that "by giving people an informal environment, we find that they're willing to speak out, ask questions, express their nosing & tasting experience, and feel involved in the session."

I ask him how far he thinks social media can go in influencing the decision making of whisky drinkers internationally.

"For me, reading other peoples' tasting notes is no substitute for actually getting your hands on the stuff," he explains, "which I guess is one of the main reasons we started a tasting group in the first place. In that vein, the types of blogs that influence me tend to be more story-focused on peoples' experiences, such as tastings they've done & enjoyed, or pairings they've tried, rather than vast catalogues of sensory descriptors."

Standing's next venture hopefully aims to replicate the ethos behind the Maltstock gathering. 'Dramboree', is a three day camping and whisky event where "everyone brings a dram they'd like to share to talk about with other people. No rush, no drinking up times, no thronging queues at exhibitors' stands."

Alongside the accessibility of whisky events, the growth of the online tasting has undoubtedly taken the industry by surprise and today it is almost inconceivable for a brand not to activate their armies of Twitter followers to help spread the good word about their latest releases.

One whisky enthusiast who has capitalised on this front is Steve Rush, founder of the Whisky Wire blog and host of a slew of

Steve Rush, founder of the Whisky Wire blog

teractive Twitter-focused tastings. The premise of the Twitter tasting is to send whisky samples to a preselected list of bloggers, writers and whisky fans, who are encouraged to sample them at a designated time and tweet their comments, effectively turning Twitter into a live chat /tasting room.

"I was motivated by the fact that not everyone can get to whisky festivals/tastings, be it for geographical or other reasons, and this was a great opportunity to bring like-minded people together, not just bloggers, from the UK and around the world," explains Rush.

I'm keen to find out what his impressions are of an industry, which, in places, hasn't fully embraced the concept of using social media in its communications strategy.

"From a brand perspective, websites and social media channels are now the modern equivalent of the shop front window," he points out. "Those not engaging and interacting socially are effectively running a business with their shutters pulled down. There are still many whisky brands that need to wake up, be less cynical and understand the benefits of well-run social media and related gatherings."

The concept of the Twitter tasting has drawn criticism from some areas of the whisky community, partly due to the fact that it could be conceived as helping to serve a cliquey minority, but it's an argument that Rush is quick to dispel.

"It's vitally important that such events are run not just for the benefit of those taking part but also, and in many ways, more importantly, for those following on the night and who may either be new to whisky or the particular brand itself. There have been tastings run by others that seem to be purely focused on their participants and that have missed out on a huge opportunity to engage with followers, both existing and new to the category."

One brand, keen to capitalise on the power of social media is Glenmorangie, who recently unveiled their Cask Masters programme, which, it is hoped, will bring a totally fresh perspective to the creation and marketing of a new whisky.

Cask Masters is the first of its kind, whereby the power of whisky creation is, to an extent, placed in the hands of the consumers, who will ultimately select the style of whisky to be released from a shortlist of three cask types. Those signed up to the programme can also have a say in the development of the aesthetics of the bottle design and launch too.

Anne Phillips, Senior Brand Manager for Glenmorangie explains that "we think of it as a great opportunity for consumers to become a little more involved in an area of whisky creation that they are never normally exposed to, with a brand whose quality credentials they already know and trust."

At the time of writing this, the winning cask type had yet to be announced, but the programme's success clearly lies on not only amplifying this unique approach across the social media channels, but also by getting 'liquid to lips' and allowing consumer's palates to do the voting, rather than their fingers.

What strikes me is that for all the benefits social media brings to whisky, without the backbone of actually 'feeling' and 'experiencing' the interaction between consumers it really only provides noise for the whisky community to respond to: too loud and most consumers will simply react negatively to it, too quiet and it will just be lost in the sea of other digital communication strategies brands are floating into cyberspace.

The heartening fact is that as a spirit, an experience with whisky can never truly be synthesised or replicated digitally. It is, and shall always remain, the most social of lubricants, whatever situation it is placed in – real-time or online.

Neil Ridley is a regular contributor to Whisky Magazine and Imbibe, and he is also the co-editor of irreverent whisky blog www.caskstrength.net, recently nominated for several online awards. As well as being Drinks Editor for The Chap, Neil has written articles on whisky and other spirits for Aston Martin Magazine and The Evening Standard, as well as providing his opinion on tasting panels for the likes of The Spirits Business and the World Whisky Awards.

On The
Whisky
Road

In 2004 Hans Offringa published an entertaining book called The Road to Craigellachie, subtitled A voyage of discovery through the world of Scotch whisky. It's a decade later and we thought it was time for Hans to give us an update. Join him on the road as he re-visits some of his favourite spots in Scotland.

or a writer it is impossible to say no to such a request. But where to start? So much has happened since 2004. I was lucky to broaden my horizon, thoroughly investigating American and Irish whiskeys, albeit that Scotch will always be my first love. I felt privileged to have the help of American, Irish and Scottish colleagues, with several of whom I've been working closely for many years now. So where to take you? What about the latest edition of the Speyside Festival, with a small detour here and there? The Spirit of Speyside, as it has been known for a while, had its 14th edition this year and so far I have not missed a single one.

In my early days of travels to Scotland I would usually fly into Edinburgh, Glasgow or Aberdeen, rent a car and set off on my self-chosen quest. In more recent years, I tend to take the ferry from IJmuiden, near Amsterdam, to Newcastle. It is a very comfortable trip, if the weather holds. You can bring your own car, dine on board, enjoy the nightclub or the casino, go to bed for a good night's sleep and wake up the next morning entering the harbour of Newcastle while enjoying a good breakfast.

I prefer to take the cross-country road to Edinburgh instead of the coastal route. Usually I stop at the border to look at the beautiful standing stones marking the end of England and the beginning of Scotland. After a chat with the ubiquitous piper I continue my trip and pass Edinburgh. Then I head for the A9 and stop for lunch somewhere around Pitlochry, in a beautiful little hollow called Moulin. It boasts an excellent inn, one of the oldest in Scotland, and a little brewery. Try their local Braveheart Ale. It sounds corny but it really tastes good.

A stone's throw away is Edradour, the smallest commercial distillery in the country and a beauty for the eye. When entering the tiny "valley" one cannot do otherwise than fall in love with the whitewashed buildings and their distinct red trimmings. Its owner Andrew Symington takes good care of this little gem among distilleries, which gives the traveller the opportunity to see how a traditional farm distillery would have looked like in the 19th century. Is it a time warp? Well, yes and no. Looking at the tiny stills and ditto wash back, yes! But considering the fact that Symington also owns an independent bottling company called Signatory, there is more than meets the eye.

Moulin Inn and Brewery in Pitlochry

Now let's not dwell too long here. I need to get to The Glenlivet in time, for it is at this distillery that the annual gala dinner will be held to celebrate the opening of the festival. The A9 is a busy road, the major link between the Highlands and the South, so I try to avoid becoming entangled in heavy traffic. Therefore I choose the A924 and at Kirkmichael turn onto the B950, which brings me straight to the A93.

The latter road is an excellent alternative to the A9 and takes me through Glen Shee with breathtaking views over the wide valley, hillsides dotted with sheep (future haggis, I sometimes call them) and a meandering stream that sparkles and glitters when the sun shines upon it. The valley plays a never-ending game with the clouds, resulting in constantly moving patches of shadow and light on the high hills in the distance. I park the car at a small bay in the middle of the valley, get out and get lucky. For 10 minutes no other car passes. Nature is overwhelming and challenges the mind.

Shortly before the attractive village Braemar, the valley ends. Braemar is not only well-known to hikers and hill walkers, it also annually hosts one of the largest Highland Games in Scotland, on the first Saturday in September. A real spectacle with events such as Highland Dancing, Piping, Tossing the Caber, Putting the Stone, Throwing the Hammer, Sprinting, Relay Race, Hill Race, Long Leap and Tug of War.

I get carried away, reminiscing and still having to drive quite a ways. Just before

Glenlivet Distillery

Balmoral Castle I turn left on a single-track road (the B976) that will take me to the A939 north, passing Corgarff Castle, conquering the highland moors, and finally turning on the B9008, just before the village of Tomintoul.

This narrow road will take me through the famous Glen of the Livet. After a wee while I can see the eponymous distillery, lying on my left next to Minmore House. It has to wait for I must check in at the Delnashaugh Inn, a bit further up the road, and change gear. My friend Kevin Smith, the proprietor of this "restaurant with rooms", as he prefers to call his place, kindly drives me back to The Glenlivet. It gives me the opportunity to enjoy a few drams during and after dinner.

The Speyside Festival hub

The following morning I head for Dufftown to meet Mike Lord, the proprietor of The Whisky Shop, opposite the town's distinctive square bell tower. This is probably the most important hub during the Speyside Festival. Many attendees make appointments here to meet likeminded friends. Over the years the festival also has been doubling as an international reunion of whisky aficionados, from Alaska to Australia.

Remember the short stop at the tiny artisanal distillery in Perthshire? No bigger contrast than Dufftown's, and some even say Scotland's, most famous distillery, Glenfiddich, where single malt is made on truly industrial scale. The tours are still free which amazes me every time I visit. The ten of thousands yearly visitors could easily bring in an interesting extra bit of income, since most distilleries charge for tours. However, this distillery, run by descendants of founder William Grant, doesn't want yo money for the tour, but prefers you spend on whisky and whisky paraphernalia in the well-stocked shop.

Those who want to see distilleries normally not opened for the public, can go cherry-picking. For instance the famous Mortlach welcomes visitors during this week. It is eve possible to book a tour to see all working distilleries in Dufftown. Similar tours are held in Rothes, home to Glen Grant, with it astonishing gardens, Speyburn, Glen Spey and Glenrothes. To the latter an interesting ghost story is attached and tours usually ends with "a toast to the ghost".

Further up on the road lies Elgin, capital of the region, home to the distilleries of Linkwood, Glen Moray and Glen Elgin. Worth seeing are the remains of Elgin Cathedral, once destroyed by fire by the Wolf of Badenoch, who had a serious quarrel with the residing bishop. These imposing ruins are a welcome change of scenery from the ubiquitous distilleries.

The remains of Elgin Cathedral

Cragganmore warehouses

ouble back on the road that took me to
gin, heading for Ballindalloch Castle, of
ich part is open to visitors. That's what I
o like about the Speyside Festival. There
so much to do and it need not necessarily
a visit to a distillery. Approximately 150
ents are "crammed" into 5 days and it is
ays a challenge deciding what to attend
d what not.

My visit to the castle is a professional one,
interview with the owners of the castle,
ich has been in the same family for more
an 600 years. I've known Mrs Clare Russell-
acPherson-Grant and her husband Oliver
r some years and am looking forward to
eing them again. We talk about Clare's
o succesful cooking books and Oliver
ives me around the beautiful golf course
at was built on the estate not so long ago.
emphasises that it is an open golf course,
for the whisky enthusiast who also plays
lf, it is a nice alternative for visiting a
tillery. By the way, the whisky business
not alien to the Russells. Clare's great-
andfather was the founder of nearby
agganmore in 1869, the first to make use
the then brand new railroad in this part
Scotland. At the time this small, beautiful
tillery even had its own private siding.
old warehouse still shows the connection
Cragganmore and Ballindalloch Estate.
Time flies in this centuries old setting and
ave to move on. A stone's throw away is
enfarclas, the fiercely independent whisky
tiller, one of the few still in family hands.
day however, I will not visit the Grants,
ce I have an appointment at another
nic distillery.

The importance of wood

The Macallan, in the village of Craigellachie,
is a must-go-to, at least for me. I've been
visiting here since 1990, have made many
friends and even hold my own maturing
cask of The Macallan single malt in one of
the old warehouses. Everyone who is seriously interested in wood maturation and its
intricacies should make an effort to visit this
distillery. He or she won't be disappointed.

The attic of one of the older warehouses
contains a beautiful exhibition concentrated
around oak wood and flavours. One can see
American and European oak, barrels and
casks of various sizes. Instructive panels
explain the differences between the sorts
and what this means for flavours and
aromas. Along one of the walls is a series of
large glass "bulbs", each containing a specific scent, known to be found in whisky,
inviting you to try and find out for yourself
what green apples, chocolate or vanilla
smell like in a concentrated form.

In the vicinity there is a plethora of small
hotels and B&Bs, from Dufftown to Elgin.
I prefer staying in Craigellachie, either in
the eponymous hotel or in the Highlander
Inn across the road. Usually I will look up
my friend Lesley Ann Parker. She represents
various famous Scottish artists and during
the festival some of them reside in her little
gallery across from the Highlander Inn. Ian
Gray displays his paintings and bard Robin
Laing signs his books and CD's. Later he will
perform in the Craigellachie hotel. An evening with Robin is very entertaining and I
join for at least one evening. Afterwards we
end up in the Fiddichside Inn, on the other

Glen Coe (above), Loch Earn (below left) and overlooking Ballindalloch Estate (below right)

side of the village. It is generally assumed to be the smallest pub in Scotland and you need to see it to confirm it.

This year I will not stay the full five days for the festival. I had planned to go up north, to add a new trophy to my ever-growing collection of miniature bottles (I only collect miniatures of distilleries I actually visited). For some reason I'd never been to Dalmore distillery before, passing it many times when heading for Orkney. So I set my sails to Inverness and from there took the A9 up north.

Dalmore is located just outside the village of Alness. It is a very interesting place to visit, as you will see when you enter the still house. The pot stills are among the most unusual ones I have seen in my life. To fully enjoy Dalmore's beautiful setting, you should hire a boat and sail away from the shore, further on up the Cromarty Firth, and then turn. On a sunny day it is a stunning view!

No such thing for me, I have to head on to meet another interesting character, going by the intriguing name Jon Beach. He jointly runs the Fiddler's Inn with his father on the western shore of Loch Ness, in the village of Drumnadrochit. Their bar has been named Whisky Bar of the Year 2013 and I have to check it out myself. Jon does not disappoint me. When I enter the bar he has a special welcome dram ready for me – The Spring-bank Blues Edition – one I exclusively had bottled for The Netherlands two years ago. It shows Jon knows how to acquire special single malts. The walls are adorned with

A view of Dalmore Distillery from the Cromarty Firth

...em and I won't even estimate how many ...fferent ones there are.

The mighty ruins of Urquhart Castle, some ...n minutes south, jut out straight into Loch ...ss. It is an excellent place to view the ...mous loch, actually standing in it, and ...ke pictures in northerly, easterly as well as ...utherly direction.

...e next day, after a delightful full Scottish ...eakfast, I head south and pass Loch Lochy, ...rt William and Loch Linnhe, before making ...e sharp turn into Glen Coe – The Valley of ...eeping. That awesome place that makes ...u humble and realise what a tiny frag- ...ent in the world you are. Glen Coe, where ...e Campbells massacred the MacDonalds ...ter having been hosted by the latter for ...fortnight. But also Glen Coe, a challenge ...hill climbers and walkers, a joy to the eye ...the photographer. In short, a glen that ...veth and taketh.

...I pass the summit of Rannoch Moor and ...ave the glen, heading south. At Crianlarich ...urn left onto the A85, following the river ...ochart, driving through Glen Ogle, where ...ce a fighter jet crashed into the moun- ...ins. At Lochearnhead I turn left and ten ...inutes later I arrive in St. Fillans.

This beautiful village and some of its 300 inhabitants have greatly inspired me when writing The Road, more than a decade ago. Although it is tiny, it boasts three hotels and a dozen B&B's. For those who like hill walking it is an excellent base camp. I walk up the mountain, above the village, and look at the ruins of "old St. Fillans", with a magnificent view of Loch Earn.

For me this is coming home from home. I spend the night at the house of dear friends, talking about things past and present, warming the heart, whilst savou- ring a dram or two, three, warming the stomach at the same time.

The next morning I continue in easterly direction. About ten minutes later I drive through Comrie where, in the centre of the village, I turn right, over the bridge. This tiny road that will eventually bring you to Braco, is somewhat like Scotland in minia- ture and a fine alternative for the main road via Crieff. At least, when you are heading for Edinburgh as I am.

A last night in the capitol of Edinburgh brings me to WHISKI, the award-winning bar on the Royal Mile. After a few pints I walk to Chambers Street to enjoy some fine live music in The Jazz Bar. The following morning it is time to go home, back to the Netherlands.

Hans Offringa is an eclectic, prolific, bilingual author and whisky connoisseur. He has written 20 books on whisky and whiskey, 3 novels and 9 non-fiction books, ranging from golf and champagne to submarines and histori- cal buildings. His numerous articles have been published across the globe in a variety of magazines and newspapers.

Photo: Hans Offringa

Fiddler's Inn - Whisky Bar of the Year 2013

Malt distilleries
of Scotland

O n the following pages,128 Scottish distilleries are described in detail. Most are active (101), while some are mothballed, decommissioned or demolished (27).

Long since closed distilleries from which whisky is very rare or practically unobtainable are described at the end together with six new and upcoming distilleries.

Japanese malt whisky distilleries are covered on pp. 210-217 and distilleries in all other countries (including Ireland and Northern Ireland) on pp. 218-257.

Distilleries that are about to be built or have not left the planning phase yet are treated in the part The Whisky Year That Was (pp. 266-270).

Explanations

Owner:
Name of the owning company, sometimes with the parent company within brackets.

Region/district:
There are four formal malt whisky regions in Scotland today; the Highlands, the Lowlands, Islay and Campbeltown. Where useful we mention a location within a region e.g. Speyside, Orkney, Northern Highlands etc.

Founded:
The year in which the distillery was founded is usually considered as when construction began. The year is rarely the same year in which the distillery was licensed.

Status:
The status of the distillery's production. Active, moth-balled (temporarily closed), closed (but most of the equipment still present), dismantled (the equipment is gone but part of or all of the buildings remain even if they are used for other purposes) and demolished.

Visitor centre:
The letters (vc) after status indicate that the distillery ha a visitor centre. Many distilleries accept visitors despite not having a visitor centre. It can be worthwhile making an enquiry.

Address:
The distillery's address.

Tel:
This is generally to the visitor centre, but can also be to the main office.

website:
The distillery's (or in some cases the owner's) website.

Capacity:
The current production capacity expressed in litres of pure alcohol (LPA).

History:
The chronology focuses on the official history of the distillery and independent bottlings are only listed in exceptional cases. They can be found in the text bodies instead.

Tasting notes:
For all the Scottish distilleries that are not permanently closed we present tasting notes of what, in most cases, can be called the core expression (mainly their best selling 10 or 12 year old).

We have tried to provide notes for official bottlings but in those cases where we have not been able to obtain them, we have turned to independent bottlers.

The whiskies have been tasted by *Gavin D Smith* (GS) and *Dominic Roskrow* (DR), well-known and experienced whisky profiles who, i.a., were assigned to write the 6th edition of Michael Jackson's Malt Whisky Companion.

There are also tasting notes for Japanese malts and these have been written by Nicholas Coldicott.

All notes have been prepared especially for Malt Whisky Yearbook 2014.

Brief distillery glossary

A number of terms occur throughout the distillery directory and are briefly explained here. We can recommend for example *A to Z of Whisky* by Gavin D Smith for more detailed explanations.

Blended malt
A type of whisky where two or more single malts are blended together. The term was introduced a few years ago by SWA to replace the previous term vatted malt. The term is controversial as those who oppose the use of it are of the opinion that it can be confused with 'blended whisky' where malt and grain is blended.

Cask strength
It has become increasingly common in recent times to bottle malt whisky straight from the cask without reducing the alcohol contents to 40, 43 or 46%. A cask strength can be anything between 40 to 65% depending on how long the cask has been matured.

Chill-filtering
A method used for removing unwanted particles and, especially used to prevent the whisky from appearing turbid when water is added. Some producers believe that flavour is affected and therefore avoid chill-filtering.

Continuous still
A type of still used when making grain whisky. The still allows for continuous distillation and re-distillation. Can also be called column still, patent still or Coffey still.

Cooling
The spirit vapours from the stills are cooled into liquids usually by a shell and tube condenser, but an older method (worm tubs) is still in use at some distilleries.

Dark grains
The draff and pot ale from the distillation process is used for making fodder pellets, so-called dark grains.

Drum maltings
The malting method used on all major malting sites today.

Dunnage warehouse
A so called traditional warehouse. The walls are made of stone and the floors of earth. The casks (up to three) are piled on top of each other.

Floor maltings
The traditional method of malting the barley on large wooden floors. This method is only used by a handful of distilleries today.

Lyne arm
The lyne arm leads the spirit vapours from the wash or spirit still to the condenser. The angle of the lyne arm has great significance for reflux and the final character of the whisky.

Mash tun
The procedure after the malt has been milled into grist is called the mashing. The mash tun is usually made of cast iron or stainless steel, but can sometimes be made of wood. The grist is mixed with hot water in order to release the sugars in the barley. The result is the wort which is drawn off through a perforated floor into the underback. The mashed grains in the mash tun are called draff and are then used for making animal feed.

Pagoda roof
A roof shaped as a pagoda which was built over the kiln to lead the smoke away from the drying peat. The pagoda roof was invented by the famous architect Charles Doig. These days pagoda roofs provide mainly aesthetical value as the majority of distilleries usually buy their malt elsewhere.

Peat
A soil layer consisting of plants which have mouldered. Used as fuel in drying the green malts when a more or less peaty whisky is to be produced. In other cases the kiln is usually heated by oil or gas.

PPM
Abbreviation for Parts Per Million. This is used to show the amount of phenols in the peated malt. Peated Islay whisky usually uses malt with 40-60 ppm, which is reduced to 10-20 ppm in the new make spirit.

Purifier
A device used in conjunction with the lyne arm which cools heavier alcohols and lead them back to the still. A handful of distilleries use this technique to make a lighter and cleaner spirit.

Racked warehouse
A modern warehouse with temperature control and built-in shelves. Casks can be stored up to a height of 12.

Reflux
When the heavier vapours in the still are cooled and fall back into the still as liquids. The amount of reflux obtained depends on the shape of the still and the angle of the lyne arm. A distillation process with high reflux gives a lighter, more delicate spirit while a small amount of reflux gives a more robust and flavour-rich whisky.

Saladin box
A method of malting barley which replaced floor maltings. It was invented by the Frenchman Charles Saladin in the late 19th century and was introduced in Scottish distilleries in the 1950s. The only distillery using the method today is Tamdhu.

Shell and tube condenser
The most common method for cooling the spirit vapours. It is a wide copper tube attached to the lyne arm of the still. Cold water is led through a number of smaller copper pipes and cools the surrounding vapours.

Spirit still
The second still, usually a little smaller that the wash still. The low wines are collected in the spirit still for redistilling. Alcohol increases to 64-68% and unwanted impurities disappear. It is only the middle fraction of the distillate (the cut or the heart) which is utilized.

Vatted malt
See blended malt.

Washback
Large tubs of stainless steel or wood in which fermentation takes place. Yeast is added to the worts and the sugars change into alcohol. The result is a wash with an alcoholic content of 6-8% which is then used for distillation.

Wash still
The first and usually largest of the stills. The wash is heated to the boiling point and the alcohol is vaporized. The spirit vapours are cooled in a condenser and the result is low wines with an alcohol content of c 21%.

Worm tub
An older method for cooling the spirit vapours in connection with distilling. This method is still used in approximately ten distilleries. The worm tub consists of a long, spiral-shaped copper pipe which is submerged in water in a large wooden tub, usually outdoors. The spirit vapours are led through the copper spiral so they can condense.

Aberfeldy

Owner:
John Dewar & Sons
(Bacardi)

Region/district:
Southern Highlands

Founded: 1896
Status: Active (vc)
Capacity: 3 500 000 litres

Address: Aberfeldy, Perthshire PH15 2EB

Tel: 01887 822010 (vc)
website: www.dewarswow.com

History:
1896 – John and Tommy Dewar embark on the construction of the distillery, a stone's throw from the old Pitilie distillery which was active from 1825 to 1867. Their objective is to produce a single malt for their blended whisky - White Label.

1898 – Production starts in November.

1917-19 – The distillery closes.

1925 – Distillers Company Limited (DCL) takes over.

1972 – Reconstruction takes place, the floor maltings is closed and the two stills are increased to four.

1991 – The first official bottling is a 15 year old in the Flora & Fauna series.

1998 – Bacardi buys John Dewar & Sons from Diageo at a price of £1,150 million.

2000 – A visitor centre opens and a 25 year old is released.

2005 – A 21 year old is launched in October, replacing the 25 year old.

2009 – Two 18 year old single casks are released.

2010 – A 19 year old single cask, exclusive to France, is released.

2011 – A 14 year old single cask is released.

Aberfeldy 12 year old

GS – Sweet, with honeycombs, breakfast cereal and stewed fruits on the nose. Inviting and warming. Mouth-coating and full-bodied on the palate. Sweet, malty, balanced and elegant. The finish is long and complex, becoming progressively more spicy and drying.

DR – The nose is a mix of fresh and clean barley, honey and a hint of smoke. The honey carries through to the palate and the pleasant finish is shaped by a touch of smoke and peppery spice.

Aberfeldy distillery was built by the Dewar's brothers on the estate belonging to the Earls of Breadalbane and the Campbell Clan. Just 10 kilometres west of Aberfeldy lies what used to be the family castle, Taymouth Castle, one of the most impressive in Scotland. Unfortunately, it was gambled away in the casinos of Monte Carlo in the 1920s, by the 7th Earl of Breadalbane and has since had a checkered history – luxury hotel, hospital for Polish troops during the Second World War and a boarding school for American children. During the last decade several attempts to restore the beauty of the castle and turning it into a luxury hotel have been started but to no avail.

The distillery has been a part of John Dewar & Sons since the start, even though the company itself has changed hands many times, but since 1998 it is being run by Bacardi. Aberfeldy single malt is not just an essential part of the Dewar's blended whisky. The distillery also illustrates its colourful heritage dating back to the Dewar brothers and this heritage is emphasized by Dewar's World of Whiskies, an excellent visitor centre where you can also bottle and buy your own exclusive Aberfeldy malts.

The equipment at Aberfeldy consists of a stainless steel mash tun, eight washbacks made of Siberian larch and two made of stainless steel and four stills. As from 2012 the distillery will be working a 7-day week carrying out 20 mashes per week and producing 2,8 million litres of alcohol. Aberfeldy single malt sells around 300,000 bottles per year. The core range consists of the *12* and *21 year old*. Single casks also appear from time to time. In 2011 it was a *14 year old* single bourbon cask with three years in a sherry hogshead while 2012 saw the release of a *16 year old* finished in a Sassicaia cask. *Aberfeldy Ramble*, a 16 year old single cask exclusive to the Whisky Shop chain, was released in 2013.

12 years old

Dewar´s White Label

Blended Scotch

Starring Aberfeldy Single Malt *in a leading role*
Producer John Dewar & Sons
Director Stephanie Macleod, Master Blender

The cornerstone for what would later become one of the most successful Scotch whisky brands was laid by John Dewar in 1846. After almost 20 years in the business as an employed or partner, John decided it was time to set up his own business as a spirits and wine merchant in Perthshire. He soon started to master the art of blending and left a prosperous legacy to his sons, John Alexander and Tommy, when he died in 1880. They would eventually develop the business to a global enterprise.

The two brothers displayed completely different personality traits, with John Alexander being the analytical, responsible and more sensible, while the younger Tommy was more enigmatic but showing great social skills. In 1891, the firm was renamed John Dewar & Sons and it was that same year they received a very special order from a country that, in time, would become their largest market – the USA. The order was sent by the famous industrialist, Andrew Carnegie, and the whisky should be sent to President Benjamin Harrison. This ignited Tommy´s interest for export and the next year he embarked on his first of two world tours promoting Dewar´s whisky to all corners of the world. On the home market, John Alexander managed to receive a Royal Warrant from Queen Victoria, the first blended whisky to achieve one.

The demand was on the increase and the brothers had now started looking for a distillery of their own. Instead of buying one, they decided to build and so, Aberfeldy was completed in 1898. One year later, during the turbulent Pattison crash when many whisky companies went bankrupt, they launched White Label which remains their core expression even to this day. The company grew with offices being opened in Sydney, Calcutta and Johannesburg and Tommy had excelled in new ways of promoting the whisky. He was the first to produce a filmed advert and in 1911 he constructed a lit up advertising display in London, using 1,400 light bulbs and six miles of electric cable. But rougher times were to follow with the advent of the first World War which was followed by the Prohibition in the USA. This was a time for consolidation and mergers and Dewar´s and Buchanan joined forces. A few years later the company teamed up with John Walker & Sons and formed Distillers Company Ltd which formed the nucleus of today´s giant, Diageo.

The two brothers died within months of each other in 1929-1930, but it was still a family member, their nephew John Arthur Dewar, who was running the operations. Together with the company´s US agent, Joseph P Kennedy (father of the president to be), he saw Prohibition being repealed and the American market virtually exploding. Soon it became the best-selling Scotch in America which it still is to this day.

In 1998, Dewar´s became a part of the Bacardi group and in 2012 it was the 7th biggest Scotch in the world with 34 million bottles being sold. The big seller in the range is *White Label* with no age statement. In 2000, *12 year old Special Reserve* was released (replacing the Ancestor from the 1950s) and it was followed by the *18 year old Founder´s Reserve* and in 2005 by the deluxe blend *Dewar´s Signature*. Recent additions to the range are *Dewar´s Legacy* and *Dewar House Experimental Batch*, a limited edition featuring different finishes.

Fruity aromas of apples and pears, leather, heather honey and a hint of smoke. On the palate toffee and vanilla develops together with more honey sweetness, malted barley and oak.

Aberlour

Owner:
Chivas Brothers Ltd
(Pernod Ricard)

Region/district:
Speyside

Founded: **Status:** **Capacity:**
1826 Active (vc) 3 800 000 litres

Address: Aberlour, Banffshire AB38 9PJ

Tel: **website:**
01340 881249 www.aberlour.com

History:
1826 – James Gordon and Peter Weir found the first Aberlour Distillery.

1827 – Peter Weir withdraws and James Gordon continues alone.

1879 – A fire devastates most of the distillery. The local banker James Fleming constructs a new distillery upstream the Spey river.

1892 – The distillery is sold to Robert Thorne & Sons Ltd who expands it.

1898 – Another fire rages and almost totally destroys the distillery. The architect Charles Doig is called in to design the new facilities.

1921 – Robert Thorne & Sons Ltd sells Aberlour to a brewery, W. H. Holt & Sons.

1945 – S. Campbell & Sons Ltd buys the distillery.

1962 – Aberlour terminates floor malting.

1973 – Number of stills are increased from two to four.

1975 – Pernod Ricard buys Campbell Distilleries.

2000 – Aberlour a'bunadh is launched. A limited 30 year old cask strength is released.

2001 – Pernod Ricard buys Chivas Brothers and merges Chivas Brothers and Campbell Distilleries under the brand Chivas Brothers.

2002 – A new, modernized visitor centre is inaugurated in August.

2008 – The 18 year old is also introduced outside France.

2013 – Aberlour 2001 White Oak is released.

Sales of Aberlour single malt increased in 2012 by 6% and reached 2,8 million bottles and the brand thereby defended its position as the seventh most sold single malt in the world. The increase was impressive if you take into account that exports of Scotch to France, where Aberlour is the most sold single malt, decreased by 25% under 2012. Part of the reason for that was a 15% tax raise and many importers had been stocking up towards the end of 2011, but fact remains that the Scotch volumes in France have fallen to levels last seen in 2004.

The distillery is equipped with one 12 tonnes semi-lauter mash tun, six stainless steel washbacks (painted white) and two pairs of stills. There are five warehouses on site (three racked and two dunnage) but only two racked, holding a total of 27,000 casks, are used for maturation. About half of the production is used for single malts.

The packaging of the whole range was upgraded in 2010 to achieve a more consistent look. The core range of Aberlour includes *10, 12, 16* and *18 year old* – all of them matured in a combination of ex-bourbon and ex-sherry casks. Another core expression is *Aberlour a'bunadh* which is based entirely on ex-Oloroso casks. It is always bottled at cask strength and up to 46 different batches have been released by August 2013. In France, a *10 year old Sherry Cask Finish* and the *15 year old Select Cask Reserve* (previously named Cuvée Marie d'Ecosse) are available. Two 'exclusives' are available for the duty free market – a *12 year old* sherry matured and a *15 year old* Double Cask matured. A new version of the *12 year old*, this time non chill-filtered, was introduced to the French market at the beginning of 2012 and was later also launched in other markets. Spring 2013 saw the release of a rather unusual expression – *Aberlour 2001 White Oak*. Not only was it a vintage but it has been matured solely in American white oak.

Aberlour 12 year old

GS – The nose offers brown sugar, honey and sherry, with a hint of grapefruit citrus. The palate is sweet, with buttery caramel, maple syrup and eating apples. Liquorice, peppery oak and mild smoke in the finish.

DR – The nose combines horse chestnut casing then sweet melon and fresh spearmint, the taste is beautifully fresh and clean, with mint and gentle fruit.

12 years old

Allt-a-Bhainne

wner:
hivas Brothers Ltd
Pernod Ricard)

Region/district:
Speyside

ounded: Status:
975 Active

Capacity:
4 000 000 litres

ddress: Glenrinnes, Dufftown,
anffshire AB55 4DB

el:
1542 783200

website:
-

istory:
975 – The distillery is founded by Chivas
rothers, a subsidiary of Seagrams, in order to
ecure malt whisky for its blended whiskies.
he total cost amounts to £2.7 million.

989 – Production has doubled.

001 – Pernod Ricard takes over Chivas
rothers from Seagrams.

002 – Mothballed in October.

005 – Production restarts in May.

The decision to build Allt-a-Bhainne and two years earlier
its sister distillery, Braeval, was made by Edgar Bronfman
Sr – the second generation of one of Canada's wealthiest
and most powerful families. His father, the legendary Sam
Bronfman, had made a fortune in the spirits business
during prohibition and bought the spirits producer Seagram's in 1928. Sam realised that as soon as the prohibition
would be repealed, the demand for whisky of a better
quality would rise. He was therefore determined to secure
his own production facilities in Scotland and bought Chivas
Brothers in 1949 and the Strathisla distillery the year thereafter. Sam died in 1971 and his son, Edgar Sr., realised that
Seagram's had to continue building stocks of Scotch whisky
for their blends. A decision was made to quickly build two
distilleries, Braeval and Allt-a-Bhainne.

Deerstalker 12 year old

S – Cereal and toffee on the sherbety nose,
ith mildly metallic notes. The palate is light,
vith fresh fruits. Medium length and warming
n the finish.

R – Autumn fields and damp hay on the
ose, a richer, sweeter earth and heathery
aste on the palate and a gentle rounded
nish.

The latter soon became associated with
one of Seagram's biggest sellers, 100
Pipers blended Scotch. Even if recent years
have seen a decline in sales figures, the
brand still sells 20 million bottles per year.
Allt-a-Bhainne, situated in the beautiful
area in the Cromdale Hills between Tomintoul and Dufftown, is equipped with a
traditional 9 tonnes mash tun with rakes
and ploughs. The rest of the equipment consists of eight stainless steel
washbacks and two pairs of stills. In
order to make the distillery more energy efficient, thermal compressors
were installed in 2011. The distillery
is a busy place running 7 days a week
with 25 mashes resulting in 4 million
litres of alcohol per year. Chivas
Brothers has no distillery on Islay so,
to cover their need of peated whisky
for their blends, they need to resort
to other solutions. During the last
few years 50% of the production at
Allt-a-Bhainne has therefore been
peated spirit with a phenol content
in the malted barley of 10ppm.
There are no official bottlings of Allt-
a-Bhainne single malt but is has been
used for bottlings of Deerstalker
from time to time.

Deerstalker 12 year old

Ardbeg

Owner:
The Glenmorangie Co
(Moët Hennessy)

Region/district:
Islay

Founded: **Status:** **Capacity:**
1815   Active (vc) 1 300 000 litres

Address: Port Ellen, Islay, Argyll PA42 7EA

Tel: **website:**
01496 302244 (vc)   www.ardbeg.com

History:

1794 – First record of a distillery at Ardbeg. It was founded by Alexander Stewart.

1798 – The MacDougalls, later to become licensees of Ardbeg, are active on the site through Duncan MacDougall.

1815 – The current distillery is founded by John MacDougall, son of Duncan MacDougall.

1853 – Alexander MacDougall, John's son, dies and sisters Margaret and Flora MacDougall, assisted by Colin Hay, continue the running of the distillery. Colin Hay takes over the licence when the sisters die.

1888 – Colin Elliot Hay and Alexander Wilson Gray Buchanan renew their license.

1900 – Colin Hay's son takes over the license.

1959 – Ardbeg Distillery Ltd is founded.

1973 – Hiram Walker and Distillers Company Ltd jointly purchase the distillery for £300,000 through Ardbeg Distillery Trust.

1974 – Widely considered as the last vintage of 'old, peaty' Ardbeg. Malt which has not been produced in the distillery's own maltings is used in increasingly larger shares after this year.

1977 – Hiram Walker assumes single control of the distillery. Ardbeg closes its maltings.

1979 – Kildalton, a less peated malt, is produced over a number of years.

1981 – The distillery closes in March.

1987 – Allied Lyons takes over Hiram Walker and thereby Ardbeg.

Only one Ardbeg core bottling holds an age statement and most of last year's limited expressions are also released without age, but one can assume that most of the whisky was distilled from 1997 and onwards, when the current owners bought the distillery. The distillery was closed from 1981-1989 and production from 1989-1997 was intermittent. Although casks from the 1960s, the 1970s and also from the 1990s were included in the purchase, both the quality and availability was inconsistent. For a couple of years after the take-over, Glenmorangie bought as many casks of Ardbeg as they could, for instance, from Diageo and William Grants, but the vast majority of stock was then used in the "first" Ardbeg 10 year old released in 2000, before the current Ardbeg Ten was introduced in 2008.

The distillery is equipped with a stainless steel semilauter mash tun, six washbacks made of Oregon pine with a fermentation time of 55 hours and one pair of stills. A purifier is connected to the spirit still to help create the special fruity character of the spirit. The heavily peated Ardbeg enjoys a cult status among the whisky aficionados around the world and it is now the fourth best selling Islay malt. Over the last five years sales of Ardbeg single malt has increased by almost 50% to nearly 700,000 bottles. To cope with future demand, the distillery has, as from 2013, gone from running 5 days per week to 24/7 production and this will increase capacity to 1,3 million litres of alcohol.

The core range consists of the *10 year old, Uiegedail* (influenced by sherry casks), *Blasda* (lightly peated, just 8ppm), *Corryvreckan* (matured in a mix of ex-bourbon American oak and French new oak) and *Supernova* (the peatiest release ever from Ardbeg with a phenol level well in excess of 100ppm). Recent limited releases have included *Rollercoaster*, a vatting of one cask from each year between 1997 and 2006, *Alligator*, where some of the whisky had been matured in heavily charred barrels and *Galileo*, a 12 year old with a combination of different casks, all filled in 1999. The core element in the whisky came from Marsala casks. Ardbeg releases a special bottling every year which pertains to the Islay Festival. In 2012 it was somewhat special as the owners had introduced an Ardbeg Day to be held every year around 1st of June. That year's Feis Ile bottling was also named *Ardbeg Day* and was a blend of two vintages matured in ex-bourbon casks and then finished for six months in sherry casks. For 2013 the special bottling was called *Ardbog*, a whisky matured for at least 10 years in a combination of ex-bourbon barrels and Manzanilla sherry butts

History (continued):

1989 – Production is restored. All malt is taken from Port Ellen.

1996 – The distillery closes in July and Allied Distillers decides to put it up for sale.

1997 – Glenmorangie plc buys the distillery for £7 million (whereof £5.5 million is for whisky in storage). On stream from 25th June. Ardbeg 17 years old and Provenance are launched

1998 – A new visitor centre opens.

2000 – Ardbeg 10 years is introduced. The Ardbeg Committee is launched and has 30 000 members after a few years.

2001 – Lord of the Isles 25 years and Ardbeg 1977 are launched.

2002 – Ardbeg Committee Reserve and Ardbeg 1974 are launched.

2003 – Uigeadail is launched.

2004 – Very Young Ardbeg (6 years) and a limited edition of Ardbeg Kildalton (1300 bottles) are launched. The latter is an un-peated cask strength from 1980.

2005 – Serendipity is launched.

2006 – Ardbeg 1965 and Still Young are launched. Distillery Manager Stuart Thomson leaves Ardbeg after nine years. Almost There (9 years old) and Airigh Nam Beist are released.

2007 – Ardbeg Mor, a 10 year old in 4.5 litre bottles is released.

2008 – The new 10 year old, Corryvreckan, Rennaissance, Blasda and Mor II are released.

2009 – Supernova is released, the peatiest expression from Ardbeg ever.

2010 – Rollercoaster and Supernova 2010 are released.

2011 – Ardbeg Alligator is released.

2012 – Ardbeg Day and Galileo are released.

2013 – Ardbog is released.

Ardbeg 10 year old

GS – Quite sweet on the nose, with soft peat, carbolic soap and Arbroath smokies. Burning peats and dried fruit, followed by sweeter notes of malt and a touch of liquorice in the mouth. Extremely long and smoky in the finish, with a fine balance of cereal sweetness and dry peat notes.

DR – Intense smoke and tar on the nose but with some distinctive sweet lemon notes, a mouth-coating palate with honeyed but firey peat, completely balanced and impressive, and a long smoke tail at the finish.

Uigeadail

Supernova

Ardbog

10 years old

Corryvreckan

Ardmore

Owner:
Beam Inc.

Region/district:
Highland

Founded: 1898
Status: Active
Capacity: 5 400 000 litres

Address: Kennethmont, Aberdeenshire AB54 4NH

Tel: 01464 831213
website: www.ardmorewhisky.com

History:
1898 – Adam Teacher, son of William Teacher, starts the construction of Ardmore Distillery which eventually becomes William Teacher & Sons´ first distillery. Adam Teacher passes away before it is completed.

1955 – Stills are increased from two to four.

1973 – A visitor centre is constructed.

1974 – Another four stills are added, increasing the total to eight.

1976 – Allied Breweries takes over William Teacher & Sons and thereby also Ardmore. The own maltings (Saladin box) is terminated.

1999 – A 12 year old is released to commemorate the distillery's 100th anniversary. A 21 year old is launched in a limited edition.

2002 – Ardmore is one of the last distilleries to abandon direct heating (by coal) of the stills in favour of indirect heating through steam.

2005 – Jim Beam Brands becomes new owner when it takes over some 20 spirits and wine brands from Allied Domecq for five billion dollars.

2007 – Ardmore Traditional Cask is launched.

2008 – A 25 and a 30 year old are launched.

Ardmore Traditional

GS – A nose of smoked haddock and butter, plus sweet, fruity malt and spices. Sweet and initially creamy on the palate, spices, peat smoke, tobacco and vanilla emerge and blend together. The finish is long and mellow.

DR – Unique and remarkable mix of burnt meat savouriness on the nose, and a delicatessen of flavours on the palate, smoked vanilla, burnt fruit and a distinctive and highly addictive sweet and savoury mix towards the peated finish.

It took many years before Ardmore became known for its single malt. Founded by the Teacher family the distillery was constructed to supply malt whisky for the Teacher´s blend. During the Allied ownership (1975-2005) Teacher´s was still in the focus and no attempts were made to launch a single malt Ardmore. It was not before 2007, when Jim Beam had taken over ownership, that the current core bottling, Traditional, was launched. With the exception of a few limited, older expressions nothing more happened and Traditional is still the only widely available, official bottling. Normally we associate peated whisky with Islay and some of the other islands. Many years ago, whisky from Speyside was also more or less peated but the only distillery in the region that has consistently held on to this tradition over the years, is Ardmore. The malted barley used at the distillery has a phenol specification of 12-14 ppm but there is also an unpeated version being produced called Ardlair, which is used by other companies as a blending malt. For 2013 the share of Ardlair will equate to about 40% of the total production.

Ten years ago, Ardmore was one of the last distilleries in Scotland to abandon the practice of directly firing the stills using coal. Such a dramatic change can easily change the character of the whisky and the owners had to put in a lot of work changing other parameters, such as the cut points of the spirit distillation, in order to maintain the style.

The distillery is equipped with a large (12,5 tonnes) cast iron mash tun, 14 Douglas fir washbacks and four pairs of stills equipped with sub-coolers to give more copper contact. At the moment, Ardmore is doing 25 mashes per week resulting in 5,4 million litres.

The core expression is the un-chill filtered *Traditional* with no age statement, but is generally made up using a range of ex-bourbon casks from six to thirteen years old. After vatting, it is filled into quarter casks and matured for another year before being bottled. In 2008 a *25 year old* was launched for the UK and duty free, while a *30 year old* was released for the American market.

Ardmore Traditional Cask

Teacher´s Highland Cream

Blended Scotch

Starring   Ardmore Single Malt *in a leading role*
Producer   William Teacher & Sons
Director   Ron Welsh, Master Blender

William Teacher had a rough start in life. Before his first birthday, his father who was a sailor was lost at sea and by the age of seven he started working in a spinning-mill near Glasgow. At the age of 19, he was employed by a small grocer and managed to get the shop a licence to sell wines and spirits. He married the owner´s daughter and opened up a second shop. During the 1850s he expanded the business, opening up a number of Teacher´s Dram Shops and eventually became the largest pub owner in Glasgow. He was later joined by his sons, Adam and William, who both showed an interest in blending whisky. Already in 1863, Teacher´s blended whisky was sold but the brand name Teacher´s Highland Cream was not registered until 1884.

By the end of 1890, several of the big blending companies decided to build their own distilleries, like Dewar's (Aberfeldy), Buchanan (Glentauchers) and W & A Gilbey (Knockando). Teacher´s was no exception and in 1898 they founded Ardmore distillery which, even today, is of vital importance to the blend. The brand had become a success in the home market and at the beginning of the 1900s, the whisky was exported to several countries including America.

Until 1913 all whisky bottles were sealed with a traditional wine cork for which you needed a corkscrew to open it. That year Dewar´s presented what they called the "self-opening bottle" which basically meant a cork with a wooden cap – the same way in which whisky bottles of today are closed. The impact was tremendous and the innovation was advertised with the slogan: "Bury the Corkscrew".

The demand for Teacher´s had increased over the years and in 1960 the company bought Glendronach distillery. Two years

later they built a blending and bottling plant in Glasgow and in 1972, the sales in the UK alone had reached 12 million bottles for the first time. The company had managed to stay as an independent, family-owned company through the 1920s when several of the big blending companies merged to form Distillers Company. In 1976 however, the era of the Teacher´s family (at least as owners) came to an end when the company was sold to Allied Breweries.

Allied was bought in a joint venture between Pernod Ricard and Fortune Brands (Jim Beam) in 2005 and Teacher´s among others, fell under the auspices of Jim Beam. At that time, Teacher´s was the 10th biggest Scotch in the world a position which they still hold. In 2012, 26 million bottles were sold mainly in the UK, where it is the 5th best selling Scotch, and in India and Brazil. Teacher´s has been the market leader in India for a decade but independent analysts say that it lost the position to 100 Pipers in 2012, while the company claims they are still in the lead.

The core expression is *Teacher´s Highland Cream* without age statement. In 1997, the 12 year old *Teacher´s 50* was launched in India to commemorate 50 years of independence

for the country. *Teacher´s Origin* with a higher share of malt whisky was released in 2010 and it was followed in 2012 by *Teacher´s 25 year old* and also by *Teacher´s Single Malt* which is a bottling of Ardmore malt whisky.

A full-bodied blend where smoke mixes with malted barley, leather and butterscotch. The peat is present but subtle on the palate together with toffee, clove, cinnamon and liquorice.

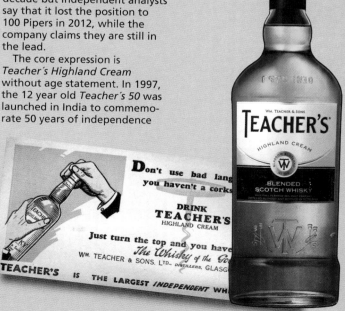

Arran

Owner:
Isle of Arran Distillers

Region/district:
Islands (Arran)

Founded: **Status:**
1993 Active (vc)

Capacity:
750 000 litres

Address: Lochranza, Isle of Arran KA27 8HJ

Tel:
01770 830264

website:
www.arranwhisky.com

History:
1993 – Harold Currie founds the distillery.

1995 – Production starts in full on 17th August.

1997 – A visitor centre is opened by the Queen.

1998 – The first release is a 3 year old.

1999 – The Arran 4 years old is released.

2002 – Single Cask 1995 is launched.

2003 – Single Cask 1997, non-chill filtered and Calvados finish is launched.

2004 – Cognac finish, Marsala finish, Port finish and Arran First Distillation 1995 are launched.

2005 – Arran 1996 and two finishes, Ch. Margaux and Grand Cru Champagne, are launched.

2006 – After an unofficial launch in 2005, Arran 10 years old is released as well as a couple of new wood finishes.

2007 – Four new wood finishes and Gordon's Dram are released.

2008 – The first 12 year old is released as well as four new wood finishes.

2009 – Peated single casks, two wood finishes and 1996 Vintage are released.

2010 – A 14 year old, Rowan Tree, three cask finishes and Machrie Moor (peated) are released.

2011 – The Westie, Sleeping Warrior and a 12 year old cask strength are released.

2012 – The Eagle and The Devil's Punch Bowl are released.

2013 – A 16 year old and a new edition of Machrie Moor and released.

Arran 14 year old

GS – Very fragrant and perfumed on the nose, with peaches, brandy and ginger snaps. Smooth and creamy on the palate, with spicy summer fruits, apricots and nuts. The lingering finish is nutty and slowly drying.

DR – The precocious ten year old becomes a testy teenager. If the 12 year old was a diversion this is right on track - with sweet, fresh and zesty nose, and rich creamy and rounded palate defined by vanilla, lemon and cream soda. The finish is long and full.

It is impossible not to be impressed with the distillery's location on the northern part of the Island of Arran, just outside the beautiful village of Lochranza and with a pair of Golden Eagles breeding on the mountain behind. No wonder the distillery is a popular destination harbouring 60,000 visitors yearly. The whisky itself has also reached great success given the relatively short existence of the distillery. For 2012 the company could show a turnover of £3,6 million and a handsome profit of £348,000.

The distillery is equipped with a semi-lauter mash tun, five Oregon pine washbacks and two stills. There are three warehouses and planning permission has been sought for one more palletized warehouse. The total production capacity is 750,000 litres and the plan for 2013 is to do 400,000 litres. For many years now, the distillery has been producing a share of peated spirit every year. For 2013 it will be 40,000 litres from malt peated to 20ppm which will be used for future releases of Machrie Moor and another 20,000 litres of heavily peated spirit (50ppm).

The core range consists of *The Arran Malt Original* without age statement, *10, 12 cask strength* and *14 years old* and finally *Robert Burns Malt*. Limited releases for 2013 include a *16 year old* which will be followed by a 17 year old in 2014 and, finally, an 18 year old in 2015 which will become a permanent part of the range. In June 2013, the second chapter of *The Devil's Punch Bowl*, a vatting of some of the oldest casks from the distillery appeared and September saw the release of the 4th edition of the peated *Machrie Moor*, this time slightly more peated (20ppm). An unusual limited expression from late 2012 was the 8 year old *Arran Malt Orkney Bere*. It was made from bere, the oldest cultivated barley in Scotland and used for whisky production until the 20th century.

Finally, the single malt range is completed with three different cask finishes – *Amarone, Port* and *Sauternes*. The distillery also produces two blends (*Robert Burns* and *Lochranza*) and a cream liqueur called *Arran Gold*.

14 years old

Auchentoshan

Owner:
Morrison Bowmore
(Suntory)

Region/district:
Lowlands

Founded: 1823

Status: Active (vc)

Capacity: 1 750 000 litres

Address: Dalmuir, Clydebank, Glasgow G81 4SJ

Tel: 01389 878561

website: www.auchentoshan.com

History:

1800 – First mention of the distillery Duntocher, which may be identical to Auchentoshan.

1823 – An official license is obtained by the owner, Mr. Thorne.

1903 – The distillery is purchased by John Maclachlan.

1941 – The distillery is severely damaged by a German bomb raid.

1960 – Maclachlans Ltd is purchased by the brewery J. & R. Tennant Brewers.

1969 – Auchentoshan is bought by Eadie Cairns Ltd who starts major modernizations.

1984 – Stanley P. Morrison, eventually becoming Morrison Bowmore, becomes new owner.

1994 – Suntory buys Morrison Bowmore.

2002 – Auchentoshan Three Wood is launched.

2004 – More than a £1 million is spent on a new, refurbished visitor centre. The oldest Auchentoshan ever, 42 years, is released.

2006 – Auchentoshan 18 year old is released.

2007 – A 40 year old and a 1976 30 year old are released.

2008 – New packaging as well as new expressions - Classic, 18 year old and 1988.

2010 – Two vintages, 1977 and 1998, are released.

2011 – Two vintages, 1975 and 1999, and Valinch are released.

2012 – Six new expressions are launched for the Duty Free market.

2013 – Virgin Oak is released.

The Duty Free market is very much in the focus for Auchentoshan at the moment. Six new bottlings were released last year and one third of the sales are in that segment. The goal is to get into the top 10 of single malts in Global Travel Retail within a couple of years. Overall sales have increased significantly over the last few years and more than 800,000 bottles were sold in 2012 – an increase of 30% compared to the previous year.

Auchentoshan is the only distillery in Scotland doing 100% triple distillation. This procedure means, among other things, having a very narrow spirit cut. They start collecting the middle cut at 82% and stop at 80%, long before any other distillery starts collecting. The equipment consists of a semilauter mash tun, seven Oregon pine washbacks and three stills. In 2013, the plan is to do 1,7 million litres of alcohol – the highest level for the last 20 years and more or less its maximum capacity.

In recent years the process of turning by-products from the distillation into useful products, has been very much focused on anaerobic digestion where organic material is converted by microorganisms in the absence of air. Plants using this technique can, for example, be found at Bruichladdich, Dailuaine and Roseisle. Come the end of 2012, the owners of Auchentoshan followed suit when they filed a planning application with the local council to build a plant where biogas would be used to provide heat and power for the distillery.

The core range consists of *Classic, 12 years, Three Wood, 18 years* and *21 years*. Six new expressions for the duty free market were released in 2012; *Springwood, Heartwood, Cooper's Reserve, Silveroak, Solera* and *Vintage 1974*. In 2013, a *Vintage 1975* was added to the range. Another new expression was released in August 2013, *Auchentoshan Virgin Oak*. As the name indicates, the whisky has been matured in charred oak casks that have held neither bourbon nor sherry before.

12 years old

Auchentoshan 12 year old

GS – The nose features fruit & nut chocolate, cinnamon and oak. Smooth and sweet in the mouth, with citrus fruits and cloves. Drying gently in a gingery finish.

DR – Toffee, rose water and Milk Chocolate Crisp on the nose, grape and crisp apple on the palate before a spicy fruity interplay in a lengthy finish.

Auchroisk

Owner: Diageo

Region/district: Speyside

Founded: 1974

Status: Active

Capacity: 5 900 000 litres

Address: Mulben, Banffshire AB55 6XS

Tel: 01542 885000

website: www.malts.com

History:
1972 – Building of the distillery commences by Justerini & Brooks (which, together with W. A. Gilbey, make up the group IDV) in order to produce blending whisky. In February the same year IDV is purchased by the brewery Watney Mann which, in July, merges into Grand Metropolitan.

1974 – The distillery is completed and, despite the intention of producing malt for blending, the first year's production is sold 12 years later as single malt thanks to the high quality.

1986 – The first whisky is marketed under the name Singleton.

1997 – Grand Metropolitan and Guinness merge into the conglomerate Diageo. Simultaneously, the subsidiaries United Distillers (to Guinness) and International Distillers & Vintners (to Grand Metropolitan) form the new company United Distillers & Vintners (UDV).

2001 – The name Singleton is abandoned and the whisky is now marketed under the name of Auchroisk in the Flora & Fauna series.

2003 – Apart from the 10 year old in the Flora & Fauna series, a 28 year old from 1974, the distillery's first year, is launched in the Rare Malt series.

2010 – A Manager's Choice single cask and a limited 20 year old are released.

2012 – A 30 year old from 1982 is released.

A relatively unknown single malt brand today, Auchroisk has seen better days. It was launched in 1986 under the name Singleton since the Scottish name was deemed unpronounceable by the customers. This lasted until 2000 when the whisky was launched in the Flora & Fauna series as a 10 year old under the distillery name and the name Singleton was later used for three other Diageo single malts – from Glen Ord, Glendullan and Dufftown.

Apart from producing malt whisky for Diageo blends, Auchroisk has another important role to play in the company. The site is the location for maturing whiskies from many other Diageo distilleries and also for part of the blending. In order to achieve this there are ten, huge racked warehouses with the capacity of storing 250,000 casks. And the buck doesn't stop there – a planning application has been submitted for another four, very large warehouses to be built just east of the existing ones which may double the warehousing capacity.

Auchroisk distillery is equipped with a 12 tonnes stainless steel semilauter mash tun, eight stainless steel washbacks and four pairs of stills. The character of Auchroisk new-make used to be nutty but changed radically in 2011/2012 to become green and grassy, only to become nutty again. Although this is something that a producer would never do with a distillery marketed mainly as a single malt, it is not uncommon with whiskies destined to become a part of a blend. It all depends on which type the producer requires in the interim. A nutty character means shorter fermentation time (53 hours) and consequently more whisky can be produced. For 2013, the target is 5,9 million litres.

Apart from producing whisky, mainly for the J&B blend, Auchroisk is also a backup for production of Gordon's gin, should any problems occur at the Cameronbridge distillery.

The core range from Auchroisk is simply the *10 year old Flora & Fauna* bottling. Recent limited bottlings include a *20 year old* from 1990 and a *30 year old*, both launched as a part of the Special Releases.

Auchroisk 10 year old

GS – Malt and spice on the light nose, with developing nuts and floral notes. Quite voluptuous on the palate, with fresh fruit and milk chocolate. Raisins in the finish.

DR – Young and zesty and citrusy on the nose, warming tangerine and citrus fruits and a touch of salt on the palate, medium long malty finish.

30 years old

Aultmore

Owner:
John Dewar & Sons
(Bacardi)

Region/district:
Speyside

Founded: 1896
Status: Active
Capacity: 3 030 000 litres

Address: Keith, Banffshire AB55 6QY

Tel: 01542 881800
website: -

History:

1896 – Alexander Edward, owner of Benrinnes and co-founder of Craigellachie Distillery, builds Aultmore.

1897 – Production starts.

1898 – Production is doubled; the company Oban & Aultmore Glenlivet Distilleries Ltd manages Aultmore.

1923 – Alexander Edward sells Aultmore for £20,000 to John Dewar & Sons.

1925 – Dewar's becomes part of Distillers Company Limited (DCL).

1930 – The administration is transferred to Scottish Malt Distillers (SMD).

1971 – The stills are increased from two to four.

1991 – UDV launches a 12-year old Aultmore in the Flora & Fauna series.

1996 – A 21 year old cask strength is marketed as a Rare Malt.

1998 – Diageo sells Dewar's and Bombay Gin to Bacardi for £1,150 million.

2004 – A new official bottling is launched (12 years old).

Aultmore 12 year old

GS – Gentle spice and fudge notes on the fragrant nose. Fresh fruits and restrained vanilla in the mouth. Nutty and drying in a medium-length finish.

DR – Orange blossom and flowers on the nose, lemon and lime Starburst on the palate, with late sherbet spicy and drying and more-ish finish. Altogether, zesty and very pleasant.

The primary task for Aultmore distillery is to produce malt whisky for the blended whisky Dewar's White Label. The brand has been the number one Scotch in the USA since 1980 when it took over the lead from J&B Rare. The success on the American market began in 1933 when Prohibition was repealed and the introduction almost resembled a well orchestrated military manoeuvre. Dewar's agent in the USA, Joseph P Kennedy (the father of former President John Kennedy) had, through his contacts, received notice in advance regarding when the Prohibition would be repealed. A vast number of boats which were anchored just off the New York coast were filled with cases of Dewar's and the moment the news broke, the boats were ordered to enter the harbour with their cargo.

Aultmore distillery was built as early as 1896 but when you travel the A96 and look to your left, a mile before you reach Keith, you see a very modern, shining, white, complex of buildings. The distillery was completely rebuilt at the beginning of the 1970s and nothing is left of the old buildings.

Since 2008 production has been running seven days a week which, for 2013, means 16 mashes per week and 2,9 million litres of alcohol in the year. A 10 tonne Steinecker full lauter mash tun, six washbacks made of larch with a fermentation time of 56 hours and two pairs of stills are operated. The stillhouse control system was modernised in 2008. All the warehouses were demolished in 1996; in fact, Dewar's no longer has any maturation capacity at any of its distilleries. Aultmore was one of the first distilleries to build a dark grains plant in order to process pot ale and draff into cattle feed. It became operational in 1977 but closed its doors again in 1985. It then reopened in 1989 but was finally taken out of production in 1993.

Most of the output is used in Dewar's blended whiskies, but a *12 year old* official bottling has been for sale since 2004.

12 years old

Balblair

Owner:
Inver House Distillers
(Thai Beverages plc)

Region/district:
Northern Highlands

Founded: **Status:** **Capacity:**
1790 Active (vc) 1 800 000 litres

Address: Edderton, Tain, Ross-shire IV19 1LB

Tel: **website:**
01862 821273 www.balblair.com

History:
1790 – The distillery is founded by John Ross.

1836 – John Ross dies and his son Andrew Ross takes over with the help of his sons.

1872 – New buildings replace the old.

1873 – Andrew Ross dies and his son James takes over.

1894 – Balnagowan Estate signs a new lease for 60 years with Alexander Cowan. He builds a new distillery, a few kilometres from the old.

1911 – Cowan is forced to cease payments and the distillery closes.

1941 – Balnagowan Estate goes bankrupt and the distillery is put up for sale.

1948 – The lawyer Robert Cumming from Keith buys Balblair for £48,000.

1949 – Production restarts.

1970 – Cumming sells Balblair to Hiram Walker.

1988 – Allied Distillers becomes the new owner through the merger between Hiram Walker and Allied Vintners.

1996 – Allied Domecq sells the distillery to Inver House Distillers.

2000 – Balblair Elements and the first version of Balblair 33 years are launched.

2001 – Thai company Pacific Spirits (part of the Great Oriole Group) takes over Inver House.

2004 – Balblair 38 years is launched.

2005 – 12 year old Peaty Cask, 1979 (26 years) and 1970 (35 years) are launched.

2006 – International Beverage Holdings acquires Pacific Spirits UK.

2007 – Three new vintages replace the entire former range.

2008 – Vintage 1975 and 1965 are released.

2009 – Vintage 1991 and 1990 are released.

2010 – Vintage 1978 and 2000 are released.

2011 – Vintage 1995 and 1993 are released.

2012 – Vintage 1975, 2001 and 2002 are released. A visitor centre is opened.

2013 – Vintage 1983, 1990 and 2003 are released.

From being one of those brands that rarely came to people´s minds when asked to name their favourite whisky, Balblair has stepped out of anonymity in the last couple of years. To further confirm this, a very elegant and contemporary visitor centre and shop were inaugurated in late 2011.

The distillery is equipped with a stainless steel mash tun, six Oregon pine washbacks and one pair of stills. There is actually a third still but it has not been used since 1969. The spirit is matured in eight dunnage warehouses with a capacity of 26,000 casks. The production has increased to 21 mashes per week which means that they have now reached their capacity of 1,8 million litres of alcohol. In 2011 and 2012, part of the production was heavily peated spirit with a phenol specification of 52ppm in the barley. In 2013, however, there will be no peated production.

Since the transition to vintages six years ago, sales have increased slowly but surely and during 2012, 75,000 bottles were sold. Apart from being released as a brand of its own, Balblair malt plays an important part in the owner´s Hankey Bannister blend. It sold 3 million bottles in 2012 and the range was expanded in summer 2013 with the release of Hankey Bannister Heritage Blend, an attempt to recreate the more peated versions from the 1920s.

The current Balblair core range consists of four vintages – 1975, 1989, 1997 and 2002 but three of them will be replaced by new expressions during autumn 2013; 1983 (replacing the 1975), second release of 1990 (replacing 1989) and 2003 (replacing 2002). For the duty free market a new 1996 was released in 2012 and there is also a limited release of 1965. Once stock has been depleted it will be replaced by a Vintage 1969. A limited 1990 Islay cask for the whisky retailer Master of Malt was released in 2013 and finally, you can bottle your own exclusive Balblair 1992 at the distillery visitor centre.

Balblair 2002

Balblair 2002

GS – Fizzy lemonade, banana skins, and violets on the nose, with soft caramel developing in time. Fruit and nut milk chocolate on the palate, with ripe apples and vanilla. Long, floral, and lively in the finish.

Balmenach

Owner:
Inver House Distillers
(Thai Beverages plc)

Region/district:
Speyside

Founded: Status:
1824   Active

Capacity:
2 800 000 litres

Address: Cromdale, Moray PH26 3PF

Tel:
01479 872569

website:
www.inverhouse.com

History:

1824 – The distillery is licensed to James MacGregor who operated a small farm distillery by the name of Balminoch.

1897 – Balmenach Glenlivet Distillery Company is founded.

1922 – The MacGregor family sells to a consortium consisting of MacDonald Green, Peter Dawson and James Watson.

1925 – The consortium becomes part of Distillers Company Limited (DCL).

1930 – Production is transferred to Scottish Malt Distillers (SMD).

1962 – The number of stills is increased to six.

1964 – Floor maltings replaced with Saladin box.

1992 – The first official bottling is a 12 year old.

1993 – The distillery is mothballed in May.

1997 – Inver House Distillers buys Balmenach from United Distillers.

1998 – Production recommences.

2001 – Thai company Pacific Spirits takes over Inver House at the price of £56 million. The new owner launches a 27 and a 28 year old.

2002 – To commemorate the Queen's Golden Jubilee a 25-year old Balmenach is launched.

2006 – International Beverage Holdings acquires Pacific Spirits UK.

2009 – Gin production commences.

Deerstalker 18 year old

GS – An intriguing and inviting nose, with herbal notes, eucalyptus, heather and hints of sherry. Rich and warming on the palate, big-bodied, with well harmonised malt and sherry flavours prevailing. The finish is long and sophisticated.

DR – Pine needles, lemon and grapefruit and flu powder on the nose, rich sherry and a trace of sulphur on the palate, with savoury lemon and a traces of peat. A medium and citrusy finish.

Balmenach is the only one of Inver House's five distilleries that is not marketed by its single malt. Instead, it forms an integral part of the owner's flagship blend – Hankey Bannister. The brand was introduced more than a century ago but Inver House acquired it as late as in 1988. There are currently five different versions of Hankey Bannister, the oldest being 40 years. The success for the brand has been impressive, not least in emerging markets like Eastern Europe and South America and the latest sales figures reveal an increase by volume of 30% to almost 3 million bottles. Balmenach distillery is equipped with an old cast iron mash tun but a semi-lauter gear was fitted into it in 2006. There are six washbacks made of Douglas fir with a 52 hour fermentation period and three pairs of stills connected to worm tubs for cooling the spirit vapours. The character of Balmenach is quite heavy, something that the worm tubs, with less copper contact, are responsible for. The distillery has recently increased production and is now working a 7 day week, doing 20 mashes per week and 2,8 million litres of alcohol annually. Since 2012, a small part of the production is peated. The three dunnage warehouses hold 9,500 casks at the moment.

Since 2009, apart from whisky, gin has been produced at Balmenach distillery. Purchased neutral spirit is pumped through a vaporiser and then to the berry chamber where the vapours travel upwards passing through five trays with six traditional gin botanicals and five non traditional Celtic botanicals – rowan berry, heather, bog myrtle, dandelion and coul blush apple. The latter is actually Britain's most northerly apple. Caorunn is today the third most sold premium gin in the UK.

The only official bottling of the whisky so far is the *12 year old Flora & Fauna* from the previous owner and this is now becoming increasingly difficult to find. There are, however, other Balmenach products on the market. One is produced by an independent company called Aberko in Glasgow under the name Deerstalker.

Deerstalker 18 years

Balvenie

Owner:
William Grant & Sons

Region/district:
Speyside

Founded: **Status:**
1892 Active (vc)

Capacity:
6 400 000 litres

Address: Dufftown, Keith,
Banffshire AB55 4DH

Tel:
01340 820373

website:
www.thebalvenie.com

History:
1892 – William Grant rebuilds Balvenie New House to Balvenie Distillery (Glen Gordon was the name originally intended). Part of the equipment is brought in from Lagavulin and Glen Albyn.

1893 – The first distillation takes place in May.

1957 – The two stills are increased by another two.

1965 – Two new stills are installed.

1971 – Another two stills are installed and eight stills are now running.

1973 – The first official bottling appears.

1982 – Founder's Reserve, in an eye-catching Cognac-reminiscent bottle, is launched.

1990 – A new distillery, Kininvie, is opened on the premises.

1996 – Two vintage bottlings and a Port wood finish are launched.

2001 – The Balvenie Islay Cask, with 17 years in bourbon casks and six months in Islay casks, is released.

2002 – A 50 year old is released.

2004 – The Balvenie Thirty is released to commemorate Malt Master David Stewart's 30th anniversary at Balvenie.

2005 – The Balvenie Rum Wood Finish 14 years old is released.

2006 – The Balvenie New Wood 17 years old, Roasted Malt 14 years old and Portwood 1993 are released.

2007 – Vintage Cask 1974 and Sherry Oak 17 years old are released.

2008 – Signature, Vintage 1976, Balvenie Rose and Rum Cask 17 year old are released.

2009 – Vintage 1978, 17 year old Madeira finish, 14 year old rum finish and Golden Cask 14 years old are released.

2010 – A 40 year old, Peated Cask and Carribean Cask are released.

2011 – Second batch of Tun 1401 is released.

2012 – A 50 year old and Doublewood 17 years old are released.

2013 – Triple Cask 12, 16 and 25 years are launched for duty free.

The Balvenie Doublewood 12 year old

GS – Nuts and spicy malt on the nose, full-bodied, with soft fruit, vanilla, sherry and a hint of peat. Dry and spicy in a luxurious, lengthy finish.

DR – Red fruits and berries, a hint of smoke on the nose, on the palate mouth filling, rich and fruity and, surprisingly, with a peat presence. Lots of sherry and some toffee in the finish.

Balvenie has for some time been one of the best known brands of single malt and the development during the couple of last years continue to impress. Since 2003 the sales have risen by 90% and from 2010 alone the increase is 22%. During 2012, 2,7 million bottles were sold, which means that they passed Laphroaig on the sales list and is currently in 8th place with both Aberlour and Glen Grant within reach of being surpassed.

The distillery is equipped with a full lauter mash tun, nine wooden and five stainless steel washbacks. The number of wash stills was increased to five and spirit stills to six, divided into two still rooms in 2008. Balvenie is one of few distilleries still doing some of their own maltings (around 15%) and there is also a coppersmith and a cooperage. For 2013, the production plan is to do 6,4 million litres of alcohol which is an all-time high for the distillery. Both bourbon (80%) and sherry casks (20%) are used.

The core range consists of *Doublewood 12 years, Doublewood 17 years, Carribean Cask 14 years, Single Barrel 12 years First Fill* (new since 2013 and bottled at the higher strength 47,8%), *Single Barrel 15 years, Portwood 21 years, 30 years, 40 years* and the extremely rare (only 88 bottles) *50 years old*. The Balvenie Signature 12 years, which was introduced in 2008, has now been discontinued.

Among the limited releases there is the highly successful *Tun 1401* which was first introduced in 2010. The ninth batch (exclusive to America) was released in autumn 2013 and every batch is a blend of casks of varying age selected by Balvenie Malt Master David Stewart. There is also a *Tun 1858* reserved for Taiwan. The Duty Free range still has the *Portwood 21 years* bottled at a higher strength and in spring 2013 the first Balvenie range created exclusively for duty free was launched – *Triple Cask 12, 16 and 25 years old*. These have been created by vatting together whiskies from first fill bourbon, re-fill bourbon and sherry casks and then marrying them.

Doublewood 17 years

Grant´s Family Reserve

lended Scotch

arring   Balvenie Single Malt *in a leading role*
oducer   William Grant & Sons
rector   Brian Kinsman, Master Blender

istory is steeped with Grants playing significant roles for otch whisky – John and James ant who founded Glen Grant tillery in 1840 and another hn Grant who took over Glen- rclas in 1865 and whose de- endants still own and manage e distillery. A third family, bea- g the name Grant, entered e arena a little later and is pro- bly the most famous whisky mily today. William Grant was rn in 1836 and started his reer in the whisky business as ook keeper at Mortlach distil- y. He quickly moved through e ranks and soon became the tillery manager and after 20 ars at the distillery he decided start his own.

Together with his seven sons d his two daughters, he unded Glenfiddich distillery d the first distillation was on ristmas Day of 1887. William ant & Sons was established d 12 years later the first blen- d whiskies from the company ere offered to the market. lliam Grant´s son in law, arles Gordon, was the first esman and in 1909 he spent year in Australia and the Far st securing new markets for eir products. Before that, one William´s sons, John Grant, d introduced Grant´s whisky the western part of the world en he closed a deal with e Hudson Bay Company of nada. By 1914 the company´s isky was sold in more than 30 untries. Meanwhile, another o distilleries had been built ose to Glenfiddich in Dufftown Balvenie and Convalmore – to cure the supply of malt whisky. After the Second World War, otch whisky became the tipple the world and the rivalry tween the different brands as extremely competitive. The ant family decided they had do something that would stinguish their brand from the hers. The designer, Hans Schle-

ger, a pre-war refugee from Germany, was called in and was assigned the task of designing a new bottle. He decided on a three-cornered shape and the famous triangular bottle was introduced in 1957. Seven years later the same bottle was also used for the Glenfid- dich single malt.

Over the years, the Grant´s blended Scotch had been sold under different names; Grant´s Family Reserve, Grant´s Best Procurable (the name of the company´s premium expression until 1973 when it changed name to Grant´s Royal) and Grant´s Stand Fast. By 1973 worldwide sales exceeded 12 million bottles for the first time and six years later the brand had sold that same volume in the UK alone! It is the fourth most po- pular blended Scotch today and sold 55 million bottles in 2012.

For many years the only of- fering from the owners was the *Grant´s Family Reserve* without age statement and this is still their biggest seller. In 2001 two cask finishes were introduced (which is unusual for blends). *Grant´s Ale Cask* had been finished for four months in barrels that had previously con- tained ale and *Grant´s Sherry Cask Finish* had received the same treat- ment in sherry casks. In 2003 the *12 year old* and the *18 year old* were laun- ched and in 2010 the *25 year old* was released as a duty free exclusive (but later released

for domestic markets as well). This exclusive bottling includes whisky from the first distillations at Girvan distillery – the Grant´s grain distillery. Completing the Grant´s range is the *Distillery Edition*, a combination of ex- bourbon and ex-Oloroso sherry casks, bottled at 50%.

Malted barley is present on the nose together with heathered honey and dark chocolate. Soft and sweet on the palate with vanilla, toffee, pears and the slightest hint of peat.

Ben Nevis

Owner:
Ben Nevis Distillery Ltd
(Nikka, Asahi Breweries)

Region/district:
Western Highlands

Founded: **Status:** **Capacity:**
1825   Active (vc) 1 800 000 litres

Address: Lochy Bridge, Fort William PH33 6TJ

Tel: **website:**
01397 702476   www.bennevisdistillery.com

History:
1825 – The distillery is founded by 'Long' John McDonald.

1856 – Long John dies and his son Donald P. McDonald takes over.

1878 – Demand is so great that another distillery, Nevis Distillery, is built nearby.

1908 – Both distilleries merge into one.

1941 – D. P. McDonald & Sons sells the distillery to Ben Nevis Distillery Ltd headed by the Canadian millionaire Joseph W. Hobbs.

1955 – Hobbs installs a Coffey still which makes it possible to produce both grain and malt whisky.

1964 – Joseph Hobbs dies.

1978 – Production is stopped.

1981 – Joseph Hobbs Jr sells the distillery back to Long John Distillers and Whitbread.

1984 – After restoration and reconstruction totalling £2 million, Ben Nevis opens up again.

1986 – The distillery closes again.

1989 – Whitbread sells the distillery to Nikka Whisky Distilling Company Ltd.

1990 – The distillery opens up again.

1991 – A visitor centre is inaugurated.

1996 – Ben Nevis 10 years old is launched.

2006 – A 13 year old port finish is released.

2007 – 1992 single cask is released.

2010 – A 25 year old is released.

2011 – McDonald's Traditional Ben Nevis is released.

Ben Nevis 10 year old

GS – The nose is initially quite green, with developing nutty, orange notes. Coffee, brittle toffee and peat are present on the slightly oily palate, along with chewy oak, which persists to the finish, together with more coffee and a hint of dark chocolate.

DR – Grape skins, over-ripe pear on the nose, baked apple and liquorice roots on the palate, pleasant malty finish.

In 1918, Masataka Taketsuru, a young Japanese chemist came to Scotland to study how whisky was made. He stayed for more than two years and did internships at several distilleries. Once back in Japan in 1920, he helped the founder of Suntory, Shinjiro Torii to build the first Japanese whisky distillery, Yamazaki. In 1934, Taketsuru decided to try his own hand at things and founded a company which would later become Nikka, as well as the Yoichi distillery. Taketsuru, who is often described as the father of Japanese production, died in 1979 and ten years later his adopted son, Takeshi Taketsuru, came to Scotland with the express idea of buying Ben Nevis distillery. Today Ben Nevis is an important supplier of whisky for Nikka's blends and one third of the newmake is sent directly to Japan, first and foremost to be part of the popular blend Nikka Black.

Ben Nevis is equipped with one lauter mash tun, six stainless steel washbacks and two made of Oregon pine and two pairs of stills. Fermentation is 48 hours in the steel washbacks and 96 hours in the wooden ones. Over the last couple of years production has increased and the plan for 2013 is to do 1,5 million litres. Part of that will be heavily peated.

Since 1996 the core of the range has been a *10 year old*. Some one-off bottlings have appeared at regular intervals, such as a *13 year old Port finish* and a *1992 single cask*. In 2010, a limited release was made of a *25 year old* which sold out quickly. *MacDonald's Traditional Ben Nevis*, an attempt to replicate the style of Ben Nevis single malt from the 1880s was introduced as a limited expression but has now become a part of the core range. The character is peatier than the core 10 year old version. The most recent limited bottling is a *15 year old single sherry cask* bottled at cask strength and released in December 2012. There is also a blended malt, the *8 year old MacDonald's Glencoe* and *The Dew of Ben Nevis* blended Scotch.

10 years old

BenRiach

Owner:
Benriach Distillery Co

Region/district:
Speyside

Founded: **Status:** **Capacity:**
1897 Active 2 800 000 litres

Address:
Longmorn, Elgin, Morayshire IV30 8SJ

Tel: **website:**
01343 862888 www.benriachdistillery.co.uk

History:
1897 – John Duff & Co founds the distillery.

1903 – The distillery is mothballed.

1965 – The distillery is reopened by the new owner, The Glenlivet Distillers Ltd.

1978 – Seagram Distillers takes over.

1983 – Production of peated Benriach starts.

1985 – The number of stills is increased to four.

1999 – The maltings is decommissioned.

2002 – The distillery is mothballed in October.

2004 – Intra Trading, buys Benriach together with the former Director at Burn Stewart, Billy Walker. The price is £5.4 million.

2004 – Standard, Curiositas and 12, 16 and 20 year olds are released.

2005 – Four different vintages are released.

2006 – Sixteen new releases, i.a. a 25 year old, a 30 year old and 8 different vintages.

2007 – A 40 year old and three new heavily peated expressions are released.

2008 – New expressions include a peated Madeira finish, a 15 year old Sauternes finish and nine single casks.

2009 – Two wood finishes (Moscatel and Gaja Barolo) and nine single casks are released.

2010 – Triple distilled Horizons and heavily peated Solstice are released.

2011 – A 45 year old and 12 vintages are released.

2012 – Septendecim 17 years and ten new vintages are released.

2013 – Vestige 46 years is released. The maltings are working again.

BenRiach 12 year old

GS – Malt, orange and pineapple on the nose, floral with vanilla notes. Soft fruits, brittle toffee and honey on the smooth palate, with a finish of spicy milk chocolate.

DR – Classic Speyside nose, with a rich blend of fruits, vanilla and honey. On the palate ripe fruits are balanced by crisp barley and sweet honey, and the finish is balanced, rounded and pleasant.

In 2013, BenRiach joined a small, elite band of distilleries which have their own malting floors. This technique was abandoned many years ago by the vast majority of distilleries in favour of buying malt from large, commercial maltsters. The last time the malting floors at BenRiach were used was in 1998 and, since the takeover in 2004 by Billy Walker and his partners, the new owners have been discussing whether or not to start using them again. Finally, trials were made in October 2012 and the first malting to be used for distillation came in September 2013.

BenRiach distillery is equipped with a traditional cast iron mash tun with a stainless steel shell, eight washbacks made of stainless steel with a fermentation time between 48 and 66 hours and two pairs of stills. The production for 2013 will be 2,4 million litres of alcohol (which includes 150,000 litres of peated spirit but no triple distillation this year) with 60% being sold to Chivas Brothers for their blends. At BenRiach the spirit aimed for single malt releases is diluted to the standard 63,5% before being filled into casks, while the quantity destined for blends is filled at 68-69%.

The core range of BenRiach is *Heart of Speyside* (no age), *12, 16, 20, 25* and *30 years old* in what the distillery calls Classic Speyside style and *Birnie Moss, Curiositas 10 year old, Septendecim 17 year old* and *Authenticus 25 year old* as the peated varieties. There are *five different wood finishes* (12-15 years) in the Classic Speyside style and another three (*Heredotus, Arumaticus* and *Maderensis*) in the peated style. In 2010 two specials were released – *Horizons*, a 12 year old triple distilled and *Solstice*, a 15 year old, heavily peated port finish. The latter was replaced in 2012 with a 17 year old. Every year a number of different *single cask* bottlings are released and *batch number 10* was launched in July 2013. The twelve bottlings, ranging from 1975 to 2005, included one from 1998 which was triple distilled. Last but not least, from one of the two remaining casks from 1966, the *46 year old Vestige* was bottled and released in July 2013. The cask only yielded 62 bottles.

12 year old

Benrinnes

Owner:
Diageo

Region/district:
Speyside

Founded: 1826 **Status:** Active **Capacity:** 3 500 000 litres

Address: Aberlour, Banffshire AB38 9NN

Tel: 01340 872600 **website:** www.malts.com

History:
1826 – The first Benrinnes distillery is built at Whitehouse Farm by Peter McKenzie.

1829 – A flood destroys the distillery.

1834 – A new distillery, Lyne of Ruthrie, is constructed a few kilometres from the first one. The owner, John Innes files for bankruptcy and William Smith & Company takes over.

1864 – William Smith & Company goes bankrupt and David Edward becomes the new owner.

1896 – Benrinnes is ravaged by fire which prompts major refurbishment. David Edward dies and his son Alexander Edward takes over.

1922 – John Dewar & Sons takes over ownership.

1925 – John Dewar & Sons becomes part of Distillers Company Limited (DCL).

1955/56 – The distillery is completely rebuilt.

1964 – Floor maltings is replaced by a Saladin box.

1966 – The number of stills doubles to six.

1984 – The Saladin box is taken out of service and the malt is purchased centrally.

1991 – The first official bottling from Benrinnes is a 15 year old in the Flora & Fauna series.

1996 – United Distillers releases a 21 year old cask strength in their Rare Malts series.

2009 – A 23 year old (6,000 bottles) is launched as a part of this year's Special Releases.

2010 – A Manager's Choice 1996 is released.

Benrinnes 15 year old

GS – A brief flash of caramel shortcake on the initial nose, soon becoming more peppery and leathery, with some sherry. Ultimately savoury and burnt rubber notes. Big-bodied, viscous, with gravy, dark chocolate and more pepper. A medium-length finish features mild smoke and lively spices.

DR – Cucumber, water melon and some caramel on the nose, sherried and full palate with some figs and harsher notes. The finish is medium long and complex.

Driving around in the heartland of Speyside close to the small towns of Aberlour and Craigellachie, you'll find that of all the distilleries in the area, whatever road you take there is one distillery which will almost always catch your eye, and that is Benrinnes. Even when you drive down the road to Macallan it is Benrinnes with its large, red chimney that catches your eye situated far away on the slopes on Benrinnes mountain. This is an excellent photo opportunity if you happen to be in the area.

The distillery was already founded in 1826 but the building we see today, dates back to the 1950s. With its pungent, meaty style the whisky is one of the key malts in many well-known blends.

A major upgrade was made in autumn 2012 which include a full automation of the process and a new control room where one operator can handle all the work. The equipment consists of one semilauter mash tun, eight washbacks made of Oregon pine with a fermentation time of 65 hours and six stills in an unusually large still house. The composition of stills is rare in the way that there are two wash stills and four spirit stills and until a few years ago, they were run three and three with a partial triple distillation. This regime has been abandoned and one wash still will now serve two spirit stills. The spirit vapours are cooled using six green, cast iron worm tubs which contributes to the character.

Since last year, the distillery is working a 7-day week which translates to 3,5 million litres of alcohol per year. The lion's share of Benrinnes' production is used in blended whiskies – J&B, Johnnie Walker and Crawford's 3 Star – and there is only one official single malt, the *Flora & Fauna 15 years old*. In autumn 2009, a *23 year old* from 1985 was released as part of Diageo's annual Special Releases and in May 2010 there was another new release, a *Manager's Choice* from *1996*, drawn from a refill bourbon cask.

Flora & Fauna 15 years old

Whisky Around the World

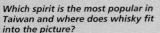

TAIWAN

Ho-cheng Yao is a certified Malt Maniac
and also the founder of Taiwan Single Malt Whisky Tasting
Association. He became a Keeper of the Quaich in 2006
and has been enroled with many whisky projects
both in Taiwan and internationally.

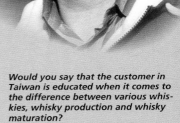

Which spirit is the most popular in Taiwan and where does whisky fit into the picture?

Whisky is actually the most popular spirit here. Besides that, Chinese white liquor and brandy are, eventhough a bit old fashioned, still popular in many occations.

What types of whisky are the most popular in Taiwan?

Quite different to most other countries, malt whisky represents almost half of the whisky consumption in Taiwan. Of course it includes both blended malt and single malt. Unsurprisingly almost 90% of the whisky consumed is Scotch whisky.

When would you say people in Taiwan started to get seriously interested in whisky? What triggered it and how has that interest developed?

Our selection of drinks used to be quite simple until the government opened up the market in the early 1990s. In the beginning of the free import people used to drink brandy but switched to whisky around 2000.

Which brands of Scotch are the most popular in Taiwan?

In terms of blended whisky, Johnnie Walker Black Label is probably the leading brand, while Royal Salute 21 year old is doing very well in the premier market and Scotttish Leader is the number one in the value category. Macallan is definitely the leading single malt brand but sales of The Singleton of Glen Ord has incresaed rapidly in the past 5 years and is now very close to Macallan. Peated whisky has become increasingly popular in the last few years, especially among the connoiseurs, and Ardbeg is without a doubt the most popular peated whisky.

How is whisky sold in Taiwan, is there a wide variety of brands and is it easy to find the brand you want?

Yes, we have a huge selection to choose from. Almost all the brands are available, even from quite a few independent bottlers.

How is whisky marketed in Taiwan?

Before 2005, nobody cared about consumer education or tastings. importers focused solely on distribution channels to bring out the products to as many customers as possible. Now things have changed – consumers have more knowledge, they can´t be as easily manipulated and they demand more information. There is also a unique cooperation between importers, distributors and retailers where they all help each other. However, competition can sometimes be quite stiff. It takes time too build a position and even for famous brands, it is not always easy to get a foot-hold on the Taiwanese market. Johnnie Walker Red Label for instance is struggling to get an acceptance by the Taiwanese customers.

Is whisky considered a luxury drink compared to other spirits?

No, I would say it's an everyday drink.

Is there a clearly defined group of customers buying whisky?

Not really. While it is true that most consumers are men, people from almost every group of the society drink whisky.

Is whisky something you drink at home or in a bar or restaurang?

Mainly at restaurants during business events but more and more people start to enjoy it in a bar or at home.

Are there special occasions when whisky is preferred?

Whisky is very good with Chinese food and people like to drink it during dinner. They have it either straight or on the rocks. Many times during a meal, people will say cheers to each other, and it means bottom up most of the time. (So we use very small glasses)!

How is whisky enjoyed in Taiwan?

Most people prefer it straight or with ice. Very few dilute it with water. On the other hand, more and more can accept the Highball way, which means mixing with soda water and ice cubes.

Would you say that the customer in Taiwan is educated when it comes to the difference between various whiskies, whisky production and whisky maturation?

Most whisky drinkers are well aware of the differences between blended whisky and single malt, although not many can recognize the different brands. A majority of the consumers believe that older and darker whisky is better.

How many producers of whisky do you have in Taiwan and how would you describe the future for domestic whisky in your country?

We have two whisky distilleries. One is Taiwan Tobacco and Liquor Corporation, which is the original government owned monopoly agency. The other is the recently famous Kavalan, owned by the King Car Group. Located on the way to the beautiful eastern part of Taiwan, the owners have been very successful attracting visitors to enjoy a free distillery tour and free drinks. The products so far from Taiwan Tobacco and Liquor Corporation, have been regarded quite cheap and of low quality. Seeing the success of Kavalan however, the company is now putting more effort into their own production and recent products seem quite good. There are no real signs at the moment of more distilleries opening up.

What are your thoughts on the future for Scotch whisky in Taiwan?

Cognac has been selling well, mainly to Chinese tourists. Chinese white liquor is also doing well here in Taiwan, especially a high quality brand made by our own Kiman distillery. Having said that, I still think Scotch whisky will the leading spirit in Taiwan in five years from now.

Benromach

Owner:
Gordon & MacPhail

Region/district:
Speyside

Founded: **Status:** **Capacity:**
1898   Active (vc)   500 000 litres

Address: Invererne Road, Forres,
Morayshire IV36 3EB

Tel: **website:**
01309 675968   www.benromach.com

History:
1898 – Benromach Distillery Company starts
the distillery.

1911 – Harvey McNair & Co buys the distillery.

1919 – John Joseph Calder buys Benromach
and sells it to recently founded Benromach
Distillery Ltd owned by several breweries.

1931 – Benromach is mothballed.

1937 – The distillery reopens.

1938 – Joseph Hobbs buys Benromach through
Associated Scottish Distillers and sells it on to
National Distillers of America (NDA).

1953 – NDA sells Benromach to Distillers
Company Limited (DCL).

1966 – The distillery is refurbished.

1968 – Floor maltings is abolished.

1983 – Benromach is mothballed in March.

1993 – Gordon & McPhail buys Benromach
from United Distillers.

1998 – The distillery is once again in operation.
A 17 year old is released to commemorate this
and the distillery's 100th anniversary.

1999 – A visitor centre is opened.

2004 – The first bottle distilled by the new
owner is released under the name 'Benromach
Traditional' in May. Other novelties (although
distilled in UD times) include a 21 year Tokaji
finish and a Vintage 1969.

2005 – A Port Wood finish (22 years old) and a
Vintage 1968 are released together with the
Benromach Classic 55 years.

2006 – Benromach Organic is released.

2007 – Peat Smoke, the first heavily peated
whisky from the distillery, is released.

2008 – Benromach Origins Golden Promise is
released.

2009 – Benromach 10 years old is released.

2010 – New batches of Peatsmoke and Origins
are released.

2011 – New edition of Peatsmoke, a 2001
Hermitage finish and a 30 year old are
released.

2013 – A Sassicaia Wood Finish is released

Benromach 10 year old

GS – A nose that is initially quite smoky, with
wet grass, butter, ginger and brittle toffee.
Mouth-coating, spicy, malty and nutty on the
palate, with developing citrus fruits, raisins
and soft wood smoke. The finish is warming,
with lingering barbecue notes.

DR – Lemon custard creams, apricots and then
pine table polish on the nose, spicy virgin oak,
refreshing sharp barley and pine needles on
the palate, and a complex and intriguing spicy
and wood shaving finish.

Since 1896 Gordon & MacPhail has, through focused work
and long-range planning, managed to establish themselves
as the foremost independent bottler in the industry. The
same attitude has characterized their efforts as distillery
owners. Benromach was acquired in 1993 but five years
passed before they were ready to start producing. Ever sin
ce, they have been running on approximately 25% of the
maximum capacity in order to be able to build a customer
base harmoniously. Now they can enjoy the fruits of their
labour. In 2012 alone, sales figures increased by 40% and i
June 2013 the owners announced that more than £1m will
be invested in doubling the production by hiring one more
distiller (as there are only two people working at the distillery at the moment). In addition, they will also hire a bran
manager and build two, new warehouses. Furthermore,
a brand new bottling line has been installed at the Elgin
headquarters, not only to take care of the
increased demand for Benromach, but also
to promote the vast range of other brands.
Benromach is the smallest working distillery in Speyside and is equipped with a 1,5
tonnes semi-lauter mash tun with a copper
dome. There are four washbacks made of
larchwood from the old washbacks and
resized to accommodate 11,000 litres and
one pair of stills. Almost the entire production is destined to be sold as single
malt and only a very small amount is
used for Gordon & MacPhail blends.
The core range consists of *Traditional*
(around 6 years old), *10 year old*, *Cask
Strength* (currently a 2002 vintage), *30
year old*, *Vintage 1969*, *Vintage 1976*
and *Classic 55 years old*. There are also
special editions; *Organic* – the first
single malt to be fully certified organic
by the Soil Association, *Peatsmoke*
– produced using peated barley and
currently a 2004 at 53ppm and *Origins*
– highlighting how differences in the
process can produce different whiskies.
The most recent expressions of Origins
are *Batch 4, Port Pipes* and *Batch 5,
Golden Promise barley*. There is also
a *Port Wood Finish* and a new 2013
version of the *Sassicaia Wood Finish*.

10 year old

Bladnoch

Owner:
Co-ordinated
Development Services

Region/district:
Lowlands

Founded: 1817
Status: Active (vc)
Capacity: 250 000 litres

Address: Bladnoch, Wigtown,
Wigtonshire DG8 9AB

Tel: 1988 402605
website: www.bladnoch.co.uk

History:
1817 – Brothers Thomas and John McClelland found the distillery.

1825 – The McClelland brothers obtain a licence.

1878 – John McClelland's son Charlie reconstructs and refurbishes the distillery.

1905 – Production stops.

1911 – Dunville & Co. from Ireland buys T. & J. McClelland Ltd for £10,775. Production is intermittent until 1936.

1937 – Dunville & Co. is liquidated and Bladnoch is wound up. Ross & Coulter from Glasgow buys the distillery after the war. The equipment is dismantled and shipped to Sweden.

1956 – A. B. Grant (Bladnoch Distillery Ltd.) takes over and restarts production with four new stills.

1964 – McGown and Cameron becomes new owners.

1966 – The number of stills is increased from two to four.

1973 – Inver House Distillers buys Bladnoch.

1983 – Arthur Bell and Sons take over.

1985 – Guiness Group buys Arthur Bell & Sons which, from 1989, are included in United Distillers.

1988 – A visitor centre is built.

1993 – United Distillers mothballs Bladnoch in June.

1994 – Raymond Armstrong from Northern Ireland buys Bladnoch in October.

2000 – Production commences in December.

2003 – The first bottles from Raymond Armstrong are launched, a 15 year old cask strength from UD casks.

2004 – New varieties follow suit: e. g. 13 year olds 40% and 55%.

2008 – First release of whisky produced after the take-over in 2000 - three 6 year olds.

2009 – An 8 year old of own production and a 9 year old are released.

2011 – Distiller´s Choice is released.

2012 – Peated Distiller´s Choice is released.

2013 – A 12 year old from the new production and a 22 year old single cask are released.

Bladnoch 8 year old

GS – Bright, fresh and citric, with lemon, cereal, soft toffee and nuts on the nose. Medium in body, the palate is gingery and very lively, with vanilla, hot spices and hazelnuts. The finish offers persistently fruity spice.

Bladnoch is the southernmost of the Scottish distilleries, situated a mile outside Wigtown. It was mothballed by United Distillers (later Diageo) in 1993 and then sold the year after to Raymond Armstrong, a builder from Northern Ireland, on the condition that it should not be used for whisky production. However, in 2000, after lobbying from Armstrong and the local community, Diageo gave permission for Bladnoch to start producing again.

Armstrong commenced the resurrection and in 2000 the first distillation was made. The distillery is equipped with a stainless steel semi-lauter mash tun, six washbacks made of Oregon pine (of which only three are in use) and one pair of stills. Due to the increase in production costs (barley, casks and fuel), the owners took a decision in 2009 to cease production for the time being. Of the 11 warehouses on site, Bladnoch uses only one for its own purposes while the others are rented to other distilleries. The latter is also an important contribution to finances of the business. Nearly 50,000 casks from other companies are stored at Bladnoch which yields a yearly income of more than £500,000.

Until five years ago, all official bottlings came from the previous owner´s production. These included 13 to 20 year olds. In 2008 the first release from stock distilled under the current ownership appeared. Three *6 year old cask strengths* were released – a bourbon matured, a sherry matured and one lightly peated from a bourbon barrel. All these have since appeared in older versions with a *10 year old* lightly peated and sherry matured, as well as an *11 year old* sherry matured being released in spring/summer 2012. In 2013, a sherry matured *12 year old* was released at both 46% and 55% and there was also an *11 year old*, peated expression. In summer 2013, a *22 year old* single bourbon cask bottled at cask strength was released. The range has mostly been about single casks bottled but the first step to a core range was made in 2011, when *Distiller´s Choice* with no age statement, bottled at 46%, was launched. This was followed up in 2012 with a *Peated Distiller´s Choice*.

8 year old

Blair Athol

Owner:
Diageo

Region/district:
Eastern Highlands

Founded: | **Status:** | **Capacity:**
1798 | Active (vc) | 2 500 000 litres

Address: Perth Road, Pitlochry,
Perthshire PH16 5LY

Tel:
01796 482003

website:
www.malts.com

History:
1798 – John Stewart and Robert Robertson found Aldour Distillery, the predecessor to Blair Athol. The name is taken from the adjacent river Allt Dour.

1825 – The distillery is expanded by John Robertson and takes the name Blair Athol Distillery.

1826 – The Duke of Atholl leases the distillery to Alexander Connacher & Co.

1860 – Elizabeth Connacher runs the distillery.

1882 – Peter Mackenzie & Company Distillers Ltd of Edinburgh (future founder of Dufftown Distillery) buys Blair Athol and expands it.

1932 – The distillery is mothballed.

1933 – Arthur Bell & Sons takes over by acquiring Peter Mackenzie & Company.

1949 – Production restarts.

1973 – Stills are expanded from two to four.

1985 – Guinness Group buys Arthur Bell & Sons.

1987 – A visitor centre is built.

2003 – A 27 year old cask strength from 1975 is launched in Diageo's Rare Malts series.

2010 – A distillery exclusive with no age statement and a single cask from 1995 are released.

Blair Athol 12 year old

GS – The nose is mellow and sherried, with brittle toffee. Sweet and fragrant. Relatively rich on the palate, with malt, raisins, sultanas and sherry. The finish is lengthy, elegant and slowly drying.

DR – The nose is rich and full, with orange and citrus fruit. The palate, too, is big and chunky, with some tannin and spice in the mix, and with water, parma violet notes.

Blair Athol distillery is one of the most visited in Scotland and there are good reasons why 35,000 people come here every year. It is conveniently situated in the small town of Pitlochry on the busy A9 between Edinburgh and Inverness. It is a beautiful distillery covered with vines and one of few built in the 1800s. It is also the spiritual home of the famous blend Bell's and the owners, Diageo, have put in a tremendous amount of work promoting both Bell's and Blair Athol single malt. The visitor centre is Diageo's second busiest after Talisker.

This area in Perthshire was known for its many distilleries and in the 18th century there were at least 30 illegal stills in and around Pitlochry. After the Excise Act of 1823 where was stated that a licence to distil was required, you could still find six distilleries in the small town of Logierait just south of Pitlochry.

For the greater part of the summer in 2010, Blair Athol distillery was closed for refurbishing and the equipment now consists of an 8 tonnes semi-lauter mash tun, six washbacks made of stainless steel (which used to be four wooden and four made of steel) and two pairs of stills. The distillery is running seven days a week with 16 mashes giving a production of 2,5 million litres of spirit. The part of the spirit which goes into Bell's is matured mainly in bourbon casks, while the rest is matured in sherry casks. Blair Athol distillery had been a supplier of malt whisky for Bell's for several decades before it became a part of Arthur Bell & Sons in 1933. Today, every fifth bottle of blended whisky sold in the UK is Bell's. The output today is still used for Bell's whisky and the only official bottling used to be the *12 year old Flora & Fauna*. In 2010, a *first fill sherry* bottled at *cask strength* and without age statement was also released as a distillery exclusive.

Flora & Fauna 12 years

Bell's Original

...ended Scotch

...rring Blair Athol Single Malt *in a leading role*
...ducer Diageo
...ector Caroline Martin, Master Blender

...he company that would become the seed for Arthur ...l & Sons many years later was ...nded in 1825 by Thomas San...man. He was related to the ...ous port family, Sandeman, ...d he opened a small wine ...d spirit shop in Perth acting ...inly as agents for Sandeman's ...t. When he died in 1837 ...business was taken over by ...company clerk, James Roy. ...ee years later, Roy employed ...fifteen year old Arthur Bell ...a travelling salesman. Bell ...monstrated great skill in his ...rk and was made a partner in ...51. Three years later, the firm ...s the first to offer blended ...isky to the London custo...rs. Unfortunately, it was not ...uccess. The Londoners were ...t used to the heavy character ...Scotch and in 1871 Arthur ...ll withdrew from the London ...rket only to return in the late ...30s.

...From then on the company ...adually managed to build up ...market that later would see ...eir whisky soar to the number ...e spot in the UK market. The ...st blended whiskies that Ar...ur Bell could offer, contained ...alt from Blair Athol distillery, ...mong others, but it would take ...ong time before the distil...y would become part of the ...mpany.

...Eventually Arthur brought ...two sons, Arthur Kinmond ...nown as A.K.) and Robert Duff ...D.) into the business resul...g in Arthur Bell & Sons being ...rmed in 1895. It was left to the ...o sons to explore the export ...portunities and while A.K. tra...lled to Australia, R.D. went to ...uth Africa. Their whisky was ...ld under many names but, so ...r, none of the brands mentio...d the name Bell. Arthur Bell ...as a member of the Sandema...an Glassite Church, a Christian ...ct with strict rules not least ...ncerned with how to do busi...ess. Bell's views on advertising

and promoting his own name was that if a product didn't speak for itself, then it is not worth producing. It was not until 1904, four years after Arthur Bell's death, that the first bottle would appear clearly stating Bell's as a brand on the label.

Arthur Bell & Sons slowly built their reputation as blenders but they didn't play in the same league as The Big Three (Buchanan's, Johnnie Walker and Dewar's) that would later expand to The Big Five (when Haig and Mackie & Co joined the club). In 1932, the first two distilleries were bought (Blair Athol and Dufftown), later adding Inchgower and Bladnoch. In 1978, Bell's became the most sold whisky in the UK – a position that the brand has kept ever since.

Since the 1920s, the Scotch whisky industry has seen fluctuations or mergers between the big companies, but Bell's managed to keep its independence until 1985 when the company was absorbed by Guinness who wanted to be a part of the whisky business. Only two years later Guinness merged with DCL to form the giant United Distillers (later to become Diageo).

As of today Bell's holds spot number 9 of the world's most sold blends with 30 million bottles being sold in 2012. The range of Bell's is very small – in fact, the only blend is *Bell's Original* without age statement,

which replaced the 8 year old version in 2008. In addition to that, there is a blended malt version called *Bell's Special Reserve* in the UK market.

Floral and light on the nose with malted barley coming through. Sweet cereals on the palate with caramel, vanilla, walnuts and green and grassy flavours. Spicy finish.

Bowmore

Owner:
Morrison Bowmore
Distillers (Suntory)

Region/district:
Islay

Founded: 1779

Status:
Active (vc)

Capacity:
2 000 000 litres

Address: School Street, Bowmore, Islay,
Argyll PA43 7GS

Tel:
01496 810441

website:
www.bowmore.com

History:
1779 – Bowmore Distillery is founded by
John Simpson and becomes the oldest Islay
distillery.

1837 – The distillery is sold to James and
William Mutter of Glasgow.

1892 – After additional construction, the
distillery is sold to Bowmore Distillery
Company Ltd, a consortium of English
businessmen.

1925 – J. B. Sheriff and Company takes over.

1929 – Distillers Company Limited (DCL) takes
over.

1950 – William Grigor & Son takes over.

1963 – Stanley P. Morrison buys the distillery
for £117,000 and forms Morrison Bowmore
Distillers Ltd.

1989 – Japanese Suntory buys a 35% stake in
Morrison Bowmore.

1993 – The legendary Black Bowmore is
launched. The recommended price is £100
(today it is at least ten times that if it can be
found). Another two versions are released
1994 and 1995.

1994 – Suntory now controls all of Morrison
Bowmore.

1995 – Bowmore is nominated 'Distiller of the
Year' in the International Wine and Spirits
competition.

The single malt from Bowmore, the oldest distillery on Isla
is truly riding a wave of success. With no less than 20 diffe
rent expressions currently available, sales have increased b
15% during 2012 when 2,2 million bottles were sold. The
recent focus on the duty free market has proven to be ver
successful. Another successful initiative was the recruitme
of Rachel Barrie, as their master blender. Rachel has been
with Morrison Bowmore almost two years, after a successful career within the industry. Another distinguished
Bowmore profile, is distillery manager Eddie MacAffer wh
was awarded Global Distillery Manager of the year for 201
by Whisky Magazine's Icons of Whisky.

Bowmore is one of only a few Scottish distilleries with its
own malting floor, with 40% of the malt requirement
produced in-house. The remaining part is bought from
Simpsons. Both parts have a phenol specification of 25ppm
and are mixed before mashing. The distillery has a stainles
steel semi-lauter mash tun, six washbacks of Oregon pine
and two pairs of stills. The 27,000 casks are stored in two
dunnage and one racked warehouse. The building closest
to the sea, dating back to the 1700s, is probably the oldest
whisky warehouse still in use in Scotland. In 2013, they wil
be doing six short fermentations and seven long per week,
which adds up to 1,8 million litres of alcohol in the year.

The core range for domestic markets includes *Legend* and
Small Batch Reserve (both bourbon matured and with no
age statement), *12 years*, *Darkest 15 years*, *18 years* and *25
years*. The duty free line-up contains *Surf*, *Enigma*, *Marine
17 year old*, *100 Degrees Proof* (replacing the Bowmore
Cask Strength), *Springtide* (matured in Oloroso casks) and
finally *Vintage 1984* (released in May 2013 and replacing
last year's *Vintage 1983*). Limited releases for 2012 include
yet another release of *Laimrig* which has matured in ex-
bourbon casks with an added finish in Oloroso sherry butts
a *Vintage 1985* and a *30 year old Bowmore Sea Dragon*,
launched in Asia to celebrate the Year of the Dragon. The
beginning of 2013 saw the release of a version of *Tempest*
for the US market under the name *Dorus Mor*, which is a
first fill bourbon maturation bottled at 55,1%. In June, a *2.
year old Port Cask Matured* (not a finish but full maturatio
in port pipes) was released followed in October by *Devil's
Casks* which is part of the Small Batches series. It is a 10 yea
old from first fill sherry butts and bottled at 56,9%. Exclusively available at the distillery visitor centre is the *14 year
old Mashmen's Collection* and, finally, a *50 year old*, distilled in 1961 was announced for release later in the year.

996 – A Bowmore 1957 (38 years) is bottled
40.1% but is not released until 2000.

99 – Bowmore Darkest with three years
ish on Oloroso barrels is launched.

00 – Bowmore Dusk with two years finish in
ordeaux barrels is launched.

01 – Bowmore Dawn with two years finish
Port pipes is launched.

02 – A 37 year old Bowmore from 1964 and
atured in fino casks is launched in a limited
ition of 300 bottles (recommended price
,500).

03 – Another two expressions complete the
ood trilogy which started with 1964 Fino
1964 Bourbon and 1964 Oloroso.

04 – Morrison Bowmore buys one of the
ost outstanding collections of Bowmore
ngle Malt from the private collector Hans
mmer. It totals more than 200 bottles and
cludes a number of Black Bowmore.

05 – Bowmore 1989 Bourbon (16 years) and
71 (34 years) are launched.

06 – Bowmore 1990 Oloroso (16 years)
nd 1968 (37 years) are launched. A new and
pgraded visitor centre is opened.

07 – Dusk and Dawn disappear from the
nge and an 18 year old is introduced. New
ackaging for the whole range. 1991 (16yo)
rt and Black Bowmore are released.

08 – White Bowmore and a 1992 Vintage
ith Bourdeaux finish are launched.

09 – Gold Bowmore, Maltmen´s Selection,
imrig and Bowmore Tempest are released.

10 – A 40 year old and Vintage 1981 are
leased.

11– Vintage 1982 and new batches of
mpest and Laimrig are released.

12 – 100 Degrees Proof, Springtide and
ntage 1983 are released for duty free.

13 – The Devil´s Casks, a 23 year old Port
ask Matured and Vintage 1984 are released.

Bowmore 12 year old

5 – An enticing nose of lemon and gentle
ine leads into a smoky, citric palate, with
otes of cocoa and boiled sweets appearing in
e lengthy, complex finish.

R – Rich peat and seaweed and the merest
nt of characteristic palma violets on the
ose, smoked fish in butter, menthol cough
veets and lemon on the palate, sweet peat
the finish.

Springtide   *The Devil's Casks*   *23 year old Port Matured*

12 years old   *15 years old Darkest*   *Mariner*

Braeval

Owner:
Chivas Brothers Ltd
(Pernod Ricard)

Region/district:
Speyside

Founded: 1973

Status: Active

Capacity: 4 000 000 litres

Address: Chapeltown of Glenlivet,
Ballindalloch, Banffshire AB37 9JS

Tel: 01542 783042

website: -

History:
1973 – The Chivas and Glenlivet Group founds Braes of Glenlivet, the name which will be used for the first 20 years. The Glenlivet, Tomintoul and Tamnavulin are the only other distilleries situated in the Livet Glen valley. Production starts in October.

1975 – Three stills are increased to five.

1978 – Five stills are further expanded to six.

1994 – The distillery changes name to Braeval.

2001 – Pernod Ricard takes over Chivas Brothers.

2002 – Braeval is mothballed in October.

2008 – The distillery starts producing again in July.

Deerstalker 10 year old

DR – Grass and violin bow on the nose, zippy sherbet and citrus fruit on the palate, with a clean and refreshing finish.

The Braes of Glenlivet where Braeval distillery lies, is not only one of the more remote places in the Highlands, but it is also exceptionally beautiful, filled with exciting histo about smugglers and illicit distillers. Furthermore, the are is also linked to the history of the oppression of Catholics after the Protestant reformation. A law from 1700 prohibited Catholics from practising their religion and priests, in particular, were being persecuted. Many took refuge i isolated parts of the Highlands and close to where the di tillery lies today, Scalan, a college where young men coul train to be priests, was secretly built. It was closed in 17 when a new law granted the Catholics their rights again. Even today, the Braes serves as a home to many Catholics and from the top of the distillery roof you look down at large Catholic church which was built in the late 1800s.

Braeval distillery is both impressive and surprisingly attractive, despite that it is modern and was built to function as a typical working distillery. At 1665 feet above sea level, it is also the highest situated distillery in Scotland. If you wish to visit this stunning area even though the distillery doesn't accept visitors, take the A95 from the B9008 towards Glenlivet distillery. About a mile south of Tamnavulin you will find the small hamlet Auchnarrow. There you take a narrow road towards Chapeltown which will lead you to the distillery.

Braeval distillery is equipped with a stainless steel mash tun with traditional rakes and a copper dome (even though there were talks about installing a modern Briggs mash tun last year), 13 stainless steel washbacks with a fermentation time of 70 hours and six stills. There are two wash stills with aftercoolers and four spirit stills and with the possibility of doing 26 mashes per week, the distillery can produce 4 million litres per year. There are no official bottlings but Braeval single malt has from time to time been used for bottling of Deerstalker.

Deerstalker 10 year

New Websites To Watch

stshotwhiskyreviews.com

van den Ende hails from The Netherlands but has
n living in Sao Paulo, Brazil since 1994. At the end of
1 he started his blog by presenting tasting notes and
ughts regarding the subject of whisky. He is diligent,
ents well written facts and he samples everything
n cheap supermarket blends to rare single cask bott-
s. And besides, he is refreshingly honest - if he thinks a
sky is bad he´ll say just that!

isky-discovery.blogspot.com

whisky lovers teaming up and starting a blog about
favourite subject is not all that new, but this is the
time that it is a father and daughter show. Dave
thington and his daughter, Kat, tour around whisky
ws and tastings in the UK and deliver well written and
essional judgments. Comparing the notes from Dave
Kat, as well as reading the reports from various shows
events, make this a highly entertaining blog.

whisky-emporium.com

An Englishman living in Germany, Keith Wood, is one of
the famous Malt Maniacs but he has also created his own
website which is a treasure trove for whisky geeks. The
foundation comprises of more than 1,000 tasting notes
which cover whiskies from all over the world . But there is
so much more than that here. Essays about Whisky & Chocolate and Collecting Whisky, as well as many other topics
even including vintage cars - another of Keith´s interests.

whiskiesrus.blogspot.com

An Australian by birth, Clint Anesbury has been living in
Japan for a long time and is well suited to cover one of
the most exciting whisky scenes in the world right now.
Read about the developments and changes within the
Japanese whisky industry or enjoy the many tasting notes
of well-known and rare Japanese whiskies. And if you
plan to go to Japan you will find the practical information
on retailers and whisky bars a great help.

Some Old Favourites

vw.maltmadness.com

all-time favourite with something for everyone.
aged by malt maniac Johannes van den Heuvel.

vw.maltmaniacs.net

unch of knowledgeable whisky lovers dissect, debate,
ck and praise the phenomena of the whisky world.

vw.whiskyadvocateblog.com

Hansell is well situated with his contacts in the busi-
to write a first class blog on every aspect of whisky.

vw.whiskyfun.com

e Valentin, one of the Malt Maniacs, is almost always
with well written tasting notes on new releases.

vw.nonjatta.com

og by Stefan van Eycken with a wealth of interesting
rmation on Japanese whisky and Japanese culture.

vw.whiskyreviews.blogspot.com

y does this video blog with tastings and field reports
n educational yet easy-going and entertaining way.

vw.caskstrength.net

and Neil won a Drammie Award for this blog and
ervedly so. Initiated, entertaining and well written.

vw.edinburghwhiskyblog.com

as, Chris and company review new releases, interview
ustry people and cover news from the whisky world.

vw.whiskycast.com

best whisky-related podcast on the internet and one
sets the standard for podcasts in other genres as well.

vw.whiskywhiskywhisky.com

active forum for whisky friends with lots of daily com-
ts on new whiskies, industry news, whisky events etc.

vw.whiskyintelligence.com

best site on all kinds of whisky news. The first whisky
site you should log into every morning!

vw.whisky-news.com

rt from daily news, this site contains tasting notes,
llery portraits, lists of retailers, events etc.

vw.dramming.com

es a wide-angle view of the whisky world including
reports, whisky ratings, whisky business, articles etc.

vw.guidscotchdrink.com

ing notes is one part of this site but the highlights are
many comments on current events and trends.

www.whiskyforum.se

Swedish whisky forum with more than 1,800 enthusiasts.
Excellent debate as well as more than 2,000 tasting notes.

www.whisky-pages.com

Top class whisky site with features, directories, tasting
notes, book reviews, whisky news, glossary and a forum.

www.whiskynotes.be

This blog is almost entirely about tasting notes (and lots
of them, not least independent bottlings) plus some news.

www.whiskyforeveryone.com

Educational site, perfect for beginners, with a blog where
both new releases and affordable standards are reviewed.

blog.thewhiskyexchange.com

Tim Forbes from The Whisky Exchange writes about new
bottlings as well as the whisky industry in general.

recenteats.blogspot.com

Steve Ury serves tasty bits of information (and entertainment) from the world of whisky and other spirits.

www.whiskymarketplace.com

This is divided into three parts - well written tasting notes,
whisky price comparison site and Whisky Marketplace TV.

www.whisky-distilleries.net

Ernie Scheiner describes more than 130 distilleries in both
text and photos and we are talking *lots* of great images!

www.connosr.com

This whisky social networking community is a virtual
smorgasbord for any whisky lover!

www.jewmalt.com

An excellent blog by Joshua Hatton who also acts as an independent bottler, check out www.singlecasknation.com.

www.canadianwhisky.org

Davin de Kergommeaux presents reviews, news and views
on all things Canadian whisky. High quality content.

www.whiskyisrael.co.il

Gal Granov is definitely one of the most active of all bloggers. Well worth checking out daily!

spiritsjournal.klwines.com

Reviews about whiskies and the whisky industry in general
by David Driscoll from the US retailer K&L Wines.

www.thewhiskywire.com

Steve Rush mixes reviews of the latest bottlings with
presentations of classics plus news, interviews etc.

Bruichladdich

Owner:
Rémy Cointreau

Region/district:
Islay

Founded: 1881

Status: Active (vc)

Capacity: 1 500 000 litres

Address: Bruichladdich, Islay, Argyll PA49 7UN

Tel: 01496 850221

website: www.bruichladdich.com

History:
1881 – Barnett Harvey builds the distillery with money left by his brother William III to his three sons William IV, Robert and John Gourlay.

1886 – Bruichladdich Distillery Company Ltd is founded and reconstruction commences.

1889 – William Harvey becomes Manager and remains on that post until his death in 1937.

1929 – Temporary closure.

1936 – The distillery reopens.

1938 – Joseph Hobbs, Hatim Attari and Alexander Tolmie purchase the distillery for £23 000 through the company Train & McIntyre.

1938 – Operations are moved to Associated Scottish Distillers.

1952 – The distillery is sold to Ross & Coulter from Glasgow.

1960 – A. B. Grant buys Ross & Coulter.

1961 – Own maltings ceases and malt is brought in from Port Ellen.

1968 – Invergordon Distillers take over.

1975 – The number of stills increases to four.

1983 – Temporary closure.

1993 – Whyte & Mackay buys Invergordon Distillers.

1995 – The distillery is mothballed in January.

1998 – In production again for a few months, and then mothballed.

2000 – Murray McDavid buys the distillery from JBB Greater Europe for £6.5 million.

A year has now passed since Bruichladdich was sold to the French spirits group, Rémy Cointreau. There were fans wh argued that the company had sold its soul to a mega com pany which quickly would change Bruichladdich´s image from an entrepreneurial brand to "just another whisky". These fears have been allayed and have not come true. Th whisky is still produced and matured on Islay and the bott ling hall has even been expanded by the new owners whi resulted in a need to recruit more employees. From Janua 2013, production has doubled to 1,5 million litres of alcok and new, interesting products have been launched during the year. Two persons have been in the forefront during the last decade; Mark Reynier, the founder of the compar and the driving force who has now left the company, whi Jim McEwan has decided to stay on for another three yea Jim has been in the industry for 50 years now, the last twelve at Bruichladdich, and he is the one who has set the agenda as to what should be produced and bottled.

The distillery is equipped with a cast iron, open mash tun from 1881, six washbacks of Oregon pine and two pairs o stills. They have also installed the only functioning Lomor still in the industry which was brought to Bruichladdich from Inverleven distillery. The still is being used for the pr duction of Botanist Gin, a new addition to Bruichladdich´s range. All whisky produced is based on Scottish barley, 40 of which comes from Islay.

There are three main lines in Bruichladdich's production; unpeated *Bruichladdich*, moderately peated *Port Charlott* and the heavily peated *Octomore*. The owners have over the years released a huge amount of bottlings but a core range has now emerged; *Scottish Barley* (signature bottlir and new for 2013), *Laddie Ten*, *Laddie 16* and *Laddie 22*. There is also *Islay Barley 2007 Rockside Farm* (replacing la: year´s *Islay Barley Dunlossit*), *Bere Barley 2006 2nd edition* (made from an old barley variety) and *The Organic Scottis Barley* (100% organic barley and exclusive to Duty Free). *Black Art 4* is a limited edition (this time a 23 year old) which has matured in American oak and various wine cas In 2012 *Port Charlotte* was released as a *10 year old*, whic will now become a core expression. New releases for 201: are *Port Charlotte Scottish Barley* and the limited *PC11 ca strength*. Last year, Octomore was also launched as a 10 year old but this has now been discontinued. New, but lir ted expressions for 2013 are instead, two 5 year olds with phenol specification for the barley of 167ppm – *Octomore Scottish Barley 6.1* (matured in American oak) and *Octom re 6.2* (matured in Limousin oak and exclusive to Duty Fre

History (continued):

2001 – Jim McEwan from Bowmore becomes
Production Director. The first distillation
(Port Charlotte) is on 29th May and the first
distillation of Bruichladdich starts in July. In
September the owners' first bottlings from the
old casks are released, 10, 15 and 20 years old.

2002 – The world's most heavily peated whisky
produced on 23rd October when Octomore
80ppm) is distilled.

2003 – Bruichladdich becomes the only
distillery on Islay bottling on-site.

2004 – Second edition of the 20 year old (nick-
named Flirtation) and 3D, also called The Peat
Proposal, are launched.

2005 – Several new expressions are launched
the second edition of 3D, Infinity (a mix of
1989, 1990, 1991 and Port Charlotte), Rocks,
Legacy Series IV, The Yellow Submarine and
the Twenty 'Islands'.

2006 – Included in a number of new releases
in autumn is the first official bottling of Port
Charlotte; PC5.

2007 – New releases include Redder Still,
Legacy 6, PC6 and an 18 year old.

2008 – More than 20 new expressions
including the first Octomore, Bruichladdich
2001, PC7, Golder Still and two sherry matured
from 1998.

2009 – New releases include Classic, Organic,
Black Art, Infinity 3, PC8, Octomore 2 and
X4+3 - the first quadruple distilled single malt.

2010 – PC Multi Vintage, Organic MV,
Octomore/3_152, Bruichladdich 40 year old are
released.

2011 – The first 10 year old from own
production is released as well as PC9,
Octomore 4_167, Ancien Regime and
Rennaisance.

2012 – Ten year old versions of Port Charlotte
and Octomore are released as well as Laddie
16 and 22, Bere Barley 2006, Black Art 3 and
DNA4. Rémy Cointreau buys the distillery.

2013 – Scottish Barley, Islay Barley Rockside
Farm, Bere Barley 2nd edition, Black Art 4, Port
Charlotte Scottish Barley, Octomore 06.1 and
06.2 are released.

The Laddie Ten

TS – Asparagus tips, raw potatoes and fresh
salmon on the nose, with a hint of peat. Black
pepper and rock pools on the palate, plus pipe
tobacco notes. Wood smoke and more black
pepper.

Port Charlotte 10

Octomore 06.2

Islay Barley 2007
Rockside Farm

Bere Barley 2006
2nd edition

Scottish Barley

The Laddie Ten

Bunnahabhain

Owner:		Region/district:
Burn Stewart Distillers (Distell Group Ltd)		Islay

Founded:	Status:	Capacity:
1881	Active (vc)	2 700 000 litres

Address: Port Askaig, Islay, Argyll PA46 7RP

Tel:	website:
01496 840646	www.bunnahabhain.com

History:

1881 – William Robertson of Robertson & Baxter, founds the distillery together with the brothers William and James Greenless, owners of Islay Distillers Company Ltd.

1883 – Production starts in earnest in January.

1887 – Islay Distillers Company Ltd merges with William Grant & Co. in order to form Highland Distilleries Company Limited.

1963 – The two stills are augmented by two more.

1982 –The distillery closes.

1984 – The distillery reopens. A 21 year old is released to commemorate the 100th anniversary of Bunnahabhain.

1999 – Edrington takes over Highland Distilleries and mothballs Bunnahabhain but allows for a few weeks of production a year.

2001 – A 35 year old from 1965 is released in a limited edition of 594 bottles during Islay Whisky Festival.

2002 – As in the previous year, Islay Whisky Festival features another Bunnahabhain – 1966, a 35 year old in sherry casks. Auld Acquaintance 1968 is launched at the Islay Jazz Festival.

2003 – In April Edrington sells Bunnahabhain and Black Bottle to Burn Stewart Distilleries (C. L. World Brands) at the princely sum of £10 million. A 40 year old from 1963 is launched.

2004 – The first limited edition of the peated version is a 6 year old called Moine.

2005 – Three limited editions are released - 34 years old, 18 years old and 25 years old.

2006 – 14 year old Pedro Ximenez and 35 years old are launched.

2008 – Darach Ur is released for the travel retail market and Toiteach (a peated 10 year old) is launched on a few selected markets.

2009 – Moine Cask Strength is released during Feis Isle.

2010 – The peated Cruach-Mhòna and a limited 30 year old are released.

2013 – A 40 year old is released.

Bunnahabhain 12 year old

GS – The nose is fresh, with light peat and discreet smoke. More overt peat on the nutty and fruity palate, but still restrained for an Islay. The finish is full-bodied and lingering, with a hint of vanilla and some smoke.

DR – Ginger and barley candy on the nose, then sweet and sour mix on the palate, lots of sweetness but with a distinctive savoury and earthy undertow.

Bunnahabhain is the star of the Burn Stewart Distillers group of distilleries. Burn Stewart, in turn, was until recently owned by the Trinidad based company CL World Brands which was a part of the hugely diversified CL Financial conglomerate. CL Financial was hit hard by the economic crisis in 2009 and the government of Trinidad & Tobago had to intervene to keep the company afloat. Since then there have been many rumours that Burn Stewart was up for sale. In spring 2013 it so happened that the South African drinks giant, Distell, (Amarula Cream and Three Ships Whisky) bought the company for £160 million.

The distillery is equipped with a 12,5 tonnes traditional stainless steel mash tun, six washbacks made of Oregon pine and two pairs of stills. The fermentation time varies between 48 and 110 hours. The stills are quite big but only filled to 47% which gives more copper contact for the spirit and produce a lighter whisky. The production for 2013 will be 1,5 million litres of which 20% will be peated (35ppm).

Bunnahabhain single malt is an important part of the blended Scotch Black Bottle but more and more effort has been put into building the single malt brand as well.

The core range consists of *12, 18* and *25 years old*. A mix of bourbon and sherry casks are used – for the 12 year old it is 25% ex sherry and 75% ex bourbon, whereas for the 18 year old the ratio is 40/60 and for the 25 year old 10/90. Part of the core range is also the peated 10 year old *Toiteach*. Limited releases for spring 2013 include a *40 year old* (only 750 bottles) and an even older version (*45 years*) which is due for release at the end of 2013. There are also two travel retail exclusives – *Darach Ur* with no age statement and *Cruach-Mhòna* which is made up of young, heavily peated Bunna-habhain matured in ex bourbon casks along with 20-21 years old matured in ex sherry butts. For Islay Festival 2013, a *10 year old* matured in 2nd fill sherry casks was launched.

12 years old

Caol Ila

Owner: **Region/district:**
Diageo   Islay

Founded: **Status:**   **Capacity:**
1846   Active (vc)   6 500 000 litres

Address: Port Askaig, Islay, Argyll PA46 7RL

Tel: **website:**
01496 302760   www.malts.com

History:

1846 – Hector Henderson founds Caol Ila.

1852 – Henderson, Lamont & Co. is subjected to financial difficulties and Henderson is forced to sell Caol Ila to Norman Buchanan.

1863 – Norman Buchanan encounters financial troubles and sells to the blending company Bulloch, Lade & Co. from Glasgow.

1879 – The distillery is rebuilt and expanded.

1920 – Bulloch, Lade & Co. is liquidated and the distillery is taken over by Caol Ila Distillery.

1927 – DCL becomes sole owners.

1972 – All the buildings, except for the warehouses, are demolished and rebuilt.

1974 – The renovation, which totals £1 million, is complete and six new stills are installed.

1999 – Experiments with a completely unpeated malt are performed.

2002 – The first official bottlings since Flora & Fauna/Rare Malt appear; 12 years, 18 years and Cask Strength (c. 10 years).

2003 – A 25 year old cask strength is released.

2005 – A 25 year old Special Release is launched.

2006 – Unpeated 8 year old and 1993 Moscatel finish are released.

2007 – Second edition of unpeated 8 year old.

2008 – Third edition of unpeated 8 year old.

2009 – The fourth edition of the unpeated version (10 year old) is released.

2010 – A 25 year old, a 1999 Feis Isle bottling and a 1997 Manager's Choice are released.

2011 – An unpeated 12 year old and the unaged Moch are released.

2012 – An unpeated 14 year old is released.

2013 – Unpeated Stitchell Reserve is released.

Caol Ila 12 year old

GS – Iodine, fresh fish and smoked bacon feature on the nose, along with more delicate, floral notes. Smoke, malt, lemon and peat on the slightly oily palate. Peppery peat in the drying finish.

DR – Barbecued fish and seaweed on the nose, oily bacon-fat, squeezed lemon and sweet smoke on the palate, immensely satisfying citrusy seaside barbecue of a finish.

When Caol Ila, the biggest distillery on Islay, was closed for an upgrade during five months in 2011, the owners were forced to buy peated spirit from the nearby Bunnahabhain to augment their stock for future needs. That shows how important Caol Ila peated single malt is for several of the Diageo blends, not least Johnnie Walker Black Label and Double Black. However, the big producers monitor their stock continuously to see what they will need in 3-10 years' time and in 2012, ten percent of the production was unpeated spirit with a nutty character. This share increased to more than 30% in 2013.

The upgrade in 2011 meant a new 13,5 tonnes full lauter mash tun, as well as two new washbacks. The fermentation time is 60 hours except for the unpeated version when it is increased to 80 hours. A new control system was also installed in the still house and the total investment amounted to £3,5m. Apart from the new mash tun, the equipment now consists of eight wooden washbacks, two made of stainless steel and three pairs of stills. During 2013 the distillery will be operating 49 weeks, doing 26 mashes per week which amounts to 6,5 million litres of alcohol.

Not too long ago, Caol Ila was rarely seen in whisky shops. Everything went to blends but the increasing interest in peated whisky prompted Diageo to offer more of the Caol Ila single malt to the market and, today, the brand sells an impressive 600,000 bottles per year. The core range consists of *12, 18* and *25 years old, Distiller's Edition Moscatel finish* and *Cask Strength*. In 2011, *Caol Ila Moch*, the first official bottling from the distillery without an age statement or distillation year, was released. The first *14 year old* of the *unpeated* Caol Ila was released in 2012 and, in conjunction with the 2013 Islay Festival, a *15 year old*, described as a triple-cask matured and bottled at cask strength, was launched. Later in the year, a limited release of an unpeated Caol Ila was released called *Stitchell Reserve* named after the distillery manager Billy Stitchell who is retiring this year.

*Caol Ila
Stitchell Reserve*

Cardhu

Owner:
Diageo

Region/district:
Speyside

Founded: **Status:** **Capacity:**
1824 Active (vc) 3 400 000 litres

Address:
Knockando, Aberlour, Moray AB38 7RY

Tel:
01479 874635 (vc)

website:
www.discovering-distilleries.com

History:
1824 – John Cumming applies for and obtains a licence for Cardhu Distillery.

1846 – John Cumming dies and his son Lewis takes over.

1872 – Lewis dies and his wife Elizabeth takes over.

1884 – A new distillery is built to replace the old.

1893 – John Walker & Sons purchases Cardhu for £20,500.

1908 – The name reverts to Cardow.

1960-61 – Reconstruction and expansion of stills from four to six.

1981 – The name changes to Cardhu.

1998 – A visitor centre is constructed.

2002 – Diageo changes Cardhu single malt to a vatted malt with contributions from other distilleries in it.

2003 – The whisky industry protests sharply against Diageo's plans.

2004 – Diageo withdraws Cardhu Pure Malt.

2005 – The 12 year old Cardhu Single Malt is relaunched and a 22 year old is released.

2009 – Cardhu 1997, a single cask in the new Manager's Choice range is released.

2011 – A 15 year old and an 18 year old are released.

2013 – A 21 year old is released.

Cardhu 12 year old

GS – The nose is relatively light and floral, quite sweet, with pears, nuts and a whiff of distant peat. Medium-bodied, malty and sweet in the mouth. Medium-length in the finish, with sweet smoke, malt and a hint of peat.

DR – Honeycomb and chocolate Crunchie bar on the nose, fluffy over-ripe apples, toffee, boiled sweets on the palate, delightful clean and crisp finish.

There was a time, not too long ago, when Cardhu was among the top five single malts in the world selling almos[t] 4 million bottles in a year. In 2012 it managed to just sque[e]ze into the top ten list with 2 million bottles. It was also th[e] only one of the Top 10 brands which decreased in volume during that year and Singleton of Glen Ord managed to take over the position of most sold single malt within Diageo. So what had happened during the decade that triggered this development? The biggest reason could be attributed to the simple fact that Cardhu single malt large[ly] has been dependant on a single market, Spain. During the last decade the country's import of Scotch whisky decrease[d] by more than 40%, partially due to the worsening econom[y] but also due to competition from other spirits. However, Cardhu is not solely dependent on the single malt sales, it is also one of the most important components of Johnnie Walker and the distillery with its visitor centre is the spiritual home of the world's best selling blended Scotch.

The distillery is equipped with an 8 tonnes stainless steel full lauter mash tun with a copper dome, ten washbacks (four made of Scottish larch, two of stainless steel and four of Douglas fir), all with a fermentation time of 75 hours and three pairs of stills. During 2013, Cardhu will be working a seven-day week with a production of 3,4 million litres of alcohol. For several years, the core range was just the *12 year old*. In 2011 two more expressions were released in France and Spain by way of a *15* and an *18 year old*. Since 2006 there is also a *Special Cask Reserve* with no age statement in these two countries. This expression, which has been matured in rejuvenated bourbon casks, has recently started to appear in other markets and it can also be found in the distillery visitor centre shop. In September 2013, a *21 year old* Cardhu bottled at 54,2% was launched as a part of the Diageo Special Releases.

21 years old

Johnnie Walker Red Label

Blended Scotch

Starring Cardhu Single Malt *in a leading role*
Producer Diageo
Director Jim Beveridge, Master Blender

John Walker (1805-1857) was just 14 years old when his father, Alexander died and left £637 which John's guardians invested in a grocery shop in Kilmarnock. A few years later, the shop had been expanded to also sell whisky and this marked the starting point of what would later become the world´s most famous whisky brand. His son, Alexander, entered the business around 1850 and when the Spirit Act of 1860, which allowed for the mixing of grain and malt whisky, came into force, Alexander was one of the first on board the bandwagon. He registered Walker's Old Highland Whisky in 1867 and a few years later, the conspicuous rectangular bottle that we see today, was launched. But the Walker´s were not satisfied with supplying just the home market and looked elsewhere to grow the brand. By the late 1880s, Walker´s Kilmarnock whisky was the leading brand in Sydney and, at the same time, they also started selling to South Africa which, in a few years, took over as Walker´s largest export market. The brand had become so popular that securing its own production of malt whisky became essential. Cardhu distillery was acquired in 1893 and this is today the spiritual home of Johnnie Walker.

When Alexander had died in 1889, the third generation, Alexander II and George, took over. The product range was revised and three expressions were introduced – Old Highland Whisky, Special Old Highland and Extra Special Old Highland. Just a few years later, in 1909, Special Old Highland was re-named *Red Label* and the more robust Extra Special Old Highland was given the name *Black Label*. Since then, the famous Striding Man, created by the cartoonist, Tom Browne, was used to promote the brand. For a few years there was also a White Label but it was soon phased out. The Striding Man was depicted on American bottles in 1937 and first became global in 1951.

The 1920s was a time when many of the whisky producers sought co-operation and, since then, acquisitions and mergers became considerably more common. Buchanan and Dewar´s had already joined forces in 1915 but the last of The Big Three, John Walker & Sons was still acting independently. In 1925, however, what would become known as The Big Amalgamation, was realized which meant that a large number of producers, including the Walkers, created a mega company under the name DCL, which, in turn, became the predecessor to the largest drinks company of our time, Diageo.

After the end of the second World War, *Johnnie Walker Red Label* was the world's most sold whisky – an achievement they have been able to hold on to even until today. In 2012, a total of 215 million bottles of Johnnie Walker (which includes all the varieties) were sold. The range has been expanded over the years; *Blue Label* was introduced in 1992, *Gold Label*, based on a recipe from 1920, was launched in 1995, the only blended malt in the range, *Green Label*, came in 1997 (at first called Johnnie Walker Pure Malt) and the super premium version *King George V* was first bottled in 2008.

Recent additions to the range are *XR 21*, 21 years old and exclusive to duty free, *Double Black*, a smokier version of Black Label and the 18 year old *Platinum Label*, which was created to slot in between the 12 year old Black Label and the ultra premium Blue Label.

A rustic and fragrant nose with notes of honey, leather, pears and a hint of peat. Malted barley comes through on the palate together with ginger, heather and berries. Touch of peat in the semi-sweet finish.

Clynelish

Owner:
Diageo

Region/district:
Northern Highlands

Founded: 1967

Status: Active (vc)

Capacity: 4 800 000 litres

Address: Brora, Sutherland KW9 6LR

Tel: 01408 623003 (vc)

website: www.malts.com

History:

1819 – The 1st Duke of Sutherland founds a distillery called Clynelish Distillery.

1827 – The first licensed distiller, James Harper, files for bankruptcy and John Matheson takes over.

1846 – George Lawson & Sons become new licensees.

1896 – James Ainslie & Heilbron takes over.

1912 – James Ainslie & Co. narrowly escapes bankruptcy and Distillers Company Limited (DCL) takes over together with James Risk.

1916 – John Walker & Sons buys a stake of James Risk's stocks.

1931 – The distillery is mothballed.

1939 – Production restarts.

1960 – The distillery becomes electrified.

1967 – A new distillery, also named Clynelish, is built adjacent to the first one.

1968 – 'Old' Clynelish is mothballed in August.

1969 – 'Old' Clynelish is reopened as Brora and starts using a very peaty malt.

1983 – Brora is closed in March.

2002 – A 14 year old is released.

2006 – A Distiller's Edition 1991 finished in Oloroso casks is released.

2009 – A 12 year old is released for Friends of the Classic Malts.

2010 – A 1997 Manager's Choice single cask is released.

Clynelish 14 year old

GS – A nose that is fragrant, spicy and complex, with candle wax, malt and a whiff of smoke. Notably smooth in the mouth, with honey and contrasting citric notes, plus spicy peat, before a brine and tropical fruit finish.

DR – Fresh green fruit and unripe melon on the nose, sweet almost fizzy lemon sherbet on the palate, a wispy hint of peat and pepper, and satisfying and balanced finish.

The history of Clynelish distillery involves one of the most controversial figures in Scottish history – George Granville Leveson-Gower. Known as the 1st Duke of Sutherland, he founded the distillery (at that time known as Brora) in 1819, but it is for his actions between 1811 and 1820 that he has become infamous. The Duke, at this time the wealthiest man in the country, was convinced that more money could be made from the vast area of land he owned through breeding sheep rather than from farming. He therefore forced 15,000 farmers from their land and relocated them to the coast to take up fishing. His actions became known as The Highland Clearances and a 100 ft statue of the Duke, with the rather ironic inscription "To a judicious, kind and liberal landlord" was erected one year after his death and can still be seen a couple of miles south of the distillery.

Clynelish is a modern distillery which was built in 1967 right next to the much older Brora (which used to be called Clynelish). The two distilleries were operating together for 14 years but the character of the single malts are completely different, with Brora being much more peated (at least some of the bottlings). Clynelish is equipped with a cast iron full lauter mash tun from 1967, eight wooden washbacks, two stainless steel washbacks and three pairs of stills. Some 6,000 casks are stored in the old Brora warehouses but most of the production at Clynelish is matured elsewhere. In 2013, the distillery will be working a 7-day week producing 4,8 million litres of alcohol. Clynelish is the signature malt in Johnnie Walker Gold Label Reserve, a no age statement version of the previous 18 year old expression which has now been phased out.

The Clynelish single malt sells around 100,000 bottles per year. Official bottlings include a *14 year old* and a *Distiller's Edition* with an Oloroso Seco finish. There is also an *American oak cask strength* exclusively available in the distillery shop exclusive.

14 years old

Cragganmore

Owner:
Diageo

Region/district:
Speyside

Founded: **Status:** **Capacity:**
1869 Active (vc) 2 200 000 litres

Address: Ballindalloch, Moray AB37 9AB

Tel: **website:**
01479 874700 www.malts.com

History:
1869 – John Smith, who already runs Ballindalloch and Glenfarclas Distilleries, founds Cragganmore.

1886 – John Smith dies and his brother George takes over operations.

1893 – John's son Gordon, at 21, is old enough to assume responsibility for operations.

1901 – The distillery is refurbished and modernized with help of the famous architect Charles Doig.

1912 – Gordon Smith dies and his widow Mary Jane supervises operations.

1917 – The distillery closes.

1918 – The distillery reopens and Mary Jane installs electric lighting.

1923 – The distillery is sold to the newly formed Cragganmore Distillery Co. where Mackie & Co. and Sir George Macpherson-Grant of Ballindalloch Estate share ownership.

1927 – White Horse Distillers is bought by DCL which thus obtains 50% of Cragganmore.

1964 – The number of stills is increased from two to four.

1965 – DCL buys the remainder of Cragganmore.

1988 – Cragganmore 12 years becomes one of six selected for United Distillers' Classic Malts.

1998 – Cragganmore Distillers Edition Double Matured (port) is launched for the first time.

2002 – A visitor centre opens in May.

2006 – A 17 year old from 1988 is released.

2010 – Manager's Choice single cask 1997 and a limited 21 year old are released.

Cragganmore 12 year old

GS – A nose of sherry, brittle toffee, nuts, mild wood smoke, angelica and mixed peel. Elegant on the malty palate, with herbal and fruit notes, notably orange. Medium in length, with a drying, slightly smoky finish.

DR – The nose has honey, soft fruits and sweet spring meadow notes and is very inviting, and on the palate soft barley, summer fruits and a sweetness lead up to an almost tangy finish.

Even though James Watson & Co, blenders from Dundee, never owned Cragganmore, the company has played an important part in the history of the distillery. In 1888, during a whisky boom, the company started buying the bulk of Cragganmore's production and kept doing that for many years to come. James Watson & Co, was a major player in the business and owners of distilleries such as Glen Ord, Parkmore and Pulteney. The company took a major blow in summer of 1906 when one of their bonded warehouses in Dundee with 1 million gallons of spirit caught fire but the company managed to continue its business. After several changes in ownership, with closures and re-openings, James Watson and Co finally ceased to operate in 1981. Cragganmore distillery is beautifully tucked away in the Spey valley, close to the A95 with Glenfarclas being its closest neighbour on the other side of the road. In 1988 it became one of the original six Classic Malts. The distillery is equipped with a 6,8 tonnes stainless steel full lauter mash tun. There are also six washbacks made of Oregon pine with a 50-60 hour fermentation time and two pairs of stills. The two spirit stills are most peculiar with flat tops, which had already been introduced during the times of the founder, John Smith. The stills are attached to worm tubs on the outside for cooling the spirit vapours. The distillery is currently doing 16 mashes per week which means a production of 2,2 million litres during 2013. Cragganmore single malt plays an important part in two blended whiskies; White Horse and Old Parr. The latter was first introduced in 1909 and is very popular in Japan and Latin America. During the last 10 years of sales, the brand has increased by more than 200% and in 2012 it sold 15 million bottles.

The core range of Cragganmore is made up of a *12 year old* and a *Distiller's Edition* with a finish in Port pipes. Two limited bottlings appeared in 2010; a *single sherry cask* distilled in *1997* released as part of the Manager's Choice series and a *21 year old* launched as a part of the Special Releases.

12 years old

Craigellachie

Owner:
John Dewar & Sons
(Bacardi)

Region/district:
Speyside

Founded: 1891
Status: Active
Capacity: 4 000 000 litres

Address: Aberlour, Banffshire AB38 9ST

Tel: 01340 872971
website: -

History:
1891 – The distillery is built by Craigellachie–Glenlivet Distillery Company which has Alexander Edward and Peter Mackie as part-owners. The famous Charles Doig is the architect.

1898 – Production does not start until this year.

1916 – Mackie & Company Distillers Ltd takes over.

1924 – Peter Mackie dies and Mackie & Company changes name to White Horse Distillers.

1927 – White Horse Distillers are bought by Distillers Company Limited (DCL).

1930 – Administration is transferred to Scottish Malt Distillers (SMD), a subsidiary of DCL.

1964 – Refurbishing takes place and two new stills are bought, increasing the number to four.

1998 – United Distillers & Vintners (UDV) sells Craigellachie together with Aberfeldy, Brackla and Aultmore and the blending company John Dewar & Sons to Bacardi Martini.

2004 – The first bottlings from the new owners are a new 14 year old which replaces UDV's Flora & Fauna and a 21 year old cask strength from 1982 produced for Craigellachie Hotel.

Craigellachie 14 year old

GS – Citrus fruits, cereal and even a whiff of smoke on the nose. Comparatively full-bodied, with sweet fruits, malt and spice on the palate, plus earthy notes and a touch of liquorice in the slightly smoky and quite lengthy finish.

DR – Intriguing and deep mix of light fruits on the nose, a spicy bite then clean and smooth mouth feel, and a soft finish.

In 1998, Craigellachie became a small piece of the puzzle which was to be one of the biggest corporate acquisitions of that time. Guinness and Grand Metropolitan had just merged to form a new giant, Diageo, and in order to approve the acquisition, the US and European competition authorities demanded that Diageo sell Dewar's whisky portfolio (including Craigellachie and four other distilleries) as well as Bombay gin. Some 20 companies competed for the brands and in the end, Bacardi was victorious but at the enormous price of £1,15bn. Diageo had no problem parting with Dewar's as they already had two global Scotch blends in their range – Johnnie Walker and J&B. To have to sell Bombay Sapphire on the other hand, was a bitter disappointment to the owners. With a growth of 30% per year, the young brand would have been perfect for their portfolio.

The Craigellachie distillery derives its name from the huge cliff which dominates the landscape and actually means "rocky hill". The village dates back to the mid 18th century with the distillery being built around a century and a half later. The founder, Peter Mackie, soon made Craigellachie single malt an important part of his famous blend White Horse.

The distillery is equipped with a modern Steinecker full lauter mash tun, installed in 2001, which replaced the old open cast iron mash tun. There are also eight washbacks made of larch with a fermentation time of 56-60 hours and two pairs of stills. The spirit vapours from the stills are condensed through worm tubs. The tub itself can last for many years but the worms (the copper pipes where the spirit is condensed) need to be replaced every 5 to 10 years. Production during 2013 will be 21 mashes per week and with the help of a shorter silent season, the staff has managed to increase production to 3,9 million litres of alcohol.

Most of the production goes into Dewar's blends but a *14 year old* has been on the market since 2004 and this is the only official bottling.

14 years old

Dailuaine

Owner: **Region/district:**
Diageo   Speyside

Founded: **Status:**   **Capacity:**
1852   Active   5 200 000 litres

Address: Carron, Banffshire AB38 7RE

Tel: **website:**
01340 872500   www.malts.com

History:
1852 – The distillery is founded by William Mackenzie.

1865 – William Mackenzie dies and his widow leases the distillery to James Fleming, a banker from Aberlour.

1879 – William Mackenzie's son forms Mackenzie and Company with Fleming.

1891 – Dailuaine-Glenlivet Distillery Ltd is founded.

1898 – Dailuaine-Glenlivet Distillery Ltd merges with Talisker Distillery Ltd and forms Dailuaine-Talisker Distilleries Ltd.

1915 – Thomas Mackenzie dies without heirs.

1916 – Dailuaine-Talisker Company Ltd is bought by the previous customers John Dewar & Sons, John Walker & Sons and James Buchanan & Co.

1917 – A fire rages and the pagoda roof collapses. The distillery is forced to close.

1920 – The distillery reopens.

1925 – Distillers Company Limited (DCL) takes over.

1960 – Refurbishing. The stills increase from four to six and a Saladin box replaces the floor maltings.

1965 – Indirect still heating through steam is installed.

1983 – On site maltings is closed down and malt is purchased centrally.

1991 – The first official bottling, a 16 year old, is launched in the Flora & Fauna series.

1996 – A 22 year old cask strength from 1973 is launched as a Rare Malt.

1997 – A cask strength version of the 16 year old is launched.

2000 – A 17 year old Manager´s Dram matured in sherry casks is launched.

2010 – A single cask from 1997 is released.

2012 – The production capacity is increased by 25%.

Dailuaine 16 year old

GS – Barley, sherry and nuts on the substantial nose, developing into maple syrup. Medium-bodied, rich and malty in the mouth, with more sherry and nuts, plus ripe oranges, fruitcake, spice and a little smoke. The finish is lengthy and slightly oily, with almonds, cedar and slightly smoky oak.

DR – Rich and full nose, with plum, apricot jam and some treacle toffee. The palate is very full, rich, rounded and sweet with apricot and red berries. The finish is medium, fruity and sweet.

Dailuaine distillery has cemented its place in whisky history thanks to a new innovation that was tested here for the first time in 1889. At that time the architect, Charles Cree Doig, constructed the first pagoda roof (as it was named later) to make it easier to ventilate the smoke coming from the kiln. Unfortunately, the roof collapsed in 1917 but the same design can still be seen today at many of the distilleries around Scotland (and abroad), although the vast majority of them these days are just ornamental and without any practical significance.

The Dailuaine site has been a busy one over the last two years. Adjacent to the distillery lays a bio plant which has been completely upgraded during 2012. The idea of the bio plant is to, through anaerobic digestion, convert spent lees and waste water from the distillation process into clean, processed water and at the same time produce biogas to provide heat and energy for the distillery. The new plant can take care of 1,000 m³ of dilutes (from Dailuaine and many other distilleries in the area) per day.

Dailuaine distillery, nicely tucked away at the Spey River, is equipped with a stainless steel full lauter mash tun, eight washbacks made of larch, plus two new stainless steel ones placed outside and three pairs of stills. All the condensers are made of copper but, until a few years ago, some of them were made of stainless steel to help achieve a sulphury style of new make. Since then the style has changed and they are now alternating between nutty and green/grassy. For 2013 it is green/grassy which demands a clear wort from the mash tun and a long fermentation (75 hours) in the washbacks. Around 4,7 million litres of alcohol will be produced in 2013. Dailuaine is one of many distilleries whose main task is to produce malt whisky which is to become part of blended Scotch. The only official bottling is the *16 year old* in the Flora & Fauna series. In April 2010 a limited ex-sherry *single cask* from *1997* was released as part of the Manager´s Choice series.

Flora & Fauna 16 years old

Dalmore

Owner:
Whyte & Mackay Ltd
(United Spirits)

Region/district:
Northern Highlands

Founded: 1839
Status: Active (vc)
Capacity: 3 700 000 litres

Address: Alness, Ross-shire IV17 0UT

Tel: 01349 882362
website: www.thedalmore.com

History:

1839 – Alexander Matheson founds the distillery.

1867 – Three Mackenzie brothers run the distillery.

1886 – Alexander Matheson dies.

1891 – Sir Kenneth Matheson sells the distillery for £14,500 to the Mackenzie brothers.

1917 – The Royal Navy moves in to start manufacturing American mines.

1920 – The Royal Navy moves out and leaves behind a distillery damaged by an explosion.

1922 – The distillery is in production again.

1956 – Floor malting replaced by Saladin box.

1960 – Mackenzie Brothers (Dalmore) Ltd merges with Whyte & Mackay and forms the company Dalmore-Whyte & Mackay Ltd.

1966 – Number of stills is increased to eight.

1982 – The Saladin box is abandoned.

1990 – American Brands buys Whyte & Mackay.

1996 – Whyte & Mackay changes name to JBB (Greater Europe).

2001 – Through management buy-out, JBB (Greater Europe) is bought from Fortune Brands and changes name to Kyndal Spirits.

2002 – Kyndal Spirits changes name to Whyte & Mackay.

2004 – A new visitor centre opens.

2007 – United Spirits buys Whyte & Mackay. 15 year old, 1973 Cabernet Sauvignon and a 40 year old are released.

2008 – 1263 King Alexander III and Vintage 1974 are released.

2009 – New releases include an 18 year old, a 58 year old and a Vintage 1951.

2010 – The Dalmore Mackenzie 1992 Vintage is released.

2011 – More expressions in the River Collection and 1995 Castle Leod are released.

2012 – The visitor centre is upgraded and Constellaton Collection is launched.

2013 – Valour is released for duty free.

Dalmore 12 year old

GS – The nose offers sweet malt, orange marmalade, sherry and a hint of leather. Full-bodied, with a dry sherry taste though sweeter sherry develops in the mouth along with spice and citrus notes. Lengthy finish with more spices, ginger, Seville oranges and vanilla.

DR – Orange jelly and squidgy fruit on the nose, an impressive full confectionery and fruit salad taste on the softest of peat beds, and a wonderful and warming finish.

Dalmore distillery, located on the north shore of the Cromarty Firth was due for an exceptional upgrade recently. The plans began to take shape at the end of 2011 to triple its capacity to around 10 million litres. Several of the old buildings would be demolished and new ones would be constructed. Planning applications were sent in to Highland Council in spring 2012 but then suddenly the plans were stopped. Diageo announced at the beginning of 2013 that they were about to buy the majority of United Spirits in India, owners of Whyte & Mackay of which Dalmore is a part. If that deal were to become a reality, it would most certainly mean that Diageo, for competitive reasons, would be forced to sell Whyte & Mackay and therefore the expansion has been put on hold.

The distillery is equipped with a semi-lauter mash tun, eight washbacks made of Oregon pine and four pairs of stills. The spirit stills have water jackets which allow cold water to circulate between the reflux bowl and the neck of the stills, thus increasing the reflux. The owners expect to produce 3,7 million litres during 2013. The whisky is normally unpeated but for the last few years, a heavily peated spirit has been produced. However, during 2013 there will be no peated production.

A new and excellent visitor centre was opened in 2011, highlighting for instance the importance of wood. They also sell a distillery exclusive bottling which currently is a *1995 Matusalem sherry finish*.

The core range consists of *12, 15, 18 year old, 1263 King Alexander III* and *Cigar Malt*. In spring 2013 *Dalmore Valour* was released as a duty free exclusive. It has been matured in three different casks (bourbon, Oloroso sherry and port). Dalmore has also become known for some very exclusive bottlings, including the 30 year old *Dalmore Ceti*, the one bottle of *Zenith* which was sold through an auction and the *Constellation Collection*.

12 years old

Whisky Around the World
ITALY

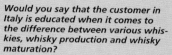

Davide Terziotti is a well-known whisky blogger (angelshare.it) and moderator of the singlemaltwhisky.it forum. He regularly arranges craft beer and whisky tastings and courses and he has participated in several judging panels.

Which spirit is the most popular in Italy and where does whisky fit into the picture?

The national spirit is Grappa which has had an interesting development in the last twenty years moving from a cheap and rough product to a smooth and elegant drink. Besides that, vodka and rum are the top spirits, not least because they are used in drinks. Whisky has a long history in Italy but is wrongly perceived as a luxury and "old fashion" product. The overall picture for spirits in Italy, is that consumption has decreased by 85% in 40 years.

What types of whisky are the most popular in Italy?

Even if Italy has a good tradition when it comes to single malt, blended Scotch is number one. Some bourbon brands are also very popular and easy to find, like Jack Daniels.

When would you say people in Italy started to get seriously interested in whisky? What triggered it and how has that interest developed?

In the 1960s and 1970s, whisky, and in particular single malt, started to become popular. The book "Single Malt Whisky – an Italian passion" by Umberto Angeloni is certainly an evidence of that. There is a long tradition of collecting whisky in Italy (Giaccone, D'Ambrosio and Begnoni for instance) and we also have a range of top rated independent bottlers who helped initiate the interest – Samaroli, Silver Seal, Intertrade/High Spirits and, recently, Wilson & Morgan.

Which brands of Scotch are the most popular in Italy?

I would say Macallan, Glen Grant, Laphroaig, Lagavulin and Ardbeg for single malts and J&B, Johnnie Walker, Ballantine's and Chivas for blends.

How is whisky sold in Italy, is there a wide variety of brands and is it easy to find the brand you want?

Almost all the main brands are available and around 80% of them are quite easy to find. The problem is to find the rarer and limited versions as they are seldom distributed in Italy and when they are, it is in very limited quantities.

How is whisky marketed in Italy?

Distributors and producers will of course advertise and use web marketing but it feels like, rather than pushing whisky, they concentrate on cheaper products that sell easier. Festivals, blogs and whisky clubs on the other hand, have done a great job in the last years promoting whisky.

Is whisky considered a luxury drink compared to other spirits?

Yes, the general idea is that whisky is a drink for men over 60 with a wallet full of euros and who usually drink it in front of an open fire after an expensive dinner. This is unfortunately also the picture that is used for marketing and advertising. Festivals and clubs on the other hand are having tastings trying to show that you can find good whiskies for 30 euros and the results so far seem positive.

Is whisky something you drink at home or in a bar or restaurant?

I think a lot of people drink whisky at home because prices at retailers and supermarkets are quite low. Restaurants with a good spirit menu are still not that common and often too expensive. A publican will typically charge you 8 euros for a (double) dram of a low tier single malt.

Are there special occasions when whisky is preferred?

The perception of whisky as an exclusive drink will push people to drink it for a special occasion, for instance Christmas or an anniversary. Many times it is also enjoyed after a dinner or as a night cap.

How is whisky enjoyed in Italy?

I would say that, unfortunately, a lot of people still drink it with ice in a tumbler. Putting some water in your whisky is often frowned upon. In mixology bourbon is largely used.

Would you say that the customer in Italy is educated when it comes to the difference between various whiskies, whisky production and whisky maturation?

An old TV advertisment stated that a blend is a symphony while a malt whisky is just a single note. The knowledge of the general consumer is at the same level and this goes for people working with whisky as well. The wine sommelier training courses cover all spirits in just one lesson. I hope distributors will invest more in training for sales people and retailers. That's why the clubs, blogs and festivals are trying to fill this lack of education.

How many producers of whisky do you have in Italy and how would you describe the future for domestic whisky in your country?

In the past there were some grappa producers that tried to distill cereals but nothing relevant. There is however a brand new distillery called Puni in Val Venosta, Sud Tyrol. They built a great distillery using Scottish equipments and the spirit I've tried is very promising. Their first whisky will be released in 2015. I don't think others will follow soon.

What are your thoughts on the future for Scotch whisky in Italy?

Popularity has diminished for several years and the availability has decreased in favour of other spirits. Still, I see some very positive indicators of a growing interest at the moment; we have the long running Milano Whisky Festival and also a new one in Rome (Spirit of Scotland), tastings and masterclasses are becoming more and more popular and the work done by these festival organizers but also by associations, bloggers and whisky enthusiasts is starting to show some results.

Dalwhinnie

Owner:
Diageo

Region/district:
Northern Highlands

Founded: **Status:** **Capacity:**
1897 Active (vc) 2 200 000 litres

Address: Dalwhinnie, Inverness-shire PH19 1AB

Tel: **website:**
01540 672219 (vc) www.malts.com

History:
1897 – John Grant, George Sellar and Alexander Mackenzie from Kingussie commence building the facilities. The first name is Strathspey and the construction work amounts to £10,000.

1898 – Production starts in February. The owner encounters financial troubles after a few months and John Somerville & Co and A P Blyth & Sons take over in November and change the name to Dalwhinnie.

1905 – America's largest distillers, Cook & Bernheimer in New York, buys Dalwhinnie for £1,250 at an auction. The administration of Dalwhinnie is placed in the newly formed company James Munro & Sons.

1919 – Macdonald Greenlees & Williams Ltd headed by Sir James Calder buys Dalwhinnie.

1926 – Macdonald Greenlees & Williams Ltd is bought by Distillers Company Ltd (DCL) which licences Dalwhinnie to James Buchanan & Co.

1930 – Operations are transferred to Scottish Malt Distilleries (SMD).

1934 – The distillery is closed after a fire in February.

1938 – The distillery opens again.

1968 – The maltings is decommissioned.

1986 – A complete refurbishing takes place.

1987 – Dalwhinnie 15 years becomes one of the selected six in United Distillers' Classic Malts.

1991 – A visitor centre is constructed.

1992 – The distillery closes and goes through a major refurbishment costing £3.2 million.

1995 – The distillery opens in March.

1998 – Dalwhinnie Distillers Edition 1980 (oloroso) is introduced for the first time. The other five in The Classic Malts, each with a different finish, are also introduced as Distillers Editions for the first time.

2002 – A 36 year old is released.

2003 – A 29 year old is released.

2006 – A 20 year old is released.

2010 – A Manager's Choice 1992 is released.

2012 – A 25 year old is released.

Dalwhinnie 15 year old

GS – The nose is fresh, with pine needles, heather and vanilla. Sweet and balanced on the fruity palate, with honey, malt and a very subtle note of peat. The medium length finish dries elegantly.

DR – Full honey and sweet peat on the nose, a rich creamy mouthfeel and a delicious honey and exotic fruits mix all layered on soft peat foundations.

Dalwhinnie is visited by 30,000 people every year and there are some good reasons for that – a well-known single malt brand, an excellent visitor centre and, not least, the location. Travelling on the busy A9 from Perth to Inverness on the outskirts of the Cairngorm wilderness, you can clearly see it from the road. Beware though, by the time you see the distillery on your left, you've already missed the turnoff for the distillery (which is clearly signposted).

Dalwhinnie is one of Diageo's best selling single malts (actually number six after Cardhu, Talisker, Lagavulin and two of the Singletons – Glen Ord and Dufftown)) and sold around 1 million bottles in 2012. But Dalwhinnie single malt also has another role to play, namely as the signature malt of Buchanan's blended Scotch. The brand has been around since the 1890s but has become increasingly popular in recent years, not least in Latin America and the USA where it was the fastest growing blend last year. A total of 20 million bottles were sold globally in 2012.

Dalwhinnie distillery is equipped with a full lauter mash tun, six wooden washbacks and just the one pair of stills. From the stills, the lyne arms lead out through the roofs to the wooden wormtubs outside. The style they are looking for in the newmake is sulphury – something that will disappear when it is ready to be bottled. This character is enhanced by the lack of copper contact in the wormtubs but also through the wide spirit cut (the part of the distillation which goes into casks to mature). In keeping with other distilleries that produce a sulphury, heavy newmake (Mortlach, Dailuaine and Benrinnes), the single malt from Dalwhinnie has to mature a couple more years than the usual 10-12 years in order for all the flavours to develop.

The core range is made up of a *15 year old* and a *Distiller's Edition*. In autumn 2012 a limited *25 year old* was launched as a part of the Special Releases.

15 years old

Deanston

Owner:
Burn Stewart Distillers
(Distell Group Ltd)

Region/district:
Southern Highlands

Founded:
1965

Status:
Active (vc)

Capacity:
3 000 000 litres

Address: Deanston, Perthshire FK16 6AG

Tel:
01786 843010

website:
www.deanstonmalt.com

History:
1965 – A weavery from 1785 is transformed into Deanston Distillery by James Finlay & Co. and Brodie Hepburn Ltd (Deanston Distillery Co.). Brodie Hepburn also runs Tullibardine Distillery.

1966 – Production commences in October.

1971 – The first single malt is named Old Bannockburn.

1972 – Invergordon Distillers takes over.

1974 – The first single malt bearing the name Deanston is produced.

1982 – The distillery closes.

1990 – Burn Stewart Distillers from Glasgow buys the distillery for £2.1 million.

1991 – The distillery resumes production.

1999 – C L Financial buys an 18% stake of Burn Stewart.

2002 – C L Financial acquires the remaining stake.

2006 – Deanston 30 years old is released.

2009 – A new version of the 12 year old is released.

2010 – Virgin Oak is released.

2012 – A visitor centre is opened.

Deanston 12 year old

GS – A fresh, fruity nose with malt and honey. The palate displays cloves, ginger, honey and malt, while the finish is long, quite dry and pleasantly herbal.

DR – Fresh and young crystallized barley on the nose with some cut hay and grass. On the palate it's a fruit sandwich, with orange and yellow fruits at first, then a cough candy honey and aniseed centre, and orange marmalade late on. The finish is intensely fruity with some spice.

Since last year, more people have had the opportunity to get an in-depth knowledge of Deanston distillery through their visitor centre which opened in May 2012. Part of the tour includes a film from the 1920s which is projected on a huge, white distillery wall showing one of the water wheels (at that time the biggest in Europe) in action. A total of 8 wheels were demounted by 1937 but were replaced by turbines and Deanston is the only Scottish distillery that is self-sufficient as regards electricity. Originally a weavery built in 1785, Deanston was transformed into a distillery in 1965. Most of the buildings are new but there is an amazing weaving shed from the 19th century which is now being used as a warehouse. The distillery has new owners since spring 2013 when the South African drinks giant, Distell, bought Burn Stewart Distillers (including Bunnahabhain and Tobermory) for £160 million.

The distillery equipment consists of a traditional open top cast iron mash tun, eight stainless steel washbacks and two pairs of stills with ascending lyne arms. During 2013, the distillery will be doing 11-13 mashes per week and producing 2,5 million litres of alcohol. Starting in 2000, a small part of organic spirit has been produced yearly. The single malt from Deanston has no artificial colouring and it is also unchillfiltered. The core range is a *12 year old* and *Virgin Oak*. The latter is a non-age statement malt with a finish in virgin oak casks. There is also a *30 year old* which is exclusive to the USA. A 12 year old bottling for Marks & Spencer was recently discontinued. The long awaited, first version of *Organic Deanston* was released in late 2013. For those who travel to the distillery there is a reward in the form of three distillery exclusive bottlings – *Toasted Oak, Spanish Oak* and the limited *1974 Vintage*. An additional expression was added in 2013 by way of a *10 year old* sherry maturation which you can fill by yourself in the shop.

12 years old

Dufftown

Owner:
Diageo

Region/district:
Speyside

Founded: 1896
Status: Active
Capacity: 6 000 000 litres

Address: Dufftown, Keith, Banffshire AB55 4BR

Tel: 01340 822100
website: www.malts.com

History:
1895 – Peter Mackenzie, Richard Stackpole, John Symon and Charles MacPherson build the distillery Dufftown-Glenlivet in an old mill.

1896 – Production starts in November.

1897 – The distillery is owned by P. Mackenzie & Co., who also owns Blair Athol in Pitlochry.

1933 – P. Mackenzie & Co. is bought by Arthur Bell & Sons for £56,000.

1968 – The floor maltings is discontinued and malt is bought from outside suppliers. The number of stills is increased from two to four.

1974 – The number of stills is increased from four to six.

1979 – The stills are increased by a further two to eight.

1985 – Guinness buys Arthur Bell & Sons.

1997 – Guinness and Grand Metropolitan merge to form Diageo.

2006 – The Singleton of Dufftown 12 year old is launched as a special duty free bottling.

2008 – The Singleton of Dufftown is made available also in the UK.

2010 – A Manager's Choice 1997 is released.

2013 – A 28 year old cask strength and two expressions for duty free - Unité and Trinité - are released.

Singleton of Dufftown 12 year old

GS – The nose is sweet, almost violet-like, with underlying malt. Big and bold on the palate, this is an upfront yet very drinkable whisky. The finish is medium to long, warming, spicy, with slowly fading notes of sherry and fudge.

DR – Honeycomb and tinned peach and apricot in syrup on the nose, sharp and spicy clean barley on the palate, with some bitter orange notes towards the finish.

Not too long ago, Dufftown was the biggest of all the Diageo distilleries in terms of capacity. In a couple of years it will only be number six. Roseisle has been built and another with the same capacity has been decided upon. Caol Ila has been upgraded and Glen Ord and Teaninich are next in line. Nevertheless, Dufftown has the capacity of producing an impressive 6 million litres. The distillery is equipped with a 13 tonnes full lauter mash tun, 12 stainless steel washbacks and three pairs of stills. All stills also have sub coolers. The style of Dufftown single malt is green and grassy which is achieved by a clear wort from the mash tun and long fermentation (75 hours minimum) in the washbacks. Add to that a slow distillation and the fact that the stills are filled with small volumes to allow as much copper contact as possible and you have its character. Dufftown has been working 24/7 since 2007 and during 2013 they will be doing 6 million litres of alcohol.

On the site there is also an evaporator plant as well as a bio plant. In the afore-mentioned the pot ale (being the residue from the wash still) is transformed into 140 tonnes of syrup every week, which then goes to the farmers to be spread on the fields. The bio plant takes care of the spent lees, the very last part of the spirit distillation. These mainly consist of water and a certain amount of copper that needs to be separated before being released into the cycle of nature again. The two plants don't just service Dufftown but also the neighbouring distilleries of Mortlach and Glendullan. Most of the production goes into blended whiskies, especially Bell's. The core range consists of Singleton of Dufftown 12, 15 and 18 year old. In spring 2013, two new bottlings were released exclusive for Duty Free – Singleton of Dufftown Unité and Singleton of Dufftown Trinité, both without age statement. Later that year, the first official cask strength (52,3%) bottling was released, Singleton of Dufftown 28 years.

Trinité

Edradour

Owner:
Signatory Vintage
Scotch Whisky Co. Ltd

Region/district:
Southern Highlands

Founded: 1825 **Status:** Active (vc) **Capacity:** 130 000 litres

Address: Pitlochry, Perthshire PH16 5JP

Tel: 01796 472095 **website:** www.edradour.com

History:

1825 – Probably the year when a distillery called Glenforres is founded by farmers in Perthshire.

1837 – The first year Edradour is mentioned.

1841 – The farmers form a proprietary company, John MacGlashan & Co.

1886 – John McIntosh & Co. acquires Edradour.

1933 – William Whiteley & Co. buys the distillery.

1982 – Campbell Distilleries (Pernod Ricard) buys Edradour and builds a visitor centre.

1986 – The first single malt is released.

2002 – Edradour is bought by Andrew Symington from Signatory for £5.4 million. The product range is expanded with a 10 year old and a 13 year old cask strength.

2003 – A 30 year old and a 10 year old are released.

2004 – A number of wood finishes are launched as cask strength.

2006 – The first bottling of peated Ballechin is released.

2007 – A Madeira matured Ballechin is released.

2008 – A Ballechin matured in Port pipes and a 10 year old Edradour with a Sauternes finish are released.

2009 – Fourth edition of Ballechin (Oloroso) is released.

2010 – Ballechin #5 Marsala is released.

2011 – Ballechin #6 Bourbon and a 26 year old PX sherry finish are relased.

2012 – A 1993 Oloroso and a 1993 Sauternes finish as well as the 7th edition of Ballechin (Bordeaux) are released.

2013 – Ballechin Sauternes is released.

Photo: © Ernst J. Scheiner, The Gateway To Distilleries

For many years dating from the 1920s to the 1960s, Edradour single malt was a part of one of the most famous blended Scotch at the time, The King's Ransom. The brand was owned by William Whiteley who bought the distillery in 1933 but when he sold his company to two Americans five years later, organised crime suddenly became a part of the Edradour history. The new owners, Irving Haim and Phil Kastel, had close relationships with the notorious mafia leader, Frank Costello, and it was actually Costello who gave them a loan of $325,000 to buy the company. Costello's profit in the taking was that he got commission on every bottle of King's Ransom sold in the States.

Today, under the ownership of Andrew Symington, Edradour, has preserved its artisanal nature and is one of the most visited distilleries in Scotland. The distillery is equipped with an open, traditional cast iron mash tun dating from 1910 with a mash size of 1,15 tonnes. The two washbacks are made of Oregon pine and two stills are connected to a more than 100 year old wormtub. In 2013 they will be doing 6 mashes per week and 130,000 litres of alcohol in the year of which 26,000 litres will be heavily peated.

The core expression is the *10 year old* and the *12 year old*, sherry matured *Caledonia Selection*. A series of wood finishes under the name *Straight From The Cask* (SFTC), are all bottled at cask strength and some of them are nowadays fully matured in various types of casks. The current range is *Burgundy, Port, Marsala, Sherry, Chardonnay, Sauternes* and *Chateauneuf du Pape*. In addition to this, there is a range of whiskies, aged *10-12 years*, bottled at 46% with a full maturation in casks that previously contained burgundy, sauternes, chardonnay and ruby port. The first release of the heavily peated *Ballechin* was in 2006 and the eighth and final bottling in this series was a *Sauternes* maturation released in summer 2013. From end of 2014 a Ballechin 10 year old will become a permanent part of the core range.

Caledonia 12 years old

Edradour 10 year old

GS – Cider apples, malt, almonds, vanilla and honey ar present on the nose, along with a hint of smoke and sherry. The palate is rich, creamy and malty, with a persistent nuttiness and quite a pronounced kick of slightly leathery sherry. Spices and sherry dominate the medium to long finish.

DR – Lemon and lime, rich fruits and some mint on the nose, sharp grape, berries and honey on the palate, and a lingering and pleasant fruity finish with hints of smoke.

Fettercairn

Owner:
Whyte & Mackay Ltd
(United Spirits)

Region/district:
Eastern Highlands

Founded: 1824
Status: Active (vc)
Capacity: 2 300 000 litres

Address: Fettercairn, Laurencekirk,
Kincardineshire AB30 1YB

Tel: 01561 340205
website: www.fettercairndistillery.co.uk

History:
1824 – Sir Alexander Ramsay founds the distillery.

1830 – Sir John Gladstone buys the distillery.

1887 – A fire erupts and the distillery is forced to close for repairs.

1890 – Thomas Gladstone dies and his son John Robert takes over. The distillery reopens.

1912 – The company is close to liquidation and John Gladstone buys out the other investors.

1926 –The distillery is mothballed.

1939 – The distillery is bought by Associated Scottish Distillers Ltd. Production restarts.

1960 – The maltings discontinues.

1966 – The stills are increased from two to four.

1971 – The distillery is bought by Tomintoul-Glenlivet Distillery Co. Ltd.

1973 – Tomintoul-Glenlivet Distillery Co. Ltd is bought by Whyte & Mackay Distillers Ltd.

1974 – The mega group of companies Lonrho buys Whyte & Mackay.

1988 – Lonrho sells to Brent Walker Group plc.

1989 – A visitor centre opens.

1990 – American Brands Inc. buys Whyte & Mackay for £160 million.

1996 – Whyte & Mackay and Jim Beam Brands merge to become JBB Worldwide.

2001 – Kyndal Spirits, a company formed by managers at Whyte & Mackay, buys Whyte & Mackay from JBB Worldwide.

2002 – The whisky changes name to Fettercairn 1824.

2003 – Kyndal Spirits changes name to Whyte & Mackay.

2007 – United Spirits buys Whyte & Mackay. A 23 year old single cask is released.

2009 – 24, 30 and 40 year olds are released.

2010 – Fettercairn Fior is launched.

2012 – Fettercairn Fasque is released.

Fettercairn Fior

GS – A complex, weighty nose of toffee, sherry, ginger, orange and smoke. More orange and smoke on the palate, with a sherried nuttiness and hints of treacle toffee. Mild, spicy oak and a touch of liquorice in the lengthy finish.

DR – A big whisky from the off, earthy and rustic on the nose, with bitter orange, cocoa, nuts and burnt toffee on the nose, full mouth feel with toasty orange marmalade, chocolate and peat. The finish includes wood, burnt toffee and spice.

The Gladstone family, including the four times Prime Minister, William Gladstone, were the owners of Fettercairn distillery for more than a century until 1939 when it was sold. The nearby Fasque Estate still belongs to the family and has also given name to one of Fettercairn´s whiskies.
Fettercairn has formed the backbone of the bulk whisky production for the owners, Whyte & Mackay, producing whisky earmarked for Tesco, Asda and many other customers. This aspect of the business has now been downsized which has given Fettercairn a chance to show its qualities as a single malt during the last four to five years.
Fettercairn distillery is equipped with a traditional cast iron mash tun with a copper canopy, eight washbacks made of Douglas fir and two pairs of stills. One feature makes it unique among Scottish distilleries – when collecting the middle cut, cooling water is allowed to trickle along the outside of the spirit still necks and is collected at the base for circulation towards the top again. This is done in order to increase reflux and thereby produce a lighter and cleaner spirit. For 2013 the production is 22 mashes per week, reaching 2 million litres of alcohol for the year. During the last couple of years the owners have produced around 200,000 litres of heavily peated spirit (55ppm) but there will be no peated production in 2013.
There are 14 dunnage warehouses on site and the oldest whisky is from 1965. Two quarter casks and three hogsheads from 1965 were re-racked into a sherry butt in 2003.
The core range consists of *Fettercairn Fior* without age statement and three older whiskies – *24, 30* and *40 year old*. The greatest part of Fior comprises of whiskies aged 14 and 15 years with an addition of 5 year old peated whisky. In 2011 another whisky without age statement was launched as an exclusive for Tesco. It is called *Fettercairn Fasque* and contains slightly younger whiskies than Fior and only 5% is peated whisky. There is also a new distillery exclusive bottling, a *10 year old* first matured in American oak sherry quarter casks and then transferred to first fill bourbon barrels.

Fettercairn Fior

Glenallachie

Owner:
Chivas Brothers
(Pernod Ricard)

Region/district:
Speyside

Founded: Status: Capacity:
1967   Active   4 000 000 litres

Address: Aberlour, Banffshire AB38 9LR

Tel: website:
01542 783042   -

History:

1967 – The distillery is founded by Mackinlay, McPherson & Co., a subsidiary of Scottish & Newcastle Breweries Ltd. William Delmé Evans is architect.

1985 – Scottish & Newcastle Breweries Ltd sells Charles Mackinlay Ltd to Invergordon Distillers which acquires both Glenallachie and Isle of Jura.

1987 – The distillery is decommissioned.

1989 – Campbell Distillers (Pernod Ricard) buys the distillery, increases the number of stills from two to four and takes up production again.

2005 – The first official bottling for many years is a Cask Strength Edition from 1989.

When Glenallachie was built by Charles Mackinlay & Co, the company had already been bought by Scottish & Newcastle Breweries. Founded in 1847 by Charles Mackinlay, the company had been a key player in the industry for more than a century. They introduced The Original Mackinlay, a blend which had risen in ascendency and quickly became so popular that Sir Ernest Shackleton asked them to supply the official whisky for his expedition to the South Pole in 1907. Exactly 100 years later, crates with bottles of The Original Mackinlay intact were discovered at Shackleton's camp at Cape Royd. The contents were analyzed and replicas were created and launched by Whyte & Mackay in 2011. Glenallachie distillery, situated just outside Aberlour and in the shadow of Ben Rinnes, is equipped with a 9,4 tonnes semi-lauter mash tun, six washbacks made of mild steel but lined with stainless steel, plus another two washbacks brought in from the now demolished Caperdonich in 2011. There are two pairs of lantern-shaped stills while the spirit stills are of the onion model. Thanks to the new washbacks, the production capacity has increased by 30% to 4 million litres. The spirit is filled into bourbon casks and matured in 12 racked and two palletised warehouses.

The most important role for the whisky from Glenallachie is to form the backbone of the blended Scotch Clan Campbell. It was established during the 1930s by Campbell Distillers, but it wasn't until Pernod Ricard took over the brand that sales had escalated. By 1985 Clan Campbell was one the best selling Scotch whiskies in France and in 2012 it sold almost 20 million bottles globally.

Currently, the only official bottling from Glenallachie is the *16 year old cask strength* matured in first fill Oloroso casks and released in 2005. This has been for sale at Chivas' visitor centres, together with the other releases in the cask strength range.

Glenallachie 16 year old 56,7%

GS – Major Sherry influence right through this expression, starting with warm leather and a hint of cloves on the fragrant nose, progressing through a Christmas pudding palate, featuring sultanas, dates and lots of spice, to a lengthy, sherried, leathery finish.

1989 16 years old

Glenburgie

Owner:
Chivas Brothers
(Pernod Ricard)

Region/district:
Speyside

Founded: 1810
Status: Active
Capacity: 4 200 000 litres

Address: Glenburgie, Forres,
Morayshire IV36 2QY

Tel: 01343 850258
website: -

History:
1810 – William Paul founds Kilnflat Distillery. Official production starts in 1829.

1870 – Kilnflat distillery closes.

1878 – The distillery reopens under the name Glenburgie-Glenlivet, Charles Hay is licensee.

1884 – Alexander Fraser & Co. takes over.

1925 – Alexander Fraser & Co. files for bankruptcy and the receiver Donald Mustad assumes control of operations.

1927 – James & George Stodart Ltd buys the distillery which by this time is inactive.

1930 – Hiram Walker buys 60% of James & George Stodart Ltd.

1936 – Hiram Walker buys Glenburgie Distillery in October. Production restarts.

1958 – Lomond stills are installed producing a single malt, Glencraig. Floor malting ceases.

1981 – The Lomond stills are replaced by conventional stills.

1987 – Allied Lyons buys Hiram Walker.

2002 – A 15 year old is released.

2004 – A £4.3 million refurbishment and reconstruction takes place.

2005 – Chivas Brothers (Pernod Ricard) becomes the new owner through the acquisition of Allied Domecq.

2006 – The number of stills are increased from four to six in May.

Glenburgie distillery may have been founded in 1810 as Kilnflat distillery but the one we see today is actually one of the youngest in Scotland! Back in 2003, the owners at the time, Allied Domecq, found the distillery in great need of refurbishment. After having studied several alternatives they realised that it would be best to simply tear the whole distillery down and build a new one. The only building that was salvaged was the old customs' house which is currently being used as a tasting room. The new distillery was functional just over a year later, with all the equipment fitted on one level in a gigantic room.

When the construction of the new distillery started, Allied Domecq was the second biggest spirits and wine company in the world after Diageo. Two years later when the distillery was set for production, the company didn't even exist. At this time, the name of the game in the drinks industry was growth through acquisition. Try as it may, Allied failed dismally at this when they tried to buy Seagrams in partnership with Diageo in 2000. The same deal was successfully carried through in 2003 by Diageo and Pernod Ricard and the latter then absorbed Allied two years later.

The distillery is now equipped with a 7,5 tonne full lauter mash tun, 12 stainless steel washbacks and three pairs of stills. Most of the equipment is new but four stills, the mill and the boiler were brought in from the old distillery. In older days the fermentation time used to be around 70 hours but has now been reduced to 52. All the stills are efficiently heated using external heat exchangers. The majority of the production is filled into bourbon casks and part thereof are matured in four dunnage, two racked and two palletised warehouses.

The single malt from Glenburgie is one of the most important parts of the Ballantine´s blend. The only official bottling of Glenburgie single malt is a *17 year old cask strength* with the current edition distilled in 1994.

Glenburgie 10 year old G&M

GS – Fresh and fruity on the nose, with toasted malt and a mildly herbal note. Soft fruits and mild oak on the palate, while the finish is subtly drying, with a touch of ginger.

DR – Classic sherry, barley and prickly wood on the nose, sweet and gentle red berry on the palate, and a warming mouth-filling soft and pleasant finish.

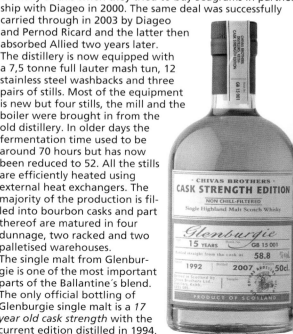

15 years old cask strength

Ballantine´s Finest

Blended Scotch

Starring Glenburgie Single Malt *in a leading role*
Producer Chivas Brothers
Director Sandy Hyslop, Master Blender

The man who had given his name to one of the world´s most famous whisky brands, George Ballantine, was the son of a farmer. At the tender age of thirteen he was already being employed as an assistant at a Grocer & Spirit dealer in Edinburgh. George, however, wanted to start his own business and only five years later he established himself as a Wine Merchant & Grocer. In the mid 1800s, whisky had also become an important part of the business. In 1865 he delegated the responsibility of the business in Edinburgh to one of his sons, Archibald, and moved to Glasgow to open up another store. George retired in 1881 and died ten years later, leaving the company in the capable hands of his son, George Jr.

Ballantine´s Finest became established as a brand in 1910 and nine years later the time had come for the founding family to exit the scene. The company was then sold to two entrepreneurs, Jimmy Barclay and R. A. McKinlay, whose goal it was to develop the family business as an international competitor and a front-runner on the American market. They were off to a tough start to say the least. Only two months after the agreement was signed, the Volstead Act was passed which prohibited the sales of alcohol. This did not deter the partners however and especially Jimmy Barclay found ways to use the situation to the advantage of the company. He teamed up with Jack Kriendler and Charlie Berns, the owners of the famous 21 Club. They formed a distribution company called 21 Brands and in 1933 when Prohibition was repealed, they were in a position where the American market could be conquered.

In those days, most Scotch blends were quite young, but in 1927 Ballantine´s were selling both a 17 year old and a 30 year old. They were also innovative when it came to maturation, using American White Oak, which was not common among producers of Scotch whiskies until 20 years later. Hiram Walker took over in 1936 and at the same time they acquired two distilleries which currently remain to be of the utmost importance for the character of Ballantine´s – Glenburgie and Miltonduff.

In the 1950s, Ballantine´s had become one of the most popular brands in USA, but eventually the brand saw diminishing market share giving way to Cutty Sark and J&B, two brands that appealed to the American palate with its lighter flavour. The owners set their eyes on Europe instead and in 1986 it had become the largest blended whisky brand on the continent. One year later, Allied Lyons became new owners and with them, the malt whisky from yet another distillery, Ardmore, was allowed to influence the blend.

Since 2007, when it surpassed J&B, Ballantine´s has been the no. 2 best selling Scotch in the world. At the same time it is also the number one in Europe and the no. 2 ultra-premium Scotch whisky in Asia. In 2012, the brand sold 75 million bottles. The core expression, *Ballantine´s Finest* without age statement, accounts for about 90% of the sales, while the *12, 17, 21, 30* and *40 year*

old make up the rest. Recently there have also been three *limited expressions of the 17 year old* which were created by Master Blender, Sandy Hyslop, to highlight three of the core malt whiskies – Glenburgie, Miltonduff and Scapa.

Robust and lightly peated nose with notes of hay and pears. Sweet and fruity with red apples, vanilla, chocolate, caramel and leather. Ends on a peppery note.

Glencadam

Owner:
Angus Dundee Distillers

Region/district:
Eastern Highlands

Founded: 1825
Status: Active
Capacity: 1 300 000 litres

Address: Brechin, Angus DD9 7PA

Tel: 01356 622217
website: www.glencadamdistillery.co.uk

History:

1825 – George Cooper founds the distillery.

1827 – David Scott takes over.

1837 – The distillery is sold by David Scott.

1852 – Alexander Miln Thompson becomes the owner.

1857 – Glencadam Distillery Company is formed.

1891 – Gilmour, Thompson & Co Ltd takes over.

1954 – Hiram Walker takes over.

1959 – Refurbishing of the distillery.

1987 – Allied Lyons buys Hiram Walker Gooderham & Worts.

1994 – Allied Lyons changes name to Allied Domecq.

2000 – The distillery is mothballed.

2003 – Allied Domecq sells the distillery to Angus Dundee Distillers.

2005 – The new owner releases a 15 year old.

2008 – A re-designed 15 year old and a new 10 year old are introduced.

2009 – A 25 and a 30 year old are released in limited numbers.

2010 – A 12 year old port finish, a 14 year old sherry finish, a 21 year old and a 32 year old are released.

2012 – A 30 year old is released.

Glencadam 10 year old

GS – A light and delicate, floral nose, with tinned pears and fondant cream. Medium-bodied, smooth, with citrus fruits and gently-spiced oak on the palate. The finish is quite long and fruity, with a hint of barley.

DR – Fruity and treacle toffee nose, sweet, fruity and with uncluttered malt on the palate, and a clean medium long fruity finish.

Glencadam distillery is owned by Angus Dundee Distillers which is controlled by the Hillman family. The Hillmans are by no means new to the whisky business. Sidney Hillman founded Burn Stewart in 1948, who today are the owners of Bunnahabhain, Tobermory and Deanston distilleries but at that time working as a small whisky broker. For some years it was trading as Ballantyne Stewart & Co but after a legal dispute with George Ballantine & Co, Hillman was forced to change the name. Sidney´s son, Terry, started working for the company and in 1988 Burn Stewart was bought by Bill Thornton and Billy Walker (of BenRiach fame) among others. Terry Hillman decided to start a new business, Angus Dundee Distillers, and after a while acquired two distilleries, Tomintoul in 2000 and Glencadam in 2003. The core of Angus Dundee´s business today is to produce and sell blended Scotch and they have a huge range of brands in their portfolio.

Glencadam distillery is equipped with a 5 tonnes traditional cast iron mash tun from the eighties. There are six stainless steel washbacks (four with wooden tops and two with stainless steel ones) with a fermentation time of 52 hours and one pair of stills. The external heat exchanger on the wash still is from the fifties and perhaps the first in the business. On site are two dunnage warehouses from 1825, three from the 1950s and one modern, racked. The distillery is currently working seven days a week, which enables 16 mashes per week and 1,3 million litres of alcohol per year. Glencadam is not only a busy distillery, but also hosts a huge filling and bottling plant with 16 large tanks for blending malt and grain whisky.

The core range consists of a 10 year old, a 15 year old and a 21 year old (introduced in 2010). Recent limited editions included two finishes (a 12 year old port and a 14 year old Oloroso sherry) as well as a 32 year old single cask – all released in 2010. This was followed by a 30 year old released in June 2012.

15 years old

Glendronach

Owner:
Benriach Distillery Co

Region/district:
Speyside

Founded: **Status:**
1826   Active (vc)

Capacity:
1 400 000 litres

Address: Forgue, Aberdeenshire AB54 6DB

Tel: **website:**
01466 730202   www.glendronachdistillery.com

History:

1826 – The distillery is founded by a consortium. James Allardes is one of the owners.

1837 – The major part of the distillery is destroyed in a fire.

1852 – Walter Scott (from Teaninich) takes over.

1887 – Walter Scott dies and Glendronach is taken over by a consortium from Leith.

1920 – Charles Grant buys Glendronach for £9,000 and starts production three months later.

1960 – William Teacher & Sons buys the distillery.

1966-67 – The number of stills is increased to four.

1976 – A visitor centre is opened.

1976 – Allied Breweries takes over William Teacher & Sons.

1996 – The distillery is mothballed.

2002 – Production is resumed on 14th May.

2005 – Glendronach 33 years old is launched. The distillery closes to rebuild from coal to indirect firing by steam. Reopens in September. Chivas Brothers (Pernod Ricard) becomes new owner through the acquisition of Allied Domecq.

2008 – Pernod Ricard sells the distillery to the owners of BenRiach distillery.

2009 – Relaunch of the whole range - 12, 15 and 18 year old including limited editions of a 33 year old and five single casks.

2010 – A 31 year old, a 1996 single cask and a total of 11 vintages and four wood finishes are released. A visitor centre is opened.

2011 – The 21 year old Parliament and 11 vintages are released.

2012 – A number of vintages are released.

2013 – Recherché 44 years and a number of new vintages are released.

Glendronach Original 12 year old

GS – A sweet nose of Christmas cake fresh from the oven. Smooth on the palate, with sherry, soft oak, fruit, almonds and spices. The finish is comparatively dry and nutty, ending with bitter chocolate.

DR – Sherry, red berries, vanilla and traces of mint-flavoured toffee on the nose, an intriguing palate of cranberry and blueberry, a peaty carpet and some pepper, and a medium savoury and peaty finish.

In 2007, GlenDronach was a neglected brand especially if one considers past times when, in its glory days, it was famous for its excellent sherried whiskies. But enter Billy Walker and company in 2008 and the GlenDronach single malt is back on track with an exciting range and increasing sales figures. In 2012, most of the 250,000 bottles that were sold, were exported.

The distillery equipment consists of a small (3,7 tonnes) cast iron mash tun with rakes, nine washbacks where six are made of Oregon pine, while the final three were recently replaced using Scottish larch, two wash stills with heat exchangers and two spirit stills. The expectation is to produce 1,3 million litres of alcohol in 2013. Glendronach was the last Scottish distillery to fire the stills with coal. This traditional process had continued until September 2005 when indirect heating, using steam coils, replaced it.

The new owners took possession of 9,000 casks of whisky when they bought the distillery which are now maturing in three dunnage and three racked warehouses. Some 50% of the production is destined for own releases and the rest is sold to Pernod Ricard for their blended whiskies.

The core range is the *8 years Octarine* (46%), *12 years Original* (43%, a combination of PX and Oloroso sherry casks), *15 years Revival* (46% Olorosomatured), *18 years Allardice* (46%, Olorosomatured) and *21 years Parliament* (48%, a combination of PX and Oloroso sherry casks). There are two *wood finishes* (Sauternes and Tawny Port) and in line with the last couple of years, several *single casks* (all sherry) were also released in 2013; in July eight vintages from 1971 to 2002 and more releases followed in November. The owners also released their first *cask strength* expression in larger quantities (12,000 bottles) and this was followed up by another two batches in 2013. The *44 year old Recherché* (a single Oloroso sherry butt) which was announced already in autumn 2012 was finally released in July 2013 and represents the oldest GlenDronach still left in the warehouses.

Parliament 21 years old

Glendullan

Owner:
Diageo

Region/district:
Speyside

Founded: **Status:** **Capacity:**
1897 Active 5 000 000 litres

Address: Dufftown, Keith, Banffshire AB55 4DJ

Tel: **website:**
01340 822100 www.malts.com

History:
1896-97 – William Williams & Sons, a blending company with Three Stars and Strahdon among its brands, founds the distillery.

1902 – Glendullan is delivered to the Royal Court and becomes the favourite whisky of Edward VII.

1919 – Macdonald Greenlees buys a share of the company and Macdonald Greenlees & Williams Distillers is formed.

1926 – Distillers Company Limited (DCL) buys Glendullan.

1930 – Glendullan is transferred to Scottish Malt Distillers (SMD).

1962 – Major refurbishing and reconstruction.

1972 – A brand new distillery is constructed next to the old one and both operate simultaneously during a few years.

1985 – The oldest of the two distilleries is mothballed.

1995 – The first launch of Glendullan in the Rare Malts series is a 22 year old from 1972.

2005 – A 26 year old from 1978 is launched in the Rare Malts series.

2007 – Singleton of Glendullan is launched in the USA.

2013 – Singleton of Glendullan Liberty is released for duty free.

Singleton of Glendullan 12 year old

GS – The nose is spicy, with brittle toffee, vanilla, new leather and hazelnuts. Spicy and sweet on the smooth palate, with citrus fruits, more vanilla and fresh oak. Drying and pleasingly peppery in the finish.

DR – The nose has a mix of fruits including grapefruit melon and even banana, the taste is moreish, with the citrus and melon notes coming through. Warm and pleasant finish.

Until a few years ago, the whisky from this Dufftown distillery was in obscurity. Admittedly it was the favourite whisky of King Edward VII and Betty Boothroyd, the first female Speaker in the House of Commons, chose it as the speaker´s whisky but sales figures were generally low. Then it was relaunched in the Singleton series together with Glen Ord and Dufftown and, although it has been the least successful of the three, sales figures are nevertheless impressive in the USA. In 2012 the owners, Diageo, announced that another huge distillery would be built and three sites were suggested to house this new distillery. Glendullan was one of them but, in the end, Teaninich in the Northern Highlands was the chosen one.

Glendullan distillery is equipped with a full lauter stainless steel mash tun from Abercrombie's, installed in 2010. The equipment also consists of 8 washbacks made of larch and three pairs of stills. In spring 2013 another two washbacks made of stainless steel were installed outside in front of the main entrance and there is space to add another two in the future. A new boiler replacing the 47 year old one was also added. At the same time the distillery went from a five day week to a seven day week which meant that all fermentations are now 75 hours, instead of having both short and long fermentations. Capacity has now increased to 5 million litres of pure alcohol. The character of the spirit is green and grassy, a style which has proven very useful for blended Scotch. But the conversion of the site is yet to be finished – a bio plant which takes care of the spent lees (the water containing copper that comes last in the spirit run) will be ready to use in 2014.

The core bottling is *Singleton of Glendullan 12 year old* which is aimed at the American market. In summer 2013, the un-aged *Singleton of Glendullan Liberty* was launched for duty free.

The Singleton of Glendullan

Glen Elgin

Owner:
Diageo

Region/district:
Speyside

Founded:
1898

Status:
Active

Capacity:
2 700 000 litres

Address: Longmorn, Morayshire IV30 3SL

Tel:
01343 862100

website:
www.malts.com

History:

1898 – The bankers William Simpson and James Carle found Glen Elgin.

1900 – Production starts in May but the distillery closes just five months later.

1901 – The distillery is auctioned for £4,000 to the Glen Elgin-Glenlivet Distillery Co. and is mothballed.

1906 – The wine producer J. J. Blanche & Co. buys the distillery for £7,000 and production resumes.

1929 – J. J. Blanche dies and the distillery is put up for sale again.

1930 – Scottish Malt Distillers (SMD) buys it and the license goes to White Horse Distillers.

1964 – Expansion from two to six stills plus other refurbishing takes place.

1992 – The distillery closes for refurbishing and installation of new stills.

1995 – Production resumes in September.

2001 – A 12 year old is launched in the Flora & Fauna series.

2002 – The Flora & Fauna series malt is replaced by Hidden Malt 12 years.

2003 – A 32 year old cask strength from 1971 is released.

2008 – A 16 year old is launched as a Special Release.

2009 – Glen Elgin 1998, a single cask in the new Manager´s Choice range is released.

Glen Elgin 12 year old

GS – A nose of rich, fruity sherry, figs and fragrant spice. Full-bodied, soft, malty and honeyed in the mouth. The finish is lengthy, slightly perfumed, with spicy oak.

DR – Ginger, crystallised barley sweet and a complex array of fruit on the nose, a beautiful balanced taste with light fruit, sweet spice and a zesty freshness and mouth filling finish.

The architect behind Glen Elgin was Charles Cree Doig (1855-1918) who is said to have been involved in more than 100 distillery constructions and was the inventor of the pagoda roof that was sometimes called the Doig ventilator. This ingenious design which leads smoke away from the kiln is the most obvious symbol for a distillery in Scotland, even if many distilleries lack it today. In 1897-98, Doig started the work on three distilleries – Glencawdor which is close to Nairn (demolished in 1930), Knockando and Glen Elgin. The latter came to be his last new distillery even though he continued to draw plans for alterations and extensions for several years to come.

The distillery is equipped with an 8,2 tonnes Steinecker full lauter mash tun from 2001, nine washbacks made of larch and six small stills. Three of the washbacks were instal-led as late as 2012 in the extended tun room which meant that the production capacity would increase by 50%. After the site moved from a 5 day operation to 7 days, the fermentation time went from a combination of short and longs to an even 90 hours for all. The stills are con-nected to six wooden worm tubs where the spirit vapours are condensed. The wormtubs placed in the yard are some of the most beautiful in the industry but, unfortunately, a stainless steel cooling tower was recently placed right in front of them. During 2013, there will be 16 mashes per week which means a production of 2,7 million litres.

The whisky from Glen Elgin has for a long time been an essential part of the blended whisky, White Horse. Introduced in 1890, the brand is currently selling 12 million bottles per year, especially in Japan, Brazil, Africa and USA.

The only official bottling is a *12 year old* but older expressions (up to 32 years) have been released in limited numbers during the last decade.

12 years old

Glenfarclas

Owner:
J. & G. Grant

Region/district:
Speyside

Founded: 1836

Status: Active (vc)

Capacity: 3 400 000 litres

Address: Ballindalloch, Banffshire AB37 9BD

Tel: 01807 500257

website: www.glenfarclas.co.uk

History:
1836 – Robert Hay founds the distillery on the original site since 1797.

1865 – Robert Hay passes away and John Grant and his son George buy the distillery for £511.19s on 8th June. They lease it to John Smith at The Glenlivet Distillery.

1870 – John Smith resigns in order to start Cragganmore and J. & G. Grant Ltd takes over.

1889 – John Grant dies and George Grant takes over.

1890 – George Grant dies and his widow Barbara takes over the license while sons John and George control operations.

1895 – John and George Grant take over and form The Glenfarclas-Glenlivet Distillery Co. Ltd with the infamous Pattison, Elder & Co.

1898 – Pattison becomes bankrupt. Glenfarclas encounters financial problems after a major overhaul of the distillery but survives by mortgaging and selling stored whisky to R. I. Cameron, a whisky broker from Elgin.

1914 – John Grant leaves due to ill health and George continues alone.

1948 – The Grant family celebrates the distillery's 100th anniversary, a century of active licensing. It is 9 years late, as the actual anniversary coincided with WW2.

Although not founded by the Grant family, Glenfarclas distillery has been in the family for nearly 150 years. In the summer of 2013 it was time for George Grant, the 6th generation, to take up his position in the board of directors. Joining the company in 2000, George has been working as the sales director for the last few years and has been largely instrumental for the steady sales increase. As a family business they are restrictive when it comes to revealing numbers, but they have declared a sales increase over the last five years of 75% and now sell more than 700,000 bottles in over 70 markets. The owners have always avoided discounting their products but, on the other hand, they are known for extremely competitive prices on their older (30 and 40 years) bottlings.

The distillery is equipped with a 16,5 tonnes semi-lauter mash tun and twelve stainless steel washbacks with a fermentation time of 48 hours. The three pairs of stills are some of the biggest in Scotland and the wash stills are equipped with rummagers. This is a copper chain rotating at the bottom of the still to prevent solids from sticking to the copper, something that otherwise easily happens when you have a direct fired still. There are 30 dunnage warehouses on-site with another four being built during 2013. Glenfarclas uses an unusually large share of sherry butts, mainly Oloroso. The distillery is working 7 days a week with only a three week silent season resulting in 3 million litres. The Glenfarclas core range consists of *10, 12, 15, 21, 25, 30* and *40 years old*, as well as the *105 Cask Strength*. There is also a *17 year old* destined for the USA, Japan and the Duty Free market. Also in the core range, is the lightly sherried *Glenfarclas Heritage* without age statement. It was originally launched for the French hypermarket trade but is now also available in other countries. There have also been bottlings of *Heritage* at *60%* and limited vintage versions. Limited releases during 2012 included the oldest whisky ever released by the owners – a *58 year old* single sherry cask, a *43 year old* with some of the maturation in a cognac cask and a *20 year old* version of the *Glenfarclas 105*. Early 2013 saw the release of a new *18 year old* for Duty Free, as well as a *25 year old quarter cask*. The latter was a vatting of the last remaining quarter casks in the warehouses. To follow up on the cognac cask expression from 2013, a *31 year old Port cask* maturation was released for the UK and France. The owners continue to release bottlings in their *Family Casks* series with vintages from 1952 and onwards and with a 1998 being added this year. Finally, the release of a *60 year old* due in 2014 has already been announced.

1949 – George Grant senior dies and sons George Scott and John Peter inherit the distillery.

1960 – Stills are increased from two to four.

1968 – Glenfarclas is first to launch a cask-strength single malt. It is later named Glenfarclas 105.

1972 – Floor maltings is abandoned and malt is purchased centrally.

1973 – A visitor centre is opened.

1976 – Enlargement from four stills to six.

2001 – Glenfarclas launches its first Flower of Scotland gift tin which becomes a great success and increases sales by 30%.

2002 – George S Grant dies and is succeeded as company chairman by his son John L S Grant.

2003 – Two new gift tins are released (10 years old and 105 cask strength).

2005 – A 50 year old is released to commemorate the bi-centenary of John Grant's birth.

2006 – Ten new vintages are released.

2007 – Family Casks, a series of single cask bottlings from 43 consecutive years, is released.

2008 – New releases in the Family Cask range. Glenfarclas 105 40 years old is released.

2009 – A third release in the Family Casks series.

2010 – A 40 year old and new vintages from Family Casks are released.

2011 – Chairman's Reserve and 175th Anniversary are released.

2012 – A 58 year old and a 43 year old are released.

2013 – An 18 year old for duty free is released as well as a 25 year old quarter cask.

Glenfarclas 10 year old

GS – Full and richly sherried on the nose, with nuts, fruit cake and a hint of citrus fruit. The palate is big, with ripe fruit, brittle toffee, some peat and oak. Medium length and gingery in the finish.

DR – Creamy sherry and bitter oranges on the nose, rich fruit cake and red berries on the palate with a pleasant spice and barley interplay and long and warming finish.

105 Cask Strength
(Duty Free version)

25 year old Quarter cask

105 Cask Strength
20 years old

18 years old

The Family Casks
1959

10 years old

Heritage

40 years old

Glenfiddich

Owner:
William Grant & Sons

Region/district:
Speyside

Founded: **Status:**
1886   Active (vc)

Capacity:
13 000 000 litres

Address: Dufftown, Keith, Banffshire AB55 4DH

Tel:
01340 820373 (vc)

website:
www.glenfiddich.com

History:
1886 – The distillery is founded by William Grant, 47 years old, who had learned the trade at Mortlach Distillery. The equipment is bought from Mrs. Cummings of Cardow Distillery. The construction totals £800.

1887 – The first distilling takes place on Christmas Day.

1892 – William Grant builds Balvenie.

1898 – The blending company Pattisons, largest customer of Glenfiddich, files for bankruptcy and Grant decides to blend their own whisky. Standfast becomes one of their major brands.

1903 – William Grant & Sons is formed.

1957 – The famous, three-cornered bottle is introduced.

1958 – The floor maltings is closed.

1963 – Glennfiddich becomes the first whisky to be marketed as single malt in the UK and the rest of the world.

1964 – A version of Standfast's three-cornered bottle is launched for Glenfiddich in green glass.

1969 – Glenfiddich becomes the first distillery in Scotland to open a visitor centre.

1974 – 16 new stills are installed.

2001 – 1965 Vintage Reserve is launched in a limited edition of 480 bottles. Glenfiddich 1937 is bottled (61 bottles).

For William Grant & Sons, 2011 was a momentous year. No only did Glenfiddich become the first single malt brand in history to sell more than 1 million cases (12 million bottles in a year, but the company also recorded annual sales of more than £1bn for the first time. Glenfiddich has been th world's number one single malt for many years now and it is also the leader in the home market UK with 1,4 million bottles sold in 2012. In the USA, the brand is number three (after Glenlivet and Macallan) with 1,6 million bottles and, in an important, emerging market like India, 50% of all single malts sold (500,000 bottles) were Glenfiddich.

Glenfiddich distillery is equipped with two big, stainless steel, full lauter mash tuns (11,2 tonnes but charged with 9,5 tonnes), 24 Douglas fir washbacks and eight new stainless steel washbacks which were installed in late 2012. The fermentation is 72 hours. One still room holds 5 wash and 10 spirit stills and the other 5 and 8 respectively. The wash stills are all onion-shaped while half of the spirit stills are o the lantern model while the rest have a boiling ball. All the stills in still house No. 1 have been internally fired for the past three years. The stills in still house No. 2, however, are still directly fired using gas. To keep up with demand, the owners have managed to increase production to a record breaking 13 million litres during 2013.

The core range consists of 12, 15 (blended using a solera system), 18, 21 (also called Gran Reserva and finished in rum casks), Rich Oak 14 year old and 15 year old Distillery Edition (bottled at 51%). Some older expressions have also been released over the years – 30, 40 and 50 years old.

A new range for Duty Free called Age of Discovery was introduced in 2011. The 2013 release in the range was a 19 year old Red Wine cask finish. Early 2012 saw the Malt Master's Edition and later in the year two expressions for Duty Free were launched; the 12 year old Glenfiddich Millennium Vintage and Glenfiddich 125th Anniversary Edition The latter was a blend of peated and unpeated whisky with a maturation in a mix of ex-bourbon and ex-sherry casks. A new programme called Cask of Dreams was introduced in 2012 where 11 empty American oak casks toured the States before being shipped to Scotland to be filled with Glenfiddich single malt. After three months the bottles were sold exclusively in the USA. The programme was later expanded to Canada and Scandinavia. An extremely limited release in 2013 was a 1987 Anniversary Vintage single cask, 25 years old and bottled at cask strength. Finally, Glenfiddich Ultimate, a 38 year old was launched in China in April 2013.

History (continued):

2002 – Glenfiddich Gran Reserva 21 years old, finished in Cuban rum casks is launched. Caoran Reserve 12 years is released. Glenfiddich Rare Collection 1937 (61 bottles) is launched and becomes the oldest Scotch whisky on the market.

2003 – 1973 Vintage Reserve (440 bottles) is launched.

2004 – 1991 Vintage Reserve (13 years) and 1972 Vintage Reserve (519 bottles) are launched.

2005 – Circa £1.7 million is invested in a new visitor centre.

2006 – 1973 Vintage Reserve, 33 years (861 bottles) and 12 year old Toasted Oak are released.

2007 – 1976 Vintage Reserve, 31 years is released in September.

2008 – 1977 Vintage Reserve is released.

2009 – A 50 year old and 1975 Vintage Reserve are released.

2010 – Rich Oak, 1978 Vintage Reserve, the 6th edition of 40 year old and Snow Phoenix are released.

2011 – 1974 Vintage Reserve and a 19 year old Madeira finish are released.

2012 – Cask of Dreams and Millenium Vintage are released.

2013 – A 19 year old red wine finish and 1987 Anniversary Vintage are released.

Glenfiddich 12 year old

NS – Delicate, floral and slightly fruity on the nose. Well mannered in the mouth, malty, elegant and soft. Rich, fruit flavours dominate the palate, with a developing nuttiness and an elusive whiff of peat smoke in the fragrant finish.

PR – Classic rich fruit and peerless clean barley nose, fruit bowl and sharp malt palate and pleasant and warming lengthy finish.

1987 Anniversary Vintage   *15 year old Distillery Edition*   *Age of Discovery 19 years Red Wine*

12 years old   *Rich Oak*   *18 years old*

121

Glen Garioch

Owner:
Morrison Bowmore
(Suntory)

Region/district:
Eastern Highlands

Founded: 1797

Status: Active (vc)

Capacity: 1 000 000 litres

Address: Oldmeldrum, Inverurie,
Aberdeenshire AB51 0ES

Tel: 01651 873450

website: www.glengarioch.com

History:

1797 – Thomas Simpson founds Glen Garioch.

1837 – The distillery is bought by John Manson & Co., owner of Strathmeldrum Distillery.

1908 – Glengarioch Distillery Company, owned by William Sanderson, buys the distillery.

1933 – Sanderson & Son merges with the gin maker Booth's Distilleries Ltd.

1937 – Booth's Distilleries Ltd is acquired by Distillers Company Limited (DCL).

1968 – Glen Garioch is decommissioned.

1970 – It is sold to Stanley P. Morrison Ltd.

1973 – Production starts again.

1978 – Stills are increased from two to three.

1982 – Becomes the first distillery to use gas from the North Sea for heating.

1994 – Suntory controls all of Morrison Bowmore Distillers Ltd.

1995 – The distillery is mothballed in October.

1997 – The distillery reopens in August.

2004 – Glen Garioch 46 year old is released.

2005 – 15 year old Bordeaux Cask Finish is launched. A visitor centre opens in October.

2006 – An 8 year old is released.

2009 – Complete revamp of the range - 1979 Founders Reserve (unaged), 12 year old, Vintage 1978 and 1990 are released.

2010 – 1991 vintage is released.

2011 – Vintage 1986 and 1994 are released.

2012 – Vintage 1995 and 1997 are released.

2013 – Virgin Oak, Vintage 1999 and 11 single casks are released.

Glen Garioch, situated in the small town of Oldmeldrum west of Aberdeen, is the easternmost distillery in Scotland and one of the oldest. Over the years it has been connecte to various, unusual projects, for example, in 1977 when heat from the distillation was used to heat greenhouses which could cultivate tomatoes etc. – a progressive approach in those days. For some time in the 1920s it was als the key malt in two blended whiskies called AM and PM, intended for drinking before and after lunch respectively. The distillery is equipped with a 4,4 tonne full lauter mash tun, eight stainless steel washbacks with a fermentation time of 48 hours and one pair of stills. There is also a third still which has not been used for a long time. The spirit is tankered to Glasgow, filled into casks and returned to the distillery's four warehouses. During 2013 the production will increase to 15 mashes per week and a little more than one million litres in the year.

The entire range from Glen Garioch was revamped four years ago and it looks as if this change is now also showing in sales. Around 200,000 bottles were sold in 2012 which is an increase by 20% compared to 2011.

The core range is *1797 Founder's Reserve* (without age statement) and a *12 year old*, both of them bottled at the rather unusual strength of 48% and non-chillfiltered. There have also been a number of limited cask strength vintages released over the years; in 2010 *1978, 1990* and *1991*, in 2011 *1986* and *1994* and in 2012 *1995* and *1997*. For 2013 there was a *Vintage 1999* matured in Oloroso sherry casks and *Virgin Oak* – the first release of a Glen Garioch fully matured in virgin American white oak. Furthermore, no less than 11 different *single casks* were launched through World Duty Free with each bottling only available at one designated airport in the UK. The 11 bottlings vary in age between 12 and 33 years.

12 years old

Glen Garioch 12 years old

GS – Luscious and sweet on the nose, peaches and pineapple, vanilla, malt and a hint of sherry. Full-bodied and nicely textured, with more fresh fruit on the palate, along with spice, brittle toffee and finally dry oak notes.

DR – Surprisingly floral and light on the nose, with fruity sweetness. The taste includes tinned sweet pear, vanilla and caramel with some earthiness as an undercarpet. There is some spice in the finale.

Glenglassaugh

Owner:
Glenglassaugh Distillery Co
(BenRiach Distillery Co.)

Region/district:
Speyside

Founded: **Status:** **Capacity:**
1875 Active (vc) 1 100 000 litres

Address: Portsoy, Banffshire AB45 2SQ

Tel:
1261 842367

website:
www.glenglassaugh.com

History:
1873-75 – The distillery is founded by Glenglassaugh Distillery Company.

1887 – Alexander Morrison embarks on renovation work.

1892 – Morrison sells the distillery to Robertson & Baxter. They in turn sell it on to Highland Distilleries Company for £15,000.

1908 – The distillery closes.

1931 – The distillery reopens.

1936 – The distillery closes.

1957-59 – Reconstruction takes place.

1960 – The distillery reopens.

1986 – Glenglassaugh is mothballed.

2005 – A 22 year old is released.

2006 – Three limited editions are released - 19 years old, 38 years old and 44 years old.

2008 – The distillery is bought by the Scaent Group for £5m. Three bottlings are released 21, 30 and 40 year old.

2009 – New make spirit and 6 months old are released.

2010 – A 26 year old replaces the 21 year old.

2011 – A 35 year old and the first bottling from the new owners production, a 3 year old, are released.

2012 – A visitor centre is inaugurated and Glenglassaugh Revival is released.

2013 – BenRiach Distillery Co buys the distillery and Glenglassaugh Evolution and a 30 year old are released.

Glenglassaugh Evolution

GS – Peaches and gingerbread on the nose, with brittle toffee, icing sugar, and vanilla. Luscious soft fruits dipped in caramel figure on the palate, with coconut and background stem ginger. The finish is medium in length, with spicy toffee.

When Glenglassaugh re-opened in 2008 after 22 years of silence, it came as a major surprise to most people. Quite frankly, the surprise wasn´t less when it was further announced in March 2013 that the distillery had been sold again and this time to BenRiach, with Billy Walker at the helm. Scaent Group, the company behind the resurgence, made an admirable achievement when they brought the distillery back to life by recruiting whisky veterans, Stuart Nickerson and Graham Eunson. After five years it became evident though that it wasn´t in the owners plans to make further, big investments. Before the distillery was offered to the market, Billy Walker made an offer and, in spite of a couple of other suitors, managed to buy the distillery for an undisclosed sum.

The equipment of the distillery consists of a Porteus cast iron mash tun with rakes, four wooden washbacks and two stainless steel ones (the last two were recommissioned in early 2013) and one pair of stills. After BenRiach took over the production, the pace has increased considerably and during 2013 they expect to do 8 mashes per week ending up with 600,000 litres of pure alcohol. For seven weeks, a peated spirit (30ppm) has also been produced. There are four racked and one dunnage warehouse on site and the old maltings have recently been converted into another warehouse. Glenglassaugh has already gained a large amount of devoted followers and in 2012 a visitor centre was inaugurated. The core range is *Revival*, a 3 year old with a 6 months Oloroso finish and *Evolution*, slightly older, matured in American oak and bottled at 50% (used to be cask strength). There is also a *30 year old* from older stock. Limited expressions have included two series called *The Chosen Few* and *The Massandra Connection* but they have now been discontinued. The first release from the new owners was a *30 year old* in September and there is also a 40 year old in the pipeline.

Evolution

Glengoyne

Owner:
Ian Macleod Distillers

Region/district:
Southern Highlands

Founded: | **Status:**
1833 | Active (vc)

Capacity:
1 100 000 litres

Address: Dumgoyne by Killearn,
Glasgow G63 9LB

Tel:
01360 550254 (vc)

website:
www.glengoyne.com

History:
1833 – The distillery is licensed under the name Burnfoot Distilleries by the Edmonstone family.

1876 – Lang Brothers buys the distillery and changes the name to Glenguin.

1905 – The name changes to Glengoyne.

1965-66 – Robertson & Baxter takes over Lang Brothers and the distillery is refurbished. The stills are increased from two to three.

2001 – Glengoyne Scottish Oak Finish (16 years old) is launched.

2003 – Ian MacLeod Distillers Ltd buys the distillery plus the brand Langs from the Edrington Group for £7.2 million.

2005 – A 19 year old, a 32 year old and a 37 year old cask strength are launched.

2006 – Nine "choices" from Stillmen, Mashmen and Manager are released.

2007 – A new version of the 21 year old, two Warehousemen's Choice, Vintage 1972 and two single casks are released.

2008 – A 16 year old Shiraz cask finish, three single casks and Heritage Gold are released.

2009 – A 40 year old, two single casks and a new 12 year old are launched.

2010 – Two single casks, 1987 and 1997, released.

2011 – A 24 year old single cask is released.

2012 – A 15 and an 18 year old are released as well as a Cask Strength with no age statement.

2013 – A 25 year old and a limited 35 year old are launched.

Glengoyne 15 year old
GS – A nose of vanilla, ginger, toffee, vintage cars leather seats, and sweet fruit notes. The somewhat oily palate features quite lively spices, raisins, hazelnuts, and oak. The finish is medium in length and spicy to the end, with cocoa powder.

You often hear names like Macallan, Glenmorangie and Highland Park being mentioned when dedication to sherry casks is discussed. Glengoyne most certainly also belongs to this group. The owners, Ian Macleod Distillers, select the oak trees in Spain and let the wood air dry in Galicia and Asturias for two years. It is then shipped to Jerez for another two years of drying, made into casks and filled with Oloroso sherry for a final two years. Another detail that makes the production of Glengoyne stand out, and that is repeatedly used in the marketing, is the extremely slow distillation in order to get as much copper contact as possible which enhances the fruity character of the whisky Glengoyne distillery is equipped with a traditional mash tun with rakes, six Oregon pine washbacks and the rather unusual combination of one wash still and two spirit stills. Both short (56 hours) and long (110 hours) fermentations are practised. In 2013, the production will be split between 12 and 16 mashes per week which constitutes 920,000 litres of alcohol – the biggest volume since the new owners took over in 2003. During these 10 years, sales have increased by 150% to 480,000 bottles in 2012. During the last five years, a total of £3m have been invested in the site alone, which was earmarked for new warehouses and an upgraded visitor centre. Glengoyne is now one of the most visited distilleries in Scotland attracting 50,000 people every year. The range of Glengoyne single malts changed dramatically during autumn 2012. The *10, 12* and *21 years old* will continue to be in the range and new expressions are the *15* and *18 year old*, the latter replacing the 17 year old. There is also a new *Cask Strength* without age statement, replacing the 12 year old cask strength. A further addition to the range was launched in autumn 2013 by way of a *25 year old*. The line-up for duty free remains unchanged – the unaged *Burnfoot* and *15 year old Distiller's Gold*. Limited releases for 2013 include a *35 year old* at the beginning of summer, as well as a couple of single casks.

15 years old

Recommended Books

ually, several books about whisky are published
ch year, but during the past year it has been
usually quiet. So let´s rather focus on a number
books that should be on
ery whisky lover's bookshelf.
st and foremost, there is the
tegory of books that try (and
metimes succeed) to take
omprehensive approach
the topic at hand – whisky
tory, production, different
es of whisky, how
taste whisky and
detailed review of
e world's different
oducers. The three
st books that have
en published during
e past few years are
ve Broom´s The World
las of Whisky, Whisky
us written by Gavin D
nith and Dominic Roskrow
d Let Me Tell You About
hisky with Neil Ridley and
vin D Smith as authors.
nother type of book descri-
s the flavour of different
niskies with Jim Murray´s annual Whisky Bible

as the most famous.
Other examples are
Ian Buxton´s 101
Whiskies To Try Before
You Die and Domi-
nic Roskrow´s 1001
Whiskies You Must
Taste Before You Die.
There are books that
concentrate on
certain types of
whisky – Davin de
Kergommeaux´s
Canadian Whisky
- the Portable Ex-
pert and Andrew
Jefford´s classic
about Islay, Peat
Smoke and Spirit.
Finally, two new
books that deserve
attention; Single
Minded subtitled A
Modest Guide To
Really Good Whisky
by Johanna Ngoh and
the directory,
A World Guide To Whisk(e)y
Distilleries compiled by Eric Abram Zandona.

The World Atlas of Whisky	101 Whiskies To Try Before You Die	Peat Smoke and Spirit
ISBN 978-1845335410	ISBN 978-0755360833	ISBN 978-0747245780
Whisky Opus	1001 Whiskies You Must Taste Before You Die	Single Minded
ISBN 978-1405394741	ISBN 978-1844037100	ISBN 978-0991809400
Let Me Tell You About Whisky	Canadian Whisky - the Portable Expert	A World Guide To Whisk(e)y Distilleries
ISBN 978-1862059658	ISBN 978-0771027437	ISBN 978-0983638940

Recommended Magazines

Whisky Advocate	Whisky Magazine	Der Whisky-Botschafter	Whisky Magazine
www.whiskyadvocate.com	www.whiskymag.com	www.whiskybotschafter.com	www.whiskymag.fr
Whisky Passion	Allt om Whisky	Whisky Time	Whisky & Bourbon
www.whiskypassion.nl	www.alltomwhisky.se	www.whiskytime-magazin.com	www.livetsgoda.se

Glen Grant

Owner: Campari Group

Region/district: Speyside

Founded: 1840

Status: Active (vc)

Capacity: 6 200 000 litres

Address: Elgin Road, Rothes, Banffshire AB38 7BS

Tel: 01340 832118

website: www.glengrant.com

History:

1840 – The brothers James and John Grant, managers of Dandelaith Distillery, found the distillery.

1861 – The distillery becomes the first to install electric lighting.

1864 – John Grant dies.

1872 – James Grant passes away and the distillery is inherited by his son, James junior (Major James Grant).

1897 – James Grant decides to build another distillery across the road; it is named Glen Grant No. 2.

1902 – Glen Grant No. 2 is mothballed.

1931 – Major Grant dies and is succeeded by his grandson Major Douglas Mackessack.

1953 – J. & J. Grant merges with George & J. G. Smith who runs Glenlivet distillery, forming The Glenlivet & Glen Grant Distillers Ltd.

1961 – Armando Giovinetti and Douglas Mackessak found a friendship that eventually leads to Glen Grant becoming the most sold malt whisky in Italy.

1965 – Glen Grant No. 2 is back in production, but renamed Caperdonich.

The distillery manager of Glen Grant is one of the legends within the whisky industry. Dennis Malcolm was actually born on the distillery grounds in 1946. Aged 15, he started his career at Glen Grant as an apprentice cooper and with short interruptions as a manager of Glenlivet and Balmenach, among others, he has stayed loyal to Glen Grant. To celebrate his 50 plus years in the business, the limited Five Decades bottling, made up of whiskies from five different decades (the oldest from 1965 and the youngest from 200? was released in summer 2013.

During the same year that Dennis Malcolm started at Glen Grant, an Italian by the name of Armando Giovinetti visite the distillery. He was impressed by what he saw and obtained the licence to sell Glen Grant single malt on the Italian market. Soon Italy had become the biggest export market for Glen Grant and still remains so today. In recent times the whisky market in Italy has admittedly declined, but the owners of Glen Grant have been compensated to a certain extent by increased sales particularly in France and USA. In 2012, 3 million bottles were sold worldwide.

The owners of Glen Grant, Campari Group are investing greatly in the distillery as is evident from the brand new and extremely efficient bottling hall, at a cost of £5m. It was inaugurated in April 2013, has a capacity of 12,000 bottles an hour and all Glen Grant expressions are now bottled on site. Other than that, the distillery is equipped with a 12,3 tonnes semi-lauter mash tun, ten Oregon pine washbacks with a minimum fermentation time of 48 hours and four pairs of stills. The wash stills are peculiar in that they have vertical sides at the base of the neck and all eigh stills are fitted with purifiers. This gives an increased reflux and creates a light and delicate whisky. In 2013, the production will be in the region of 3,2 million litres. Bourbon casks are used for maturation and the share of sherry butts is less than 10% (mainly used for the 10 year old).

Some 50% of the production goes into blended whisky, especially Chivas Regal. The Glen Grant core range of singl malts consists of *Major's Reserve* with no age statement bu probably around 7 years old, a *5 year old* sold in Italy only, a *10 year old* and the recently introduced *16 year old*. Recent limited editions include the 170th *Anniversary Edition* from 2010, a *25 year old* from sherry butts in 2011 and the aforementioned *Five Decades* launched in 2013. There is also a single cask available at the excellent visitor centre. The 4th edition of this is a *20 year old*, slightly peated from having been matured in an Islay cask.

History (continued):

1972 – The Glenlivet & Glen Grant Distillers merges with Hill Thompson & Co. and Longmorn-Glenlivet Ltd to form The Glenlivet Distillers. The drum maltings ceases.

1973 – Stills are increased from four to six.

1977 – The Chivas & Glenlivet Group (Seagrams) buys Glen Grant Distillery. Stills are increased from six to ten.

2001 – Pernod Ricard and Diageo buy Seagrams Spirits and Wine, with Pernod acquiring the Chivas Group.

2006 – Campari buys Glen Grant for €115 million in a deal that includes the acquisition of Old Smuggler and Braemar for another €15 million.

2007 – The entire range is re-packaged and re-launched and a 15 year old single cask is released. Reconstruction of the visitor centre.

2008 – Two limited cask strengths - a 16 year old and a 27 year old - are released.

2009 – Cellar Reserve 1992 is released.

2010 – A 170th Anniversary bottling is released.

2011 – A 25 year old is released.

2012 – A 19 year old Distillery Edition is released.

2013 – Five Decades is released and a bottling hall is built.

Glen Grant 10 year old

GS – Relatively dry on the nose, with cooking apples. Fresh and fruity on the palate, with a comparatively lengthy, malty finish, which features almonds and hazelnuts.

DR – Sweet banana and toffee, vanilla and pear on the nose, sweet barley, crystallised pineapple on the palate with a touch of honey and finally a cinnamon and spice note at the finish.

16 years old

25 years old

Five Decades

10 years old

The Major's Reserve

Glengyle

Owner:
Mitchell's Glengyle Ltd

Region/district:
Campbeltown

Founded: **Status:**
2004 Active

Capacity:
750 000 litres

Address: Glengyle Road, Campbeltown,
Argyll PA28 6LR

Tel:
01586 551710

website:
www.kilkerran.com

History:
1872 – The original Glengyle Distillery is built by William Mitchell.

1919 – The distillery is bought by West Highland Malt Distilleries Ltd.

1925 – The distillery is closed.

1929 – The warehouses (but no stock) are purchased by the Craig Brothers and rebuilt into a petrol station and garage.

1941 – The distillery is acquired by the Bloch Brothers.

1957 – Campbell Henderson applies for planning permission with the intention of reopening the distillery.

2000 – Hedley Wright, owner of Springbank Distillery and related to founder William Mitchell, acquires the distillery.

2004 – The first distillation after reconstruction takes place in March.

2007 – The first limited release - a 3 year old.

2009 – Kilkerran "Work in progress" is released.

2010 – "Work in progress 2" is released.

2011 – "Work in progress 3" is released.

2012 – "Work in progress 4" is released.

2013 – "Work in progress 5" is released and this time in two versions - bourbon and sherry.

Kilkerran Work in Progress V (Bourbon)
GS – Vanilla, cinnamon, milk chocolate, ripe apples and ultimately slightly smoky mango notes on the nose. Spicy on the palate, with blood orange and a hint of peat smoke. The medium-length finish is drying, with a wisp of smoke.

Kilkerran Work in Progress V (Sherry)
GS – Ripe green grapes and figs on the nose, followed by honey and plain chocolate. Quite full on the palate, softly fruity, with soft toffee and a hint of brine. Drying significantly in the finish, with cocoa powder, liquorice and lots of spice.

Glengyle and Springbank share the same owner, and since the first release of Kilkerran single malt from Glengyle in 2007, sales and marketing have been handled by the same people who work with Springbank, Longrow and Hazelburn. In 2013, however, it was time for Glengyle to step out of the shadow of its much older sibling. From now on Glengyle will be operated as a separate company with its own staff. The owners hope that this will increase awareness and focus on the brand. By the way, the name Kilkerran is used for the whisky, as Glengyle was already in use for a vatted malt produced by Loch Lomond Distillers.

Glengyle was one of 17 distilleries in Campbeltown forced to close during the 1920s – a decade which saw the town lose its former glory as the whisky capital of the world. The distillery is equipped with a 4 tonnes semilauter mash tun, four washbacks made of boat skin larch and one pair of stills. The stills were bought from a closed distillery, Ben Wyvis. Malt is obtained from the neighbouring Springbank whose staff also runs operations. Its present capacity is 750,000 litres, but the plan for 2013 is to produce only 30,000 litres. Although the bottlings so far haven't shown it, there is a lot of experimentation going on at Glengyle using different wood maturations, peated barley and even quadruple distillation. The first core expression of Kilkerran single malt will be a 12 year old to be released in 2016 but, every year since 2009, the owners have released a limited edition called Work in Progress which will showcase what the distillery is capable of. In June 2013 it was time for the 9 year old Kilkerran *Work in Progress 5* and for the first time two versions were released – the one being *bourbon wood* and the other a *sherry wood*. When the distillery turns 10 in 2014 it has also been decided that there will be a release of no less than six limited 10 year old single malts, all bottled from the first six casks (and from different wood types) that were filled in 2004.

Kilkerran - Work in Progress V Bourbon

Glen Keith

Owner:
Chivas Brothers
(Pernod Ricard)

Region/district:
Speyside

Founded: 1957
Status: Active
Capacity: 6 000 000 litres

Address: Station Road, Keith,
Banffshire AB55 3BU

Tel: 01542 783042
website: -

History:

1957 – The Distillery is founded by Chivas Brothers (Seagrams).

1958 – Production starts.

1970 – The first gas-fuelled still in Scotland is installed, the number of stills increases from three to five.

1976 – Own maltings (Saladin box) ceases.

1983 – A sixth still is installed.

1994 – The first official bottling, a 10 year old, is released as part of Seagram's Heritage Selection.

1999 – The distillery is mothballed.

2001 – Pernod Ricard takes over Chivas Brothers from Seagrams.

2012 – The reconstruction and refurbishing of the distillery begins.

2013 – Production starts again.

Glen Keith 10 year old

GS – Soft heather and honey on the nose with a hint of banana. The palate is quite flat and light and the finish is soft and smooth with a honeyed aftertaste.

In 1999, Glen Keith was mothballed after only 41 years of production. The distillery, built on the site of the old Mill of Keith corn mill, had over the years been a virtual test lab for various production methods, including triple distillation, trials making malt whisky in a column still, research on new strains of yeast and the making of heavily peated whiskies. The reason for the latter was that Seagram's, the owners at that time, needed a smoky whisky for their blends but lacked a distillery on Islay. Instead of buying the smoky whisky they tried to shift the production to Glen Keith. After 13 years of silence the current owners, Chivas Brothers, saw that the growing demand for Scotch in Asia demanded increased production within the group and the work to restart the distillery was started during the spring of 2012. The old Saladin maltings were demolished and part of that area now holds a new building with a highly efficient (four hour mash cycle) Briggs 8 tonnes full lauter mash tun and six stainless steel washbacks. In the old building there are nine new washbacks made of Oregon pine and six, old (but refurbished) stills. All stills are equipped with external heat exchangers and have both vertical condensers and subcoolers. These stills have extremely long lyne arms and the desired character of the new make spirit is fruity. The distillery was re-opened in April 2013 and has the capacity to do an impressive 6 million litres with the possibility of producing 40 mashes per week. Glen Keith distillery has always worked in symbiosis with nearby Strathisla distillery (also owned by Chivas Brothers) even when Glen Keith was closed. Strathisla uses the boiler at Glen Keith and the newmake from Strathisla is brought to Glen Keith for filling. The only official bottling used to be a *10 year old*. It is no longer being bottled by the owners but can still be found in some whisky shops

10 years old

Glenkinchie

Owner:
Diageo

Region/district:
Lowlands

Founded: 1837
Status: Active (vc)
Capacity: 2 500 000 litres

Address: Pencaitland, Tranent,
East Lothian EH34 5ET

Tel: 01875 342004
website: www.malts.com

History:
1825 – A distillery known as Milton is founded by John and George Rate.

1837 – The Rate brothers are registered as licensees of a distillery named Glenkinchie.

1853 – John Rate sells the distillery to a farmer by the name of Christie who converts it to a sawmill.

1881 – The buildings are bought by a consortium from Edinburgh.

1890 – Glenkinchie Distillery Company is founded. Reconstruction and refurbishment is on-going for the next few years.

1914 – Glenkinchie forms Scottish Malt Distillers (SMD) with four other Lowland distilleries.

1939-45 – Glenkinchie is one of few distilleries allowed to maintain production during the war.

1968 – Floor maltings is decommissioned.

1969 – The maltings is converted into a museum.

1988 – Glenkinchie 10 years becomes one of selected six in the Classic Malt series.

1998 – A Distiller's Edition with Amontillado finish is launched.

2007 – A 12 year old and a 20 year old cask strength are released.

2010 – A cask strength exclusive for the visitor centre, a 1992 single cask and a 20 year old are released.

Glenkinchie 12 year old

GS – The nose is fresh and floral, with spices and citrus fruits, plus a hint of marshmallow. Notably elegant. Water releases cut grass and lemon notes. Medium-bodied, smooth, sweet and fruity, with malt, butter and cheesecake. The finish is comparatively long and drying, initially rather herbal.

DR – The nose is light and flowery, with wet meadow notes and cucumber, the palate is pure barley with a touch of star anise spice and an earthy note.

During the first decade of the 20th century, the Scotch whisky industry survived one of its toughest crises ever. The general economy was bad and when Lloyd George and his government in 1909 decided to raise the duty on spirits (and not on wine and beer) to help pay for social services to the citizens, the industry was forced down on its knees. This called for organisation and structure to avoid overproduction and falling prices. James Gray, the owner of Glenkinchie at that time, persuaded four other Lowland distilleries that they should merge to form Scottish Malt Distillers Ltd so that they could weather the storm together. A similar cooperation had already been created 30 years earlier when six grain distilleries had formed Distiller's Company Limited. DCL had grown from strength to strength over the years and in 1925 they acquired SMD. This constellation would, many years later, become the core of the biggest drinks company in the world, namely Diageo.

The proximity to Edinburgh makes Glenkinchie an attractive distillery to visit and every year more than 40,000 visitors frequent this distillery. Glenkinchie single malt has also become well-known due to the fact that it was selected as one of the six original Classic Malts in 1988. Glenkinchie is equipped with a full lauter mash tun (9 tonnes), six wooden washbacks and one pair of stills. Steeply descending lyne arms give very little reflux and condensation of the spirit vapours takes place in a cast iron worm tub. Since 2008, the distillery has been working 7 days and 14 mashes per week which amounts to 2,5 million litres of alcohol per year. Three dunnage warehouses on site have 10,000 casks maturing, the oldest dating from 1952.

The core range consists of a *12 year old* and a *Distiller's Edition 14 years old*. There is also a *cask strength* without age statement sold exclusively at the visitor centre. Recent limited editions include a Manager's Choice *1992 single cask* and a *20 year old cask strength* distilled in 1990, both released in 2010.

12 years old

Whisky Around the World

UKRAINE

Alexey Savchenko has been a member of the Ukrainian Club of Whisky Connoisseurs since 2004 and in 2010 he became president of the organisation. He is also the owner of a Scottish restaurant in Kiev, the Whisky Corner, whiskycorner.kiev.ua.

Which spirit is the most popular in Ukraine and where does whisky fit into the picture?

The most popular Ukrainian spirit is, without any doubt, vodka and *samogon* (similar to the American moonshine or Irish poteen). Already in the 5th century, Ukraine was known for the production of *samogon*. The massive consumption of vodka, on the other hand, started during the Soviet Union period. In 1936, the production of vodka became regulated and standards for the spirit were enforced. From that time vodka has been the most affordable spirit and nowadays vodka plays a very important role in our culture. Whisky is in fourth place after vodka, wine and cognac.

What types of whisky are the most popular in Ukraine?

The most popular type in Ukraine is blended whisky but people have also started to get interested in American straight whiskey.

When would you say people in Ukraine started to get seriously interested in whisky? What triggered it and how has that interest developed?

During the Soviet Union era it was not easy to travel outside Ukraine. After independence had been proclaimed, people started to travel more frequently, bringing home whisky from their journey. It started with blends but as many Ukrainians started to earn more money, single malt Scotch became an item as well. Single malts started to appear on the market right after the millennium but at that time the category was represented by just a few distilleries. Starting from 2008 the number of brands has grown significantly and today you can find official releases from around 60 different distilleries as well as bottlings from some of the independent bottlers – Gordon & MacPhail, Douglas Laing and Duncan Taylor. Another factor that has influenced the whisky culture in Ukraine are the whisky clubs that have been formed in recent years

Which brands of Scotch are the most popular in Ukraine?

No surprises when it comes to single malts – Macallan, Glenmorangie, The Glenlivet, Glenfiddich and Laphroaig. The most popular blended Scotch is Johnnie Walker Red Label followed by Chivas Regal and Johnnie Walker Black. Jack Daniels and Jameson are also selling well. These are whiskies that young people can afford and they are also the base for cocktails in bars.

How is whisky sold in Ukraine, is there a wide variety of brands and is it easy to find the brand you want?

Nowadays the variety of brands is really good, but supply can be a problem. It is very difficult to find some of the rarer or more limited releases such as Port Ellen. Ukrainian law does not make it easy for importers. To be able to import alcohol, you need to have a licence which will cost you $60,000 per year. There are also many restrictions and regulations, for instance you need to present a selection of the bottles every time you make an import to be examined.

How is whisky marketed in Ukraine?

There are just a few producers actively advertising or doing commercials on the television – Jameson for instance. The rest use BTL marketing and social networks.

Is whisky considered a luxury drink compared to other spirits?

At least single malt Scotch is definitely considered a luxury. The price for a dram of Scotch in Ukraine is twice as high compared to for example Scotland. Vodka is cheap!

Is there a clearly defined group of customers buying whisky?

I would say the typical consumer is male, over 35 and with an income above average. Having said that, there are also many women drinking whisky nowadays and they usually mix it with Coca Cola or use it in cocktails.

Is whisky something you drink at home or in a bar or restaurant?

There are just a handful of bars or restaurants in the Ukraine that specialise in good whisky. I am the owner of one of them, the Whisky Corner restaurant which is in Kiev. We have almost 600 different whiskies which is very unique in Ukraine.

How is whisky enjoyed in Ukraine?

Ukrainians drink blended whisky mainly with ice, cola or juices. Single malt on the other hand is almost always enjoyed neat.

Would you say that the customer in Ukraine is educated when it comes to the difference between various whiskies, whisky production and whisky maturation?

The Ukrainian consumer has not yet reached the level where they will understand the finer nuances in a whisky but every year knowledge is increasing. In our restaurant we explain to our guests the differences in production between vodka, cognac, whisky and other spirits. We also educate them in the history of whisky, about the importance of maturation and the differences between the various distilleries. Everything is of course accompanied by tastings. Very often we try to play on contrast, for example Speyside versus Islay.

Do you have any whisky distilleries in Ukraine and do you see any future for domestic whisky in your country?

At the moment there are no whisky distilleries in Ukraine but I hope we will have some in the future. Right now it is way more profitable to import whisky from Scotland rather than producing it yourself.

Glenlivet

Owner:
Chivas Brothers
(Pernod Ricard)

Region/district:
Speyside

Founded:
1824

Status:
Active (vc)

Capacity:
10 500 000 litres

Address: Ballindalloch, Banffshire AB37 9DB

Tel:
01340 821720 (vc)

website:
www.theglenlivet.com

History:
1817 – George Smith inherits the farm distillery Upper Drummin from his father Andrew Smith who has been distilling on the site since 1774.

1840 – George Smith buys Delnabo farm near Tomintoul and leases Cairngorm Distillery. His son William takes over operations at Upper Drummin.

1845 – George Smith leases three other farms, one of which is situated on the river Livet and is called Minmore.

1846 – William Smith develops tuberculosis and his brother John Gordon moves back home to assist his father. Sales of Smith's Glenlivet increases steadily and neither Upper Drummin nor Cairngorm Distillery can meet demand.

1858 – George Smith buys Minmore farm, which he has leased for some time, and obtains permission from the Duke of Gordon to build a distillery.

1859 – Upper Drummin and Cairngorm close and all equipment is brought to Minmore which is renamed The Glenlivet Distillery.

1864 – George Smith cooperates with the whisky agent Andrew P. Usher and exports the whisky with great success.

1871 – George Smith dies and his son John Gordon takes over.

Two years ago, as the first single malt brand in the world, Glenfiddich managed to sell more than 1 million cases (12 million bottles) in a year. Now it seems that Glenlivet may follow suit in the not so distant future. Sales figures for 2012 came in at 900,000 cases – an increase by 15% in the last year and no less than 135% in the last decade. This puts the brand as the second most popular single malt in the world and the most sold in the USA where it has been number one since the 1970s.

A substantial expansion to the distillery was completed in 2010 with an 80% increase in capacity. After the expansion, the equipment has been divided into two still rooms. In the old still house there are eight stills, eight wooden washbacks and the old mash tun (which has been mothballed). The new still house has a brand new, Briggs mash tun with six arms (13 tonnes capacity), eight new Oregon pine washbacks with a fermentation time of 50 hours and three pairs of stills. The maximum capacity is 42 mashes per week and 10.5 million litres of alcohol per year.

Glenlivet's core range is the *12 year old*, the *15 year old French Oak Reserve, 18 year old, 21 year old Archive* and *Glenlivet XXV*. A special range of unchillfiltered whiskies is called Nadurra and it comes in three expressions; *Nadurra 16 year old* at *cask strength*, the same for *duty free* but bottled at *48%* and *Nadurra Triumph 1991*. Apart from Nadurra, another four expressions are earmarked for the Duty Free market: *First Fill Sherry Cask 12 years old, 15 years old, Glenlivet Master Distiller's Reserve* and *18 year old Batch Reserve* – a variation of the core 18 year old. In 2012, the Cellar Collection range was continued with the *1980 Vintage*, while the *12 year old Excellence* was released as an exclusive for Hong Kong. In spring 2013 *Glenlivet Alpha* was released in a black bottle with the alcohol strength (of 50%) as the only information. The idea was to get people to speculate what the content could be, based on their personal knowledge and experiences. Six weeks later, it was revealed that the whisky had been matured in casks that had previously contained only Scotch whisky and no other spirits or wines – a first for Glenlivet! A series of limited expressions of Glenlivet for select markets called *Single Cask Editions* was introduced in 2005 with The Glenlivet Atlantic. The subsequent releases have been given their names in alphabetical order and in 2013, the 17 year old *The Glenlivet Quercus* was launched exclusively to the Whisky Shop chain as well as the 18 year old *The Glenlivet Tombae* which was released at the Changi Airport in Singapore.

History (continued):

1880 – John Gordon Smith applies for and is granted sole rights to the name The Glenlivet. All distilleries wishing to use Glenlivet in their names must from now hyphenate it with their brand names.

1890 – A fire breaks out and some of the buildings are replaced.

1896 – Another two stills are installed.

1901 – John Gordon Smith dies.

1904 – John Gordon's nephew George Smith Grant takes over.

1921 – Captain Bill Smith Grant, son of George Smith Grant, takes over.

1953 – George & J. G. Smith Ltd merges with J. & J. Grant of Glen Grant Distillery and forms the company Glenlivet & Glen Grant Distillers.

1966 – Floor maltings closes.

1970 – Glenlivet & Glen Grant Distillers Ltd merges with Longmorn-Glenlivet Distilleries Ltd and Hill Thomson & Co. Ltd to form The Glenlivet Distillers Ltd.

1978 – Seagrams buys The Glenlivet Distillers Ltd. A visitor centre opens.

1996/97 – The visitor centre is expanded, and a multimedia facility installed.

2000 – French Oak 12 years and American Oak 12 years are launched

2001 – Pernod Ricard and Diageo buy Seagram Spirits & Wine. Pernod Ricard thereby gains control of the Chivas group.

2004 – This year sees a lavish relaunch of Glenlivet. French Oak 15 years replaces the previous 12 year old.

2005 – Two new duty-free versions are introduced – The Glenlivet 12 year old First Fill and Nadurra. The 1972 Cellar Collection (2,015 bottles) is launched.

2006 – Nadurra 16 year old cask strength and 1969 Cellar Collection are released. Glenlivet sells more than 500,000 cases for the first time in one year.

2007 – Glenlivet XXV is released.

2009 – Four more stills are installed and the capacity increases to 8.5 million litres. Nadurra Triumph 1991 is released.

2010 – Another two stills are commissioned and capacity increases to 10.5 million litres. Glenlivet Founder´s Reserve is released.

2011 – Glenlivet Master Distiller´s Reserve is released for the duty free market.

2012 – 1980 Cellar Collection is released.

2013 – The 18 year old Batch Reserve and Glenlivet Alpha are released.

Glenlivet 12 year old

GS – A lovely, honeyed, floral, fragrant nose. Medium-bodied, smooth and malty on the palate, with vanilla sweetness. Not as sweet, however, as the nose might suggest. The finish is pleasantly lengthy and sophisticated.

DR – Freshly chopped apple, rhubarb and crisp barley on the nose, soft rounded and beautiful mouth feel with green fruit and gooseberries and a delicate, rounded and medium long finish.

18 years old   21 Archive   The Glenlivet XXV   1980 Cellar Collection

Batch Reserve 18 years   The Glenlivet Alpha

12 years old   15 years old   Master Distiller´s Reserve

Glenlossie

Owner: **Region/district:**
Diageo   Speyside

Founded: **Status:**   **Capacity:**
1876   Active   2 700 000 litres

Address: Birnie, Elgin, Morayshire IV30 8SS

Tel: **website:**
01343 862000   www.malts.com

History:
1876 – John Duff, former manager at Glendronach Distillery, founds the distillery. Alexander Grigor Allan (to become part-owner of Talisker Distillery), the whisky trader George Thomson and Charles Shirres (both will co-found Longmorn Distillery some 20 years later with John Duff) and H. Mackay are also involved in the company.

1895 – The company Glenlossie-Glenlivet Distillery Co. is formed. Alexander Grigor Allan passes away.

1896 – John Duff becomes more involved in Longmorn and Mackay takes over management of Glenlossie.

1919 – Distillers Company Limited (DCL) takes over the company.

1929 – A fire breaks out and causes considerable damage.

1930 – DCL transfers operations to Scottish Malt Distillers (SMD).

1962 – Stills are increased from four to six.

1971 – Another distillery, Mannochmore, is constructed by SMD on the premises. A dark grains plant is installed.

1990 – A 10 year old is launched in the Flora & Fauna series.

2010 – A Manager's Choice single cask from 1999 is released.

Glenlossie 10 year old

GS – Cereal, silage and vanilla notes on the relatively light nose, with a voluptuous, sweet palate, offering plums, ginger and barley sugar, plus a hint of oak. The finish is medium in length, with grist and slightly peppery oak.

DR – Powdery and light, with salt and pepper on the nose, big, earthy and spicy palate; savoury and full, with a long and mouth-coating finish.

Glenlossie is located just south of Elgin in an area that is like a veritable bee's nest of distilleries. No less than seven other distilleries are situated within a radius of merely 4 kilometres; to the west Miltonduff, to the north Glen Moray and Linkwood, to the south BenRiach, Longmorn and Glen Elgin and on the same site as Glenlossie, there is Mannochmore, built as late as in 1971. Glenlossie was founded almost 100 years before that and the malt whisky has, over the years, earned a reputation amongst blenders to be one of the best there is to work with when creating a blended Scotch. Glenlossie has always been an integral part of Haig's and Dimple, both brands emanating from the Haig family which could probably be called Scotland's oldest whisky dynasty. Already in 1667, Robert Haig was rebuked for distilling on the Sabbath! The golden years of Haig whisky were from 1930-1970 when it was the brand leader in the UK. Ever since the sales have decreased but, despite that, about 5 million bottles are still being sold every year.

Glenlossie distillery is equipped with one stainless steel full lauter mash tun (8,2 tonnes) installed in 1992, eight washbacks made of larch and three pairs of stills. The spirit stills are also equipped with purifiers between the lyne arms and the condensers are used to increase the reflux which, in turn, gives Glenlossie newmake its light and green/grassy character. In February 2013, the distillery moved to a 7-day week production which enables them to do 17 mashes per week and 2,7 million litres of alcohol per year – a substantial increase compared to previous years. Except for the two distilleries, a dark grains plant and a newly constructed bio plant (see Mannochmore for more information) the site also holds fourteen warehouses (12 racked and 2 dunnage) that can store 250,000 casks of maturing whisky. To Glenlossie Bonds, as it is called, casks are sent from a number of Diageo's distilleries in the vicinity.

The only official bottling of Glenlossie available today is a *10 year old*. During 2010 a first fill bourbon cask distilled in *1999* was released as a part of the Manager's Choice range.

Flora & Fauna 10 years

Whisky Around the World

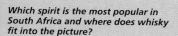

SOUTH AFRICA

Karen Chaloner was born in Zimbabwe and has worked in the drinks industry for 20 years. She co-founded the Whisky Live Festival, South Africa (www.whiskylivefestival.co.za) and was previously Marketing Manager of Johnnie Walker and J&B. She was also the co-founder of the College of Whisky and has been appointed a Keeper of the Quaich.

Which spirit is the most popular in South Africa and where does whisky fit into the picture?

Traditionally South Africa has always been a brandy market; the brandy consumption far outweighed whisky. However whisky has completely overtaken brandy in a big way and is now the biggest category by both value and volume.

What types of whisky are the most popular in South Africa?

Standard and premium Scotch blends remain the favourite choice right now with a great move towards trading up from standard to premium Scotch.

When would you say people in South Africa started to get seriously interested in whisky? What triggered it and how has that interest developed?

During the Apartheid and sanctions era many international whisky brands weren't so easy to get hold of – hence the rise in brandy sales. South Africa has always been a large producer of wine and brandy and thus was far more available than whisky. This all ended in 1994 when South Africa transferred to a majority rule system. Things really started to change for whisky with the rapid rise of the growing middleclass and along with the re-entry of a number of whisky brands back into the country.

Which brands of Scotch are the most popular in South Africa?

Bell's, the Johnnie Walker range, J&B, Black & White, VAT 69, The Famous Grouse, Chivas Regal, Glenlivet, Glenfiddich, Glenmorangie, Singleton and The Macallan are the most popular Scotch brands in the country.

How is whisky sold in South Africa, is there a wide variety of brands and is it easy to find the brand you want?

Generally the big blended well-known Scotch whiskies are widely available in the country; it is the more specialized smaller and independent single malts that are harder to get hold of.

Ten years ago whisky in South Africa was predominantly sold through the mass retailers, wholesalers and independent retailers. With the consumer becoming more knowledgeable, there has been a definite rise in specialised online whisky sales and even a few specialist whisky stores have opened.

Is whisky considered a luxury drink compared to other spirits?

It is considered premium and if you are seen drinking at the top end of the scale it would indeed be luxury. Whisky is associated with an international and successful lifestyle. We are seeing an increasing demand for premium and super premium whiskies and I actually read somewhere recently that Soweto is thought to be the most lucrative per capita market for Johnnie Walker Blue Label in the world!

Is there a clearly defined group of customers buying whisky?

Long gone are the days when whisky was the preserve of old men wearing moth-eaten tartans and dusty old slippers. With huge efforts made by the whisky industry and ourselves to smash all the barriers to entry into the world of whisky, whisky is now exciting, fun, youthful and sexy. The consumers are younger, 25-40 years old, educated and successful and are more educated about the subject.

Are there special occasions when whisky is preferred?

Whisky remains a chosen drink for any celebratory occasion whether it is a promotion, special holiday, birth of a child and popular amongst the emerging market at funerals. However with the massive growth seen in this country it has also become an every day preferred drink.

How is whisky enjoyed in South Africa?

Because South Africa is a hot country, mostly over ice with a dash of water. With the younger generation, whose palates still prefer a sweet taste, there is definitely a lot of mixing going on.

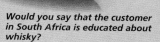

Would you say that the customer in South Africa is educated about whisky?

Back in 2003 when we launched the first FNB Whisky Live Festival, the South African consumer had no idea there were so many whiskies out there. The questions the consumers are asking now are a lot more sophisticated and in-depth. Most consumers understand age and the difference between a single malt and a blend as well as the difference between an Irish, Scottish and American whisky.

How many producers of whisky do you have in South Africa and how would you describe the future for domestic whisky in your country?

The major producer of whisky in South Africa is Distell; the company owns two South African home-grown brands that are giving established whisky countries like Scotland and Ireland a run for their money. There are a few craft distillers such as Moritz Kallmeyer who owns Drayman's Brewery and Distillery in Pretoria. He is a fantastic character and has been producing a range of home-made whiskies and beer for a while.

What are your thoughts on the future for Scotch whisky in South Africa?

I think we are going to see an increased demand for premium, super-premium and craft whiskies from both international and domestic sources. What's more, the average whisky drinker in South Africa is becoming increasingly educated and therefore more demanding in their whisky tastes and styles. Hopefully we will see more niche Scotch whiskies enter the market on the back of this trend and as existing whisky enthusiasts expand their repertoire of brands and tastes.

Glenmorangie

Owner:
The Glenmorangie Co
(Moët Hennessy)

Region/district:
Northern Highlands

Founded: **Status:**   **Capacity:**
1843   Active (vc)   6 000 000 litres

Address: Tain, Ross-shire IV19 1PZ

Tel: **website:**
01862 892477 (vc)   www.glenmorangie.com

History:
1843 – William Mathesen applies for a license for a farm distillery called Morangie, which is rebuilt by them. Production took place here in 1738, and possibly since 1703.

1849 – Production starts in November.

1880 – Exports to foreign destinations such as Rome and San Francisco commence.

1887 – The distillery is rebuilt and Glenmorangie Distillery Company Ltd is formed.

1918 – 40% of the distillery is sold to Macdonald & Muir Ltd and 60 % to the whisky dealer Durham. Macdonald & Muir takes over Durham's share by the late thirties.

1931 – The distillery closes.

1936 – Production restarts in November.

1980 – Number of stills increases from two to four and own maltings ceases.

1990 – The number of stills is doubled to eight.

1994 – A visitor centre opens. September sees the launch of Glenmorangie Port Wood Finish which marks the start of a number of different wood finishes.

1995 – Glenmorangie's Tain l´Hermitage (Rhone wine) is launched.

1996 – Two different wood finishes are launched, Madeira and Sherry. Glenmorangie plc is formed.

Today, Glenmorangie is the fourth most sold single malt in the world but, in 1918, when Roderick Macdonald bought the distillery he wasn´t interested in the brand as such. Macdonald set up his own business in 1893 and soon established a blended Scotch brand called Highland Queen which would become one of the leading brands for a major part of the 1900s. The success of the blend prompted Macdonald to secure whisky production of his own and his eyes fell on Glenmorangie. In the 1980s the priorities shifted when Glenmorangie started being marketed as single malt and Highland Queen was left to its own demise. Today, both brands are owned by French companies – Glenmorangie by LVMH since 2004 and Highland Queen by Picard since 2008.

Following a major expansion in 2009, the distillery is now equipped with a full lauter mash tun with a charge of 10 tonnes, 12 stainless steel washbacks with a fermentation time of 52 hours and six pairs of stills. They are the tallest in Scotland and the still room is one of the most magnificent to be seen. Production for 2013 has increased to 32 mashes per week which equates to 6 million litres in the year which is more or less its full capacity. The newmake is always filled into bourbon barrels. For some of the expressions it is later re-racked into different casks for extra maturation.

Glenmorangie single malt sold almost five million bottles in 2012 of which a quarter was sold in the UK where it is the number two brand after Glenfiddich. Sales in the USA, where Glenmorangie until a few years ago was relatively unknown, has grown phenomenally from 450,000 bottles in 2008 to more than one million in 2012.

The core range consists of *Original* (10 year old), *18* and *25 year old*. There are three 12 year old wood finishes: *Quinta Ruban* (port), *Nectar D´Or* (Sauternes) and *Lasanta* (sherry). Added to the core range are *Astar* and *Signet*. Astar has matured in designer casks while Signet is an unusual piece of work with one portion of the whisky (20%) having been made using chocolate malt. A series of bottlings, called Private Edition, started in 2009 with the release of the sherried *Sonnalta PX* and was followed up a year later with lightly peated *Finealta*. In 2012, *Artein*, which is a mix of 15 and 21 year old whiskies which have been extra matured in Sassicaia wine casks was launched and spring 2013 saw the fourth release by way of *Ealanta*, a 19 year old fully matured in virgin American oak. Previous limited expressions include *Glenmorangie Pride*, 28 years old with a second maturation of ten years in Sauternes barriques.

History (continued):

1997 – A museum opens.

2001 – A limited edition of a cask strength port wood finish is released in July, Cote de Beaune Wood Finish is launched in September and Three Cask (ex-Bourbon, charred oak and ex-Rioja) is launched in October for Sainsbury's.

2002 – A Sauternes finish, a 20 year Glenmorangie with two and a half years in Sauternes casks, is launched.

2003 – Burgundy Wood Finish is launched in July and a limited edition of cask strength Madeira-matured (i. e. not just finished) in August.

2004 – Glenmorangie buys the Scotch Malt Whisky Society. The Macdonald family decides to sell Glenmorangie plc (including the distilleries Glenmorangie, Glen Moray and Ardbeg) to Moët Hennessy at £300 million. A new version of Glenmorangie Tain l´Hermitage (28 years) is released and Glenmorangie Artisan Cask is launched in November.

2005 – A 30 year old is launched.

2007 – The entire range gets a complete makeover with 15 and 30 year olds being discontinued and the rest given new names as well as new packaging.

2008 – An expansion of production capacity is started. Astar and Signet are launched.

2009 – The expansion is finished and Sonnalta PX is released for duty free.

2010 – Glenmorangie Finealta is released.

2011 – 28 year old Glenmorangie Pride is released.

2012 – Glenmorangie Artein is released.

2013 – Glenmorangie Ealanta is released.

Glenmorangie Original

GS – The nose offers fresh fruits, butterscotch and toffee. Silky smooth in the mouth, mild spice, vanilla, and well-defined toffee. The fruity finish has a final flourish of ginger.

DR – Rounded honey and light tangerine on the nose, much weightier on the palate, with vanilla, honey, oranges and lemons nudging alongside some tannins and soft peat, all coming together in a rich and warming finish.

Signet   Astar   Ealanta

Original (10 years old)   18 years old   Nectar D´Or

Glen Moray

Owner: **Region/district:**
La Martiniquaise (COFEPP)   Speyside

Founded: **Status:**   **Capacity:**
1897   Active (vc)   3 300 000 litres

Address: Bruceland Road, Elgin,
Morayshire IV30 1YE

Tel: **website:**
01343 542577   www.glenmoray.com

History:
1897 – West Brewery, dated 1828, is
reconstructed as Glen Moray Distillery.

1910 – The distillery closes.

1920 – Financial troubles force the distillery to
be put up for sale. Buyer is Macdonald & Muir.

1923 – Production restarts.

1958 – A reconstruction takes place and the
floor maltings are replaced by a Saladin box.

1978 – Own maltings are terminated.

1979 – Number of stills is increased to four.

1996 – Macdonald & Muir Ltd changes name
to Glenmorangie plc.

1999 – Three wood finishes are introduced
- Chardonnay (no age) and Chenin Blanc (12
and 16 years respectively).

2004 – Louis Vuitton Moët Hennessy buys
Glenmorangie plc and a 1986 cask strength, a
20 and a 30 year old are released.

2005 – The Fifth Chapter (Manager's Choice
from Graham Coull) is released.

2006 – Two vintages, 1963 and 1964, and a
new Manager's Choice are released.

2007 – New edition of Mountain Oak is
released.

2008 – The distillery is sold to La Martiniquaise.

2009 – A 14 year old Port finish and an 8 year
old matured in red wines casks are released.

2011 – Two cask finishes and a 10 year old
Chardonnay maturation are released.

2012 – A 2003 Chenin Blanc is released.

2013 – A 25 year old port finish is released.

Glen Moray 12 year old

GS – Mellow on the nose, with vanilla, pear
drops and some oak. Smooth in the mouth,
with spicy malt, vanilla and summer fruits. The
finish is relatively short, with spicy fruit.

DR – Maltesers and soft vanilla ice cream on
the nose, full and rich sweet malt, a touch of
vanilla and hints of tannin on the palate and a
pleasant and pleasing finish.

The owners of Glen Moray distillery since 2008, La Martiniquaise, the second largest spirits company in France, had
plans to build another malt distillery next to their huge
grain distillery, Starlaw, near Bathgate. The reason being
the huge success in sales for their two major blends, Label 5
and Sir Edwards, in France. However, the plans were changed and subsequently the capacity at Glen Moray was increased by over 40% as from January 2013. It will probably
not stop there – planning applications for further expan-
sions have already been filed with Moray Council where the
old maltings would be replaced by another building with a
new mash tun and more washbacks and stills. This second
expansion could be a reality as soon as 2015.

The Starlaw plant, which opened in 2010, has the capacity
of producing 25 million litres of grain whisky and there
is also a maturation, blending and bottling plant on site
which already opened in 2004.

Thanks to the recent expansion, Glen
Moray is now equipped with a stainless
steel mash tun, four stainless steel washbacks plus another five new ones which
are outside. There are now three pairs
of stills and the distillery is producing at
full capacity for 51 weeks, seven days
a week. In 2009, the distillery, for the
first time, produced a share of whisky
from peated malt with around 40ppm
phenols. The volume for 2013 will be
200,000 litres and it will mainly be
used in the owner's Label 5 blended
whisky, as well as for another of
their fast growing brands, Glen
Turner – a blended malt which sells
one million bottles per year.

The core range consists of *Classic,
10 year old Chardonnay cask, 12
years old* and *16 years old*. In 2012
a Glen Moray from *2003* with a full
maturation in Chenin Blanc cask
was released as a distillery exclusive
and this was replaced by a *1977*
single cask in 2013. A *25 year old*
with one year's finish in *port* pipes
was already announced in 2012 but
the 3,400 bottles were not released
until summer 2013.

12 years old

Glen Ord

Owner:
Diageo

Region/district:
Northern Highlands

Founded: 1838

Status:
Active (vc)

Capacity:
5 000 000 litres

Address: Muir of Ord, Ross-shire IV6 7UJ

Tel:
01463 872004 (vc)

website:
www.malts.com

History:

1838 – Thomas Mackenzie founds the distillery and licenses it to Ord Distillery Co.

1847 – The distillery is put up for sale.

1855 – Alexander MacLennan and Thomas McGregor buy the distillery.

1870 – Alexander MacLennan dies and the distillery is taken over by his widow who marries the banker Alexander Mackenzie.

1877 – Alexander Mackenzie leases the distillery.

1878 – Alexander Mackenzie builds a new still house and barely manages to start production before a fire destroys it.

1882 – Mackenzie registers the name Glenoran to be used for whisky from Glen Ord.

1896 – Alexander Mackenzie dies and the distillery is sold to the blending company James Watson & Co. for £15,800.

1923 – John Jabez Watson, James Watson's son, dies and the distillery is sold to John Dewar & Sons. The name is changed from Glen Oran to Glen Ord.

1925 – Dewar's joins Distillers Company Ltd.

1961 – Floor maltings is abandoned in favour of a Saladin box.

1966 – The two stills are increased to six.

1968 – To augment the Saladin box a drum maltings is built.

1983 – Malting in the Saladin box ceases.

1988 – A visitor centre is opened.

2002 – A 12 year old is launched.

2003 – A 28 year old cask strength is released.

2004 – A 25 year old is launched.

2005 – A 30 year old is launched as a Special Release from Diageo.

2006 – A 12 year old Singleton of Glen Ord is launched.

2010 – A Singleton of Glen Ord 15 year old is released in Taiwan.

2011 – Two more washbacks are installed, increasing the capacity by 25%.

2012 – Singleton of Glen Ord cask strength is released.

2013 – Singleton of Glen Ord Signature is launched.

Singleton of Glen Ord 12 year old

GS – Honeyed malt and milk chocolate on the nose, with a hint of orange. These characteristics carry over onto the sweet, easy-drinking palate, along with a biscuity note. Subtly drying, with a medium-length, spicy finish.

DR – Red fruits and blackcurrant, mince pies, red apple and sherry on the nose, enjoyable taste of apple, prune and cinnamon, and a delightful and more-ish finish.

To build a completely new single malt brand and after seven years reaching over 2 million bottles sold annually, as well as putting it on the Top Ten list of most sold malt whiskies in the world, is a remarkable achievement. This is what's happened with Singleton of Glen Ord, a brand which is now exclusively sold in Asia. But Glen Ord malt is also an important part of almost every Diageo blended whisky (only 15% goes to single malt bottlings) so it is small wonder that the owners have had to increase the production capacity. In 2010/2011 a new mash tun was installed as well as two extra washbacks. But that's not all! Another expansion worth £25 million has been put in motion and will be finished during the second half of 2014. This means one more mash tun, ten new washbacks and another six stills, raising the capacity to 10 million litres of alcohol per year. When everything is in place, the equipment specification will be – two 12,5 tonnes full lauter mash tuns, 20 wooden washbacks (two of the existing stainless steel ones will be replaced by wood) and 12 stills.

A major part of the site is occupied by the Glen Ord Maltings which was built in 1968. Equipped with 18 drums and with a capacity of 37,000 tonnes per year it produces malt for several other Diageo distilleries. The distillery is situated 15 miles west of Inverness in the fertile Black Isle and with one of the best visitor centres in the industry, it is well worth a visit.

Singleton of Glen Ord is an exclusive to Southeast Asia, in particular Taiwan and Singapore. The core range is the Singleton of Glen Ord 12, 15 and 18 year old. There have also been two limited ones, 32 and 35 year old and a cask strength, bottled at 58,1% and released in May 2012. The latest addition is Singleton of Glen Ord Signature, released for duty free in June 2013.

The Singleton of Glen Ord

Glenrothes

Owner: The Edrington Group
(the brand is owned by Berry Bros)

Region/district: Speyside

Founded: 1878 **Status:** Active **Capacity:** 5 600 000 litres

Address: Rothes, Morayshire AB38 7AA

Tel: 01340 872300 **website:** www.theglenrothes.com

History:

1878 – James Stuart & Co., licensees of Macallan since 1868, begins planning a new distillery in Rothes. Robert Dick, William Grant and John Cruickshank are partners in the company. Stuart has financial problems so Dick, Grant and Cruickshank terminate the partnership, form William Grant & Co. and continue the building of the distillery in Rothes.

1879 – Production starts in May.

1884 – The distillery changes name to Glenrothes-Glenlivet.

1887 – William Grant & Co. joins forces with Islay Distillery Co. (owners of Bunnahabhain Distillery) and forms Highland Distillers Company.

1897 – A fire ravages the distillery in December.

1898 – Capacity doubles.

1903 – An explosion causes substantial damage.

1963 – Expansion from four to six stills.

1980 – Expansion from six to eight stills.

1989 – Expansion from eight to ten stills.

1999 – Edrington and William Grant & Sons buy Highland Distillers.

2002 – Four single cask malts from 1966 and 1967 are launched.

2005 – A 30 year old is launched together with Select Reserve and Vintage 1985.

2006 – 1994 and 1975 Vintage are launched.

2007 – A 25 year old is released as a duty free item.

2008 – 1978 Vintage and Robur Reserve are launched.

2009 – The Glenrothes John Ramsay, two vintages (1988 and 1998), Alba Reserve and Three Decades are released.

2010 – Berry Brothers takes over the brand while Edrington remains owner of the distillery.

2011 – Editor's Casks are released.

2013 – 2001 Vintage and the Manse Brae range are released.

The location of Glenrothes is quite unique. The distillery stands right in the middle of the small town of Rothes in Speyside and as you drive up to the distillery you have the Burn of Rothes on your left hand and to the right lies Rothes Cemetery with the tombstones all blackened by fungi which thrive from the evaporated alcohol vapour from the distillery. The distillery is owned and operated by Edrington but the single malt brand itself is in the hands of Berry Bros & Rudd (BBR).

The distillery is equipped with a stainless steel full lauter mash tun from the 1970s – probably one of the first in the business. Ten washbacks made of Oregon pine are in one room, whilst an adjacent modern tun room houses eight new stainless steel washbacks. The wash from the different types of washbacks are always mixed before distillation. With the new 7 day week, all fermentations are 58 hours. The magnificent, cathedral-like still house has five pairs of stills performing a very slow distillation. In 2013 the distillery is producing 5,2 million litres of alcohol.

The core expression of Glenrothes is the *Select Reserve* and the *Alba Reserve*, but it is the vintages that have brought fame to Glenrothes. The most recent vintages are *1988, 1995, 1998* and (released in spring 2013) *Vintage 2001*. The duty free range include *Robur Reserve, Three Decades* (with whiskies from the seventies, eighties and nineties) and a *25 year old*. A new range for duty free, *Manse Brae*, was introduced in autumn 2013. The names of the three whiskies celebrate the spiritual home of Glenrothes; *Manse Reserve* (unaged), *Elder's Reserve* (18 years) and *Minister's Reserve* (21 years). Finally, another new range called *The Glenrothes Extra-ordinary Cask* was introduced in autumn 2012 with the first expression being a *Vintage 1970*. The cask did not come from distillery stock but was sourced by Ronnie Cox, the brand's heritage director, from a private collector in Scotland.

2001 Vintage

Glenrothes Select Reserve

GS – The nose offers ripe fruits, spice and toffee, with a whiff of Golden Syrup. Faint wood polish in the mouth, vanilla, spicy and slightly citric. Creamy and complex. Slightly nutty, with some orange, in the drying finish.

DR – On the nose, oranges dominating a fruit bowl of flavours that includes berries among the citrus. The palate is wonderfully rounded and complete, a masterclass in fruit, wood and spice balance, and the finish is a total joy, perfectly weighted and balanced.

Cutty Sark

Blended Scotch

Starring Glenrothes Single Malt *in a leading role*
Producer Edrington
Director Kirsteen Campbell, Master Blender

Most of the big Scotch blended brands were already established in the late 1800s but Cutty Sark stems from a later date. It was created in 1923 by Berry Bros & Rudd, the oldest and one of the most renowned wine and spirits merchants in the world. In the 1920s the company was run by Francis and Walter Berry, who were second cousins, and their younger partner, Hugh Rudd. Francis had been visiting USA regularly since 1909 and had managed to create a loyal clientele for the company's products. When Prohibition hit the States in 1920, the company faced the risk of losing a substantial part of their business. Francis met with the legendary whisky smuggler, captain Bill McCoy, in the Bahamas where McCoy would explain what type of whisky would appeal to the thirsty Americans. Not only that - McCoy had all the contacts to be able to get the whisky into the country.

Francis Berry gave a whisky blender in Scotland, James Stanhard, the assignment to compose a light and pale blend which would appeal to the American palate. The whisky was named after one of the last tea clippers to be built and one of the fastest while the artist, James McBey, was commissioned to do the label. The colour in McBey's label was originally cream, but later turned out to be yellow due to a printing error and they've retained that colour ever since.

Cutty Sark became an instant success and after the Second World War, sales had escalated. By 1961 the brand had become the category leader in the US. Sales have since slowed, but it is still in the top ten in America. The brand has expanded into new territory and is now popular in Spain, Greece and India. Early on, the Berry Brothers formed an alliance with Edrington, who today are the owners of the

Famous Grouse brand, as well as the Macallan, Highland Park and Glenrothes distilleries.

BBR were the owners of the Cutty Sark brand and were responsible for the sales and marketing, while Edrington stood for production, blending and bottling. By 2010, the Berry Brothers, who wanted to concentrate on the exclusive segment of the wine & spirits business, realised that, in order to grow the brand, it would be better suited in a larger company's portfolio. A deal was concluded with Edrington where they took over Cutty Sark, while Berry Brothers became owners of the Glenrothes single malt brand (not the distillery).

Today Cutty Sark is selling eleven million bottles per year which means that sales have dropped by 50% in just ten years. A major relaunch of the brand was started in 2012 which included a new expression and new packaging and the brand seems destined for increased sales.

The basis of the range is *Cutty Sark* without age statement. There are also a *12, 15* and *25 year old*. The latter is called *Tam O'Shanter* and has been named after the narrative poem written by Robert Burns. Finally two more bottlings were recently added to the range – *Cutty Storm* (in 2012) which features a higher

proportion of older single malts and *Cutty Prohibition* (in 2013), a more powerful version and bottled at 50%. The latter was launched to commemorate the 90th anniversary of the brand and 80 years since the repeal of Prohibition.

A light and gentle blend with citrus, apples and sweet grain on the nose. Smooth mouthfeel with barley, honey, vanilla and a touch of jasmine tea.

Glen Scotia

Owner:
Loch Lomond Distillery Co

Region/district:
Campbeltown

Founded: **Status:** **Capacity:**
1832   Active   750 000 litres

Address: High Street, Campbeltown, Argyll PA28 6DS

Tel: **website:**
01586 552288   www.glenscotia-distillery.co.uk

History:

1832 – The family Galbraith founds Scotia Distillery (the year 1835 is mentioned by the distillery itself on labels).

1895 – The distillery is sold to Stewart Galbraith.

1919 – Sold to West Highland Malt Distillers.

1924 – West Highland Malt Distillers goes bankrupt and one of its directors, Duncan MacCallum, buys the distillery.

1928 – The distillery closes.

1930 – Duncan MacCallum commits suicide and the Bloch brothers take over.

1933 – Production restarts.

1954 – Hiram Walker takes over.

1955 – A. Gillies & Co. becomes new owner.

1970 – A. Gillies & Co. becomes part of Amalgated Distillers Products.

1979–82 – Reconstruction takes place.

1984 – The distillery closes.

1989 – Amalgated Distillers Products is taken over by Gibson International and production restarts.

1994 – Glen Catrine Bonded Warehouse Ltd takes over and the distillery is mothballed.

1999 – Production restarts 5th May through J. A. Mitchell & Co., owner of Springbank.

2000 – Loch Lomond Distillers runs operations with its own staff from May onwards.

2005 – A 12 year old is released.

2006 – A peated version is released.

2012 – A new range (10, 12, 16, 18 and 21 year old) is launched.

Glen Scotia 12 year old

GS – Nougat and a suggestion of fresh newsprint on the nose. Quite full-bodied, with a palate of mixed nuts and peaches in brandy. The finish is slightly waxy, with fruit and nut chocolate.

The history of Glen Scotia is one of frequent changes of ownership and intermittent production but also a history of extraordinary resilience. When the famous whisky traveller and writer, Alfred Barnard, came to Campbeltown in 1886 (at that time called The Whisky Capital of the World), he had no less than 21 distilleries to visit. Then came the dark 1920s when no less than 17 distilleries were forced to close permanently. When Rieclachan stopped production in 1934, there were only two survivors left – Springbank and Glen Scotia. The latter struggled on gamely, but since the 1990s it has been in the shadow of Springbank which by then had reached cult status. However, the last couple of years have shown some measure of change, firstly, through an extensive refurbishing and from the end of last year a completely new range of whiskies.

Glen Scotia, which lies hidden away between modern high-rise buildings, is equipped with a traditional cast iron mash tun, six new washbacks made of stainless steel (which used to be Corten steel) and one pair of stills. Fermentation time is usually 48 hours but can be as long as up to five days. The production in 2013 started off with 12,000 litres of lightly peated malt (15ppm) followed by the same amount of heavily peated (50ppm) and for the rest of the year, 375,000 litres of unpeated whisky will be produced. This is an extensive increase in comparison to last year´s 100,000 litres.

The owners of Glen Scotia also have Loch Lomond distillery, as well as the affiliate, Glen Catrine Bonded Warehouse which was established in 1974, under their wings. It is today one of the largest bottling plants in Scotland with an annual production of 40 million bottles of whisky, vodka, gin, rum and brandy. The whole conglomerate is owned by the Bulloch family which is headed by Sandy Bulloch.

The core range, which used to consist of just the one 12 year old, was completely revamped in November 2012 and there is now a *10, 12, 16, 18* and *21* year old in completely new packaging.

12 years old

Glen Spey

Owner: Region/district:
Diageo   Speyside

Founded: Status: Capacity:
1878   Active   1 400 000 litres

Address: Rothes, Morayshire AB38 7AU

Tel: website:
01340 831215 www.malts.com

History:
1878 – James Stuart & Co. founds the distillery which becomes known by the name Mill of Rothes.

1886 – James Stuart buys Macallan.

1887 – W. & A. Gilbey buys the distillery for £11,000 thus becoming the first English company to buy a Scottish malt distillery.

1920 – A fire breaks out.

1962 – W. & A. Gilbey combines forces with United Wine Traders and forms International Distillers & Vintners (IDV).

1970 – The stills are increased from two to four.

1972 – IDV is bought by Watney Mann who is then acquired by Grand Metropolitan.

1997 – Guiness and Grand Metropolitan merge to form Diageo.

2001 – A 12 year old is launched in the Flora & Fauna series.

2010 – A 21 year old is released as part of the Special Releases and a 1996 Manager´s Choice single cask is launched.

Glen Spey 12 year old
GS – Tropical fruits and malt on the comparatively delicate nose. Medium-bodied with fresh fruits and vanilla toffee on the palate, becoming steadily nuttier and drier in a gently oaky, mildly smoky finish.

DR – Delicate and floral on the nose, a complex mix of flavours on the palate with orange, citrus fruits, honey, vanilla and cinnamon in the mix.

Until a few years ago, the sign in front of Glen Spey distillery in Rothes read Glen Spey Distillery and (in larger type) Spey Royal. Today, Spey Royal has been exchanged for J&B Rare. In both cases they tell the story about the blended whiskies where Glen Spey malt whisky plays a significant role. Spey Royal, introduced as a brand by W & A Gilbey in the early 20th century, has had its strongest market in Thailand over the past 20 years. In the late 1990s it was the leader in the country in the standard Scotch segment with an 80% share. Just a few years later it was down to 20% having not only been surpassed by 100 Pipers, but also by some of Diageo´s other brands like Benmore and Johnnie Walker Red Label. J&B on the other hand, plays in a different division. Even if the brand has battled over the last couple of years, it still remains the fifth most popular Scotch in the world with almost 50 million bottles sold in 2012.

Glen Spey distillery, hidden away in a side street in Rothes, is equipped with a semi-lauter mash tun, eight stainless steel washbacks and two pairs of stills where the spirit stills are equipped with purifiers to obtain a lighter character of the spirit. The distillery is producing on a 5-day week basis and this means that they practise short fermentations (just 46 hours) during the weekdays and long fermentations (100 hours) over the weekend. To even out the differences in the character, the two versions are always mixed before distillation. For 2013 a production of 1,4 million litres is planned (18 mashes per week). Almost the entire production of Glen Spey malt is intended for different blends, not least that of J&B. The core expression is the *12 year old Flora & Fauna* bottling. In 2010, two limited releases were made – a *single cask* from new American Oak, distilled in *1996*, was released as a part of the Manager´s Choice series and later, as part of the yearly Special Releases, a *21 year old* with a maturation in ex-sherry American oak was also launched.

12 years old

Glentauchers

Owner:
Chivas Brothers
(Pernod Ricard)

Region/district:
Speyside

Founded: **Status:** **Capacity:**
1897   Active   4 200 000 litres

Address: Mulben, Keith,
Banffshire AB55 6YL

Tel: **website:**
01542 860272   -

History:
1897 – James Buchanan and W. P. Lowrie, a whisky merchant from Glasgow, found the distillery.

1898 – Production starts.

1906 – James Buchanan & Co. takes over the whole distillery and acquires an 80% share in W. P. Lowrie & Co.

1915 – James Buchanan & Co. merges with Dewars.

1923-25 – Mashing house and maltings are rebuilt.

1925 – Buchanan-Dewars joins Distillers Company Limited (DCL).

1930 – Glentauchers is transferred to Scottish Malt Distillers (SMD).

1965 – The number of stills is increased from two to six.

1969 – Floor maltings is decommissioned.

1985 – DCL mothballs the distillery.

1989 – United Distillers (formerly DCL) sells the distillery to Caledonian Malt Whisky Distillers, a subsidiary of Allied Distillers.

1992 – Production recommences in August.

2000 – A 15 year old Glentauchers is released.

2005 – Chivas Brothers (Pernod Ricard) become the new owner through the acquisition of Allied Domecq.

Glentauchers 1991 Gordon & MacPhail

GS – Fresh and floral aromas, with sweet fruits and peppery peaches. Medium to full-bodied in the mouth, with cereal and sweet spice. The finish is medium to long.

DR – Deep plum and sherry on the nose, then cocoa and blackcurrant. The palate is soft, with plum, raisin and green banana, and the finish is banana and date cake.

For part of its history, Glentauchers was owned by Allied Spirits, the spirits division of Allied Breweries, one of the largest brewing companies in the UK. Brewers started to become interested in owning distilleries in the mid 1960s and 70s when Scottish & Newcastle took over Charles MacInlay & Co, Watney Mann bought International Distillers & Vintners, Whitbread acquired Long John International and Allied Breweries bought William Teacher's. One reason for the interest in whisky and other distilled spirits was that 50% of the pubs in the UK at this time were owned by the six biggest brewers. So, it made sense to control as much of the products sold in their pubs as possible. However, in 1989 the government decided to put an end to this monopoly by legislating a new law, Beer Orders, restricting a brewer to own no more than 2,000 pubs. At this time Allied Breweries, for example, had around 7,000 pubs under their control. Glentauchers is one of Chivas Bros least known distilleries and from the very start, the distillery's role has been to produce malt whisky for blends and today it is an important part of Ballantine's. The distillery is equipped with a 12 tonnes stainless steel full lauter mash tun installed in 2007 with the copper dome from the old mash tun fitted on top. There are six washbacks made of Oregon pine with a fermentation time of 52 hours and tree pairs of stills with sub-coolers fitted in 2007. Since 2006 the distillation is what you would call balanced, i. e. one wash still and one spirit still work together and they have their own designated low wines and feints receiver. The production recently increased from six to seven days, which means 18 mashes per week and a total of 4 million litres per year. In 1910 trials with continuous distillation of malt whisky using columns stills were carried out at Glentauchers. The only distillery in Scotland practising this today for part of its production is Loch Lomond. An official 15 year old was released by Allied Domecq some years ago but the current owners have not yet released any bottlings.

Gordon & MacPhail Glentauchers 1990

Whisky Around the World

INDIA

Keshav Prakash is the founder of The Vault (www.vaultfinespirits.com), an India based import house of artisanal, hand-crafted spirits. Focused on building the culture of fine spirits appreciation, The Vault is also a platform for world-class experiences curated by Charles MacLean, Dave Broom, Tomas Estes and Fluid Movement of London.

Which spirit is the most popular in India and where does whisky fit into the picture?

Whisky is the most consumed spirit in India. A majority of the whisky produced is molasses based, un-aged, local production that is debated as not being whisky by a few. The fact is India consumed about 165 million 9 liter cases of it in 2012.

What types of whisky are the most popular in India?

Locally distilled 'whisky' has about 98% market share followed by blended Scotch, single Scotch malt and US whiskey.

When would you say people in India started to get seriously interested in whisky? What triggered it and how was that interest developed?

Historically India has been a land of local brews and distills – Feni, Arrack, Toddy, Mahua etc... Whisky was introduced in India by the British who also imparted modern and large scale distilling knowledge to Indians. A classic example of this is the Kasauli distillery in Solan, Himachal Pradesh, that still uses much of the original equipment from the ex-brewery set up by Edward Dyer in the late 1820.

Which brands of Scotch are the most popular in India?

Johnnie Walker, Chivas and Teachers are the most popular blended Scotch brands, while Glenfiddich and Glenlivet top the malt Scotch category.

How is whisky sold in India, is there a wide variety of brands and is it easy to find the brand you want?

Excise is a state matter in India, hence each state has a slightly different policy. There are over one hundred local whisky brands, some restricted to a particular state. In off-trade, whisky, or for that matter any other spirit, is sold over the counter at small private or government controlled vends depending on state laws. In the on-trade, whisky is usually sold by the pegs in premium bars and by the 'quarter' in smaller permit rooms. Except in major metros and large cities, finding a brand of your choice can be challenging indeed.

How is whisky marketed in India?

Across India, advertising of spirits is prohibited and marketing of spirits is challenging. Most 'advertising' is done surrogate, for example sponsorship of events under the brand name without mentioning the spirit category. There are hardly any organised platforms such as whisky shows, clubs etc. in comparison to the market size.

Is whisky considered a luxury drink compared to other spirits?

For each of the consumer classes, whisky is an aspirational drink. We pay high local taxes and about 160% customs duty on imported spirits, so single malts are considered a luxury.

Is there a clearly defined group of customers buying whisky?

Whisky is the most consumed spirit category in India and is available in several price points from very cheap to Ultra-Premium. It is also a common spirit category across social and economic classes in metros such as Delhi and Mumbai and in cities like Bengaluru, Pune etc.

Is whisky something you drink at home or in a bar or restaurant?

The social/family acceptance of drinking varies vastly between different socio-economic classes. Middle-aged plus, elite, urban Indians like to entertain guests at home, while the younger elite drinkers follow a more global pattern of drinking in bars. A majority of super premium and premium whisky is consumed at home while standard and cheap whisky, consumed by the middle and lower classes, sells more in bars.

Are there special occasions when whisky is preferred?

Indian food is so good that it does not need any pairing with spirits! On a serious note, we do not have that culture. A blended whisky is an after-work drink of choice for many. Urban India celebrates special occasions with Indian sweets and whisky.

How is whisky enjoyed in India?

Whisky is mostly consumed as a long drink with soda and ice. The discerning urban drinker prefers malts over ice. There are very few who are into tasting whiskies.

Would you say that the customer in India is educated when it comes to the difference between various whiskies and whisky production?

The ratio of discerning, informed consumers to that of over all whisky drinkers is very small, almost non-existent. There is so much that needs to be done in this area.

How many producers of whisky do you have in India and how would you describe the future for domestic whisky in your country?

There are over 150 distillers/producers of whisky in India. We are a young nation, over half of our population is under 30 years of age. There will be a lot of consumers in the immediate future and this will only boost whisky production in India. We will notice major multi-national brands establishing a manufacturing base in India to cater to this market.

What are your thoughts on the future for Scotch whisky in India?

There has been a slow growth for standard Indian whisky when compared to CAGR 08-12 of 20+% for Imported Whiskies and CAGR 08-12 of 30+% for Scotch Malt. The growth of premium, imported whiskies will be around 15-20% year on year. Should the EU trade body and the Scotch Whisky Association convince the Government of India to reduce the import tarrifs on spirits, then it will be one big party for this industry!

Glenturret

Owner:
The Edrington Group

Region/district:
Southern Highlands

Founded: **Status:** **Capacity:**
1775 Active (vc) 340 000 litres

Address: The Hosh, Crieff, Perthshire PH7 4HA

Tel: **website:**
01764 656565 www.thefamousgrouse.com

History:
1775 – Whisky smugglers establish a small illicit farm distillery named Hosh Distillery.

1818 – John Drummond is licensee until 1837.

1826 – A distillery in the vicinity is named Glenturret, but is decommissioned before 1852.

1852 – John McCallum is licensee until 1874.

1875 – Hosh Distillery takes over the name Glenturret Distillery and is managed by Thomas Stewart.

1903 – Mitchell Bros Ltd takes over.

1921 – Production ceases and the buildings are used for whisky storage only.

1929 – Mitchell Bros Ltd is liquidated, the distillery dismantled and the facilities are used as storage for agricultural needs.

1957 – James Fairlie buys the distillery and re-equips it.

1959 – Production restarts.

1981 – Remy-Cointreau buys the distillery and invests in a visitor centre.

1990 – Highland Distillers takes over.

1999 – Edrington and William Grant & Sons buy Highland Distillers for £601 million. The purchasing company, 1887 Company, is a joint venture between Edrington (70%) and William Grant (30%).

2002 – The Famous Grouse Experience, a visitor centre costing £2.5 million, is inaugurated.

2003 – A 10 year old Glenturret replaces the 12 year old as the distillery's standard release.

2007 – Three new single casks are released.

2013 – An 18 year old bottled at cask strength is released as a distillery exclusive.

Glenturret 10 year old

GS – Nutty and slightly oily on the nose, with barley and citrus fruits. Sweet and honeyed on the full, fruity palate, with a balancing note of oak. Medium length in the sweet finish.

DR – Full and rich honeyed nose, oily and fruity palate with some appealing rootsy savouriness. Something of the farmyard about it.

Glenturret is considered by many to be Scotland's oldest working distillery, having already been established in 1775 but records show that there may have been illicit distilling going on since 1717. In the mid 1920s it seemed as if the life of the distillery had come to an end. It was closed and later dismantled only to be resurrected by James Fairlie in the late 1950s. His son, Peter, also started at the company and when Highland Distillers (later re-named Edrington) took over the distillery, Peter Fairlie began a successful, career with the new company. This included repositioning The Macallan brand globally and simultaneously developing a visitor centre for the different distilleries in the group. One of them was Glenturret's The Famous Grouse Experience, inaugurated in 2002 and which today attracts 100,000 visitors every year.

With so much emphasis on Famous Grouse, it is easy to overlook the Glenturret distillery itself. Not only is it the oldest working distillery but is also a very traditional one at that. The mash tun, for example, is a stainless steel, open tun and the only one left in Scotland where the mash is stirred by hand and where the draff at the end of the process must be removed manually. There are eight Douglas fir washbacks with a minimum fermentation time of 48 hours and one pair of stills with vertical condensers.

In the last couple of years, production has been 160,000 litres per year (with 8-10 mashes per week). The main part, 150,000 litres, has been the heavily peated (80ppm in the barley) Ruadh Maor which is used for blended whisky. The remaining 10,000 litres are put aside for Glenturret single malt.

There is only one official bottling in the core range, the *10 year old*. A limited edition of three single casks was released in 2007 but not much has happened since these new releases. In August 2013, however, an *18 year old* ex sherry butt was bottled at 59,8% and released exclusively at the distillery visitor centre.

10 years old

The Famous Grouse

Blended Scotch

Starring **Glenturret Single Malt** *in a leading role*
Producer **Edrington**
Director **Gordon Motion, Master Blender**

The Gloag family's part of the whisky history starts with Matthew Gloag and his wife, Margaret, setting up a small licensed grocer's shop in Perth in the 1820s. Matthew's wife was running the business and in 1835 Matthew joined her. The focus was now on wines and Matthew was so successful that he was handed the honour of supplying the wines for the royal banquet in 1842 when Queen Victoria visited Perth. When he died in 1860, the business was passed on to the youngest son William, and it was also he who steered the business towards whisky and blending.

William was joined by his nephew, Matthew, and one year after William had died in 1896, one of today's most famous whisky brands was born – The Famous Grouse. Actually it was not until 1905 that the word Famous was added to the name – at the beginning it was simply known as The Grouse. The reason for choosing that name was that Matthew wanted to create a brand that appealed to the sporting gentlemen visiting The Highlands for hunting and fishing. Matthew retired in 1910, leaving the business in the capable hands of his son, Matthew William. Thereafter, Famous Grouse's history differed vastly from many of the other blended Scotch of the time. Most brands used the Prohibition in the USA to build their position on the international market. The Famous Grouse, on the other hand, continued to be more or less a local brand being sold mainly in Scotland.

Matthew Frederick Gloag, the last family member to run the business, died in 1970. Matthew Gloag & Sons was sold to Highland Distilleries (nowadays called Edrington). Highland Distilleries saw the potential of Famous Grouse and quickly started to market the brand to a large number of export markets. By 1980 Famous Grouse had become the most sold blended whisky in Scotland (and still is today) and sales volumes rose quickly in other parts of the world. Today, the brand occupies the sixth place among the world's most sold blended Scotch and sold 37 million bottles in 2012. In 2002 a spiritual home for the brand, The Famous Grouse Experience, was established at Glenturret distillery and almost 100,000 visitors frequent the distillery annually.

The range includes the biggest seller, *The Famous Grouse* without age statement and a 12 year old version called *Gold Reserve*. In 2007 the line-up was extended by the peated *Black Grouse* followed in 2008 by the blended grain whisky, *Snow Grouse*, and in 2009 by the deluxe version, *Naked Grouse*. A peatier version of the Black Grouse, *The Black Grouse Alpha*, was released in 2012 for Duty Free. Over the years the range has also included a variety of finishes – bourbon, sherry, port and Scottish oak.

Famous Grouse was also among the first to bet on the blended malt category of whiskies in 2000. The interest for this type of whisky increased rapidly and by 2006, Famous Grouse blended malt with its different expressions, sold more than 2 million bottles, especially in Asia. Just a few years later, the interest had decreased considerably and volumes were only around 350,000 bottles. The owners decided to withdraw Famous Grouse vatted malt from all markets, except Taiwan where it is still popular. The most important malt whiskies in the Famous Grouse "recipe" are Macallan, Highland Park and Glenrothes – all three distilleries owned by Edrington but Bunnahabhain also plays an important role.

Light and sweet with notes of herbs, barley, vanilla and citrus. Smooth and creamy on the palate with orange marmalade, fruit cake and vanilla fudge coming through.

147

Highland Park

Owner:
The Edrington Group

Region/district:
Highlands (Orkney)

Founded: 1798

Status: Active (vc)

Capacity: 2 500 000 litres

Address: Holm Road, Kirkwall, Orkney KW15 1SU

Tel: 01856 874619

website: www.highlandpark.co.uk

History:

1798 – David Robertson founds the distillery. The local smuggler and businessman Magnus Eunson previously operated an illicit whisky production on the site.

1816 – John Robertson, an Excise Officer who arrested Magnus Eunson, takes over production.

1826 – Highland Park obtains a license and the distillery is taken over by Robert Borwick.

1840 – Robert´s son George Borwick takes over but the distillery deteriorates.

1869 – The younger brother James Borwick inherits Highland Park and attempts to sell it as he does not consider the distillation of spirits as compatible with his priesthood.

1876 – Stuart & Mackay becomes involved and improves the business by exporting to Norway and India.

1895 – James Grant (of Glenlivet Distillery) buys Highland Park.

1898 – James Grant expands capacity from two to four stills.

1937 – Highland Distilleries buys Highland Park.

1979 – Highland Distilleries invests considerably in marketing Highland Park as single malt which increases sales markedly.

1986 – A visitor centre, considered one of Scotland's finest, is opened.

For more than 75 years now, Highland Park has been a part of Edrington (or its predecessor, Highland Distillers) and the company has one of the more interesting stories in the history of Scotch. Co-founded by William A Robertson in 1887, Highland Distillers became one of the main players in the industry and this attracted several bids to the company. Seagram´s made an attempt to acquire the company in both 1947 and 1955, but both offers were rejected by the three grand-daughters of William Robertson – Agnes, Ethel and Elspeth. In 1961 they were advised to create a combination of a holding company (Edrington Holdings) and a charitable trust (The Robertson Trust) to protect their interests, but bidders were still queuing up. In 1999, right under the noses of big companies like Remy Cointreau, Pernod Ricard and Seagram´s, Edrington bought the remaining shares in Highland Distillers and the continued, Scottish ownership of Highland Park and the other distilleries in the group was secured. Highland Park single malt is one of the most respected Scotch whiskies and the distillery is known not least for their dedication to sherry casks. The oak is left to air dry for four years in Spain and thereafter it is filled with sherry for two to three years. The owners spend £10m on wood alone every year.

The distillery is equipped with a semi-lauter mash tun, twelve Oregon pine washbacks with a fermentation time of between 50 and 80 hours and two pairs of stills. The mash tun has a 12 tonnes capacity but is only filled to 50% of its capacity. The plan for 2013 is to produce 2 million litres. The core range of Highland Park consists of *12, 15, 18, 21,* (new since 2012), *25, 30,* and *40 years old.* Vintages have for many years been the orientation regarding limited releases and bottlings for duty free. This has now changed and the vintages have all been replaced by expressions without year or (in most cases) age statements. For duty free, the range will mirror the Viking heritage which is of great importance to Orkney and Highland Park. *Svein, Einar* and *Harald* were released in spring 2013 and were followed by *Sigurd, Ragnvald* and *Thorfinn* in autumn. Highlighting the Vikings is also a new range which comprises of four expressions called Valhalla Collection. The first bottling was the *16 year old Thor* in 2012 and it was followed by *Loki 15 years* in 2013. Loki is unusual since the malted barley, for once, has been dried using peat from the mainland. Two specials for Sweden were released – a *cask strength* in spring 2013 a *10 year old Ambassador´s Choice* in the autumn. More bottles of the *50 year old* (first released in 2010) were also announced for release in January 2014.

History (continued):

1997 – Two new Highland Park are launched, an 18 year old and a 25 year old.

1999 – Highland Distillers are acquired by Edrington Group and William Grant & Sons.

2000 – Visit Scotland awards Highland Park "Five Star Visitor Attraction".

2005 – Highland Park 30 years old is released. A 16 year old for the Duty Free market and Ambassador´s Cask 1984 are released.

2006 – The second edition of Ambassador´s Cask, a 10 year old from 1996, is released. New packaging is introduced.

2007 – The Rebus 20, a 21 year old duty free exclusive, a 38 year old and a 39 year old are released.

2008 – A 40 year old and the third and fourth editions of Ambassador´s Cask are released.

2009 – Two vintages and Earl Magnus 15 year are released.

2010 – A 50 year old, Saint Magnus 12 year old, Orcadian Vintage 1970 and four duty free vintages are released.

2011 – Vintage 1978, Leif Eriksson and 18 year old Earl Haakon are released.

2012 – Thor and a 21 year old are released.

2013 – Loki and a new range for duty free, The Warriors, are released.

Loki

Einar

Thor

Highland Park 12 year old

GS – The nose is fragrant and floral, with hints of heather and some spice. Smooth and honeyed on the palate, with citric fruits, malt and distinctive tones of wood smoke in the warm, lengthy, slightly peaty finish.

DR – Honey, peat and marmalade fruit in balance on the nose, then on the palate a big mouth feel with dark chocolate, chilli, sharp barley and honey, concluding with a monster pot pouri of a finish.

12 years old

18 years old

21 years old

Inchgower

Owner:
Diageo

Region/district:
Speyside

Founded: 1871
Status: Active
Capacity: 2 900 000 litres

Address: Buckie, Banffshire AB56 5AB

Tel: 01542 836700
website: www.malts.com

History:
1871 – Alexander Wilson & Co. founds the distillery. Equipment from the disused Tochineal Distillery, also owned by Alexander Wilson, is installed.

1936 – Alexander Wilson & Co. becomes bankrupt and Buckie Town Council buys the distillery and the family's home for £1,600.

1938 – The distillery is sold on to Arthur Bell & Sons for £3,000.

1966 – Capacity doubles to four stills.

1985 – Guinness acquires Arthur Bell & Sons.

1987 – United Distillers is formed by a merger between Arthur Bell & Sons and DCL.

1997 – Inchgower 1974 (22 years) is released as a Rare Malt.

2004 – Inchgower 1976 (27 years) is released as a Rare Malt.

2010 – A single cask from 1993 is released.

Inchgower 14 year old

GS – Ripe pears and a hint of brine on the light nose. Grassy and gingery in the mouth, with some acidity. The finish is spicy, dry and relatively short.

DR – Rootsy, fresh cut grass and hay nose, light grassy and hay-like palate, and incredibly delicate barley-like nose, with a very delicate dusting of spice.

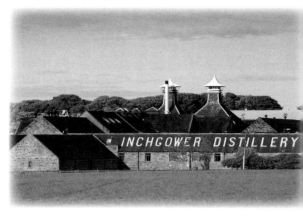

Last year a "race" developed among three distillery sites as to which one would be the ideal place for the new, huge distillery that Diageo was going to build. It was going to be between Inchgower, Glendullan and Teaninich. The latter was chosen but it is not unlikely that within a couple of years we could see another mega distillery at Inchgower. When the decision was announced, Diageo CEO at the time, Paul Walsh, declared that given a continued interest in Scotch from Asian markets, a third distillery could be built. Diageo already owns a huge site facing the North Sea next to the existing Inchgower.

Inchgower distillery itself was the target of an extensive upgrade in 2012 and was closed for 16 weeks. Back in full operation it will produce for 51 weeks which gives almost 3 million litres of pure alcohol. The distillery is equipped with a cast iron (but lined with stainless steel) semilauter mash tun, six wooden washbacks and 2 pairs of stills. Almost 100% of the production goes to blends (Johnnie Walker and Bell's in particular) and the distillation regime is tailored to produce a nutty spirit. This means cloudy worts, short fermentation (53 hours) and a quick distillation to give as little copper contact as necessary. There is also a sharp decline on the lyne arms of the stills in order to keep reflux to a minimum. Most of the production is matured elsewhere, but there are also five dunnage and four racked warehouses on site with room for 60,000 casks.

Inchgower is situated on the south side of Moray Firth and is difficult to miss as it is situated just at the A98 near the small fishing port of Buckie. If one is driving from Elgin towards Banff it is even easier to spot as the name appears on the roof. If you continue to the east, you will soon find two other coastal distilleries – Glenglassaugh and Macduff.

Besides the official *Flora & Fauna 14 years old* there have been a few limited bottlings of Inchgower single malt. In 2010, for example, a *single sherry cask* distilled in *1993* was released.

Flora & Fauna 14 years old

Jura

Owner: Whyte & Mackay (United Spirits)

Region/district: Highlands (Jura)

Founded: 1810

Status: Active (vc)

Capacity: 2 200 000 litres

Address: Craighouse, Isle of Jura PA60 7XT

Tel: +1496 820240

website: www.isleofjura.com

History:

1810 – Archibald Campbell founds a distillery named Small Isles Distillery.

1853 – Richard Campbell leases the distillery to Norman Buchanan from Glasgow.

1867 – Buchanan files for bankruptcy and J. & K. Orr takes over the distillery.

1876 – The licence is transferred to James Ferguson & Sons.

1901 – The distillery closes and Ferguson dismantles the distillery.

1960 – Charles Mackinlay & Co. embarks on reconstruction and extension of the distillery. Newly formed Scottish & Newcastle Breweries acquires Charles Mackinlay & Co.

1963 – The first distilling takes place.

1978 – Stills are doubled from two to four.

1985 – Invergordon Distilleries acquires Charles Mackinlay & Co., Isle of Jura and Glenallachie from Scottish & Newcastle Breweries.

1993 – Whyte & Mackay (Fortune Brands) buys Invergordon Distillers.

1996 – Whyte & Mackay changes name to JBB (Greater Europe).

2001 – The management of JBB (Greater Europe) buys out the company from the owners Fortune Brands and changes the name to Kyndal.

2002 – Isle of Jura Superstition is launched.

2003 – Kyndal reverts back to its old name, Whyte & Mackay. Isle of Jura 1984 is launched.

2004 – Two cask strengths (15 and 30 years old) are released in limited numbers.

2006 – The 40 year old Jura is released.

2007 – United Spirits buys Whyte & Mackay. The 18 year old Delmé-Evans and an 8 year old heavily peated expression are released.

2008 – A series of four different vintages, called Elements, is released.

2009 – The peated Prophecy and three new vintages called Paps of Jura are released.

2010 – Boutique Barrels and a 21 year old Anniversary bottling are released.

2012 – The 12 year old Jura Elixir is released.

2013 – Camas an Staca, 1977 Juar and Turas-Mara are released.

Jura 10 year old

GS – Resin, oil and pine notes on the delicate nose. Light-bodied in the mouth, with malt and drying saltiness. The finish is malty, nutty, with more salt, plus just a wisp of smoke.

DR – The nose is sweet condensed milk, the palate an intriguing mix of earthy malt and tangy spice, with a medium sweet and spice finish.

Jura single malt has experienced tremendous sales growth over the past three years, almost bringing the brand into the Top 10. Even if sales in the UK dropped during 2012, it is still the third biggest malt whisky in the country (after Glenfiddich and Glenmorangie) and global sales in 2012 were impressive with 1,5 million bottles being sold.

Jura distillery is equipped with one semi-lauter mash tun, six stainless steel washbacks and two pairs of stills. Until April 2011 they were working a 5 day week with a fermentation time of 60 hours. They have since then increased to a 7 day production and the fermentation time has changed to 54 hours. At the moment they are doing 28 mashes per week producing 2,2 million litres of alcohol in the year. Since the restart of the distillery in 1963, Jura single malt has been unpeated, but in 2002 the first expression containing peated whisky was introduced and today they produce peated spirit (55ppm) for eight weeks of the year. The distillery visitor centre was upgraded in 2011 and, despite its remote location, almost 10,000 visitors come here annually.

The core range consists of *Origin* (10 years), *Diurach's Own* (16 years), *Superstition* (with a part of peated Jura), as well as the peated *Prophecy*. Jura *Elixir*, a 12 year old matured in both American and European oak, was released in 2012 as an exclusive for Sainsbury's. Recent limited releases include the *1977 Juar* with a one year finish in port pipes and the 30 year old *Camas an Staca* which was matured in American white oak for 27 years with the final three years being spent in Amoroso sherry casks. This year's *Whisky Festival bottling* was a combination of sherried and peated Jura, matured in a vintage 1963 sherry butt to celebrate the 50th anniversary of the first distillation after the distillery was resurrected. *Turas-Mara*, a duty free exclusive with no age statement was released in May 2013 and the launch of a *40 year old* in spring 2014 was also announced.

10 years old

Kilchoman

Owner:
Kilchoman Distillery Co.

Region/district:
Islay

Founded: 2005
Status: Active (vc)
Capacity: 150 000 litres

Address: Rockside farm, Bruichladdich, Islay PA49 7UT

Tel: 01496 850011
website: www.kilchomandistillery.com

History:
2002 – Plans are formed for a new distillery at Rockside Farm on western Islay.

2005 – Production starts in June.

2006 – A fire breaks out in the kiln causing a few weeks´ production stop but malting has to cease for the rest of the year.

2007 – The distillery is expanded with two new washbacks.

2009 – The first single malt, a 3 year old, is released on 9th September followed by a second release.

2010 – Three new releases and an introduction to the US market. John Maclellan from Bunnahabhain joins the team as General Manager.

2011 – Kilchoman 100% Islay is released as well as a 4 year old and a 5 year old.

2012 – Machir Bay, the first core expression, is released together with Kilchoman Sherry Cask Release and the second edition of 100% Islay.

2013 – Loch Gorm and Vintage 2007 are released.

Kilchoman Machir Bay

GS – A nose of sweet peat and vanilla, undercut by brine, kelp and black pepper. Filled ashtrays in time. A smooth mouth-feel, with lots of nicely-balanced citrus fruit, peat smoke and Germolene on the palate. The finish is relatively long and sweet, with building spice, chili and a final nuttiness.

DR – Down by the seaside after a storm, with salt and fresh seaweed in the breeze, chimney smoke drifting. On the palate the distillery hits its stride, with sweet honey and lemon, peat smoke and coastal saltiness all in evidence. Nice balance between sugar and spice. A savoury, earthy, medium long and balanced finish.

It is full steam ahead for Kilchoman, the youngest distillery on Islay, and several investments have been made recently to keep up with increased production and demand. In June 2013 a new warehouse holding 9,000 casks was completed and more automated bottling equipment was installed to ensure that all bottling is done on site. Kilchoman lies a few miles northwest of Bruichladdich, just a stone´s throw from the Atlantic.

The distillery has its own floor maltings with a quarter of the barley requirements coming from fields surrounding the distillery. The malt is peated from 20 to 25 ppm and the remaining malt (50 ppm) is bought from Port Ellen. Other equipment includes a stainless steel semi-lauter mash tun, four stainless steel washbacks with an average fermentation time of 100 hours and one pair of stills. The distillery is currently running at near full capacity which translates to 140,000 litres of alcohol. The spirit is filled into fresh and refill bourbon casks (80%) and fresh sherry butts (20%). Kilchoman increased its sales in 2012 by 45% to 80,000 bottles and the owners hope to sell 120,000 bottles in the UK during 2013, as well as to 35 export markets worldwide.

The *Inaugural Release*, bourbon-matured for 3 years with a six months Oloroso finish, was launched in September 2009. This was followed up by a number of expressions and in 2011 it was time for the first *Kilchoman 100% Islay* where all the barley used, came from the own farm and had been malted at the distillery. The first general release in larger quantities was *Machir Bay*, and this is now the distillery´s core expression. Other re-occurring, although limited releases are 100% Islay (3rd edition in July 2013) and *Loch Gorm*. The latter, released for the first time in spring 2013, will be a range of sherry cask maturations. Recent limited releases include the 6 year old *Vintage 2007* (in September 2013) and a variety of single casks bottled at cask strength.

Machir Bay

Kininvie

Owner:
William Grant & Sons

Region/district:
Speyside

Founded: **Status:**
1990   Active

Capacity:
4 800 000 litres

Address: Dufftown, Keith,
Banffshire AB55 4DH

Tel: **website:**
01340 820373   -

History:
1990 – Kininvie distillery is inaugurated on 26th June and the first distillation takes place 18th July.

2001 – A bottling of blended whisky containing Kininvie malt is released under the name Hazelwood Centennial Reserve 20 years old.

2006 – The first expression of a Kininvie single malt is released as a 15 year old under the name Hazelwood.

2008 – In February a 17 year old Hazelwood Reserve is launched at Heathrow's Terminal 5.

Kininvie distillery only consists of one still house which is made of white, corrugated metal and neatly tucked away behind Balvenie. The owners, William Grant & Sons, built it as a working distillery which produces malt whisky for the increasingly popular Grant's blended whiskies. When the owners built the new distillery, Ailsa Bay, in Girvan in 2007 and notched up 6 million litres per year, it was assumed that Kininvie's importance would lessen. The fact that production closed in October 2010 and the distillery remained silent during 2011, led many to believe that it would be a permanent closure, but the distillery opened up again in 2012 and during 2013 it will be producing 2,5 million litres of alcohol. If not technically, then from a personnel perspective, this is more or less the capacity for the distillery. It is operated by staff from Glenfiddich and Balvenie and more production would mean either reducing production at these distilleries or recruiting more stillmen.

The distillery is equipped with a stainless steel full lauter mash tun which is placed next to Balvenie's in the Balvenie distillery. Ten Douglas fir washbacks can be found in two separate rooms next to the Balvenie washbacks. Three wash stills and six spirit stills are all heated by steam coils. Kininvie malt whisky is frequently sold to other companies for blending purposes under the name Aldundee. Kininvie malt is mainly used for the Grant's blend but is also a major part of the blended malt, Monkey Shoulder. The first time that Kininvie appeared as an official single malt bottling was in 2006, when a *Hazelwood 15 year old* was launched to celebrate the 105th birthday of Janet Sheed Roberts. She was the last surviving grand-daughter of William Grant who founded Glenfiddich distillery. In 2008 it was time for a *17 year old* to celebrate her 107th birthday. A bottling under the name Hazelwood 110 was given to employees of Wm Grant in 2011 to celebrate Mrs. Roberts' 110th birthday, but this was a blend and not a single malt. Mrs Roberts passed away in April 2012.

Hazelwood Reserve 17 year old

GS – New leather and creamy nougat on the nose. Developing molasses notes with time. Rich, leathery and spicy on the palate, with oranges and milk chocolate. Lengthy and elegant in the finish.

*Hazelwood Reserve
17 years old*

Knockando

Owner:
Diageo.

Region/district:
Speyside

Founded: **Status:** **Capacity:**
1898 Active 1 400 000 litres

Address: Knockando, Morayshire AB38 7RT

Tel: **website:**
01340 882000 www.malts.com

History:

1898 – John Thompson founds the distillery. The architect is Charles Doig.

1899 – Production starts in May.

1900 – The distillery closes in March and J. Thompson & Co. takes over administration.

1904 – W. & A. Gilbey purchases the distillery for £3,500 and production restarts in October.

1962 – W. & A. Gilbey merges with United Wine Traders (including Justerini & Brooks) and forms International Distillers & Vintners (IDV).

1968 – Floor maltings is decommissioned.

1969 – The number of stills is increased to four.

1972 – IDV is acquired by Watney Mann who, in its turn, is taken over by Grand Metropolitan.

1978 – Justerini & Brooks launches a 12 year old Knockando.

1997 – Grand Metropolitan and Guinness merge and form Diageo; simultaneously IDV and United Distillers merge to United Distillers & Vintners.

2010 – A Manager's Choice 1996 is released.

Knockando 12 year old

GS – Delicate and fragrant on the nose, with hints of malt, worn leather, and hay. Quite full in the mouth, smooth and honeyed, with gingery malt and a suggestion of white rum. Medium length in the finish, with cereal and more ginger.

DR – Beeswax, honey and gentle peat on the nose, the palate is altogether bolder, with pepper and earthy peat in evidence mixing it with very sweet crystallised barley and a sweet and rounded finish.

The two key markets for Knockando single malt are France and Spain and they are also two of the most important export countries in the world for Scotch whisky. France is actually the biggest market for Scotch in terms of volume (in terms of value it´s USA) and Spain comes in at place number four. It is therefore somewhat unsettling for the owners of Knockando that the exports to France had fallen by 25% in 2012 and in Spain the decline was 20%. The situation in Spain is actually even worse – Scotch sales have dropped by 50% in the last decade while France has increased by 15%. In spite of this Knockando´s sales figures were pretty steady during that period with approximately 650,000 bottles being sold per year. Instead, they are the blends like J&B that have taken a fall in sales.

The distillery is equipped with a small (4,4 tonnes), semi-lauter mash tun, eight Douglas fir washbacks and two pairs of stills. Knockando has always worked a five-day week with 16 mashes per week, 8 short fermentations (50 hours) and 8 long (100 hours). In 2013 this will mean a production of 1,4 million litres of alcohol. The spirit is tankered away to Auchroisk and Glenlossie and some of the casks are returned to the distillery for maturation in two dunnage and two racked warehouses.

The blended Scotch J&B consists of 42 different whiskies and at the very heart of the whisky you will find Knockando single malt. J&B was established as a brand in the 1930s and was tailored to suit the taste of American consumers taste for a lighter whisky. It was introduced to the Spanish market in 1962 and today it is the market leader in the country. Knockando single malt is bottled according to vintage but the label also carries an age statement. The core range consists of four expressions, all of them being a mix of bourbon and sherry maturation; *12 year old, 15 year old Richly Matured, 18 year old Slow Matured* and the *21 year old Master Reserve*. In 2011 a *25 year old* matured in first fill European oak was released as part of the Special Releases range.

12 years old

J&B Rare

Blended Scotch

Starring Knockando Single Malt *in a leading role*
Producer Diageo
Director Caroline Martin, Master Blender

Long before any of the other well-known whisky companies were established, the corner stone for Justerini & Brooks was laid and that can be attributed to one of the most unlikely characters in the whisky history. Giacomo Justerini travelled from Bologna in Italy in 1749 to London to pursue the opera singer Margherita Bellini with whom he had fallen in love. The love was not reciprocated, but luckily for Justerini he had brought his uncle's liqueur recipe with him and decided to stay in London to set up a wine & spirits business. He met with George Johnson and they founded the firm Johnson & Justerini. Justerini returned to Italy in 1760 and in 1779 the firm was reported to have sold usquebaugh (Scotch whisky) in London. George Johnson was run down by a runaway horse in 1785 and died, leaving the company to his son, Augustus.

In 1830 the company was sold to Alfred Brooks who decided to keep Justerini in the company name but would add his own. The main business at the time was sales of wine but blended Scotch became an increasingly bigger part and in the late 1800s Club was launched. Like many other whisky producers J&B used the Prohibition years to build a network on the US market and when Prohibition was repealed in 1933 it was time to benefit from the contacts that they had established.

The one who came to play the biggest part was Charlie Guttman, a former prohibition enforcement officer. He had set up The Buckingham Corporation in 1933, together with Jake Culhane in order to import Cutty Sark. In 1937 the two companions went their separate ways and Guttman established the Paddington Corporation and acquired the licence for J&B instead. By now the brand we know today, J&B Rare, had

become established, but long time had passed before the sales figures started to impress. In 1955, 300,000 bottles were exported to USA. In 1962 there were 12 million bottles and only four years later it had doubled to 24 million.

Meanwhile, Justerini & Brooks had merged with Twiss & Browning & Hallowes and later with W. & A. Gilbey to form International Distillers & Vintners. In 1972 this constellation was absorbed by Grand Metropolitan which 20 years later merged with Guinness to form Diageo. J&B was now part of the biggest spirits business in the world and had advanced to become the second biggest Scotch in the world, selling 80 million bottles per year.

Part of its success was the introduction to the Spanish market in 1962 where it became the category leader. Just more than 10 years ago J&B had started a downward spiral, partially due to the deteriorating economy in Spain. Sales in 2012 were down to 55 million bottles and the brand is now holding fourth place, having been passed by both Ballantine's and Chivas Regal. There are around 40 different malt whiskies in J&B and apart from Knockando, Glen Spey and Strathmill play a significant role. The core expression is *J&B Rare* with no age statement and the only other bottling in the range is the *J&B 15 year old Reserve*. The latter is mostly

sold in Asia, South America and a few European countries. Other varieties in recent years have all been withdrawn – amongst others *J&B Ultima* which was a limited version released in 1994 and made up of whiskies from 128 distilleries (116 malts and 12 grains).

Citrus and barley dominate the nose aided by vanilla. The palate is sweet with oranges, heather, pear drops and a whiff of peat. The finish is quite peppery and ends in sweet marzipan notes.

Knockdhu

Owner:
Inver House Distillers
(Thai Beverages plc)

Region/district:
Highland

Founded: **Status:** **Capacity:**
1893 Active 1 900 000 litres

Address: Knock, By Huntly,
Aberdeenshire AB54 7LJ

Tel: **website:**
01466 771223 www.ancnoc.com

History:
1893 – Distillers Company Limited (DCL) starts construction of the distillery.

1894 – Production starts in October.

1930 – Scottish Malt Distillers (SMD) takes over production.

1983 – The distillery closes in March.

1988 – Inver House buys the distillery from United Distillers.

1989 – Production restarts on 6th February.

1990 – First official bottling of Knockdhu.

1993 – First official bottling of anCnoc.

2001 – Pacific Spirits purchases Inver House Distillers at a price of $85 million.

2003 – Reintroduction of anCnoc 12 years.

2004 – A 14 year old from 1990 is launched.

2005 – A 30 year old from 1975 and a 14 year old from 1991 are launched.

2006 – International Beverage Holdings acquires Pacific Spirits UK.

2007 – anCnoc 1993 is released.

2008 – anCnoc 16 year old is released.

2011 – A Vintage 1996 is released.

2012 – A 35 year old is launched.

2013 – A 22 year old and Vintage 1999 are released.

anCnoc 12 year old

GS – A pretty, sweet, floral nose, with barley notes. Medium bodied, with a whiff of delicate smoke, spices and boiled sweets on the palate. Drier in the mouth than the nose suggests. The finish is quite short and drying.

DR – Complex and layered nose, with delicate peat, green fruits and pear. On the palate, full savoury peatiness then tingling yellow fruity follow through and fairydust finale.

Apart from good whisky, distilleries produce different kinds of by-products that need to be taken care of. One of them is spent lees, the residue left in the spirit still after distillation. Because it contains copper, it has to be treated so as not to contaminate the environment. An ingenious way of doing so in a biological fashion has recently been implemented at Knockdhu distillery. They have created a wetland area where the cupreous water is led through gravity to six, lined cells (circa 25 x 15 metres). Each cell has been planted with 17 different species of plants and, in particular, iris which has an ability to bind and neutralize copper. Once the spent lees have reached the sixth cell, the water is copper free. It also means that this process has taken 8-10 tankers per week off the road which otherwise would have transported the waste to a treatment plant.

Knockdhu distillery is equipped with a 5 tonnes stainless steel lauter mash tun, eight washbacks made of Oregon pine (two new ones since last year) and one pair of stills. For 2013 they plan to do 1,9 million litres of spirit of which 400,000 litres will be heavily peated (45ppm). The spirit is filled mainly into bourbon casks with an additional 15% of sherry butts. The casks are stored in one racked and three dunnage warehouses. The biggest markets for anCnoc (as the single malt is called) are UK, USA, Sweden and Germany and 180,000 bottles were sold in 2012.

The core range of a *12* and *16 year old* was complemented in early 2013 by a *22 year old*, predominantly matured in ex-bourbon casks but with a small influence from Oloroso sherry as well. Every year a new vintage is released and for 2012 it was a *1998* which was replaced by a *1999* in autumn 2013. Another limited release in 2012 was a *35 year old* – the oldest expression yet to be released by the owner, and more bottles were released in 2013. In 2012, InverHouse also commissioned the illustrator, *Peter Arkle*, to produce a series of limited edition packaging for a new series of anCnoc without age statement. Three different expressions were made in 2012 and another two in 2013.

22 years old

Whisky Around the World

BRAZIL

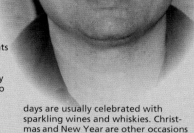

Living in Brazil, Alexandre Campos spent seven years in the UK where his passion for Scotch whisky took off. Back in Brazil, he was invited to be a member in the group that started the website Single Malt Brasil (singlemalt.com.br) with the purpose of educating Brazilian consumers about whisky. Attached to the site, Single Malt Brasil also runs the biggest specialised whisky retailer in the country, lojadewhisky.com.br.

...hich spirit is the most popular in ...azil and where does whisky fit into ...e picture?

...chaça is the most popular spirit ...th 82% of the spirits' market in ...lume and 55% in value. Whisky ...presents only 3.5% of the Brazilian ...rits' market in volume, but 15.5% ...value.

...hat types of whisky are the most ...pular in Brazil?

...nded scotch is by far the most ...portant category with 70% of the ...isky market in volume, followed ...locally produced whiskies with ...% of the market. The other types ...whisky are marginal in terms of ...umes.

...en would you say people in Brazil ...rted to get seriously interested in ...isky? What triggered it and how ...s that interest developed?

...cording to historical documents, ...isky has been imported to Brazil ...ce 1850. The British presence in ...uth America since the last century ...s helped to forge a drinking cul-...e around whisky in the continent ...d Brazil is not an exception. The ...oximity to USA and the influence ...American culture is another factor ...reasing the awareness of bourbon.

...ich brands of Scotch are the most ...pular in Brazil?

...ivas Regal and Johnnie Walker by ...The reality is that Brazilian market ...till dominated by cheap blended ...otch whiskies such as Johnnie ...alker Red Label, Ballantine's Finest, ...mous Grouse Finest, Grant's Family ...serve and Teacher's.

...w is whisky sold in Brazil?

...hty percent of the sales of spirits ...cluding whisky) in Brazil is done ...ough on-trade channels, such as ...rs, discos and restaurants. There is ...ly one store specialised in whisky ...d spirits in Brazil, the online busi-...ss Single Malt Brasil (www.loja-...whisky.com.br). The other retailers ...liquor stores sell any kind of drinks ...h as wines, beers and cachaças.

How is whisky marketed in Brazil?

Predominantly through advertisments on TV and internet. Social media is another important tool to promote whisky in Brazil. There are no whisky shows in Brazil and no perspective to host one soon. The availability of single malts is restricted and Brazilians would not go to a whisky show to taste what they find in their local supermarkets. Most cities have whisky clubs, however they are promoted and built around the brands Johnnie Walker and Chivas Regal.

Is whisky considered a luxury drink compared to other spirits?

Absolutely and whilst there is nothing wrong to position whisky as luxury product, there is a misconception as to what can be regarded a luxury in terms of whisky in Brazil. A whisky considered a premium product in the USA or Europe may be sold for 3 or 4 times more in Brazil under the idea of a "super-premium" whisky. I don´t see any acceptable explanations that justify a price of $300 for 10 year old Scotch single malt.

Is there a clearly defined group of customers buying whisky?

Since whisky is an expensive drink in Brazil, customers usally are between 35 and 60 years old coming from up-per-middle and upper classes. These people also see whisky as a status symbol. Younger consumers usually drink cheap Scotch blends used with mixers in cocktails.

Is whisky something you drink at home or in a bar or restaurant?

Most of the whisky is consumed in bars and restaurants, but this scenario is changing and will change even more in the future. A strict law was passed last year to prevent drinking and driving. There is now a zero tole-rance and this encourages people to instead enjoy whisky in their homes.

Are there special occasions when whisky is preferred?

Whisky is the spirit of choice on many special occasions. Weddings and birth-days are usually celebrated with sparkling wines and whiskies. Christmas and New Year are other occasions when the consumption increases.

How is whisky enjoyed in Brazil?

Living in a tropical country, Brazilians usually drink whisky with mixers and ice. Aficionados familiar with single malts prefer to drink their whiskies neat or with a small splash of water. In the northeast of Brazil people mix whisky with coconut water.

Would you say that the customer in Brazil is educated about whisky?

The basic knowledge about this spirit is very poor. Brazilians choose their whisky by brands and not by aspects and elements behind flavour profile or maturation. The level of under-standing about whisky in Brazil is far from what is found in Europe and USA. Therefore, they are easy preys for marketing abuses and overpri-ced products. The result is that an ordinary blended Scotch is priced 5-7 times higher than in Scotland.

How many producers of whisky do you have in Brazil and how would you describe the future for domestic whisky in your country?

Cachaça is the Brazilian spirit and I don´t see any future for whisky pro-duction in Brazil. Locally produced whisky has an awful reputation and is in general channeled towards the lower classes.

What are your thoughts on the future for Scotch whisky in Brazil?

I think there is a bright future, espe-cially for single malts and bourbon. Forecasts show that the market for these products will grow about 10% a year in the next five years. However, this growth depends on the perfor-mance of the Brazilian economy.

Lagavulin

Owner:
Diageo

Region/district:
Islay

Founded: 1816
Status: Active (vc)
Capacity: 2 450 000 litres

Address: Port Ellen, Islay, Argyll PA42 7DZ

Tel: 01496 302749 (vc)
website: www.malts.com

History:
1816 – John Johnston founds the distillery.

1825 – John Johnston takes over the adjacent distillery Ardmore founded in 1817 by Archibald Campbell and closed in 1821.

1835 – Production at Ardmore ceases.

1837 – Both distilleries are merged and operated under the name Lagavulin by Donald Johnston.

1852 – The brother of the wine and spirits dealer Alexander Graham, John Crawford Graham, purchases the distillery.

1867 – The distillery is acquired by James Logan Mackie & Co. and refurbishment starts.

1878 – Peter Mackie is employed.

1889 – James Logan Mackie passes away and nephew Peter Mackie inherits the distillery.

1890 – J. L. Mackie & Co. changes name to Mackie & Co. Peter Mackie launches White Horse onto the export market with Lagavulin included in the blend. White Horse blended is not available on the domestic market until 1901.

1908 – Peter Mackie uses the old distillery buildings to build a new distillery, Malt Mill, on the site.

The whisky that started the whole trend of drinking peated whisky in the 1990s is back on track! Until 2000, Lagavulin single malt was the most sold whisky from Islay. For inventory reasons it then lost its leading position when in 2001 it was surpassed by Laphroaig and the year thereafter by Bowmore. Admittedly, it is still only third behind the other two but sales have been increasing steadily in recent years and the brand now sells around 1,4 million bottles per year. In order to avoid the shortage of mature whisky a decade ago, the owners have been producing 24/7 for a number of years now. By adding 80 kilos to the mash charge and shortening the silent season, the production will this year increase to 2,45 million litres of alcohol.

If you stand outside the distillery and look to the east side of Lagavulin Bay, you will see the ruins of Dunyvaig Castle. Originating from the 13th century, this was the naval base of The Lord of the Isles. In the 12th century, Somerled, a man of both Celtic and Norse blood, founded a dynasty which soon would become one of the most influential in medieval Scotland. In 1336 Good John of Islay became the first to assume the title Lord of the Isles and this era ended with John MacDonald II in 1493. The castle then shifted ownership between the MacDonald's and the Campbell's until 1677, when most of the castle was demolished.

The distillery is equipped with a stainless steel full lauter mash tun, ten washbacks made of larch with a 55 hour fermentation and two pairs of stills. The spirit stills are filled to 95% of its capacity during distillation which is very unconventional. The result is that the spirit vapour's diminished contact with the copper produces a more robust spirit. Bourbon hogsheads are used almost without exception for maturation and all of the new production is stored on the mainland. There are only around 16,000 casks on Islay, split between warehouses at Lagavulin, Port Ellen and Caol Ila. The core range of Lagavulin is unusually narrow and only consists of *12 year old cask strength*, *16 year old* and the *Distiller's Edition*, a Pedro Ximenez sherry finish. In 2010 a *distillery exclusive bottling*, available only at the distillery, was added to the range which basically was a slightly older cask strength version of the Distiller's Edition. In autumn 2012, a *21 year old* from first fill sherry casks was launched. This was only the second time the owners had released a 21 year old Lagavulin. The Islay Festival special release for 2013 was an *18 year old* matured in European oak and bottled at cask strength. As in recent years, a new edition of the *12 year old* was released in autumn 2013 as a Special Release and it was accompanied by a *37 year old* distilled in 1976, the oldest official bottling so far.

History (continued):

1924 – Peter Mackie passes away and Mackie & Co. changes name to White Horse Distillers.

1927 – White Horse Distillers becomes part of Distillers Company Limited (DCL).

1930 – The distillery is administered under Scottish Malt Distillers (SMD).

1952 – An explosive fire breaks out and causes considerable damage.

1960 – Malt Mills distillery closes and today it houses Lagavulin's visitor centre.

1974 – Floor maltings are decommissioned and malt is bought from Port Ellen instead.

1988 – Lagavulin 16 years becomes one of six Classic Malts.

1998 – A Pedro Ximenez sherry finish is launched as a Distillers Edition.

2002 – Two cask strengths (12 years and 25 years) are launched.

2006 – A 30 year old is released.

2007 – A 21 year old from 1985 and the sixth edition of the 12 year old are released.

2008 – A new 12 year old is released.

2009 – A new 12 year old appears as a Special Release.

2010 – A new edition of the 12 year old, a single cask exclusive for the distillery and a Manager´s Choice single cask are released.

2011 – The 10th edition of the 12 year old cask strength is released.

2012 – The 11th edition of the 12 year old cask strength and a 21 year old are released.

2013 – A 37 year old and the 12th edition of the 12 year old cask strength are released.

Lagavulin 12 year old

GS – Soft and buttery on the nose, with dominant, fruity, peat smoke, grilled fish and a hint of vanilla sweetness. More fresh fruit notes develop with the addition of water. Medium-bodied, quite oily in texture, heavily smoked, sweet malt and nuts. The finish is very long and ashy, with lingering sweet peat.

DR – A monster truck nose with rich smoke, lychee and unripe pear, with prickly smoke and banana skin notes on the palate, and a superb long dark chocolate and smoky finish.

37 years old   *Distiller´s Edition*

Dunyvaig Castle

16 years old   *12 years old*   *Distillery Exclusive no age*

Laphroaig

Owner: **Region/district:**
Beam Inc.   Islay

Founded: **Status:**   **Capacity:**
1810   Active (vc)   3 300 000 litres

Address: Port Ellen, Islay, Argyll PA42 7DU

Tel: **website:**
01496 302418   www.laphroaig.com

History:

1810 – Brothers Alexander and Donald Johnston found Laphroaig.

1815 – Official year of starting.

1836 – Donald buys out Alexander and takes over operations.

1837 – James and Andrew Gairdner found Ardenistiel a stone's throw from Laphroaig.

1847 – Donald Johnston is killed in an accident in the distillery when he falls into a kettle of boiling hot burnt ale. The Manager of neighbouring Lagavulin, Walter Graham, takes over.

1857 – Operation is back in the hands of the Johnston family when Donald's son Dugald takes over.

circa 1860 – Ardenistiel Distillery merges with Laphroaig.

1877 – Dugald, being without heirs, passes away and his sister Isabella, married to their cousin Alexander takes over.

1907 – Alexander Johnston dies and the distillery is inherited by his two sisters Catherine Johnston and Mrs. William Hunter (Isabella Johnston).

1908 – Ian Hunter arrives in Islay to assist his mother and aunt with the distillery.

1924 – The two stills are increased to four.

1927 – Catherine Johnston dies and Ian Hunter takes over.

Laphroaig single malt is the biggest seller from Islay and judging by the sales figures for 2012 the brand will keep the lead with good margin to the runner up Bowmore. After three years (2008-2010) where sales only increased by a mere 2%, sales have picked up significantly. The years 2010-2012 saw an increase by 20% to 2,7 million bottles being sold in 2012 and the strong sales figures continued well into the first half of 2013.

Laphroaig is one of very few distilleries with its own maltings. Four malting floors hold 7 tonnes each and together they account for 15% of the requirements. The balance comes from Port Ellen maltings or is imported from the mainland. Own malt and malt from different suppliers is always blended before mashing. The own malt has a phenol specification of 40-60ppm while bought malt lies between 35 and 45ppm.

The distillery is equipped with a stainless steel full lauter mash tun and six washbacks that are also made of stainless steel. Three years ago the manager, John Campbell, introduced smaller mashes (5,5 tonnes instead of 8,5) in order to increase flexibility and capacity. Two mashes will now fill one washback which yields five wash still charges. The distillery uses an unusual combination of three wash stills and four spirit stills and the spirit is matured in three dunnage and five racked warehouses. During 2013, they will be working full time producing 3,2 million litres of alcohol.

The core range consists of *10 year old, 10 year old cask strength* (batch five released 2013), *Quarter Cask, Triple Wood, 18 year old* and *25 year old*. The 10 year old and the Quarter Cask have now been removed from the Duty Free market and instead a new range has been implemented; *Laphroaig PX*, without age statement but made up of whiskies between 5 and 10 years old with maturation both in hogsheads and quarter casks and with a finish in Pedro Ximenez sherry casks, *Laphroaig QA Cask* with a double maturation in ex-bourbon barrels and new, un-charred American oak and *Laphroaig An Cuan Mor*, also a double maturation with no age statement but bottled at cask strength. The last two were introduced in 2013. Since 2008 the special bottling, in conjunction with Feis Isle, has been a variety of Cairdeas. The festival bottling for 2013 was no exception; *Cairdeas Port Wood Edition* has been matured in ex-bourbon barrels with a finish in port pipes and is bottled at 51,3%. Another new limited release for 2013 was a *25 year old cask strength*.

1928 – Isabella Johnston dies and Ian Hunter becomes sole owner.

1950 – Ian Hunter forms D. Johnston & Company

1954 – Ian Hunter passes away and management of the distillery is taken over by Elisabeth "Bessie" Williamson, who was previously Ian Hunters PA and secretary. She becomes Director of the Board and Managing Director.

1967 – Seager Evans & Company buys the distillery through Long John Distillery, having already acquired part of Laphroaig in 1962. The number of stills is increased from four to five.

1972 – Bessie Williamson retires. Another two stills are installed bringing the total to seven.

1975 – Whitbread & Co. buys Seager Evans (now renamed Long John International) from Schenley International.

1989 – The spirits division of Whitbread is sold to Allied Distillers.

1991 – Allied Distillers launches Caledonian Malts. Laphroaig is one of the four malts included.

1994 – HRH Prince Charles gives his Royal Warrant to Laphroaig. Friends of Laphroaig is founded.

1995 – A 10 year old cask strength is launched.

2001 – 4,000 bottles of a 40 year old, the oldest-ever Laphroaig, are released.

2004 – Quarter Cask, a mix of different ages with a finish in quarter casks (i. e. 125 litres) is launched.

2005 – Fortune Brands becomes new owner.

2007 – A vintage 1980 (27 years old) and a 25 year old are released.

2008 – Cairdeas, Cairdeas 30 year old and Triple Wood are released.

2009 – An 18 year old is released.

2010 – A 20 year old for French Duty Free and Cairdeas Master Edition are launched.

2011 – Laphroaig PX and Cairdeas - The Ileach Edition are released. Triple Wood is moved to the core range and replaced in duty free by Laphroaig PX.

2012 – Brodir and Cairdeas Origin are launched.

2013 – QA Cask, An Cuan Mor, 25 year old cask strength and Cairdeas Port Wood Edition are released.

Laphroaig 10 year old

GS – Old-fashioned sticking plaster, peat smoke and seaweed leap off the nose, followed by something a little sweeter and fruitier. Massive on the palate, with fish oil, salt and plankton, though the finish is quite light and increasingly drying.

DR – Salt, peat, seaweed and tar in a glorious and absorbing nose, then structured and rock like barley with waves of tarry peat washing over them, then a long phenolic and peaty finish.

10 year old cask strength

Quarter Cask

Triple Wood

PX Cask

QA Cask

10 year old

Cairdeas Port Wood

An Cuan Mor

Linkwood

Owner:
Diageo

Region/district:
Speyside

Founded: **Status:** **Capacity:**
1821 Active 5 600 000 litres

Address: Elgin, Morayshire IV30 3RD

Tel: **website:**
01343 862000 www.malts.com

History:

1821 – Peter Brown founds the distillery.

1868 – Peter Brown passes away and his son William inherits the distillery.

1872 – William demolishes the distillery and builds a new one.

1897 – Linkwood Glenlivet Distillery Company Ltd takes over operations.

1902 – Innes Cameron, a whisky trader from Elgin, joins the Board and eventually becomes the major shareholder and Director.

1932 – Innes Cameron dies and Scottish Malt Distillers takes over in 1933.

1962 – Major refurbishment takes place.

1971 – The two stills are increased by four. Technically, the four new stills belong to a new distillery referred to as Linkwood B.

1985 – Linkwood A (the two original stills) closes.

1990 – Linkwood A is in production again for a few months each year.

2002 – A 26 year old from 1975 is launched as a Rare Malt.

2005 – A 30 year old from 1974 is launched as a Rare Malt.

2008 – Three different wood finishes (all 26 year old) are released.

2009 – A Manager's Choice 1996 is released.

2013 – Expansion of the distillery including two more stills.

Linkwood 12 year old

GS – Floral, grassy and fragrant on the nutty nose, while the slightly oily palate becomes increasingly sweet, ending up at marzipan and almonds. The relatively lengthy finish is quite dry and citric.

DR – Sweet and squidgy with over-ripe melon and soft pear on the nose, and a delightful palate of marzipan, vanilla, green apples and a touch of spice. The finish is balanced, pleasant and very enticing.

Linkwood distillery, situated on the outskirts of Elgin, was closed from February to July 2011 to fit in a new mash tun as well as installing a new control system but that was just the first part of a major upgrade. In April 2013 the distiller closed again for 12 weeks and this time the capacity was expanded. The old distillery buildings facing Linkwood Road were demolished and an extension of the current sti house was constructed to house two more stills (actually two old ones from the old stillhouse that were refurbishe and six new wooden washbacks. The modern part of the distillery was built in 1971 and it worked together with th older part where worm tubs were used for cooling until 1995.

The complete set up is now one full lauter mash tun, 11 wooden washbacks (80,000 litres but only filled with 57,000) and three pairs of stills. New cooling towers were also added working with a closed system which renders the dam behind the distillery as redundant where cooling is concerned. The new capacity is a staggering 5,6 million litres of alcohol and the greater part is used for Diageo's different blended whiskies where it plays an important role in major brands such as Johnnie Walker and White Horse but Linkwood single malt is also much sought after.

To be able to achieve the desired green/grassy character of the newmake, they try to get the wort as clear as possible, the fermentations are long (75 hours), the large stills are only filled just above the man door to enhance the copper contact and the spirit stills are allowed to rest for a minimum of one hour between runs to allow for the regeneration of the copper.

The core expression is a *12 year old Flora & Fauna*. In 2008 a limited edition of three unusual *26 year old* bottlings were released. For the last 14 years, all of them finished in three different types of casks – port, rum and sweet red wine. A 15 year old Linkwood from independent bottler Gordon & MacPhail is also widely available.

12 years old

Loch Lomond

Owner:
Loch Lomond
Distillery Co.

Region/district:
Western Highlands

Founded: **Status:** **Capacity:**
1965 Active 4 000 000 litres

Address: Lomond Estate, Alexandria G83 0TL

Tel: **website:**
1389 752781 www.lochlomonddistillery.com

History:

1965 – The distillery is built by Littlemill Distillery Company Ltd owned by Duncan Thomas and American Barton Brands.

1966 – Production commences.

1971 – Duncan Thomas is bought out and Barton Brands reforms as Barton Distilling (Scotland) Ltd.

1984 – The distillery closes.

1985 – Glen Catrine Bonded Warehouse Ltd buys Loch Lomond Distillery.

1987 – The distillery resumes production.

1993 – Grain spirits are also distilled.

1997 – A fire destroys 300,000 litres of maturing whisky.

1999 – Two more stills are installed.

2005 – Inchmoan and Craiglodge are launched for the first time. Both are 4 years old from 2001. Inchmurrin 12 years is launched.

2006 – Inchmurrin 4 years, Croftengea 1996 (9 years), Glen Douglas 2001 (4 years) and Inchfad 2002 (5 years) are launched.

2010 – A peated Loch Lomond with no age statement is released as well as a Vintage 1966.

2012 – New range for Inchmurrin released – 12, 15, 18 and 21 years.

Loch Lomond Blue Label

GS – The nose yields American cream soda, cereal, lemonade and ginger. More cereal on the palate, with digestive biscuits and a yeasty note. Bubble gum, oats and yeast in the relatively lengthy finish.

Inchmurrin 12 year old

GS – Pear drops and white chocolate on the nose. Slightly floral, with a little ginger. Quite viscous on the palate, with caramel and almonds. Drying significantly in the medium-length finish.

Loch Lomond Distillers have done well during the last year. Accounts for 2011/2012 show pre-tax profits increasing by 34% to £9m while turnover rose by 14% to £36m. Even so, many rumours have done the rounds during the spring of 2013 to the effect that Loch Lomond would be up for sale. One company that has been linked to the discussions is the investment group Exponent which bought Quorn Foods in 2011. The current owners, headed by the whisky tycoon Sandy Bulloch and his family, started the company in the mid 1980s and together with their other company, Glen Catrine Bonded Warehouse, they have managed to build a large and versatile spirits company.

Loch Lomond distillery is equipped with one full lauter mash tun complemented by ten 25,000 litres and eight 50,000 litres washbacks, all of which are made of stainless steel. There are two traditional copper pot stills and four copper stills where the swan necks have been exchanged with rectifying columns. Two of the latter are used to produce Inchmurrin and the spirit still has 13 bubble cap trays which increases reflux and enhances the control of the distillation which gives Inchmurrin a distinctly different taste compared to Loch Lomond single malt. Furthermore, there is one Coffey still used for continuous distillation where, for example, the Rhosdhu single malt is produced. As if this was not enough, an additional distillery with continuous stills producing grain whisky is housed in the same building. For the grain side of production there are twelve 100,000 litres and eight 200,000 litres washbacks. The total capacity is 4 million litres of malt spirit and 18 million litres of grain. Loch Lomond produces a broad range of whiskies with two main brands. *Loch Lomond* with *Blue Label* (no age statement), *Black Label* (18 year old and peated), *Green Label* (no age and peated) and *Loch Lomond Single Blend*. The second brand is *Inchmurrin* where a new range was introduced in late 2012; *12, 15, 18* and *21 years old*. There have also been other releases in their Distillery Select range but the range has now been discontinued.

Loch Lomond Blue Label

Longmorn

Owner:
Chivas Brothers
(Pernod Ricard)

Region/district:
Speyside

Founded: 1894 **Status:** Active **Capacity:** 4 500 000 litres

Address: Longmorn, Morayshire IV30 8SJ

Tel: 01343 554139 **website:** -

History:
1893 – John Duff & Company, which founded Glenlossie already in 1876, starts construction. John Duff, George Thomson and Charles Shirres are involved in the company. The total cost amounts to £20,000.

1894 – First production in December.

1897 – John Duff buys out the other partners.

1898 – John Duff builds another distillery next to Longmorn which is called Benriach (at times aka Longmorn no. 2). Duff declares bankruptcy and the shares are sold by the bank to James R. Grant.

1970 – The distillery company is merged with The Glenlivet & Glen Grant Distilleries and Hill Thomson & Co. Ltd. Own floor maltings ceases.

1972 – The number of stills is increased from four to six. Spirit stills are converted to steam firing.

1974 – Another two stills are added.

1978 – Seagrams takes over through The Chivas & Glenlivet Group.

1994 – Wash stills are converted to steam firing.

2001 – Pernod Ricard buys Seagram Spirits & Wine together with Diageo and Pernod Ricard takes over the Chivas group.

2004 – A 17 year old cask strength is released.

2007 – A 16 year old is released replacing the 15 year old.

2012 – Production capacity is expanded.

Longmorn 16 year old

GS – The nose offers cream, spice, toffee apples and honey. Medium bodied in the mouth, with fudge, butter and lots of spice. The finish is quite long, with oak and late-lingering dry spices.

DR – Cut flowers and mixed fruit on the nose, rounded and full fruit and honey with some wood and spice adding complexity, long and rich finish.

The history of Longmorn involves one of the more adventurous characters in the Scottish whisky history – John Duff. He already built Glenlossie distillery in 1876, immigrated in 1888 with his entire family to South Africa where he unsuccessfully tried to build a distillery in the Transvaal (now called Gauteng) before moving on to America. His attempts to start a distillery there also failed and he found himself back in Scotland in 1892 before taking up a job as distillery manager for Bon Accord in Aberdeen. Just one year later he built Longmorn distillery and five years later BenRiach. In 2012, Longmorn distillery was completely revamped and expanded. The old tun rooms were demolished and a new tun room, as well as a mash house, was built on the northern side of the still houses. The old mash house was converted into a tank room. A new 8,5 tonnes Briggs full lauter mash tun replaced the old, traditional tun and seven of the eight, old stainless steel washbacks were moved to the new tun room and an additional three were installed. There are currently four pairs of stills, all fitted with sub-coolers and the wash stills now have external heat exchangers. The production capacity has also increased by 30% to 4,5 million litres.

Longmorn has always had a mutual relationship with BenRiach distillery next door and the last one was actually named Longmorn 2 when it was built. Even today, Longmorn supplies BenRiach with water from boreholes and also takes care of the effluent. Longmorn single malt is often referred to as a hidden gem or the whisky blender's favourite, and to the owners, Chivas Brothers, the whisky has become an integral part of several of their blends, not least Chivas Regal 18 year old and Royal Salute. There is only one widely available official bottling – the 16 year old, but a cask strength version can also be found at Chivas' visitor centres. The latest version is a 1997 bottled in 2011.

16 years old

Whisky Around the World

AUSTRALIA

Chris Middleton works in the whisky industry as business analyst, trade & consumer writer, and B2B educator with knowledge programs and workshops to liquor companies. Previously, he was global brand director for one of the world's leading whiskeys' and recently established a malt whisky distillery in Australia.

Which spirit is the most popular in Australia and where does whisky fit into the picture?

1880 Australia became a whisky ation. Every year since whisky has ominated the spirits & liqueurs tegory. Today, it's still more than lf of the spirits market.

What types of whisky are the most popular in Australia?

uring the past 130 years different hisky styles and countries-of-origin ave lead the whisky pack. Blended otch dominated until the late 30s. Then Australian blended hisky held sway under high tariffs. otch rebounded as protectionism as dismantled. Now bourbon is e undisputed leader with 62% of nsumption volume, including RTD quivalence adjusted to full strength. otch has shrunk to less than 34%, sh 4% and all others less than 1%. ourbon's relentless growth only arted in 1964. Australians drink 5 times more bourbon per capita an Americans. Australia is now a ourbon nation.

What do you think caused this henomenon?

ourbon has a contemporary and bellious image, epitomising the odern values of independence and dventure. It's sweeter and more avoursome than light blended hiskies. Along with its mixer partner la, it's proven a more desirable nsory fit amongst recent genera- ons. Even the RTD phenomenon hich began in Australia was led by m Beam & Cola cans in 1984.

Which brands of Scotch are the most popular in Australia?

he top three blended scotch brands ontrol over half of the category eing Johnnie Walker, Grant's and hivas Regal. Three malt brands hold early two thirds of malt sales: Glen- ddich, The Glenlivet & Glen Moray. nd three American whiskey brands njoy three quarters of bourbon les: Jim Beam, Jack Daniels' and Vild Turkey.

Is there a wide variety of brands and is it easy to find the brand you want?

Australia is well inventoried with world whiskies, over 400 brands and thousands of line extensions. International whisky labels are ubiquitous. Premium brands are increasing their reach with growing premiumisation, followed by numerous super-premium expressions. In recent years over thirty specialist whisky bars, as well as specialist whisky retailers have begun to populate the country.

Is there a clearly defined group of customers buying whisky?

No, it's a very broad church of drinkers too. Lawyers to plumbers, from LDAs (legal drinking age Millennials) to DNDs (damn near dead Silvertails), as well as an unprecedented interest and participation by females, especially younger cohorts. The historical demographic for premium whisky, notably Scotch, once AB socio-economic quintile of males 45 plus is a fossil.

Is whisky something you drink at home or in a bar or restaurant?

Twenty percent of the whisky is sold in bars and restaurants (there are 68,000 licensed premises) while 80% is consumed at home.

How is whisky enjoyed in Australia?

Most whisky is consumed mixed and cola is by far the most popular.

Would you say that the customer in Australia is educated about whisky?

There is an increasing demand to better understand and appreciate whisky. This is evidenced in the numerous whisky shows and the growing high-end sales.

How many producers of whisky do you have in Australia and how would you describe the future for domestic whisky in your country?

Since Australia's first boutique malt whiskies were released in 1998, over a dozen local brands have been introduced. While the total malt category is only less than 2% of total whisky consumption, malts have been enjoying a meteoric rise in recent years. Amongst this 2% segment dominated by Scotch labels, Australian malts have carved out over 5% share. This year 300,000 litres will probably be distilled by the dozen active distilleries, double the production of two years ago. Some of these domestic malts are gaining a solid reputation for good quality. Public acceptance has been a slow process and distribution barriers still a business obstacle. Managing sales systems where two retail groups control 60% of off-premise sales results in the bulk of domestic whisky sold direct. The higher cost of goods means higher price points to imported malt whiskies. Australian malts are very much hands-on with small production runs, marked by younger whiskies often using small cask, warm climate maturation to accelerate extraction. Variability in production, especially wood programs offers choice (cask by cask), whereas global brands seek flavour consistency so their franchises find familiarity (bottle to bottle, year after year).

What are your thoughts on the future for Scotch whisky in Australia?

As blended Scotch loses image and flavour relevance, it's their single malts that are proving to be the winners, albeit off a small base. An interesting shift has happened in the malt whisky category. It's no longer of Scottish provenance. It's become international, defined as a transnational style with Japanese, Australian, Indian, Taiwanese, Welsh, Irish, American, Swedish and another three dozen countries producing malt whisky. Australia will foreseeably remain a whisky nation. Just different styles and segments will evolve and change with time.

Macallan

Owner:
Edrington Group

Region/district:
Speyside

Founded: 1824
Status: Active (vc)
Capacity: 9 800 000 litres

Address: Easter Elchies, Craigellachie, Morayshire AB38 9RX

Tel: 01340 871471
website: www.themacallan.com

History:

1824 – The distillery is licensed to Alexander Reid under the name Elchies Distillery.

1847 – Alexander Reid passes away and James Shearer Priest and James Davidson take over.

1868 – James Stuart takes over the licence. He founds Glen Spey distillery a decade later.

1886 – James Stuart buys the distillery.

1892 – Stuart sells the distillery to Roderick Kemp from Elgin. Kemp expands the distillery and names it Macallan-Glenlivet.

1909 – Roderick Kemp passes away and the Roderick Kemp Trust is established to secure the family's future ownership.

1965 – The number of stills is increased from six to twelve.

1966 – The trust is reformed as a private limited company.

1968 – The company is introduced on the London Stock Exchange.

1974 – The number of stills is increased to 18.

1975 – Another three stills are added, now making the total 21.

1979 – Allan Schiach, descendant of Roderick Kemp, becomes the new chairman of the board after Peter Schiach.

1984 – The first official 18 year old single malt is launched.

1986 – Japanese Suntory buys 25% of Macallan-Glenlivet plc stocks.

Macallan single malt continues to sell well, defending its third place on the global sales list after Glenfiddich and Glenlivet. From 3,5 million bottles sold in 2003 the number have continued to increase and by 2012 they had reached almost 9 million bottles. The distillery has a popular and excellent visitor centre and the distillery tour is one of the best in the industry. Small models next to the real equipment clearly explain the process and the visitors can even smell the newmake spirit as it trickles through glass pipes at the bottom of the still house. The tour includes a visit to warehouse 7, where the Story of Oak explains the importance of the casks necessary for creating the characte and flavour of the whisky.

Since 2008 the production takes place in two separate plants. The number one plant holds one full lauter mash tun, 16 stainless steel washbacks, five wash stills and ten spirit stills. The number two plant is comprised of one sem lauter mash tun (6 tonnes), six new wooden washbacks, two wash stills and four spirit stills. All the stills at Macalla are surprisingly small with sharply descending lyne arms preventing too much reflux. Warehouse capacity has increased over the last few years and a total of 186,000 casks are now being handled by 25 warehousemen. In 201 the distillery will be working 7 days a week for 49 weeks producing 9,8 million litres of alcohol.

In 2012, Macallan took the market by surprise when they announced a new series of expressions without age statement. All the whiskies in the 1824 series have been matured in ex-sherry casks but the origin of the oak and the age of the whisky will vary. With names referring to the colour of the whisky, *Gold* (a mix of refill and first fill European and American oak) was the first to be released in 2012. This was followed in spring 2013 by *Amber* (simila mix as Gold but slightly older), *Sienna* (a 50/50 split bet-ween first fill American oak and European oak) and finally *Ruby* (matured in 100% first fill European oak). Macallan´s two previous ranges remain available; *Sherry oak (12, 18, 25* and *30 years old)*, exclusively matured in ex-sherry casks and *Fine Oak (10, 12, 15, 17, 18, 21, 25* and *30 years old)* matured in a combination of ex-sherry and ex-bourbon. The duty free range holds five expressions; *Select Oak, Whisky Maker´s Edition, Estate Reserve, Oscuro* and *The Macallan Limited Release MMXII*. There is also *The Fine & Rare* range – vintages from 1926 to 1990. Recent limited editions include *The Macallan Coronation* bottling release in 2013.

1996 – Highland Distilleries buys the remaining stocks. 1874 Replica is launched.

1999 – Edrington and William Grant & Sons buys Highland Distilleries (where Edrington, Suntory and Remy-Cointreau already are shareholders) for £601 million. They form the 1887 Company which owns Highland Distilleries with 70% held by Edrington and 30% by William Grant & Sons (excepting the 25% share held by Suntory).

2000 – The first single cask from Macallan (1981) is named Exceptional 1.

2001 – A new visitor centre is opened.

2002 – Elegancia replaces 12 year old in the duty-free range. 1841 Replica, Exceptional II and Exceptional III are also launched.

2003 – 1876 Replica and Exceptional IV, single cask from 1990 are released.

2004 – Exceptional V, single cask from 1989 is released as well as Exceptional VI, single cask from 1990. The Fine Oak series is launched.

2005 – New expressions are Macallan Woodland Estate, Winter Edition and the 50 year old.

2006 – Fine Oak 17 years old and Vintage 1975 are launched.

2007 – 1851 Inspiration and Whisky Maker´s Selection are released as a part of the Travel Retail range. 12 year old Gran Reserva is launched in Taiwan and Japan.

2008 – Estate Oak and 55 year old Lalique are released.

2009 – Capacity increased by another six stills. The Macallan 1824 Collection, a range of four duty free expressions, is launched. A 57 year old Lalique bottling is released.

2010 – Oscuro is released for Duty Free.

2011 – Macallan MMXI is released for duty free.

2012 – Macallan Gold, the first in the new 1824 series, is launched.

2013 – Amber, Sienna and Ruby are released.

Macallan 12 year old Sherry Oak

GS – The nose is luscious, with buttery sherry and Christmas cake characteristics. Rich and firm on the palate, with sherry, elegant oak and Jaffa oranges. The finish is long and malty, with slightly smoky spice.

DR – Unmistakenly the sherried version of The Macallan, with a classic red berry and orange mix. The palate is plummy, with intense sherry and some toffee and cocoa notes. The finish is medium long sweet and fruity.

Macallan Gold

GS – The nose offers apricots and peaches, fudge and a hint of leather. Medium-bodied, with malt, walnuts and spices on the palate. Quite oaky in the medium-length finish.

Amber   Sienna   Ruby

Fine Oak 17 yo   1949 vintage   18 year old

The Macallan Gold   Oscuro   Whisky Maker´s Edition   Select Oak

Macduff

Owner:
John Dewar & Sons Ltd
(Bacardi)

Region/district:
Highlands

Founded: 1962
Status: Active
Capacity: 3 340 000 litres

Address: Banff, Aberdeenshire AB45 3JT

Tel: 01261 812612
website: -

History:
1962 – The distillery is founded by Marty Dyke, George Crawford and Brodie Hepburn (who is also involved in Tullibardine and Deanston). Macduff Distillers Ltd is the name of the company.

1963 – Production starts.

1965 – The number of stills is increased from two to three.

1967 – Stills now total four.

1972 – William Lawson Distillers, part of General Beverage Corporation which is owned by Martini & Rossi, buys the distillery from Glendeveron Distilleries.

1990 – A fifth still is installed.

1993 – Bacardi buys Martini Rossi (including William Lawson) and eventually transfered Macduff to the subsidiary John Dewar & Sons.

2013 – The Royal Burgh Collection (16, 20 and 30 years old) is launched for duty free.

Glen Deveron 10 year old

GS – Sherry, malt and a slightly earthy note on the nose. Smooth and sweet in the mouth, with vanilla, spice and a hint of smoke. Sweet right to the finish.

DR – The nose is a mix of crisp barley, orange, hay and a trace of smoke, and on the palate an oily and fruity combination beautifully coats the mouth before giving way to a pepper, savoury and astringent finish.

Dewar´s own five malt distilleries but only two of them are promoted as single malts of note – namely Aberfeldy and Macduff (or Glen Deveron as the whisky is called when bottled by the owners). Ten years ago, Glen Deveron was outstanding in terms of sales figures. It sold more than 400,000 bottles while Aberfeldy came in at 50,000. Today the roles have changed with Aberfeldy selling 350,000 while Glen Deveron has declined to 250,000. In the same period William Lawson´s blend, one of the fastest growing brands in the world, has increased its sales by more than 100% and this is where Glen Deveron has its most important feature as a signature malt. Nevertheless, in April 2013, the owners surprisingly launched three older Glen Deveron's under the name Royal Burgh Collection for the Duty Free market – 16, 20 and 30 years old and all bottled at 40%.

Macduff has a beautiful location being situated at the banks of the River Deveron and on the eastern outskirts of Banff on the Moray Firth coast. The distillery is equipped with a 6-roller Bühler Miag mill from 2007, a stainless steel semi-lauter mash tun, nine washbacks made of stainless steel and the rather unusual set-up of five stills (two wash stills and three spirit stills). The fifth still was installed in 1990. In order to fit the stills into the still room, the lyne arms on four of the stills are bent in a peculiar way and on one of the wash stills it is U-shaped. Because of limited space, they have chosen vertical condensers on the wash stills but horizontal condensers on the spirit stills. For maturation, a mix of sherry and bourbon casks is used. In 2013 the distillery will be doing 26 mashes per week for 46 weeks producing 3,2 million litres of alcohol.

The most common official bottling of Glen Deveron is the 10 year old but there is also a 15 year old to be found. Older versions of 8 and 12 year olds are also available. New bottlings released in 2013 for Duty Free (as mentioned above) are 16, 20 and 30 years old.

10 years old

William Lawson's

Blended Scotch

Starring Glen Deveron Single Malt *in a leading role*
Producer John Dewar & Sons
Director Stephanie Macleod, Master Blender

The vast majority of the top Scotch blends are named after the founders of the company but that, however, is not the case with Lawson's. In 1889, the brand name, as well as the company name (W. Lawson & Co.) were registered by a Dublin firm of blenders called E. & J. Burke which was founded in 1849.

Edward and John Burke were nephews of Arthur Guinness, the son of the founder of Guinness brewery and the two brothers managed to build a successful spirits company. Later they became agents for Guinness in the USA and eventually founded a brewery in New York. Edward died in 1887 and his brother, John, five years later.

So, who then was William Lawson? In contrast to the Burke brothers, there is very little known about him. He was born in Scotland in 1853, got married in 1881 and then relocated to Dublin. There he was employed by E. & J. Burke and by 1888 he had become the exports manager of the company. He must have done a great job since the company's main brand of Scotch whisky was renamed Lawson's Liqueur Whisky in 1889. The company also pioneered and patented an electrically welded cork that stopped even a single drop of whisky dripping from the bottle. By 1901, William Lawson had become a director of the company but, something obviously happened as he was dismissed in 1903. Thereafter, nothing further is known about William Lawson's fate but for the legacy of the whisky that was named after him.

During the first three decades of the 20th century fairly large quantities of William Lawson's whisky were exported to the USA but the brand never really took off. In 1963, the Italian drinks giant, Martini & Rossi, which a few years earlier had established themselves on the

Scottish whisky market through the company, Clan Munro, acquired the brand Lawson's from E. & J. Burke. Sales started to increase again but this time in Europe. The demand called for a distillery of its own and so the Macduff distillery outside Banff was purchased in 1972. Twenty years later Bacardi became the new owners when they acquired Martini & Rossi and, finally, in 1998 Bacardi bought John Dewar & Sons and gathered all their Scotch whisky interests in that company.

William Lawson's Scotch is not what you could call a global brand but it is very big in certain markets like France for example but also in Spain and Portugal. In recent years the brand has also become established in Venezuela and Ecuador, whereas in Russia it is currently the number one blended Scotch in both value and volume. It is one of the fastest growing brands in the world and while it was in 15th place on the global sales list of blended Scotch ten years ago, it has now risen to 8th place thanks to a more than 100% increase. In 2012 the brand sold 31 million bottles and is now, for the first time, close on the heels of the Bacardi group's biggest blended Scotch, Dewar's.

The range of Lawson's Scotch is not big. There used to be a *12 year old* and an *18 year old* which complemented the core expression, the unaged *William Lawson's*, but they have since, both been removed from the market. On the other hand, a new expression was launched in

spring 2013 – *William Lawson's 13 year old*.

Apart from Glen Deveron, other malt whiskies owned by Dewar's, for example, Aultmore, Craigellachie and Royal Brackla, all play their part in the William Lawson's blend.

Fresh and clean on the nose with citrus and floral notes. Surprisingly heavy on the palate with cereals, apple pie, vanilla and toffee. The finish is sweet and light.

Mannochmore

Owner:
Diageo

Region/district:
Speyside

Founded: 1971
Status: Active
Capacity: 4 500 000 litres

Address: Elgin, Morayshire IV30 8SS

Tel: 01343 862000
website: www.malts.com

History:
1971 – Scottish Malt Distillers (SMD) founds the distillery on the site of their sister distillery Glenlossie. It is managed by John Haig & Co. Ltd.

1985 – The distillery is mothballed.

1989 – In production again.

1992 – A Flora & Fauna series 12 years old becomes the first official bottling.

1997 – United Distillers launches Loch Dhu – The Black Whisky which is a 10 year old Mannochmore. A 22 year old Rare Malt from 1974 and a sherry-matured Manager´s Dram 18 years are also launched.

2009 – An 18 year old is released.

2010 – A Manager´s Choice 1998 is released.

2013 – The number of stills is increased to four.

Mannochmore 12 year old

GS – Perfumed and fresh on the light, citric nose, with a sweet, floral, fragrant palate, featuring vanilla, ginger and even a hint of mint. Medium length in the finish, with a note of lingering almonds.

DR – Buttery, with lemon, sweet dough and floral notes on the nose, oily, malty and floral on the palate and with a relatively short finish.

Some distilleries can be seen miles away when you travel in Speyside, while others are almost impossible to detect. Mannochmore definitely belongs to the latter group. From a distance you only see the huge dark grains plant and when you´re approaching it, you see its older sister distillery, Glenlossie, close to the road. To catch a glimpse of Mannochmore still house you have to enter the site (which you are not allowed to because this is strictly a working distillery and not open to visitors). Mannochmore distillery was unproductive from March to August 2013 and the reason was an extensive refurbishment and extension which now means an increase in its capacity by 30% to 4,5 million litres. A new Briggs full lauter mash tun replaced the old one made of cast iron, while eight new external washbacks were added, as well as one pair of stills. The total set up now is the 11 ton mash tun, a total of 16 washbacks (of which eight are wooden and eight are stainless steel) and four pairs of stills. When production was resumed in August, the distillery went to a 7-day week with 20-21 mashes per week.

The workforce at Glenlossie and Mannochmore used to alternate between the two distilleries with each distillery being in production for half a year at a time, but since 2007, both distilleries are producing all year round.

Next to Mannochmore lies a dark grains plant which processes pot ale (the left over from the wash stills after distillation) into a heavy syrup which is then used for cattle feed. A biomass burner was commissioned in early 2013 to convert the draff (being the residue from the mashing of the malt) of almost 20 nearby distilleries into steam which will power both distilleries and the dark grains plant.

The core range of Mannochmore is just a *12 year old Flora & Fauna*. In 2009, a limited *18 year old* matured in re-charred sherry casks, bourbon casks and new American Oak casks was released and in 2010 it was time for a sherry matured *single cask* from *1998*.

Flora & Fauna 12 years o

Miltonduff

Owner:
Chivas Brothers
(Pernod Ricard)

Region/district:
Speyside

Founded: 1824

Status: Active

Capacity: 5 800 000 litres

Address: Miltonduff, Elgin,
Morayshire IV30 8TQ

Tel: 01343 547433

website: -

History:

1824 – Andrew Peary and Robert Bain obtain a licence for Miltonduff Distillery. It has previously operated as an illicit farm distillery called Milton Distillery but changes name when the Duff family buys the site it is operating on.

1866 – William Stuart buys the distillery.

1895 – Thomas Yool & Co. becomes new part-owner.

1936 – Thomas Yool & Co. sells the distillery to Hiram Walker Gooderham & Worts. The latter transfers administration to the newly acquired subsidiary George Ballantine & Son.

1964 – A pair of Lomond stills is installed to produce the rare Mosstowie.

1974-75 – Major reconstruction of the distillery.

1981 – The Lomond stills are decommissioned and replaced by two ordinary pot stills, the number of stills now totalling six.

1986 – Allied Lyons buys 51% of Hiram Walker.

1987 – Allied Lyons acquires the rest of Hiram Walker.

1991 – Allied Distillers follow United Distillers' example of Classic Malts and introduce Caledonian Malts in which Tormore, Glendronach and Laphroaig are included in addition to Miltonduff. Tormore is later replaced by Scapa.

2005 – Chivas Brothers (Pernod Ricard) becomes the new owner through the acquisition of Allied Domecq.

Miltonduff 10 year old (Gordon & MacPhail)

GS – Fresh and fruity on the nose, with toasted malt and a mildly herbal note. Soft fruits and mild oak on the palate, while the finish is subtly drying, with a touch of ginger.

DR – Clean, honeyed and deceptively gentle on the nose, chunky malt and clean vanilla on the plate, pleasant and warming finish.

Until the mid 1990s, two of the biggest whisky companies in the world were Canadian – Hiram Walker and Seagram´s. Both were taken over from the respective founding families in the mid 1920s by two successful entrepreneurs who both seized the opportunity to use the Prohibition in the USA in order to position them well for the future. Sam Bronfman was the man who took charge of Seagram´s, while Hiram Walker was acquired by Harry Hatch. Both of these men realised the importance of producing Scotch whisky which could be used for blends. Harry Hatch was first out of the blocks when he, in 1936, acquired Miltonduff and Glenburgie distilleries including the famous brand, Ballantine´s. Bronfman on the other hand, acquired Chivas Bros and Strathisla distillery in 1949/50. The two businesses were now among the most powerful in the industry, but in 1994 Hiram Walker was sold to a British company and in 2005 it was absorbed by the French, Pernod Ricard. Seagram´s went the same route in 2001 when Pernod Ricard acquired the Scottish part (Chivas Bros) leaving the rest for Diageo.

Miltonduff single malt has been associated with Ballantine´s for a long period of time and still remains so today. For the last six years, Ballantine´s has been the global number two Scotch whisky after Johnnie Walker and sold 75 million bottles in 2012.

The distillery is equipped with an 8 tonne full lauter mash tun, 16 stainless steel washbacks and three pairs of stills. Several racked warehouses on the site hold a total of 54,000 casks. Miltonduff is one of a handful of distilleries which used Lomond stills for a period of time, 1964 to 1981. The idea behind it was to produce several types of malt whisky with the same, flexible still.

The most recent official bottling of Miltonduff is a *1997, 15 years old,*which was released in Chivas Brothers´ cask strength series and is available only at Chivas´ visitor centres.

18 years old cask strength

Mortlach

Owner:
Diageo

Region/district:
Speyside

Founded: **Status:**
1823 Active

Capacity:
3 800 000 litres

Address: Dufftown, Keith,
Banffshire AB55 4AQ

Tel:
01340 822100

website:
www.malts.com

History:
1823 – The distillery is founded by James Findlater.

1824 – Donald Macintosh and Alexander Gordon become part-owners.

1831 – The distillery is sold to John Robertson for £270.

1832 – A. & T. Gregory buys Mortlach.

1837 – James and John Grant of Aberlour become part-owners. No production takes place.

1842 – The distillery is now owned by John Alexander Gordon and the Grant brothers.

1851 – Mortlach is producing again after having been used as a church and a brewery for some years.

1853 – George Cowie joins and becomes part-owner.

1867 – John Alexander Gordon dies and Cowie becomes sole owner.

1895 – George Cowie Jr. joins the company.

1897 – The number of stills is increased from three to six.

1923 – Alexander Cowie sells the distillery to John Walker & Sons.

1925 – John Walker becomes part of Distillers Company Limited (DCL).

1930 – The administration is transferred to Scottish Malt Distillers (SMD).

1964 – Major refurbishment.

1968 – Floor maltings ceases.

1996 – Mortlach 1972 (23 years) is released as a Rare Malt. The distillery is renovated at a cost of £1.5 million.

1998 – Mortlach 1978 (20 years) is released as a Rare Malt.

2004 – Mortlach 1971, a 32 year old cask strength is released.

2009 – Mortlach 1997, a single cask in the new Manager´s Choice range is released.

Cardhu distillery may be the spiritual home of Johnnie Walker but the malt from Mortlach plays an equally important role in obtaining the character of one of the world´s best selling de luxe blends – Johnnie Walker Black Label. The brand, and its new cousin Double Black, are selling so well in especially Asia and South America, that only a tiny fraction of the production at Mortlach is bottled as a single malt. When available, the bottles are quickly swept up by fans who love the powerful, meaty, sherried taste.

The distillery is equipped with a 12 tonnes full lauter mash tun and six washbacks made of larch which each holds 90,000 litres, but are charged with 55,000 litres of wort. In the still house there are six stills in various sizes with slightly descending lyne arms. The distillation process at Mortlach, sometimes called partial triple distillation, is unique in Scotland. There are three wash stills and three spirit stills where the No. 3 pair acts as a traditional double distillation. The low wines from wash stills No. 1 and 2 are directed to the remaining two spirit stills according to a certain distribution. In one of the spirit stills, called Wee Witchie, the charge is redistilled twice and with all the various distillations taken into account, it could be said that Mortlach is distilled 2,8 times. All spirit is condensed using five worm tubs made of larch and one made of stainless steel, which adds to the powerful character.

Mortlach has an exciting future ahead. Starting 2014, another still house will be built and the equipment will be expanded with a new mash tun, another 6-8 washbacks and six more stills. The set-up of the new stills will be replicas of the existing ones so as not to compromise the character of the newmake. The new site will probably be in production by summer 2015 which means that the capacity will double to almost 8 million litres.

The only official core bottling of Mortlach is the *16 year old Flora & Fauna*. In 2013, a special vatting of different casks and bottled at 48% was made for the Spirit of Speyside Festival.

Mortlach 16 year old

GS – A rich, confident and spicy, sherried nose, with sweet treacle and pepper. Complex, elegant, yet masterful. Sherry, Christmas cake, gunpowder, black pepper on the palate. A long, relatively dry, and slightly smoky, gingery finish.

DR – Christmas cake and rich sherry nose, and a rich full plum-fruit and soft summer fruit palate. The finish is rich, full and long, with the wood making its presence felt.

Flora & Fauna 16 years

Oban

Owner:
Diageo

Region/district:
Western Highlands

Founded: **Status:**   **Capacity:**
1794   Active (vc)   780 000 litres

Address: Stafford Street, Oban, Argyll PA34 5NH

Tel: **website:**
01631 572004 (vc)   www.malts.com

History:

1793 – John and Hugh Stevenson found the distillery on premises previously used for brewing.

1794 – Start of operations.

1820 – Hugh Stevenson dies.

1821 – Hugh Stevenson's son Thomas takes over.

1829 – Bad investments force Thomas Stevenson into bankruptcy. His eldest son John takes over operations at the distillery.

1830 – John buys the distillery from his father's creditors for £1,500.

1866 – Peter Cumstie buys the distillery.

1883 – Cumstie sells Oban to James Walter Higgins who refurbishes and modernizes it.

1898 – The Oban & Aultmore-Glenlivet Co. takes over with Alexander Edwards at the helm.

1923 – The Oban Distillery Co. owned by Buchanan-Dewar takes over.

1925 – Buchanan-Dewar becomes part of Distillers Company Limited (DCL).

1930 – Administration is transferred to Scottish Malt Distillers (SMD).

1931 – Production ceases.

1937 – In production again.

1968 – Floor maltings ceases and the distillery closes for reconstruction.

1972 – Reopening of the distillery.

1979 – Oban 12 years is on sale.

1988 – United Distillers launches Classic Malts. Oban 14 year is selected to represent Western Highlands.

1989 – A visitor centre is built.

1998 – A Distillers' Edition is launched.

2002– The oldest Oban (32 years) so far is launched in a limited edition of 6,000 bottles.

2004 – A 20 year old cask strength from 1984 (1,260 bottles) is released.

2009 – Oban 2000, a single cask in the new Manager's Choice range is released.

2010 – A no age distillery exclusive is released.

2013 – A limited 21 year old is released.

Oban 14 year old

GS – Lightly smoky on the honeyed, floral nose. Toffee, cereal and a hint of peat. The palate offers initial cooked fruits, becoming spicier. Complex, bittersweet, oak and more gentle smoke. The finish is quite lengthy, with spicy oak, toffee and new leather.

DR – A mixed nose of heather, honey, pineapple and nuts, a perfectly balanced mix of grapey fruit, pineapple chunks, roast nuts and smoky undertow, and a rounded and fruity finish, drying and more-ish.

Oban is one of the six, original Classic Malts introduced in 1988 to accentuate the different whisky producing regions of Scotland. Oban was chosen to represent West Highlands and the others were Cragganmore (Speyside), Dalwhinnie (Highlands), Lagavulin (Islay), Glenkinchie (Lowlands) and Talisker (The Islands, in this case Skye). Oban is the second smallest distillery in the Diageo group (after Royal Lochnagar) and the vast majority, if not all, of the production is destined for single malt releases. The sales figures are steadily increasing and 950,000 bottles were sold in 2012. USA is by far the biggest market and has been so for years. The distillery is equipped with a 6,5 tonnes traditional stainless steel mash tun with rakes, four washbacks made of European larch and one pair of stills. Attached to the stills is a rectangular, stainless steel, double worm tub to condense the spirit vapours. One washback will fill the wash still twice. However, the character of Oban single malt is dependent on long fermentations (110 hours), hence they can only manage six mashes per week (five longs and one short). As a result of a shortened, silent season during the last couple of years, the owners have managed to keep production going for 50 weeks per year, which means 780,000 litres of alcohol. The distillery boasts one of the best visitor centres in the business with 35,000 visitors every year.

The core range consists of two expressions – a *14 year old* and a *Distiller's Edition* with a montilla fino sherry finish. In 2010 a distillery exclusive bottling, available only at the distillery, was released. It is finished in fino sherry casks and has no age statement. A rare, single cask bottling (297 bottles) of an *18 year old* Oban was released in spring 2013 to celebrate the 40th anniversary of the Royal National Lifeboat Institution station at Oban. In autumn 2013 a *21 year old* bottled at 58,5% was launched as part of the annual Special Releases. Older, limited editions include a *32 year old*, a *20 year old* and, exclusive to the American market, an *18 year old* released in 2008. Every year 300 barrels are set aside for future releases of this expression.

21 years old

Pulteney

Owner:
Inver House Distillers
(Thai Beverages plc)

Region/district:
Northern Highlands

Founded: 1826

Status: Active (vc)

Capacity: 1 800 000 litres

Address: Huddart St, Wick, Caithness KW1 5BA

Tel: 01955 602371

website: www.oldpulteney.com

History:

1826 – James Henderson founds the distillery.

1920 – The distillery is bought by James Watson.

1923 – Buchanan-Dewar takes over.

1930 – Production ceases.

1951 – In production again after being acquired by the solicitor Robert Cumming.

1955 – Cumming sells to James & George Stodart, a subsidiary to Hiram Walker & Sons.

1958 – The distillery is rebuilt.

1959 – The floor maltings close.

1961 – Allied Breweries buys James & George Stodart Ltd.

1981 – Allied Breweries changes name to Allied Lyons.

1995 – Allied Domecq sells Pulteney to Inver House Distillers.

1997 – Old Pulteney 12 years is launched.

2001 – Pacific Spirits (Great Oriole Group) buys Inver House at a price of $85 million.

2004 – A 17 year old is launched.

2005 – A 21 year old is launched.

2006 – International Beverage Holdings acquires Pacific Spirits UK.

2009 – A 30 year old is released.

2010 – WK499 Isabella Fortuna is released.

2012 – A 40 year old and WK217 Spectrum are released.

2013 – Old Pulteney Navigator is released and The Lighthouse range (3 expressions) is launched for duty free.

Old Pulteney 12 year old

GS – The nose presents pleasingly fresh malt and floral notes, with a touch of pine. The palate is comparatively sweet, with malt, spices, fresh fruit and a suggestion of salt. The finish is medium in length, drying and decidedly nutty.

DR – Honey and lemon lozenges on the nose, sweet citrus fruits, chunky malt and some traces of sea brine on the palate, an amusing sweet and sour two step at the finish.

The interest for Old Pulteney single malt has increased considerably over the last decade, especially in the UK, USA and Sweden. Today it is the second best selling single malt in the Inver House group after Speyburn with almost 500,000 bottles sold in 2012. Inver House in turn, has since 12 years ago been owned by ThaiBev, Thailand's largest brewer (Chang beer) but with interest in many other areas as well. The founder of ThaiBev is Charoen Sirivadhana-bhakdi whose life is a true rags-to-riches story. The son of a Bangkok street vendor and one of eleven children, he started working at the age of nine. Today he is the third richest man in Thailand and worth $11,7 billion.

Pulteney distillery is equipped with a brand new, stainless steel semi-lauter 5 tonnes mash tun, six washbacks, five made of Corten steel and one of stainless steel and one pair of stills. The wash still is equipped with a huge ball creating added reflux. The spirit still is equipped with a purifier (which hasn't been used for years) and both stills use stainless steel worm tubs for condensing the spirit. The plan for 2013 is to produce 1,4 million litres of alcohol.

The core range of Old Pulteney is made up of *12, 17, 21, 30* and *40 years old*. To complement the bottlings with age statements, a new series, non chill-filtered and with no age was introduced in September 2013 – *Old Pulteney Navigator*. More expressions in the range will follow in 2014. In 2010, the owners started to release a series of whiskies to celebrate the fact that the distillery is situated in Wick, at one time being the biggest herring port in Europe. All three were named after herring drifters working from Wick – *WK499 Isabella Fortuna, WK209 Good Hope* and *WK217 Spectrum*. To replace these, another three were launched in August 2013 for Duty Free, all named after lighthouses in the vicinity of the distillery. *Noss Head* is matured in ex-bourbon American oak, *Duncansby Head* is a mix of ex-bourbon and ex-sherry, while *Pentland Skerries* is matured in Spanish ex-sherry casks.

12 years old

Royal Brackla

Owner:
John Dewar & Sons
(Bacardi)

Region/district:
Highlands

Founded: 1812   **Status:** Active   **Capacity:** 4 000 000 litres

Address: Cawdor, Nairn, Nairnshire IV12 5QY

Tel: 01667 402002   **website:** -

History:
1812 – The distillery is founded by Captain William Fraser.

1835 – Brackla becomes the first of three distilleries allowed to use 'Royal' in the name.

1852 – Robert Fraser & Co. takes over the distillery.

1898 – The distillery is rebuilt and Royal Brackla Distillery Company Limited is founded.

1919 – John Mitchell and James Leict from Aberdeen purchase Royal Brackla.

1926 – John Bisset & Company Ltd takes over.

1943 – Scottish Malt Distillers (SMD) buys John Bisset & Company Ltd and thereby acquires Royal Brackla.

1966 – The maltings closes.

1970 – Two stills are increased to four.

1985 – The distillery is mothballed.

1991 – Production resumes.

1993 – A 10 year old Royal Brackla is launched in United Distillers' Flora & Fauna series.

1997 – UDV spends more than £2 million on improvements and refurbishing.

1998 – Bacardi–Martini buys Dewar´s from Diageo.

2004 – A new 10 year old is launched.

Royal Brackla 10 year old

GS – An attractive malty, fruity, floral nose, with peaches and apricots. Quite full-bodied, the creamy palate exhibits sweet malt, spice and fresh fruit. The finish is medium to long, with vanilla and gently-spiced oak.

DR – Pineapple and citrus fruits on the nose, candy barley, melon and pleasant sweet spice on the palate, medium sweet finish with a trace of green melon.

Photo: © Ernst J. Scheiner, The Gateway To Distilleries

In 1998, Royal Brackla distillery became a small pawn in the game when one of the biggest deals ever in the drinks industry was completed. The year before, Grand Metropolitan and Guinness merged to form the giant Diageo. Anti-trust authorities reacted vehemently and demanded that Diageo sells off all its interests in John Dewar & Sons so that they wouldn't have too much of a stranglehold on the Scotch whisky market. More than 20 companies vied for the bid, which, of course, pushed up the price. Bacardi-Martini was ultimately the victorious bidder with a staggering amount of £1,15bn. This enabled them to acquire the Dewar´s brand, including Bombay gin and four distilleries, among them being Royal Brackla. Apart from the deal eleven years earlier when Guinness had bought DCL for £2,35bn, this was the biggest deal so far in the business. Royal Brackla was founded in 1812 and celebrated its 200th anniversary last year with an exhibition at the nearby Nairn museum and a big party was thrown in November. An anniversary bottle was planned but will probably only be released this year. The equipment consists of a big (12,5 tonnes) full lauter mash tun from 1997. There are six wooden washbacks (but with stainless steel tops) and another two made of stainless steel which are insulated because they are placed outside. Finally, there are two pairs of stills. At the moment the distillery is running at full capacity, which means 17 mashes per week and 4 million litres of alcohol per year. This makes it the biggest distillery in the Dewar´s group.

In 1835, Royal Brackla was the first of only three Scottish distilleries to receive a royal warrant. Almost the entire output is used by the owners for their blends, Dewar´s in particular, and even if they want to release more single malt, they don´t have any stock older than 14 years. When Dewar´s bought the distillery from Diageo in 1998, no maturing whisky was included in the deal.

Today's core range consists of a *10 year old* and a limited edition of a *25 year old*. There have been indications from the owners though, that the range is about to be expanded.

10 years old

Royal Lochnagar

Owner:
Diageo

Region/district:
Eastern Highlands

Founded:
1845

Status:
Active (vc)

Capacity:
500 000 litres

Address: Crathie, Ballater,
Aberdeenshire AB35 5TB

Tel:
01339 742700

website:
www.malts.com

History:
1823 – James Robertson founds a distillery in Glen Feardan on the north bank of River Dee.

1826 – The distillery is burnt down by competitors but Robertson decides to establish a new distillery near the mountain Lochnagar.

1841 – This distillery is also burnt down.

1845 – A new distillery is built by John Begg, this time on the south bank of River Dee. It is named New Lochnagar.

1848 – Lochnagar obtains a Royal Warrant.

1882 – John Begg passes away and his son Henry Farquharson Begg inherits the distillery.

1896 – Henry Farquharson Begg dies.

1906 – The children of Henry Begg rebuild the distillery.

1916 – The distillery is sold to John Dewar & Sons.

1925 – John Dewar & Sons becomes part of Distillers Company Limited (DCL).

1963 – A major reconstruction takes place.

2004 – A 30 year old cask strength from 1974 is launched in the Rare Malts series (6,000 bottles).

2008 – A Distiller's Edition with a Moscatel finish is released.

2010 – A Manager's Choice 1994 is released.

Royal Lochnagar 12 year old

GS – Light toffee on the nose, along with some green notes of freshly-sawn timber. The palate offers a pleasing and quite complex blend of caramel, dry sherry and spice, followed by a hint of liquorice before the slightly scented finish develops.

DR – Rich fruit and honey on the nose, sophisticated mix of crystal barley, chunky fruit and delicious peat base and a warming and rounded finish.

Royal Lochnagar single malt is not very well known and often difficult to find. Not because of poor quality, on the contrary – the flavour makes it perfect for the role of signature malt in Diageo's key blend in Korea, Windsor, and most of the production goes into that. Windsor is the leading whisky in Korea but is now struggling to hold its own in a very difficult market. Because of a severe and prolonged economic slump, exports of Scotch to the country have gone down by one third since 2009. In 2002, Korea was the fourth biggest export market for Scotch and now it has fallen to place number ten. Consumers prefer cheaper alcohol like beer and vodka and sales of Windsor fell by 13% in 2012. It remains to be seen if the rejuvenated interest for Windsor in China will make up for the losses.

Royal Lochnagar lies in beautiful surroundings with Royal Deeside and the imposing Lochnagar mountain situated to the south and Balmoral, the Queen's summer residence, just a stone's throw to the north. The pretty visitor centre attracts 10,000 visitors a year, a figure that could easily be quadrupled if it had been more accessible to one of the main roads.

The distillery is equipped with a 5,4 ton open, traditional stainless steel mash tun using rakes. Fermentation takes place in two wooden washbacks, with short fermentations of 60 hours and long ones of 106 hours. The long fermentation helps create the light character that the owners are looking for. The two stills are quite small with a charge in the wash still of 6,100 litres and 4,000 litres in the spirit still. The cooling of the spirit vapours takes place in cast iron worm tubs. The whole production is filled on site (mostly into European oak casks) with around 1,000 casks stored in the only warehouse and the rest being sent to Glenlossie for maturation. Five mashes per week during 2013 will result in 500,000 litres of pure alcohol.

The core range consists of the *12 year old* and *Selected Reserve*. The latter is a vatting of selected casks, usually around 18-20 years of age. There is also a *Distiller's Edition* with a second maturation in Muscat casks. In 2010 a *single cask* distilled in *1994* was released as part of the Manager's Choice series.

12 years old

Scapa

Owner:
Chivas Brothers
(Pernod Ricard)

Region/district:
Highlands (Orkney)

Founded: 1885

Status: Active

Capacity: 1 100 000 litres

Address: Scapa, St Ola, Kirkwall,
Orkney KW15 1SE

Tel: 01856 876585

website: www.scapamalt.com

History:

1885 – Macfarlane & Townsend founds the distillery with John Townsend at the helm.

1919 – Scapa Distillery Company Ltd takes over.

1934 – Scapa Distillery Company goes into voluntary liquidation and production ceases.

1936 – Production resumes.

1936 – Bloch Brothers Ltd (John and Sir Maurice) takes over.

1954 – Hiram Walker & Sons takes over.

1959 – A Lomond still is installed.

1978 – The distillery is modernized.

1994 – The distillery is mothballed.

1997 – Production takes place a few months each year using staff from Highland Park.

2004 – Extensive refurbishing takes place at a cost of £2.1 million. Scapa 14 years is launched.

2005 – Production ceases in April and phase two of the refurbishment programme starts. Chivas Brothers becomes the new owner.

2006 – Scapa 1992 (14 years) is launched.

2008 – Scapa 16 years is launched.

Scapa 16 year old

GS – The nose offers apricots and peaches, nougat and mixed spices. Pretty, yet profound. Medium-bodied, with caramel and spice notes in the mouth. The finish is medium in length and gingery, with fat, buttery notes emerging at the end.

DR – Sweet baked banana in cream with shortbread on the nose. The taste is a delightful mix of sweet and sour, with sugar and salt sparring but kept apart by green and orange fruit. There's a late sharper note towards lengthy fruit finish.

The Canadian spirits giant, Hiram Walker, made its first entry into the Scotch market when it acquired the blended Scotch Ballantine's in 1936 and, at the same time, bought Miltonduff and Glenburgie distilleries in addition to building Dumbarton grain distillery. The demand for Ballantine's grew and the owners found it challenging to obtain all the different styles of single malts required for the character. Two engineers in the company, Alistair Cunningham and Arthur Warren, came up with the idea of constructing a new type of still that could be adjusted to produce several styles of whisky. They were called Lomond stills and, instead of a swan neck, they had a straight tube where three adjustable plates were fitted. When the position of the plates was modified you could control the character of the spirit. A total of six Lomond stills were installed; the first in 1956 at Inverleven (within the Dumbarton complex), then two more at Glenburgie in 1958, one at Scapa in 1959 and finally two were added at Miltonduff in 1964. Only two are operative today (although the plates have been removed); the Inverleven one which was brought to Bruichladdich a couple of years ago and the one at Scapa.

The equipment at Scapa distillery consists of a semi-lauter mash tun, eight washbacks (four made of Corten steel and four of stainless steel) and two stills. Scapa probably has the longest fermentation time of any distillery in Scotland. All the washbacks are filled and left for up to 160 hours before distillation begins. The distillery was in danger of being closed down in 2000 but the owners at the time, Allied Domecq decided to invest £2 million to refurbish it. Current production is about 400,000 litres of alcohol. There are three dunnage and three racked warehouses, but only the latter are in use today.

The Scapa core range is just the *16 year old*, while limited editions include a *25 year old* from 1980 and a *Vintage 1992*. There is also a *12 year old cask strength* distilled in 2000, which is sold exclusively at Chivas' visitor centres.

16 years old

Speyburn

Owner:
Inver House Distillers
(Thai Beverages plc)

Region/district:
Speyside

Founded: 1897
Status: Active
Capacity: 2 000 000 litres

Address: Rothes, Aberlour,
Morayshire AB38 7AG

Tel: 01340 831213
website: www.speyburn.com

History:
1897 – Brothers John and Edward Hopkin and their cousin Edward Broughton found the distillery through John Hopkin & Co. They already own Tobermory. The architect is Charles Doig. Building the distillery costs £17,000 and the distillery is transferred to Speyburn-Glenlivet Distillery Company.

1916 – Distillers Company Limited (DCL) acquires John Hopkin & Co. and the distillery.

1930 – Production stops.

1934 – Productions restarts.

1962 – Speyburn is transferred to Scottish Malt Distillers (SMD).

1968 – Drum maltings closes.

1991 – Inver House Distillers buys Speyburn.

1992 – A 10 year old is launched as a replacement for the 12 year old in the Flora & Fauna series.

2001 – Pacific Spirits (Great Oriole Group) buys Inver House for $85 million.

2005 – A 25 year old Solera is released.

2006 – Inver House changes owner when International Beverage Holdings acquires Pacific Spirits UK.

2009 – The un-aged Bradan Orach is introduced for the American market.

2012 – Clan Speyburn is formed.

Speyburn 10 year old

GS – Soft and elegant on the spicy, nutty nose. Smooth in the mouth, with vanilla, spice and more nuts. The finish is medium, spicy and drying.

DR – Sweet malt nose, then one of the sweetest and most easy-drinking of all malts, with the faintest touch of smoke in the mix. Like eating a bag of sugar.

Considering that Speyburn is a small distillery which is not very well-known in Europe, it has been doing exceptionally well in the United States for decades. For the time being, the brand is positioned between 5th and 10th place in the US among the most sold single malts, having to compete with giants like Glenlivet, Glenfiddich, Balvenie and Glenmorangie. Total sales for 2012 were well over 500,000 bottles and with the recent revamping of the packaging, as well as the creation of a whole new community on the internet called Clan Speyburn, the whisky seems sure to continue to increase its sales.

Speyburn distillery is equipped with an old cast iron mash tun with a copper canopy but the rakes inside were replaced in 2008 with a semilauter gear. There are six wooden washbacks, one wash still (17,300 litres) and one spirit still (13,200 litres) using stainless steel worm tubs with 104 metre long copper tubes for cooling. This constitutes a fairly small distillery but there are bigger plans in the pipeline! A planning application has been submitted for an expansion with a new mash tun, more washbacks (made of stainless steel) and two more stills. This would double the distillery's capacity! One change will be that the wash stills will be fitted with shell and tube condensers while the spirit stills will still be using worm tubs. The expansion may take some time to complete seeing that special consideration has to be taken for one of the buildings on the site, the old drum maltings, which is a listed building protected by Historic Scotland.

There are also four dunnage warehouses with 5,000 casks where the spirit intended for bottling as single malt is maturing.

The core range of Speyburn single malt is the *10 year old* and *Bradan Orach* without age statement. There is also a limited *25 year old* which was released in a new version in 2012. In 2013 the first of the Clan casks for members was released – a *1975 PX sherry single cask*.

10 years old

Speyside

Owner:
Speyside Distillers Co.
(Harvey's of Edinburgh)

Region/district:
Speyside

Founded: 1976
Status: Active
Capacity: 600 000 litres

Address: Glen Tromie, Kingussie
Inverness-shire PH21 1NS

Tel: 01540 661060
website: www.speysidedistillery.co.uk

History:

1956 – George Christie buys a piece of land at Drumguish near Kingussie.

1957 – George Christie starts a grain distillery near Alloa.

1962 – George Christie (founder of Speyside Distillery Group in the fifties) commissions the drystone dyker Alex Fairlie to build a distillery in Drumguish.

1986 – Scowis assumes ownership.

1987 – The distillery is completed.

1990 – The distillery is on stream in December.

1993 – The first single malt, Drumguish, is launched.

1999 – Speyside 8 years is launched.

2000 – Speyside Distilleries is sold to a group of private investors including Ricky Christie, Ian Jerman and Sir James Ackroyd.

2001 – Speyside 10 years is launched.

2012 – Speyside Distillers is sold to Harvey's of Edinburgh.

Speyside 12 year old

GS – A nicely-balanced nose of herbs and toasted barley. Medium-bodied, with a suggestion of peat, plus hazelnuts and oak. Toffee and orange notes in the lingering finish.

DR – Rootsy damp straw nose, a sharp and clean barley delivery on the palate with an earthy, peaty undertow, and a willowy, nutty savoury finish.

From the time George Christie, a former submarine captain, got the idea of building a distillery it took 34 years before the production started. That is part of the fascinating story of Speyside distillery near Kingussie. In the mean time, Christie had kept himself busy. He founded a grain distillery and started a career as a blender and bottler. When Christie died in 2011 he had not been the owner for many years and in September 2012, the distillery opened a new chapter when the company was acquired by Harvey's of Edinburgh with John Harvey McDonough at the helm. His ancestors have been in the whisky business since the 1770s and the company owns a single malt brand called Spey. The Spey brand, with 6 different expressions, has been exported to Taiwan since 2011 and Harvey's of Edinburgh has close relations with the Taiwanese company Vedan – the world's largest producer of monosodium glutamate. It is still uncertain what the new owner's plans for the Speyside brand are, but it could mean that it will be discontinued and the whisky used for their own Spey brand instead. They have already ceased production of the Cu Dubh single malt and the Scott's Selection range will probably be replaced by a new range called Single. Rumours also have it that there are plans to build a second distillery in Rothiemurches near Aviemore. Speyside produces on a small-scale and is set in beautiful surroundings. The distillery is equipped with a semi-lauter mash tun, four stainless steel washbacks and one pair of stills. There are no warehouses on site. Instead, the spirit is tankered away to the company's warehouses in Glasgow. The total production for 2013 will be around 500,000 litres of alcohol. Under the previous owners, three brands of single malt have been produced; *Speyside* with the core range of *12* and *15 year old*, *Drumguish* and the quaint *Cu Dubh*. Apart from the distillery at Drumguish, there is a diverse range of activities at the company's base in Rutherglen, Glasgow. Cask warehousing, a bottling plant and a blending operation are all found here.

12 years old

Springbank

Owner:
Springbank Distillers
(J & A Mitchell)

Region/district:
Campbeltown

Founded: 1828
Status: Active (vc)
Capacity: 750 000 litres

Address: Well Close, Campbeltown,
Argyll PA28 6ET

Tel: 01586 551710
website: www.springbankdistillers.com

History:

1828 – The Reid family, in-laws of the Mitchells (see below), founds the distillery.

1837 – The Reid family encounters financial difficulties and John and William Mitchell buy the distillery.

1897 – J. & A. Mitchell Co Ltd is founded.

1926 – The depression forces the distillery to close.

1933 – The distillery is back in production.

1960 – Own maltings ceases.

1969 – J. & A. Mitchell buys the independent bottler Cadenhead.

1979 – The distillery closes.

1985 – A 10 year old Longrow is launched.

1987 – Limited production restarts.

1989 – Production restarts.

1992 – Springbank takes up its maltings again.

1997 – First distillation of Hazelburn.

1998 – Springbank 12 years is launched.

1999 – Dha Mhile (7 years), the world's first organic single malt, is released.

2000 – A 10 year old is launched.

2001 – Springbank 1965 'Local barley' (36 years), 741 bottles, is launched.

2002 – Number one in the series Wood Expressions is a 12 year old with five years on Demerara rum casks. Next is a Longrow sherry cask (13 years). A relaunch of the 15 year old replaces the 21 year old.

2004 – J. & A. Mitchell's main owner, Hedley Wright, reopens Glengyle Distillery. Springbank 10 years 100 proof is launched as well as Springbank Wood Expression bourbon, Longrow 14 years old, Springbank 32 years old and Springbank 14 years Port Wood.

Frank McHardy, an icon in the industry and who has been honoured on numerous occasions for his achievements for Scotch whisky during his tenure of 50 years, has retired in July 2013. Frank started off as a shift worker at Invergordon grain distillery in 1963. Since then he has worked at several distilleries but is mainly known for his time as Master Distiller at Bushmills 1986-1996, then manager and later Director of Production at Springbank 1977-1986 and again from 1996. Frank will not leave the whisky scene entirely though, as he has promised to come back every year to run the Whisky School at Springbank. Springbank is the oldest distillery in Scotland owned by the same family (the Mitchells) and is also one of just three remaining distilleries in Campbeltown.

The distillery is equipped with an open cast iron mash tun, six washbacks made of Scandinavian larch, one wash still and two spirit stills. The wash still is unique in Scotland, as it is fired by both an open oil-fire and internal steam coils. Ordinary condensers are used to cool the spirit vapours, except in the first of the two spirit stills, where a worm tub is used. Springbank is unique in Scotland as it malts its entire need of barley using its own floor maltings. Springbank produces three distinctive single malts with different phenol contents in the malted barley. Springbank is distilled two and a half times (12-15ppm), Longrow is distilled twice (50-55 ppm) and Hazelburn is distilled three times and unpeated. Currently around 100,000 litres are produced in a year at Springbank.

The range from the distillery has changed somewhat since last year because the owners want to concentrate on age statement bottlings, at least of Springbank. The core range is *Springbank 10, 15* and *18 years, Springbank 12 year old cask strength* and *Springbank 21* (limited but with increasing quantities every year). This means that Springbank CV has been discontinued. Longrow is represented by *Longrow* (formerly known as Longrow CV), the *18 year old* and *Longrow Red*. The 2013 edition of the latter (released for the first time in September 2012) is a *12 year old* with a second maturation in *Shiraz* wine casks. Finally there is *Hazelburn* where the 8 year old and CV have both been discontinued and the *12 year old* is now the only expression. Recent limited editions include *Longrow Rundlets & Kilderkins* (an 11 year old matured in small casks of 68 and 82 litres) and a *12 year old Springbank Calvados finish*. In autumn 2013 a *9 year old Springbank Gaja Barolo* was also added to the list while *Hazelburn Rundlets & Kilderkins* has been announced for a spring 2014 release.

History (continued):

2005 – Springbank 21 years is released. The first version of Hazelburn (8 years) is released. Longrow Tokaji Wood Expression is launched.

2006 – Longrow 10 years 100 proof, Springbank 25 years, Springbank 9 years Marsala finish, Springbank 11 years Madeira finish and a new Hazelburn 8 year old are released.

2007 – Springbank Vintage 1997 and a 16 year old rum wood are released.

2008 – The distillery closes temporarily. Three new releases of Longrow - CV, 18 year old and 7 year old Gaja Barolo.

2009 – Springbank Madeira 11 year old, Springbank 18 year old, Springbank Vintage 2001 and Hazelburn 12 year old are released.

2010 – Springbank 12 year old cask strength and a 12 year old claret expression together with new editions of the CV and 18 year old are released. Longrow 10 year old cask strength and Hazelburn CV are also new.

2011 – Longrow 18 year old and Hazelburn 8 year old Sauternes wood expression are released.

2012 – New releases include Springbank Rundlets & Kilderkins, Springbank 21 year old and Longrow Red.

2013 – Longrow Rundlets & Kilderkins, a new edition of Longrow RED and Springbank 9 year old Gaja Barolo finish are released.

Springbank 10 year old

GS – Fresh and briny on the nose, with citrus fruit, oak and barley, plus a note of damp earth. Sweet on the palate, with developing brine, nuttiness and vanilla toffee. Long and spicy in the finish, coconut oil and drying peat.

DR – Raw vegetables, damp leaves, autumn forest, traces of smoke fire. Wonderful and challenging on the palate with gooseberry, apple, pear, greek yoghurt, oil, smoke and chili. Complex, tingling, savoury delight. Spicy, earthy, savoury and fun in the finale.

Longrow (NAS)

GS – Initially slightly gummy on the nose, but then brine and fat peat notes develop. Vanilla and malt also emerge. The smoky palate offers lively brine and is quite dry and spicy, with some vanilla and lots of ginger. The finish is peaty with persistent, oaky ginger.

DR – Slightly vegetal, oily and industrial, with pepper and smoke. Much better on the palate than the nose. Big fishy peaty earthy taste with gooseberry and grape, chili pepper and fresh salad. Rapier sharp in the mouth with big flavours. A long finish, with pepper and peat.

Hazelburn 12 year old

GS – A highly aromatic nose, featuring nutty toffee, sherry, dried fruits and dark chocolate. The palate is rich and spicy, with cocoa, coffe, ginger and sweet notes of caramel and orange marmalade. Long and spicy in the finish, with more caramel, coffee and chocolate.

DR – Rich and fruity nose of nectarine, peach, plums and some nuttiness. On the palate rich plums, red berries, dry sherry and drying tannins, with an intense rich and fruity finish.

Springbank 15 years

Hazelburn 12 years

Springbank 21 years

Longrow 18 years

Springbank 10 years old

Longrow (former CV)

Strathisla

Owner:
Chivas Brothers
(Pernod Ricard)

Region/district:
Speyside

Founded: | **Status:** | **Capacity:**
1786 | Active (vc) | 2 400 000 litres

Address: Seafield Avenue, Keith,
Banffshire AB55 5BS

Tel:
01542 783044

website:
www.maltwhiskydistilleries.com

History:
1786 – Alexander Milne and George Taylor found the distillery under the name Milltown, but soon change it to Milton.

1823 – MacDonald Ingram & Co. purchases the distillery.

1830 – William Longmore acquires the distillery.

1870 – The distillery name changes to Strathisla.

1880 – William Longmore retires and hands operations to his son-in-law John Geddes-Brown. William Longmore & Co. is formed.

1890 – The distillery changes name to Milton.

1940 – Jay (George) Pomeroy acquires majority shares in William Longmore & Co. Pomeroy is jailed as a result of dubious business transactions and the distillery goes bankrupt in 1949.

1950 – Chivas Brothers buys the run-down distillery at a compulsory auction for £71,000 and starts restoration.

1951 – The name reverts to Strathisla.

1965 – The number of stills is increased from two to four.

1970 – A heavily peated whisky, Craigduff, is produced but production stops later.

2001 – The Chivas Group is acquired by Pernod Ricard.

Strathisla 12 year old

GS – Rich on the nose, with sherry, stewed fruits, spices and lots of malt. Full-bodied and almost syrupy on the palate. Toffee, honey, nuts, a whiff of peat and a suggestion of oak. The finish is medium in length, slightly smoky and a with a final flash of ginger.

DR – Rich, full and fruity nose with lots of barley, then barley, currants and a touch of oak, peat and pepper, concluding with a complex and intriguing finish.

James "Jimmy" Barclay, one of the most adventurous and enigmatic profiles of the 20th century whisky industry, has played an important part in the history of Chivas Brothers and Strathisla. At the age of 16 he started working at Benrinnes distillery as a clerk and later joined Mackie & Co. to work for the legendary Peter Mackie. In 1919 he bought Georg Ballantine & Son together with R A McKinlay and expanded the brand to an international player. They sold the company to Hiram Walker in 1938, Barclay joined the board of the Canadian company but soon moved on. In 1949, he was asked by Hiram Walker´s fierce competitor, Seagram´s, to help them establish a foothold in the Scotch whisky market. He acquired Chivas Brothers, became the managing director and in 1950 bought Strathisla which has been an important part of the Chivas Regal brand both before and after. Jimmy Barclay died a wealthy man in 1963, aged 77. Strathisla distillery is one of the oldest and prettiest in Scotland and is also the spiritual home of Chivas Regal.

The excellent visitor centre attracts nearly 15,000 visitors per year. The distillery is equipped with a 5 tonnes traditional cast stainless steel mash tun with a raised copper canopy, ten washbacks made of Oregon pine with a 48 hour fermentation and two pairs of stills. The wash stills are of lantern type with descending lyne arms and the spirit stills have boiling balls and the lyne arms are slightly ascending. The spirit produced at Strathisla is piped to nearby Glen Keith distillery for filling or to be tankered away. A small amount is stored on site in two racked and one dunnage warehouse.

Pernod Ricard has only released two official bottlings of Strathisla, the *12 year old* and a *cask strength* (currently a 16 year old from 1997) which is sold only at the distillery. The packaging of the 12 year old was revamped in 2013 and at the same time, the alcohol strength was lowered to 40%.

12 years old

Chivas Regal 12 year old

Blended Scotch

Starring Strathisla Single Malt *in a leading role*
Producer Chivas Brothers
Director Colin Scott, Master Blender

The year 1801 is important to Chivas Brothers, in as much as that the phone number for their headquarter in Paisley ends with 1801. In that year John Forrest opened a licensed grocer´s shop in Aberdeen. The business flourished and in the 1820s he hired William Edward as store manager. When Forrest died in 1828, Edward took over the business and expanded it. His friend, Alexander Chivas, approached him in 1838 and asked if he would consider hiring Alexander´s cousin, James, who was unemployed. Edward agreed and when he died only three years later, the thriving business was taken over by James Chivas.

He brought in a partner but when they went their separate ways in 1857, James decided that a family run business might be the best after all and brought his brother, John on board. Chivas Brothers the company, was born! Sadly, John dies only five years later, aged 48 and years later, James brought his son, Alexander, into the business. By this time Chivas Brothers had already started blending whisky and one of their first brands was Glen-Dee. This was probably a blend of different malt whiskies but when the Spirits Act of 1860 was passed, it became legal to blend grain and malt whiskies in bond, i. e. without paying any duty before it was bottled. By this time all the big whisky companies had launched new blended whiskies and Chivas Brothers were no exception, with Strathythan and Old Vat being added to the range.

Alexander Chivas died in 1893 and he would become the last man standing from the Chivas family to run the company. The company was taken over by the clerk, Alexander J Smith. It would take until 1909 before the company launched its first whisky labelled Chivas Regal. It was a whisky without age statement and was, with great success, introduced to the American market in 1909, together with a 25 year old version. The latter was withdrawn during Prohibition only to be re-created and added to the range again in 2007.

It was in 1949, when Seagram & Co took over the company, that Chivas Regal started to take off for real. The legendary owner of Seagram's, Sam Bronfman, wanted to get a share of the Scotch whisky market and after an unsuccessful attempt at acquiring Robertson & Baxter he set his eyes on Chivas Brothers and had greater success. One year later, Strathisla distillery was bought. Strathisla malt had long been an important part of the Chivas Regal recipe and they had now ensured availability for the future. But possibly the most important thing that Sam Bronfman did, was to make Chivas Regal a *12 year old* and to invest heavily on marketing. The brand quickly established itself as one of the world's best-selling whiskies.

Admittedly, it is second in the world to Johnnie Walker Black Label in the premium category, but is number one in Europe and the biggest brand in Southeast Asia. An *18 year old* was added to the range in 1997 and (as mentioned) the *25 year old* made a comeback in 2007. In autumn 2012 a new expression was added, *The Chivas Brothers´ Blend,* aimed at the duty free market. A total of 58 million bottles were sold in 2012 which positions the brand as number three after Johnnie Walker and Ballantine´s. Except for Strathisla – Longmorn, Glenlivet and Glen Grant all play important roles in the Chivas Regal blends.

A fruity nose with apricots and oranges, honey and herbs. Creamy on the palate with vanilla and a hint of sherry and heather. More fruits and hazelnuts and a spicy finish.

Strathmill

Owner:
Diageo

Region/district:
Speyside

Founded: | **Status:** | **Capacity:**
1891 | Active | 2 300 000 litres

Address: Keith, Banffshire AB55 5DQ

Tel: 01542 883000

website: www.malts.com

History:
1891 – The distillery is founded in an old mill from 1823 and is named Glenisla-Glenlivet Distillery.

1892 – The inauguration takes place in June.

1895 – The gin company W. & A. Gilbey buys the distillery for £9,500 and names it Strathmill.

1962 – W. & A. Gilbey merges with United Wine Traders (including Justerini & Brooks) and forms International Distillers & Vintners (IDV).

1968 – The number of stills is increased from two to four and purifiers are added.

1972 – IDV is bought by Watney Mann which later the same year is acquired by Grand Metropolitan.

1993 – Strathmill becomes available as a single malt for the first time since 1909 as a result of a bottling (1980) from Oddbins.

1997 – Guinness and Grand Metropolitan merge and form Diageo.

2001 – The first official bottling is a 12 year old in the Flora & Fauna series.

2010 – A Manager's Choice single cask from 1996 is released.

Strathmill 12 year old

GS – Quite reticent on the nose, with nuts, grass and a hint of ginger. Spicy vanilla and nuts dominate the palate. The finish is drying, with peppery oak.

DR – Butterscotch and summer flowers mixed with lemon flu powder, and some powdery, talc-like notes on the nose, the palate has some apricot and peach fruits before a wave of salt and pepper and a spicy conclusion.

Almost all the distilleries owned by Diageo today were once owned by the predecessor of Diageo, Distillers Company Limited, founded already in 1877. Strathmill (and three others) is an exception. The distillery was owned by Grand Metropolitan when they joined forces with Guinness to form Diageo in 1997. Grand Metropolitan is an excellent example of a company growing through diversification. Established as a hotel group in 1934, they entered into the catering business followed by acquisitions of several breweries and distilleries (including Strathmill) and finally finding themselves a prominent player in the fast food market, owning Burger King and Wimpy's.

The history of Strathmill distillery on the other hand has been characterised by stability and, since its inception, its goal has been to produce malt whisky for various blends. The brands have shifted through the years from more or less defunct brands such as Spey Royal, Old Master and Dunhill to the world's fifth most sold blended Scotch – J&B. The brand has admittedly fallen from the second place held as late as in 2006, but it still sold 48 million bottles during 2012!

Strathmill distillery is equipped with a stainless steel semi-lauter mash tun and six stainless steel washbacks with a combination of short (60 hours) and long (120 hours) fermentations. There are two pairs of stills and Strathmill is one of a select few distilleries still using purifiers on the spirit stills. This device is mounted between the lyne arm and the condenser and acts as a mini-condenser, allowing the lighter alcohols to travel towards the condenser and forcing the heavier alcohols to go back into the still for another distillation. The result is a lighter and fruitier spirit. In Strathmill's case both purifiers and condensers are fitted to the outside of the still house to optimise energy savings. For 2013 the production will be 2,1 million litres of pure alcohol.

The only official bottling was a *12 year old* until 2010, when a *single cask* distilled in *1996* was released as part of the Manager's Choice series.

Flora & Fauna 12 years

Whisky Around the World

FINLAND

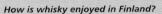

Mika Jansson, an avid whisky fan and activist for the last 25 years, is the current President of the Malt Whisky Association of Finland. He is also one of the organizers of the annual UISGE Whisky Festival. Currently Mika is trying to form an international fellowship between various whisky societies, in order to unite (whisky) hobbyists globally.

Which spirit is the most popular in Finland and where does whisky fit into the picture?

Firstly it is perhaps worth noting that the overall sales of spirits have steadily decreased in Finland since 2007, and this can be clearly seen from the sales figures published by our national Alcohol retail monopoly. In terms of sheer volume, vodka still clearly dominates the retail sales. Cognac, blended Scotch – both decreasing, but still relatively big in volume. The only categories where there has been year-on-year steady increase in sales during the last 6 years are Scotch Malt Whisky and to a slightly lesser extent, Irish Whiskey.

What types of whisky are the most popular in Finland?

Scotch Blended whisky still outsells all the other whisky categories put together, but this fact does not tell the whole story of the whisky scene here. Whilst inexpensive blends make up the bulk retail sales figures, there's been a definite increase in the number of restaurants and pubs choosing to offer high quality (malt) whiskies to better cater for their clientele, while maybe keeping only one or two blended Scotch on the shelf.

When would you say people in Finland started to get seriously interested in whisky? What triggered it and how has that interest developed?

The interest in quality whisky started to grow slowly from the end of the 1990s, and it has been on the rise since then. In the last five years we have seen single malts become a trendy hobby at an increasing rate. Sipping whisky, making tasting notes, blogging about whisky – all are on the rise more than ever before.

Which brands of Scotch are the most popular in Finland?

Traditionally Finland has been seen as a "smoky whisky" nation, but in recent years, heavily sherried whiskies have been all the rage, and have also done extremely well in competitions.

Stronger flavours do seem to please Finnish whisky fans.

How is whisky sold in Finland, is there a wide variety of brands and is it easy to find the brand you want?

The selection available in restaurants and pubs is quite good. Retail selection of our national alcohol monopoly is increasing in variety but compared to Sweden for example, selections here are still considerably smaller. There has been some real highlights here though, and by this I mean the availability of whiskies selected exclusively for the Finnish market.

How is whisky marketed in Finland?

Our legislation forbids all public promotion of alcohol above 22% vol. This ban on "promotion" extends even to sharing information such as price, and even mentioning the word "whisky" in any public context. The only legal way to promote strong spirits is within licensed pubs. Private mailing lists and various closed Facebook groups have been set up by private individuals to allow people to discuss whisky topics

Is whisky considered a luxury drink compared to other spirits?

To a certain degree yes, especially with the rising prices. It is also quite the fashionable spirit currently.

Is there a clearly defined group of customers buying whisky?

Whisky certainly is no longer only for the older males here, it attracts members of both genders, and from a wide variety of ages.

Are there special occasions when whisky is preferred?

One thing is noticeable: Whisky gets far less attention during the short summer months we have here in the North. People are too busy trying to enjoy the weather in the summer rather than sip whisky. Once the dark fall season sets in, whisky starts to attract far more people.

How is whisky enjoyed in Finland?

Most Finnish whisky enthusiasts prefer their whisky neat, with no ice or water. Some consumers with little or no whisky knowledge may still add ice, but it isn't all that popular here – unless the whiskey is from America.

Would you say that the customer in Finland is educated about whisky?

Not all by any means – but a growing group of fans, yes. Certainly there is a growing number of consumers here who wish to know more about the spirits they drink and enjoy, as people are getting more conscious of quality, production methods, etc. Days of "its all good, as long as it tastes ok" are over. Today's person seeks knowledge on products, and his/her choices are affected by this knowledge.

How many producers of whisky do you have in Finland and how would you describe the future for domestic whisky in your country?

Currently there is one larger producer (Teerenpeli), and several other small-scale makers of whisky here. Their efforts of increasing quality have produced good results, so I believe we will see at least a few Finnish whiskies gain international fame, as well as sales in Finland.

What are your thoughts on the future for Scotch whisky in Finland?

Scotch whisky is very respected here, because of its high quality and integrity as a spirit. Overall, whisky culture is growing steadily here, I see more and more people go for quality rather than quantity, and I believe this trend to continue. I think this means that Scotch whisky sales will prosper in the coming years.

Talisker

Owner:
Diageo

Region/district:
Highlands (Skye)

Founded: **Status:** **Capacity:**
1830   Active (vc)   2 600 000 litres

Address: Carbost, Isle of Skye,
Inverness-shire IV47 8SR

Tel: **website:**
01478 614308 (vc)   www.malts.com

History:

1830 – Hugh and Kenneth MacAskill, sons of the local doctor, found the distillery.

1848 – The brothers transfer the lease to North of Scotland Bank and Jack Westland from the bank runs the operations.

1854 – Kenneth MacAskill dies.

1857 – North of Scotland Bank sells the distillery to Donald MacLennan for £500.

1863 – MacLennan experiences difficulties in making operations viable and puts the distillery up for sale.

1865 – MacLennan, still working at the distillery, nominates John Anderson as agent in Glasgow.

1867 – Anderson & Co. from Glasgow takes over.

1879 – John Anderson is imprisoned after having sold non-existing casks of whisky.

1880 – New owners are now Alexander Grigor Allan and Roderick Kemp.

1892 – Kemp sells his share and buys Macallan Distillery instead.

1894 – The Talisker Distillery Ltd is founded.

1895 – Allan dies and Thomas Mackenzie, who has been his partner, takes over.

1898 – Talisker Distillery merges with Dailuaine-Glenlivet Distillers and Imperial Distillers to form Dailuaine-Talisker Distillers Company.

1916 – Thomas Mackenzie dies and the distillery is taken over by a consortium consisting of, among others, John Walker, John Dewar, W. P. Lowrie and Distillers Company Limited (DCL).

In the huge Diageo family of single malts, Talisker if definitely one of the favourite children. A lot of attention has gone into the brand during the last five to ten years and following a complete revamp of label and bottle design last year, 2013 saw investments being made in the visitor centre, as well as the release of no less than three new bottlings. The distillery on Skye attracts 60,000 visitors a year but the visitor centre, dating back to 1988, was a bit small and worn out. The owners invested £1m and by Easter of 2013 a new, expanded centre was opened which included a viewing gallery in one of the warehouses, as well as new tasting rooms. The popularity of Talisker single malt has increased rapidly in recent years. From 720,000 bottles sold ten years ago, the sales figures for 2012 had increased to almost 1,6 million bottles.

The malt is peated at 18-20 ppm which gives a phenol content of 5-7 ppm in the new make. The distillery is equipped with a stainless steel lauter mash tun with a capacity of 8 tonnes, eight washbacks and five stills (two wash stills and three spirit stills) all of them connected to wooden wormtubs. The wash stills are equipped with a special type of purifiers, using the colder outside air, and have a u-bend in the lyne arm. The purifiers and the odd bend of the lyne arms allow for more copper contact and increase the reflux during distillation.

The fermentation time is quite long (65-75 hours) and the middle cut from the spirit still is collected between 76% and 65% which gives a medium peated spirit. Only a small part of the produce is matured on the island, while the rest is tankered and taken to the mainland for storage. The distillery is currently running at full capacity.

Until last year, Talisker's core range consisted of *10 year old*, *18 year old*, *Distiller's Edition* with an Amoroso sherry finish and *Talisker 57° North* which is released in small batches. Previous limited releases of *25* and *30 year old* have now become part of the core range but the big news for 2013 was the introduction of two new permanent members of the range – *Talisker Storm* without age statement is a more intense and smoky version of the 10 year old, while *Talisker Port Ruighe* (pronounced Portree after the main town on Isle of Skye) has been given a finish in ruby port casks. But new releases did not stop there. A Duty Free exclusive called *Dark Storm*, the smokiest Talisker so far, was launched in the summer of 2013 and it has been matured in heavily charred casks. Finally, in autumn 2013, a *27 year old* was launched as part of this year's Special Releases.

1928 – The distillery abandons triple distillation.

1960 – On 22nd November the distillery catches fire and substantial damage occurs.

1962 – The distillery reopens after the fire with five identical copies of the destroyed stills.

1972 – Malting ceases and malt is now purchased from Glen Ord Central Maltings.

1988 – Classic Malts are introduced, Talisker 10 years included. A visitor centre is opened.

1998 – A new stainless steel/copper mash tun and five new worm tubs are installed. Talisker is launched as a Distillers Edition with an amoroso sherry finish.

2004 – Two new bottlings appear, an 18 year old and a 25 year old.

2005 – To celebrate the 175th birthday of the distillery, Talisker 175th Anniversary is released. The third edition of the 25 year old cask strength is released.

2006 – A 30 year old and the fourth edition of the 25 year old are released.

2007 – The second edition of the 30 year old and the fifth edition of the 25 year old are released.

2008 – Talisker 57° North, sixth edition of the 25 year old and third edition of the 30 year old are launched.

2009 – New editions of the 25 and 30 year old are released.

2010 – A 1994 Manager's Choice single cask and a new edition of the 30 year old are released.

2011 – Three limited releases - 25, 30 and 34 year old.

2012 – A limited 35 year old is released.

2013 – Four new expressions are released – Storm, Dark Storm, Port Ruighe and a 27 year old.

Talisker 10 year old

GS – Quite dense and smoky on the nose, with smoked fish, bladderwrack, sweet fruit and peat. Full-bodied and peaty in the mouthy; complex, with ginger, ozone, dark chocolate, black pepper and a kick of chilli in the long, smoky tail.

DR – Grilled oily fish in lemon oil, on the nose, dry salt and pepper on the palate, peat and pepper in a tastebud treat of a finish.

Port Ruighe

Storm

Dark Storm

57° North

1985, 27 year old

18 years old

Distiller's Edition

10 years old

Tamdhu

Owner:
Edrington Group

Region/district:
Speyside

Founded: 1896
Status: Active

Capacity:
4 000 000 litres

Address: Knockando, Aberlour,
Morayshire AB38 7RP

Tel:
01340 872200

website:
www.tamdhu.com

History:
1896 – The distillery is founded by Tamdhu Distillery Company, a consortium of whisky blenders with William Grant as the main promoter. Charles Doig is the architect.

1897 – The first casks are filled in July.

1898 – Highland Distillers Company, which has several of the 1896 consortium members in managerial positions, buys Tamdhu Distillery Company.

1911 – The distillery closes.

1913 –The distillery reopens.

1928 – The distillery is mothballed.

1948 – The distillery is in full production again in July.

1950 – The floor maltings is replaced by Saladin boxes when the distillery is rebuilt.

1972 – The number of stills is increased from two to four.

1975 – Two stills augment the previous four.

1976 – Tamdhu 8 years is launched as single malt.

2005 – An 18 year old and a 25 year old are released.

2009 – The distillery is motballed.

2011 – The Edrington Group sells the distillery to Ian Macleod Distillers.

2012 – Production is resumed.

2013 – The first official release from the new owners – a 10 year old.

Tamdhu 10 year old

GS – Soft sherry notes, new leather, almonds, marzipan and a hint of peat on the nose. Very smooth and drinkable, with citrus fruit, gentle spice and more sweet sherry on the palate. Persistent spicy leather, with a sprinkling of black pepper in the finish.

When the new owners of Tamdhu distillery, Ian Macleod Distillers, chose the timing to present their first official bottling since the takeover, they fittingly decided to do so during the Speyside Whisky Festival in early May 2013. A special, commemorative 10 year old matured in first fill Oloroso casks was released in limited numbers, simultaneously when a new core 10 year old where both first and second fill sherry casks had been used, was launched. For the first months the 10 year old was sold only in the UK bu' was later rolled out to other markets. Next year will most likely see a second release of either a 12 year old or a 15 year old.

When Ian Macleod Distillers restarted production at the distillery in early 2012, it had been mothballed since 2009. A decision was taken not to use the old Saladin maltings on site. In the first year, 1,9 million litres were produced but the speed has now been increased and the target for 2013 is 3 million litres. The distillery is equipped with a 12 tonne semilauter mash tun, nine Oregon pine washbacks with a fermentation time of 71 hours and three pairs of stills. All the washbacks date from 1973 but two of them were replaced in summer 2012. There are four dunnage and one racked warehouse on site, but considering the future plans the new owners have in mind for the brand, the intention is to have another six palletised warehouses (each with a capacity of 10,200 barrels) and a filling store ready by the end of 2013 with another three warehouses in the pipeline. Sherry butts will mainly be used for the single malts while bourbon barrels are reserved for the spirit going to blends.

The idea is to position Tamdhu as a premium malt and the core range at the moment is only the *10 year old*. The previous owners were restricted when it came to promoting the brand and the official range only consisted of a non-aged version. In 2005 an 18 and a 25 year old were introduced and there has also been a 10 year old.

10 years old

Tamnavulin

Owner:
Whyte & Mackay
(United Spirits)

Region/district:
Speyside

Founded: 1966
Status: Active
Capacity: 4 000 000 litres

Address: Tomnavoulin, Ballindalloch, Banffshire AB3 9JA

Tel: 1807 590285
website: -

History:
1966 – Tamnavulin-Glenlivet Distillery Company, a subsidiary of Invergordon Distillers Ltd, founds Tamnavulin.

1993 – Whyte & Mackay buys Invergordon Distillers.

1995 – The distillery closes in May.

1996 – Whyte & Mackay changes name to JBB (Greater Europe).

2000 – Distillation takes place for six weeks.

2001 – Company management buy out operations for £208 million and rename the company Kyndal.

2003 – Kyndal changes name to Whyte & Mackay.

2007 – United Spirits buys Whyte & Mackay. Tamnavulin is opened again in July after having been mothballed for 12 years.

Tamnavulin 12 year old

GS – Delicate and floral on the nose, with light malt and fruit gums. Light to medium bodied, fresh, malty and spicy on the palate, with a whiff of background smoke. The finish is medium in length, with lingering spice, smoke, and notes of caramel.

FR – Wet hay, celery and cucumber on the nose and a delightful exotic fruit and citrus taste and a satisfying and pleasant finish.

Tamnavulin distillery is definitely one of the lesser known in Scotland. Built as late as in 1965, with no tradition to lean back upon, no visitor centre and no bottlings from the owners – this is a distillery that whisky lovers rarely think about. On the other hand, it is quite likely that they have come across it in one of many blends where Tamnavulin plays a part. The owners, Whyte & Mackay, use it not only in their high profile blends, but also for the large quantities sold through the major supermarket chain stores.

The distillery is equipped with a full lauter mash tun with 10,7 tonnes capacity, eight washbacks (four of them made of stainless steel and the rest of Corten steel) with a fermentation time of 48 hours and three pairs of stills. Two racked warehouses (10 casks high) on site have a capacity of 35,000 casks with the oldest ones dating back to 1967, but several of the casks are from other distilleries. Two hundred casks are filled every week on site, while the rest of the production is tankered to Invergordon for filling.

During the first six months of 2013 the owners were doing 16 mashes per week but moved up to 21 mashes which will be around 3,5 million litres in the year. Unlike the last two years, there will be no peated production at Tamnavulin during 2013.

Almost the entire production goes to blended whiskies as a result of a 12 year gap between 1995 and 2007 with no production, and the fact that there is not that much stock of older whisky in the warehouse. The only recent official bottling of Tamnavulin was a *12 year old* which has now been discontinued. There is, however, a 12 year old single malt mainly sold in supermarkets called *Ben Bracken* which has been distilled at Tamnavulin.

12 years old

Teaninich

Owner:
Diageo

Region/district:
Northern Highlands

Founded: **Status:** **Capacity:**
1817 Active 4 400 000 litres

Address: Alness, Ross-shire IV17 0XB

Tel: **website:**
01349 885001 www.malts.com

History:

1817 – Captain Hugh Monro, owner of the estate Teaninich, founds the distillery.

1831 – Captain Munro sells the estate to his younger brother John.

1850 – John Munro, who spends most of his time in India, leases Teaninich to the infamous Robert Pattison from Leith.

1869 – John McGilchrist Ross takes over the licence.

1895 – Munro & Cameron takes over the licence.

1898 – Munro & Cameron buys the distillery.

1904 – Robert Innes Cameron becomes sole owner of Teaninich.

1932 – Robert Innes Cameron dies.

1933 – The estate of Robert Innes Cameron sells the distillery to Distillers Company Limited.

1970 – A new distillation unit with six stills is commissioned and becomes known as the A side.

1975 – A dark grains plant is built.

1984 – The B side of the distillery is mothballed.

1985 – The A side is also mothballed.

1991 – The A side is in production again.

1992 – United Distillers launches a 10 year old Teaninich in the Flora & Fauna series.

1999 – The B side is decommissioned.

2000 – A mash filter is installed.

2009 – Teaninich 1996, a single cask in the new Manager's Choice range is released.

Teaninich 10 year old

GS – The nose is initially fresh and grassy, quite light, with vanilla and hints of tinned pineapple. Mediumbodied, smooth, slightly oily, with cereal and spice in the mouth. Nutty and slowly drying in the finish, with pepper and a suggestion of cocoa powder notes.

DR – All about the barley this one, with clean, sweet ginger barley on the nose, and a clean and crealy palate with some orange and other citrus notes. Pleasant, clean and impressive with a wave of spices late on.

The busiest distillery site in Scotland over the next two years will probably be Teaninich in Alness (just a short distance from Dalmore). Not only will the current distillery double its capacity but Diageo has also decided to build its second mega distillery (after Roseisle in 2009) adjacent to Teaninich. The new distillery, yet to be named, will be operational as from 2015 and will be equipped with 16 stills with a capacity to produce 13 million litres of pure alcohol. The site will also include a bio-energy plant where the by-products from the distillery will be converted into energy. The total investment will be £50 million and it will create 20 new jobs.

Teaninich distillery, which lies in the rather unromantic Teaninich Industrial Estate just south of Alness village, was in the 1970s one of the largest distilleries in Scotland with a capacity of 6 million litres. With the planned upgrade (due to be finished in 2014), the distillery will be able to produce 9,5 million litres.

Two elements in the production process of Teaninich that differ from all other Scottish distilleries are the milling and the mashing. The malt is ground into fine flour without husks in an Asnong hammer mill. Once the grist has been mixed with water, the mash passes through a Meura 2001 mash filter and the wort is collected. Water is added for a second time in the filter and a second run of mash is obtained. The procedure is repeated three times until a washback is filled. Besides the mash filter, the distillery is equipped with 10 washbacks, eight made of larch and two of stainless steel, all with a fermentation time of 75 hours, and six stills. The plan for 2014 is to increase to 20 washbacks (all wooden) and 12 stills and also to upgrade the mash filter.

Teaninich is mainly produced to be a component of Johnnie Walker blended whiskies. The only official bottling used to be a *10 year old* in the Flora & Fauna series, until autumn of 2009 when a Teaninich *1996 single cask* was released in the new range Manager's Choice.

Flora & Fauna 10 years o

Tobermory

Owner:
Burn Stewart Distillers
(Distell Group Ltd)

Region/district:
Highland (Mull)

Founded: 1798
Status: Active (vc)
Capacity: 1 000 000 litres

Address: Tobermory, Isle of Mull,
Argyllshire PA75 6NR

Tel: 1688 302647
website: www.burnstewartdistillers.com

History:

1798 – John Sinclair founds the distillery.

1837 – The distillery closes.

1878 – The distillery reopens.

1890 – John Hopkins & Company buys the distillery.

1916 – Distillers Company Limited (DCL) takes over John Hopkins & Company.

1930 – The distillery closes.

1972 – A shipping company in Liverpool and the sherrymaker Domecq buy the buildings and embark on refurbishment. When work is completed it is named Ledaig Distillery Ltd.

1975 – Ledaig Distillery Ltd files for bankruptcy and the distillery closes again.

1979 – The estate agent Kirkleavington property buys the distillery, forms a new company, Tobermory Distillers Ltd and starts production.

1982 – No production. Some of the buildings are converted into flats and some are rented to a dairy company for cheese storage.

1989 – Production resumes.

1993 – Burn Stewart Distillers buys Tobermory for £600,000 and pays an additional £200,000 for the whisky supply.

2002 – Trinidad-based venture capitalists CL Financial buys Burn Stewart Distillers for £50m.

2005 – A 32 year old from 1972 is launched.

2007 – A Ledaig 10 year old is released.

2008 – A limited edition Tobermory 15 year old is released.

2013 – Burn Stewart Distillers is sold to Distell Group Ltd. A 40 year old Ledaig is released.

Tobermory 10 year old

GS – Fresh and nutty on the nose, with citrus fruit and brittle toffee. A whiff of peat. Medium-bodied, quite dry on the palate with delicate peat, malt and nuts. Medium finish with a hint of mint and a slight citric tang.

DR – Barley and crystal ginger on the nose, but the palate carries this, with a nice oily mouth feel, and creamed fruits giving way to a sharper spicier conclusion.

Ledaig 10 year old

GS – The nose is profoundly peaty, sweet and full, with notes of butter and smoked fish. Bold, yet sweet on the palate, with iodine, soft peat and heather. Developing spices. The finish is medium to long, with pepper, ginger, liquorice and peat.

DR – Peat and smoke on the nose, more fruity and malty on the palate but with a definite tarry heart, and then gristly smoke in the finish.

Burn Stewart Distillers, owners of Bunnahabhain, Deanston and Tobermory distilleries, have been doing well lately with the latest accounts showing a 30% increase in turnover and operating profits increasing by 50% to £6.9m. The whole range of single malts has been revamped and their flagship blend, Scottish Leader, is selling well, not least in Taiwan where the company opened up a branch as early as 1995. However, they have suffered as a result of an owner, CL Financial, that had been in economic difficulties for a few years now and it probably came as a relief when South African drinks giant, Distell, took over the company in spring of 2013.

It may come as a surprise to visitors to the windswept and rainy Western Isles that the island of Mull was named the driest place in the UK in March 2013. Only 1,8 inches of rain fell and forced Tobermory distillery to cease operating for a week and the same occurrence happened in summer 2012.

The distillery has alternatingly been called Tobermory and Ledaig, and single malt is released under both names with Ledaig being reserved for the peated versions with a phenol content of 30-40ppm. Peat was used in the olden days and was re-introduced in 1996 when Burn Stewart's Master Blender, Ian Macmillan, decided to recreate the old style of Tobermory single malt.

Tobermory is equipped with a traditional cast iron mash tun, four wooden washbacks and two pairs of stills with unusual S-shaped lyne arms to increase the reflux. During 2013, production will be 750,000 litres of alcohol with a 50/50 split between peated Ledaig and unpeated Tobermory. The core range from Tobermory distillery is 10 and 15 year old Tobermory and 10 year old Ledaig. A limited 40 year old Ledaig was released in 2013, as well as two bottlings exclusively available at the distillery visitor centre – a 19 year old Tobermory and a 16 year old Ledaig, both with a second maturation for over 10 years in PX sherry casks.

10 years old

Tomatin

Owner:
Tomatin Distillery Co
(Takara Shuzo Co. Ltd., Kokubu & Co., The
Marubeni Corporation)

Region/district:
Highland

Founded: 1897
Status: Active (vc)
Capacity: 5 000 000 litres

Address: Tomatin, Inverness-shire IV13 7YT

Tel: 01463 248144 (vc)
website: www.tomatin.com

History:

1897 – The Inverness businessmen behind Tomatin Spey Distillery Company found Tomatin.

1906 – Production ceases.

1909 – Production resumes through Tomatin Distillers Co. Ltd.

1956 – Stills are increased from two to four.

1958 – Another two stills are added.

1961 – The six stills are increased to ten.

1964 – One more still is installed.

1974 – The stills now total 23 and the maltings closes.

1985 – The distillery company goes into liquidation.

1986 – Two long-time customers, Takara Shuzo Co. and Okara & Co., buy Tomatin through Tomatin Distillery Co. Tomatin thus becomes the first distillery to be acquired by Japanese interests.

1997 – Tomatin Distillery Co buys J. W. Hardie and the brand Antiquary.

1998 – Okura & Co, owners of 20% of Tomatin Distillery, is liquidated and Marubeni buys out part of their shareholding.

2004 – Tomatin 12 years is launched.

2005 – A 25 year old and a 1973 Vintage are released.

2006 – An 18 year old and a 1962 Vintage are launched.

2008 – A 30 and a 40 year old as well as several vintages from 1975 and 1995 are released.

2009 – A 15 year old, a 21 year old and four single casks (1973, 1982, 1997 and 1999) are released.

2010 – The first peated release - a 4 year old exclusive for Japan.

2011 – A 30 year old and Tomatin Decades are released.

2013 – Cù Bòcan, the first peated Tomatin, is released.

Tomatin 12 year old

GS – Barley, spice, buttery oak and a floral note on the nose. Sweet and medium-bodied, with toffee apples, spice and herbs in the mouth. Medium-length in the finish, with sweet fruitiness.

DR – Strawberry cream and raspberry ripple ice cream and pecan on the nose, delicate zesty barley on the palate, with a sweet citrus and powdery spice mix contributing to a very welcoming finish. More-ish.

It is not uncommon with long-term retainers within the Scotch whisky industry, but Douglas Campbell is quite unique. The former distillery manager of Tomatin and current brand ambassador was honoured in 2011 for his 50 years at the distillery with a limited release of Tomatin Decades. Early in 2013, and in the company of Olympian gold medalists, his services to the distillery and the community of Tomatin were recognised again when he was honoured as a Member of the Order of the British Empire (MBE).

In a way, you could say that Tomatin single malt has fared the same way – from quietly going on with its business to, in the last few years, being acknowledged for its high quality whisky. Tomatin´s changed image is the direct outcome of a conscious choice where the change from producing bulk whisky for other companies to establishing a broad range of single malts under its own brand name, has paved the way. In 2012, 250,000 bottles of Tomatin were sold while the blends in the company (mainly Talisman and The Antiquary) sold over 1 million bottles.

The distillery is equipped with one 8 tonne stainless steel mash tun, 12 stainless steel washbacks with a fermentation time from 57 to 110 hours and six pairs of stills (only four of the spirit stills are used). The goal is to produce 2,2 million litres in 2013 of which 2% will be peated (18ppm). There is also a cooperage on site and Tomatin recently became the first distillery to install a boiler fired by wood pellets.

The core range of single malts consists of *12, 15, 18, 30 year old* and the recently introduced *Legacy* with no age statement which has been matured in first fill casks (90% bourbon and 10% virgin oak). In 2012 a limited *15 year old* with a maturation in a combination of bourbon and Tempranillo wine casks was released and, in summer 2013, it was time for the first official release of a peated Tomatin under the name *Cù Bòcan*. It carries no age statement and is a mix of bourbon- and sherrymatured whiskies.

Cù Bòcan

Tomintoul

Owner:
Angus Dundee Distillers

Region/district:
Speyside

Founded: 1964

Status: Active

Capacity: 3 300 000 litres

Address: Ballindalloch, Banffshire AB37 9AQ

Tel: 01807 590274

website: www.tomintouldistillery.co.uk

History:

1964 –The distillery is founded by Tomintoul Distillery Ltd, which is owned by Hay & MacLeod & Co. and W. & S. Strong & Co.

1973 – Scottish & Universal Investment Trust, owned by the Fraser family, buys the distillery. It buys Whyte & Mackay the same year and transfers Tomintoul to that company.

1974 – The two stills are increased to four and Tomintoul 12 years is launched.

1978 – Lonhro buys Scottish & Universal Investment Trust.

1989 – Lonhro sells Whyte & Mackay to Brent Walker.

1990 – American Brands buys Whyte & Mackay.

1996 – Whyte & Mackay changes name to JBB (Greater Europe).

2000 – Angus Dundee plc buys Tomintoul.

2002 – Tomintoul 10 year is launched.

2003 – Tomintoul 16 years is launched.

2004 – Tomintoul 27 years is launched.

2005 – A young, peated version called Old Ballantruan is launched.

2008 – 1976 Vintage and Peaty Tang are released.

2009 – A 14 year old and a 33 year old are released.

2010 – A 12 year old Port wood finish is released.

2011 – A 21 year old, a 10 year old Ballantruan and Vintage 1966 are released.

2012 – Old Ballantruan 10 years old is released.

2013 – A 31 year old single cask is released.

Nowadays, all whisky producers in Scotland are involved in reducing energy costs, as well as its carbon footprint. It is rare, though, to see four different distilleries with three different owners work harmoniously on a project where both economy and environment can benefit, but this is exactly what is happening with the building of a Speyside gas pipeline. The idea is, by way of a new 16-mile pipeline, to link together The Glenlivet, Tormore, Cragganmore and Tomintoul distilleries with Scotland's main gas network. The project, when finished in spring 2014, will cut the distilleries' energy bills by 30% and the conversion from fuel oil will reduce carbon emissions by up to a third.

The owners of Tomintoul, Angus Dundee Distillers, who also own Glencadam distillery, are one of Scotland's biggest exporters of whisky with a huge range of blended whisky. In 2003 they built their own blend centre at Tomintoul with 14 whisky storage vats, in order to handle the large production. They also operate a bottling and warehouse plant in Coatbridge.

Tomintoul distillery is equipped with a 11,6 tonnes semi lauter mash tun, six washbacks, all made of stainless steel and with a fermentation time of 54 hours, and two pairs of stills. There are currently 15 mashes per week, which means that capacity is used to its maximum, and the six racked warehouses have a storage capacity of 116,000 casks. The malt used for mashing is lightly peated but every year a small batch of heavily peated spirit (55ppm) is produced.

The core range consists of *10, 14, 16* and *21 years old*. The peaty side of Tomintoul is represented by *Old Ballantruan, Peaty Tang* (a vatting of 4-5 year old peated Tomintoul and 8 year old unpeated Tomintoul) and the latest addition, *Old Ballantruan 10 years old*, launched in 2012. May 2013 saw the first official single cask bottling from the distillery – a *31 year old* distilled in 1981, matured in a bourbon cask and bottled at 53,9%. Older, limited editions have included a *12 year old portwood finish*, the *1976 Vintage* and a *12 year old Oloroso finish*.

Tomintoul 10 year old

GS – A light, fresh and fruity nose, with ripe peaches and pineapple cheesecake, delicate spice and background malt. Medium-bodied, fruity and fudgy on the palate. The finish offers wine gums, mild, gently spiced oak, malt and a suggestion of smoke.

DR – Toffee and fruit on the nose then an easy, pleasant rounded and sweet barley taste before a gently fading finish.

16 years old

Tormore

Owner:
Chivas Brothers
(Pernod Ricard)

Region/district:
Speyside

Founded: **Status:** **Capacity:**
1958 Active 4 400 000 litres

Address: Tormore, Advie, Grantown-on-Spey,
Morayshire PH26 3LR

Tel: **website:**
01807 510244 -

History:
1958 – Schenley International, owners of Long
John, founds the distillery.

1960 – The distillery is ready for production.

1972 – The number of stills is increased from
four to eight.

1975 – Schenley sells Long John and its
distilleries (including Tormore) to Whitbread.

1989 – Allied Lyons (to become Allied Domecq)
buys the spirits division of Whitbread.

1991 – Allied Distillers introduce Caledonian
Malts where Miltonduff, Glendronach and
Laphroaig are represented besides Tormore.
Tormore is later replaced by Scapa.

2004 – Tormore 12 year old is launched as an
official bottling.

2005 – Chivas Brothers (Pernod Ricard)
becomes new owners through the acquisition
of Allied Domecq.

2012 – Production capacity is increased by
20%.

To say that Tormore is an unusual distillery is like saying that the Beatles was a well-known pop group – a definite understatement! Tormore looks like no other distillery in Scotland and those of you who have travelled the A95 in the middle of Speyside will probably agree. Sitting right next to the road, with its white washed walls, the green copper roofs and the extraordinary barred windows, its view is stupendous! When it was built in the 1950s by Schenley International, owners of Long John, it was decided that it should become a showpiece. The architect, Sir Albert Richardson, was given carte blanche and no expenses were saved – the total for the building came to £600,000 which, today, equates to more than £10 million. Tormore was closed from November 2011 to January 2012 for an upgrade of the distillery. Three more washbacks were installed in a separate building and this means that the production capacity has increased by 20% to 4,4 million litres of alcohol. The beautiful still room was also refurbished and all stills now have external heaters instead of steam coils inside the stills, thus reducing the energy needed by 15%. The equipment consists of one stainless steel full lauter mash tun, 11 stainless steel washbacks and four pairs of stills. Tormore single malt is known for its fruity and light character which is achieved by a clear wort, a slow distillation and by using purifiers on all the stills.
Tormore has recently become involved in a new project together with three other distilleries in the neighbourhood (Glenlivet, Cragganmore and Tomintoul) where the idea is to link all distilleries with a 16 mile gas pipeline. The project will be completed in 2014 and should cut the distilleries' energy bills by 30% and the conversion from fuel oil should further reduce carbon emissions by up to a third.
Nearly everything that is produced at Tormore goes into a variety of blended Scotch and there is only one official bottling, a *12 year old* which was intro-duced in 2004/5.

Tormore 12 year old

GS – Caramel on the nose, with hints of lemon and mint, mildly spicy, gentle and enticing. Good weight of body, and a creamy, honeyed mouth feel. Fudge and mixed spices, notably ginger, dry in the increasingly complex finish.

DR – A perfumey and delicate smell on the nose and soft but pleasant palate with macaroni cake and toasted almond in the mix, and a soft fading finish.

12 years old

Tullibardine

Owner:
Picard Vins & Spiritueux

Region/district:
Highlands

Founded: 1949
Status: Active (vc)

Capacity:
2 900 000 litres

Address: Blackford, Perthshire PH4 1QG

Tel: 01764 682252

website: www.tullibardine.com

History:

1949 – The architect William Delmé-Evans founds the distillery.

1953 – The distillery is sold to Brodie Hepburn.

1971 – Invergordon Distillers buys Brodie Hepburn Ltd.

1973 – The number of stills increases to four.

1993 – Whyte & Mackay (owned by Fortune Brands) buys Invergordon Distillers.

1994 – Tullibardine is mothballed.

1996 – Whyte & Mackay changes name to JBB Greater Europe).

2001 – JBB (Greater Europe) is bought out from Fortune Brands by management and changes name to Kyndal (Whyte & Mackay from 2003).

2003 – A consortium buys Tullibardine for £1.1 million. The distillery is in production again by December. The first official bottling from the new owner is a 10 year old from 1993.

2004 – Three new vintage malts are launched.

2005 – Three wood finishes from 1993, Port, Moscatel and Marsala, are launched together with a 1986 John Black selection.

2006 – Vintage 1966, Sherry Wood 1993 and a new John Black selection are launched.

2007 – Five different wood finishes and a couple of single cask vintages are released.

2008 – A Vintage 1968 40 year old is released.

2009 – Aged Oak is released.

2011 – Three vintages (1962, 1964 and 1976) and a wood finish are released. Picard buys the distillery.

2013 – A completely new range is launched – Sovereign, 225 Sauternes, 228 Burgundy, 500 Sherry, 20 year old and 25 year old.

Tullibardine Sovereign

GS – Floral on the nose, with new-mown hay, vanilla and fudge. Fruity on the palate, with milk chocolate, brazil nuts, marzipan, malt, and a hint of cinnamon. Cocoa, vanilla, a squeeze of lemon and more spice in the finish.

Since Picard bought Tullibardine in November 2011, we have been waiting for the inevitable restructuring of both the range of bottlings, as well as the distillery itself. In spring 2013 the time had come to launch an entirely new set up of whiskies (see below) and the visitor centre, which has 120,000 visitors annually, was given a face lift where the owners will now concentrate on smaller, but more focused tours. There are also plans for a new bottling line sometime during 2014 which will be able to take care of not only the Tullibardine single malts, but also Highland Queen and Muirhead´s – two brands owned by Picard. Both of these brands consist of blended Scotch, as well as single malts and according to law, single malt Scotch must be bottled in Scotland.

The equipment at Tullibardine consists of a 6 tonne stainless steel semi-lauter mash tun, nine stainless steel washbacks with a minimum fermentation of 52 hours and two pairs of stills. In 2013 the owners expect the distillery to run at full capacity, which translates to 2,9 million litres of alcohol in the year. The legendary distillery manager, John Black, who has been in the industry since 1958 and with Tullibardine distillery since the re-opening in 2003, retired in 2013.

The whole range of Tullibardine single malts was completely revamped in spring 2013. What used to be a mix of non aged bottlings (Aged Oak), wood finishes, vintages and single casks was replaced by a bourbon matured core expression without age statement, *Sovereign*, three wood finishes, *225 Sauternes finish*, *228 Burgundy finish* and *500 Sherry finish* and, finally, two older bottlings – *20 year old* and *25 year old*. All three wood finishes have received a second maturation for 12 months in other casks and the names refer to the sizes of these casks. The Sauternes casks came from Ch Suduiraut, the Burgundy casks previously held red wine from Chassagne Montrachet (owned by Picard) and for the Sherry finish, mainly PX casks were used.

Sovereign

The really new ones!

Abhainn Dearg

Owner:	Region/district:	
Mark Tayburn	Islands (Isle of Lewis)	
Founded:	Status:	Capacity:
2008	Active	c 20 000 litres
Address:		
Carnish, Isle of Lewis, Outer Hebrides HS2 9EX		
Tel:	website:	
01851 672429	www.abhainndearg.co.uk	

In September 2008, spirit flowed from a newly constructed distillery in Uig on the island of Lewis in the Outer Hebrides. The Gaelic name of this distillery is Abhainn Dearg which means Red River, and the founder and owner is Mark "Marko" Tayburn who was born and raised on the island.

Part of the distillery was converted from an old fish farm while some of the buildings are new. There are two 500 kg mash tuns made of stainless steel and two 7,500 litre washbacks made of Douglas fir with a fermentation time of 4 days. The two stills are modelled after an old, illicit still which is now on display at the distillery. The wash still has a capacity of 2,112 litres and the spirit still 2,057 litres. Both have very long necks and steeply descending lye pipes leading out into two wooden worm tubs. To start with Marko is using ex-bourbon barrels for maturation but is planning for ex-sherry butts as well. Some 50 tonnes of malted barley is imported while 5 tonnes is grown locally and slightly peated.

The first limited release, in October 2011, was a 3 year old unpeated whisky and beginning of 201 a cask strength version (58%) was released.

Daftmill

Owner:	Region/district:	Founded:
Francis Cuthbert	Lowlands	2005
Status:	Capacity:	website:
Active	c 65 000 litres	www.daftmill.com
Address:		Tel:
By Cupar, Fife KY15 5RF		01337 830303

Permission was granted in 2003 for a steading at Daftmill Farmhouse in Fife, just a few miles west of Cupar and dating back to 1655, to be converted into a distillery. Contrary to most other new distilleries selling shares in their enterprise, Francis Cuthbert funded the entire operation himself. The first distillation was on 16th December 2005 and around 20,000 litres are produced in a year.

It is run as a typical farmhouse distillery. The barley is grown on the farm and they also supply other distilleries. Of the total 800 tonnes that Francis harvests in a year, around 100 tonnes are used for his own whisky. The malting is done without peat at Crisp´s in Alloa. The equipment consists of a one tonne semi-lauter mash tun with a copper dome, two stainless steel washbacks with a fermentation between 72 and 100 hours and one pair of stills with slightly ascending lyne arms. The equipment is designed to give a lot of copper contact, a lot of reflux. The wash still has a capacity of 3,000 litres and the spirit still 2,000 litres.

Francis Cuthbert´s aim is to do a light, Lowland style whisky similar to Rosebank. In order to achieve this they have very short foreshots (five minutes) and the spirit run starts at 78% to capture all of the fruity esters and already comes off at 73%. The spirit is filled mainly into ex-bourbon casks, always first fill, but there are also a few sherry butts in the two dunnage warehouses.

Taking care of the farm obviously prohibits Francis from producing whisky full time. His silent season is during spring and autumn when work in the fields take all of his time. Whisky distillation is therefore reserved for June-August and November-February. During that period he manages to do 2-4 mashes per week. Even though the maturing whisky is now 8 years old, Francis himself say that the first release is still a good few years away

Ailsa Bay

Owner:		Region/district:
William Grant & Sons		Lowlands
Founded:	**Status:**	**Capacity:**
2007	Active	12 000 000 litres
Address:		**Tel:**
Girvan, Ayrshire KA26 9PT		01465 713091

Commisioned in September 2007, it only took nine months to build this distillery on the same site as Girvan Distillery near Ayr on Scotland's west coast. Until recently, it was equipped with a 12,5 tonne full lauter mash tun, 12 washbacks made of stainless steel and eight stills. In August 2013 however, it was time for a major expansion when yet another mash tun, 12 more washbacks and eight more stills were commissioned, doubling the capacity to 12 million litres of alcohol.

Each washback will hold 50,000 litres and fermentation time is between 72 and 78 hours. The stills are made according to the same standards as Balvenie's and some of them have stainless steel condensers instead of copper. That way, they have the possibility of making batches of a more sulphury spirit if desired. A unique feature is the rectangular spirit safe which sits between the two rows of stills. Each side corresponds to one specific still. Another feature is the preheater for the wash. By using this technique at Ailsa Bay, the wash enters the still preheated at 60° C.

To increase efficiency and to get more alcohol, high gravity distillation is used. The wash stills are heated using external heat exchangers but they also have interior steam coils. The spirit stills are heated by steam coils.

Four different types of spirit are produced; one lighter and sweeter, one heavier and two peated with the peatiest having a malt specification of 50ppm. A majority of the casks (60-70%) used for maturation, are refill bourbon casks and the rest is made up of first fill bourbon and sherry casks. The production is destined to become a part of Grant's blended Scotch which is currently the fourth most popular Scotch in the world with 55 million bottles sold in 2012.

Roseisle

Owner:	Region/district:
Diageo	Highlands
Founded: **Status:**	**Capacity:**
2009 Active	12 500 000 litres
Address:	**Tel:**
Roseisle, Morayshire IV30 5YP	01343 832100

Roseisle distillery is located on the same site as the already existing Roseisle maltings just west of Elgin. The distillery has won several awards for its ambition towards sustainable production. In 2012 it was named one of the world's most hi-tech distilleries by Popular Mechanics magazine due to its commitment to renewable energy.

The distillery is equipped with two stainless steel mash tuns with a 13 tonnes charge each. There are 14 huge (115,500 litres) stainless steel washbacks and 14 stills with the wash stills being heated by external heat exchangers while the spirit stills are heated using steam coils. The spirit vapours are cooled through copper condensers but on three spirit stills and three wash stills there are also stainless steel condensers attached, that you can switch to for a more sulphury spirit. During 2013 the plan is to produce 11,4 million litres of alcohol. The total cost for the distillery was £40m and how to use the hot water in an efficient way was very much a focal point from the beginning. For example, Roseisle is connected by means of two

long pipes with Burghead maltings, 3 km north of the distillery. Hot water is pumped from Roseisle and then used in the seven kilns at Burghead and cold water is then pumped back to Roseisle. The pot ale from the distillation will be piped into anaerobic fermenters to be transformed into biogas and the dried solids will act as a biomass fuel source. The biomass burner on the site, producing steam for the distillery, covers 72% of the total requirement. Furthermore, green technology has reduced the emission of carbon dioxide to only 15% of an ordinary, same-sized distillery.

During 2013 they will concentrate on producing a whisky with a light Speyside character and so far no substantial quantities of peated spirit has been distilled. For the heavy style a fermentation time of 50-60 hours is used and for the lighter style, 75 hours.

Wolfburn

Owner:	Region/district:	
Aurora Brewing Ltd	Northern Highlands	
Founded:	**Status:**	**Capacity:**
2013	Active	120 000 litres
Address:		
Henderson Park, Thurso, Caithness KW14 7XW		
Tel:	**website:**	
01465 713091	www.wolfburn.com	

The malt is unpeated and the intention is to create a smooth whisky. The experienced Shane Fraser, who used to be the distillery manager of Glenfarclas, joined the company as production manager late in 2012.

This is now the most northerly distillery on the Scottish mainland (thereby displacing Pulteney in Wick). The owners have chosen a site that is situated 350 metres from the ruins of the old Wolfburn Distillery which was founded in 1821 and closed down during the latter half of the 19th century. Planning consent was received from the authorities in Caithness in June 2012, construction work commenced in August and the first newmake came off the stills at the end of January 2013.

The distillery is equipped with a 1,1 ton semi-lauter mash tun with a copper canopy, three stainless steel washbacks (from the demolished Caperdonich distillery), one wash still (5,500 litres) and one spirit still (3,600 litres). Wolfburn uses a mix of casks: approximately one third of the spirit is laid down in ex-bourbon quarter casks, a further third is in ex-bourbon hogsheads as well as barrels, and the final third is laid down in ex-Miguel sherry butts.

Strathearn

Owner:	Region/district:
Tony Reeman-Clark, David Lang and David Wight	Southern Highlands
Founded:	**Status:**	**Capacity:**
2013	Active	c 30 000 litres
Address:		
Bachilton Farm Steading, Methven PH1 3QX		
Tel:	**website:**	
01738 840 100	www.strathearndistillery.com	

sers. For maturation, the owners will use oak octaves (50 litre casks) made of virgin French oak and virgin American oak, but ex-sherry, ex-port and ex-wine casks will also come into use at a later stage. Both peated and un-peated whisky will be produced and the first bottlings are expected to appear in September 2016.

This is something as unique as Scotland´s first micro-distillery. Admittedly, Abhainn Dearg on Isle of Lewis potentially has the same capacity but the stills at Strathearn are considerably smaller. It is the brainchild of Tony Reeman-Clark, David Lang and David Wight where the idea was ignited during a conversation at Whisky Fringe in Edinburgh a couple of years ago. In February 2013 they received the planning permission from the council and six months later, the distillery was up and running. It is situated at the 160 year old Bachilton Farm near Methven which is a few miles west of Perth. They started gin production at the beginning of August and the first whisky was distilled a couple of weeks later.

The distillery is equipped with a stainless steel mash tun, two stainless steel washbacks (2,000 litres), a 1,000 litre wash still and a 500 litre spirit still. Both stills are of the Alambic type, made in Portugal and with vertical tube copper conden-

Distilleries per owner

c = closed, d = demolished, mb = mothballed, dm = dismantled

Diageo
Auchroisk
Banff (d)
Benrinnes
Blair Athol
Brora (c)
Bushmills
Caol Ila
Cardhu
Clynelish
Coleburn (dm)
Convalmore (dm)
Cragganmore
Dailuaine
Dallas Dhu (c)
Dalwhinnie
Dufftown
Glen Albyn (d)
Glendullan
Glen Elgin
Glenesk (dm)
Glenkinchie
Glenlochy (d)
Glenlossie
Glen Mhor (d)
Glen Ord
Glen Spey
Glenury Royal (d)
Inchgower
Knockando
Lagavulin
Linkwood
Mannochmore
Millburn (dm)
Mortlach
North Port (d)
Oban
Pittyvaich (d)
Port Ellen (dm)
Rosebank (c)
Roseisle
Royal Lochnagar
St Magdalene (dm)
Strathmill
Talisker
Teaninich

Pernod Ricard
Aberlour
Allt-a-Bhainne
Braeval
Caperdonich (d)
Glenallachie
Glenburgie
Glen Keith
Glenlivet
Glentauchers
Glenugie (dm)
Imperial (d)
Inverleven (d)
Kinclaith (d)
Lochside (d)
Longmorn
Midleton

Miltonduff
Scapa
Strathisla
Tormore

Edrington Group
Glenrothes
Glenturret
Highland Park
Macallan

Inver House (Thai Beverage)
Balblair
Balmenach
Glen Flagler (d)
Knockdhu
Pulteney
Speyburn

John Dewar & Sons (Bacardi)
Aberfeldy
Aultmore
Craigellachie
Macduff
Royal Brackla

William Grant & Sons
Ailsa Bay
Balvenie
Glenfiddich
Kininvie
Ladyburn (dm)

Whyte & Mackay (United Spirits)
Dalmore
Fettercairn
Jura
Tamnavulin

Beam
Ardmore
Cooley
Kilbeggan
Laphroaig

Morrison Bowmore (Suntory)
Auchentoshan
Bowmore
Glen Garioch

Burn Stewart Distillers
(Distell Group Ltd)
Bunnahabhain
Deanston
Tobermory

Benriach Distillery Co.
Benriach
Glendronach
Glenglassaugh

Loch Lomond Distillers
Glen Scotia
Littlemill (d)
Loch Lomond

J & A Mitchell
Glengyle
Springbank

Glenmorangie Co.
(Moët Hennessy)
Ardbeg
Glenmorangie

Angus Dundee Distillers
Glencadam
Tomintoul

Ian Macleod Distillers
Glengoyne
Tamdhu

Campari Group
Glen Grant

Isle of Arran Distillers
Arran

**Signatory Vintage
Scotch Whisky Co.**
Edradour

Tomatin Distillery Co.
(Marubeni Europe plc)
Tomatin

J & G Grant
Glenfarclas

Rémy Cointreau
Bruichladdich

**Co-ordinated
Development Services**
Bladnoch

Gordon & MacPhail
Benromach

La Martiniquaise
Glen Moray

Ben Nevis Distillery Ltd (Nikka)
Ben Nevis

Tullibardine Ltd
(Picard Vins & Spiritueux)
Tullibardine

Speyside Distillers Co.
(Harvey's of Edinburgh)
Speyside

Kilchoman Distillery Co.
Kilchoman

Cuthbert family
Daftmill

Mark Tayburn
Abhainn Dearg

Aurora Brewing Ltd
Wolfburn

**Tony Reeman-Clark,
David Lang & David Wight**
Strathearn

Closed Distilleries

Brora Distillery

Brora

Owner:		Region/district:
Diageo		Northern Highlands
Founded:	**Status:**	**Capacity:**
1819	Closed	

History:

1819 – The Marquis of Stafford, 1st Duke of Sutherland, founds the distillery as Clynelish Distillery.

1827 – The first licensed distiller, James Harper, files for bankruptcy and John Matheson takes over.

1828 – James Harper is back as licensee.

1834 – Andrew Ross takes over the license.

1846 – George Lawson & Sons takes over.

1896 – James Ainslie & Heilbron takes over and rebuilds the facilities.

1912 – James Ainslie & Co. narrowly escapes bankruptcy and Distillers Company Limited (DCL) takes over together with James Risk.

1916 – John Walker & Sons buys a stake of James Risk's stocks.

1925 – DCL buys out Risk.

1930 – Scottish Malt Distillers takes over.

1931 – The distillery is mothballed.

1939 – Production restarts.

1960 – The distillery becomes electrified (until now it has been using locally mined coal from Brora).

1967 – A new distillery is built adjacent to the first one, it is also named Clynelish and both operate in parallel from August.

1968 – 'Old' Clynelish is mothballed in August.

1969 – 'Old' Clynelish is reopened as Brora and starts using a very peaty malt over the next couple of years

1983 – Brora is closed in March.

1995 – Brora 1972 (20 years) and Brora 1972 (22 years) are launched as Rare Malts.

1996 – Brora 1975 (20 years) is launched as a Rare Malt.

1998 – Brora 1977 (21 years) is launched as a Rare Malt.

2001 – Brora 1977 (24 years) is launched as a Rare Malt.

2002 – A 30 year old cask strength is released in a limited edition.

2003 – Brora 1982 (20 years) is launched as a Rare Malt.

2011 – The 10th release of Brora – a 32 year old.

2012 – The 11th release of Brora – a 35 year old.

2013 – The 12th release of Brora – a 35 year old.

Although founded under the name Clynelish distillery in 1819, it is under the name Brora that the single malt has enjoyed its newfound fame during the past two decades. The whisky has mostly appealed to peat freaks around the world but, for the first 140 years, it actually wasn't that peated. In 1967 DCL decided to build a new, modern distillery on the same site. This was given the name Clynelish and it was decided the old distillery should be closed. Shortly after, the demand for peated whisky, especially for the blend Johnnie Walker, increased and the old site re-opened but now under the name Brora and the "recipe" for the whisky was changed to a heavily peated malt. This continued from 1969 to 1973 and after that the peatiness was reduced, even if single peated batches turned up until the late seventies.

Brora closed permanently in 1983 but the buildings still stand next to the new Clynelish. The two stills, the feints receiver, the spirit receiver and the brass safe remain, while the warehouses are used for storage of spirit from Clynelish.

The first distillery was built in the time referred to as the Highland Clearances. Many land-owners wished to increase the yield of their lands and consequently went into large-scale sheep farming. Thousands of families were ruthlessly forced away and the most infamous of the large land-owners was the Marquis of Stafford who founded Clynelish (Brora) in 1819.

Since 1995 Diageo has regularly released different expressions of Brora in the *Rare Malts* series. The latest, which also became the last, appeared in 2003. In 2002 a new range was created, called *Special Releases* and bottlings of Brora have appeared ever since. In autumn 2012 the time had come for the 11th expression, a *35 year old* and the oldest ever distillery bottling of Brora. This was followed up in 2013 by another 35 year old distilled in 1977. Very few independent bottlings of Brora turn up nowadays. The latest was a 28 year old from Douglas Laing in 2009.

35 years old 1977

Banff

Owner:	Region:	Founded:	Status:
Diageo	Speyside	1824	Demolished

Banff's tragic history of numerous fires, explosions and bombings have contributed to its fame. The most spectacular incident was when a lone Junkers Ju-88 bombed one of the warehouses in 1941. Hundreds of casks exploded and several thousand litres of whisky were destroyed. The distillery was closed in 1983 and the buildings were destroyed in a fire in 1991. The distillery was owned for 80 years by the Simpson family but when their company filed for bankruptcy in 1932, it was sold to Scottish Malt Distillers which later would be a part of Diageo. When the distillery was at its largest it produced 1 million litres per year in three pairs of stills.

Recent bottlings:
There has only been one official Rare Malts bottling from 2004. A couple of expressions from 1975 were released in 2012; a 36 year old from Douglas Laing and a 37 year old from Duncan Taylor.

Caperdonich

Owner:	Region:	Founded:	Status:
Chivas Bros	Speyside	1897	Demolished

The distillery was founded by James Grant, owner of Glen Grant which was located in Rothes just a few hundred metres away. Five years after the opening, the distillery was shut down and was re-opened again in 1965 under the name Caperdonich. In 2002 it was mothballed yet again, never to be re-opened. Parts of the equipment were dismantled to be used in other distilleries within the company. In 2010 the distillery was sold to the manufacturer of copper pot stills, Forsyth´s in Rothes, and the distillery was demolished. In the old days a pipe connected Caperdonich and Glen Grant for easy transport of spirit, ready to be filled.

Recent bottlings:
An official cask strength was released in 2005. Recent independent bottlings are a 20 year old distilled in 1992 from Douglas Laing and a 30 year old (1982) from the same company. There is also Caperdonich Batch 3 from That Boutique-y Whisky Company.

Coleburn

Owner:	Region:	Founded:	Status:
Diageo	Speyside	1897	Dismantled

Like so many other distilleries, Coleburn was taken over by DCL (the predecessor of Diageo) in the 1930s. Although the single malt never became well known, Coleburn was used as an experimental workshop where new production techniques were tested. In 1985 the distillery was mothballed and never opened again. Two brothers, Dale and Mark Winchester, bought the buildings in 2004 with the intention of transforming the site into an entertainment centre. After a lengthy process, they were granted planning permission in 2010 and the reconstruction work, transforming it into a 60-bedroom hotel and a spa, has commenced.

Recent bottlings:
There has only been one official Rare Malts bottling from 2000, while Independent bottlings are also rare. One of the latest was a 36 year old released in 2006 by Signatory.

Convalmore

Owner:	Region:	Founded:	Status:
Diageo	Speyside	1894	Dismantled

This distillery is still intact and can be seen in Dufftown next to Balvenie distillery. The buildings were sold to William Grant´s in 1990 and they now use it for storage. Diageo, however, still holds the rights to the brand. In the early 20th century, experimental distilling of malt whisky in continuous stills (the same method used for producing grain whisky) took place at Convalmore. The distillery closed in 1985. One of the more famous owners of this distillery was James Buchanan who used Convalmore single malt as a part of his famous blend Black & White. He later sold the distillery to DCL (later Diageo).

Recent bottlings:
A 28 year old was released by the owners in 2005. In autumn 2013, as part of the Special Releases, Diageo released a 36 year old distilled in 1977. The latest independent bottling was a 32 year old from 1975 released by Douglas Laing in 2007.

Dallas Dhu

Owner:	Region:	Founded:	Status:
Diageo	Speyside	1898	Closed

Dallas Dhu distillery is located along the A96 between Elgin and Inverness and is still intact, equipment and all, but hasn´t produced since 1983. Three years later, Diageo sold the distillery to Historic Scotland and it became a museum which is open all year round. In spring 2013 a feasibility study was commissioned by Historic Scotland to look at the possibilities of re-starting production again. One of the founders of the distillery, Alexander Edwards, belonged to the more energetic men in the 19th century Scotch whisky business. Not only did he start Dallas Dhu but also established Aultmore, Benromach and Craigellachie and owned Benrinnes and Oban.

Recent bottlings:
There are two Rare Malts bottlings from Diageo, the latest in 1997. The latest from independents is a 1979 bottled in 2012 by Gordon & Macphail.

Glen Albyn

Owner:	Region:	Founded:	Status:
Diageo	N Highlands	1844	Demolished

Glen Albyn was one of three Inverness distilleries surviving into the 1980s. Today, there is no whisky production left in the city. The first forty years were not very productive for Glen Albyn. Fire and bankruptcy prevented the success and in 1866 the buildings were transformed into a flour mill. In 1884 it was converted back to a distillery and continued producing whisky until 1983 when it was closed by the owners at the time, Diageo. Three years later the distillery was demolished.

Recent bottlings:
Glen Albyn has been released as a Rare Malt by the owners on one occasion. It is rarely seen from independents as well. In 2010, Signatory released a 29 year old and in 2012 a 1976 was bottled by Gordon & MacPhail.

Glenesk

Owner:	Region:	Founded:	Status:
Diageo	E Highlands	1897	Demolished

Few distilleries, if any, have operated under as many names as Glenesk; Highland Esk, North Esk, Montrose and Hillside. The distillery was one of four operating close to Montrose between Aberdeen and Dundee. Today only Glencadam remains. At one stage the distillery was re-built for grain production but reverted to malt distilling. In 1968 a large drum maltings was built adjacent to the distillery and the Glenesk maltings still operate today under the ownership of Boortmalt, the fifth largest producer of malt in the world. The distillery building was demolished in 1996.

Recent bottlings:
The single malt from Glen Esk has been bottled on three occasions as a Rare Malts, the latest in 1997. It is also very rare with the independent bottlers. Last time it appeared was in 2007 when Duncan Taylor released a 26 year old distilled in 1981.

Glenlochy

Owner:	Region:	Founded:	Status:
Diageo	W Highlands	1898	Demolished

Glenlochy was one of three distilleries in Fort William at the beginning of the 1900s. In 1908 Nevis merged with Ben Nevis distillery (which exists to this day) and in 1983 (a disastrous year for Scotch whisky industry when eight distilleries were closed), the time had come for Glenlochy to close for good. Today, all the buildings have been demolished, with the exception of the kiln with its pagoda roof and the malt barn which both have been turned into flats. For a period of time, the distillery was owned by an energetic and somewhat eccentric Canadian gentleman by the name of Joseph Hobbs who, after having sold the distillery to DCL, bought the second distillery in town, Ben Nevis.

Recent bottlings:
Glenlochy has occurred twice in the Rare Malts series. Recent independent bottlings from 2012 are a 32 year old from Signatory and 33 year old from Gordon & MacPhail.

Glen Mhor

Owner:	Region:	Founded:	Status:
Diageo	N Highlands	1892	Demolished

Glen Mhor is one of the last three Inverness distilleries and probably the one with the best reputation when it comes to the whisky that it produced. When the manager of nearby Glen Albyn, John Birnie, was refused to buy shares in the distillery he was managing, he decided to build his own and founded Glen Mhor. Almost thirty years later he also bought Glen Albyn and both distilleries were owned by the Birnie family until 1972 when they were sold to DCL. Glen Mhor was closed in 1983 and three years later the buildings were demolished. Today there is a supermarket on the site.

Recent bottlings:
Glen Mhor has appeared on two ocasions as Rare Malts. In the last couple of yerars there have been a 30 year old (1982) from Douglas Laing and a 29 year old (1982) from Signatory.

Glenury Royal

Owner:	Region:	Founded:	Status:
Diageo	E Highlands	1825	Demolished

Glenury Royal did not have a lucky start. Already a few weeks after inception in 1825, a fire destroyed the whole kiln, the greater part of the grain lofts and the malting barn, as well as the stock of barley and malt. Just two weeks later, distillery worker James Clark, fell into the boiler and died after a few hours. The founder of Glenury was the eccentric Captain Robert Barclay Allardyce, the first to walk 1000 miles in 1000 hours in 1809 and also an excellent middle-distance runner and boxer. The distillery closed in 1983 and part of the building was demolished a decade later with the rest converted into flats.

Recent bottlings:
Bottled as a Rare Malt on three occasions. Even more spectacular were three Diageo bottlings released 2003-2007; two 36 year olds and a 50 year old. In early 2012 a 40 year old was released. There are few independent bottlings, the latest being a 32 year old released in 2008 by Douglas Laing.

Imperial

Owner:	Region:	Founded:	Status:
Chivas Bros	Speyside	1897	Demolished

Rumours of the resurrection of this closed distillery have flourished from time to time during the last decade. Six years ago, the owner commissioned an estate agent to sell the buildings and convert them into flats. Shortly after that, Chivas Bros withdrew it from the market. In 2012, the owners announced that a new distillery would be built on the site, ready to start producing in 2015. Demolition of the old distillery began and in spring 2013 nothing was left but some old warehouses. In over a century, Imperial distillery was out of production for 60% of the time, but when it produced it had a capacity of 1,6 million litres per year.

Recent bottlings:
The 15 year old official bottling is hard to find these days but independents are more frequent. Mackillop´s released a 22 year old in 2013 and there have also been recent bottlings of Imperial 1995 from Duncan Taylor and Signatory.

Littlemill

Owner:	Region:	Founded:	Status:
Loch Lomond Distillery Co.	Lowlands	1772	Demolished

Until 1992 when production stopped, Littlemill was Scotland´s oldest working distillery and could trace its roots back to 1772, possibly even back to the 1750s! Triple distillation was practised at Littlemill until 1930 and after that some new equipment was installed, for example, stills with rectifying columns. The stills were also isolated with aluminium. The goal was to create whiskies that would mature faster. Two such experimental releases were Dunglas and Dumbuck. In 1996 the distillery was dismantled and part of the buildings demolished and in 2004 much of the remaining buildings were destroyed in a fire.

Recent bottlings:
Official bottlings still occur - in November 2012 a 21 year old was released. Several independent bottlings were released in 2013; three from Berry Brothers (1988, 1990 and 1992), a 1991 from Douglas Laing and a 21 year old from Master of Malt.

Lochside

Owner:　　*Region:*　　*Founded:*　　*Status:*
Chivas Bros　E Highlands　1957　　Demolished

Originally a brewery for two centuries, In the last 35 years of production Lochside was a whisky distillery. The Canadian, Joseph Hobbs, started distilling grain whisky and then added malt whisky production in the same way as he had done at Ben Nevis and Lochside. Most of the output was made for the blended whisky Sandy MacNab´s. In the early 1970s, the Spanish company DYC became the owner and the output was destined for Spanish blended whisky. In 1992 the distillery was mothballed and five years later all the equipment and stock were removed. All the distillery buildings were demolished in 2005.

Recent bottlings:
There are no recent official bottlings. A handful of independent bottlings, however, appeared in 2010/2011 and in 2012, the second edition of the unusual Lochside single blend (malt and grain distilled at the same distillery) distilled in 1965 was released by Adelphi Distillery.

Millburn

Owner:　　*Region:*　　*Founded:*　　*Status:*
Diageo　　N Highlands　1807　　Dismantled

The distillery is the oldest of those Inverness distilleries that made it into modern times and it is also the only one where the buildings are still standing. It is now a hotel and restaurant owned by Premier Inn. With one pair of stills, the capacity was no more than 300,000 litres. The problem with Millburn distillery was that it could never be expanded due to its location, sandwiched in between the river, a hill and the surrounding streets. It was bought by the London-based gin producer Booth´s in the 1920s and shortly after that absorbed into the giant DCL. In 1985 it was closed and three years later all the equipment was removed.

Recent bottlings:
Three bottlings of Millburn have appeared as Rare Malts, the latest in 2005. Other bottlings are scarce. The most recent was a 33 year old distilled in 1974, released by Blackadder.

North Port

Owner:　　*Region:*　　*Founded:*　　*Status:*
Diageo　　E Highlands　1820　　Demolished

The names North Port and Brechin are used interchangeably on the labels of this single malt. Brechin is the name of the city and North Port comes from a gate in the wall which surrounded the city. The distillery was run by members of the Guthrie family for more than a century until 1922 when DCL took over. Diageo then closed 21 of their 45 distilleries between 1983 and 1985 of which North Port was one. It was dismantled piece by piece and was finally demolished in 1994 to make room for a supermarket. The distillery had one pair of stills and produced 500,000 litres per year.

Recent bottlings:
North Port was released as a Rare Malt by Diageo twice and in 2005 also as part of the Special Releases (a 28 year old). Independent bottlings are very rare - the latest (distilled in 1981) was released by Duncan Taylor in 2008.

Port Ellen

Owner:		Region/district:
Diageo		Islay
Founded:	**Status:**	**Capacity:**
1825	Dismantled	

History:

1825 – Alexander Kerr Mackay assisted by Walter Campbell founds the distillery. Mackay runs into financial troubles after a few months and his three relatives John Morrison, Patrick Thomson and George Maclennan take over.

1833 – John Ramsay, a cousin to John Morrison, comes from Glasgow to take over.

1836 – Ramsay is granted a lease on the distillery from the Laird of Islay.

1892 – Ramsay dies and the distillery is inherited by his widow, Lucy.

1906 – Lucy Ramsay dies and her son Captain Iain Ramsay takes over.

1920 – Iain Ramsay sells to Buchanan-Dewar who transfers the administration to the company Port Ellen Distillery Co. Ltd.

1925 – Buchanan-Dewar joins Distillers Company Limited (DCL).

1929 – No production.

1930 – The distillery is mothballed.

1967 – In production again after reconstruction and doubling of the number of stills from two to four.

1973 – A large drum maltings is installed.

1980 – Queen Elisabeth visits the distillery and a commemorative special bottling is made.

1983 – The distillery is mothballed.

1987 – The distillery closes permanently but the maltings continue to deliver malt to all Islay distilleries.

1998 – Port Ellen 1978 (20 years) is released as a Rare Malt.

2000 – Port Ellen 1978 (22 years) is released as a Rare Malt.

2001 – Port Ellen cask strength first edition is released.

2011 – The 11th release of Port Ellen - a 32 year old from 1979.

2012 – The 12th release of Port Ellen - a 32 year old from 1979

2013 – The 13th release of Port Ellen - a 34 year old from 1978.

When Port Ellen closed in 1983 it was one of three Islay distilleries owned by Diageo (then DCL). The other two were Lagavulin and Caol Ila who had been operating uninterruptedly for many years. Port Ellen, mothballed since 1930, had only been producing for 16 years since re-opening, which made it easy for the owners to single out which Islay distillery was to close when malt whisky demand decreased. It was also the smallest of the three, with an annual output of 1,7 million litres of alcohol. The stills were shipped abroad early in the 1990s, possibly destined for India, and the distillery buildings were destroyed shortly afterwards. The whisky from Port Ellen is so popular, however, that rumours of distilling starting up again, do flourish from time to time.

Today, the site is associated with the huge drum maltings that was built in 1973. It supplies all Islay distilleries and a few others, with a large proportion of their malt. There are seven germination drums with a capacity of handling 51 tonnes of barley each. Three kilns are used to dry the barley and for every batch, an average of 6 tonnes of peat are required which means 2,000 tonnes per year. The peat was taken from Duich Moss until 1993 when conservationists managed to obtain national nature reserve status for the area in order to protect the thousands of Barnacle Geese that make a stop-over there during their migration. Nowadays the peat is taken from nearby Castlehill.

Besides a couple of versions in the *Rare Malts* series, Diageo began releasing one official bottling a year in 2001 and in autumn 2013 it was time for the 13th release and the oldest so far – a *34 year old* from refill American and European oak, distilled in 1977. Port Ellen is a favourite with independent bottlers as well. Some of the most recent ones are two from 1982 released by Douglas Laing and a 1979 bottled by Mackillop's Choice.

34 years old

Pittyvaich

Owner: Region: Founded: Status:
Diageo   Speyside   1974   Demolished

The life span for this relatively modern distillery was short. It was built by Arthur Bell & Sons on the same ground as Dufftown distillery which also belonged to them and the four stills were exact replicas of the Dufftown stills. Bells was bought by Guinness in 1985 and the distillery was eventually absorbed into DCL (later Diageo). For a few years in the 1990s, Pittyvaich was also a back up plant for gin distillation (in the same way that Auchroisk is today) in connection with the production of Gordon´s gin having moved from Essex till Cameronbridge. The distillery was mothballed in 1993 and has now been demolished.

Recent bottlings:
An official 12 year old Flora & Fauna can still be obtained and in 2009 a 20 year old was released by the owners. Recent independents include an 18 year old from Douglas Laing and a 23 year old rum finish by Cadenheads, both released in 2008.

Rosebank

Owner: Region: Founded: Status:
Diageo   Lowlands   1798   Dismantled

When Rosebank in Falkirk was mothballed in 1993, there were only two working malt distilleries left in the Lowlands – Glenkinchie and Auchentoshan. The whisky from the distillery has always had a great amount of supporters and there was a glimmer of hope that a new company would start up the distillery again. At the beginning of 2010 though, most of the equipment was stolen and furthermore, Diageo has indicated that they are not interested in selling the brand. The buildings are still intact and most of them have been turned into restaurants, offices and flats. The whisky from Rosebank was triple distilled.

Recent bottlings:
The official 12 year old Flora & Fauna can still be found and in autumn 2011 a 21 year old Special Release appeared. The latest independent bottling was released in 2013, a 22 year old from Mackillop´s Choice.

St Magdalene

Owner: Region: Founded: Status:
Diageo   Lowlands   1795   Dismantled

At one time, the small town of Linlithgow in East Lothian had no less than five distilleries. St Magdalene was one of them and also the last to close in 1983. The distillery came into ownership of the giant DCL quite early (1912) and was at the time a large distillery with 14 washbacks, five stills and with the possibility of producing more than 1 million litres of alcohol. Ten years after the closure the distillery was carefully re-built into flats, making it possible to still see most of the old buildings, including the pagoda roofs.

Recent bottlings:
These include two official bottlings in the Rare Malts series. In 2008/2009 a handful of independent releases appeared, all of them distilled in 1982 and released by Ian MacLeod, Douglas Laing, Blackadder, Signatory and Berry Brother. The latest were two 28 year olds from Douglas Laing and Mackillop´s released in 2011.

Ben Wyvis

Owner: *Region:*   *Founded:*   *Status:*
Whyte & Mackay   N Highlands   1965   Dismantled

The large grain distillery, Invergordon, today producing 36 million litres of grain whisky per year, was established in 1959 on the Cromarty Firth, east of Alness. Six years later a small malt distillery, Ben Wyvis, was built on the same site with the purpose of producing malt whisky for Invergordon Distiller's blends. The distillery was equipped with one mash tun, six washbacks and one pair of stills. Funnily enough the stills are still in use today at Glengyle distillery. Production at Ben Wyvis stopped in 1976 and in 1977 the distillery was closed and dismantled.

Bottlings:
There have been only a few releases of Ben Wyvis. The first, a 27 year old, was released by Invergordon in 1999, followed by a 31 year old from Signatory in 2000 and finally a 37 year old from Kyndal (later Whyte & Mackay) in 2002. It is highly unlikely that there will be more Ben Wyvis single malt to bottle.

Inverleven

Owner: *Region:*   *Founded:*   *Status:*
Chivas Bros   Lowlands   1938   Demolished

Dumbarton was the largest grain distillery in Scotland when it was built in 1938. It was mothballed in 2002 and finally closed in 2003 when Allied Domecq moved all their grain production to Strathclyde. On the same site, Inverleven malt distillery was built, equipped with one pair of traditional pot stills. In 1956 a Lomond still was added and this still (with the aid of Inverleven's wash still), technically became a second distillery called Lomond. Inverleven was mothballed in 1991and finally closed. The Lomond still is now working again since 2010 at Bruichladdich distillery.

Bottlings:
The first official bottling of Inverleven came as late as in 2010 when Chivas Bros released a 36 year old in a new range called Deoch an Doras. The latest independent was a 34 year old released by Signatory in 2011. The whisky from the Lomond still was bottled in 1992 by the Scotch Malt Whisky Society.

Glen Flagler / Killyloch

Owner: *Region:*   *Founded:*   *Status:*
Inver House   Lowlands   1964   Closed

In 1964 Inver House Distillers was bought by the American company, Publicker Industries, and that same year they decided to expand the production side as well. Moffat Paper Mills in Airdrie was bought and rebuilt into one grain distillery (Garnheath) and two malt distilleries (Glen Flagler and Killyloch). A maltings was also built which, at the time, became the biggest in Europe. The American interest in the Scotch whisky industry faded rapidly and Killyloch was closed in 1975, while Glen Flagler continued to produce for another decade.

Bottlings:
Glen Flagler was bottled as an 8 year old by the owners in the 70s. The next release came in the mid 1990s when Signatory released both Glen Flagler and Killyloch (23 year old) and finally in 2003 when Inver House bottled a Glen Flagler 1973 and a Killyloch 1967. A peated version of Glen Flagler, produced until 1970, was called Islebrae.

Kinclaith

Owner: *Region:*   *Founded:*   *Status:*
Chivas Bros   Lowlands   1957   Demolished

This was the last malt distillery to be built in Glasgow and was constructed on the grounds of Strathclyde grain distillery by Seager Evans (later Long John International). Strathclyde still exists today and produces 40 million litres of grain spirit per year. Kinclaith distillery was equipped with one pair of stills and produced malt whisky to become a part of the Long John blend. In 1975 it was dismantled to make room for an extension of the grain distillery. It was later demolished in 1982.

Bottlings:
There are no official bottlings of Kinclaith. The latest from independents came in 2009 when Signatory released a 40 year old distilled in 1969. In 2005, Duncan Taylor and Signatory both released 35 year old bottlings.

Glenugie

Owner: *Region:*   *Founded:*   *Status:*
Chivas Bros   E Highlands   1831   Demolished

Glenugie, positioned in Peterhead, was the most Eastern distillery in Scotland, producing whisky for six years before it was converted into a brewery. In 1875 whisky distillation started again, but production was very intermittent until 1937 when Seager Evans & Co took over. Eventually they expanded the distillery to four stills and the capacity was around 1 million litres per year. After several ownership changes Glenugie became part of the brewery giant, Whitbread, in 1975. The final blow came in 1983 when Glenugie, together with seven other distilleries, was closed never to open again.

Bottlings:
The first official bottling of Glenugie came as late as in 2010 when Chivas Bros (the current owners of the brand) released a 32 year old single sherry cask in a new range called Deoch an Doras. Recent independent bottlings include a 33 year old with 8 years Oloroso finish from Signatory, released in 2011.

Ladyburn

Owner: *Region:*   *Founded:*   *Status:*
W Grant & Sons   Lowlands   1966   Dismantled

In 1963 William Grant & Sons built their huge grain distillery in Girvan in Ayrshire. Three years later they also decided to build a malt distillery on the site which was given the name Ladyburn. The distillery was equipped with two pairs of stills and they also tested a new type of continuous mashing. The whole idea was to produce malt whisky to become a part of Grant's blended whisky. The distillery was closed in 1975 and finally dismantled during the 1980s. In 2008 a new malt distillery opened up at Girvan under the name Ailsa Bay.

Bottlings:
The latest official bottling from the owners was a 27 year old distilled in 1973 and released in 2001. Independent bottlings have appeared occasionally, sometimes under the name Ayrshire. The most recent was a 36 year old, released by Signatory in 2012.

Single malts from
Japan

by Nicholas Coldicott

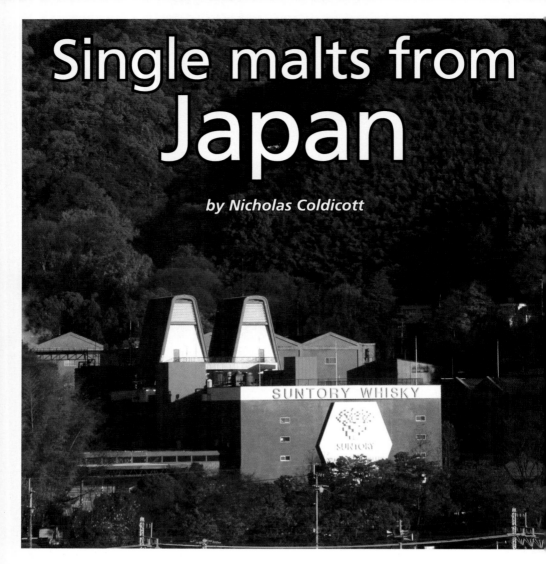

It was a year of greetings and goodbyes in the Japanese whisky world. It began with a welcome of sorts. A newspaper in Okayama Prefecture, southern Japan, reported that a local company that makes sake, shochu, umeshu and beer had begun distilling malt.

Miyashita Shuzo switched the stills on in June 2012, and by the end of the year had put 1,000 liters of new make into casks. They started again in August 2013, but at time of writing had no production target for the year.

President Koichi Miyashita says the company's 90th anniversary is approaching (2015), they decided they wanted to try to make something new, and they thought they could use much of their shochu equipment to make whisky. The company is beginning with a shochu still, but Miyashita says they are considering investing in a more traditional whisky-making setup.

They are aging the spirit in new oak, sherry butts and brandy casks, and plan to use old shochu casks (some of which began as sherry casks). Miyashita plans to release his first whisky in 2015, and though he has yet to decide whether to release it as single malt, single cask or blended, he says he's aiming for an easy-to-drink, "distinctly Okayama" style.

Young at heart

The first farewell of 2013 was to a pair of 10 year old single malts – Suntory's Hakushu and Yamazaki – but their demise is more a sign of the maker's success than its struggles. The 10 year olds had passed the mantle of gateway into Suntory's single malt world to the no-age-statement (NAS) versions that appeared in May 2012. And though Suntory spokespeople are guarded on issues of stock, it seems fair to assume that supply is more of a problem than demand these days.

The company is aiming squarely at the premium market abroad, and we're still less than ten years into the domestic whisky drinking resurgence, so Suntory blenders doubtless appreciate the flexibility that comes when you drop the age statement. But there's something else at play in Japan. As Suntory's annual mission statement said, the aim is to move whisky from the smoky bar to the living room, dining room and izakaya.

The highball boom, focused on the budget Kakubin blend, proved that there's a big thirst in Japan for sprightly, affordable whiskies.

At White Oak , where even 10 year old stock is in very short supply, the NAS is pretty much the only way they're going to get single malts out. Their Akashi NAS will be the only standard malt in the line-up for the foreseeable future.

Nikka were years ahead of the trend with their NAS single malt Yoichi and Miyagikyo, but in September of 2013 they added a version of their Taketsuru blended malt (or pure malt as they prefer to call it). Nikka calls Taketsuru their "flagship brand", and sales are booming (helped, surely, by the 17 years old winning last year's WWA for Best Blended). The company says sales for the full range (12, 17 and 21 years) over the first six months of 2013 were up 7% year-on-year.

The NAS debuted in the autumn of 2013, bottled at 43% and available in four sizes (50ml, 180ml, 500ml, 700ml). Nikka says the "key malts" in the Taketsuru NAS will be drawn from sherry casks and remade hogsheads.

Suntory rising

The Japanese whisky industry leader has been in a bullish mood in its 90th year of whisky making. Sales figures just keep on rising, with the latest report showing sales up 3% in 2012 from a year earlier. The domestic whisky market as a whole rose 1%

The Hakushu push paid big dividends, with sales up a staggering 310%. Yamazaki sales were up a modest-by-comparison 27%.

Suntory say their focus for the coming year will be approachability. They'll highlight smaller bottle sizes in their marketing campaigns, and now that Japanese drinkers are well acquainted with the highball, Suntory will make rocks the focus of their campaigns, suggesting consumers try mizuwari or whisky soda over ice in a rocks glass. Suntory won the Distiller of the Year awards at both the International Spirits Challenge and the

San Francisco World Spirits Competition. The company announced that it would be leveraging these awards, and the usual haul of gold medals, to prise open more international markets. With growth looking inevitable, they announced a plan to add four new stills to their Yamazaki distillery, and cut the ribbon on a new grain facility on the Hakushu site.

Trophy cabinets

The judges for the World Whiskies Awards sent some trophies Japan's way again. It can't have surprised anyone to see Suntory's Hibiki on the list of winners. The 21 year old has now taken the Best Blended prize three times in the last four years. It also won the trophy for best world whisky at the International Spirits Challenge.

Hibiki's victory was business as usual, but Japan's other award came straight out of the blue. Japan's smallest distillery (in terms of capacity) pulled off the biggest surprise when it grabbed the Best Blended Malt award for their Mars Maltage 3 Plus 25. That world-beating bottle was composed of whiskies from two distilleries that each lasted less than a decade. The Hombo Shuzo executives surely never imagined collecting such an accolade when they pulled the plug on whisky making in 1969 and again in 1992.

Company president Osamu Hombo told Japan's Asahi Shimbun that they began making whisky in 1949, but the award feels like a new "start line" for them, and they see it as their job to help make Japanese whisky more global. Distillery manager Kenji Taniguchi says the award was proof that Nagano was a good place to age whisky.

We may find out this year if it's a good place to distil it too. The first spirit made at Shinshu hits the magic three years in 2014. Though there's nothing officially on the release schedule, it would be a surprise if they passed up the chance to show off their (latest) first whisky proper. But as Taniguchi acknowledged in an interview with Japanese drinks magazine Taru, there's a lot more pressure on them now.

Nicholas Coldicott is the former editor-in-chief of Eat magazine, former drink columnist for The Japan Times and former contributing editor at Whisky Magazine Japan. He currently works for Japan's national broadcaster, NHK, and writes a drink column for CNNgo.com.

Chichibu

Owner: Venture Whisky   **Founded**: 2008
Location: Saitama Prefecture
Capacity: 80,000 litres
Malt whisky range: Occasional limited releases.

Japan's newest distillery is well on its way to being the first to produce a whisky born and bottled in its backyard. Around 10% of Chichibu's barley is grown locally, and the team is experimenting with local peat. The distillery has a malting floor and bottling plant onsite. The team is training with a local cooper to learn how to make and maintain their own casks, and even the washbacks are made of local wood: the Japanese oak known as mizunara. Most of the team members are local, too, hailing either from Saitama Prefecture or nearby Tokyo. So it's hardly a surprise that Akuto has his eye on producing the Saitama version of Kilchoman's 100% Islay.

The Chichibu process is more hands-on than in many distilleries. The mashman uses a wooden paddle to stir, and the stillman opens the spirit safe and samples the distillate to decide when to cut. The two stills are small with steep arms for a rich spirit. The distillate is aged, without temperature controls, in Chichibu's seesawing climate. Akuto says the fluctuations let the casks breathe more deeply and speed up the aging process. He uses more than 20 kinds of cask, including ones that once held Cognac, Madeira and rum, as well, of course, as ones made from mizunara.

The first release (in 2011) was called, naturally, The First. Then came The Floor Malted, made from barley the team had malted on a visit to a malt-ster in England. In 2012 came the first peated version, followed by a series of very limited releases of whisky aged in Port pipes and 'chibidaru' quarter casks. At time of writing, Akuto says he's planning to release a 2013 Pea-ted, the first 5 year old Chichibu, and some "non-vintage" styles.

They're currently distilling for ten months of the year, taking two months off at the peak of summer. The final two months before the break are devoted to peated malt.

Tasting note:
Chibidaru 2013
A vatting of 4 year old whiskies aged in quarter casks. Astoundingly mature for its age. There's quince and baked apple on the nose. It's quite tight on the tongue, with lots of wood, until you add a splash of water, then almonds, spices and a butteriness emerges.

Fuji Gotemba

Owner: Kirin Holdings   **Founded**: 1973
Location: Shizuoka Prefecture
Capacity: 12,000,000 litres (including grain whisky)
Malt whisky range: Fujisanroku 18 years old.

Japan's biggest distillery is also one of its most inconspicuous. Owner Kirin hasn't followed fellow drink giants Suntory and Asahi (Nikka) in building a world-beating single malt portfolio. It has focused instead on filling bottles at the cheaper end of the whisky market with brands such as Emblem, Boston Club, Ocean Lucky Gold and Robert Brown.

They issue just two whiskies that identify themselves as products of the distillery: an 18 year old single malt called Fujisanroku, bottled at 43%, and a blended, also called Fujisanroku, bottled at 50% and available in 600 ml or whopping 4-litre plastic bottles.

The distillery sits at the foot of Mount Fuji, and was originally opened as a collaboration between Kirin, Seagram, Chivas and Four Roses. Kirin took full control in 2002.

It has pot and column stills to produce malt and grain whisky. Unlike every other Japanese distilleries, Fuji Gotemba sticks exclusively to one kind of wood: American oak. Kirin wanted easy warehouse management, but they sacrificed much of the depth and variety that has made Japanese whisky so successful.

Japan's thirst for highballs has helped boost sales of Kirin's blends, especially the Fujisanroku, and that seems to be where Kirin is happy to stay. The company's solitary single malt offering is a rare sight on bar or liquor store shelves, even in Japan.

Hakushu

Owner: Suntory **Founded**: 1973
Location: Yamanashi Prefecture
Capacity: Undisclosed (estimated 3,000,000 litres)
Malt whisky range: Hakushu Single Malt NAS, 12, 18 and 25 years old plus regular limited releases.

Hakushu was once the biggest distillery in the world. Back in the Bubble years of the 1980s when people in Japan were guzzling whisky, there were 36 stills running in the forested foothills of Mt Kaikomagatake, reportedly turning out 30 million litres a year. There are just 12 now, but the place is growing again. Two years ago they added four washbacks, taking the total to 18. Last year they announced that a new grain facility on the site was in full swing. Suntory makes most of its grain whisky at a facility in Chita, near Nagoya, in central Japan. The new Hakushu extension has boosted the company's grain production capacity by just 10%, but a spokesperson says it's a more flexible, experimental facility that can use various kinds of source materials. There's no decision yet on how they'll use the spirit that emerges.

Suntory trimmed the Hakushu line-up by ending production of the 10 year old, but issued a limited edition Sherry Cask Hakushu for the domestic market. Whisky drinkers in the US got their first taste of the Heavily Peated Hakushu that appears most years in Japan.

Hakushu single malts have been the focus of a premium highball campaign in Japan as Suntory tries to tempt highball fans upmarket. The company erected heavily branded pop-up bars in Japan, offering variations on Hakushu 12 years old and soda. The marketing makes much of Hakushu's verdant setting, 700 metres above sea level in the Japanese Alps, as well as the local spring water that's also bottled as the top-selling "Minami Alps Tennensui".

Tasting note:
Hakushu 12 year old
A clean nose of pepper and wood shavings. On the palate, forest floor, bamboo, pepper, fresh apple, with an elegant smokiness. The pepper stays with the long finish.

Hanyu

Owner: Toa Shuzo **Founded**: 1941
Location: Saitama Prefecture
Capacity: Dismantled
Malt whisky range: Limited single cask, single malt and other bottlings.

Japanese whisky fans could be forgiven for getting a little teary eyed in January 2013, as four releases appeared to mark the end of an era. The final four bottles in the astonishingly popular Ichiro's Malt card series appeared on, and quickly disappeared from, liquor store shelves. The seven of spades, six of hearts, five of diamonds and ace of clubs completed the 52-release run of bottles bearing playing card motifs.

The series was a marketing masterstroke, helping consumers remember their favourites and making single cask whiskies approachable for neophytes. It also brought acclaim and awards to a once obscure distillery.

Hanyu only made whisky for 17 years. Those years coincided with a downturn in domestic whisky consumption, and preceded international interest in Japanese malts. The place was dismantled in 2004, and Ichiro Akuto, grandson of the Hanyu founder and now owner of Chichibu distillery, snapped up the 400 or so casks from the warehouse. He had some fun with the whisky, too, finishing much of it for a couple of years in madeira, cream sherry, oloroso, port, cognac, bourbon or Japanese oak casks.

Though the 52-card deck is complete, there is talk of one final release in the series: the Joker. Akuto says he hasn't made a decision on that yet. "We're now sampling every cask. We'll release the Joker if we find a good one for it," he says. Given that there are still around 100 casks of Hanyu whisky untapped, the smart money says we'll see a Joker sometime in 2014. If not, the whisky will come trickling out one way or another, and the Hanyu story will reach its conclusion.

Tasting note:
Ichiro's Malt Four of Spades (Distilled 2000, bottled 2010; Hogshead with mizunara finish)
A nose of spice and cypress. More prickly and spicy on the palate, with ginger and a pleasant bitterness. Ends long and dry.

Karuizawa

Owner: Kirin Holdings   **Founded**: 1956
Location: Nagano Prefecture
Capacity: Dismantled
Malt whisky range: Single cask and Asama vatted malt.

Karuizawa might just be the world's liveliest defunct distillery. It's been 12 years since anyone made whisky there, but its profile has never been higher. When Kirin bought fellow drink company Mercian in 2007, it acquired the already mothballed Karuizawa distillery, but showed no interest in reviving operations there. Several people helped spread the love of the sherry-rich whisky by buying and bottling some Karuizawa casks, including Ichiro Akuto, now owner of Chichibu distillery. But it's U.K.-based distributor Number One Drinks that's done the most to make the place famous. The company began with a series of releases under their Noh and Vintage labels. Then, in 2011, they bought up the last few hundred casks and have been releasing the contents at a prodigious rate.

For those with bottomless bank accounts, the highlight of the past year was the launch of the oldest single cask Japanese whisky ever bottled. The liquid sat for 52 years in a 250-litre sherry cask, and filled just 41 bottles. Each one sold for ¥2million (about US$20,000). That eye-watering price tag almost made the other blockbuster release seem reasonable. Nearly 150 bottles of a 50 year old single cask Karuizawa was set for release in the autumn of 2013. The price hadn't been fixed at time of writing.

A couple of years ago, Number One vatted 77 of the younger casks, selected by a Japanese blender and whisky writer Dave Broom, then poured it all into sherry butts. The first release appeared in mid-2012 under the name Asama. The second spent another year in the butts and was released in mid-2013. Number One Drinks' David Croll says the rest of the Karuizawa stock is all spoken for, and they're sending it out as fast as they can bottle it. Keep your eyes on La Maison du Whisky, The Whisky Exchange or Magny if you want some.

Tasting note:
Asama Vatted Malt (50,5%)
A higher strength version of the vatting we reviewed last year, and with an extra year in the cask, both of which have done the drink a lot of good. Nice stewed fruits on the nose. There's quite a bit going on when you sip it: cereal, saltiness and some mushrooms along with the sherry notes you'd expect.

Miyagikyo

Owner: Nikka Whisky   **Founded**: 1969
Location: Miyagi Prefecture
Capacity: 3,000,000 litres
Malt whisky range: NAS, 10, 12, 15 years old and occasional 20 years and single cask releases.

In 2013 Nikka announced that it would finally be shipping Miyagikyo to the United States. It's the last of the four big single malts to make it to those shores. They're beginning with what's arguably the most approachable expression of this fragrant malt, the 12 year old. It will be bottled at 45%.

Nikka was the first of Japan's whisky makers to open a second distillery. By the late 1960s, founder Masataka Taketsuru needed to boost production capacity. Rather than expanding Yoichi, he decided to build a new facility that would produce something lighter, fruitier and more elegant. He reportedly spent three years searching for the right spot, until he found a secluded, humid location in Miyagi Prefecture on Japan's main island of Honshu. Nestled between mountains and encircled by rivers, it had the purity of air and water he was looking for.

The distillery was named after the nearby city of Sendai until 2001, when Asahi bought the company and renamed it Miyagikyo. It had four stills when it first opened, but expanded in 1979, 1989 and 1999. It now has eight pot stills and 22 steel washbacks. The stills are all large and have boil bulbs, and the malt that goes into them is unpeated or very lightly peated, to produce a light, fruity spirit. There are also two sets of Coffey stills, brought in when an earthquake struck their original home in Nishinomiya, Hyogo Prefecture. Nikka sells a single grain whisky without an age statement, as well as a Coffey Malt.

Japan's massive earthquake of 2011 rattled Miyagikyo, but the distillery suffered only minor damage.

Tasting note:
Miyagikyo No Age Statement
The nose suggests fresh peach juice. There's more going on when you sip it – pine, fudge, raisins, varnish. It benefits from a splash of water to calm the astringency.

Shinshu

Owner: Hombo Shuzo **Founded**: 1985
Location: Nagano Prefecture
Capacity: 25,000 litres
Malt whisky range: Komagatake 10 years old

If Shinshu began last year as one of Japan's lesser-known distilleries, the obscurity sure didn't last long. In March, the folks at Whisky Magazine announced the winners of their annual World Whiskies Awards, with Shinshu as one of the surprise winners. Managing Director Kenji Taniguchi collected the Best Blended Malt Whisky award for "Mars Maltage 3 Plus 25", a drink that tells (most of) the peculiar story of Japan's most elevated distillery.

Owner company Hombo Shuzo began life in 1872 as a cotton processor. They branched out into shochu in 1909, then added a whisky license forty years later. Production started on the southern island of Kyushu and in 1960, they built a winery and whisky distillery in Yamanashi, west of Tokyo, and asked a Japanese whisky legend to help them design it. Kiichiro Iwai was one of the backers

of Nikka Whisky founder Masataka Taketsuru's pivotal 1918 research trip to Scotland. He used Taketsuru's report to create a more traditional whisky distillery. But it proved to be a short-lived venture, and they turned off the stills before the decade was out.

In 1985 they moved the equipment to Nagano Prefecture and tried again. This time they lasted 7 years and halted production when the economic bubble burst. But the indefatigable Hombo team launched their third whisky era in February 2011. They entered the World Whiskies Awards for the first time last year, and triumphed with a vatting of three year olds from the Kyushu and Yamanashi distilleries, aged a further 25 years at Shinshu. The award had a predictable effect on sales. The first 1,500 bottles had sold in trickles over two years. The remaining 2,500 sold in a flash. For now, there's just one malt whisky on offer, the Komagatake 10 years old.

Blender Koki Takehira says they have just two stills, but produce 108 styles of spirit by varying the malt, yeasts and casks.

Tasting note:
Mars Maltage 3 plus 25 pure malt
The aromatic nose made me think of Gewürztraminer with its Turkish Delight and marzipan. There's also a touch of rubber. On the tongue, lavender, vanilla and raisins. Medium, subtle finish.

White Oak Distillery

Owner: Eigashima Shuzo **Founded**: 1919
Location: Hyogo Prefecture
Capacity: 60,000 litres
Malt whisky range: NAS, limited 15 years old Akashi single malt.

The White Oak distillery has a quiet little coastal home, a quick hop west of Kobe, facing the Seto Inland Sea. Owner company Eigashima Shuzo team distills for just two months a year, and spends the other months making sake, shochu, umeshu, brandy and wine.

White Oak is, technically, Japan's oldest distillery. It received its whisky license in 1919, four years before the first spirit emerged from the Yamazaki stills. But current president Mikio Hiraishi says it took at least 40 more years before they made use of that license. They focused on blends at first, but released their first single malt in 2007, and have been sending out limited runs each year as their stock matures. Things reached their pinnacle in 2013 with the first 15 year old, released under their Akashi label. It was notable for being what we believe is the first whisky ever finished in konara oak, (*Quercus serrata*). The wood is a cousin of the better known mizunara, but reportedly even harder to work with. The people at White Oak took a cask that once held shochu and poured a 12 year old sherry-aged malt into it. Three years later... it's so deep and dark that it's hard to tell exactly what effect the Japanese wood had.

White Oak are planning to release a 5 year old single cask, taken from a sherry butt, in late 2013. After that it might be a quiet time for White Oak single malts. Most of the stock is less than 5 years old, and much of it still goes into blends. The mainstay of the single malt portfolio will be the no-age statement Akashi, bottled at 46%. It first appeared in 2012 with a run of 4,000 bottles. Demand was high enough to convince them to increase that output to 6,500 this year.

Tasting note:
Akashi 15 years old
An unusual whisky, to be sure. It wallops you right from the nose with something between molasses and creosote. On the palate, it's more of the same, though you can find some apricots buried somewhere. It's a monster, with an enormous finish, and if there's any influence from the konara cask, I'm not sure what it is.

Yamazaki

Owner: Suntory   **Founded**: 1923
Location: Osaka Prefecture
Capacity: Undisclosed (estimated 6,000,000 litres)
Malt whisky range: NAS, 12, 18, 25 years old and regular limited bottlings.

The true birthplace of Japanese whisky. Suntory founder Shinjiro Torii chose a humid little valley between Osaka and Kyoto as the site of Japan's first whisky distillery. The marketing blurbs talk of the purity of the local water, but it can't have hurt to have been right in the middle of the country and close to several major cities.

Yamazaki fans in Japan saw their options shrink in 2013 with the disappearance of the 10 year old from the line-up, but the drinkers in the United States finally got the chance to try the award-winning 25 year old. It's the oldest Japanese standard release to reach the US market, and cements Yamazaki's place as the most global of Japanese distilleries.

Suntory periodically issues limited releases of Yamazaki for the Japanese market, usually a vatting of spirits aged in one kind of cask (mizunara, sherry butt, barrel, puncheon). In 2013 the offered a very limited heavily peated Yamazaki, bottled at 48%.

The company's most exciting news of the year was its plan to expand Yamazaki. The company will install 4 more pot stills, taking the total to 16. The 40% boost in capacity will be the first expansion there in 45 years.

It may also increase the variety that Yamazaki is capable of producing. Those current 12 stills, some with boil balls, some without, some direct fired, some using steam, some with steep arms, some with straight ones, already produce a miscellany of styles that gives the blenders plenty to work with. Who would bet against the new stills offering even more diversity?

Tasting note:
Yamazaki 12 year old
On the nose, very fresh fruits, peaches, apricots, milk chocolate. On the palate, plump and sweet, with tropical fruits, straddling the line between fresh and dried. It's a very elegant whisky, but has lots of body.

Yoichi

Owner: Nikka Whisky   **Founded**: 1934
Location: Hokkaido
Capacity: 2,000,000 litres
Malt whisky range: NAS, 10, 12, 15, 20 years old and occasional single cask releases.

When Japanese whisky pioneer Masataka Taketsuru departed from Yamazaki in the 1930s and went in search of a location for Japan's second distillery, he headed north until he found a site he thought perfect for the more rugged spirit he wanted to make. Yoichi, on Japan's northernmost island of Hokkaido, had access to water, coal, peat and wood, and is just a kilometre from the sea which may or may not lend it a salty note.

It's often described as Japan's most traditional distillery, meaning it hews closest to the methods Taketsuru observed while working at Scotland's Longmorn, Hazelburn and Bo'ness distilleries. But even Scotland's distilleries have given up on heating their still with a coal fire, as Yoichi still does.

The six stills are fairly straight to create the kind of bold spirit that Taketsuru must have been drinking in Scotland. The varying angles of the lyne arms offer some diversity, as do the differing peat levels (0ppm, 4ppm and 35-50ppm). The on-site coopers work with new oak, sherry butts and bourbon barrels.

The distillery released its first single malt, a 12 year old, in 1984. The label bore the distillery's original name: Hokkaido. Yoichi was the first Japanese whisky to grab global attention when the 10 year old won "Best of the Best" at the 2001 World Whisky Awards. Since then the distillery has built an enviable collection of medals and trophies, including a World's Best Single Malt title for a limited release 20 years old at the WWAs in 2008.

It also gives the heft to Nikka's multi-award winning Taketsuru blended malts. Yoichi's visitors centre offers the chance to buy single cask bottles that aren't available anywhere else.

Tasting note:
Yoichi 15 year old
A wonderful aroma of campfires, brazil nuts and dried figs. In the mouth, it's oily and a little salty, with a big body. Buttered nuts, chocolate and more dried fruit. It's got smoke, but doesn't punch you with phenol. Wonderfully balanced.

Meet the Blender

SHINJI FUKUYO
CHIEF BLENDER, SUNTORY

Shinji Fukuyo has been Suntory's chief blender since 2009. His tenure has already been marked with a haul of trophies, including World Whisky Awards for the Yamazaki 1984 and Yamazaki 25 Years Old, as well as a spike in domestic whisky consumption. Nick Coldicott sat down with him over a glass of Yamazaki.

Tell me about your career at Suntory.

I joined the company in 1984. I started in quality control at the Hakushu distillery. Then I moved to production planning, and then covered maturation. In 1992 I moved to the blending team as a blender. Between 1996 and 2002, I worked in Scotland, the last four years at Morrison Bowmore. I became manager of the blending team in 2006, and chief blender three years later.

What were the biggest differences between the process in Scotland and Japan?

The Scotch industry is so big, and there's a lot of communication between distilleries and companies. Not only competition, but also some arrangement, particularly whisky stock arrangements. It's a big difference from Japan. The Scotch industry has big lobbying power. That's another difference with Japan. And in Japanese maturation, there's much more acidity than in Scotch whisky I think. Hot summer, 35 degrees. Cold winter, maybe minus 3 or 4. In Scotland, maybe minus 5 to 15 or 20. We get a much deeper maturation here, from my understanding.

The Suntory blends are well established, so there can't have been much room for personal expression when you took over from predecessor Seiichi Koshimizu.

Mr Koshimizu and myself use almost the same whiskies. It's impossible to change drastically. Maybe Mr Koshimizu recognises differences between him and myself. And also I have some idea of some differences. But there are no arguments about it. Limited editions are another story. That's an opportunity to try a new style or new character. And every year we revisit our blending formulas, then, according to our sales forecast for the next 20 years, we review things.

I hear there's a new Suntory blend, Toki, on the horizon. That must be a chance to show a Fukuyo character.

Ah yes it is. But that's a work in progress. We've been working on it for about a year and a half, but there's a lot more to do before it's ready.

What's the biggest challenge as a Suntory blender?

There are a lot of things to do. Not only deciding formulas, but also managing the inventory, and casks, malting the barley, quality control, consumer communication. But I like it.

The Yamazaki 25 years old is composed only of sherry-aged whiskies. Is it hard to keep consistency through each release?

Oh yes. Every time we have to change the ratio. If you bring a 25 years old from two years ago, maybe you can find some difference. The style is the same, but to keep it exact is very difficult. Sherry-matured whisky is particularly uneven, cask to cask. We usually check sherry casks after 8 or 10 years. We check every individual cask and then categorise: this is a good maturation, this is a little bit weaker, this one is very dark but too woody, something like that. Then we make some plan to use each category of whisky.

Your blending room is impressive. Do you know how many styles you have?

I often get this question, but which unit should I categorise? For example, in the case of 12 years old Yamazaki, maybe our blending formula, we use between 7 and 11 (components), but that doesn't mean 5 types of whisky. One line contains many types of whisky. That's why it's very difficult to say how many types. We have different types of casks, different conditions of warehouses, different types of malted barley, different shapes of pot stills. In general we just say roughly 100 kinds of whisky, but it's very difficult to say which 100.

Is it hard to get casks these days?

American oak casks are very easy to get. Mizunara is very limited. We can make only 50-100 casks a year. We work with Tokyo University, which has huge forests in Hokkaido. But they allow us only maybe 10 trees per year. We also purchase from the timber market, where the prices are (makes a "very high" gesture). Good sherry butts are not available in the market. We order new casks, but Spanish oak needs maybe one year for drying after it's cut, then they put sherry in it, keep for 2 or 3 years, dump the casks, then they come to Japan. So there's a 4-year time lag. And Spanish people are very kind and good guys, but sometimes they lose our casks or something like that, so every year I go to Spain and count casks, check the wine, and how much is in it. It's very important to become amigos.

You mature whisky in Hakushu, Yamazaki and Ohmi. Is there a difference in character between the locations?

Yes, maturation is faster in the west (Yamazaki and Ohmi) than east (Hakushu), and some texture or character is a bit different. The west side has a higher temperature. That's why we use refill or big casks, like puncheons and butts. It's milder, softer. The east is crispy.

Yamazaki is celebrating its 90th anniversary this year, but the whiskies are just beginning to build their reputation abroad. These must be exciting times.

Yes, looking from abroad, we're just starting. We're very lucky because over the last 10 years, we got some awards, and foreign whisky lovers and journalists became interested in Japanese whisky. As a volume of sales, it's still very small. But we now have a very good opportunity to go out in the world.

Distilleries
around the globe

Puni Distillery, Italy

In this book, we have always covered distilleries from Scotland and Japan in separate chapters. The reason is, of course, that the absolute largest part of all malt whisky which is produced in the world derives from these two countries but, furthermore, that Scotch and Japanese malt whisky have the highest overall quality in the world. This, however, doesn't mean that there's a lack of examples of whisky in the ensuing 38 pages that can match the best whiskies in the world. Here are also whiskies that have been manufactured in unorthodox ways and which, for that reason, can hardly be compared to traditionally manufactured single malt. In spite of this, many of them maintain a very high quality. These innovators furthermore add excitement to a whole category of spirits that would, in time, risk getting caught in a rut.

The number of distilleries in this chapter is increasing every year and the only thing we can say for certain is that we haven't succeeded in covering them all this year either. It is impossible to keep abreast of every new distillery project around the world and sometimes it is also hard to determine if they are producing malt whisky in the strictest sense of the word. One thing is clear though, and that is that this year we have a record breaking number of distilleries outside of Scotland and Japan that produce malt whisky – in fact, no less than 171! Moreover, this year we have the pleasure of welcoming a number of new countries to the family of malt whisky producers – namely Norway, Israel and Italy.

USA represents the largest growth with 46 distilleries this year. In the early days of micro distilleries, it was mainly brewers and producers of eau de vie from fruit who decided to try their skills at producing whisky. This has now changed and more and more ventures are being set up with the specific goal of distilling whisky. Most of them are small but a handful have reached (or are about to reach) a capacity where it becomes questionable if you can still refer to them as micro distilleries. One example is Balcones where a newly started expansion may result in a capacity of close to 1 million litres in a couple of years. However, while the label micro distilleries often refer to small volumes it is perhaps better to use the term craft or artisanal distilleries which better reflects the often groundbreaking and innovative methods of producing the spirit, rather than how many litres they are putting in barrels.

There are other countries where the emergence of whisky producers is also strong; France and Germany, for example, where most of the producers tend to produce only for their home market and very little collaboration is visible between the different distilleries. In other countries, distilleries are seeking to conquer bigger markets and are embroiled in joint ventures to establish their own geographical category of whisky, for instance, Sweden and Australia (in particular Tasmania). The number of high, quality producers in these countries has now reached such levels that, before long, we shall use the term Swedish whisky and Tasmanian whisky in the same way that we today speak of Japanese whisky.

While this chapter mainly revolves around producers with small volumes, there are also some large distilleries with a capacity that can match the bigger competitors in Scotland. Midleton and Cooley in Ireland and Bushmills in Northern Ireland are obvious examples. So we also have Penderyn in Wales, St George in England, Amrut and John Distilleries in India, Kavalan in Taiwan, James Sedgwick in South Africa and Mackmyra in Sweden.

A few of these have been around for centuries but all of them have released whiskies that have earned due recognition and respect amongst the whisky aficionados and they have the muscles in terms of sheer production capacity to make a difference in the world of whisky.

EUROPE

Austria _____

DISTILLERY: Whiskydistillery J. Haider, Roggenreith
FOUNDED: 1995
OWNER/MANAGER: Johann & Monika Haider
www.roggenhof.at

In the small village of Roggenreith in northern Austria, Johann and Monika Haider have been distilling whisky since 1995 and three years later, the first Austrian whisky was released. In 2005, they opened up a Whisky Experience World with guided tours, a video show, whisky tasting and exhibitions. Today, more than 75,000 visitors find their way to the distillery every year and the owners have even built a helipad. Roggenhof was the first whisky distillery in Austria and over the years production has steadily increased to 30,000 litres. The capacity currently stands at 100,000 litres per annum. The wash is allowed to ferment for 72 hours before it reaches either of the two 450 litre Christian Carl copper stills. The desired strength is reached in one single distillation, thanks to the attached column. The new make is filled in casks made of the local Manhartsberger Oak.

The current range of single malts made from barley is Single Malt J.H, Special Single Malt "Karamell" J.H. which is made from dark roasted malt, both bottled at 41% and two older versions bottled at 46% – Single Malt Selection J.H. and Special Single Malt Selection J.H. There is also the limited edition, Special Single Malt Peated J.H., as well as three rye whiskies. The very latest addition for 2013 is a very limited 6 year old which has matured in a Winsky barrel, Winsky being a grape brandy which is also produced at the distillery.

DISTILLERY: Reisetbauer, Kirchberg-Thening
FOUNDED: 1994 (whisky since 1995)
OWNER/MANAGER: Julia & Hans Reisetbauer
www.reisetbauer.at

This is a family-owned farm distillery near Linz in northern Austria specialising in brandies and fruit schnapps. Since 1995, a range of malt whiskies are also produced. The distillery is equipped with five 350 litre stills. All stills are heated, using hot water rather than

Johann Haider, owner of Destillerie J. Haider

steam, which, according to Hans Reisetbauer, allows for a more delicate and gentle distillation. The 70 hour-long fermentation takes place in stainless steel washbacks. Approximately 20,000 litres of pure alcohol destined for whisky making are produced annually, using local barley to make the unpeated malt. Casks are sourced locally from the best Austrian wine producers. The current range of whiskies includes a 7 year old single malt which consists of a vatting of whiskies aged in casks that have previously contained Chardonnay and Trockenbeerenauslese, a 12 year old which has undergone maturation in Trockenbeerenauslese barrels and a Vintage 1998.

Other distilleries in Austria

Destillerie Weutz
St. Nikolai im Sausal, founded in 2002
www.weutz.at

A family distillery with a history of producing schnapps and liqueur from fruits and berries. In 2004 Michael Weutz started cooperation with the brewer Michael Löscher and since then Weutz has added whisky to its produce based on the wash from the brewery. Since 2004, 14 different malt whiskies have been produced. Some of them are produced in the traditional Scottish style: Hot Stone, St. Nikolaus and the peated Black Peat. Others are more unorthodox, for example Green Panther in which 5% pumpkin seeds are added to the mash, and Franziska based on elderflower. Annual production is currently at approximately 14,000 litres and for maturation casks made of French Limousin and Alliere oak are used.

Old Raven
Neustift, founded in 2004
www.oldraven.at

In 2004, a distillery was added to the Rabenbräu brewery by Andreas Schmidt. More than 250,000 litres of beer are produced yearly and the wash from the brewery is used for distillation of the 2,000 litres of single malt whisky every year. Old Raven, which is triple distilled, comes in three expressions – Old Raven, Old Raven Smoky and Old Raven R1 Smoky. The last one was filled into a PX sherry cask which had been used to mature Islay whisky.

Wolfram Ortner Destillerie
Bad Kleinkirchheim, founded in 1990
www.wob.at

Fruit brandies of all kinds make up the bulk of Wolfram Ortner´s produce, as well as cigars, coffee and other luxuries. For the last years he has also been producing malt whisky. New oak of different kinds (Limousin, Alolier, Nevers, Vosges and American) is used for the maturation process. His first single malt, WOB DÖ MALT Vergin, began selling in 2001 and an additional product line, in which Ortner mixes his whisky with other distillates such as orange/moscatel, is called WOB Mariage.

Destillerie Rogner
Rappottenstein, founded in 1997
www.destillerie-rogner.at

This distillery in Waldviertel in the northeast part of Austria has produced spirits from fruits and berries for more than a decade. Recently, Hermann Rogner has also added whisky to the range. Two of them are called Rogner Waldviertel Whisky 3/3 with the last figures referring to barley, wheat and rye being used for one of the expressions and three different kinds of malted barley for the other.

Waldviertler Granit Destillerie
Waidhofen/Thaya, founded in 1995
www.granitdestillerie.at

The distillery has from 1995 established a comprehensive product portfolio of liquers and schnapps from all kinds of delectable berries and fruit. Whisky production started in 2006 and the owner, Günther Mayer, has not only released two different smoked single malts, but is also working with rye and dinkel.

Keckeis Destillerie
Rankweil, founded in 2003
www.destillerie-keckeis.at

Like so many other Austrian distilleries, it started with schnapps and eau de vie from fruit, in Keckeis' case, mostly pears and apples. Whisky production started in 2008 and today one expression of single malt is for sale. Part of the barley has been smoked with beech and maturation takes place in small ex-sherry casks made of French Limousin oak.

Destillerie Hermann Pfanner
Lauterach, founded in 1854
www.pfanner-weine.com

Founded as an inn and brewery more than 150 years ago, the production soon turned to distillation of eau de vie and schnapps. In 2005, the current owner, Walter Pfanner, started whisky production and today 10,000 litres per year are filled into casks previously used for maturing sherry and sweet wines.

Broger Privatbrennerei
Klaus, founded in 1976 (whisky since 2008)
www.broger.info

The production of whisky is supplementing the distillation and production of eau de vie from apples and pears. For their whisky, Broger buys peated malt from Crisp in the UK and unpeated malt from Germany. The distillery is equipped with a 1,000 litre mash tun, a 150 litre Christian Carl still and a 1,000 litre washback. The total volume of whisky produced in a year is 700 litres. The current range of whiskies consists of three expressions; Triple Cask which is a blend of whiskies matured in bourbon, sherry and madeira casks, Medium Smoked which has been smoked using beech wood and finally Burn Out, a heavily peated whisky.

Destillerie Weidenauer
Kottes, founded in 1854
www.weidenauer.at

The distillery's ancestry dates back to 1838 but it was the present owner, Oswald Weidenauer, that led the company to a production of note. He was the one who in 1997 broadened the range to include whisky. Weidenauer's speciality is something as rare as whiskey distilled from oats. He even uses spelt and the range also includes a single malt from barley.

Belgium

DISTILLERY: The Owl Distillery, Grâce Hollogne
FOUNDED: 1997
OWNER/MANAGER: Etienne Bouillon (manager), Christian Polis & Pierre Roberti
www.belgianwhisky.com
www.thebelgianowl.com

In October 2007, Belgium's first single malt, 'The Belgian Owl', was released. The next bottling came in 2008 but was exclusively reserved for private customers. The first commercial bottling was introduced in November 2008. A limited cask strength expression, 44 months old, was released in 2009 and more cask strength versions have followed. In 2013, there were several releases, 3 to 4 years old with most of them bottled at 46%, but also a couple of cask strength expressions. The distillery is equipped with a mash tun holding 2,1 tonnes per mash, one washback with a fermentation time of 60-100 hours and two stills (11,000 and 8,000 litres respectively) that had previously been used at the now demolished Caperdonich distillery in Rothes, Speyside. At the same time, production has moved to a new location in Fexhe-le-Haut-Clocher, close to where their barley is grown. For 2013, they intend to produce 23,000 litres of pure alcohol.

The stills from the demolished Caperdonich distillery in Rothes, Scotland came to good use at The Owl Distillery in Belgium

DISTILLERY: Het Anker Distillery, Blaasfeld
FOUNDED: 1471 (whisky since 2003)
OWNER/MANAGER: Charles Leclef (owner)
www.hetanker.be

Charles Leclef started out as a brewer and currently maintains this role at Brouwerij Het Anker. He also experimented with distillation of his own beer into whisky with some assistance from a nearby genever distiller. The first bottles under the name Gouden Carolus Singe Malt appeared on the market in 2008.

Thereafter, Leclef concentrated on the next step in his project, namely, building a distillery of his own with pot stills. The location chosen was not at the brewery in Mechelen, but at Leclef´s family estate, Molenberg, at Blaasfeld. The distillery eventually started producing in October 2010. The stills have been made by Forsyth´s in Scotland with a wash still capacity of 3,000 litres and a spirit still of 2,000 litres. The wash for the distillation is made at the brewery in Mechelen and it is basically a Gouden Carolus Tripel beer without hops and spices and with a fermentation time of four to five days. Around 100,000 litres of alcohol are produced per year and the first release of this new whisky will be in December 2013. The distillery will, at the same time be open to the public for visits and guided tours.

Czech Rebublic _____

DISTILLERY: Gold Cock Distillery
FOUNDED: 1877
OWNER/MANAGER: Rudolf Jelinek a.s
www.rjelinek.cz

The distilling of Gold Cock whisky started already in 1877. Today it is produced in two versions – a 3 year old blended whisky and a 12 year old malt. Production was stopped for a while but after the brand and distillery were acquired by R. Jelinek a.s., the leading Czech producer of plum brandy, the whisky began life anew.

The malt whisky is double distilled in 500 litre traditional pot stills. The new owner has created a small whisky museum which is also home to the club Friends of Gold Cock Whisky with private vaults, where any enthusiast can store his bottlings of Gold Cock.

Denmark _____

DISTILLERY: Braunstein, Køge
FOUNDED: 2005 (whisky since 2007)
OWNER/MANAGER: Michael & Claus Braunstein
www.braunstein.dk

Denmark's first micro-distillery was built in an already existing brewery in Køge, just south of Copenhagen. Unlike many other brewery/whisky distillery enterprises, the owners consider the whisky production to be on equal terms with beer production, even in financial terms.

The wash comes from the own brewery. A Holstein type of still, with four plates in the rectification column, is used for distillation and the spirit is distilled once. For five winter months, peated whisky (+60ppm) is produced, while the rest of the year is devoted to unpeated varieties. Peated malt is bought from Port Ellen, unpeated from Simpsons, but as much as 40% is from ecologically grown Danish barley. The lion's share of the whisky is stored on ex-bourbon (peated version) and first fill Oloroso casks (unpeated) from 190 up to 500 litres.

The Braunstein brothers filled their first spirit casks in 2007 and have produced 50,000 litres annually since then. Their first release and the first release of a malt whisky produced in Denmark was in 2010 – a 3 year old single Oloroso sherry cask called Edition No. 1 which was followed the same year by Library Collection 10:1, bottled at 46%. The first Braunstein whisky from 100% ecologically grown barley, was released as Edition No. 3 in 2011. The most recent releases are Library Collection 13:1 (peated with an Oloroso maturation) and Edition No: 4 (peated and bourbon matured). Library Collection 13:2 (peated and sherry matured but with a rum finish) and Edition No: 5 (peated and sherry matured) are scheduled for a December 2013 release.

The owners of Braunstein Distillery - Claus and Michael Braunstein

DISTILLERY: Stauning Whisky, Stauning
FOUNDED: 2006
OWNER/MANAGER: Stauning Whisky A/S
www.stauningwhisky.dk

The first Danish purpose-built malt whisky distillery entered a more adolescent phase in 2009, after having experimented with two small pilot stills bought from Spain. Two, new Portuguese-made stills of 1,000 and 600 litres respectively were installed and the distillery was able to produce 6,000 litres of alcohol annually. More stills were installed in 2012 and they now have two wash stills and two spirit stills and a yearly production of 15,000 litres.

The aim has always been to be self-sustaining and Danish barley is bought and turned into malt on an own malting floor. The germinating barley usually has to be turned 6-8 times a day, but Stauning has constructed an automatic "grain turner" to do the job. Two core expressions were decided on – Peated Reserve and Traditional Reserve – and the peat for the first one is acquired from one of few remaining peat bogs in Denmark. In June 2012 the first edition of the two versions were released with slightly more than 700 bottles of each. The distillery has now established a core range including Traditional and Peated single malts as well as a Young Rye. Two limited versions were released in 2013 – both of them peated but with different finishes, Oloroso and Pedro Ximenez. An interesting release was announced for later in the year where the Traditional has been given a finish in one of their own rye casks.

Other distilleries in Denmark

Ørbæk Bryggeri
Ørbæk, founded in 1997 (whisky since 2007)
www.oerbaek-bryggeri.nu

Niels Rømer and his son, Nicolai, have since 1997 run Ørbæk Brewery on the Danish island of Fyn. It is now one of many combinations of a micro-brewery and a micro-distillery where the wash from the brewery is used to produce whisky. In June 2009 the first barrels of Isle of Fionia single malt were filled and the first release was made exactly three years later. The whisky, in keeping with Ørbæk's beer, is ecological and two different expressions are produced – Isle of Fionia and the peated Fionia Smoked Whisky. It is matured in ex-bourbon barrels from Jack Daniels and ex-sherry casks. The spirit production (a mix of whisky and rom) is very small and in 2013, twenty casks will be filled. There are exciting plans to convert an old railway workshop into a new and bigger distillery, but it is unlikely to happen before 2015.

Fary Lochan Destilleri
Give, founded in 2009
www.farylochan.dk

This distillery, owned by Jens Erik Jørgensen, is situated in Jutland. The first cask was filled in December 2009 and the owner has recently increased the production from 10,000 bottles per year to 14,000. Jens Erik Jørgensen imports most of the malted barley from the UK, but he also malts some Danish barley by himself. A part of his own malted barley is dried using nettles instead of peat to create a special flavour. After mashing, it is fermented for five days in a 600 litre stainless steel washback. Distillation is performed in two traditional copper pot stills from Forsyth´s in Scotland – a 300 litre wash still and a 200 litre spirit still but there are plans to invest in one more still, 1,500 litres. The spirit is matured in ex-bourbon barrels, some of which have been remade into quarter casks. The first whisky, lightly smoked, was released in September 2013.

Trolden Distillery
Kolding, founded in 2011
www.trolden.com

The distillery is a part of the Trolden Brewery which started in 2005. Michael Svendsen, the owner, uses the wash from the brewery and ferments it for 4-5 days before a double distillation in a 325 litre alembic pot still. The spirit is filled in bourbon casks and production is quite small as brewing beer is the main task. The first release of the whisky will be in December 2014.

Braenderiet Limfjorden
Sillerslev Havn, founded in 2013
www.braenderiet.dk

The latest distillery to come on stream in Denmark. The owner, Ole Mark, started production in June 2013 and the plan is to to do 1,000 to 1,500 litres the first year. Mashing and fermentation is carried out at a local brewery while distillation takes place in alembic type stills. The plan is to do both peated and unpeated single malt as well as rye. The first whisky will be released in 2016.

England

DISTILLERY: St. George´s Distillery, Roudham, Norfolk
FOUNDED: 2006
OWNER/MANAGER: The English Whisky Co.
www.englishwhisky.co.uk

St. George´s Distillery near Thetford in Norfolk was started by father and son, James and Andrew Nelstrop, and came on stream on 12th December 2006. This made it the first English malt whisky distillery for over a hundred years. Customers, both in the UK and abroad, have had the opportunity to follow the development of the whisky via releases of new make, as well as 18 months old spirit,

Two Danish single malts from Stauning and Fary Lochan

both peated and unpeated. These were called Chapters 1 to 4. Finally, in December 2009, it was time for the release of the first legal whisky called Chapter 5 – unpeated and without chill filtering or colouring. This was a limited release but, soon afterwards, Chapter 6 was released in larger quantities. The next expression (Chapter 8) was a limited release of a lightly peated 3 year old, followed in June 2010 by Chapter 9 (with the same style but more widely available). Chapter 7, a 3 year old with 6 months finish in a rum cask, was launched in autumn 2010 together with Chapter 10, which has a sherry cask finish. The next bottling, Chapter 11, appeared in July 2011. This was the heaviest peated expression so far (50ppm) aged between 3 and 4 years matured in bourbon casks. October 2012 saw the release of the sherry cask matured Chapter 12. After some hesitation whether or not they should release a Chapter 13, the owners decided to do it as a limited Halloween whisky and it was launched on Friday the 13th September 2013 at 13.00. Later that autumn Chapter 14, basically an older version of Chapter 6, and Chapter 15, similar to Chapter 11 but twice the age, were released. The whole idea with the Chapters is that they are released as batches (never more than four casks per bottling) either quarterly or once a year. Chapter 6 is at the moment the biggest seller followed by 9 and 11. In summer 2013 a new series was introduced called The Black Range. The thought is to have a more consistent product, predominantly for export and retail chains. Two expressions are available – Classic and Peated, both bourbon matured and bottled at 43%. In between the Chapter releases there are also very limited bottlings of the so called Founder´s Private Cellar. These are unique casks chosen by the founding chairman James Nelstrop.

Around 55,000 bottles were sold in 2012 and important markets are Benelux, France, Scotland, Japan, Singapore and England. In 2013 they entered three new, important markets - USA, China and Canada.

The distillery is equipped with a stainless steel semi-lauter mash tun with a copper top and three stainless steel washbacks with a fermentation time of 85 hours. There is one pair of stills, the wash still with a capacity of 2,800 litres and the spirit still of 1,800 litre capacity. First fill bourbon barrels are mainly used for maturation but the odd sherry, madeira and port casks have also been filled. Non-peated malt is bought from Crisp Malting Group and peated malt from Simpson´s Malt in Berwick-upon-Tweed. Around 60% of production is unpeated and the rest is peated. Around 120,000 bottles will be produced during 2013.

Other distilleries in England

The London Distillery Company
London, founded in 2012
www.thelondondistillerycompany.com

The London Distillery Company is London´s first whisky distillery since Lea Valley closed its doors for the final time more than a century ago. Founded in 2011 by whisky expert, Darren Rook, and former microbrewery owner, Nick Taylor, and located in Battersea, the distillery started distilling gin at the beginning of February 2013. The owners have one still designated for gin called Christina and a second still, Matilda, was installed in February and will be used for whisky production. The first release was towards the end of March 2013 and was called Dodd´s Gin and Darren and company hope to start production of whisky sometime in October 2013. With the help of chief distiller, Andrew MacLeod Smith, they envisage to produce small batch whiskies from low yield barley strains that have long been abandoned by the industry, for example, Golden Promise and Maris Otter.

Adnams Copper House Distillery
Southwold, founded in 2010
www.adnams.co.uk

Famous for their beer since 1872, the owners of Adnams Brewery in Suffolk installed a new brewhouse in their Sole Bay Brewery in 2008. Left with a redundant, old building, they decided to convert it into a distillery. Equipment was ordered from the famous German manufacturer, Carl GmbH; a 1,000 litre beer stripping still and an 850 litre copper pot still with a rectification column with 42 plates attached. Distillation began towards the end of

Two of the most recent releases from St George´s in Norfolk

Darren Rook from the London Distillery Company

ecember 2010 and apart from whisky – gin, vodka and osinthe are also produced. There are some interesting eatures at the Copper House Distillery which will affect ne final spirit. For the fermentation they use brewer´s east which has been abandoned by almost all the Scot- sh distilleries, but adds a different and fruitier character the spirit. The distillation resembles American bourbon roduction in part as they are using a beer stripping still hich results in low wines that are high in alcohol (85- 0%). The low wines are then distilled twice in the pot ill where the 16 meter high rectification column with its ates give added reflux, making the spirit exceptionally nooth and clean. Finally, for the maturation, they use ew oak which adds to the aromas and flavours.

The first two whiskies from the distillery will be relea- ed at the beginning of December 2013 – one is a single alt matured in new French oak, while the other has een made from three grains (barley, wheat and oats) nd matured in new American oak.

inland

STILLERY: Teerenpeli, Lahti
OUNDED: 2002
WNER/MANAGER: Anssi Pyysing
www.teerenpeli.com

he first Teerenpeli Single Malt was sold as a 3 year old late 2005, though solely at the owner's restaurant in ahti. Four years later, the first bottles of a 6 year old ere sold in the Teerenpeli Restaurants and later that ear also in the state owned ALKO-shops. In spring 2011, was time for an 8 year old, which was introduced at Vhisky Live in London. This is a mix of whisky from both ourbon and sherry casks. In late 2012, a 100% sherry natured version called Teerenpeli Distiller´s Choice Kaski vas released.

Teerenpeli is equipped with one wash still (1,500 litres) nd one spirit still (900 litres) and the average fermen- ation time in the washback is 70 hours. Lightly peated nalt obtained locally is used and the whisky matures in x-sherry and ex-bourbon casks from Speyside Coope- age. In August 2010 a new mash tun was installed and ter that month a new visitor centre was opened. The

projected production for 2013 is 30,000 litres but accor- ding to the owners the plan is to increase even further.

France

DISTILLERY: Glann ar Mor, Pleubian, Bretagne
FOUNDED: 1999
OWNER/MANAGER: Jean Donnay
www.glannarmor.com

The owner of Glann ar Mor Distillery in Brittany, Jean Donnay, already started his first trials back in 1999. He then made some changes to the distillery and the process and regular production commenced in 2005. The distillery is very much about celebrating the traditional way of dis- tilling malt whisky. The two small stills are directly fired and Donnay uses worm tubs for condensing the spirit. He practises a long fermentation in wooden washbacks and the distillation is very slow. For maturation, first fill bour- bon barrels and ex-Sauternes casks are used and when the whisky is bottled, there is neither chill filtration nor caramel colouring. The full capacity is 50,000 bottles per year. In the last twelve months sales have grown signifi- cantly and Jean Donnay has been forced to employ more people to keep up with demand. Apart from France the whisky is now selling also in the UK, Sweden, Denmark, Germany, The Netherlands, Italy, Singapore, Taiwan and Canada.

There are two versions of the whisky from Glann ar Mor – the unpeated Glann ar Mor matured in bourbon barrels and the peated Kornog matured in either bour- bon barrels or Sauternes casks. The first release, in 2008, was a 3 year old Glann ar Mor followed in 2009 by a Kornog bottled at cask strength. The most recent releases of the two expressions bottled at 46% are Kornog Taouarc´h Trived 13 BC and Glann ar Mor 2L Gwech 13. Limited bottlings are released regularly with Kornog Saint Ivy 2013 (58,6%) and Kornog Sant Erwan 2013 (50%) as the most recent. Apart from the Glann ar Mor venture, Jean Donnay has also specialised in double ma- turation Single Malts. The "Celtique Connexion" range includes whiskies distilled and matured in Scotland, then further matured at the company's seaside warehouse. The whiskies can be found at *www.tregorwhisky.com*

The beautiful still room at Glann ar Mor distillery in Bretagne

DISTILLERY: Distillerie Warenghem, Lannion, Bretagne
FOUNDED: 1900 (whisky since 1994)
OWNER/MANAGER: Gilles Leizour
www.distillerie-warenghem.com

Leon Warenghem founded the distillery at the beginning of the 20th century and in 1967 his grandson, Paul-Henri Warenghem, took over together with his associate, Yves Leizour. They moved the distillery to its current location on the outskirts of Lannion in Brittany. Today, the distillery is owned by the Leizour family and it was Gilles Leizour, taking over in 1983, who added whisky production to the repertoire. The first whisky, a blend called WB, was released in 1987 and in the ensuing year, the first single malt distilled in France, Armorik, was launched.

The distillery is equipped with a 6,000 litres semi lauter mash tun, four stainless steel washbacks and two, traditional copper pot stills (a 6,000 litres wash still and a 3,500 litres spirit still). The company currently produces 100,000 litres of pure alcohol per year and 30% thereof is grain spirit for their blends.

The single malt core range consists of Armorik Edition Original and Armorik Sherry Finish. Both are around 4 years old, bottled at 40%, have matured in ex-bourbon casks plus a few months in sherry butts for the Sherry Finish and are sold in supermarkets in France. Armorik Classic, a mix of 4 to 8 year old whiskies from bourbon and sherry casks and the 7 year old Armorik Double Maturation which has spent time in both new oak and sherry wood are earmarked for export. Both are unchillfiltered and bottled at 46%. Armorik Millesime 2002 is a limited although re-occurring release and the latest expression, released in June 2013, was 11 years old and matured in an Oloroso sherry cask. Finally, there are three blended whiskies; WB Whisky Breton which is 3-4 years old with 25% malt and 75% grain whisky, Galleg with the same age but 50% malt whisky and Breizh which is slightly older and 50% malt whisky. A total of 250,000 bottles were sold last year.

Other distilleries in France

Distillerie Claeyssens de Wambrechies
Wambrechies, Nord-Pas-de-Calais, founded in 1817 (whisky since 2000)
www.wambrechies.com

Claeyssens distillery is one of the oldest in France, tracing its history back to 1817 and located in a building classified as a historic monument in 1999. Located in the town of Wambrechies near Roubaix, the distillery was originally famous for its genever, a traditional gin-like spirit consumed in the north of France, in Belgium and in Holland. In 2000, the distillery started to produce single malt whisky, launching Wambrechies 3 year old in 2003, and an 8 year old version in 2009. In the spring of 2013, two 12 year old bottlings (the oldest French whisky to date) were released: one aged in madeira casks and the other in sherry casks, both bottled at 40%.

Distillerie Meyer
Hohwarth, Alsace, founded in 1958 (whisky since 2007)
www.distilleriemeyer.fr

The Meyer distillery was founded in 1958 by Fridolin Meyer, a fruit wholesaler who thought it would be an excellent way to make money from his unsold fruit. Together with his son Jean-Claude who joined the company in 1975, Meyer soon became one of the most awarded distillers in France. At the beginning of the 2000's, Jean-Claude Meyer helped the Venturini family in Corsica to start producing whisky under the P&M brand, and this convinced him to produce his own whisky. In 2007, they launched two no-age statement whiskies: one blend and one single malt. More than 5 000 casks are currently maturing in the new warehouse built in 2012. Mainly sold in supermarkets in the Alsace area, Meyer's is probably one of the best selling French whiskies. There are currently three different versions – Meyer´s Pur Malt (a single malt), Meyer´s Hohwarth Blend Superieur and, new since summer 2013, Oncle Meyer´s Blend Superieur.

Armorik Millesime 10 year old and Double Maturation

Warenghem still room

Distillerie Kaerilis
Belle-Île, Bretagne, founded in 2011
www.kaeriliswhisky.com

In 2006, Fabien Mueller started out, like many others in the industry, as an independent bottler, in this case with a range of whiskies distilled in Scotland and finished on Belle-Île, a small island a few kilometers off the south-coast of Brittany. In 2011, he also began to operate a small distillery located at the back of a shop in Le Palais, the main city of the island starting out with just one still – a bain-marie model from Müller -- and some Bourbon barrels. The first bottles will be available in November 2014. Fabien Mueller has plans to grow his own barley and one day releasing a 100% Kaerilis whisky (Kaer-ilis in Breton means Belle-Île).

Distillerie Gilbert Holl
Ribeauvillé, Alsace, founded in 1979 (whisky since 2004)
www.gilbertholl.com

In 1979, Gilbert Holl came across distillation by chance with a friend and began to distill occasionally in the back of his wine and spirits shop. He bought his first still in 1982 in order to produce eaux-de-vie with his own fruit: cherry plums, raspberries and cherries. It wasn't until the beginning of 2000 that he finallly started using his very small still (150l) to make whisky. His very first bottling, Lac'Holl, was put on sale in 2004 and was joined in 2007 by Lac'Holl Junior and in 2009 by Lac'Holl Vieil Or. Production of this light bodied whisky remains very limited.

Distillerie Bertrand
Uberach, Alsace, founded in 1874 (whisky since 2002)
www.distillerie-bertrand.com

Distillerie Bertrand is an independent affiliate of Wolfberger, the large wine and eaux-de-vie producer. The manager, Jean Metzger, gets his malt from a local brewer and then distils it in Holstein type stills. Two different types of whisky are produced. One is a single malt at 42.2%, non-chill filtered and with maturation in both new barrels and barrels which have previously contained the fortified wine Banyuls. The other is a single cask at 43.8% matured only in Banyuls barrels. The first bottles, aged 4 years, were released in late 2006 and the annual production is around 7,000 bottles with 5,000 bottles currently being sold per year.

Distillerie Lehmann
Obernai, Alsace, founded in 1850 (whisky since 2008)
www.distillerielehmann.com

The story of the Lehmann distillery starts in 1850 when the family of the actual owner set up a still in Bischoff-heim. Yves Lehmann inherited the facility in 1982 but decided to move all the equipment to a new distillery in 1993. In 2001, he bought two Rump stills (1,200 litres and 600 litres) and started to produce single malt whisky which he ages exclusively in French white wine casks. The first bottling, aged for 7 years in Bordeaux casks and bottled at 40%, was launched in 2008 under the brand Elsass Whisky ("Alsace" in the Alsacian dialect). A second bottling, aged for 8 years in Sauternes casks and bottled at 50%, followed soon after, whilst a third, aged entirely in Coteaux-du-Layon casks has yet to be bottled.

Distillerie Hepp
Uberach, Alsace, founded in 1972 (whisky since 2005)
www.distillerie-hepp.com

A town with only 1000 inhabitants but two whisky distilleries, Uberach means "beyond the river" in the Alsacian dialect. A family-owned distillery, Hepp started producing single malt whisky in 2005, on the initiative of the then owner's son, Yannick. Although there is currently only one official expression, a no-age statement bottled at 42% under the brand Tharcis Hepp, Hepp also supplies the independant bottler Denis Hanns with liquid for Authentic Whisky Alsace AWA, a range of single cask whiskies finished in Alsacian wine (riesling, gewurtztra-miner and pinot gris) and brandy (kirsch and cherry plum) casks.

Distillerie Grallet Dupic
Rozelieures, Lorraine, founded in 1860 (whisky since 2007)
www.maisondelamirabelle.com

Hubert Grallet had been distilling cherry plums for many years when his daughter married a barley farmer, Christophe Dupic: following a dare issued during a well-lubricated dinner, they decided to try their hand at whisky production, and launched the Glen Rozelieures brand in 2007, changing it to G. Rozelieures after being menaced by the SWA. Two versions are currently available – one aged in sherry casks, the other lightly peated and aged in Sauternes casks. Rozelieures is also bottled for the chain of En Passant Par La Lorraine boutiques under the brand name Lughnasadh ("August" in Gaelic).

Brûlerie du Revermont
Nevy sur Seille, Franche-Comté,
founded in 1991 (whisky since 2003)
www.marielouisetissot-levin.com

For many years, the Tissot family were itinerant distillers offering their services to the many wine producers in the Franche-Comté area. Relying upon a very unique distillation set-up – three Blavier pot stills, designed and built in the early 1930's for the perfume industry – they have been producing single malt whisky since 2003. Whilst the whisky was originally distilled to order by Bruno Mangin of the Rouget de Lisle Brewery, Pascal & Joseph Tissot launched their own whisky brand Prohibition in 2011. Aged in "feuillettes" (114 litre half-casks coopered specially for Macvin and Vin de Paille wines), the whisky is reduced to 42% and bottled un-coloured cask by cask.

Rouget de Lisle
Bletterans, Franche-Comté,
founded in 1994 (whisky since 2006),
www.brasserie-rouget-lisle.com

Rouget de Lisle (named after the man who wrote the lyrics to the French national anthem La Marseillaise) is a micro-brewery created by Bruno Mangin and his wife. Having made a first unsuccessful attempt to distill in 1998, they tried again In 2006, commissioning the Brûlerie du Revermont to do it for them. This proved to be a good idea and the first Rouget De Lisle single malt whisky was released in 2009. In 2012, Bruno Mangin bought his own still, a Sofac Armagnac still with a capacity of 1, 500 litres. Current bottlings are from the numerous casks he filled during his association with the Tissot family and which lie maturing in his own warehouse. The very first 100% Rouget de Lisle whisky won't be available until some time towards the end of 2015.

Distillerie Brunet
Cognac, Poitou-Charentes,
founded in 1920 (whisky since 2009)
www.drinkbrenne.com

With more than 5 000 stills in operation, the Poitou-Charentes region in Cognac boasts the highest concentration of distillers in the world. But apart from cognac there is whisky produced here as well. The Brunet distillery, owned by Stéphane Brunet, was founded in 1920 but started to distill whisky in 2006. His whisky, Tradition Malt, was launched in 2009 and has already found its way to the USA where it is sold under the Brenne brand name created by Allison Patel, a whisky connoisseur and spirits enthusiast who expertly associated the fame of cognac. Each version, bottled at 80° proof (40%) comes from a single cask.

Brasserie Michard

Limoges, Limousin, founded in 1987 (whisky since 2011)
www.bieres-michard.com

The Limousin area is very well known for its forests of oak trees cherished by the cognac industry, but not really for its eaux-de-vie, nor for its whisky. However, that could change thanks to Michard, a brewery founded in 1987 by Jean Michard. On the initiative of his daughter, Julie, he bottled his first single malt in 2011. Using their own unique yeast, the first batch of their whisky is highly original and very fruity. Available in an 800 bottle limited edition, it will be followed by a second batch some time in late 2013 or early 2014.

Distillerie de Northmaen

La Chapelle Saint-Ouen, Haute-Normandie, founded in 1997 (whisky since 2005)
www.northmaen.com

Northmaen is a craft brewery founded in 1997 by Dominique Camus and his wife. Every year since 2005, they have bottled and sold Thor Boyo, a 3 year old single malt, distilled in a small mobile pot still. In 2009, they released a 5 year old cask strength (59%) version and, in 2013, the oldest version to date – an 8 year old bottled at 44% under the brand name Sleipnir.

Distillerie Castan

Villeneuve sur Vère, Midi-Pyrénées, founded in 1946 (whisky since 2013)
www.distillerie-castan.com

Castan distilling activities can be traced back to 1941 when Gilbert Castan bought a mobile still. His son, Jacques, will go down in history as the last itinerant distiller of its county since his son Sébastien Castan, the third generation, decided in 2010 to permanently locate the still in a distillery. That same year, he distilled his first whisky and aged the spirit in ex-Gaillac wine casks, launching it in May 2013 as Villanova Berbie, the first in a series of biannual bottlings, some of them peated.

Domaine des Hautes-Glaces

Saint Jean d´Hérans, Rhône-Alpes, founded in 2009 (whisky since 2013)
www.hautesglaces.com

Jérémy Bricka and Frédéric Revol have decided to produce whisky from the barley to the bottle! Apart from growing their own barley, all the parts of whisky production take place at the distillery – malting, brewing, distillation, maturation and bottling. All the barley (and also some rye) is ecologically grown. Their first whisky won´t be released until 2015 but at the moment you can buy their new make and single malt spirits.

The new Blaue Maus distillery

Germany

DISTILLERY: Whisky-Destillerie Blaue Maus, Eggolsheim-Neuses
FOUNDED: 1980
OWNER/MANAGER: Robert Fleischmann
www.fleischmann-whisky.de

This is the oldest single malt whisky distillery in Germany and it celebrated its 30th anniversary in 2013. This was also a celebration of the first German single malt whisky which was distilled in 1983. It took, however, 15 years before the first whisky, Glen Mouse 1986, appeared. Fleischmann uses unpeated malt and the whisky mature for approximately eight years in casks of fresh German Oak. A completely new distillery became operational in April 2013. All whisky from Blaue Maus are single cask and there are currently around ten single malts in the range, for example Blaue Maus, Spinnaker, Krottentaler, Schwarzer Pirat, Grüner Hund, Austrasier and Old Fahr. Some of them are released at cask strength while others are reduced to 40%. To celebrate the 30th anniversary, some limited releases were made in June 2013 – for example, Blaue Maus and Spinnaker, both in 20 and 25 year old versions.

DISTILLERY: Slyrs Destillerie, Schliersee
FOUNDED: 1928 (whisky since 1999)
OWNER/MANAGER: Florian Stetter
www.slyrs.de

Lantenhammer Destillerie in Schliersee, Bavaria was founded in 1928 and was producing mainly brandy until 1999 when whisky took preference, and in 2003 Slyrs Destillerie was founded. The malt, smoked with beech, comes from locally grown grain and the spirit is distilled twice at low temperatures in the 1,500 litre stills. Maturation takes place in charred 225-litre casks of new American White Oak from Missouri. Investments in three new fermentation tanks (washbacks) and a malt silo during 2009/2010 increased the capacity to 60,000 bottles.

The non chill-filtered whisky is called Slyrs after the original name of the surrounding area, Schliers. Around 40,000 bottles are sold annually. The core expressions are a 3 year old bottled at 43% and a cask strength version. In March 2013, two limited versions were released – one with a finish in PX sherry casks and the other with a finish in Oloroso casks. The owners also envisage releasing a 12 year old in 2015. Slyrs whisky is available in several European countries and is also exported to the USA and Australia.

The limited Slyrs Sherry Edition PX cask

DISTILLERY: Hammerschmiede, Zorge
FOUNDED: 1984 (whisky since 2002)
OWNER/MANAGER: Alexander Buchholz
www.hammerschmiede.de

In keeping with many other small whisky producers on mainland Europe, Hammerschmiede's main products are liqueurs, bitters and spirits from fruit, berries and herbs. But whisky distilling was only embarked on in 2002 and whisky production has now increased remarkably to 4,000 bottles per year. The first bottles were released in 2006 under the name Glan Iarran. Today, all whisky produced has changed name to Glen Els. After experimenting with various single cask releases, a distinct range of whiskies evolved. Glen Els Journey is the core expression, together with Ember, which is woodsmoked and Unique Distillery Edition which is always from a sherry cask. Journey and Ember are made from a combination of different casks (Sherry, Port, Malaga, Madeira and red Bourdeaux). These whiskies are complemented by the Woodsmoked Malts, a range of single cask bottlings where the whisky is always smoked but has matured in a variety of casks – PX sherry, ruby port, moscatel, Amarone, Sauternes, Marsala etc. Finally, there is the Alrik by Glen Els which according to the owner, Alexander Buchholz, is the ultimate woodsmoked malt, always matured in a PX sherry cask and released once a year. The term woodsmoked should not be confused with peat which is rarely used in German whisky production. Instead, the malted barley gets a smoky flavour from burning alder and beech for 4-36 hours while drying the malt.

Other distilleries in Germany

Spreewälder Feinbrand- & Likörfabrik
Schlepzig, founded in 2004 (whisky production)
www.spreewaldbrennerei.de

The product range consists of different kinds of beers, eau-de-vie and rum, and since 2004 malt whisky is also included. The distillery is equipped with a 650 litre still with eight trays in the fractionating column and is fired by using gas. The annual production of whisky and rum has now increased to 15,000 litres per year. French Oak casks, that have previously contained wine made of Sylvaner and Riesling grapes, are used for maturation, as well as new Spessart oak casks. Torsten Römer released his first whisky; Sloupisti, as a 3 year old in 2007. Recent bottlings have been older and there is also a cask

strength version. Since 2011, 40 casks per year are filled and bigger volumes are expected to be released as from 2014.

Bayerwald-Bärwurzerei und Spezialitäten-Brennerei Liebl
Kötzting, founded in 1970 (whisky since 2006)
www.coillmor.com

In 1970 Gerhard Liebl started spirit distillation from fruits and berries and in 2006 his son, Gerhard Liebl Jr., built a completely new whisky distillery. Maturation takes place in first or second fill ex-bourbon barrels, except for whisky destined to be bottled as single casks. Sherry, Port, Bordeaux and Cognac casks are used here. About 10,000 litres of whisky are produced per year and in 2009 the first 1,500 bottles bearing the name Coillmór were released in three different expressions – American White Oak, Sherry single cask and Bordeaux single cask. The most recent releases include a 5 year old Bourdeaux single cask and a peated 5 year old matured in sherry casks.

Brennerei Höhler
Aarbergen, founded in 1895 (whisky since 2001)
www.brennerei-hoehler.de

The main produce from this distillery in Hessen consists of different distillates from fruit and berries. The first whisky, a bourbon variety, was distilled in 2001 and released in 2004. Since then, Karl-Holger Höhler has experimented with different types of grain (rye, barley, spelt and oat). A couple of the more recent releases of his Whesskey (so called since it is from the province Hessen) are a Cara-Aroma Single Malt and single malts made from smoked (and not peated) barley.

Stickum Brennerei (Uerige)
Düsseldorf, founded in 2007
www.stickum.de

Uerige Brewery, which celebrated its 150th anniversary last year, was completed with a distillery in 2007. The wash comes from their own brewery, of course, and the distillation takes place in a 250 litre column still. For the maturation they not only use new oak but also bourbon, sherry and port casks. The distillery produces 1,200 litres per year of their whisky BAAS and the first bottling (a 3 year old) was released in December 2010. The whisky is sold in Germany but could also, surprisingly, be found in Whisky Shop in San Francisco (July 2012).

Preussische Whiskydestillerie
Mark Landin, founded in 2009
www.preussischerwhisky.de

Cornelia Bohn, one of few female whisky producers in Germany, purchased a closed-down distillery in 2009 in the Uckermark region, one hour's drive from Berlin. The distillery had been operational for 100 years up until WWII when Russian soldiers took it apart and the last copper stills disappeared in the 1950s. She installed a 550 litre copper still with a 4-plate rectification column attached and brought in malt from a malting in Bamberg. Some of the malt is smoked (not peated) using beechwood. The fermentation is done with all the solids from the mashing still left in the washbacks, to get a more full-bodied and robust result. The spirit is distilled very slowly five to six times and is then matured in casks made of new, toasted American oak, as well as new German Spessart oak. Since February 2013 only organic barley is used for the distillation. The first whisky was released as a 3 year old in December 2012 and was followed by three more in 2013 – March, June and November.

Glen Els Journey from Hammerschmiede and the first Preussicher Whisky

Kleinbrennerei Fitzke
Herbolzheim-Broggingen
founded in1874 (whisky since 2004)
www.kleinbrennerei-fitzke.de

The main commerce for this old distillery is the production of schnapps, eau de viex and vodka, but they also distil 900 litres of whisky from different grains. Mashing, fermentation and distillation all take place at the distillery and for maturation they use 30 litres oak casks. For the first six months they use virgin oak and thereafter the spirit is filled into used barrels for another two and a half years. The first release of the Schwarzwälder Whisky single malt was in 2007 and new batches have been launched ever since. New, malted whiskies for 2013 have been distilled using buckwheat, sorghum and emmer wheat.

Rieger & Hofmeister
Fellbach, founded in 1994 (whisky since 2006)
www.rieger-hofmeister.de

Marcus Hofmeister´s stepfather, Albrecht Rieger, started the distillery and when Marcus entered the business in 2006 he expanded it to also include whisky production. The mashing is done in a keg with a mixer, the mash is then fermented in a stainless steel tank for five days before distillation. Marcus selects a middle cut starting at 80% and coming off at 70% and maturation takes place in casks from local wine producers. The first release of this Schwäbischer Whisky was in 2009 and currently there are two expressions in the range – a single malt matured in Pinot Noir casks and a Malt & Grain (50% wheat, 40% barley and 10% smoked barley) from Chardonnay casks. By the end of 2012 a malted rye was distilled and at the beginning of 2013 a lightly peated malt from barley.

Kinzigbrennerei
Biberach, founded in 1937 (whisky since 2004)
www.kinzigbrennerei.de

Martin Brosamer is the third generation in the family and he is also the one who expanded the production in 2004 to include whisky. The total production of whisky is 2,000 litres annually. In the beginning, Martin filled small casks (50 litres) made of new oak but has progressively moved to larger casks. The first release in 2008 was Badische Whisky, a blend made from wheat and barley. Two years later came Biberacher Whisky, the first single malt and in 2012, the range was expanded with Schwarzwälder Rye Whisky and the smoky single malt Kinzigtäler Whisky.

Destillerie Kammer-Kirsch
Karlsruhe, founded in1961 (whisky since 2006)
www.kammer-kirsch.de

Like for so many distilleries, production of spirits from various fruits and berries is the main focus for Kammer-Kirsch and they are especially known for their Kirschwasser from cherries. In 2006 they started a cooperation with the brewery, Landesbrauerei Rothaus, where the brewery delivers a fermented wash to the distillery and they continue distilling a whisky called Rothaus Black Forest Single Malt Whisky. The whisky was launched in 2009 and every year in March a new batch is released. Bourbon casks are used for maturation and besides the "original" version; there is a special edition with a wood finish. In 2011 a Glendronach sherry cask was used to enhance the whisky and in 2012 it was a Madeira cask. Around 6,000 bottles are produced every year.

Obsthof am Berg
Kriftel, founded in 1983 (whisky since 2009)
www.obsthof-am-berg.de, www.gilors.de

Holger and Ralf Heinrich are the third generation running this distillery and their focal point is to produce spirits from fruits and berries. In 2009 the two brothers

started whisky production and the first release of their 3 year old single malt Gilors was in 2012. The whisky is non chillfiltered and the majority of the production is unpeated. For maturation they use 100-250 litre ex-sherry and ex-port casks and several new expressions were launched during 2013. The yearly production is 1,200 litres.

AV Brennerei
Wincheringen, founded in 1824 (whisky since 2006)
www.avadisdistillery.de

For generations, the Vallendar family have been making schnapps and edelbrände on a farm in an area where France, Luxembourg and Germany's borders meet. Since 2006 the brothers Andreas and Carlo Vallendar, also produce malt whisky. Around 2,000 bottles per annum are available for purchase and the oak casks from France have previously been used for maturing white Mosel wine. Threeland Whisky is a 3 year old and the range also consists of three finishes – Oloroso, Port and Bourbon

Birkenhof-Brennerei
Nistertal, founded in 1848 (whisky since 2002)
www.birkenhof-brennerei.de

The traditional production of edelbrände made from a delightful variety of fruits and berries was complemented with whisky production in 2002. The first release was a 5 year old rye whisky under the name Fading Hill in 2008. This was followed a year later by a single malt. The most recent single malt bottling is from April 2013 – a single ex-bourbon cask distilled in 2008.

Brennerei Faber
Ferschweiler, founded in 1949
www.faber-eifelbrand.de

Established as a producer of eau-de vie from fruits and berries, Ludwig Faber – the third generation of the owners – has included whisky production during the last few years. The only whisky so far is a single malt that has matured for 6 years in barrels made of American white oak.

Steinhauser Destillerie
Kressbronn, founded in 1828 (whisky since 2008)
www.weinkellerei-steinhauser.de

The distillery is situated in the very south of Germany, near Lake Constance, close to Austria. The main products are spirits which are derived from fruits, but whisky also has its own niche. The first release was the single malt Brigantia which was released in November 2011. It was triple distilled and only 111 bottles were released. That was followed by 212 bottles in December 2012. The ultimate goal is to release a 12 year old in 2020 under the name of Constantia.

Weingut Simons
Alzenau-Michelbach, founded in 1879 (whisky since 1998)
www.feinbrenner.eu

The owner, Severin Simon, produces wine from his own vineyards, spirits from fruit as well as gin, vodka and whisky. Until recently all the whisky was produced in a 150 litre still but a new still from Arnold Holstein was recently installed, raising the whisky production from 300 litres per year to 3-5,000 litres. A pure pot still whisky has since been released and the first whisky from 100% malted barley was distilled in January 2013 and is due for release in 2016.

Nordpfälzer Edelobst & Whiskydestille
Winnweiler, founded in 2008
www.nordpfalz-brennerei.com

This fairly new distillery owned by Bernhard Höning is based on the production of spirits from fruits but also distilling whisky. The first release was in 2011, a 3 year old single malt by the name Taranis with a full maturation in a Sauternes cask. In October 2013 a 4 year old from ex-bourbon casks with an Amarone finish was launched and by the end of the year a second distillery was operational.

Brennerei Ziegler
Freudenberg, founded in 1865
www.brennerei-ziegler.de

Like so many other distilleries in Germany, Ziegler has distillation of spirits from fruits and berries as their main business, but has also added a small whisky production. One characteristic that distinguishes itself from most other distilleries is that the maturation takes place not only in oak casks, but also in casks made of chestnut! Their current bottling is a 3 year old called Aureum 1865 Single Malt.

Destillerie Drexler
Arrach, whisky since 2007
www.drexlers-whisky.de

The main business for Reinhard Drexler is the production of spirits from herbs, fruits and berries. In between he also finds the time to produce malt whisky and from August 2013 also rye whisky. The first release was Bayerwoid in 2011 which was followed up by the 3 year old No. 1 Single Cask Malt Whisky in 2012. The whisky matures in fresh American oak and casks that have previously been used for sherry, bourbon and cognac.

Märkische Spezialitäten Brennerei
Hagen, whisky since 2010
www.msb-hagen.de

Under the brand name Bonum Bono, Klaus Wurm and Christian Vormann produce spirits and liqueurs from various fruits. In autumn 2010 they added whisky to the range. The spirit is distilled four times, matured in ex-bourbon barrels in the distillery warehouse for 12 months and then brought to a cave with low temperature and high humidity 20 kilometres from the distillery for further maturation. The first releases have been new

make and aged spirit while the first 3 year old whisky, Tronje van Hagen, is due for release at the beginning of November 2013.

Sylter Offshore
Handewitt, founded in 2011
www.sylter-whisky.com

This whisky comes from the island of Sylt, off the coast of Northern Germany in the North Sea, but ironically, there is no distillery on the island. Instead the spirit is distilled at the Dolleruper distillery in Dollerup on the mainland. The wash is brought in from a brewery in Flensburg, distilled in Holstein stills and filled in casks. For the first 18 months, new oak is used and for the final 18 months, the spirit is re-racked into ex-sherry casks. The casks are then transferred to Sylt for maturation. The idea is that the marine climate and temperature fluctuations will have a positive influence on the spirit. During 2013, 600 litres will be produced. The first single malt will be released in 2014 but young spirit is already for sale!

Republic of Ireland _____

DISTILLERY: Midleton Distillery, Midleton, Co. Cork
FOUNDED: 1975
OWNER/MANAGER: Irish Distillers (Pernod Ricard)
www.irishdistillers.ie

Midleton is by far the biggest distillery in Ireland and the home of Jameson´s Irish Whiskey. The distillery we see today is barely 40 years old but Jameson´s as a brand is of a far older date. John Jameson, the founder, moved from Scotland to Ireland in 1777 and became part-owner in a distillery called Bow Street Distillery in Dublin. Some years later he became the sole owner and renamed the company John Jameson & Son.

In 1966, John Jameson & Son with their distillery in Bow Street merged with John Power & Son and Cork Distillery Company to form Irish Distillers Group. It was decided that the production of the three companies

Part of the impressive Midleton still room

should move to Midleton Distillery in Cork, founded by the Murphy brothers in 1825 and the Bow Street Distillery was closed in 1971. Four years later an ultra modern distillery was built next to the old Midleton distillery and this is what we can see today while the old distillery has been turned into a visitor attraction.

The production at Midleton is divided in two – grain whiskey and single pot still whiskey. The first part is needed for the blends where Jameson´s is the biggest seller. Single pot still whiskey on the other hand is unique to Ireland and has really nothing to do with the vessel used for the distillation but refers to the mash where circa 60% is unmalted barley and the rest is malted. This part of the production is also used for the blends but is being bottled more and more on its own.

Midleton distillery is equipped with mash tuns both for the barley side and the grain side. There are 14 washbacks for grain and 10 for barley and finally three, very large copper pot stills and 5 column stills. The hugely increased demand for Irish whiskey, and for Jameson´s in particular, has forced the owners to heavily expand their capacitiy. The expansion, which will double the capacity and will be ready during 2013, includes a completely new brew house, another 24 washbacks, a new still house with three more pot stills and six new, larger columns replacing the existing. A new maturation facility with 40 warehouses is also currently being built in Dungourney, not far from Midleton. The investment for the whole expansion will be €200m.

Of all the brands produced at Midleton, Jameson´s blended Irish whiskey is by far the biggest. In 2012 the brand sold 48 million bottles and apart from the core expression with no age statement, there are 12 and 18 year olds, Black Barrel, Gold Reserve and a Vintage. Other blended whiskey brands include Paddy, Powers, the exclusive Midleton Very Rare and Tullamore Dew. The latter is produced for the brand owners William Grants who are planning to move that production to a distillery of their own by 2014. In recent years, Midleton has invested increasingly in their second category of whiskies, single pot still, and that range now includes Redbreast (12 and 15 year old), Green Spot, Yellow Spot, Powers John´s Lane and Barry Crocket Legacy. In spring 2013, no less than 10 single cask single pot still bottlings were released with whiskey distilled between 1991 and 1999.

DISTILLERY: Cooley Distillery, Cooley, Co. Louth
FOUNDED: 1987
OWNER/MANAGER: Beam Inc.
www.kilbeggandistillingcompany.com

In the late 1980s the Irish whiskey business was nothing less than a monopoly. From a country where, in the mid 18th century, there were more than 1,000 legal and illegal whiskey distilleries, the numbers had been reduced to two, both of which were owned by the mighty Irish Distillers Group. The one who came to change that picture was John Teeling, a man who's background was very diverse. He holds a doctorate from Harvard Business School but has also been involved with diamond mines in Botswana, oil fields in Iraq and gold deposits in Iran. He bought a disused distillery, restarted it under the name Cooley and managed to create a strong brand. So strong that it attracted interest from a number of stakeholders and in December 2011 it was announced that Beam Inc. had bought the distillery for $95m. A large part of Cooley´s production had been sold to other companies and supermarkets, but Beam announced that this will cease in order to concentrate on their own brands instead. As the time passed after the acquisition it became increasingly clear that the most important part of the takeover for Beam's was the Kilbeggan blended whiskey brand that had already reached some level of success on the American market. Cooley distillery is equipped with one mash tun, four malt and six grain washbacks all made of stainless steel, two copper pot stills and two column stills. There is a production capacity of 650,000 litres of malt spirit and 2,6 million litres of grain spirit.

The Cooley range of whiskies consists of several brands. Connemara single malts, which are all more or less peated, consist of a no age, a 12 year old, a cask strength, sherry finish and the heavily peated Turf Mor. The latter two are part of a series of limited expressions called The Small Batch Collection. A new member of this range for 2011, replacing the sherry finish, was Bog Oak with the whiskey maturing in 2000 year old oak found in the Irish bog. The rest of Cooley´s single malt range includes Tyrconnel no age, Tyrconnel 15 year old single cask and Tyrconnel wood finishes, as well as Locke's 8 years old. A number of blended whiskeys are also produced, as is a single grain, Greenore 8 years old. An 18 year old version of the latter was recently released.

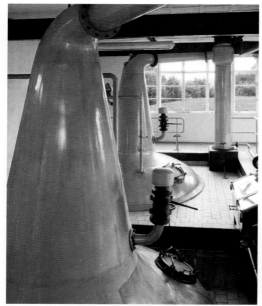

Stills at Cooley distillery

The warehouse at Kilbeggan distillery

DISTILLERY: Kilbeggan Distillery,
Kilbeggan, Co. Westmeath
FOUNDED: 1757
OWNER/MANAGER: Beam Inc.
www.kilbegganwhiskey.com

Kilbeggan distillery has now been producing for six years since its sensational re-birth in 2007. It was the owners of Cooley distillery with John Teeling at the forefront, who decided to bring the distillery back to life and it is now the oldest producing whiskey distillery in the world. The distillery, which lies in the town Kilbeggan on the N6 and just an hour's drive west of Dublin, was bought by John Teeling and his Cooley Distillery way back in 1988. Eventually, the new owner decided to reinstate the distillery to its former glory and to start distilling again. Meanwhile, a blended Kilbeggan whiskey, a brand taken over simultaneously with the distillery, was selling with great success. In December 2011, Cooley Distillery was taken over by Beam Inc. and they are now also the owners of Kilbeggan. It is no secret that Beam's biggest interest lies in the Kilbeggan blended whiskey brand which is very popular in the USA. Since most of the production for the Kilbeggan blend is confined to Cooley distillery in Riverstown, it remains to be seen what will now happen to Kilbeggan distillery.

At the moment, the distillery is equipped with a wooden mash tun, four Oregon pine washbacks and two stills with one of them being 180 years old. The production at the distillery spans over a wide range of techniques and whiskey varieties including malt whiskey, pure pot still whiskey (malted and unmalted barley mixed), rye whiskey from pot stills and triple distillation.

The first single malt whiskey release (a 3 year old bottled at 40%) from the new production came in June 2010 and a second batch, 5 years old, was released in 2012. The blended range of Kilbeggan includes a no age statement and an 18 year old. There has also been a release of Poitín (unaged spirit) under the name of Cooley but distilled at Kilbeggan.

Other distilleries in Ireland

The Dingle Whiskey Distillery
Milltown, Dingle, Co. Kerry, founded in 2012
www.dinglefoundingfathers.com

Permission to build a distillery in Dingle, County Kerry, was applied for in 2008 and was granted in 2009. The people whose brainchild it was, Porterhouse Brewing Company, with Oliver Hughes at the helm and Jerry O'Sullivan, managing director of Southbound Properties, planned to convert an old creamery into a distillery. In 2010, the former business partners went their separate ways and Oliver Hughes found a new location, the old Fitzgerald sawmills. Aided by the whisky consultant, John McDougall, they set about transforming the site into a distillery. Three pot stills and a combined gin/vodka still were installed in June 2012 and the first production of gin and vodka was in October. Whisky distillation began in December and the plan is to produce 100,000 bottles per year. The first products that were launched were Dingle Original Gin and DD Vodka. The triple distilled whisky under the brand names, Dingle Green and Dingle Gold, will not be available until at least 2016/2017. Oliver Hughes owns pubs in Ireland, London and New York and the idea is to turn these bars into Dingle Whiskey Bars.

Alltech/Carlow Distillery
Bagenalstown, founded in 2012
www.carlowbrewing.com

To be quite honest, there is no official name for this distillery (at least not yet) but since it is a joint venture between the American company, Alltech, and the Irish Carlow Brewing Company, we decided to call it Alltech/Carlow distillery. Alltech is an American biotechnology company which specialises in animal nutrition and feed supplements. They purchased Lexington Brewing Company in Kentucky in 1999 and added whisky production in 2008. Then in 2012, the owner, Dr. Pearse Lyons, of Irish descent, initiated a co-operation with the Irish brewer, Carlow, where two copper stills made at Vendome Copper in Kentucky were shipped to Ireland and set up in the Carlow Craft Brewing House. The wash still has a capacity of 1,900 litres and the spirit still 1,000 litres. Both have columns attached and distilling began in November 2012. At the moment the production is targeted at whiskey made of 100% malted barley but there are plans to do an Irish single pot still whiskey with both malted and unmalted barley as well. The capacity is 210,000 litres per year but, within a year, it will have more than doubled to 500,000 litres.

Mark Coffman from Alltech in the United States, Seamus O'Hara from Carlow Brewing Company and Jack O'Shea from Alltech Ireland.

Italy

DISTILLERY: Puni Destillerie, Glurns, South Tyrol
FOUNDED: 2012
OWNER/MANAGER: Ebensperger family
www.puni.com

In a country which embraced whisky in the early 1950s, it seemed a bit odd that there were no domestic production of the spirit. The lack of a whisky distillery in Italy was rectified in February 2012 when the first spirit was distilled at Puni distillery in South Tyrol in the north of Italy. It is owned and run by the Ebensperger family with Albrecht, the father, and one of his sons, Jonas, as the front figures. There are at least two things that distinguish this project from most others. One characteristic is the design of the distillery – a 13-metre tall cube made of red brick. The other is the raw material that they are using. They are making malt whisky but malted barley is only one of three cereals in the recipe. The other two are malted rye and malted wheat. The family calls it Triple Malt and it is their intention to use this combination of cereals for their main line of whiskies. Potential single malts or even single rye whiskies will in the future just be released as limited expressions.

The distillery is equipped with five washbacks made of local larch and the fermentation time is 84 hours. There is one wash still (3,000 litres) and one spirit still (2,000 litres), both made at Forsyth´s in Scotland. The capacity is 80,000 litres of alcohol in a year. For maturation, mainly ex-Bourbon barrels and ex-Marsala casks are being used. Some of the casks are maturing in old bunkers from the Second World War.

The first two spirit products have already been released although the first whisky (3 years old at least) is expected to be launched in autumn 2015. Puni Pure (which was first called Puni White) is a "white dog" or new make spirit, while Puni Alba (previously named Puni Red) has been matured for more than a year in Marsala casks.

Albrecht and Jonas Ebensperger from Puni Distillery

Liechtenstein

DISTILLERY: Brennerei Telser, Triesen
FOUNDED: 1880 (whisky production since 2006)
OWNER/MANAGER: Telser family
www.brennerei-telser.com

The first distillery in Liechtenstein to produce whisky is not a new distillery. It has existed since 1880 and is now run by the fourth generation of the family. Traditions are strong and Telser is probably the only distillery in Europe still using a wood fire to heat the small stills (150 and 120 litres). Like so many other distilleries on mainland Europe, Telser produces mainly spirits from fruits and berries, including grappa and vodka.

For whisky, the distillery uses a mixture of three different malts (some peated) which are fermented and distilled separately. After an extremely long fermentation (lasting 10 days), the spirit is triple distilled (still containing the solids from the mashing and fermentation) and the three different spirits are blended and filled into Pinot Noir barriques and left to mature for a minimum of three years in a 500 year old cellar with an earth floor resembling the dunnage warehouses of Scotland.

The first bottling of Telsington was distilled in May 2006 and released in July 2009. Since then, another four releases have been made, the latest (the 4 year old Telsington V) in October 2012 and a Telsington VI is under way during 2013. There are also plans to release a cask strength version as well as peated expressions.

The Netherlands

DISTILLERY: Zuidam Distillers, Baarle Nassau
FOUNDED: 1974 (whisky since 1998)
OWNER/MANAGER: Zuidam family
www.zuidam.eu

Zuidam Distillers was started in 1974 as a traditional family distillery producing liqueurs, genever, gin and vodka. The first release of a whisky, which goes by the name Millstone, was from the 2002 production and it was bottled in 2007 as a 5 year old. The current range is a 5 year old which comes in both peated and unpeated versions, American oak 10 year old, French Oak 10 year old and Sherry oak 12 year old. There is also a Millstone 100% Rye.

The whisky is double distilled in two 1,000 litre pot stills made by Kothe & Holstein in Germany. The malt is sourced both locally and abroad and there are three stainless steel mash tuns. Fermentation is slow (five days) and takes place at a low temperature. The spirit is matured in new barrels made of American White Oak, but ex bourbon and ex Oloroso sherry casks are also used. Fermentation capacity was increased in 2012 to cope with the rising demand and in 2013 another two washbacks (10,000 litres each) were installed, as well as a new mash tun. According to the owners it is also planned to increase the distillation capacity. The total production capacity at the moment is 280,000 litres of pure alcohol.

Other distilleries in The Netherlands

Us Heit Distillery
Bolsward, founded in 2002
www.usheitdistillery.nl

This is one of many examples where a beer brewery also contains a whisky distillery. Frysk Hynder, as the whisky is called, was the first Dutch whisky and made its debut in 2005 at 3 years of age. The barley is grown in surrounding Friesland and malted at the distillery. The owner of the brewery and distillery, Aart van der Linde, has even developed a malting technique which he describes on a separate website - *www.mouteryfryslan. nl.* Some 10,000 bottles are produced annually and the whisky is matured in various casks - sherry, bourbon, red wine, port and cognac.

Northern Ireland

DISTILLERY: Bushmill´s Distillery,
Bushmills, Co. Antrim
FOUNDED: 1784
OWNER/MANAGER: Diageo
www.bushmills.com

The owners of Bushmill´s usually claim that the distillery is the oldest in the world, dating back to 1608. This is not entirely true as the license issued by James I that year was for the district and not a specific distillery. Be that as it may, this is the second biggest of the Irish distilleries after Midleton with a capacity to produce 4,5 million litres of alcohol a year. In 1972 the distillery became a part of Irish Distillers Group which thereby gained control over the entire whiskey production in Ireland. Irish Distillers were later (1988) purchased by Pernod Ricard which in turn resold Bushmill´s on to Diageo in 2005 at a price tag of €295.5 million. Since the take-over, Diageo has invested heavily into the distillery as well as the brand, resulting in a new mash tun, new stills, more warehouses and a new bottle design. Bushmills now has ten stills and since 2008, the production runs seven days a week which means 4.5 million litres a year. Two kinds of malt are used, one unpeated and one slightly peated. The distillery uses triple distillation, which is the traditional Irish method. It is worth noting though, that this practise wasn´t used at Bushmills until the 1930s.

The Millstone 12 year old Sherry Cask

Bushmills´ core range of single malts consists of a 10 year old, a 16 year old Triple Wood with a finish in Port pipes for 6-9 months and a 21 year old finished in Madeira casks for two years. There is also a 12 year old Distillery Reserve which is sold exclusively at the distillery and the 1608 Anniversary Edition. Black Bush and Bushmills Original are the two main blended whiskeys in the range. With 7,8 million bottles sold, Bushmill´s is the third most sold Irish whiskey after Jameson (48 million bottles) and Tullamore Dew (8,4 million bottles). In order to speed up the sales volumes, Bushmills recently introduced a honeyed version, Bushmills Irish Honey and at the same time launched a completely revised web site in order to appeal more to younger drinkers.

Other distilleries in Northern Ireland

Echlinville Distillery
Kircubbin, Co. Down, founded in 2013
www.feckinwhiskey.com

Shane Braniff, who launched the Feckin Irish Whiskey brand in 2005, has had plans for a distillery of his own for some time now. Feckin Irish Whiskey, which has become popular in USA, has so far been produced at Cooley Distillery but when Beam Inc. bought the distillery in 2012, the new owners decided not to supply whiskey to independent bottlers. Shane had already started the building of the new distillery located near Kircubbin on the Ards Peninsula and some of the equipment was already in place when they were granted a license by Customs and Excise in May 2013. Only a few weeks later, the first spirit was distilled. When completed, the distillery will include a visitor centre, restaurant, bar and museum.

Norway

DISTILLERY: Agder Brenneri, Grimstad
FOUNDED: 1952 (whisky since 2009)
OWNER/MANAGER: K. G. Puntervold AS
www.agderbrenneri.no

The company was founded in 1952 by Karl Gustav Puntervold and for more than 50 years it mainly produced wine from apples and other fruits. The company was taken over by Karl Gustav´s son, Ole, in 1977. In July 2005 the state monopoly in terms of production of spirits in Norway was abolished and Ole decided to take advantage of that. He started to produce aquavit, among other products, and the first products were launched during autumn 2005. Whisky production started in 2009 and Ole currently uses a Holstein still from Germany for the distillation. In November 2012 the first single malt produced in Norway was released (1,750 bottles). It was a single ex-sherry butt called Audny and in spring 2013 another 1,750 bottles were released.

Spain

DISTILLERY: Distilerio Molino del Arco, Segovia
FOUNDED: 1959
OWNER/MANAGER: Distilerias y Crianza del Whisky, (DYC)
www.dyc.es

Spain´s first whisky distillery is definitely not a small artisan distillery like so many others on these pages.

Established by Nicomedes Garcia Lopez already in 1959 (with whisky distilling commencing three years later), this is a distillery with capacity for producing eight million litres of grain whisky and two million litres of malt whisky per year. In addition to that, vodka and rum are produced and there are in-house maltings which safeguard malted barley for the production. The distillery is equipped with six copper pot stills and there are 250,000 casks maturing on site. The blending and bottling plant which used to sit beside the distillery is now relocated to the Anis Castellana plant at Valverde del Majano.

The big seller when it comes to whiskies is a blend simply called DYC which is around 4 years old. It is supplemented by an 8 year old blend and, since 2007, also by DYC Pure Malt, i. e. a vatted malt consisting of malt from the distillery and from selected Scottish distilleries. A brand new expression was also launched in 2009 to commemorate the distillery's 50th anniversary – a 10 year old single malt, the first from the distillery. A recent extension of the range is DYC Red One which is a cherry infused blended whisky.

DYC has an interesting liaison with a Scottish distillery which dates back to the early seventies. It bought Lochside Distillery north of Dundee in 1973 to safeguard malt whisky requirements and retained it until it stopped production in 1992. During that time DYC was acquired by Pedro Domecq, which, in turn, was acquired by Allied Lyons, which eventually changed its name to Allied Domecq. When the latter was bought by Pernod Ricard in 2005, a small share, including DYC, went to Beam Global.

Other distilleries in Spain

Destilerias Liber
Padul, Granada, founded in 2001
www.destileriasliber.com

This distillery is quite a bit younger than its competitor in Segovia, DYC. Destilerias Liber was founded towards the latter part of 2001 and did not start production until late 2002. Like so many other, newly established distilleries, they started distilling rum, marc and vodka – spirits that do not require maturation and can also instantaneously generate cash to the company. For the whisky production, the spirit is double distilled after a fermentation of 48-72 hours. Maturation takes place in sherry casks. The only available whisky on the market is a 5 year old single malt called Embrujo de Granada.

Sweden

DISTILLERY: Mackmyra Svensk Whisky, Valbo
FOUNDED: 1999
OWNER/MANAGER: Mackmyra Svensk Whisky AB
www.mackmyra.se

Mackmyra´s first distillery was built in 1999 and ten years later the company revealed plans to build a brand new facility in Gävle, a few miles from the present distillery at Mackmyra. Come 2012, the distillery was ready and the first distillation took place in spring of that year. The total investment, which includes a whisky village to be built within a ten year period, is expected to amount to approximately £50 million and the capacity of the two distilleries is 1,2 million litres of alcohol per year. The construction of the new distillery is quite extraordinary and with its 37 metre structure it is perhaps one of the tallest distilleries in the world. The reason for its exceptional height is that it is a gravity fed distillery with malt and water coming in at the top of the building and then the entire production process "works itself" downwards to reach the stills at the bottom. Since April 2013, all the

distillation takes place at the new gravitation distillery, while the old distillery will be used for special runs and marketing activities.

Mackmyra whisky is based on two basic recipes, one resulting in a fruity and elegant whisky, the other being more peaty. The peatiness does not stem from peat, but from juniper wood and bog moss. The whisky is matured in a variety of casks, which includes Swedish oak.

The first release in 2006/2007 was a series of six called Preludium. The first "real" launch was in June 2008 – 'Den Första Utgåvan' (The First Edition) and this is still part of the core range. The other two expressions in the core range are Brukswhisky, launched in 2010 and matured in first fill bourbon casks with an addition of whisky matured in sherry casks and Swedish oak and Svensk Rök. The latter is the first peated release from the distillery and was introduced in September 2013. A series of limited editions called Special was introduced in 2009 and the final bottling was Special:10 Kaffegök which was released in spring 2013. Another range of limited editions called Moment was introduced in December 2010 and consists of exceptional casks selected by the Master Blender Angela D`Orazio. Thirteen bottlings have so far been released in that series. The latest was Mareld from June 2013, a peated version with a sherry finish.

The owners also sell their newmake under the name Vit Hund (White Dog) as well as a honey flavoured whisky liqueur called Bee. Currently the whisky is sold in several European countries, Canada and the USA.

DISTILLERY: Spirit of Hven, Hven
FOUNDED: 2007
OWNER/MANAGER: Backafallsbyn AB
www.hven.com

The second Swedish distillery to come on stream, after Mackmyra, was Spirit of Hven, a distillery situated on the island of Hven right between Sweden and Denmark. The first distillation took place in May 2008.

Henric Molin, founder and owner, is a trained chemist and very concerned about choosing the right oak for his casks. The oak is left to air dry for three to five years before the casks are loaned to, especially, wine producers in both the USA and Europe. Around 70% of the casks are

Brukswhisky and Svensk Rök – two of Mackmyra´s core expressions

made of American White oak (*Quercus alba*) while the rest are of Spanish Red oak (*Quercus falcata*) and (a few percent) of Japanese Mizunara oak (*Quercus mongolica*). The distillery is equipped with a 0,5 ton mash tun, six washbacks made of stainless steel and one pair of stills – wash still 2,000 litres and spirit still 1,500 litres.

A long fermentation time of 90-120 hours is used in order to achieve a more full flavoured product with high citric notes and a nutty character. Part of the barley is malted on site and for part of it he uses Swedish peat, sometimes mixed with seaweed and sea-grass, for drying. Around 15,000 litres of whisky is distilled per year and other products include rum made from sugar beet, vodka, gin, aquavit and calvados.

The distillery was expanded in summer 2013 with a new warehouse, an upgraded bottling line and a new spirits laboratory. In the new lab, Henric will have the possibility of examining not only 300 hunderd different types of oak, but also monitoring how spirit matures in other types of wood. He is also installing an instrument for performing GCMS (gas chromatography/mass spectrometry) in his laboratory. Using a new application, he will be able to determine which flavour compounds will appear during the different stages of production.

The first whisky to hit the market, was the lightly peated Urania which was released in 2012. The second launch, in early 2013, was the start of a new series of limited releases called The Seven Stars. The first was called Dubhe which is the second brightest star in the Big Dipper and in the following six years there will be a new expression yearly named after the other stars in the constellation. Dubhe, a 5 year old bottled at 45%, is lightly peated and a vatting of 26 casks; 15 made of American oak that had only held vodka prior to whisky being filled, 9 made of French oak that had been used to mature red Italian wine and finally 2 that were made of the rare Japanese Mizunara oak.

DISTILLERY: Smögen Whisky AB, Hunnebostrand
FOUNDED: 2010
OWNER/MANAGER: Pär Caldenby
www.smogenwhisky.se

In August 2010, Smögen Whisky on the west coast of Sweden, produced its first spirit and thus became the country's third whisky distillery, following Mackmyra and Spirit of Hven. Pär Caldenby – a lawyer, whisky enthusiast and the author of Enjoying Malt Whisky is behind it all. He has designed the facilities himself and much of the equipment is constructed locally. The distillery is equipped with three washbacks (1,600 litres each), a wash still (900 litres) and a spirit still (600 litres). The distillery has the capacity to produce 35,000 litres of alcohol a year. Pär practices a slow distillation with unusually long foreshots (45 minutes) in order not to get a newmake with too many fruity esters. The maturation takes place in casks made of new, toasted French Oak but some of them will also have held sherry. Ex-bourbon barrels made of American white oak and Sauternes cask are also used. The cask size ranges from 28 to 500 litres. Heavily peated malt is imported from Scotland and the vision is to produce an Islay-type of whisky. In summer 2011, the first production from own barley, grown at the distillery, was made. The first release, bottled at cask strength and un chill-filtered, is planned for late 2013 or early 2014 and will probably be around 1,500 – 2,000 bottles.

DISTILLERY: Box Destilleri, Bjärtrå
FOUNDED: 2010
OWNER/MANAGER: Ådalen Destilleri AB
www.boxwhisky.se

The company was founded in 2005 by Mats and Per de Vahl who, during their travels to Scotland, had been inspired to start their own distillery in Sweden. Buildings from the 19th century that had previously been used both as a box factory (hence the distillery name) and a power-plant, were restructured and equipped with a four-roller Boby mill, a semilauter mash tun with a capacity of 1,5 tonnes and three stainless steel washbacks holding 8,000 litres each. The wash still (3,800 litres) and the spirit still (2,500 litres) were both ordered from Forsyth´s in Scotland. The first distillation was made in November 2010 and the distillery has a capacity of 115,000 litres.

Box Destilleri is making two types of whisky – fruity/unpeated and peated. As regards the former, the malted barley comes from Sweden, whereas the peated malt is imported from Belgium where it has been dried using

Dubhe 5 year old – the latest from Spirit of Hven

One of the stills at BOX distillery

peat from Islay. The distillery manager, Roger Melander, wants to create a new make which is as clean as possible through a very slow distillation process with lots of copper contact in the still. The flavour of the spirit is also impacted by the effective condensation using what might be the coldest cooling water in the whisky world, 2 to 6°C, from a nearby river. A fermentation time of 72-96 hours also affects the character. A majority of the casks, from 500 litres down to 40 litres, are first fill bourbon but Oloroso casks, virgin oak and casks made from Hungarian oak have also been filled. A variety of spirit bottlings under the name Försmak (Foretaste) have been released and in autumn 2013 a box of five different spirits, Advanced Master Class, was released. The idea was to showcase differences in flavour owing to malt variety, distillation cut points, cask toasting levels etc. The first whisky will be released in June 2014.

Other distilleries in Sweden

Grythyttan Whisky
Lillkyrka, founded in 2010
www.grythyttanwhisky.se

The company was founded as a result of the initiative of Benny Borgh in 2007 at a farm dating back to the 13th century, which is situated about 180 km west of Stockholm. The company has around 800 share-holders and the distillery came on stream in October 2010. In common with most Swedish distilleries, the stills (900 litres wash still and 600 litres spirit still) were made at Forsyth's in Scotland and the three washbacks are made of Oregon pine. The owners already have plans to build a substantially larger distillery but the time frame has yet to be decided upon.

Three different malt varieties are used; unpeated Swedish malt imported from Scotland, medium peated (16ppm) and heavily peated (50ppm). For maturation they use ex-sherry casks, ex-bourbon barrels from Maker's Mark, as well as new Swedish oak. The capacity of the distillery is 24,000 litres per year. The distillery has a visitor centre and they are also selling new make spirit and future casks. The first whisky, a 3 year old unpeated from ex-sherry casks and bottled at cask strength, will be released for Christmas 2013.

Norrtelje Brenneri
Norrtälje, founded in 2002 (whisky since 2009)
www.norrteljebrenneri.se

This distillery, situated 70 kilometres north of Stockholm, was founded on a farm which has belonged to the owner's family for five generations. The production consists mainly of spirits from ecologically grown fruits and berries. Since 2009, a single malt whisky from ecologically grown barley is also produced. The whisky is double distilled in copper pot stills (400 and 150 litres respectively) from Christian Carl in Germany. Most of the production is matured in 250 litre Oloroso casks with a finish of 3-6 months in French oak casks which have previously held the distillery's own apple spirit. The character of the whisky will be fruity and lightly peated (6ppm) and the first bottling may appear in 2013.

Gammelstilla Whisky
Torsåker, founded in 2005
www.gammelstilla.se

Less than 30 kilometres from the better known Mackmyra lies another distillery since 2011 – Gammelstilla. The company was already founded in 2005 by three friends but today there are more than 200 shareholders. Unlike most of the other Swedish whisky distilleries, they chose to design and build their pot stills themselves. The wash still has a capacity of 500 litres and the spirit still 300 litres and the annual capacity is 20,000 litres per year. The mashing and fermentation takes place in a brewery which has moved into the same facilities. The first distil-

lation took place in April 2012 with a plan to launch the first bottlings in four years.

Gotland Whisky
Romakloster, founded in 2011
www.gotlandwhisky.se

The company behind this distillery was already founded in 2004 with the intention of building a distillery at a farmstead near Klinte. The plans were changed and it was decided to build the distillery at the present location instead, a decommissioned sugar works south of Visby. The distillery is equipped with a wash still (1,600 litres) and a spirit still (900 litres) – both made by Forsyth's in Scotland. The local barley is ecologically grown and malted on site. The floor malting is made easier through the use of a malting robot of their own construction which turns the barley. The whisky is matured in a warehouse situated four metres underground. The goal is to produce two kinds of single malts, unpeated and peated and the capacity is 60,000 litres per year. The distillery came on stream in May 2012 and the plan is to release the first whisky, under the name Isle of Lime, in 2015.

Switzerland

DISTILLERY: Whisky Castle, Elfingen, Aargau
FOUNDED: 2002
OWNER/MANAGER: Ruedi Käser
www.whisky-castle.com

The first whisky from this distillery in Elfingen, founded by Ruedi Käser, reached the market in 2004. It was a single malt under the name Castle Hill. Since then the range of malt whiskies has been expanded and today include Castle Hill Doublewood (3 years old matured both in casks of chestnut and oak), Whisky Smoke Barley (at least 3 years old matured in new oak), Fullmoon (matured in casks from Hungary) and Terroir (4 years old made from Swiss barley and matured in Swiss oak). All these are bottled at 43%. Adding to these are Cask Strength (5 years old and bottled at 58%) and Edition Käser (71% matured in new oak casks from Bordeaux). Other expressions include Girl's Choice, which is a light, 3 year old whisky aged in white wine barrels, Port Cask, which is 4 years old with a full maturation in port pipes and bottled at 50% and Chateau with a maturation in Sauternes casks.

A couple of years ago, Ruedi's son, Raphael, was brought into the business with the express goal of releasing older whiskies and narrowing down the range of expressions. New, open top fermenters were installed in 2010 to add fresher and fruitier notes to the newmake. The owners have also cut down on the number of casks made from new oak and have added a variety of other casks to influence the spirit. The new style of whisky will be available in about two years' time, but some trials may be released earlier. Another goal is to use only local, organically grown grain. The yearly production is between 8,000 and 10,000 litres and on the premises one can have a complete visitor's experience, which includes a restaurant as well as a shop.

DISTILLERY: Brauerei Locher, Appenzell, Appenzell Innerrhoden
FOUNDED: 1886 (whisky since 1999)
OWNER/MANAGER: Locher family
www.säntisspirits.ch, www.saentismalt.ch

This old, family-owned brewery started to produce whisky on a small scale in 1999 when the Swiss government changed laws and allowed for spirit to be distilled from grain. From 2005, larger volumes have been produced.

The whole production takes place in the brewery where there is a Steinecker mash tun holding 10,000 litres. The spirit ferments in stainless steel vats and, for distillation, Holstein stills are used. Brauerei Locher is unique in using old (70 to 100 years) beer casks for the maturation. The core range consists of three expressions; Säntis, bottled at 40%, Dreifaltigkeit which is slightly peated having matured in toasted casks and bottled at 52% and, finally, Sigel which has matured in very small casks and is bottled at 40%. A new range of limited bottlings under the name Alpstein was recently launched. After a few years in a beer cask, these whiskies have received a further maturation in casks that previously held bourbon, port or sherry. In spring 2013, Säntis Malt Cask No 1144 (57,5%) was released. Instead of using a former beer cask this has been matured for 8 years in a Pinot Noir cask.

Other distilleries in Switzerland

Langatun Distillery
Langenthal, Bern, founded in 2007
www.langatun.ch

The distillery was built in 2005 and under the same roof as the brewery Brau AG Langenthal (which was already established in 2001). The reason for this co-habitation was to access a wash for distillation and thereby avoiding investments in mashing equipment. The casks used for maturation are all 225 litres and Swiss oak (Chardonnay), French oak (Chardonnay and red wine) and ex sherry casks are used. The first whisky was produced in 2007 by way of the 3 year old single malt, Olde Deer. In 2011 the whisky underwent a name change to Old Deer and a peated version was launched under the name Old Bear. Both of them are now bottled as 5 year olds and are available at 40% and 64% respectively. The latest new whisky was a single cask rye, Old Eagle, released in March 2013.

Bauernhofbrennerei Lüthy
Muhen, Aargau, founded in 1997 (whisky since 2005)
www.swiss-single-malt.ch

This farm distillery started in 1997 by producing distillates

Säntis Malt from Locher distillery

from fruit, as well as grappa, absinthe and schnapps. The range was expanded to include whisky in 2005 which was distilled in a mobile pot still distillery. Lüthy's ambition is to only use grain from Switzerland in his production. Since it was impossible to obtain peated malt from Swiss barley, he decided to build his own floor maltings in 2009. The first single malt expression to be launched in 2008, was Insel-Whisky, matured in a Chardonnay cask. It was followed by Wyna-Whisky from a sherry cask and Lenzburg-Whisky, another Chardonnay maturation in 2009. Starting in 2010, the yearly bottling was given the name Herr Lüthy and the fourth release from these was in 2012, a Chardonnay maturation.

Brennerei Stadelmann
Altbüron, Luzern, founded in 1932 (whisky since 2003)
www.schnapsbrennen.ch

Established in the 1930s this distillery was mobile for its first 70 years. The current owner's grandfather and father would visit farmers and distil local fruits and berries. Hans Stadelmann took over in 1972 and in 2001 decided to build a stationary distillery. The distillery was equipped with three Holstein-type stills (150-250 litres) and the first whisky was distilled for a local whisky club in 2003. In 2005 the first Luzerner Hinterländer Single Malt was released, although not as a whisky since it was just 1 year old. A year later the first 3 year old was bottled for the whisky club under the name Dorfbachwasser and finally, in 2010, the first official bottling from the distillery in the shape of a 3 year old single malt whisky was released. In autumn 2011, the fourth release was made, a 3 year old matured in a Merlot cask. The first whisky from smoked barley was distilled in 2012.

Etter Distillerie
Zug, founded in 1870 (whisky since 2007)
www.etter-distillerie.ch

This distillery was started in 1870 by Paul Etter and has been in the family ever since. Today it is the third and fourth generations who are running it. Their main produce is eau de vie from various fruits and berries. A sidetrack to the business was entered in 2007 when they decided to distil their first malt whisky. The malted barley was bought from a brewery (Brauerei Baar), distilled at Etter, filled into wine casks and left to mature in moist caves for a minimum of three years. The first release was made in 2010 under the name Johnett Single Malt Whisky and the second, distilled in 2008, was released during the autumn of 2012.

Spezialitätenbrennerei Zürcher
Port, Bern, founded in 1954 (whisky from 2000)
www.lakeland-whisky.ch

The first in the Zürcher family to distil whisky was Heinz Zürcher in 2000, who released the first 1,000 bottles of Lakeland single malt in 2003. Daniel and Ursula Zürcher took over in 2004. They continued their uncle's work with whisky and launched a second release in 2006. The main focus of the distillery is specialising in various distillates of fruit, absinth and liqueur. The latest barrel of Lakeland single malt was released in 2009 as a 3 year old, but the Zürchers are working on the release of older whiskies in the future. The wash for the whisky is bought from Rugenbräu brewery in Interlaken and maturation takes place in Oloroso sherry casks.

Whisky Brennerei Hollen
Lauwil, Baselland, founded in 1999 (for whisky distillation)
www.swiss-whisky.ch, www.single-malt.ch

The first Swiss whisky was distilled at Hollen 1st July 1999. The whisky is stored on French oak casks, which have been used for white wine (Chardonnay) or red wine (Pinot Noir). Most bottlings are 4 years old and contain

42% alcohol. A 5 year old has also been released, which has had three years in Pinot Noir casks followed by two years in Chardonnay casks. Other expressions include a peated version and a cask strength Chardonnay-matured. In 2009 the first 10 year old was released and there has also been a 9 year old double wood. Annual production amounts to roughly 30,000 bottles.

Brennerei Hagen
Hüttwilen, Thurgau, founded in 1999
www.distillerie-hagen.ch

A triple distilled malt whisky is produced by Ueli Hagen in the small village of Hüttwilen in the northernmost part of Switzerland. The spirit is matured in bourbon barrels and the first produce was sold in 2002 as a 3 year old. Ueli Hagen produces mainly schnapps and absinth and distills around 300 bottles of malt whisky a year, a number he expects to double.

Wales _____

DISTILLERY: Penderyn Distillery, Penderyn
FOUNDED: 2000
OWNER/MANAGER: Welsh Whisky Company Ltd
www.welsh-whisky.co.uk

In 1998 four private individuals started The Welsh Whisky Company and two years later, the first Welsh distillery in more than a hundred years started distilling.

A new type of still, developed by David Faraday for Penderyn Distillery, differs from the Scottish and Irish procedures in that the whole process from wash to new make takes place in one single still. But that is not the sole difference. Every distillery in Scotland is required by law, to do the mashing and fermenting on site. At Penderyn, though, the wash is bought from a regional beer brewer and transported to the distillery on a weekly basis. Even though the distillery has been working 24 hours a day to keep up with the increasing demand, it

Independence from Penderyn´s new Icons of Wales range

became obvious in 2012 that they had to do something to increase its capacity. In August 2013, a second still (almost a replica of the first still) was commissioned and the plan is to add another two pot stills, as well as their own mashing equipment early in 2014. The expansion, worth £1m, will triple the production and will also allow the company to experiment with new styles and expressions of single malts.

The first single malt was launched in March 2004. The core range consists of Penderyn Madeira Finish, Penderyn Sherrywood and Penderyn Peated. From 2014, a new addition will be Penderyn Portwood Finish. A special version for the French market (and the company´s biggest seller there) is Penderyn 41, bourbon matured with a Madeira finish. Limited releases in 2012 were a portwood matured expression bottled at 41% and non chill-filtered, Penderyn Grand Slam 2012 which celebrated the success of Wales rugby team in beating all other nations in the annual six nations tournament and Red Flag, the first in a new series of 50 called Icons of Wales. This new range was expanded in 2013 with another two expressions – Independence (a madeira finish like Red Flag) and Dylan, celebrating the centenary of the Welsh poet, Dylan Thomas.

In 2012 Penderyn sold 140,000 bottles with 75% of the sales in the UK and the rest were exported with France as the biggest market. A visitor centre opened in 2008 and attracted 33,000 visitors last year.

NORTH AMERICA

USA _____

DISTILLERY: Stranahans Whiskey Distillery, Denver, Colorado
FOUNDED: 2003
OWNER/MANAGER: Proximo Spirits
www.stranahans.com

Stranahans, founded by Jess Graber and George Stranahan, became a victim of its own success in 2009. In order to keep up with demand, the owners not only had to find a new location, but also needed to bring the mashing in-house instead of being dependent on local breweries. The solution was to move to the closed Heavenly Daze Brewery in Denver in May 2009.

In December 2010, the next significant step in the history of the distillery was taken when the New York based Proximo Spirits (makers of Hangar 1 Vodka and Kraken Rum among others) acquired the company. Their intentions were to increase production even further with the addition of three new stills from Vendome. A surprising decision was also made to withdraw Stranahans Colorado Whiskey from all other markets but Colorado. The owners claim that they want to build up a significant stock before delivering nationally (and also internationally) again.

The whiskey is always made in batches aged from two to five years. Every batch has approximately 5,000 bottles and until autumn of 2013, 110 batches have been released. Except for the core expression, a single barrel is launched once a year under the name Snowflake. The special release for 2013 was Mount Shavano Malbec which had been finished in fresh Malbec casks from a local winery.

DISTILLERY: Clear Creek Distillery, Portland, Oregon
FOUNDED: 1985
OWNER/MANAGER: Stephen McCarthy
www.clearcreekdistillery.com

Steve McCarthy was one of the first to produce malt whiskey in the USA and, like many other, smaller distilleries, they started by distilling eau-de-vie from fruit, especially pears, and then expanded the product line into whiskey. They began making whiskey in 1996 and the first bottles were on the market three years later. There is only one expression at the moment, McCarthy's Oregon Single Malt 3 years old. Steve has for a long time expressed the desire to launch an 8 year old, but so far it has simply not been possible to save adequate quantities due to the high demand.

The whiskey is reminiscent of an Islay and, in fact, the malt is purchased directly from Islay with a phenol specification of 30-40 ppm. Steve expanded the number of pot stills to four a couple of years ago to try and catch up with demand. Maturation takes place in ex-sherry butts with a finish in new Oregon White Oak hogsheads.

Steve has doubled the production of whiskey every year since 2004 which does not, however, seem to be enough to satisfy demand. He only bottles twice a year and the next release is scheduled for October 2013.

DISTILLERY: Charbay Winery & Distillery, St. Helena, California
FOUNDED: 1983
OWNER/MANAGER: Miles and Marko Karakasevic
www.charbay.com

Charbay, which is celebrating its 30th anniversary this year, was founded by Miles Karakasevic – a legend in American craft distilling – and the distillery is now run by his son Marko, the 13th generation in a winemaking and distilling family. With a wide range of products such as wine, vodka, grappa, pastis, rum and port, the owners decided in 1999 to also enter in to whiskey making. That year they took 20,000 gallons of Pilsner and double distilled it in their Charentais pot still. From this distillation, a year old called Double-Barrel Release One (comprising of two barrels) was launched in 2002. There were 840 bottles at cask strength and non-chill filtered. The whis-

key was quite unique since a ready beer, hops and all, rather than wash from a brewery was used.

It took six years before Release II appeared in 2008, this time with a production of 22 barrels and in 2013 it was time for Release III. At 14 years old, it had spent the first six years in charred, new American oak. The reaming eight years it was allowed to mature in stainless steel tanks. This was followed by yet another release where the whiskey had matured for a full 14 years in the same barrel.

In October 2011, a 14 month old Charbay IPA Whiskey (the whole maturation process taking place in French oak) was released, together with a Charbay IPA Light Whiskey (one day on oak and then filled into stainless steel tanks). New releases which followed in 2012 were Charbay R5 Whiskey matured in French oak for 21 months and Charbay R5 Clear Whiskey. R5 stands for the Racer 5 beer from Bear Republic that they are using.

DISTILLERY: St. George Distillery, Alameda, California
FOUNDED: 1982
OWNER/MANAGER: Jörg Rupf/Lance Winters
www.stgeorgespirits.com

The distillery is situated in a hangar at Alameda Point, the old naval air station at San Fransisco Bay. It was founded by Jörg Rupf, a German immigrant, who came to California in 1979 and who was to become one of the forerunners when it came to craft distilling in America. In 1996, Lance Winters joined him and today he is Distiller, as well as co-owner. In 2005, the two were joined by Dave Smith who today has the sole responsibility for the whisky production.

The main produce is based on eau-de-vie which is produced from locally grown fruit, and vodka under the brand name Hangar One. Whiskey production was picked up in 1996 and the first single malt appeared on the market in 1999. Like in so many other craft distilleries, the wash is not produced in-house. St George's obtains theirs from Sierra Nevada Brewery. Some of the malt used, has been dried with alder and beech but is non-peated. Maturation is in bourbon barrels (80%), French Oak (15%) or port pipes (5%). St. George Single Malt used to be sold as a three year old, but nowadays comes to the market as a blend of whiskeys aged from 5 to 12 years. The latest

Lance Winters, co-owner of St George's Distillery and Dave Smith, responsible for the distillery's whisky production

release was Lot 13 and every lot is around 3-4,000 bottles. In 2012, the distillery´s 30th anniversary was celebrated with the production of 715 bottles of a single malt that had spent the previous six months in pear brandy barrels.

DISTILLERY: Edgefield Distillery, Troutdale, Oregon
FOUNDED: 1998
OWNER/MANAGER: Mike and Brian McMenamin
www.mcmenamins.com

Mike and Brian McMenamin started their first pub in Portland, Oregon in 1983. It has now expanded to a chain of more than 60 pubs and hotels in Oregon and Washington. More than 20 of the pubs have adjoining microbreweries (the first opened in 1985) and it is now the fourth-largest chain of brewpubs in the United States.

The chain's first distillery opened in 1998 at their huge Edgefield property in Troutdale and their first whiskey, Hogshead Whiskey (46%), was bottled in 2002. Hogshead is still their number one seller and the production has increased to nearly 70 barrels per year. Starting with the releases in 2012, the character of the whiskey will be more complex and a touch sweeter. The reason for this is that Head Distiller James Whelan back in 2008 started to use three different malted barley recipes for the wash. He also began aging the spirit in both heavily and lightly charred barrels. Another part of the range is the Devil´s Bit, a limited bottling released every year on St. Patrick´s Day. For 2013 it was a blend of a 12 year old wheat whiskey and a 14 year old single malt.

A second distillery was opened in 2011 at the company´s Cornelius Pass Roadhouse location in Hillsboro. A 19th century Charentais alambic still has been acquired and the initial focus will be on whiskey and then moving on to brandy and gin. The first release from the Hillsboro distillery was an un-aged whiskey called The White Owl in 2012 and it was followed by a gin in 2013.

DISTILLERY: Prichard´s Distillery, Kelso, Tennessee
FOUNDED: 1999
OWNER/MANAGER: Phil Prichard
www.prichardsdistillery.com

When Phil Prichard started his business in 1999, it became the first legal distillery for 50 years in Tennessee. Today,

it is the third largest in the state after giants Jack Daniel's and George Dickel. In 2012 the capacity was tripled with the installation of a new 1,500 gallon mash cooker and three additional fermenters. The plan is to increase the capacity even further by adding a 1,500 gallon wash still and turning the old 550 gallon wash still into a spirit still. In late 2012, Phil Prichard also announced plans for opening a second distillery at the Fontanel in Nashville sometime during 2013.

Prichard produces around 20,000 cases per year with different kinds of rum as the main track. The first single malt was launched in 2010 and later releases usually have been vattings from barrels of different age (some up to 10 years old). The whiskey range also includes rye, bourbon and Tennessee whiskey. Their bourbon range was expanded in late 2011 with the innovative Double Chocolate Bourbon where Prichard has infused the essence of chocolate beans into the bourbon.

DISTILLERY: Lexington Brewing & Distilling Co., Lexington, Kentucky
FOUNDED: 1999
OWNER/MANAGER: Pearse Lyons
www.lyonsspirits.com

Most of the producers of malt whiskey in the USA have a background in brewing, winemaking or distilling other spirits. This also applies to Lexington Brewing & Distilling Company, as whiskey production is derived from their production of Kentucky Ale. Dr Pearse Lyons' background is interesting – being the owner, the founder and a native of Ireland, he used to work for Irish Distillers in the 1970s. In 1980 he changed direction and founded Alltech Inc, a biotechnology company specializing in animal nutrition and feed supplements. Alltech purchased Lexington Brewing Company in 1999, with the intent to produce an ale that would resemble both an Irish red ale and an English ale. In 2008, two traditional copper pot stills from Scotland were installed with the aim to produce Kentucky´s first malt whiskey. North American 2-row malted barley is mashed in a lauter mash tun and fermented using a yeast designed by Alltech. The first single malt whiskey was released in August 2010 under the name Pearse Lyons Reserve and in autumn 2011 it was time for a release of their Town Branch bourbon

The new Town Branch distillery in Lexington

with the rather unusual mash bill of 51% corn and 49% malted barley.

In autumn 2012 the stills were relocated from the brewery to a new stand alone distillery building right across the street. The new distillery, with a capacity of 150,000 litres of pure alcohol per year, is also a part of the Kentucky Bourbon Trail experience. Two new stills that were made at Vendome Copper and Brass Company in Louisville Kentucky, were shipped to Ireland end of August 2012 to become part of a new distillery located at Carlow Brewing Company in Bagenalstown, Co Carlow.

DISTILLERY: RoughStock Distillery, Bozeman, Montana
FOUNDED: 2008
OWNER/MANAGER: Kari & Bryan Schultz
www.montanawhiskey.com

Unlike many other American micro distilleries which rely on obtaining mash from a nearby brewery, RoughStock buys its 100% Montana grown and malted barley and then mill and mash it themselves in a 1,000 gallon mash cooker. The mash is not drained off into a wash, but brought directly from the mash tun into two 1,000 gallon open top wooden fermenters for a 72 hour fermentation before distillation in two Vendome copper pot stills (500 and 250 gallons). Maturation is on a mix of quarter casks and 225 litre barrels made from new American oak. The distillery moved to a new location in early 2011 and, one year later, two new stills and two Douglas fir fermenters were installed, increasing the capacity significantly.

In 2009, the first bottles of RoughStock Montana Pure Malt Whiskey, the first legally made whiskey in Montana's history since Prohibition, were released. Since then a single barrel bottled at cask strength has been added (Black Label Montana Whiskey) and apart from whiskey made from 100% malted barley, the product range also includes Spring Wheat Whiskey, Sweet Corn Whiskey and Straight Rye Whiskey. In November 2013 a Montana Bourbon Whiskey was added to the range.

DISTILLERY: Tuthilltown Spirits, Gardiner, New York
FOUNDED: 2003
OWNER/MANAGER: Ralph Erenzo & Brian Lee
www.tuthilltown.com

This is the first whiskey distillery in the State of New York since Prohibition. Just 80 miles north of New York City, Ralph Erenzo and Brian Lee produce bourbon, single malt whiskey, rye whiskey, rum, vodka and gin. Erenzo bought the 18th century property in 2001 with the intention of turning it into a rock climbers ranch, but neighbours objected. A change in the law in New York State made it possible to start a micro-distillery. Erenzo thus changed direction and started distilling instead. Erenzo and Lee built the distillery, acquired licences and learned the basic craft over the following two years.

The first products came onto the shelves in 2006 in New York and the whiskey range now consists of Hudson Baby Bourbon, a 2-4 year old bourbon made from 100% New York corn and the company´s biggest seller by far, Four Grain Bourbon (corn, rye, wheat and malted barley), Single Malt Whiskey (aged in small, new, charred American oak casks), Manhattan Rye and New York Corn Whiskey. The spirits range also include Half Moon Orchard Gin (made from wheat and apples), Indigenous Vodka and Tuthilltown Cassis.

A cooperative venture was announced between Tuthilltown and William Grant & Sons (Grants, Glenfiddich, Balvenie et al) in 2010, in which W Grants acquired the Hudson Whiskey brand line in order to market and distribute it around the world. Tuthilltown Spirits remains an independent company that will continue to produce the different spirits. The produce from Tuthilltown currently sells in all 50 states, in Europe, Australia and Hong Kong.

DISTILLERY: Rebecca Creek Distillery, San Antonio, Texas
FOUNDED: 2010
OWNER/MANAGER: Steve Ison and Mike Cameron
www.rebeccacreekdistillery.com

With a background in the insurance business, Mike Cameron and Steve Ison started Rebecca Creek Distillery in 2010. Fermenters and a mash system were bought from Newland Systems in Canada and the 3,000 litre copper pot still, together with the column, was made by the well-known Christian Carl in Germany. The malted barley is sourced from Cargill in Sheboygan, Wisconsin and for maturation charred American oak is used.

The first product to be launched was Enchanted Rock Vodka. The first year alone, 30,000 cases of vodka were sold. First whiskey to be released was Rebecca Creek Fine Texas Whiskey, a blended whiskey which was launched in autumn 2011. Steve and Mike plan for a release of their Single Malt Whiskey sometime during 2013.

At the moment, the production capacity for vodka is 100,000 cases per year and for whiskey 10-20,000 cases, but the owners have even bigger plans, namely, to become the largest craft distillery in North America with a yearly production of 150,000 cases of vodka and 75,000 cases of whiskey.

DISTILLERY: Balcones Distillery, Waco, Texas
FOUNDED: 2008
OWNER/MANAGER: Chip Tate
www.balconesdistilling.com

Chip Tate, the founder of Balcones distillery, is one of the most creative whisky producers in America today. All the equipment in the current distillery was manufactured by Chip and his partners and the creativity is also reflected in the first whiskies that were produced. He was the first to use Hopi blue corn for distillation. Four different expressions of blue corn whiskey have been released so far – Baby Blue, bottled at 46%, followed by True Blue which is a cask strength version. The third variety is called Brimstone Smoked Whiskey but the smoky flavours do not derive from drying the grain using smoke but it is, instead, the whisky itself that is treated with smoke from Texas scrub oak. The fourth release was True Blue 100,

Chip Tate – President and Head Distiller at Balcones distillery

a 100 proof bottling of True Blue. Chip´s biggest seller however, is his Texas Single Malt Whisky. Like his other whiskies it is un chill-filtered and without colouring. Chip has also implemented a method of maturing his whiskies on a rotating scheme in casks of different sizes and woods. The final maturation is always made in bigger barrels. Balcones whisky is typically not aged for more than two years but there are plans to also release older versions. To celebrate the distillery's 5th anniversary, four single barrel releases were made in 2013 including a straight Bourbon bottled at 64,2%, Brimstone Resurrection which is slightly older than the original Brimstone and bottled at full cask strength, a Straight Single Malt and a Straight Corn Whisky.

The demand for Balcones whiskies has grown rapidly and Chip Tate has already expanded the distilling capacity. The big step though, will be a completely new distillery which will be built 5 blocks from the current site and the plan is to start production by early 2015. The expansion has been made possible thanks to a new group of investors and the capacity will initially be 120,000 litres of pure alcohol using two new stills from Forsyth's in Scotland. Eventually the number of stills will increase to 12.

DISTILLERY: Corsair Artisan, Bowling Green, Kentucky and Nashville, Tennessee
FOUNDED: 2008
OWNER/MANAGER: Darek Bell, Andrew Webber and Amy Lee Bell
www.corsairartisan.com

The two founders of Corsair Artisan, Darek Bell and Andrew Webber, were based in Nashville when they came up with the idea in 2008 to start up a distillery. At that time Tennessee law didn´t allow this, so the first distillery was opened across the border in Bowling Green, Kentucky. Two years later, the legislation in Tennessee had changed and a second distillery and brewery were opened up in Nashville. Apart from producing 16 different types of beer, the brewery is also where the wash for all the whisky production takes place. In Nashville, they also have a 240 gallon antique copper pot still. For those spirits in the range that require a second distillation, the low wines are taken to Bowling Green and the custom made 50 gallon still from Vendome Copper.

Corsair Artisan has a wide range of spirits – gin, vodka, absinthe, rum and whiskey. The number of different whiskies released is growing constantly and Corsair Artisan is most likely the distillery in the USA which experiments the most with different types of grain. The range includes Triple Smoke Single Malt Whiskey (made from three different types of smoked malt with an addition of chocolate malt), Wry Moon (unaged 100% rye whiskey), Ryemageddon (an aged version of Wry Moon), Grainiac (a bourbon made from 9 different grains), Insane in the Grain (a 12 grain bourbon!), Triticale Whiskey (made from triticale, a crossing between wheat and rye), Amarillo (a hopped bourbon), Rasputin (a hopped malt whiskey), Quinoa Whiskey and Pumpkin Spice Moonshine (a malt whiskey where different spices and pumpkin are added after fermentation).

Other distilleries in USA

Dry Fly Distilling
Spokane, Washington, founded in 2007
www.dryflydistilling.com

Dry Fly Distilling was the first grain distillery to open in Washington since Prohibition. The first batch of malt whisky was distilled in 2008. The owners expect to produce 200-300 cases of malt whisky annually, but the first bottling will probably not be released until 2017/2018. However, several other types of whisky have been released recently – Bourbon 101, Straight Cask Strength Wheat Whiskey, Port Finish Wheat Whiskey, Peated Wheat Whiskey and Straight Triticale Whiskey (triticale is a hybrid of wheat and rye).The original equipment

consisted of one still, a Christian Carl manufactured in Germany. In autumn of 2008 another still was installed, as well as two additional fermenters, which raised its capacity to 10,000 cases per annum. Another three fermenters were added recently.

Virginia Distillery
Lovingston, Virginia, founded in 2008
www.vadistillery.com

Founded in 2008, the company has over the years struggled to find funding for the distillery. The plan was originally to start distilling in spring of 2009 but things took longer than expected. As of summer 2011, the building was complete and the copper pot stills were in place. The equipment now consists of a 2 tonne mash tun, a 10,000 litre wash still and an 8,000 litre spirit still. The intention is to start distillation by spring of 2014. Meanwhile, the owners have created a series of vatted malt whiskies called "Eades Anticipation Series" where they select two different Scotch single malts, marry them and then let them go through a second maturation in wine barrels. A new release in autumn 2012 was Virginia Highland Malt where a 6 year old Highland malt was finished in a Virginia wine barrel.

Triple Eight Distillery
Nantucket, Massachusetts, founded in 2000
www.ciscobrewers.com

In 1995 Cisco Brewers was established and five years later it was expanded with Triple Eight Distillery. The Nantucket facility consists of a brewery, winery and distillery. Apart from whiskey, Triple Eight also produces vodka, rum and gin. Whiskey production was moved to a new distillery in May 2007. The first 888 bottles (5 barrels) of single malt whiskey were released on 8th August 2008 as an 8 year old. To keep in line with its theme, the price of these first bottles was also $888. The whiskey is named Notch (as in "not Scotch"). More releases have followed, one being a 10 year old in 2011.

Nashoba Valley Winery
Bolton, Massachusetts, founded in 1978 (whiskey since 2003)
www.nashobawinery.com

Nashoba Valley Winery is mainly about wines but over the last decade, the facilities have been expanded with a brewery and a distillery. The owner, Richard Pelletier, produces a wide range of spirits including vodka, brandy and grappa. Since 2003 malt whiskey is also being distilled. The malt is imported and the wash is produced at his own brewery. The whiskey is matured in a combination of ex bourbon barrels and American and French Oak casks, which have previously contained wine.

In autumn 2009, Stimulus, the first single malt was released. The second release of a 5 year old came in 2010 and it is Richard´s intention to release a 5 year old once a year. At the same time he has also put aside whiskey to be sold as a 10 year old and, eventually, as a 15 year old. The first 10 year old is due in 2014 and during that same year he will also bottle a rye whiskey, as well as a corn whiskey. At the moment they are producing about 20 barrels per year.

Woodstone Creek Distillery
Cincinnati, Ohio, founded in 1999
www.woodstonecreek.com

Don and Linda Outterson opened a farm winery in Lebanon, Ohio in 1999 and relocated to the present facilities in 2003 where a distillery was added to the business. The first whiskey, a five grain bourbon (white and yellow corn, malted barley, malted rye, and malted wheat), was released in July 2008 and the second in November. Both bourbons were made of malted grains (no enzymes), 51% corn, sweet mash and without chill-filtering and colouring. In 2010, the Outtersons released a peated 10 year old single malt from malted barley which they call "The Murray Cask", named after Jim Murray who praised it in his Whisky Bible. In 2012 this was followed up by a 12 year old unpeated single malt whiskey, Ridge Runner (a five-grain bourbon white dog) and a blended whiskey. The last one is made from 5% malted wheat, malted barley and malted rye which is mixed with 95% unmalted wheat distillate. The malted whiskey is 8 years old while the unmalted is 3 years. The reason behind this release was to be able to have something on offer for the customers who wished to purchase a more affordable product.

High Plains Distillery
Atchison, Kansas, founded in 2004
www.highplainsinc.com

Former process engineer, Seth Fox, is mainly known for his Most Wanted Vodka of which he sells over 13,000 cases a year in Kansas, Missouri and Texas. The product range was expanded in late 2006 also to include a Most Wanted Kansas Whiskey (reminiscent of a Canadian whisky) and Kansas Bourbon Mash. Fox continued in 2007 to produce his first single malt whiskey made from malted barley but it has not been released yet. He also produces Pioneer Whiskey and a premium vodka called Fox Vodka which is filtered five extra times. The two stills were bought second-hand from Surrey in England. When High Plains opened, it was the first legal distillery in Kansas since 1880. In 2009 he expanded the facility in order to accommodate a production of 70-80,000 cases per year, compared to previous 20,000.

Cedar Ridge Distillery
Swisher, Iowa, founded in 2003
www.crwine.com

Jeff Quint and his wife Laurie started Cedar Ridge Vineyards in downtown Cedar Rapids in 2003 and expanded the business soon afterwards to also include a distillery. After a while they moved to the present location in Swisher, between Cedar Rapids and Iowa City, where they now have two stills in the distillery part. The first whis-

key, a bourbon, was released on 1 July 2010. Malt whiskey production started in 2005 and in May 2013 the time had come for the launch of the first single malt. Four 15 gallon ex-bourbon barrels were bottled after having a finish in different secondary casks (port, rum, sherry and bourbon). The bourbon finish was furthermore peated. Another four casks were released in August (port, cherry wood, madeira and Hungarian oak). Another new release for 2013 was a wheat whiskey.

House Spirits Distillery
Portland, Oregon, founded in 2004
www.housespirits.com

In the absolute vicinity of House Spirits in Portland, another five distilleries have been established, producing vodka, gin, rum and brandy and the area is now called Distillery Row. The main products for House Spirits are Aviation Gin and Krogstad Aquavit but the owners, Christian Krogstad and Matt Mount, also have big plans in store for whiskey.
The first three expressions were released locally in 2009 and this was followed up by more bottlings in 2010 and 2011, which included a blended whiskey called Slab Town Whiskey. In November 2012 it was time for the advent of the first, widely available single malt under the name of Westward Whiskey. It is a 2 year old, double pot distilled and matured in 2-char new American oak. The first batch was 12 barrels but the owners are setting their sights on producing around 200 barrels in 2015.

New Holland Brewing Co.
Holland, Michigan, founded in 1996 (whiskey since 2005)
www.newhollandbrew.com

This company started as a beer brewery, but after a decade, it opened up a micro-distillery as well, and the wash used for the beer is now also used for distilling whiskey. There is a variety of malts for mashing and the house ale yeast is used for fermentation. Until August 2011, the spirit was double distilled in a 225 litre, self-constructed pot still. At that time, the capacity increased tenfold mainly as a result of the installation of a 3,000-litre still. This still had been built in 1932 and hasn't been used since the early 1940s but was then restored.
The first cases of New Holland Artisan Spirits were released in 2008 and among them were Zeppelin Bend, a 3 year old (minimum) straight-malt whiskey which is now their flagship brand. In 2010, the single malt Double Down Barley 6 months old and aged in five and eight gallon casks was released. A rye and a bourbon released in 2011 and 2012 respectively, saw the release of batch number 2 of Double Down Barley. Later that year, a novelty was introduced – Beer Barrel Bourbon which was a matured bourbon that was given a finish for 90 days in New Hollands own Dragon's Milk beer barrels.

DownSlope Distilling
Centennial, Colorado, founded in 2008
www.downslopedistilling.com

The three founders were brought together by their interest and passion for craft-brewing when they started the distillery in 2008 and in 2009 they finally got their licence to start distilling. The distillery is equipped with two stills – one very elegant, copper pot still made by Copper Moonshine Stills in Arkansas and a vodka still of an in-house design. The first products to be launched in August 2009 were a vodka made from sugar cane and a white rum. More vodkas and rums were to follow and in April 2010 the first whiskey, Double-Diamond Whiskey, was released. It is made from 65% malted barley and 35% rye and matured in three different barrels in a solera style. The first malt whiskey (a single barrel), available only at the distillery, was released in November 2011. The whiskey had spent two years in a burgundy cask. It was followed by the Irish Immigrant All Malt Whiskey in February 2013. A vatting of 2 year old Double Diamond

The first single malts from Cedar Ridge and House Spirits

Whiskey and 2 year old Single Malt has also been released as well as a malt/rye whiskey aged in a 40 year old French cognac barrel.

Copper Fox Distillery
Sperryville, Virginia, founded in 2000
www.copperfox.biz

Copper Fox Distillery was founded in 2000 by Rick Wasmund. In 2005 they moved to another site where they built a new distillery and began distilling in January 2006. Rick Wasmund has become one of the most unorthodox producers of single malt. He does his own floor malting of barley and it is dried using smoke from selected fruitwood. After mashing, fermentation and distillation, the spirit is filled into oak barrels, together with plenty of hand chipped and toasted chips of apple and cherry trees, as well as oak wood. Adding to the flavour, Wasmund also believes that this procedure drastically speeds up the time necessary for maturation. The first bottles of Wasmund´s Single Malt were just four months old but the current batches are more around 12-16 months. Occasionally he does older bottlings of up to 42 months. Other expressions in the distillery range include Copper Fox Rye Whiskey with a mash bill of 2/3 Virginia rye and 1/3 malted barley and two unaged spirits – Rye Spirit and Single Malt Spirit.

Ballast Point Brewing & Distilling
San Diego, California, founded in 1996 (whiskey since 2008)
www.ballastpoint.com

Building on Jack White´s Home Brew Mart, Jack and Yuseff Cherney founded Ballast Point Brewing Company in 1996. Distilling started in 2008 and it became the first craft distillery in San Diego. The equipment consists of two hybrid pot/column stills – one 200 gallon for gin production and a second 500 gallon for whiskey and rum. The first product to appear on the market was Old Grove gin in 2009. Three Sheets (white) Rum, Three Sheets Barrel Aged Rum and Fugu Vodka have been released thereafter. Two different whiskeys are also produced; a single malt Devil´s Share Whiskey and Devil´s Share Bourbon, both of them maturing in virgin American oak with a

heavy (#3) char for a minimum of three years. They were released for the first time during the summer of 2013.

Bull Run Distillery
Portland, Oregon, founded in 2011
www.bullrundistillery.com

Founded by former brewer, Lee Medoff, an experienced man in the industry, the distillery made its first distillation in early autumn of 2011. The distillery is equipped with two pot stills (800 gallons each) and the plan, to start with, is to use local breweries for the production of the wash but in the future they may be installing their own mashing equipment. The main focus is on 100% Oregon malted barley whiskey but the first release isn´t expected until 2015 when the whiskey will be three years old. Spirits currently for sale include Medoyeff Vodka, a rum from Hawaiian turbinado sugar, a straight bourbon which is also available at barrel strength, as well as with different finishes and an aged aquavit.

Rogue Ales & Spirits
Newport, Oregon, founded in 2009
www.rogue.com

The company started in 1988 as a combined pub and brewery. Over the years the business gradually expanded and now consists of one brewery, two combined brewery/pubs, two distillery pubs (Portland and Newport) and five pubs scattered over Oregon, Washington and California. The main business is still producing Rogue Ales, but apart from whiskey, rum and gin are also distilled.

Two malt whiskies have been released so far. The first, Dead Guy Whiskey, was launched in December 2009 and is based on five different types of barley. It is distilled twice in a 150 gallon Vendom copper pot still and the spirit is matured for one month in charred barrels made of American Oak. The second expression was released in June 2010 under the name Chatoe Rogue Oregon Single Malt Whiskey (the name was recently changed to Rogue Farms Single Malt). It is made from barley grown and floormalted on Rogue´s own farm in Tygh Valley. Part of the malt is smoked using local alder and maple wood chips and the spirit is matured for three months.

Sons of Liberty Spirits Co.
South Kingstown, Rhode Island, founded in 2010
www.solspirits.com

Michael Reppucci started the distillery with the help of the renowned David Pickerell who was Master Distiller for Maker´s Mark for 13 years. This distillery is equipped with a stainless steel mash tun, stainless steel, open top fermenters and one 950 litre combined pot and column still from Vendome. Newly charred American oak barrels are used for maturation. Sons of Liberty is first and foremost a whiskey distillery but the first products that were launched were two versions of Loyal 9 Vodka – Mint/Cucumber and Dark Chocolate/Vanilla Bean. In December 2011 the double distilled Uprising American Whiskey was launched, made from an unhopped stout beer. It was followed by the limited 1765 Collection, a slightly older version of Uprising. Summer 2013 saw the first release of a whiskey made from a hopped IPA flavoured with pumpkin, vanilla, cinnamon and orange peel.

Cut Spike Distillery (formerly Solas Distillery)
La Vista, Nebraska, founded in 2009
www.solasdistillery.com

Lucky Bucket Brewery was opened in 2008 and the sister company Solas Distillery one year later. The founders were Zac Triemert, Brian McGee and Jason Payne but Triemert left the company in May 2012. The remaining owners then decided to shift focus and concentrate more on the distillation side. The first product from Solas distillery to hit the market in 2009 was Joss Vodka while the Cuban-style Chava Rum was released in 2011. In February

Devil´s Share from Ballast Point and Uprising from Sons of Liberty

2010 single malt whiskey was distilled and the first 140 bottles were launched in August 2013. Every month 140 bottles will be released until November 2014 when volumes are going to increase. Cut Spike Single Malt Whiskey is two years old and bottled at 43%.

Green Mountain Distillers
Stowe, Vermont, founded in 2001
www.greendistillers.com

Tim Danahy and Howie Faircloth, previously in the beer brewing business, started Green Mountain Distillers in 2001. It is an unusual distillery in respect of being Certified Organic. The first product to hit the shelves was Sunshine Vodka in 2004, which became a huge success and was followed in summer 2009 with two new versions – Organic Lemon and Organic Orange. Two years earlier, Green Mountain Distillers had also released Maple Syrup Liqueur. However, a 100% organic malt whiskey has always been uppermost in their minds. The first batches were already distilled in September 2004, but unlike many other distillers in the USA, Tim and Howie decided to let it mature for quite a number of years and, at the moment, there has been no release.

Santa Fe Spirits
Santa Fe, New Mexico, founded in 2010
www.santafespirits.com

Colin Keegan, originally from Newcastle in England, was working as an architect when he decided to become a distiller of spirits. Santa Fe Spirits is one of only two distilleries in New Mexico and is the only one producing whiskey. Colin is collaborating with Santa Fe Brewing Company which supplies the un-hopped beer that is fermented and distilled in a 1,000 litre copper still from Christian Carl in Germany. The whiskey gets a hint of smokiness due to a special and (as of yet) undisclosed type of malt. The first product, Silver Coyote released in spring 2011, was an unaged malt whiskey which was followed in November by an apple brandy and in spring 2012, Expedition Vodka was launched. Autumn of 2012 saw the release of Wheeler´s Western Dry Gin and the first release of an aged (2 years) malt whiskey is expected late in 2013. Colin´s goal is to produce 24,000 bottles of whiskey a year and the same amount of other spirits.

Journeyman Distillery
Three Oaks, Michigan, founded in 2010
www.journeymandistillery.com

Before opening his own distillery, Bill Welter rented one month of still time at Koval Distillery in Ravenswood to make sure he had an aged rye whiskey (Ravenswood Rye) available when his own distillery was opened. The range of whiskies distilled on his own premises now include a wheat whiskey, a bourbon, Silver Cross Whiskey (equal parts of rye, wheat, corn and barley), W.R. Whiskey (un-aged rye) and Kissing Cousins (bourbon finished in

a Cabernet Sauvignon barrel). There is also gin, vodka and rum. The first, limited release of a single malt was in October 2013. Bill currently produces 10,000 gallons of whiskey annually and the spirit is matured in new, charred American white oak, ranging from five to 55 gallon size. Journeyman also happens to be one of only a few 100% organic distilleries.

Immortal Spirits
Medford, Oregon, founded in 2008
www.immortalspirits.com

In the beginning, this distillery could be seen mainly as a labour of love by two home brewers, Jesse Gallagher and Enrico Carini, but they had their minds set on something bigger. The two stills (a 1,200 gallon pot still and an 88 gallon still for limited release runs) are designed and fabricated by themselves and the wash used to come from a local brewery. Recently, however, a 2,000 gallon mash tun and three 2,000 gallon fermenters were installed so not only will all of the production be handled at the distillery but the volumes would have increased substantially with a possibility to do 3-4 barrels per day. Jesse and Enrico plan on releasing a small amount of a 2 year old single malt by the end of 2013, whilst the larger part of the production will probably be matured for an additional 6-8 years.

Blue Ridge Distilling Co.
Bostic, North Carolina, founded in 2010
www.blueridgedistilling.com

After a career in commercial diving and salvage, Tim Ferris opted for a change. He took the crew from his company, Defiant Marine, and opened up a distillery in 2010. The equipment consists of a lauter mash tun, stainless steel fermenters and a modified Kothe still. For maturation they use 24 months air dried, toasted American oak. At least for the time being, their minds are totally set on single malt whisky and for 2013 they plan to produce 10,000 cases with production doubling the following year. The first distillation was in June 2012 and already in December the first bottles of Defiant Single Malt Whisky were released.

Defiant single malt from Blue Ridge Distilling Co.

The still at Journeyman Distillery

Batch 206 Distillery
Seattle, Washington, founded in 2011
www.batch206.com

A consortium of Seattle business owners started this distillery in downtown Seattle in 2011 and its first distillation was in February 2012. In November 2011 Rusty Figgins, known from the Ellensburg distillery which he had sold, started as the Master Distiller at Batch 206. Accompanying him he also had his own brand of malt whisky, Gold Buckle Club, which in the future will be produced under his supervision at this new distillery. The first products from Batch 206 to hit the shelves were Batch 206 Vodka, Counter Gin and See 7 Stars Moonshine. The distillery is also producing bourbon, rye and, since summer 2013, rum. For the whiskey, they are doing some of the mashing themselves, but are also working with a brewery which delivers un-fermented wort. Distillation takes place in a 1,000-litre pot-and-column still from Kothe in Germany. Batch 206 distillery produces around 12 barrels of whiskey every month

Deerhammer Distilling Company
Buena Vista, Colorado, founded in 2010
www.deerhammer.com

The location of the distillery at an altitude of 2,500 metres with drastic temperature fluctuations and virtually no humidity, have a huge impact on the maturation of the spirit. Owners Lenny and Amy Eckstein found that their first whiskey was ready to be released after only 9 months´ maturation in December 2012 and it was sold out in January. The next bottling of the Down Time single malt was in June 2013. There is also an unaged version called Whitewater Whiskey. The distillery was upgraded in summer 2013 with more fermenters, a bigger mash tun and one more still. The spirit is double distilled with a very narrow middle cut and matured in 30 gallon barrels made of new American oak.

Deerhammer´s Down Time and Leviathan II from Lost Spirits

Hillrock Estate Distillery
Ancram, New York, founded in 2011
www.hillrockdistillery.com

Jeffrey Baker seems to have planned this brand-new distillery ten years ago. That is when he bought the 100-ac farm where the distillery is now situated and another 100 acres nearby. In 2011 the time was right for this MD of a banking firm in New York to take the next step. A 250 gallon pot still was ordered from Vendome, five fermentation tanks were installed and the first spirit wa distilled in November 2011. What makes this distillery really unique, at least in the USA, is that they are not ju malting their own barley – they are floor malting it. Thi a technique that has been abandoned even in Scotland, except for a handful of distilleries. The malt is dried in a kiln for two to three days and then goes into the mash tun. The first release from the distillery was in Septembe 2012, the Solera Aged Bourbon and in June 2013 it was time for the first Single Malt whiskey. At that time a coo peration with George Washington´s Distillery at Mount Vernon was also presented – George Washington´s Rye Whiskey. It was distilled at Hillrock but also contained a small amount of whiskey produced at Mount Vernon. To help Jeffrey set up the distillery and to take on the role as Master Distiller, the legendary David Pickerell of Maker´s Mark fame was called in.

Lost Spirits Distillery
Prunedale, California, founded in 2009
www.lostspirits.net

Before opening up their own whiskey distillery near Monterey, Bryan Davis and Joanne Haruta managed an absinthe distillery in Spain. Back in California, they built this highly original distillery themselves. The still is place outside and it is of a design called log-and-copper which means that it is made of both oak wood and copper. From the very start, their goal was to make peated, single malt whisky. In the beginning, Bryan and Joanne chose late harvest Cabernet casks (sweet wine) from Napa Valley for maturation but they have ventured into other types of wood as well. In 2012 the first two expressions were released – Leviathan I (peated at 110ppm) an Seascape (55ppm). This was followed up in 2013 with the launch of Leviathan II, Paradiso (one single cask bottled for Germany) and Ouroboros. The latter was made from California grown barley using California peat and was matured in ex-sherry Hungarian oak.

High West Distillery
Park City, Utah, founded in 2007
www.highwest.com

Even though the distillery has not yet been established for more than a few years the owner, David Perkins, has already made a name for himself mainly because of the releases of several rye whiskies. None of these have beer distilled at High West distillery though. Perkins has instead bought casks of mature whiskies and blended them himself. The first (released in 2008) was Rendezvous Rye, a mix of two whiskies (16 and 6 years old). Since then, he has also released a 16 year old and a 21 year old rye. Summer 2011 saw the release of a 12 year old rye and Double Rye which is a mix of a 2 year old and a 16 year old whiskey. One year later, Bourye and Son of Bourye were released – both created by blending bourbon and rye whiskies. That year Camofire, which is a blend of Straight Bourbon, Straight Rye and peated Blended Malt Scotch Whiskey, also saw the light of day. Meanwhile, Perkins has been distilling vodka from oats and he has also released an unaged oat whiskey made from his own production called Western Oat which contains 85% oats and 15% malted barley. A single malt from 100% barley is also in the pipeline. High West Distillery is currently working on a joint project with Blue Shy Ranch to build a combined luxury guest ranch and distillery in Wanship, Utah. The plan is to be up and running end of 2013.

ackney Bend Distillery
w Haven, Missouri, founded in 2011
ww.pinckneybend.com

e founders of this distillery all pooled their vast expe-
nce as artisan brewers when they decided to build a
stillery. Most of the mashing and fermentation take
ace at the local Second Shift Brewery in New Haven.
en distillery has four small stills, the biggest of which
a 60 gallon Vendome copper still. For maturation, the
vners are still experimenting with different types of
sks from 15 gallon barrels to a variety of types made
om Missouri oak. The main purpose for the distillery
to produce malt whiskey, but in order to finance this,
ey also distil spirits that don't require maturation – gin,
dka and brandies. The first whiskey release was an
aged corn whiskey followed by a 6 months old in July
13. The first malt whiskey will probably be bottled in
14.

estland Distillery
attle, Washington, founded in 2011
ww.westlanddistillery.com

like most of the new craft distilleries in the USA
oducing whiskey, Westland Distillery will not (at least
r the foreseeable future) distil other spirits to finance
e early stages of production. Until November 2012,
estland was a medium sized craft distillery where they
ought in the wash from a nearby brewery and had
e capacity of doing 60,000 litres of whiskey per year.
uring the summer of 2013 the owners, the Lamb family,
oved to another location which is equipped with a
000 litre brewhouse, five 10,000 litre fermenters and
vo Vendome stills (7,560 and 5,670 litres respectively).
ne capacity is now 260,000 litres per year which makes
estland Distillery an unusually large distillery. The malt
r the production is sourced both locally as well as from
ngland and the casks are predominantly heavy char new
merican oak. Trials are also being conducted with ex-
ourbon, ex-sherry and ex-port casks.
The first bottlings of their core expression, American
ngle Malt Whiskey, were released in autumn 2013
gether with a couple of limited bottlings.

Long Island Spirits
Baiting Hollow, New York, founded in 2007
www.lispirits.com

Long Island Spirits is the first distillery on the island
since the 1800s. The starting point for The Pine Barrens
Whisky, the first single malt from the distillery, is a
finished ale with hops and all. The beer is distilled twice
in a potstill and matures for one year in a 10 gallon new
American white oak barrel. The whisky was released in
April 2012 and was followed up in 2013 with a bourbon
called Rough Rider. The big seller for the owner Richard
Stabile, is not a whisky however, but LiV Vodka, made
100% from potatoes and selling 5,000 cases per year.

Parliament Distillery
Sumner, Washington, founded in 2011
www.parliament-distillery.com

This small craft distillery, producing 10,000 gallons in
2013, and founded by Jarrett Tomal and Flynn Hunting-
ton has yet to release a 100% single malt whiskey. The
first product instead was Ghost Owl Moonshine which
consists of 35-51% of their own malt whiskey, 10% very
young rye and the balance is made up of 4 year old
bourbon. A local brewery prepares the wort which is
fermented for 2-3 days at the distillery and double distilled in a 570 litre alambic still and a 130 litre column still.
The spirit is then matured in 20 litre American oak casks
with a #4 char.

Van Brunt Stillhouse
Brooklyn, New York, founded in 2012
www.vanbruntstillhouse.com

To the Whisky Trail in Scotland and the Kentucky Bourbon Trail you can now add The Brooklyn Spirits Trail in
New York where no less than 11 distillers have teamed
up to showcase their different spirits. One of them is Van
Brunt Stillhouse, owned by Daric Schlesselman and located near the Red Hook waterfront. They made their first
release of Van Brunts American Whiskey in December
2012, a mix of malted barley, wheat and a hint of corn
and rye. This was followed by a malt whiskey from 100%
malted barley. Other products include rum and grappa
and they are also planning for a rye and a bourbon.

Westland Distillery still house

The stills at Van Brunt Stillhouse

Civilized Spirits

Traverse City, Michigan, founded in 2009
www.civilizedspirits.com

Jon Carlson and Greg Lobdell developed a passion for craft beer and artisan spirits whilst they were attending the University of Michigan. Years later they founded Northern United Brewing Company which is the parent company of Civilized Spirits. The spirits are produced at a distillery on Old Mission Peninsula, just outside Traverse City, and it opened in 2009. The still is a 1,000 litre pot still with a 24-plate column attached. The whiskey side of the business includes Civilized Single Malt (at least 3 years old), Civilized Whiskey (made from locally grown rye) and Civilized White Dog Whiskey (an unoaked wheat whiskey). Rum and gin are also produced.

Dark Corner Distillery

Greenville, South Carolina, founded in 2011
www.darkcornerdistillery.com

Joe Fenten, founder and owner of this distillery in downtown Greenville, uses a handmade 80 gallon copper pot still for all his distillations. His main focus is on different varieties of whiskey (2,000 gallons will be produced during 2013) which includes a moonshine corn whiskey, South Carolina's first bourbon and a malted wheat whiskey. The range also includes gin and absinthe.

Square One Brewery & Distillery

St. Louis, Missouri, founded in 2006
www.squareonebrewery.com

Steve Neukomm has been working with micro-breweries since 1999. In 2006 he opened a combined brewery and restaurant in St. Louis and two years later he was granted Missouri's first micro-distilling licence. Apart from rum, gin, vodka and absinthe, Steve also produces J.J. Neukomm Whiskey, a malt whiskey made from toasted malt and cherry wood smoked malt.

Canada _____

DISTILLERY: Glenora Distillery, Glenville, Nova Scotia
FOUNDED: 1990
OWNER/MANAGER: Lauchie MacLean
www.glenoradistillery.com

Situated in Nova Scotia, Glenora was the first malt whisky distillery in Canada. The first launch of in-house produce came in 2000 but a whisky called Kenloch had been sold before that. This was a 5 year old vatting of some of Glenora's own malt whisky and whisky from Bowmore Distillery on Islay. The first expression, a 10 year old, came in September 2000 and was named Glen Breton and this is still the core expression under the name Glen Breton Rare. Since then several expressions have been launched, among them single casks and sometimes under the name Glenora. In 2008 a 15 year old version was available from the distillery only and in 2011 a 17 year old version was released. Recent releases have included a 14 year old and a 19 year old and for the first time these aged varities have been exported as well, in this case to Spain and France. A new expression, Glen Breton Ice (10 years old), the world's first single malt aged in an ice wine barrel, was launched in 2006. Interest was massive and more bottlings (aged 15 and 17 years) were released after that. A 15 year old version of Glen Breton single malt was released under the name Battle of the Glen in June 2010. The release commemorated the distillery's victorious outcome of the ten year-long struggle with Scotch Whisky Association. Finally, a limited 20 year old expression was recently launched for sale at the distillery only.

DISTILLERY: Shelter Point Distillery, Vancouver Island, British Columbia
FOUNDED: 2009
OWNER/MANAGER: Patrick Evans
www.shelterpointdistillery.com

Patrick Evans was born and raised on a dairy farm just 20 kilometres from the distillery site. In 2005 he and his family decided to switch from the dairy side of farming to growing crops and they bought the Shelter Point Farm just north of Comox on Vancouver Island, a stone's throw from the ocean. Eventually the idea to transform the farm into a distillery was raised and with the help of some Scottish investors headed by Andrew Currie, who co-founded Arran Distillery in Scotland in the early 1990 the construction work began. The buildings were completed in 2009 and in May 2010 all the equipment was in place. This includes a one tonne mash tun, five washbacks made of stainless steel (5,000 litres each) and one pair of stills (a 5,000 litre wash still and a 4,000 litre spirit still). Both stills and the spirit safe were made by Forsyth in Scotland while the rest was manufactured in Canada. The idea was to start distillation in September 2010 but federal, provincial and local licensing requirements, multiple inspections and one mechanical complication after another, delayed the start by eight months and the first casks were only filled in June 2011. To assist with the start up, Patrick Evans asked Mike Nicholson to join him and his operating manager, Jim Marinus. Mike is an incredibly experienced distiller having worked for many years in Scotland at Lagavulin, Caol Ila and other distilleries. The barley used for the distillation is grown on the farm and being a true farm distillery also means that a lot of time is devoted to other duties, besides distillation. For now, only half of the capacity is being used which still amounts to 150,000 litres of alcohol per year. There are also plans to eventually install their own maltings on site. Legally, a whisky could be released in summer 2014 as a three year old, but the owners have not yet decided when to launch their first whisky.

DISTILLERY: Still Waters Distillery, Concord, Ontario
FOUNDED: 2009
OWNER/MANAGER: Barry Bernstein, Barry Stein
www.stillwatersdistillery.com

Barry Bernstein and Barry Stein started their careers in the whisky business as Canada's first independent bottlers, importing casks from Scottish distilleries and selling the whisky across Canada. The next step came in January 2009 when they opened Still Waters distillery in Concord, on the northern outskirts of Toronto. The distillery is equipped with a 3,000 litre mash tun, two 3,000 litre washbacks and a Christian Carl 450 litre pot still. The still also has rectification columns for brandy and vodka production. The plan is to install a second, larger still for wash distillations and a couple of more washbacks in a year. The focus is on whisky but Bernstein and Stein also produce vodka, brandy and gin. Their first release was a triple distilled, single malt vodka and they have also released a Canadian whisky with distillate sourced from

*Stalk & Barrel
from Still Waters Distillery*

ther producers. Their first single malt, named Stalk & Barrel Single Malt, was released in April 2013. It was cask strength (61.3%), unchillfiltered and with no colouring. During 2013 they will be doing 6-10 releases depending on demand.

ther distilleries in Canada

ctoria Spirits
ctoria (Vancouver Island), British Columbia, founded in 08 (whisky since 2009)
ww.victoriaspirits.com

is family-run distillery actually has its roots in a winery led Winchester Cellars, founded by Ken Winchester ack in 2002. Bryan Murray, the owner of Victoria Spirits, me in as an investor, but soon started to work with en on the distilling part of the business. Before Ken left e business in 2008, he took part in introducing Victoria n, which currently is the big-selling product with 10,000 ttles a year. The Murray family left the wine part of e business in order to increase the spirits role and the ext product on the list was a single malt whisky. The st batch was distilled in late 2009 by Bryan's son, Peter unt, using wash from a local brewery owned by Matt illips. Since then whisky has been distilled on a few casions.

mberton Distillery
mberton, British Columbia, founded in 2009 (whisky nce 2010)
ww.pembertondistillery.ca

is is one of the most recently established distilleries Canada. Distilling started in July 2009, with vodka roduced from potatoes being their first product. The ganically grown potatoes are sourced locally and the stillery itself is a Certified Organic processing facility. ler Schramm uses a copper pot still from Arnold lstein and the first vodka, Schramm Vodka, was unched in 2009. During the ensuing year, Tyler started s first trials, distilling a single malt whisky using organic alted barley from the Okanagan Valley. He filled four -bourbon barrels with unpeated spirit and another five ere filled in 2011. At that time he also produced five arrels of lightly peated new make. The first release of is whisky will probably not take place for another two three years.

AUSTRALIA
& NEW ZEALAND

ustralia

STILLERY: Bakery Hill Distillery, North Balwyn, ictoria
OUNDED: 1998
WNER/MANAGER: David Baker
www.bakeryhilldistillery.com.au

nce 2008, when Bakery Hill Distillery completed the stallation of a 2,000 litre brewery, David Baker has had tal control of all the processes from milling the grain bottling the matured spirit. The first spirit at Bakery ll Distillery was produced in 2000 and the first single alt was launched in autumn 2003. Three different rsions are available – Classic and Peated (both matured ex-bourbon casks) and Double Wood (ex-bourbon and a finish in French Oak). As Classic and Peated are also available as cask strength bottlings, they can be considered two more varieties. Most of the spirit is matured in ex-bourbon American oak from Jack Daniels and the 225 litre hogsheads are rebuilt into 100 litre barrels. Recently David started doing trials with three new wood finishes but an eventual release is still a couple of years away. The whisky is double-distilled in a copper pot still.
For the last couple of years David has concentrated on building stock. The interest from the home market has increased significantly and last year he was forced to put a temporary halt to exporting his whisky just to keep up with domestic demand.

With the Bakery Hill Distillery being situated in the southern part of Australia, the climate is very different to that of Scotland. The overall ambient temperatures are much higher while the air mass is much drier. These factors influence the rate of flavour development and whisky character, and David Baker is constantly experimenting with a wide variety of oak to find the optimal path.

DISTILLERY: Lark Distillery, Hobart, Tasmania
FOUNDED: 1992
OWNER/MANAGER: Bill Lark
www.larkdistillery.com.au

In 1992, Bill Lark was the first person for 153 years to take out a distillation licence in Tasmania. Since then he has not just established himself as a producer of malt whiskies of high quality, but has also helped to off-set several new distilleries.

Bill Lark's original establishment in Kingston was moved to Hobart in 2001. In 2006 a new distillery was constructed on a farm at Mt Pleasant, 15 minutes' drive from Hobart. The farm grows barley for Cascade Brewery and at the moment that is where Lark Distillery gets its malt from. Bill's intentions are to set up his own floor maltings but recently he became involved in a new distillery in Tasmania, Redlands Estate Distillery, where they have started floor malting the barley and in the future the capacity will be sufficient to also supply Lark distillery. The "old site" down in Hobart by the waterfront is now a cellar door and a showcase for the Lark whisky with a shop, café and whisky bar with over 100 different single malts. There are also plans to build a visitor centre at the distillery at Mt Pleasant.

The core product in the whisky range is the Single Cask Malt Whisky at 43% but Bill Lark has also released a Distillers Selection at 46% and a Cask Strength at 58%, both of which are also single cask. The range is completed by a malt whisky liqueur called Slainte and a Pure Malt Spirit at 45%. The whisky is double-distilled in a 1,800 litre wash still and a 600 litre spirit still and then matured in 100 litre "quarter casks". In 2012 Lark distillery celebrated its 20th anniversary with a unique bottling where samples of the distillery's first 150 releases were married together in the first barrel of Para Port laid down by the renowned Seppeltsfield Wine in Barossa Valley in 1878!

The demand for Lark single malt has grown rapidly in recent years, also outside of Australia and the whisky can now be found in the USA, Singapore, Hong Kong, the UK, France, Germany, Netherlands and Spain.

DISTILLERY: Tasmania Distillery, Cambridge, Tasmania
FOUNDED: 1996
OWNER/MANAGER: Patrick Maguire
www.tasmaniadistillery.com

Three generations of whisky can trace its origin to Tasmania Distillery. The first was distilled between 1996 and 1998 and, according to the current owner, Patrick Maguire, the quality is so poor that he does not want to bottle it. The second generation was distilled from November 1999 to July 2001 and today is bottled under the name Sullivan's Cove. The third generation is the whisky distilled from 2003 until the present day under Patrick and his partners' ownership and which hasn't been bottled yet.

The distillery obtains wash from Cascade Brewery in Hobart and the spirit is then double distilled, although there is only one still at the distillery. The distillery recently entered a cooperation with Moo Brew brewery located in MONA (Museum of Old and New Art), the world famous art museum in Hobart. Sales figures increased by 40% in 2012 and the owners have now increased the production to 160 casks of 200 litres each of non chill-filtered whisky, which is then matured in American oak bourbon casks and French oak port pipes.

The range comprises of Sullivan's Cove Single Cask, bottled at 47,5% and matured in either bourbon casks or port casks and Sullivan's Cove Double Cask (40%) which is a marriage of port and bourbon casks. The age has increased over the years and currently they are bottling 12 and 13 year old whisky.

In 2010, Patrick bought a disused train tunnel, a few kilometres from the distillery, and all the maturing stock was moved there in late 2013. And the tunnel provides a cooler and more even temperature, not to be taken on lightly in this part of the world, where great differences in temperature occur during the year.

Around 75% of the production is sold in Australia and the biggest export markets are USA and Canada. Sullivan's Cove is also available in several European countries, as well as in Singapore, Hong Kong, Japan and Dubai.

DISTILLERY: Old Hobart Distillery, Blackmans Bay, Tasmania
FOUNDED: 2005
OWNER/MANAGER: Casey Overeem
www.oldhobartdistillery.com

Even though Casey Overeem did not start his distillery until 2007, he had spent several years experimenting with different types of distillation which were inspired by travels to Norway and Scotland. The distillery (previously known as Overeem Distillery) came on stream in 2007. The mashing is done at Lark distillery where Overeem

Overeem Port Cask Matured bottled at cask strength

also has his own washbacks and the wash is made to his specific requirement, i. a. with his own yeast. In every mash, a mix of 50% unpeated barley and 50% slightly peated is used. The peat smoke is added to the barley when it has been malted and not during the drying of the malt which is the most common. The wash is then transported to Old Hobart Distillery where the distillation takes place in two stills (wash still of 1,800 litres and spirit still of 600 litres). The spirit is matured in casks that have previously contained either port, bourbon or sherry. In 2013 Overeem increased the production to 10,000 bottles. The first release in November 2011 consisted of four different expressions, all single casks and distilled in 2007; two bottled at 60% from port and sherry casks and two bottled at 43%, also from port and sherry. The plan is to launch a bourbon cask matured later in 2013, both at 43% and 60%. The whisky is sold in Australia but export orders have also been shipped to Belgium, the Netherlands, the UK and Sweden.

DISTILLERY: Hellyers Road Distillery, Burnie, Tasmania
FOUNDED: 1999
OWNER/MANAGER: Betta Milk Co-op
www.hellyersroaddistillery.com.au

Hellyer's Road Distillery is the largest single malt whisky distillery in Australia with a capacity of doing 100,000 litres per year. The Tasmanian barley is malted at Cascade Brewery in Hobart and peat from Scotland is used for the peated expressions. Batches of 6,5 tonnes of grist are loaded into the mash tun and then the wash is fermented for 65 hours. There is only one pair of stills but they compensate for numbers by size. The wash still has a capacity of 40,000 litres and the spirit still 20,000 litres and they practise a really slow distillation. The foreshots take around 4-5 hours and the middle cut will last for 24 hours, which is six to seven times longer compared to practice in Scotland. Another interesting fact is that the pots on both stills are made of stainless steel while heads, necks and lyne arms are made of copper. Maturation takes place in ex-bourbon casks but they also use Tasmanian red wine barrels for part of it.

There are five varieties of Hellyers Road Single Malt Whisky in the range: Original (with no age statement) and a peated bottled at cask strength are only available to visitors at the distillery. Original 10 year old, Slightly Peated and a Pinot Noir finish are more readily available. There is also a Hellyer's Road Roaring 40's reserved for export. In 2014 the range will be further complemented with Hellyer's Road 12 year old.

At the moment, the whisky is exported to the UK, France, Switzerland, Belgium, Denmark, Sweden and Canada.

DISTILLERY: Great Southern Distilling Company, Albany, Western Australia
FOUNDED: 2004
OWNER/MANAGER: Great Southern Distilling Company Pty Ltd/Cameron Syme
www.distillery.com.au

The distillery was built in Albany on the south-western tip of Australia in 2004 with whisky production commencing in late 2005. Throughout the initial years, production of whisky, brandy, vodka and gin took place in a series of sheds on the outskirts of Albany. A move was made in October 2007 to a new, custom-built distillery with a visitor centre at Princess Royal Harbour.

For the distillation, one wash still (1,900 litres) and one spirit still (580 litres) are used and a 600 litre copper pot antique gin still has also been installed. The fermentation time is unusually long – 7 to 10 days and for maturation a mix of ex-bourbon, ex-house brandy and ex-sherry barrels are used. When casks are used for finishes, they are the ex-bourbon barrels that were shipped to Australia in the 1920s and 30s and then used to mature port or sherry for 70 to 80 years. Production was doubled in 2012 to 12,000 es and will increase to 16,000 litres in 2013 to finally ich 25,000 litres by 2016.

he first expression of the whisky, called Limeburners, s released in 2008 and this is still the core expression. 2010, the first peated version of Limeburners was re- sed. The whiskies are bottled either at barrel strength %) or diluted to 43% for the unpeated and 48% for e peated version. A new addition to the range was eased in 2012 – Tiger Snake, an Australian sour mash isky based on corn, malted barley and rye.

TILLERY: Nant Distillery, Bothwell, Tasmania
UNDED: 2007
VNER/MANAGER: Keith Batt
ww.nantdistillery.com.au

nt distillery, in Bothwell in the Central Highlands Tasmania, started when Queensland businessman, ith Batt, bought the property in 2004. He embarked refurbishing the Historic Sandstone Water Mill on e estate that was built in 1823 and converted it into a isky distillery. The first distillation took place in 2008. rley has been grown on the estate since 1821 and the n is to start with floor malting on site.

he distillery is equipped with a 1,800 litre wash still, 00 litre spirit still and wooden washbacks for the fer- ntation. Quarter casks of 100 litres, which previously d port, sherry and bourbon, are used for maturation. duction has increased recently and they are now lay- down 48 barrels per month. The first bottlings were eased in June 2010 and since 2012 the range consists Nant Single Malt Whisky matured in either bourbon, erry or port casks and bottled at 43%. There are also k strength version (63%) of all three.

n 2012, Keith expanded the business to include two nt Whisky Cellar & Bars – one in Hobart and the other Brisbane. The bars are dedicated to all things whisky d offer single malts from Scotland as well as Tasmanian isky. This is just the beginning of an unusual business n which will see 20 more bars opening in Australia d abroad within the next two years. By Christmas 2013, ey expect to open in Sydney and London.

ther distilleries in Australia

w World Whisky Distillery
endon Fields, Melbourne, Victoria,
unded in 2008
ww.newworldwhisky.com.au

fore David Vitale started this distil-
y (which until recently was known
Victoria Valley Distillery), he
rked with sales and marketing at
k Distillery and Bill Lark has also
en part in the start-up of Victo-
Valley. The distillery is fitted
o an old Qantas maintenan-
hangar at Essendon Fields,
lbourne's original airport.
e stills (an 1,800 litre wash
l and a 600 litre spirit still)
re bought from Joadja
eek Distillery in Mittagong
d currently the yearly
oduction is around 20,000
es. There are also 860 bar-
s of maturing whisky stored
the warehouse.
David uses a variety of cask
es for maturation (50, 100
d 200 litres) but all have
eviously contained sherry.
e first whisky, a blend of 12
ferent casks and bottled at
%, was released in Australia
February 2013 under the
me Starward.

Starward from New World Whisky

William McHenry and Sons Distillery
Port Arthur, Tasmania, founded in 2011
www.mchenrydistillery.com.au

William McHenry was working as an employee at a biotech company in Sydney in 2006 when he first started considering a distillery of his own. In 2011 the decision was taken and he moved to Tasmania with his family. The copper still was delivered in October of that year and in January 2012 he started distilling. The distillery is equipped with a 500 litre copper pot still with a surroun- ding water jacket to get a lighter spirit. The plan is to do 400 litres of newmake per month and the spirit is filled into first-fill bourbon barrels from Maker's Mark, both 100 and 200 litres. William is hoping for a first release in 2014. In June 2013 he built a new 200 m² bond store to be able to increase production. To facilitate the cash flow, he produces a triple distilled vodka and sloe gin.

Timboon Railway Shed Distillery
Timboon, Victoria, founded in 2007
www.timboondistillery.com

The small town of Timboon lies 200 kilometres southwest of Melbourne. Here Tim Marwood established his combi- nation of a distillery and a restaurant in 2007 in a reno- vated railway goods shed. Using a pilsner malted barley, Marwood obtains the wash (1,000 litres) from the local Red Duck microbrewery. The wash is then distilled twice in a 600 litre pot still. For maturation, resized (20 litres) and retoasted ex-port, tokay and bourbon barrels are used. The first release of a whisky, matured in port barrels, was made In 2010 and the latest expression is a bourbon maturation.

Black Gate Distillery
Mendooran, New South Wales, founded in 2012
www.blackgatedistillery.com.au

This boutique distillery was opened by Brian and Genise Hollingworth in January 2012. They have already a range of vodkas and liqueurs for sale and rum as well as single malt whisky is currently maturing in ex-sherry casks. The first release of a single malt will probably be in the beginning of 2015. For the first whisky distillation they used wash from a local brewer but both mashing and fermentation is now taking place at the distillery.

Redlands Estate Distillery
Plenty, Tasmania, founded in 2013
www.redlandsestate.com.au

Redlands Estate in Derwent Valley, just 35 minutes from Hobart, dates back to the early 1800s and was run mainly as a hop and grain farm. A few years ago Peter and Elizabeth Hope bought the rundown property with the goal to restore it and turn it back into a working farm. Part of the plans included a distillery. The first spirit was double distilled in March 2013 in a 900 litre copper pot still and there are plans to install yet another and bigger still (2,000 litre) in the future. The barley used is grown on the estate and it is also floor malted on site. Initially, around 60 barrels will be produced yearly. One of the shareholders of the distillery is the well known Bill Lark.

Castle Glen Distillery
The Summit, Queensland, founded in 2009
www.castleglenaustralia.com.au

Established as a vineyard in 1990 by the current owner Cedric Millar, Castle Glen moved on to open up also a brewery and a distillery in 2009. Apart from wine and beer, a wide range of spirits are produced including rum, vodka, gin, absinthe and various eau de vies. Castle Glen is also the only whiskey (they use this spelling) distillery in Queensland. Malted barley is imported from Switzerland and the first whiskey, Castle Glen Limited Edition, was released as a 2 year old in early 2012.

New Zealand

DISTILLERY: New Zealand Malt Whisky Co, Oamaru, South Island
FOUNDED: 2000
OWNER/MANAGER: Extra Eight
www.thenzwhisky.com
www.milfordwhisky.co.nz

In 2001, Warren Preston bought the entire stock of single malt and blended whisky from the decommissioned Wilsons Willowbank Distillery in Dunedin. The supplies that Preston acquired consisted of 400 casks of single malt whisky including production dating back to 1987. Before he bought it, the whisky was sold under the name Lammerlaw, but Preston renamed it Milford. Preston also had plans to build a distillery in Oamaru. In February 2010, however, his company was evicted from its premises and one month later the company was placed in receivership. In October 2010, rescue came in the form of a syndicate of nine international investors led by Tasmanian-based businessman Greg Ramsay who had been involved in the funding of distilleries in both Australia and Scotland. Their capital injection revived the company and plans to build a distillery still exist. The plan has been to either build the distillery in Oamaru or Dunedin (where the former chief post office was a possible location) at the far end on the South Island but external investors have shown an interest in establishing it in Auckland on the North Island. The hope is still to have a distillery in production by 2015.

With the new ownership, the range of expressions from the old stock has increased and the following bottlings can now be found; Milford Single Malt (10, 15, 18 and 20 years old), South island Single Malt (18 and 21 years), Dunedin Doublewood (6 years in American oak and 4 years in French red wine casks), single casks from 1988, 1989, 1990 and 1993, Diggers & Ditch (a blended malt with whiskies from both New Zealand and Tasmania) and The Water of Leith (a 10 year old blend). The most recent release was a 24 year old from 1987 – the year the All Blacks won the Rugby World Cup.

ASIA

India

DISTILLERY: Amrut Distilleries Ltd., Bangalore
FOUNDED: 1948
OWNER/MANAGER: Jagdale Group
www.amrutdistilleries.com
www.amrutwhisky.co.uk

The family-owned distillery, based in Bangalore, south India, started to distil malt whisky in the mid-eighties. The equivalent of 50 million bottles of spirits (including rum, gin and vodka) is manufactured a year, of which 1,4 million bottles is whisky. Most of the whisky goes to blended brands, but Amrut single malt was introduced in 2004. It was first introduced in Scotland, can now be found in more than 20 countries and has recently been introduced to the American market. Funnily enough, it took until 2010 before it was launched in India and currently it is only sold in Bangalore. In 2012 total sales of Amrut single malt on the export market were 13,000 cases compared to total sales for the company of 4,2 million cases of spirits. The turnover that year was $35 million.

The distillery is equipped with two pairs of stills, each with a capacity of 5,000 litres. The barley is sourced from the north of India, malted in Jaipur and Delhi and final distilled in Bangalore and the whisky is bottled without chill-filtering or colouring. The conditions for maturatic differ from the Scottish environment. The temperature the summer is close to 40°C and it rarely falls below 20° in winter. Hence the much larger evaporation, between 10-16% per year. This, in turn, means that it is not cost efficient to mature the whisky for more than four years The Amrut family of single malts has grown considerab in recent years and ingenuity is great when it comes to new limited releases. The core range consists of unpeat and peated versions bottled at 46%, a cask strength an a peated cask strength and finally Fusion which is base on 25% peated malt from Scotland and 75% unpeated Indian malt. Special releases include Two Continents, where maturing casks have been brought from India to Scotland for their final period of maturation, Intermediate Sherry Matured where the new spirit has mature in ex-bourbon or virgin oak, then re-racked to sherry butts and with a third maturation in ex-bourbon casks, Kadhambam which is a peated Amrut which has mature in ex Oloroso butts, ex Bangalore Blue Brandy casks and then finally in ex rum casks, Amrut Herald (released in 2011) with four years bourbon maturation in India and a final 18 months on the German island of Helgoland and finally Portonova (also from 2011) with a maturatic in bourbon casks, then 9 months in port pipes and back to bourbon casks for the last 8 months. Autumn 2011 also saw the release of new editions of Kadhambam (this time unpeated) and Two Continents. In 2013, the third batch of Portonova was released and this will now be an annual bottling for Europe and USA. The biggest surprise for 2013 was however the release of Amrut Greedy Angels, 8 years old and the oldest Amrut so far. This an astonishing achievement in a country where the hot and humid climate causes major evaporation during maturation. When the two casks were filled in 2004, the held 360 litres but over the years, 274 litres were lost to evaporation. In spring 2013, 144 bottles were filled at 50%.

Greedy Ange
from Amru

DISTILLERY: McDowell's, Ponda, Goa
FOUNDED: 1988 (malt whisky)
OWNER/MANAGER: UB Group
www.unitedspirits.in

In 1826 the Scotsman, Angus McDowell, established himself as an importer of wines, spirits and cigars in Madras (Chennai) and the firm was incorporated in 1898. In the same town another Scotsman, Thomas Leishman, founded United Breweries in 1915. Both companies were bought by Vital Mallya around 1950 and today United Breweries (in which the spirits division consists of United Spirits) is the second largest producer of alcohol in the world after Diageo. Vijay Mallya, the son of Vital, is acting as chairman since 1983.

United Spirits has more than 140 brands in their portfolio including Scotch whisky, Indian whisky, vodka, rum, brandy and wine. Since last year, 21 of the brands are called "millionaire brands", i.e. brands selling more than one million cases a year. A total of 123,7 million cases were sold in 2012. The absolute majority of United Spirits' whiskies are Indian whisky, i. e. made of molasses. The major brands in the group are huge sales-wise with McDowell's No.1 whisky as the top seller (19,5 million cases in 2012). There is also a blended Scotch whisky, Black Dog Whisky. Single malt sales are negligible compared to these figures. McDowell's Single Malt is made at the distillery in Ponda (Goa) and sells 20,000 cases each year. It has matured for 3-4 years in ex-bourbon casks. In 2007 United Spirits Limited acquired the Scottish whisky-maker, Whyte & Mackay, (with Whyte & Mackay blends and Dalmore, Jura and Fettercairn distilleries) for £595m. In 2013, Diageo bought 25% of the shares in United Spirits which made them the biggest shareholder.

DISTILLERY: John Distilleries Jdl, Goa
FOUNDED: 1992
OWNER/MANAGER: Paul P John
www.pauljohnwhisky.com

Paul P John, who is today the chairman of the company, started in 1992 by making a variety of spirits including Indian whisky made from molasses. Their biggest seller today is Original Choice which is a blend of extra neutral alcohol distilled from molasses and malt whisky from their own facilities. The brand, which was introduced in 1995/96 has since made an incredible journey. It is today the world's seventh most sold whisky with sales of 130 million bottles in 2012. John Distilleries owns three distilleries and produces brands from 18 locations in India with its head office in Bangalore. In autumn 2012 the company released their first single malt which was a bourbonmatured single cask bottled at cask strength and around 5 years old. In the following months more single cask expressions became available, some of

Brilliance from John Distilleries

them matured in ex-sherry casks. In May 2013 it was time for two more widely available core expressions, both made from Indian malted barley and distilled in copper pot stills in their distillery in Goa. Brilliance was unpeated and bourbon-matured while Edited, also matured in bourbon casks, had a small portion of peated barley in the recipe. The peat was brought in from Scotland but the malting process took place in India. There are plans to release a highly peated version as well by the end of 2013. Brilliance and Edited have no age statements but are probably quite young. It has to be remembered that the conditions in Scotland, with a cool climate and an evaporation loss (Angel´s Share) of 1.5% per year, are quite different to those in Goa with temperatures reaching 40ºC and an Angel´s Share of 10% per year. Maturation therefore is much quicker in India.

Israel

DISTILLERY: The Milk & Honey Distillery, Tel Aviv
FOUNDED: 2013
OWNER/MANAGER: Simon Fried, Amit Dror et al.
www.mh-distillery.com

Usually we only enter distilleries that have already started to produce in this section of the Malt Whisky Yearbook but, since this is the first whisky distillery project in Israel, we shall make an exception. The owners hope to start distillation in late 2013. The project began when five friends met up in a bar in Tel Aviv in 2012. The driving force of the consortium, being the friends Amit Dror and Simon Fried, sought help from the well-known whisky consultant, Jim Swan, to devise an equipment specification. They decided upon a traditional pot still (3,500 litres) but with a column attached. The plan is to start by producing a wide variety of products like vodka, brandy, rum and locally inspired liqueurs and then branching out towards whisky somewhere around mid 2014. The owners will also be experimenting with maturation in a wide variety of climates from dry deserts to hot and humid coastal areas.

Pakistan

DISTILLERY: Murree Brewery Ltd., Rawalpindi
FOUNDED: 1860
OWNER/MANAGER: Bhandara family
www.murreebrewery.com

Murree Brewery in Rawalpindi started as a beer brewery supplying the British Army. The assortment was completed with whisky, gin, rum, vodka and brandy. The core range of single malt holds two expressions – Murree´s Classic 8 years old and Murree´s Millenium Reserve 12 years old. In 2005 an 18 year old single malt was launched and the following year their oldest expression so far, a 21 year old, reached the market. There is also a Murree´s Islay Reserve, Vintage Gold, which is a blend of Scotch whisky and Murree single malt and a number of local, blended whiskies such as Vat No. 1, Lion and Dew of Himalaya. The brewery makes its own malt (using both floor maltings and Saladin box) and produces 2,6 million litres of beer every year and approximately 440,000 litres of whisky.

Muslims are prohibited by their religion to drink alcohol, so it is not surprising that in a country where 97% are Muslims, the whisky market is quite small. Only about 3 million litres per year are sold, mainly to the Christian, Hindu and Parsee minorities.

Taiwan

DISTILLERY: Yuan Shan Distillery, Yuanshan, Yilan County
FOUNDED: 2005
OWNER/MANAGER: King Car Food Industrial Co.
www.kavalanwhisky.com

The first whisky distillery in Taiwan lies in the north-eastern part of the country, in Yilan County, just one hour from Taipei. The area is flat between two mountain ranges and it was built in record time with construction lasting just eight months. The first distillation took place on 11th March 2006.

The distillery is equipped with a 5 ton semi-lauter stainless steel mash tun with copper top and eight closed stainless steel washbacks with a 60-72 hour fermentation time. The malted barley is imported with Baird's of Inverness as the main supplier. There are two pairs of lantern-shaped copper stills with descending lye pipes. The capacity of the wash stills is 12,000 litres and of the spirit stills 7,000 litres. After 10-15 minutes of foreshots, the heart of the spirit run takes 2-3 hours. The spirit vapours are cooled using tube condensers but due to the hot climate, subcoolers are also used. The total capacity of this unit is 1,3 million litres per year.

The warehouse is five stories high with the first four floors palletised and the top floor more of a traditional dunnage warehouse. The casks are tied together four and four due to the earthquake risk. The climate in Taiwan is very hot and humid and on the top floors of the warehouse the temperature can reach 42° C. Hence the angel's share is quite dramatic – no less than 15% is lost every year. The warehouse has the capacity to hold 60,000 casks and there is a need for more warehousing capacity within the near future. Predominantly American white oak is used since the owners have found that it is the type of wood that works the best for maturation in a subtropical climate.

The brand name for the whisky produced at Yuan Shan distillery is Kavalan. The name derives from the earliest tribe that inhabited Yilan, the county where the distillery is situated. Since the first bottling was released in Decem-ber 2008, the range has been expanded and now holds more than ten different expressions. The big seller is Classic Kavalan, bottled at 40%. In 2011, an "upgraded" version of the Classic was launched in the shape of King Car Conductor. This was the first whisky from Kavalan to be bottled under the company name and is a mix of eight different types of casks, unchillfiltered and bottled at 46%. A port finished version called Concertmaster was released in 2009 and later that year two different single cask bottlings were launched under the name Solist – one ex-bourbon and one ex-Oloroso sherry. It was these two expressions that made the rest of the world aware of Taiwanese whisky. They are still in the range with new editions being released continuously. More expressions in the Solist series were added – Solist Fino with a fino sherry maturation and Solist Vinho where Portuguese wine barriques had been used. End of 2012, two varieties of the Solist but bottled at 46% were launched – Kavalan Bourbon Oak and Kavalan Sherry Oak – together with Kavalan Podium. The latter is a vatting of whiskies from new American oak and a selection of re-fill casks. Finally, the latest expression is Kavalan Distillery Reserve Peaty Cask, a lightly peated expression released in 2013 and exclusively available at the distillery visitor centre and the Kavalan showrooms. All the whiskies in the Kavalan range are at least four years old.

The most important market apart from Taiwan is mainland China. The strategy has been to open up showrooms where visitors can attend master classes, taste the whisky for free and, of course, buy from the whole range. End of 2012 and 2013 marked the start of the export of Kavalan to the rest of the world and the whisky is now available in several European countries (including the UK, France, Belgium, Sweden, Denmark, Germany, Italy, Poland and Switzerland), Australia, Singapore, Hong Kong and Canada. By the end of 2013 it will also be found in USA, South Africa, Russia and South Korea.

There is an impressive visitor centre on site and it was awarded Whisky Visitor Attraction of the Year in 2011 by Whisky Magazine. No less than one million visitors come here per annum, which is roughly the same number as all Scottish distilleries' visitor centres together. The owning company, King Car Group, with 2,000 employees, was already founded in 1956 and runs businesses in several fields; biotechnology and aquaculture, among others. It is also famous for its ready-to-drink coffee, Mr. Brown, which is also exported to Europe.

Yuan Shan Distillery - home of Kavalan whisky

AFRICA

outh Africa _____

STILLERY: James Sedgwick Distillery,
ellington, Western Cape
OUNDED: 1886 (whisky production since 1990)
WNER/MANAGER: Distell Group Ltd.
ww.threeshipswhisky.co.za

stell Group Ltd. was formed in 2000 by a merger
etween Stellenbosch Farmers' Winery and Distillers
orporation although the James Sedgwick Distillery was
ready established in 1886. The company produces a
ge range of wines and spirits including the popular
eam liqueur Amarula Cream. James Sedgwick Distillery
as been the home to South African whisky since 1990.
e distillery has undergone a major expansion recently
d is now equipped with one still with two columns for
oduction of grain whisky, two pot stills for malt whisky
d one still with six columns designated for neutral
irit. There are also two mash tuns and 23 washbacks.
ain whisky is distilled for nine months of the year,
alt whisky for two (always during the winter months
ly/August) and one month is devoted to maintenance.
vo new warehouses have been built and a total of six
arehouses now hold 150,000 casks.
In Distell's whisky portfolio, it is the Three Ships brand,
troduced in 1977, that makes up for most of the sales.
e range consists of Select and 5 year old Premium
lect, both of which are a blend of South African and
otch whiskies. Furthermore, there is Bourbon Cask
nish, the first 100% South African blended whisky and
e 10 year old single malt. The latter was launched for
e first time in 2003 and it wasn't until autumn 2010
at the next batch was released. It sold out quickly and
nother 8,000 bottles were launched in October 2011
d a third batch appeared in December 2012. Fans will
ow have to wait until late 2015/early 2016 before the
ext release is due. The reason for this is that the success
the release in 2003 took the owners by surprise and
ere was no stock reserved for single malt bottlings. The
oduction all went to their blends. It wasn't until 2005
at the planning started again for future single malt
leases.
Apart from the Three Ships range, Distell also produces
vo 3 year old blended whiskies, Harrier and Knight,
well as South Africa's first single grain whisky, Bain's
ape Mountain. In 2013 the Distell Group acquired the
ottish whisky group Burn Stewart Distillers inclduing
unnahabhain, Tobermory and Deanston distilleries.

ther distilleries in South Africa

rayman's Distillery
verton, Pretoria, founded in 2006
ww.draymans.com

eing a full-time beer brewer since 1997, Moritz Kall-
eyer began distilling malt whisky in July 2006. Until
vo years ago, production was small, but operations
ave now been expanded to two pot stills. The new wash
ill has a capacity of 1,500 litres with the old spirit still
olding 800 litres. The wash is fermented for up to ten
ays in the washback, to allow the malolactic fermen-
tion to transfer its character to the spirit. The whisky
atures in French oak casks which have previously held
d wine from the Cape area. Kallmeyer's first whisky
as released as a 4 year old in autumn 2010 under the
ame Drayman's Highveld Single Malt and there has also
een the release of a second batch. Other products in-
ude Mampoer, which is a local brandy, a honey liqueur
d fruit schnapps. The main source of income, however,
mes from production of craft beers.

SOUTH AMERICA

Brazil _____

DISTILLERY: Union Distillery, Veranópolis
FOUNDED: 1972
OWNER/MANAGER: Union Distillery Maltwhisky Do
Brasil Ltda
www.maltwhisky.com.br

The company was already founded in 1948 as Union of
Industries Ltd to produce wine. In 1972 they started to
produce malt whisky and two years later the name of the
company was changed to Union Distillery Maltwhisky do
Brasil. In 1986 a co-operation with Morrison Bowmore
Distillers was established in order to develop the technology at the Brazilian distillery. Most of the production is
sold as bulk whisky to be part of different blends, but the
company also has its own single malt called Union Club
Whisky.

Argentina _____

DISTILLERY: La Alazana Distillery, Golondrinas,
Patagonia
FOUNDED: 2011
OWNER/MANAGER: Pablo Tognetti, Nestor Serenelli
www.laalazanawhisky.com

The first whisky distillery in Argentina concentrating
solely on malt whisky production was founded in 2011
and the distillation started in December that year.
Located in the Patagonian Andes
in the South of Argentina, it is owned and run by Pablo Tognetti, an
old time home brewer, and his son-
in-law Nestor Serenelli. The distillery is equipped with a lauter mash
tun and four 1,100 litre washbacks
all made of stainless steel. The one
550 litre pot still is made of copper
and takes care of both distillation
runs. A second still (1,300 litres) is
currently being built and will be in
production early 2014. This will also
allow for a dubbling of the production to 8,000 litres a year.
The owners are aiming for
a light and fruity whisky and
for maturation they use a mix
of 200 litre toasted Malbec
casks, ex-bourbon casks and
fresh PX sherry casks. Apart
from the bourbon casks and
the yeast, eveything needed
for the production is sourced
locally. A warehouse holding
100 casks has recently been
built and the plan is to add
more warehouses as well as
a visitor centre by the end of
2013. Following Argentinian
legislation, whisky can be
released after two years and
the first (limited) release will
be made in December 2013.
A general release of the La
Alazana single malt is planned
for December 2014.

First bottling from La Alazana

Still Going Up
The Whisky Year That Was

The figures for 2012 – small gain in value but volumes dropping

When the Scotch Whisky Association presented the export figures for 2012 in April 2013 the headlines read "Scotch Whisky Exports Hit Record Level" and that was true – never had the total value been higher. But a closer look at the figures did not create a pretty picture. The rise in value was barely 1% and total volumes have actually dropped by 5%. Part of the reason is that the figures for 2011 were quite extreme and difficult to match and also that large parts of the world still suffer from an economic downturn.

When looking at it from a longer time perspective – the total value of Scotch export has increased by 51% since 2007, while volumes have gone up by 5%. In the same period bottled single malt had increased 71% by value and 35% by volume while the corresponding figures for blended Scotch were +44% and -2% respectively.

The total value of exported Scotch in 2012 had increased by 0,95% to £4,27bn while volumes had dropped by 5% to the equivalent of 1,19bn 70 cl bottles. With values up and volumes down it is obvious that the average bottle has become more expensive. Since 2006 we have been analyzing the revenue per bottle for the producers. In that year they earned £2,38 per bottle and this has now increased to £3,59 in 2012.

The picture for 2012, if broken down into malt and blends, is as follows:

SINGLE MALT - EXPORT
Value: +4% to £778m
Volume: -3% to 97m bottles

BLENDED SCOTCH - EXPORT
Value: -4% to £3,2bn
Volume: -5% to 858m bottles

TOTAL SCOTCH - EXPORT
Value: +1% to £4,27bn
Volume: -5% to 1190m bottles

NB. The figures show export in bottles. Bulk export is not included except in the Total.

Looking at the detailed figures for each of the 8 regions, only one showed increasing volumes (Africa) while all but three (EU, rest of Europe and Middle East) showed increasing value.

Even though figures are dropping, The European Union (excluding the UK) is still the biggest market for Scotch whisky. In terms of volume 35% of the exports land in this region while the value is marginally less (31%). France is the biggest market and has been for many years. In 2012, however, figures dropped considerably with value down by 19% to £434m and volume slipping by 25% to 154 million bottles. A major reason for the negative performance was an excise tax increase in 2012 which led many buyers to stock up in 2011. The second biggest market in the EU, Spain couldn't show any impressive figures either, but

...his is due to a continuous, unfavourable financial climate. Value was down by 25% and volume by 0%. Germany, the number three market, showed strength on the other hand with an increase in value by 13% and in volume by 5%. After the top io follow three countries in the Eastern part of the Union – Poland, Estonia and Latvia. All three markets have grown rapidly in recent years but at east when it comes to the two Baltic countries, a substantial part of the volume is exported to Russia. The UK is a big, although not growing market for Scotch and is second only to France in Europe.

The second biggest region is Asia and with a line-up of emerging markets, it is closing in on EU every year. 2012 was not exceptional, however, with volumes dropping by 5% and value only increasing by 2%. The biggest importer, both in terms of value and volume, is Singapore but one must bear in mind that the country serves as a hub for further export to neighbouring countries. If we look at markets where most of the imported Scotch is consumed within the country, Taiwan is exceptional. With a population of only 23 million it is by far the most important market in the region ahead of much bigger countries such as india, China and South Korea. India and China have both been identified by producers of Scotch as the two most interesting markets for the future but while India has a tradition of drinking brown spirits, not least whisky, China is a white spirits market where the tradition of drinking domestic spirits like baijiu is strong. Scotch exports to India have increased in terms of volume by an impressive 275% since 2005 and the value rose by 17% in 2012. The volume increase for China since 2005 is a mere 12%. One country that finds itself in limbo is South Korea, once the biggest market in Asia. Due to a persistent, sluggish economy, volumes have dropped by 32% since 2005 and the downturn continued in 2012.

The third biggest region is North America where the USA accounts for 73% of the volume and 83% of the value. USA is furthermore the number one market in the world in terms of value. The region showed impressive figures during 2012, gaining 15% in value and the USA alone imported Scotch to the value of £758m – for the first time breaking through the £700m barrier.

Number four of the regions is Central and South America, an important (and growing) market for blended Scotch. The region as a whole was down 1% in terms of volume and up 3% in terms of value. The two biggest markets are Brazil and Venezuela but, while the former has shown a steady increase by 160% since 2000, Venezuela has performed a rollercoaster ride over the years with big fluctuations from year to year. In 2012 export value to Venezuela had increased by 23% while Brazil headed in the other direction with a decrease of 16%.

Africa is still unchartered whisky territory with the exception of South Africa. However, more and more companies are expanding into the region and exports to some of the countries, especially Angola, Nigeria and Morocco, are growing rapidly. South Africa accounts for up to two-thirds of the continent's whisky import and even though value had dropped by 2% in 2012, it still ranks as the 7th biggest market in the world in terms of value.

Next is the Middle East, a growing region even though both volumes and value decreased in 2012. The biggest market in the region is the United Arab Emirates representing 45% of the volume, but Lebanon also imports decent volumes.

Australasia is a region where Australia accounts for almost 90% of the total of 30 million bottles of Scotch. Export of Scotch to Australia has remained fairly constant over the past 15 years with volumes ranging between 25 and 30 million bottles per year. Value has increased though, matching the growing interest for single malt and in 2012 the value went up by 11%.

Exports to non-EU members are dominated by Turkey and Switzerland. The figures for all countries in this segment showed a decrease in

Super premium whiskies, like Ballantine's aged range, is part of the success for Scotch whisky in China

Photo: Pernod Ricard

2012 by 12% in volumes but an increase by the same numbers in terms of value.

Eastern Europe, finally, showed a remarkable decline during 2012 which can be deemed surprising, considering it is regarded as one of the emerging markets for Scotch and has shown a steady increase in recent years. The reason being, as mentioned previously, that a part of the import to Russia is made via Latvia and Estonia and is therefore reflected in the statistics of these countries. While Russia had decreased by 35% in value during 2012, the corresponding figures for Latvia and Estonia were 48% and 28% respectively. Several countries in Eastern Europe showed double digit increases during 2012 (Ukraine, Georgia, Azerbaijan and Armenia) and several producers have shown an increasing interest for the region.

Judging by the first six months of 2013, it seems like Scotch whisky exports are back on track compared to the very modest increase in 2012. Sales from January to June increased by 11% while volumes grew by 9%. In USA, Scotch's biggest market, sales soared by 29%. Other countries showing double digit growth were Mexico (67%), Brazil (42%), Germany (28%), Australia (26%) and The Netherlands (21%). Even Spain, which has been a sluggish market for years, increased (11%). But there were also countries bucking the positive trend. Several important markets in Asia have dropped in the first six months – China (-20%), Taiwan (-18%), Japan (-13%) and South Korea (-9%). Part of the decline in China was offset by a 19% increase in sales to Singapore which serves as a distribution hub to other Asian countries.

What about the future for Scotch whisky?

When the worst economic depression since the 1930s had hit the world in 2008, Scotch whisky showed impressive resilience and even during the protracted recession which has since followed, the industry has been able to report growth. Judging by the increases in volumes of production that the producers have recorded recently and the plans for even more, it seems obvious that there is optimism among industry representatives that there are prosperous times ahead for Scotch whisky.

There are several reasons for this positive view. The most important is a growing middle class with a rising disposable income in developing economies. This new generation can demonstrate its wealth by buying premium Scotch and aspiration is the key growth driver in countries, for example, like China and Russia. Other factors include successful trade negotiations resulting in lowering duty tariffs and protection for Scotch whisky by achieving Geographical Indication (GI) status in countries such as Malaysia, Thailand, China, South Korea and India. The status makes it illegal for any member state to produce or sell whisky outside of Scotland using the name Scotch whisky.

The fastest growing markets for Scotch whisky are Southeast Asia, Latin America, Eastern Europe and Africa. This is where the emerging markets can be found but does this mean that established markets such as Europe and North America are of no interest to the producers? On the contrary – they may be mature, but Europe is still the biggest market for Scotch, both in terms of volume and value and North America slides into place number three just behind Asia. It is therefore important to be pro-active, if not to create growth, then at least to maintain the market share that you have.

However, several key executives in the industry are more offensive than that. They claim that there certainly are opportunities for growth, but in order to do that it takes innovation. In the case of Scotch whisky, innovation could mean following in the footsteps of the American Bourbon industry, by adding flavoured variants.

In Scotland this is like navigating through a minefield as the Scotch Whisky Association's regulations strictly prohibit adding anything to Scotch other than the three key ingredients – water, barley (or other cereals) and yeast. Dewar's recently introduced a spirit called Dewar's Highlander Honey where whisky had been infused with honey. This is exactly what Jim Beam, Wild Turkey, Jack Daniel's and Bushmills have already done but unlike these producers, Dewar's can't call their products whisky. Edrington announced in May 2013 that they were testing three new flavoured products in Sweden – Famous Grouse Citrus, Vanilla and Spice. All three have been infused with flavouring compounds but, again, the spirit cannot be called whisky.

Opinions are divided in the industry but several companies have suggested that a change in the rules could be beneficial to the business. A spokesperson for Diageo commented on the SWA regulations about flavouring by posing the question "...whether we should deregulate that aspect at some stage" while an Edrington director was more cautious stating "We must be innovative within those regulations". Still it is an undisputed fact that in the USA, half of the volume growth for spirits in 2012 comprised of the flavoured versions and the flavoured segment now accounts for nearly 30% of the total volumes.

The big players

Diageo

At first glance, Diageo's increase in net profit for the fiscal year ending 30 June 2013 seems extraordinary – plus 25%! The reason though has to do with tax rates. Last year, the taxation for the company was a staggering 33% but that was just a one off, exceptional write-off of future tax deductions. For 2012/2013, the company was down to its normal rate of 16,9% tax. The overall results came in just slightly lower compared to last year. Net sales were up 5% to £11,4bn and operating profit increased by 8% to £3,53bn. The total number of cases sold was 165 million which can be compared to United Spirits' 124 million cases.

The best regions during the year have been

orth America (net sales +5%), Latin America 15%) and the emerging markets in Africa and astern Europe (+10%). Southern Europe continues to be a challenge with an 11% decrease in et sales while Germany, Austria and Benelux all lowed double digit increases. Sales in Asia Pacific ontinue to increase (3%) but at a much slower ace than before. China, Taiwan, Japan and ustralia were all performing well, while Korea nd Thailand fared disappointingly.

Whisky represents 40% of Diageo´s net sales but s much as 68% of the net sales growth during he year. The number one brand is, of course, ohnnie Walker, the most sold Scotch whisky in he world. Figures from IWSR showed that 18 milon cases (216 million bottles) were sold during he calendar year 2012. The company´s figures for scal year 2012/2013 were even more impressive 20 million cases (240 million bottles). Emerging arkets accounted for more than 75% of the rand´s growth. Another Scotch blend which is oing very well at the moment is Buchanan´s, sold ainly in Latin America and the USA. Volumes ere up by 11% and net sales by 25% and the rand sold around 23 million bottles. One brand hat is experiencing some difficulty is J&B. In he last two years, volumes have dropped by 3% to 48 million bottles. Diageo doesn´t have single malt Scotch among the top five in the orld unless you choose to see The Singleton, hich is a collective name for whiskies from three istilleries, as one brand. Sales of the range have evertheless increased rapidly over the last few ears, especially Singleton Glen Ord which is sold Asia. Cardhu single malt continued to decrease, hile both Talisker and Lagavulin have delivered steady growth.

Paul Walsh, who has been Diageo´s CEO for the ast 13 years, stepped down 1 July 2013 and Ivan Menezes was appointed as the new Chief Executive. Walsh will stay in the company for another ear to support Menezes in certain parts of his

duties, not least in relation to the recent acquisition of 25% of the shares in United Spirits, which makes Diageo the majority share holder. Read more about that deal on page 266.

Pernod Ricard
Due to a less buoyant market compared to 2011/2012, Pernod Ricard´s figures for the year ending June 2013 came in slightly lower than the previous year. Net sales increased by 4% to €8,58bn while net profits increased by 3% to €1,21bn. The main reasons for the slowdown in growth is China where sales increased 9%, lower than expected, Thailand and Korea, two markets that are challenging all producers at the moment and Western Europe where Spain continues to disappoint and France saw a decline in sales by 7%. The markets who, on the contrary, showed strength were the Americas (+7%) with USA, in particular, and to some extent Mexico performing well. Even in Asia many countries were pleased with their performances. Local whiskies in India increased by 16% with Chivas Regal and Glenlivet recording good figures. Sales in China were up 9% but, as mentioned, these figures are lower than the year before. Eastern Europe (in particular Russia, Poland and Ukraine) saw sales increasing by 11% and Africa/Middle East grew by 12%.

If we look at the different brands, and whisky in particular, Ballantine´s is still the top seller in the group in terms of volumes despite a decline of 4% to 71 million bottles. Chivas Regal comes in at second place with a value growth of 5% while volumes remained flat (59 million bottles). Jameson Irish whiskey was one of last year´s climbers with a 17% increase in value and volumes rising by 10% to reach 52 million bottles. The real star however, was Glenlivet, showing record growth with value up by 22% and volumes by 18%. The IWSR figures for the calendar year 2012, show sales of 900,000 cases of Glenlivet, while Pernod Ricard´s figures for the fiscal year 2012/2013 in-

Ivan Menezes, the new CEO of Diageo

Photo: Diageo

Laurent Lacassagne, the new CEO of Chivas Brothers

Photo: Pernod Ricard

dicate that volumes have soared beyond the magical 1 million case level, only the second Scotch malt whisky to achieve this after the performance of Glenfiddich a couple of years ago.

A change of leadership was announced for Pernod Ricard´s Scotch whisky operations, Chivas Brothers. The past seven years´ CEO, Christian Porta, has been appointed head of Pernod Ricard Europe and his successor is Laurent Lacassagne who joined the company in 1988.

United Spirits

United Spirits, the spirits division of United Breweries Group, can look back on a fiscal year ending March 2013 where net profits had slipped while net sales had increased. Net profits fell by 6,4% to Rs. 3,21 billion and net sales increased by 12,3% to Rs. 86,1 billion. The total number of cases sold (an important measure of value for United Spirits) was 123,7 million cases compared to 120,2 million the previous year, while the number of "millionaire brands", i.e. brands selling more than one million cases a year, was 21. United Spirits has more than 140 brands in its portfolio which include Scotch whisky, Indian whisky, vodka, rum, brandy and wine. The absolute majority of United Spirits´ whiskies are Indian whisky, i. e. whisky made of molasses. The major brands in the group are saleswise exceptional, with McDowell´s No.1 whisky as the top seller (19,5 million cases in 2012), followed by Bagpiper, Old Tavern, Hayward´s and Director´s Special.

United Spirits as a company is going through a tremendous time of change at the moment. Since the early 1950s the company has been controlled by members of the Mallya family with Vijay Mallya as the CEO and chairman since 1983. During the last five years, discussions regarding a co-operation and part-ownership between United Spirits and Diageo, the world´s leading drinks company, have been extensive. This finally came to fruition as Diageo recently took control of the company in spring 2013 (see more details on page 266 under Changes in Ownership). It seems that Mallya now, due to financial reasons, has been forced to relinquish control of his company. One main reason is the financial difficulties of another company in the Mallya conglomerate, namely Kingfisher Airline. The airline has large debts and has been grounded since October 2012 and the lenders are now calling the shots. Since becoming the major share holder, Diageo has been quick to make changes in the management of United Spirits. In August 2013 more than 100 executive officers were transferred to the holding company UB Group, while Paul Walsh, the former Diageo CEO, took his place on United Spirits board. Vijay Mallya is, at this point in time, still the CEO of the company but Diageo reserves the right to appoint a new CEO should it choose to do so.

Edrington

Looking at the figures for the fiscal year ending March 2013 must have made the owners more than pleased, particularly if you compare the

Ian Curle, Edrington´s CEO, is pleased with Macallan´s success

results to 2011/2012 which was an unusually lean year for one of the biggest players in the industry with key brands such as Macallan, Highland Park, The Famous Grouse and Cutty Sark. The turnover increased by 6,3% to £591m while profits before tax surged by 13,3% to £169m. More than 90% of total sales are now made outside the UK and the company has decided to strengthen its sales operations in four continents. Edrington Africa has already been set up and during 2013 new sales, marketing and distribution companies will be established in the USA, South East Asia and the Middle East.

If we look at how specific brands have performed during 2012 it becomes abundantly clear that Macallan continues its strong advance. Sales of the brand increased by 6% to 8,6 million bottles and during the last five years sales have grown by over 40%. Macallan is now the number 2 brand in the world in terms of value. The other single malt star in the range, Highland Park, has increased by 8% to 1,2 million bottles and has grown by 20% in value. Sales figures for The Famous Grouse blend decreased in 2011 but in 2012 the brand was back in full swing with sales rising by 10% to 37 million bottles. The Edrington Group is owned by a charitable trust, The Robertson Trust, established in 1961, which donated £14,6m to charitable causes in Scotland during 2011.

Whyte & Mackay

The company has been through a transition period ever since it was bought by Indian United Spirits in 2007 for £595m. Until then the bulk spirits trade was an important component of the activities but, after the change in ownership, the focus has shifted more towards a brand-orientated business. The two main single malts, Dalmore and Jura, get most of the attention and especially Jura single malt has presented amazing increases in sales volumes in the last three years, making it the third biggest single malt in the UK with a market share of 9%. Total sales for Jura in 2012 were 1,4 million bottles. Dalmore, which has a more executive profile, sells smaller volumes but has shown an increase in 2012 by 25% to 770,000 bottles. The blended brand Whyte & Mackay, is not among the 25 most sold in the world but has remained steady in figures, selling around 7 million bottles per year during the last decade.

The transformation of the company's concept becomes evident from the accounts that in recent years have varied widely. However, for the year ending March 2012 the figures were quite encouraging. Turnover increased by 36% to £230m while pre-tax profits rose 24% to £15,4m. The company also reported stocks of maturing whisky valued at £122m.

Speculations about the future of Whyte & Mackay have been rife since Diageo began negotiations about taking a majority stake of its parent company, United Spirits. Once the deal has been approved, it is believed that Diageo may have to put Whyte & Mackay on the market if the Office of Fair Trading and Competition Commission is of the opinion that Diageo controls too much of the Scotch whisky market. If this happens, then a couple of possible buyers could be in the running, particularly Campari and Bacardi.

Morrison Bowmore

Five years ago, the owners of Morrison Bowmore decided upon a new route for the business. Gone were the days of concentrating on bulk sales to super market chains like Asda and Tesco and, instead, they decided to concentrate on the single malts category and, in particular, the Duty Free segment. It seems as if it was a strategically correct decision. The recent financial statements have been positive, to say the least, and 2012 is no exception. Sales increased by 12% to £49.8m while pre-tax profits jumped by 39% to £8.5m. Looking at the individual brands, Bowmore increased by 15% and sold almost 2,3 million bottles in 2012, while sales of Auchentoshan single malt rose by 30% to more than 800,000 bottles.

Gruppo Campari

The sales in the Campari Group is reflected in the following four areas, namely the Americas (35% of the sales), Italy (29%), rest of Europe (26%) and rest of the world including duty free (10%). For the full year of 2012, the company showed a rise in net sales of 5,2% to €1341m, while net profits slipped by 1,6% to €156.7m. Numbers were saved by a strong performance in the USA not least by Wild Turkey bourbon (a brand that Campari acquired in 2009) where volumes had increased by 18% to almost 16 million bottles. The home market is still a problem area and sales in Italy declined by 3%. The only larger brand in the portfolio that increased was SKYY Vodka.

Campari's CEO - Bob Kunze Conzewitz

Photo: Campari

Other well known brands in the company include Aperol, Campari, Cinzano and Glen Grant single malt. The latter has experienced increasing volumes over the last two years but in 2012 it spiralled downwards again by 6,5%, mainly due to a weak Italian market – a country where Glen Grant for decades has been the biggest single malt. On the other hand, the brand is looking at growing numbers in many other markets, including America.

During the last four years, Campari has spent $850m on acquisitions and investing in brands, primarily Wild Turkey. In conjunction with last year's closing of the books, the company CEO, Bob Kunze-Concewitz, did not exclude the fact that there could be more acquisitions during 2012. This is indeed what happened. In September, Campari bought more than 80% of the shares of Lascelles de Mercado & Co, the parent company of the Appleton Estate and Wray & Nephew rum brands. The price was $415m and this was Campari's first move into the rum category. This also means that the Campari group, where the Garavoglia family owns 51% of the shares, is the eighth largest producer of premium spirits brands in the world.

LVMH

LVMH Moët Hennessy Louis Vuitton SA is the world's leading luxury goods vendor. It provides products ranging from champagne and perfumes, to designer handbags and jewellery. The Wines & Spirits business group includes brands such as Moët & Chandon Champagne and Hennessy Cognac, with Glenmorangie and Ardbeg representing Scotch whisky.

The company has since 2010 been spoiling their shareholders with impressive results despite an uncertain economic climate. The figures for 2012 were no exception. The turnover increased by 19% to €28,1bn, while operating profits reached €5921m, up by 13%.

Wine & Spirits is the second largest division in the company with a turnover in 2012 of €4137 million (+17%) and a profit of €1260 million (+14%). Champagne and cognac are the most important segments of the division with Hennessy, by far, being the largest cognac brand in the world, selling 62 million bottles during 2012.

Diageo owns 34% of the group's Wine & Spirits division (Moët Hennessy) and since 2009 rumours have surfaced regularly that Diageo would have placed a bid on the remaining 66%. Diageo's former CEO, Paul Walsh, has on more than one occasion expressed interest in buying if LVMH would consider selling. Every time, however, the LVMH majority share holder, Bernard Arnault, has declined the offer. In May 2013 rumours were bandied around again, but only days later LVMH ruled out the possibility of a sale. This time there was also a possible purchase sum mentioned – €12 billion. The interest for Diageo in securing the deal would be to add a big cognac and champagne brand to its portfolio.

Glenmorangie Company
It is true that the turnover for Glenmorangie Company rose by 10% in 2012 to £66,2m but then one has to keep in mind that there was a decrease of 20% the year before. The figures for 2012 are still lower than 2010 (£75,5m). Part of the explanation lies in the fact that the company is still affected by the changes made in 2008 when they decided to withdraw from blended whisky and bulk- and third party sales to concentrate solely on single malts. Pre-tax profits for 2012 on the other hand were impressive with an increase of 21% to £13,1m. Sales of Glenmorangie single malt went up by 14% during the year and 5,3 million bottles were sold making Glenmorangie the fourth biggest single malt brand in the world. Glenmorangie Company is a subsidiary of LVMH and apart from Glenmorangie, Ardbeg single malt is an important part of the range.

Ian Macleod Distillers
The family-owned company could record another impressive closing for the year ending September 2012. The turnover had improved by 16% to £50m and even though profits have dropped by 12% to £4,76m, the owners do not seem that perturbed. The reason for the decrease could be sought in the investments needed to get the Tamdhu distillery up and running. Ian Macleod bought the distillery from Edrington in 2011, just as they did with Glengoyne back in 2003. One million pounds have been invested in Tamdhu so far and another £2,5m have been earmarked to increase warehouse capacity. Since the take-over of Glengoyne ten years ago, sales of the single malt have more than doubled and in May 2013, it was time for the first release of a 10 year old Tamdhu single malt under the new regime. Ian Macleod also acts as an independent bottler by releasing malts from other

distilleries under the name Dun Bheagan and The Chieftain's. Isle of Skye (with four different expressions) is a blended malt and there is also a blended Scotch in the portfolio – King Robert II – which sells 6 million bottles per year and is one of the most popular brands in India.

Beam Inc.
Until 2011 Beam Inc. (at that time known as Beam Global Spirits & Wine) had been part of a company called Fortune Brands, which also had businesses in two different fields, golf and home & security. The latter two business areas were sold off and Beam continued as a company on its own. Their portfolio holds world famous brands such as Jim Beam, Maker's Mark, Canadian Club, Courvoisier and, in Scotch, Teacher's and Laphroaig.

The full year figures for 2012, the first for Beam as a pure spirits company, were surprisingly strong. Net sales were up by 7% to $2,47bn while like-for-like net profits rose by 15% to $398m. It was mainly the growth in the bourbon segment which contributed to the strong result. Jim Beam, the number one bourbon in the world, was up 10% to 76 million bottles, while sales of Maker's Mark rose by 15%, reaching close to 16 million bottles. Two of the smaller bourbon brands have also performed well – Knob Creek (+24%) and Basil Hayden's (+35%). Laphroaig also proved itself with an increase in volume by 15% reaching a total of 2,7 million bottles. Teacher's, on the other hand, was worse off. Although increasing but only with 1%, some analytics claim that the brand now has lost its number one position in the Indian market to its rival, 100 Pipers. The past year has been tough for Teacher's in India as the company is the subject of an ongoing corruption investigation. Two years ago, Beam Inc. also made its entry into the lucrative Irish whiskey segment through the acquisition of Cooley Distillery.

Since the spirits division has become an independent company, there have been persistent rumours that one of the big conglomerates in the industry would seek to buy the company. Bets have been placed on Diageo which still hasn't got a really big bourbon brand in the portfolio. Recently, analysts have rather considered Pernod Ricard as a potential buyer in order to strengthen its position on the American market. The reason that a potential acquisition has taken a long time can be ascribed to the fact that if it would have taken place in 2011, this would have led to heavy taxes, but these could be avoided once a two-year period has elapsed, i.e. sometime during autumn 2013.

Inver House Distillers
Inver House Distillers, a part of International Beverage Holdings which is the international arm of ThaiBev, recorded impressive numbers for 2011, mainly due to the brilliant success of their blended Scotch brand, Hankey Bannister. When the company filed their report for 2012, sales figures were still impressive with an increase of 13% to £91m. Pre-tax profits, on the other hand, fell by

Johnnie Walker - still in the lead

ten climbers, seven hail from India while from the rest, two are from Scotland (The Famous Grouse and William Lawson´s) and one from America (Wild Turkey).

Johnnie Walker is, of course, the undisputed leader amongst blended Scotch whiskies. Their market share continues to increase and they now possess 20% of the total blended Scotch sales. Still at number two, a spot which they have maintained since 2007, is Ballantine´s with 70 million bottles sold. In spot number three we find Chivas Regal (59 million bottles) which has been climbing since last year, not so much because of a modest increase, but mainly because of the decreasing numbers of its nearest rivals, Grant´s (55 million) and J&B (48 million). Thereafter we find Famous Grouse (37 million) which has surpassed Dewar's (36 million) thanks mainly to the steady increase over the recent years. William Peel, the biggest Scotch in France, comes in at eighth place (32 million bottles) closely followed by the fast growing William Lawson´s (31 million bottles) and in tenth place, yet another Scotch with French overtones, Label 5 (28 million).

So what is the picture for single malts? Overall, they managed to increase their volumes in 2012, more so than the blended Scotch. Of the top 25, 19 single malts were climbers whilst the comparative figure for blended Scotch was 12 brands. Glenfiddich, which in 2011 became the first brand that managed to sell more than 1 million cases (12 million bottles) in one year is, of course, still the world's most sold single malt Scotch with 12,7 million bottles. The second place is currently held by Glenlivet which in 2010 was 30% behind Glenfiddich. A year later the gap had narrowed to 25% and in 2012 to 15%. Glenlivet sold 10,8 million bottles and could, in the foreseeable future, be the next brand that will pass the dream sales target of 1 million cases in a year. Macallan

21% to £12,3m. The main reason for this was the company´s investment in building stock reserves for the future. If Hankey Bannister was the star of 2011, then 2012 was Old Pulteney´s year. The single malt brand saw volumes rise by 16% while sales value increased by almost 25%.

The big brands

In 2009 the Indian whisky, Bagpiper, assumed the position as the world's most sold whisky and pushed Johnnie Walker into second place. The two years that followed, Johnnie Walker resumed the lead up to 2012, only to be surpassed by yet another Indian whisky, this time McDowell´s No. 1, which increased its volume by no less than 21% from 2011. McDowell´s No. 1 sold 234 million bottles in comparison to Johnnie Walker´s 227 millions. On the list of the top ten most sold whiskies in the world, no less than eight brands are from India. The only non-Indian whisky except for Johnnie Walker that can compete, is Jack Daniel's. When looking at the top 30 brands, it is India that is dominating (with14 brands) and Scotland (11 brands). The brands that are increasing quickly are to a great extent Indian too. Amongst the top

Glenfiddich - the first single malt to reach 1 million cases in a year

has certainly increased but is somewhat behind its former rival regarding the second place with 8,6 million bottles sold in 2012. An impressive increase noticeable from last year's results puts Glenmorangie fairly unchallenged in fourth place with 5,3 million bottles. The Singleton came in at fifth place (3,25 million bottles) but that includes all three versions – Glen Ord (with the lion's share), Glendullan and Dufftown. Due to a steady decrease on the whisky market in Italy, Glen Grant has now fallen to sixth place with 3,2 million bottles. The seventh spot through to the tenth spot is being held by the same four brands as last year, namely Aberlour (2,8 million), Balvenie (2,7 million), Laphroaig (2,6 million) and Cardhu (2,1 million). The only difference is that Laphroaig and Balvenie have exchanged places.

As always, this ranking shows just the Scotch whisky brands. If we look at whiskies produced in North America, the number one spot is held by Jack Daniel's (Tennessee whiskey) with 128 million bottles, followed by Jim Beam (Bourbon) with 76 million bottles, Crown Royal (Canadian) 59 million bottles, Seagram's 7 Crown (American blended whiskey) 29 million bottles and Black Velvet (Canadian) with 25 million bottles – the same top five and in exactly the same order as last year.

As mentioned before, Indian whiskies are dominating the top ten lists and the different brand rankings change considerably, more so than within the Scotch whisky top ten. Last year's number one and two have changed places this year, with McDowell's No. 1 being the leader with 234 million bottles, followed by Officer's Choice (217 million). The latter has, in spite of this, made an impressive journey since 2007 with a total increase of 175%. At one time being the most sold whisky in the world, Bagpiper has now slipped to third place with 169 million bottles, while Royal Stag defends its fourth place with 154 million. Finally, Old Tavern, is in fifth place with 139 million bottles.

Changes in ownership - mergers and acquisitions

The acquisition in the whisky world that has drawn the most attention the past year is, by far, Diageo's' move to buy a part of the Indian spirits giant, United Spirits. For years now, rumours have flourished regarding discussions between the two companies concerning a possible collaboration. There have also been times when representatives have actively engaged in discussions that have yielded nothing. Things started to change in 2011 when it became clear that United Spirits' main owner, Vijay Mallya, had financial problems in other parts of his business, mainly the Kingfisher Airline. On the one hand it appeared as if he would be forced to sell part of his empire, while Diageo, on the other hand, was of course very much interested in gaining better access to the important Indian market. In November 2012, Diageo announced that they had agreed to

acquire a 53,4% controlling stake in United Spirits for US$2.05bn but that the acquisition would be done in phases. The first step was an open offer to United Spirits' public shareholders to acquire 26% of the shares. This proposition was supposed to be made at the beginning of January 2013, but was delayed several times and was not presented to the market until April. The outcome for Diageo was disappointing as only 0,4% of the shares were secured. By the end of May, another 10% were bought through a preferential allotment agreement and at the beginning of July another 14,98% were bought from the mother company of United Spirits, namely, United Breweries. This makes Diageo the biggest shareholder in United Spirits and, in terms of an agreement reached with United Breweries, they agreed to vote in Diageo's direction until either June 2018 or until Diageo owns more than 50% of United Spirits. Diageo is now in control of the Indian company and it came at a cost of US$871m.

The deal means, of course, that Diageo now has secured many important distribution channels in India, but there may be other implications. Whyte & Mackay (including four malt distilleries and one grain distillery in Scotland) is owned by United Spirits since 2007 and it remains to be seen if Diageo's control of United Spirits (and indirectly Whyte & Mackay) is in breach of the rules on competition. The UK's Office of Fair Trading will investigate this and it may result in Diageo being forced to sell off Whyte & Mackay. A potential buyer that has been mentioned would be the Campari Group (owner of, for instance, Glen Grant and Wild Turkey).

Burn Stewart Distillers, owners of the blended Scotch Scottish Leader, as well as three distilleries – Bunnahabhain, Deanston and Tobermory – have spent the last five years in uncertainty. The company was bought in 2002 by Trinidad based CL Financial, originally an insurance company but through diversifying, became involved in a number of different business fields. A financial crisis in 2009 led to the fact that the Trinidadian government more or less took over the entire company, with the exception of CL World Brands, the part of the company dealing with wine and spirits. In April 2013, it was announced that the South African Distell Group had acquired Burn Stewart at a cost of £160m. Distell is South Africa's biggest whisky producer with brands such as Three Ships whisky. Since 2007 both companies have cooperated on the African market and Distell is hoping that the acquisition will provide it with greater access to Taiwan, where Burn Stewart is well positioned.

Many of the comments regarding Distell's acquisition of Burn Stewart revolve around the positive aspects that the new owner has an anchorage in the whisky world and the same goes for another distillery changing owners, namely Glenglassaugh. It came as a surprise for most people when the take-over was announced in March 2013, BenRiach Distillery Company, owners of BenRiach and GlenDronach distilleries acquired Glen-

If everything goes according to plan, Ardnamurchan distillery will be producing end of 2013

assaugh distillery for an undisclosed sum. The
othballed Glenglassaugh had been bought in
008 by the Scaent Group involving owners from
ussia, Sweden and The Netherlands, but when
enRiach took over in 2013, the seller was
umière Holdings and nobody really knew who
ere left of the original owners. Lumière Holdings
cquired Glenglassaugh in 2012 and the company
as interests in a wide range of businesses in
ithuania, Russia and the Czech Republic. It soon
ecame clear that the owners neither would,
or could make the investments necessary to lift
lenglassaugh to the next level as a brand nor as
distillery. Billy Walker of BenRiach and his long-
anding associates South African whisky entre-
reneurs Geoff Bell and Wayne Kieswetter, saw
he opportunity and managed to secure the ow-
ership more or less under the radar, even though
here was at least one other interested party.

New, revived
and planned distilleries

Ardnamurchan Distillery
he success for the independent bottler, Adelphi
istillery, has forced the owners to build their
wn distillery. The chosen site at Glenbeg in
rdnamurchan is 1,5 miles west of the company´s
eadquarter at Glenborrodale Castle and this
neans that it will become the most westerly distil-
ery in mainland Scotland. Most of the buildings
vere complete by August 2013 and the equip-
nent started to arrive in September – one mash
un, 7 washbacks (4 made of wood and 3 stainless
teel), one wash still (10,000 litres) and one spirit
till (6,000 litres). The goal is to produce 100,000
tres of alcohol in the first year (2014) with a pos-
ibility of increasing production to 300,000 litres.
he distillery will be self-sufficient with malted
arley by way of its own floor maltings and com-

missioning of the distillery is scheduled for mid
December. Graeme Bowie, assistant manager at
Balblair distillery, was hired as distillery manager
in May. In June, the company was granted an
award of £1,7m by the Scottish Government to
help finance the project.

The owners are planning for three different styles of whisky; the first one will be similar to their
current brand, Fascadale, which has usually been
drawn from bourbon casks from either Talisker or
Highland Park. The second style will be more sherried, while the third will probably be a heavier
peated whisky.

John Fergus & Co.
Many of the distilleries currently under construction in Scotland are small and most of them
would be labelled microdistilleries. The one that is
planned by John Fergus & Co in Glenrothes in Fife
is not. The plan is to be able to produce 4 million
litres per year and the market being targeted is
India, where demand for Scotch is booming. John
Fergus & Co, based in Milnathort south of Perth,
was registered as late as 2011 and the managing
director is Ian Palmer who, until recently, was the
manager of Glen Turner distillery and bottling
plant, owned by French La Martiniquaise. Planning permission for the new distillery, which is
located next to Fife airport, was approved in
January 2013 and it is expected that production
will start early in 2014. June 2013 saw the company being granted an award of £1,5m by the
Scottish Government to help finance the project.
The total cost is estimated to be £8m.

Tullamore Dew Distillery
When William Grant & Sons acquired the second
biggest Irish whiskey brand in the world, Tullamore Dew, in 2010, rumours started to flourish
that they also planned to build a new distillery.

David Thomson is supervising the installation of the spirit still at Annandale distillery

Until the 1950s, Tullamore Dew had been distilled at Daly's Distillery in Tullamore. When it closed, production was temporarily moved to Power's Distillery in Dublin, and was later moved to Midleton Distillery, where it currently is still produced. In March 2012, Grant's could report that they were in the final stages of negotiations to acquire a site at Clonminch, situated on the outskirts of Tullamore. Construction began in May 2013 and the owners hope to have the distillery ready for production by summer 2014. The construction will be executed in three phases where the first is a pot still distillery with the possibility to distil 1,8 million litres per year. This will be increased in 2019 to 3,6 million litres and, finally, in 2021 a grain distillation unit will be added which will have the capacity of doing 8 million litres of grain spirit. Since Tullamore Dew whiskey comprises of malt whiskey, pot still whiskey and grain whiskey it would appear that William Grant's will rely heavily on Midleton distillery for its need of grain whiskey at least for eight more years. The total cost for the new plant will be €35m.

Annandale Distillery
In May 2010 consent was obtained from Dumfries & Galloway Council for the building of the new Annandale Distillery. The old one was closed in 1921 and in December 2008 the site was bought by Professor David Thomson and his wife, Teresa Church, with the aim to resurrect this, the southernmost distillery in Scotland. Work on the restoration began in June 2011 with the two, old sandstone warehouses being restored to function as two-level dunnage warehouses. The mash house and the tun room were completely reconstructed while a new still house was built in what used to be the mill house in the Johnnie Walker days. David also has plans to start using the old maltings as well, to malt locally sourced barley,

but that will probably not be for another five years. Meanwhile, the old maltings with the kiln and original pagoda roof, will house a visitor centre and the owners hope to attract 50,000 visitors to the distillery once it is up and running.

As for the equipment (the original ones have all disappeared), this has been made by Forsyth's in Rothes. In 2010, Malcolm Rennie, who managed Kilchoman distillery on Islay, joined the company as Distillery Manager and, together with Jim Swan, he has created the design. The equipment will consist of one semi-lauter mash tun (2,5 tonnes), six wooden washbacks (12,000 litres each), one wash still (12,000 litres), one intermediate still and one spirit still (4,000 litres each). The capacity will be 250,000 litres per annum and the plan is to start distillation by Easter 2014.

Kingsbarns Distillery
The plans for this distillery near St Andrews in Fife, have been on the table since 2009 and many people have been involved over the years. The driving force has been Doug Clement who has worked tirelessly to get the necessary funds to make the plans become a reality. In January 2013 his dream was realised when the Scottish Government awarded a grant of £670,000 and this, in turn, led to an investor agreeing to inject £3m into the project. The new owner is the independent bottler, Wemyss Malts, which is based in Edinburgh.

A farmhouse from the late 18th century will now be converted into a distillery and a visitor centre. The site lies just south of St Andrew's and it is the owners' hope that the location will also attract visitors who, otherwise, would only have come to the area just to play golf. Construction work began in summer 2013 and the owners hope to be able to start production sometime in autumn 2014. The distillery will be equipped with one

5 ton mash tun, four washbacks (with room to add a further two), one wash still and one spirit still. The capacity will be 500,000 litres of alcohol and local barley will be used to produce a fruity, lowland style whisky.

Duncan Taylor Distillery
Duncan Taylor is one of two big independent bottlers (Douglas Laing being the other) that does not have its own distillery. In 2007, they acquired an old granary built in 1899 just outside Huntly with the express purpose of transforming it into a distillery. Following the financial crisis in 2008/2009, the plans were put on hold. Instead, the company focused on setting up its own import company in Pasadena, California, as well as investing in a brand new bottling facility in Huntly. In summer 2013, however, the work on the distillery was in full swing with contractors paving a new road for the diggers and trucks. The plan is to dismantle the old building brick by brick, then to install the distilling equipment and finally to reassemble the building. The owners are planning for a distillery with a capacity of 1,1 million litres, with one wash still (16,000 litres) and one spirit still (12,000 litres), as well as column stills and a gin still. No final date has been set for the start of the production but as the owners say: "This is a long term project and it will take a number of years before we start production".

Falkirk Distillery
The construction of the first distillery in Falkirk, since Rosebank was closed in 1993, came to a halt temporarily in autumn of 2009 after the plans had been approved by the local council in spring of that year. Objections were raised by Historic Scotland that the distillery would be built too close to the Antonine Wall. The Wall was built in 142 AD to stop Caledonian tribes attacking the Romans and it was given World Heritage Status in 2008. However, in May 2010 Scottish ministers gave the final approval, arguing that the distillery would not interfere with the wall but could boost tourism to the area instead. Falkirk Distillery Company, owned by Fiona and Alan Stewart, is behind the £5m project. Apart from the distillery,the facilities will include a visitor centre, restaurant and shops and could create up to 80 jobs. Very little news has come from the company in the last years but in June 2013, it was awarded a grant of £444,000 by the Scottish Government and the owners now hope to start construction work shortly.

Barra Distillery
The classic film, Whisky Galore, based on the equally classic novel by Sir Compton Mackenzie, was filmed on the island of Barra in the Outer Hebrides. It is a story of the SS Politician which was stranded in 1941 and 264,000 bottles of whisky which were among her cargo were lost. The island where the ship went missing was in fact Eriskay, a smaller island to the north of Barra, but Peter Brown still wants to build a distillery on Barra and is convinced that the connection with the film location will be favourable for the business. Future casks have been sold to the public since early 2008 and most of the plans regarding building and construction are ready. In July 2010, Peter Brown bought all the shares owned by Andrew Currie (of Arran Distillery fame) who had been part of the project since its inception. The original idea was to start building in autumn of 2009, but the recession has made funding difficult and the future for the distillery is now uncertain.

Lakes Distillery
Headed by Paul Currie, who is the co-founder of

Doug Clement and William Wemyss start the build at Kingsbarns Distillery in Fife

Photo: Wemyss Malts

Isle of Arran distillery, a consortium of private investors will be embarking on a plan to build the first whisky distillery in the Lake District for more than 100 years. The distillery will be housed in a Victorian farm which has been converted near Bassenthwaite Lake and the owners hope to start production in December 2013. The £2,5m distillery will be equipped with two stills (around 3-4,000 litres each) for the whisky production and a third still for the distillation of gin. A combination of copper and steel condensers will allow for greater permutations when it comes to the flavour of the spirit. The capacity will be 300,000 litres of pure alcohol and for the first year a production of 85,000 litres is envisaged. A visitor centre is scheduled to open in spring 2014. In 2007, Paul´s brother, Andrew, made an attempt to open the Barley Bridge distillery near Kendal in Cumbria but the plans were thwarted due to lack of funding.

Early plans
Apart from the distilleries (or proposed distilleries) that we have mentioned, there are a few more that are still in the early stages of planning or where planning approval has just recently been granted.

When the Teeling family sold Cooley and Kilbeggan Distilleries to Beam in 2012, it was not long before John Teeling and his son, Jack, started a new whiskey business as blenders and bottlers. The company name is Teeling Whiskey and John and Jack were soon accompanied by the younger son, Stephen. The family now has plans to build a distillery of their own in Dublin. The family´s involvement in the whiskey industry started in 1782 when Walter Teeling owned a distillery on Marrowbone Lane in Dublin and, if all goes according to plans, the family could be distilling again in Dublin by the end of 2014 or beginning of 2015.

The Teeling family is also involved in another distillery project of an even bigger magnitude. The newly formed Irish Whiskey Company (IWC) which has the Teeling family as majority owners, signed an agreement with Diageo in August 2013 where it has taken over the Great Northern Brewery in Dundalk. Diageo will be moving the brewing operation to Dublin and the IWC has the intention of restructuring the site into Great Northern Distillery at a cost of €35m. The new owners envisage three different business opportunities when taking over; producing own-label whiskey, making bulk whiskey for bottlers without their own distilleries and distilling grain whiskey for smaller pot still distilleries. Once the new distillery is up and running, it will be the second biggest distillery in Ireland after Midleton, with the capacity to produce 3 million litres of pot still whiskey and 8 million litres of grain spirit. The IWC will take over the site at the beginning of 2014 and the plan is to start production towards the end of that year.

There are a lot of distillery projects underway in Ireland at the moment. One is the Dublin Whiskey Company, founded by Marie Byrne, Edmond O´Flaherty and Patrick O´Brien. They are currently rebuilding a former mill in Dublin´s Liberties less than 500 meters from St Patrick´s Cathedral and making it into a whiskey distillery. The idea is to produce single pot still whiskey and the distillery, equipped with a 10,000 litre wash still and a 6,00 litre spirit still, will be able to produce 1 million litres per year. The owners hope to start production in January 2014.

The Northern Irish producer of cream liqueurs, Niche Drinks, are looking to build a new plant in Londonderry for their existing operation and the plans also include a new whiskey distillery. Planning permission was granted in May 2013 and the total investment will amount to £15m. The owners hope that the new plant will create 10 new jobs to add to the 90 people already employed by the company.

Slane Castle, north of Dublin, has been famous since the 1980s for hosting rock concerts with many of the biggest stars. But the Conyngham family, who owns the estate, has also in recent years established a whiskey brand which has become popular in USA, Slane Castle Whiskey. Until recently, the whiskey has been produced at the Cooley Distillery but when Beam Inc. took over the distillery in 2012 they also stopped selling whiskey to independent bottlers. This made the Conyngham family decide to build their own distillery on the estate. The planning application was approved in June 2013 and the plans include production of triple distilled single malt, triple distilled single pot still and blended whiskey. The latter means that the distillery will be equipped with a column still for the production of grain whiskey, apart from pot stills for malt whiskey. The barley (of which the main bulk will come from the estate) will be malted on site in a Saladin box and the capacity of the distillery will be one million litres of alcohol.

Peter Lavery, lottery millionaire and founder of The Belfast Distillery Company, has started to transform the former Crumlin Road jail into a whiskey distillery. Three stills have been ordered from Forsyth´s in Rothes and the capacity will be 300,000 litres of alcohol. The whole investment is expected to be around £5m and if everything is going according to plans, the distillery could be producing by 2014. Since 2011, Lavery is already selling whiskey produced by Cooley Distillery under the brand names Danny Boy and Titanic.

Ballindalloch Castle is one of the most impressive in Scotland. Built in 1546 it lies right in the middle of "whisky country", in Speyside, not far from Glenlivet and Glenfarclas distilleries. The previous owners of the castle have been involved in the whisky industry, from 1923 to 1965, when they owned part of Cragganmore distillery, not far away from the castle. The current owners of the estate, the Lady Laird Mrs Clare Macpherson-Grant Russel and her husband, Oliver Russel, now have plans to put Ballindalloch on the whisky map again. The idea is to build a distillery on the grounds and in June 2013, the Scottish Government awarded a grant of £1,2m to help fund the project.

Pernod Ricard´s future distillery on the old Imperial site in Carron, Speyside

In 2010, Alasdair Day launched a new blended Scotch whisky by the name of The Tweeddale. To be entirely accurate, it wasn´t a new whisky, but a recreation of a whisky manufactured in the 19th century. A company called J & A Davidson launched the brand and in 1895, Alasdair´s great grandfather, Richard Day, joined the company and eventually took over the business. When Richard Day retired after World War II, the business ceased trading and the brand fell into oblivion. Alasdair inherited the old company´s cellar book and based on the recipes noted there, he was able to recreate the whisky and in August 2013 the fourth batch of The Tweeddale (14 years old) was released. Alasdair has now decided to build his own distillery in Walkerburn in the Tweed valley in the Scottish Borders – actually the first distillery in that area since 1837. The distillery will have a capacity of 100,000 litres and Alasdair is currently having discussions with investors to generate the funding for the project.

Isle of Harris Distillers is planning for a distillery on the Hebridean island of Harris. One of the men at the helm is a former director of Glenmorangie, Simon Erlanger, and the distillery will be built at Tarbert. According to Erlanger, £10m is needed of which one-third is already secured by investors. In January 2013, the project got a boost through a £1,9m grant from the Scottish Government and if the rest of the funds can be secured, a distillery could be up and running by the second half of 2014.

Gerald Michaluk, the entrepreneur behind the Arran Brewery, announced in November 2012 that he had bought the old Rosebank distillery (which closed in 1993) in Falkirk from Diageo. His plan is to turn the site into a brewery, bottling plant and micro-distillery. He has raised £1m and hopes to raise another £10m, for instance through crowd-funding. When the former distillery was sold, Diageo had written into the deeds that the site couldn't be used for distilling until 2017, but Michaluk has since asked Diageo to reconsider.

Plans to build a distillery in the Shetlands were announced in 2002 by a company called Black-wood Distillers. After a few years, it became clear that the plans would never materialize. The issue regarding a distillery has now been resuscitated by the whisky consultant, Stuart Nickerson, former distillery manager at Highland Park and Glenglassaugh. The idea is to build it at Saxa Vord on Unst, the most northerly of the islands. Nickerson says the plans are at a "very early stage of development" and if they do materialize, it will become a small boutique distillery.

Finally, rumour has it that there will soon be a ninth distillery on Islay! It is named Gartbreck and will be situated in a stunning location right by the see on Loch Indaal, three miles south of Bowmore. The plan is to start production in spring 2015 and it will most probably become the smallest distillery on Islay.

Investments

Most of the investments in the Scottish whisky industry during the past year have been about increasing production capacity by a large number of distilleries. Overall, when all the projects are completed, the increase will have raised the total capacity for Scotland´s malt whisky distilleries by 15% or 50 million litres of pure alcohol. These measures are motivated by the increased demand, particularly in the emerging markets in Asia, South America and Africa.

The main part of the investments is, not unexpectedly, made by the largest actor, Diageo, who in present time possesses 28 malt whisky distilleries. On the same site as the existing Teaninich distillery in Alness, a new mega distillery will be constructed and will be operational as from 2015. The total capacity will be 13 million litres and the investment is £50m. At the same time, Teaninich will be expanded to double its capacity (compared to today) at a cost of £12m. Several Speyside distilleries have also been refurbished during the year and several more will follow in the next year. A total investment of £30m was used to increase the capacity at Glendullan, Linkwood and Mannochmore and by summer 2015, Mortlach will have another six stills, exact replicas of the existing ones, which will double the capacity. Glen Ord, which saw the capacity increasing already a year ago, is now subject to another refurbishing which will add another 5 million litres to the capacity at a cost of £25m. But added capacity is not all – reducing energy costs and taking care of co-products from the distillation process are equally important. A new bio-energy plant, similar to the one at Dailuaine, is currently being built at Glendullan distillery. By 2014 it will be ready to take care of the copper residues which emanate from the spirit distillation.

The main competitor, Chivas Brothers, is not wasting time either. In May 2013, Glen Keith distillery was back in production after having been mothballed for 13 years. More stills were added and the capacity is now 6 million litres. Chivas Brothers has also kept many wondering about what it would do with the closed Imperial distillery in Carron. The whole site was offered for sale in 2008, but was soon withdrawn from the market. Since then, speculations have been rife whether or not the company would re-open Imperial again. However, during autumn 2012 the news broke that the distillery would be demolished to make way for a new distillery with a capacity to produce 6 million litres. In May 2013, the old Imperial buildings had all been demolished and the new distillery will be ready during 2015.

William Grant & Sons built a new malt whisky distillery, Ailsa Bay, in 2007 next to its Girvan grain distillery in Ayrshire. The capacity was quite impressive, 6 million litres, but in 2013 it was time for further expansion when eight more stills were added raising the volume to 12 million litres. The company's star distillery, Glenfiddich in Dufftown, also received increased capacity through eight new washbacks. At the same time, W Grants is working on its new Tullamore Dew distillery in Ireland which should be completed in summer 2014 at a cost of €35m.

Bottling grapevine

Three trends have become increasingly more apparent when launching new bottlings; whisky with no age statement, whisky matured in virgin oak and whisky released as duty free exclusives.

If we look at the first, this is a much debated trend, both amongst customers who sometimes feel deprived of the opportunity to compare the age (and sometimes in their view, the quality) to the price, but also within the industry where, for example, Chivas Brothers, since a few years back, have made it abundantly clear how important the age of a whisky is in their campaign "Age Matters." Other producers, on the other hand, believe that too much emphasis has been placed on the number of years that the whisky has been

maturing. Examples of new bottlings without age statement during 2013 were the three expressions to follow Macallan Gold, which was launched last year – Amber, Sienna and Ruby. Old Pulteney introduced Navigator as part of their core range and Tomatin released Legacy. Talisker launched Storm and Port Ruighe, the latter with a finish in ruby port casks. From Laphroaig came three expressions; PX (finished in PX sherry casks), QA (double matured in American oak) and An Cuan Mor (bottled at cask strength).

The second trend, maturation in casks that have not held any wine or spirit before they were filled with newmake, is of somewhat later date. We call that type of casks Virgin oak and there is always the risque that the new oak will be too dominant in the whisky. Today, more and more producers have started to experiment with this way of maturation. Rachel Barrie, Master Blender at Morrison Bowmore, is one of those who have spearheaded this technique and, during the year, we have seen both Auchentoshan Virgin Oak and Glen Garioch Virgin Oak both carrying Rachel's signature. We are now only waiting for a Bowmore Virgin Oak. Both Deanston and BenRiach have previously launched similar releases.

The third trend is that duty free sales are becoming increasingly important to the industry. During 2012/2013 we saw many examples of that; Balvenie launched a trio of whiskies called Triple Cask and aged 12, 16 and 25 years respectively. Dalmore released Valour, which had also been matured in three different casks, Glenfarclas presented an 18 year old and Glenfiddich launched the third expression in their Age of Discovery range - a 19 year old from red wine casks. Glen Garioch wagered on no less than 11 different single casks for 11 different airports in the UK, whilst Glenrothes introduced the Manse Brae range with three bottlings, the oldest having matured for 21 years. Highland Park, which has previously chosen vintage bottlings for duty free, launched a series of six bottlings with no age statement called Warriors. Jura gave us the unaged Turas-Mara while Talisker introduced Dark Storm, the peatiest Talisker so far. Several producers came up with whole ranges for travel retail like, for example, Macduff with its Royal Burgh Collection (16, 20 and 30 years old) and Old Pulteney which replaced its series named after herring drifters, with a new series named after lighthouses (Noss Head, Duncansby Head and Pentland Skerries).

Some producers have revamped their entire range, for instance Tullibardine which now consists of the unaged Sovereign, three wood finishes (Sauternes, Burgundy and Sherry) and two aged expressions (20 and 25 years). Loch Lomond distillers launched new whiskies from both of their distilleries; Glen Scotia with 10, 12, 16, 18 and 21 year old versions and Loch Lomond where Inchmurrin 12, 15, 18 and 21 year old versions are the new varieties, while Glengoyne replaced a few of their bottlings with 15, 18 and 25 year olds. Old and rare bottlings often raise interest among the enthusiasts. *Auchentoshan* released a *Vintage 1975* and the oldest bottlings so far from *Ben-Riach* (*Vestige 46 years*) and *GlenDronach* (*Recherché 44 years*) also saw the light of day. From Burn Stewart we have a *40 year old Ledaig*, as well as a *40 year old Bunnahabhain* and *Glengoyne* has launched a *35 year old*. *Glen Grant* celebrated distillery manager, Dennis Malcolm´s, 50 years in the industry with *Decades*, made up of whiskies from five different decades. *Glenrothes* released a *Vintage 1970* in a new range called *Extraordinary Casks* and from *Jura* came the *1977 Juar*, as well as the *30 year old Camas an Staca*. Finally, Inver House released its oldest *anCnoc* so far, a *35 year old*, while *Talisker 27 years* and *Lagavulin 37 years* were launched as part of Diageo´s yearly Special Releases. This was accompanied by a *28 year old Singleton of Dufftown*, a *36 year old Convalmore* and new releases of two cult whiskies – a *35 year old Brora*, as well as a *34 year old Port Ellen*.

At the other end of the spectrum – young whiskies – we find *Loch Gorm* and the *6 year old Vintage 2007* from *Kilchoman* and *Kilkerran Work in Progress V* from *Glengyle*, 9 years old and this year in two versions, bourbon and sherry. The new owners of *Tamdhu*, Ian Macleod Distillers, have released their first expression since the take-over, a *10 year old* and *Tomatin* gave us a nice surprise with its first peated expression, *Cù Bòcan*. Some producers have spoilt us with double digit releases every year, like *BenRiach* with this year´s *12 single casks* from 1975 to 2005, one of them triple distilled and *GlenDronach* with a launch of *8 single casks* (with more to follow later in the year) ranging from 1971 to 2002. The owners of *Bruichladdich* were also diligent and launched *Scottish Barley, Islay Barley Rockside Farm, Bere Barley 2nd edition, Black Art 4, Port Charlotte Scottish Barley, Octomore 06.1 and 06.2*. Finally, there was a bottling which confused many people just as it was supposed to do – *The Glenlivet Alpha*. Released in a black bottle with the alcohol strength (of 50%) as the only information, the idea was to get people to speculate what the content could be, based on their personal knowledge and experiences. Six weeks later, it was revealed that the whisky had been matured in casks that had previously contained only Scotch whisky and no other spirits or wines – a first for Glenlivet.

Tullibardine 25 year old, Balvenie Triple Cask 25 year old, Tamdhu 10 year old and Convalmore 36 year old

Independent Bottlers

*The independent bottlers play an important role
in the whisky business. With their innovative bottlings, they increase
diversity. Single malts from distilleries where the owners' themselves
decide not to bottle also get a chance through the independents.
The following are a selection of the major companies.
All tasting notes have been prepared by Gavin Smith.*

Gordon & MacPhail .... www.gordonandmacphail.com

Established in 1895 the company, which is owned by the Urquhart family, still occupies the same premises in Elgin. Apart from being an independent bottler, there is also a legendary store in Elgin and, since 1993, an own distillery, Benromach. There is a wide variety of bottlings, for example *Connoisseurs Choice* (single malts bottled at either 43 or 46%), *Private Collection* (single malts, some dating back to the 1950s, usually bottled at 45%), *MacPhail's Collection* (single malts bottled at 43%), *Distillery Labels* (a relic from a time when Gordon & MacPhail released more or less official bottlings for several producers. Currently 16 distilleries are represented in the range and the whisky is bottled at either 40 or 43%), *Rare Old* (exclusive whiskies from distilleries that are closed and sometimes even demolished. The latest release included Glenlochy 1979, Glencraig 1975, Glenugie 1970, Port Ellen 1979, St Magdalene 1975, Mosstowie 1979 and Glenury Royal 1984), *Secret Stills* (single malts from 1966 to 2000 where the distillery name in not disclosed, bottled at 45%), *Cask Strength* (a range of single malts bottled at cask strength), *Rare Vintage* (single malts, including several Glen Grant and Glenlivet bottlings going back to the 1940s) and *Speymalt* (a series of single malts from Macallan from 1938 and onwards).

In 2010, a new range was launched under the name *Generations*. To say that these are rare and old whiskies is an understatement. The first release was a Mortlach 70 year old, the world's oldest single malt ever bottled, which was followed the year thereafter by a Glenlivet 70 year old. Additional bottlings in the series have not been announced yet, but there are casks in the warehouses containing Macallan from the early 1940s!

Several blended whiskies, e. g. *Ben Alder*, *Glen Calder* and *Avonside* are also found in the company's range. Gordon & MacPhail rarely buy matured whisky from other producers. Instead, around 95% is bought as new make spirit and filled by the company. Some 7,000 casks are maturing in one racked (7 casks high) and one dunnage warehouse in Elgin, another 7,000 casks are found at various distillers around Scotland and 20,000 casks are located in the warehouses at Benromach.

Around 1,000 casks are bottled every year. The continued success for Gordon & MacPhail prompted them recently to add another bottling line in Elgin.

Caol Ila 1999, 46%

Nose: Notably marine, seaweed drying on a beach, rock pools, hints of sherry and coal tar soap.
Palate: Sweet and spicy, Germolene, then black olives and brine.
Finish: Spicy and long, smoke persists.

Benrinnes 1997, 46%

Nose: White pepper, ginger nut biscuits, honey and ripe melons.
Palate: Full-bodied and oily, with fruit and nut chocolate, vanilla and spice.
Finish: Medium in length, with cloves and ginger.

Berry Bros. & Rudd .... www.bbr.com

Britain's oldest wine and spirit merchant, founded in 1698 has been selling their own world famous blend, *Cutty Sark*, since 1923. Berry Brothers had been offering their customers private bottlings of malt whisky for years, but it was not until 2002 that they launched *Berry's Own Selection* of single malt whiskies. Under the supervision of Spirits Manager, Doug McIvor, some 30 expressions are on offer every year. Bottling is usually at 46% but expressions bottled at cask strength are also available. The super premium blended malt, *Blue Hanger*, is also inclu-

ded in the range. So far, six different releases have been made, each different from the other. The sixth edition sets itself apart from the rest as it combines both sherried malts from Speyside and peated Islay whisky. The seventh edition of Blue Hanger, ready to be launched in autumn 2013, will be exclusive to the American market. In 2012, to commemorate the centenary of the sinking of Titanic, Berry Brothers released a *Titanic Malt* drawn from a 1998 cask of Glenrothes. In 2010, BBR sold Cutty Sark blended Scotch to Edrington and obtained The Glenrothes single malt in exchange.

A visit to Berry Bros. & Rudd at 3 St James's Street in London is an extraordinary experience. The business was established in 1698 by the Widow Bourne and the company has traded from the same shop for over 300 years! Originally selling coffee, the company soon expanded into wine and started supplying the Royal Family during the reign of King George III and still continues to do so today. An odd service which started in the mid 1700s was weighing the customers on the giant coffee scale. The results were entered into ledgers which have been maintained. Even today, it still happens that certain customers are offered this service.

Berry Brothers may be a guarantee for quality whiskies among whisky aficionados, but it is equally acknowledged as one of the world's finest suppliers of great wines.

Berry's Own Selection Jura 1976, 55,1%

Nose: Sweet sherry and caramel, sultanas, cinnamon and rum baba, with an elusive wisp of smoke.
Palate: Full-bodied, very fruity, with mixed spices, pine cones and old sherry notes.
Finish: Long, nutty and luxurious.

Berry's Own Selection Bunnahabhain 2006, 60,7%

Nose: Sea salt and buttery, smoked haddock, damp fabric Elastoplast, wet ashtrays in time.
Palate: Fruity Germolene notes and peat ash.
Finish: Persistent ginger and medicinal peat.

Signatory Vintage Scotch Whisky

Founded in 1998 by Andrew and Brian Symington, Signatory lists at least 50 single malts at any one occasion. The most widely distributed range is *Cask Strength Collection* which sometimes contains spectacular bottlings from distilleries which have long since disappeared. Another range is *The Un-chill Filtered Collection* bottled at 46%. Some of the bottlings released during 2013 are (as often is the case from Signatory) quite spectacular and rare; *Craigduff 1973* (an extremely rare, peated Strathisla), *Glencraig 1976, Mosstowie 1979* and *Glen Mhor 1982*. Andrew Symington bought Edradour Distillery from Pernod Ricard in 2002.

Ian Macleod Distillers .... www.ianmacleod.com

The company was founded in 1933 and is one of the largest independent family-owned companies within the spirits industry. Gin, rum, vodka and liqueurs, apart from whisky, are found within the range and they also own Glengoyne and Tamdhu distilleries. In total 15 million bottles of spirit are sold per year. Their single malt ranges are single casks either bottled at cask strength or (more often) at reduced strength, always natural colour and un chill-filtered. *The Chieftain's* (with new bottle design) cover a range of whiskies from 10 to 50 years old while *Dun Bheagan* is divided into two series – *Regional Malts*, 8 year old single malts expressing the character from 5 whisky regions in Scotland and *Rare Vintage Single Malts*, a selection of single cask bottlings from various distilleries. There are two *As We Get It* single malt expressions – *Highland* and *Islay*, both 8 year olds and bottled at cask strength. The *Six Isles* blended malt contains whisky from all the whisky-producing islands and is bottled at 43%. One of the top sellers is the blended malt *Isle of Skye* with four expressions – *8, 12, 21* and *50 years old*. Finally, *Smokehead*, a heavily, peated single malt from Islay, was introduced in 2006. There is also a *Smokehead Extra Black 18 years old* and *Smokehead Extra Rare* (which basically is a 1 litre duty free bottling of the 12 year old). The company also has a blended Scotch portfolio which includes its biggest seller, *King Robert II* as well as *Langs Supreme* (5 years old) and *Langs Select* (12 years old).

Langs Supreme 5 year old, 40%
Nose: Sweet, juicy barley notes and a hint of caramel.
Palate: Nicely rounded, fruity and spicy – notably oranges, then drying slightly.
Finish: Medium in length, softly spiced, a little oak.

Langs Select 12 year old, 40%
Nose: Soft, with early citrus fruit, vanilla, almonds and a hint of marzipan.
Palate: Silky, with ginger, autumn berries, honey and newly-sawn timber.
Finish: Spice lingers in the fruity finish.

Blackadder International ....**www.blackadder.se**
Blackadder is owned by Robin Tucek, one of the authors of The Malt Whisky File. Apart from the *Blackadder* and *Blackadder Raw Cask*, there are also a number of other ranges – *Smoking Islay, Peat Reek, Aberdeen Distilleries, Clydesdale Original* and *Caledonian Connections*. One of the latest brands in the Blackadder family is *Riverstown* which is especially earmarked for the Asian market. The company has also been known for bottling unusual expressions of *Amrut* single malt. All bottlings are single cask, uncoloured and un chill-filtered. Most of the bottlings are diluted to 43-46% but Raw Cask is always bottled at cask strength. Around 100 different bottlings are launched each year.

Duncan Taylor ....**www.duncantaylor.com**
Duncan Taylor & Co was founded in Glasgow in 1938 and in 2001, Euan Shand bought the company and operations were subsequently moved to Huntly. The company bottles around 200 expressions per year. The range includes *Rarest of the Rare* (single cask, cask strength whiskies of great age from demolished distilleries), *Battlehill* (younger malts at 43%) and *Lonach* (vattings of two casks from same distillery to bring them up to a natural strength of over 40%). A new addition to the range is the *Dimensions* collection with single malts and single grains aged up to 39 years and bottled either at cask strength or at 46%. *Auld Reekie* is a 10 year old, vatted malt from Islay, which is similar to *Big Smoke*, although the latter is younger, more peated and available in two strengths, 40% and 60%.

In the blended Scotch category, Duncan Taylor is well represented by the *Black Bull* range. The brand was already trademarked in 1933 and Duncan Taylor took over the brand in 2001. The range consists of a *12 year old*, a *30 year old* and a *40 year old*. Recent additions to the range are a *Black Bull without age statement* and *Black Bull Special Reserve No. 2*. There have even been rumours about an upcoming *Black Bull 50 years*. Another

new blend is *Smokin'* – a vatting of peated Speyside, Islay and grain whisky from the Lowlands. This is an attempt to recreate a style similar to the blends of the prohibition era. In 2007, the owners announced their plans to build a distillery of their own in a more than 100 year old granary in Huntly. Following the financial crisis in 2008/2009, the plans were put on hold. Instead, the company focused on setting up their own import company in Pasadena, California, as well as investing in a brand new bottling facility in Huntly. In summer 2013, however, the work on the distillery was in full swing. The plan is to dismantle the old building brick by brick, installing the distilling equipment and then to reassemble the building. The owners plan for a distillery with 1,1 million litres capacity with one pair of stills, as well as column stills and a gin still. No final date for the production start has been given and the owners maintain that "it could still be a number of years".

Smokin', 40%
Nose: Smoky malt, orange and lemon, whipped cream and aerosol furniture polish.
Palate: Nutty, with wood smoke, citrus fruit, fudge and gentle spice.
Finish: Medium in length, with malt, pipe tobacco and cocoa powder.

Scottish Glory, 40%
Nose: Malt, ginger, apricots and burgeoning vanilla fudge.
Palate: Smooth, with more malt, citrus fruit and soft spices.
Finish: Medium in length, milk chocolate and lingering spicy sweetness.

Murray McDavid ....**www.murray-mcdavid.com**
Established in 1995 by Mark Reynier, Gordon Wright and Simon Coughlin. The range is highly selective and all casks have so far been chosen by Jim McEwan who has more than 50 years of experience in the whisky industry. The bottlings are vattings of four or five casks (same age) at 46% without chill filtration or tinting. The range can be divided into three categories – the *Murray McDavid* range, the *Mission* range (unusual, aged stock) and, finally, the *Celtic Heartlands* range (exceptionally old or unique casks from the sixties and seventies). In May 2013, the company was sold to Aceo Ltd, a whisky broker founded in 1999.

Wm Cadenhead & Co................**www.wmcadenhead.com**
This company was established in 1842 and is owned by J & A Mitchell (who also owns Springbank) since 1972. The single malts from Cadenheads are neither chill filtered nor coloured. The last couple of years, there have been three different ranges of whisky; *Authentic Collection* (cask strength), *Duthie's* (diluted to 46%) and *Chairman's Stock* (older and rarer whiskies). The latter two will now be phased out to make room for four new ranges developed by Mark Watt who joined the company in 2012 after having worked for Duncan Taylor for several years. The first is *Creations* which will be small batch blended malts or blended Scotch. The first two releases are *Robust Smoky Ember*, which is a 21 year old blended malt consisting of Ardbeg, Bowmore and Caol Ila and a 20 year old sherry cask blended Scotch called *Rich Fruit Sherry* with Bruichladdich, Mortlach, Cameronbridge and Invergordon in the bottle. The second new range is *Small Batch* which are single malt (or single grain) vattings of two to three casks and bottled at 46%. Some of the first releases, aged between 14 and 24 years, included Bowmore, Dailuaine, Glen Moray and Glengoyne. The third range is similar but the whiskies are bottled at

cask strength. Some of the first releases have been from closed distilleries; Convalmore 36 years, Caperdonich 35 years, Littlemill 38 years and Banff 36 years. The fourth range, which hasn't been launched yet will comprise of single cask bottled at cask strength.

A chain of ten whisky shops working under the name Cadenhead´s can be found in the UK, Denmark, The Netherlands, Germany, Poland, Italy and Switzerland.

Glenlivet 1970, 54,4%
Nose: Sultanas, milk chocolate, soft, mellow Christmas cake aromas. Old leather, wood polish and oak.
Palate: Voluptuous and insistent. A big hit of sweet, fruity sherry and lots of spice.
Finish: Slowly oak notes emerge, but fail to overwhelm.

Littlemill 1977, 40,2%
Nose: Sweet, with icing sugar, vanilla, honey, peaches in syrup. Damp grass in time.
Palate: Initially sweet and full, slightly resinous, marzipan, then bitter wood contrast.
Finish: Medium length – the marzipan and tannins fight it out.

Compass Box Whisky Co ....www.compassboxwhisky.com

Most people within the whisky industry acknowledge the fact that the cask has the greatest influence on the flavour of whisky, but none more so than the founder and owner of Compass Box, John Glaser. His philosophy is strongly influenced by meticulous selection of oak for the casks, clearly inspired by his time in the wine business. But he also has a lust for experimenting and innovation to test the limits, which was clearly shown when Spice Tree was launched in 2005. For an additional maturation, Glaser filled malt whisky in casks prepared with extra staves of toasted French oak suspended within the cask.

The company divides its ranges into a *Signature Range* and a *Limited Range*. *Spice Tree* (a blended malt), *The Peat Monster* (a combination of peated islay whiskies and Highland malts where a 10th anniversary edition was launched in September 2013), *Oak Cross* (American oak casks fitted with heads of French oak), *Asyla* (a blended whisky matured in first-fill ex-bourbon American oak) and *Hedonism* (a vatted grain whisky) are included in the former.

In the Limited range, whiskies are regularly replaced and at times only to resurface a couple of years later in new variations. Among the recent releases are *Hedonism Maximus, Peat Monster Reserve* and *Flaming Heart*. In November 2011 it became illegal to use the term vatted malt when you produced a malt whisky containing whisky from more than one distillery. Instead the term blended malt must be used. This change of terminology was heavily debated with opponents who claimed that it would create confusion for customers to distinguish between the two categories blended malt and blended Scotch (including also grain whisky). To mark the occasion, Compass Box released two limited expressions – *The Last Vatted Malt* (a vatting of 36 year old Glenallachie and 26 year old Caol Ila) and *The Last Vatted Grain* (with whiskies from Invergordon, Cameron Bridge and the two closed distilleries Carsebridge and Port Dundas).

A third range was added in summer of 2011 when *Great King Street* was launched. The range will offer blended Scotch with a 50% proportion of malt whisky and using new French oak for complexity. The first expression was called *Artist's Blend* and the next version is expected in 2014. To help the producers decide what that will be, they will use customer feedback from two experimental

batches (one lightly sherried and one peated) that were released in autumn 2013. There has also been a limited regional version of Great King Street called *New York Blend* which was released in New York in October 2012. More regional releases are expected to follow. In August 2013, the blended Scotch Delilah´s was released to commemorate the 20th anniversary of Delilah´s bar in Chicago.

Hedonism, 43% (new edition)
Nose: Initially, very ripe, fresh pineapple, vanilla, milk chocolate and finally caramel.
Palate: Viscous, sweet and soft; spicy banoffee pie.
Finish: Nutty toffee, drying slightly with oak, remaining unctuous.

Peat Monster, 46% (new edition)
Nose: Sweet peat smoke, with Jaffa oranges, wood embers, vanilla and a hint of salt.
Palate: The sweet, fruity peat dominates, with more vanilla, plus honey and a tang of brine.
Finish: Earthy, ashy, relatively long and nutty.

Creative Whisky Company .....www.creativewhisky.co.uk

David Stirk, who worked in the whisky industry for many years, started the Creative Whisky Co in 2005. He is also author of The Distilleries of Campbeltown and features in several editions of Malt Whisky Yearbook. Creative Whisky exclusively bottles single casks, divided into three series: *The Exclusive Malts* are bottled at cask strength and vary in age between 8 and 40 years. Around 20 bottlings are made annually. This is followed by the *Exclusive Range* which comprises of somewhat younger whiskies, between 8 and 16 years, bottled at either 45% or 45.8%. Finally, *Exclusive Casks* are single casks, which have been 'finished' for three months in another type of cask, e. g. Madeira, Sherry, Port or different kinds of virgin oak. Some of the most recent bottlings include *Aberlour 2000, Braeval 1994, Mortlach 1995, Clynelish 1997, Glen Grant 1992, Littlemill 1991* and *Bowmore 2001*. In spring 2013, David had a major breakthrough on the American market when ImpEx Beverages became his distributor. The first bottlings for the USA have all been exclusives and apparently California is where they will concentrate their efforts to start with.

Master of Malt ....www.masterofmalt.com

Master of Malt is one of the biggest and most innovative whisky retailers in the UK and in 2012 they were awarded Online Retailer of the Year at the World Whiskies Awards. The company also has ranges of its own bottled single malts. One range is called *Secret Bottlings* and is bottled at 40%. No distillery names appear on the labels. Instead, the region is highlighted (as 50 year old Speyside, 12 year old Lowland etc.). The bottlings are very competitively priced, not least the older ones. Master of Malt also bottles single casks at cask strength from various distilleries in their *Single Cask Range*. Some of the latest are a *21 year old Strathmill*, a *17 year old Tomintoul* and an *18 year old North British* grain. In 2011, Master of Malt invited 10 whisky bloggers to create their own whisky blends. The winning contribution was released in autumn 2011 under the name *St Isidore*. The people behind Master of Malt have also come up with the brilliant idea to sell single malts (and other spirits) in 30 ml bottles. They call it *Drinks by the Dram* and it gives the customer an opportunity to sample a whisky before they buy it. At the moment there are around 500 different drams to choose from, some of them are extremely rare whiskies from closed distilleries such as *Brora* and

Linlithgow. In September 2012 a new range was added to their assortment under the name *That Boutique-y Whisky Company*. The idea was to blend whisky from the same distillery but at different ages. Sometimes the age difference between these whiskies can be as much as 30 years and hence there is no age statement on the bottlings. The whiskies turned out to be an instant success and, within a year, no less than 60 different bottlings had been released from distilleries like *Springbank, Highland Park, Bowmore, North British* and *Invergordon*.

That Boutique-y Springbank batch 2, 53,1%

Nose: Initially, over-ripe pineapples and dry hay, cut by a sprinkling of salt. Brittle toffee and finally hand-rolling tobacco.
Palate: Oily and very fruity; more pineapple, plus peach, a hint of peat, plenty of spice and more tobacco.
Finish: Long and spicy, with a suggestion of black treacle.

That Boutique-y Invergordon, 41,6%

Nose: Vanilla, American cream soda, milk chocolate, over-ripe bananas and a sprinkling of white pepper.
Palate: Citrus fruit and vanilla pods. Sawn timber and soft spices, notably nutmeg and cloves.
Finish: Medium in length, with toffee and spice.

Glenkeir Treasures .... www.whiskyshop.com

The Whisky Shop is the biggest whisky retail chain in the UK with 22 shops – the latest, a flagship store, having been established in Piccadilly opposite the Ritz Hotel in London just before Christmas 2012. The company was founded in 1992 and was bought by the current owner, Ian Bankier, in 2004. Apart from having an extensive range of malt (and other) whiskies, they also select and bottle their own range of single malts called *Glenkeir Treasures*. Once a cask has been chosen it is re-racked into smaller oak casks which are then put out for display in each store. The whisky is bottled to order and the customer can also try the whisky in the shop before buying. Glenkeir Treasures comes in three bottle sizes – 10, 20 and 50 cl and is bottled at 40%. The current range consists of *Ben Nevis 15, Deanston 12, Ledaig 9, Macallan 18* and *Speyside 13 year old. Dalmore Zenith*, one of the rarest whiskies in the world (one bottle actually!), was on offer through an auction by Whisky Shop in 2012. The oldest whisky in the bottle was from 1926.

A Dewar Rattray Ltd .... www.adrattray.com

This company was founded by Andrew Dewar Rattray in 1868. In 2004 the company was revived by Tim Morrison, previously of Morrison Bowmore Distillers and fourth generation descendent of Andrew Dewar, with a view to bottling single cask malts from different regions in Scotland. One of its best-sellers is the 12 year old single malt named *Stronachie*. It is named after a distillery that closed in the 1930s. Tim Morrison bought one of the few remaining bottles of Stronachie and found a Highland distillery that could reproduce its character. The distillery in question was shrouded in secrecy until 2010, when it was revealed as being Benrinnes in Speyside. Each Stronachie bottling is a batch of 6-10 casks from Benrinnes. The *12 year old Stronachie* was joined in 2010 by another expression – an *18 year old*. In 2011, A Dewar Rattray introduced a new range of blended malts.

The first was a limited release named *Rattray´s Selection Batch 01* and it was followed up by *A D Rattray´s Whisky Experience - Malt 2* in 2013.

A peated, blended malt, *Cask Islay*, became available in 2011 and released again in 2013 but this time as a single malt. In April 2012 a new blend was launched under the name *Bank Note* and, although developed primarily for the US market, it is now also selling well in the UK and some export markets.

In September 2011, the company opened A Dewar Rattray´s Whisky Experience & Shop in Kirkoswald, South Ayrshire. Apart from having a large choice of whiskies for sale, there is a sample room, as well as a cask room. The plan is to have a new spirit collection from every distillery in Scotland and samples from as many different types of casks and ages from as many distilleries as possible. The Whisky Experience also provides organised tastings for individuals and groups, from half an hour speed tasting of three whiskies, to a master class of five very old and rare single casks.

Bank Note, 43%

Nose: Ginger spice, a hint of honey, vanilla and nutmeg, with lurking sweet pipe tobacco notes.
Palate: Rich mouth-feel, smooth and sophisticated, citrus fruits and soft spice.
Finish: Long and silky.

A D Rattray´s Whisky Experience – Malt 2, 40%

Nose: Initially, farmyard notes, then floral character comes through. Quite reticent.
Palate: Summer fruits, mild ginger and mixed nuts.
Finish: Medium in length, with a hint of ginger.

Scotch Malt Whisky Society .... www.smws.com

The Scotch Malt Whisky Society, established in the mid 1980s and owned by Glenmorangie Co since 2003, has more than 20,000 members worldwide and apart from UK, there are 15 chapters around the world. The idea from the very beginning was to buy casks of single malts from the producers and bottle them at cask strength without colouring or chill filtration. The labels do not reveal the name of the distillery. Instead there is a number but also a short description which will give you a clue to which distillery it is. A Tasting Panel selects and bottles around twenty new casks the first Friday of every month. The SMWS also arranges tastings at their different venues but also at other locations. The society produces an excellent, award winning members magazine called *Unfiltered*.

Adelphi Distillery .... www.adelphidistillery.com

Adelphi Distillery is named after a distillery which closed in 1902. The company is owned by Keith Falconer and Donald Houston, who recruited Alex Bruce from the wine trade to act as Marketing Director. Their whiskies are always bottled at cask strength, uncoloured and non chill-filtered. Adelphi bottles around 50 casks a year. Two of their recurrent brands are *Fascadale* (a Highland Park) and *Liddesdale* (a Bunnahabhain) which are in batches of approximately 1,500 bottles. They also have their own blended Scotch, *Adelphi Private Stock*, which is bottled at 40%. Unusual for an independent, Adelphi has an on-line shop on their website. The company affords its customers the opportunity to join the Adelphi´s Dancey Man Whisky Club which has special offerings for its members, discounts and first choice of the latest releases. In 2012, Adelphi Distillery received planning permission to build their own distillery in Ardnamurchan, a couple of miles from the company´s office. It will become the most westerly distillery in mainland Scotland and the goal is to produce 100,000 litres per year. Construction work began in summer 2013 and the intention is to start malting in November and distillation in December.

Fascadale 12 year old batch 5, 46%
Nose: Icing sugar, vanilla, milk chocolate, apricots, plus mildly smoky malt.
Palate: Full-bodied and fruity, with toffee, black pepper and a hint of peat in the background.
Finish: Medium in length, slowly drying.

Liddesdale 21 year old batch 4, 46%
Nose: A whiff of warm balloons, hand-rolling tobacco, raisins, sweet new leather and pencil shavings.
Palate: Rich, sweet, spicy notes, soft peat, sherry and fruit malt loaf.
Finish: Bold, with lingering citrus fruit.

The Whisky Agency .... www.whiskyagency.de
The man behind this company is Carsten Ehrlich, to many whisky aficionados known as one of the founders of the annual Whisky Fair in Limburg, Germany. His experience from sourcing casks for limited Whisky Fair bottlings led him to start as an independent bottler in 2008 under the name The Whisky Agency. He is currently working with three ranges; *The Whisky Agency* with 12 series of whiskies released so far – from *Butterflies* to *Bugs* – the names alluding to the motif on the labels, *The Perfect Dram* (at least 30 expressions so far) and *Specials* with some unusual bottlings, for example a Tomatin 1967 sherry butt. A recent collaboration between The Whisky Agency and The Whisky Exchange in London resulted in the bottling of a 48 year old Girvan single grain, distilled in 1964.

Wemyss Malts .... www.wemyssmalts.com
This family-owned company, a relatively newcomer to the whisky world, was founded in 2005. The family owns another three companies in the field of wine and gin. Based in Edinburgh, Wemyss Malts takes advantage of Charles MacLean´s experienced nose when choosing their casks. There are two ranges; one of which consists of single casks bottled at 46% or 55%. The name of the distillery is not used on the label; instead, the names are chosen to reflect what the whisky tastes like. For instance, some of the most recent releases are called *Melon Cocktail, Spiced Chocolate Cup* and *Salted Caramels*. All whiskies are un chill-filtered and without colouring. The other range is made up of blended malts of which there are three at the moment – *Spice King, Peat Chimney* and the recently introduced *The Hive*. When first launched in 2005 they were bottled at the age of 5. Four years later the range was expanded with 8 year olds and in 2010 with 12 year olds. All the blended malts are bottled at 40%. In October 2012, the company released its first premium blended whisky based on a selection of malt and grain whiskies aged a minimum of 15 years. The whisky is named *Lord Elcho* after the eldest son of the 5th Earl of Wemyss. The company is headed towards exciting times. In January 2013, it was announced that the company would invest £3m in the Kingsbarns distillery project in Fife. The idea to build a distillery at this 18th century farmstead, originally came from Doug Clement in

2009 and, since then, he has persistently worked on the planning and to obtain the necessary funding. With their investment, Wemyss, whose family estate isn't far from the future distillery, has now secured a new Lowland distillery which will be able to produce 150,000 litres per year from 2015.

Spice King 12 year old, 40%
Nose: Sweet and slightly smoky, with pepper, lemonade and vanilla.
Palate: Tangy, with apple pie, tobacco smoke and walnuts.
Finish: Medium length, with cinnamon and lingering citrus fruit notes.

Lord Elcho 15 year old, 40%
Nose: Sherry, vanilla, mandarin oranges, pipe tobacco and dark toffee.
Palate: Smooth and full-bodied, fruity, with caramel and cloves, plus a balancing hint of latakia tobacco and soft smoke.
Finish: Long and silky. A very stylish and satisfying blend.

Hunter Laing & Co .... www.hunterlaing.com
This is a new company which was formed after the demerger between Fred and Stewart Laing (see below). It is run by Stewart Laing and his two sons, Scott and Andrew. The relatively new company *Edition Spirits Ltd*, founded by the two sons has also been absorbed into Hunter Laing with the range of single malts called *The First Editions*.

From the demerger, the following ranges and brands ended up in the Hunter Laing portfolio; *The Old Malt Cask* (rare and old malts, bottled at 50%), *The Old and Rare Selection* (an exclusive range of old malts offered at cask strength), *Douglas of Drumlanrig* (single casks bottled at 46%) and *Sovereign* (a range of grain whiskies). The portfolio also includes blended Scotch such as *John Player Special, House of Peers* and *Langside*. A new range bearing the name *Highland Journey* is under development and will include blended malts.

Mortlach 18 year old, 50%
Nose: Initially, mildly herbal, then fruity: green banana peel and figs. Linseed oil.
Palate: Soft fruits, mixed nuts, ginger and digestive biscuits.
Finish: Slowly drying, with a hint of liquorice.

Blair Athol 20 year old, 57,8%
Nose: Cocoa powder, cloves, Christmas cake mix, plus freshly-sawn wood.
Palate: Full, with treacle, ripe Jaffa oranges and slightly smoky malt.
Finish: Lengthy, with treacle, a whiff of smoke and lingering citrus fruits.

Douglas Laing & Co ....www.douglaslaing.com
Established in 1948 by Douglas Laing, this firm has been run for many years by his two sons, Fred and Stewart. Visitors to whisky shows all around the world have met

with the two of them over the years and that is why it came as a surprise to many when they decided to go their separate ways in May 2013. Douglas Laing & Co is now run by Fred Laing and his daughter, Cara (who worked for Morrison Bowmore for instance). The other side of the business, run by Stewart and his sons, Scott and Andrew, is called Hunter Laing & Company.

The demerger resulted in a 50/50 split of the assets and Douglas Laing & Co now has the following ranges and brands in their portfolio; *Provenance* (single casks typically aged between 8 and 20 years and bottled at 46%), *Director´s Cut* (introduced in 2011, old and rare single malts bottled at cask strength), *Premier Barrel* (single malts in ceramic decanters bottled at 46%), *Clan Denny* (two blended malts, one from Islay and one from Speyside, and a selection of old single grains), *Double Barrel* (where only two malts are vatted together and bottled at 46%), a new range of single casks called *Old Particular* and finally *Big Peat*. The latter, a vatting of selected Islay malts, was introduced in 2009 and has become one of their biggest sellers. The company also has blended whiskies in its portfolio.

Big Peat (special on-line version), 50%
Nose: Smoked haddock, Elastoplast, wood-smoke, ground coffee, ginger and damp heather.
Palate: Notably sweet, with lively spices and developing nutty peatiness.
Finish: Germolene, brine and lots of spicy smoke.

Double Barrel Ardbeg/Glenrothes, 46%
Nose: Sweet, slightly citric, vanilla, muted peat smoke and old leather.
Palate: Fruity, with almonds and more overt peat coming through than on the nose.
Finish: Chilli notes, straw and lingering smoky citrus fruit

Malts of Scotland .... www.malts-of-scotland.com
This is one of the more recently established independent bottlers. Thomas Ewers from Germany, bought casks from Scottish distilleries and decided in the spring of 2009 to start releasing them as single casks bottled at cask strength and with no colouring or chill filtration. At the moment he has released circa 80 bottlings from a 5 year old Bunnahabhain to a 45 year old Lochside. He also has two expressions called *Glen First Class* (a Glenfarclas) and *Glen Peat Class* (a vatting of Ardbeg, Laphroaig and Bowmore), both bottled at 50%. Another new series is *Amazing Casks*, dedicated to very special and superior casks. According to Ewers, there are several hundreds of casks from more than 60 distilleries maturing in the warehouse.

Speciality Drinks........................www.specialitydrinks.com
Sukhinder Singh, known by most for his two very well-stocked shops in London, The Whisky Exchange, is behind this company. Since 2005 he is also a bottler of malt whiskies operating under the brand name *The Single Malts of Scotland*. He has around 50 bottlings on offer at any time, either as single casks or as batches bottled at cask strength or at 46%. In 2009 a new range of Islay malts under the name *Port Askaig* was introduced, starting with a *cask strength*, a *17 year old* and a *25 year old*. In summer 2011 the 17 year old was replaced by a *19 year old* and a *30 year old* has also been added to the range. In 2013, *cask strength* versions of the *19 year old* and the *30 year old* were released.

Elements of Islay, a series in which all Islay distilleries are, or will be, represented was introduced around the same time. The list of the product range is cleverly constructed with periodical tables in mind (see www.elements-of-islay.com) in which each distillery has a two-letter acronym followed by a batch number, for example Pe_4 (Port Ellen) and Lg_3 (Lagavulin).

Port Askaig 19 year old, 50,4%
Nose: Maritime notes, with rock salt and buttery kippers. Creosote develops in time.
Palate: Full and smoky, with citrus fruit and malt.
Finish: Slowly drying, with liquorice and lingering peat embers.

Port Askaig 30 year old, 51,1%
Nose: Soft, muted peatiness, ripe bananas, sweet heather and bracken.
Palate: Quite oily, toffee and discreet peat smoke, with lemon and lime.
Finish: Long and gentle, with more peat, slight oakiness, persistent fruit.

Mackillop´s Choice .... www.mackillopschoice.com
Mackillop's Choice, founded in 1996, is an independent bottler owned by Angus Dundee Distillers (owner of Tomintoul and Glencadam distilleries). The brand is named after Lorne McKillop who selects the casks. The whole range is single casks with no colouring or chill filtration. Some of the bottlings are at cask strength, while others are diluted to 40 or 43%. Among the latest new bottlings are Tomintoul 1976, Highland Park 1988, Laphroaig 1990 and Glen Garioch 1990.

Samaroli Srl .... www.samaroli.it
The company was founded by Silvano Samaroli in 1968 and at that time he was the only person from outside the UK who was working as an independent bottler of Scotch whisky. Over the years, Samaroli has built up a reputation as a discerning bottler, selecting only the best casks available. Some of the latest expressions bottled in 2013 include *Jura 1997, Laphroaig 1998, Glen Grant 1993, Glen Garioch 1990, Highland Park 1992* and *Caol Ila 1980*. Apart from single malts, Samaroli also produces a blended malt every year known as *No Age*. The 2013 release of *Edition No Age* is a vatting of single malts from 15 to 50 years. The whisky is diluted to 45% and that process takes a year to complete. Small amounts of water are added repeatedly and in between the whisky rests, in order to let the water and the whisky merge. There is also a blended Scotch based on single malts from Speyside and Islay and grain whisky called *1995 Samaroli Blend*. Apart from whisky, Samaroli also has an exquisite range of rums.

The Vintage Malt Whisky Company .... www.vintagemaltwhisky.com
The Vintage Malt Whisky Co. was founded in 1992 by Brian Crook who previously had twenty years experience in the malt whisky industry. In recent years, Brian has been joined in the company by his son Andrew. The company also owns and operates a sister company called The Highlands & Islands Scotch Whisky Co. The most famous brands in the range are undoubtedly two single Islay malts called *Finlaggan* and *The Ileach*. Other expressions include the blended Highland malt *Glenalmond* and, not least, a wide range of single cask single malts under the name *The Cooper´s Choice*. They are bottled at 46% or at

cask strength and are all non coloured and non chillfiltered. In 2012, the company launched a range extension called *Cooper´s Choice Golden Grains* with a selection of old single grain whiskies from closed distilleries, for example Lochside and Garnheath. The company´s whiskies are today sold in more than 25 countries.

The Ileach, 58%
Nose: Initially, pine, oily and fragrant, then iodine and smoked haddock, with a hint of honey.
Palate: Powdery peat, cloves and sweet spices.
Finish: Earthy and mildly herbal, with lingering peat smoke.

Finlaggan, 58%
Nose: Gingerbread, peat, sea kelp, Germolene and Beecham's Powders.
Palate: Soft and fruity, with lots of brine and spice, then old leather notes emerge.
Finish: Pepper, leather, wood smoke and a tang of the sea.

Sirius .... www.siriuswhiskypurveyors.com
This newly established independent bottler is a boutique brand and not one where we can expect a wide range of releases every year. It is the brainchild of Mahesh Patel, a passionate whisky collector and connoisseur, as well as the founder and CEO of The Nth Ultimate Whisky Experience in Las Vegas. Over the years, Mahesh has established valuable contacts with whisky producers in Scotland enabling him to select and buy rare casks. The first range was released in summer 2012 through The Whisky Shop chain in the UK and consisted of *Dalmore 1967, Fettercairn 1966* and two single grains – *Carsebridge 1965* and *North British 1962*. The next release will be towards the end of 2014 and, in the future, the range will probably be extended to also include rare Japanese whiskies and bourbons.

Jewish Whisky Company
www.singlecasknation.com
Jason Johnstone-Yellin and Joshua Hatton, two well-known whisky bloggers have, in alliance with Seth Klaskin, taken their first step into the world of whisky bottling. The idea with *Single Cask Nation* somewhat reminds you of Scotch Malt Whisky Society in the sense that you have to become a member of the nation in order to buy the bottlings. You can choose between three different cost levels which will give you various benefits, including one or more bottlings from the current range of whiskies. The first four bottlings that were released in 2012 were *Arran 12 years* from a Pinot Noir cask, a peated *BenRiach 17 years* from a bourbon cask, a *Glen Moray 12 years* bourbon cask and, finally, a *4 year*

old Kilchoman also bourbon matured. These were followed up in 2013 with a *6 year old Laphroaig* from a refill bourbon barrel and a *12 year old Dalmore* which had been given a 10 months finish in a PX sherry hogshead. Autumn 2013 the company also arranged two whisky events in New York state called Whisky Jewbilee which was a charitable whisky festival that offered a special festival bottling which this year was a 15 year old single barrel bourbon from Heaven Hill.

Meadowside Blending ..... www.meadowsideblending.com
The company may be a newcomer to the family of independent bottlers but the founder certainly isn´t. Donald Hart, a Keeper of the Quaich and co-founder of the well-known bottler Hart Brothers, runs the Glasgow company together with his son, Andrew. There are two sides to the business – blends sold under the name *The Royal Thistle* where the core expression is a 3 year old, as well as single malts labelled *The Maltman*. Some of the most recent single malts include *Glenturret 30 year old, Glenrothes 18 year old* and *Arran 16 year old*.

Svenska Eldvatten............................ www.eldvatten.se
This new, Swedish independent bottler, founded in 2011, is run by Tommy Andersen and Peter Sjögren. They both have extensive experience from whisky and other spirits, which they have gained from arranging tastings for many years. Through the contacts that they had established in Scotland, they managed to get hold of three high quality casks of *Bunnahabhain 1991* and *1997* and these were the first to be bottled in 2011. Since then, about fifteen single casks, bottled at cask strength, have been released including *Caol Ila 1983, Girvan 1964, Mortlach 1995* and *Bowmore 2000*. The two that were launched most recently in autumn 2013, were *Glen Moray 1991* and *Laphroaig 2005*. The owners have also released their own blended malt under the name *Glenn* (a humorous tip of the hat to their home town Gothenburg where Glenn is one of the most common names). In their range of spirits they also have aged tequila, a 6 year old Arette from Destiladora Azteca de Jalisco and rum called Caroni Trinidad Rum. They have also recently launched their own series of single cask rum under the name *The Rum Swedes*. The name of their company, Svenska Eldvatten, can be translated to Swedish Firewater.

Scotia Royale
www.lochlomonddistillery.com
At one time, Scotia Royale was a blended Scotch brand owned by A. Gillies & Co. who also were the owners of Glen Scotia distillery between 1955 and 1970. The blend was later discontinued but appears at auctions from time to time. When Glen Catrine Bonded Warehouse Ltd. took over the distillery in 1994, they also came in possesion of the brand Scotia Royale. They didn´t take advantage of it until 2012 when they, as an independent bottler introduced a range of bottlings called *Scotia Royale*. The whiskies are all bottled at cask strength and can be both single casks or small batches of several casks. The idea is to launch 30-40 different expression per year and included in the first release were *Miltonduff 1978, Laphroaig 1976, Fettercairn 1976, Dalmore 1978, Glenturret 1977, Dufftown 1978* and *Inchgower 1978*.

Whisky Shops

AUSTRALIA

The Odd Whisky Coy
PO Box 2045
Glynde, SA, 5070
Phone: +61 (0)8 8365 4722
www.theoddwhiskycoy.com.au
Founded and owned by Graham Wright who has been in the business since the mid 1990s, this on-line whisky specialist has an impressive range. They are agents for famous brands such as Springbank, Glengoyne, Benromach and Berry Brothers and arrange recurrent tastings and seminars on the subject.

World of Whisky
Shop G12, Cosmopolitan Centre
2-22 Knox Street
Double Bay NSW 2028
Phone: +61 (0)2 9363 4212
www.worldofwhisky.com.au
A whisky specialist in Double Bay, Sydney which offers a range of 300 different expressions, most of them single malts. The shop is also organising and hosting regular tastings.

AUSTRIA

Potstill
Strozzigasse 37
1080 Wien
Phone: +43 (0)664 118 85 41
www.potstill.org
Austria's premier whisky shop with over 1100 kinds of which c 900 are malts, including some real rarities. Arranges tastings and seminars and ships to several European countries. On-line ordering.

Cadenhead Austria
Alter Markt 1
5020 Salzburg
Phone: +43 (0)662 84 53 05
www.cadenhead.at
Number 8 in the famous Cadenhead's chain of whisky shops, this store was opened in March 2013 by Klaus Pinkernell from Cadenhead's Berlin. At the moment they offer 350 different whiskies, mostly single malts and they also arrange monthly tastings.

BELGIUM

Whiskycorner
Kraaistraat 16
3530 Houthalen
Phone: +32 (0)89 386233
www.whiskycorner.be
A very large selection of single malts, no less than 1100 different! Also other whiskies, calvados and grappas. The site is in both French and English. Mail ordering, but not on-line. Shipping worldwide.

Jurgen´s Whiskyhuis
Gaverland 70
9620 Zottegem
Phone: +32 (0)9 336 51 06
www.whiskyhuis.be
An absolutely huge assortment of more than 2,000 different single malts with 700 in stock and the rest delivered within the week. Also 40 different grain whiskies and 120 bourbons. Worldwide shipping

Huis Crombé
Doenaertstraat 20
8510 Marke
Phone: +32 (0)56 21 19 87
www.crombewines.com
A wine retailer which also covers all kinds of spirits. The whisky range is very nice where a large assortment of Scotch is supplemented with whiskies from Japan, the USA and Ireland to mention a few.

We Are Whisky
Avenue Rodolphe Gossia 33
1350 Orp-Jauche (Jauche)
Phone: +32 (0)471 134556
www.wearewhisky.com
A fairly new shop and on-line retailer with a range of more than 400 different whiskies. They also arrange 3-4 tasting every month.

BRAZIL

Single Malt Brasil
Kraaistraat 16
3530 Houthalen
Phone: +32 (0)89 386233
www.lojadewhisky.com.br
The biggest whisky specialist In Brazil (and one of few in the country) with a nice range of other spirits as well, especially cachaça. The sister site, singlemalt.com.br, is a great, educational site about single malt whisky.

CANADA

Kensington Wine Market
1257 Kensington Road NW
Calgary
Alberta T2N 3P8
Phone: +1 403 283 8000
www.kensingtonwinemarket.com
With 400 different bottlings this is the largest single malt assortment in Canada. Also 2,500 different wines. Regular tastings in the shop.

DENMARK

Juul´s Vin & Spiritus
Værnedamsvej 15
1819 Frederiksberg
Phone: +45 33 31 13 29
www.juuls.dk
A very large range of wines, fortified wines and spirits. Around 500 single malts. Also a good selection of drinking glasses. On-line ordering. Shipping outside Denmark.

Cadenhead´s WhiskyShop Denmark
Kongensgade 69 F
5000 Odense C
Phone: +45 66 13 95 05

Silkegade 7, kld
1113 København K
Phone: +45 33 39 95 05
www.cadenheads.dk
Whisky specialist with a very good range, not least from Cadenhead's. Nice range of champagne, cognac and rum. Arranges whisky and beer tastings. On-line ordering with worldwide shipping.

Whiskydirect.dk
Braunstein
Carlsensvej 5
4600 Køge
Phone: +45 7020 4468
www.whiskydirect.dk
On-line retailer owned by Braunstein Distillery. Aside from own produce one can find an assortment of 200 different whiskies.

Kokkens Vinhus
Hovedvejen 102
2600 Glostrup
Phone: +45 44 97 02 30

Peter Bangs Vej 74
2000 Frederiksberg
Phone: +45 38 87 86 70
www.kokkensvinhus.dk
A shop with a complete assortment of wine, spirit, coffee, tea and delicatessen. More than 500 whiskies are in stock, mostly single malts. They are specialists in independent bottlings. On-line ordering for shipments within Denmark.

ENGLAND

The Whisky Exchange (2 shops)
The Whisky Exchange
Vinopolis, 1 Bank End
London SE1 9BU
Phone: +44 (0)207 403 8688

Elixir House, Whitby Avenue
Park Royal
London NW10 7SF
Phone: +44 (0)208 838 9388
www.thewhiskyexchange.com
This is an excellent whisky shop established in 1999 and owned by Sukhinder Singh. Started off as a mail order business which was run from a showroom in Hanwell, but since some years back there is also an excellent shop at Vinopolis in downtown London. The assortment is huge with well over 1000 single malts to choose from. Some rarities which can hardly be found

anywhere else are offered much thanks to Singh's great interest for antique whisky. There are also other types of whisky and cognac, calvados, rum etc. On-line ordering and ships all over the world.

The Whisky Shop
(See also Scotland, The Whisky Shop)
Unit 1.09 MetroCentre
Gateshead NE11 9YG
Phone: +44 (0)191 460 3777

11 Coppergate Walk
York YO1 9NT
Phone: +44 (0)1904 640300

510 Brompton Walk
Lakeside Shopping Centre
Grays, Essex RM20 2ZL
Phone: +44 (0)1708 866255

7 Turl Street
Oxford OX1 3DQ
Phone: +44 (0)1865 202279

3 Swan Lane
Norwich NR2 1HZ
Phone: +44 (0)1603 618284

70 Piccadilly
London W1J 8HP
Phone: +44 (0)20 7499 6649

Unit 7 Queens Head Passage
Paternoster
London EC4M 7DY
Phone: +44 (0)207 329 5117

3 Exchange St
Manchester M2 7EE
Phone: +44 (0)161 832 6110

25 Chapel Street
Guildford GU3 3UL
Phone: +44 (0)1483 450900

Unit 35 Great Western Arcade
Birmingham B2 5HU
Phone: +44 (0)121 212 1815

64 East Street
Brighton BN1 1HQ
Phone: +44 (0)1273 327 962

3 Cheapside
Nottingham NG1 2HU
Phone: +44 (0)115 958 7080

Trentham Shopping Village
Trentham, Stoke on Trent
Staffordshire ST4 8JG
Phone: +44 (0)178 264 4483
www.whiskyshop.com
The first shop opened in 1992 in Edinburgh and this is now the United Kingdom's largest specialist retailer of whiskies with 22 outlets. The two most recent to open up were flagship stores in Piccadilly, London and in Manchester. A large product range with over 700 kinds, including 400 malt whiskies and 140 miniature bottles, as well as accessories and books. The own range 'Glenkeir Treasures' is a special assortment of selected malt whiskies. The also run The W Club, the leading whisky club in the UK where the excellent Whiskeria magazine is one of the member's benefits. On-line ordering and shipping all over the world except to the USA.

Royal Mile Whiskies
3 Bloomsbury Street
London WC1B 3QE
Phone: +44 (0)20 7436 4763
www.royalmilewhiskies.com
The London branch of Royal Mile Whiskies. See also Scotland, Royal Mile Whiskies.

Berry Bros. & Rudd
3 St James' Street
London SW1A 1EG
Phone: +44 (0)870 900 4300

Berry Bros. & Rudd's Bin End Shop
Hamilton Close, Houndmills
Basingstoke RG21 6YB
Phone: +44 (0)800 280 2440
www.bbr.com/whisky
A legendary shop that has been situated in the same place since 1698. One of the world's most reputable wine shops but with an exclusive selection of malt whiskies. There are also shops in Dublin and Hong Kong.

The Wright Wine and Whisky Company
The Old Smithy, Raikes Road, Skipton, North Yorkshire BD23 1NP
Phone: +44 (0)1756 700886
www.wineandwhisky.co.uk
An eclectic selection of near to 1000 different whiskies to choose from. 'Tasting Cupboard' of nearly 100 opened bottles for sampling with hosted tasting evenings held on a regular basis. Great 'Collector to Collector' selection of old and rare whiskies plus a fantastic choice of 1200+ wines, premium spirits and liqueurs. International mail order.

Master of Malt
8a London Road
Tunbridge Wells
Kent TN1 1DA
Phone: +44 (0)1892 888 376
www.masterofmalt.com
Independent bottler and online retailer since 1985. A very impressive range of more than 1,000 Scotch whiskies of which 800 are single malts. In addition to whisky from other continents there is a wide selection of rum, cognac, Armagnac and tequila. The website is redesigned and contains a wealth of information on the distilleries. They have also recently launched "Drinks by the Dram" where you can order 3cl samples of more than 500 diffe-rent whiskies to try before you buy a full bottle.

Whiskys.co.uk
The Square, Stamford Bridge
York YO4 11AG
Phone: +44 (0)1759 371356
www.whiskys.co.uk
Good assortment with more than 600 different whiskies. Also a nice range of armagnac, rum, calvados etc. On-line ordering, ships outside of the UK. The owners also have another website, **www. whiskymerchants.co.uk** with a huge amount of information on just about every whisky distillery in the world and very up to date.

The Wee Dram
5 Portland Square, Bakewell
Derbyshire DE45 1HA
Phone: +44 (0)1629 812235
www.weedram.co.uk
Large range of Scotch single malts (c 450) with whiskies from other parts of the world and a good range of whisky books. Run 'The Wee Drammers Whisky Club' with tastings and seminars. On-line ordering.

Hard To Find Whisky
10 Upper Gough Street
Birmingham B1 1JG
Phone: +44 (0)8456 803 489
www.htfw.com
As the name says, this family owned shop specialises in rare, collectable and new releases of single malt whisky. The range is astounding - almost 3,000 different bottlings including no less than 215 different Macallan. World wide shipping.

Mainly Wine and Whisky
3-4 The Courtyard, Bawtry
Doncaster DN10 6JG
Phone: +44 (0)1302 714 700
www.whisky-malts-shop.com
A good range with c 400 different whiskies of which 300 are single malts. Arranges tastings and seminars. On-line ordering with shipping also outside the UK.

Chester Whisky & Liqueur
59 Bridge Street Row
Chester
Cheshire CH1 1NW
Phone: +44 (0)1244 347806
www.chesterwhisky.com
A shop that specialises in single malt Scotch and American, Irish, Japanese and Welsh whisky. There is also a good range of calvados, armagnac and rum and the shop has its own house blend, Chester Cross Blended Scotch Whisky, as well as three casks for tasting and bottling in the store.

Nickolls & Perks
37 Lower High Street, Stourbridge
West Midlands DY8 1TA
Phone: +44 (0)1384 394518
www.nickollsandperks.co.uk
Mostly known as wine merchants but also has a good range of whiskies with c 300 different kinds including 200 single malts. On-line ordering with shipping also outside of UK. Since 2011, Nickolls & Perks also organize the acclaimed Midlands Whisky Festival, see **www.whiskyfest.co.uk**

Gauntleys of Nottingham
4 High Street
Nottingham NG1 2ET
Phone: +44 (0)115 9110555
www.gauntley-wine.co.uk
A fine wine merchant established in 1880. The range of wines are among the best in the UK. All kinds of spirits, not least whisky, are taking up more and more space and several rare malts can be found. The monthly whisky newsletter by Chris Goodrum makes good reading and

there is also a mail order service available.

Hedonism Wines
3-7 Davies St.
London W1K 3LD
Phone: +44 (020) 729 078 70
www.hedonism.co.uk
Located in the heart of London's Mayfair, this is a new temple for wine lovers (opened in autumn 2012) but also with an impressive range of whiskies and other spirits. They have over 1,200 different bottlings from Scotland and the rest of the world! The very elegant shop is in itself well worth a visit.

The Wine Shop
22 Russell Street, Leek
Staffordshire ST13 5JF
Phone: +44 (0)1538 382408
www.wineandwhisky.com
In addition to wine there is a good range of 300 whiskies and also calvados, cognac, rum etc. They also stock a range of their own single malt bottlings under the name of 'The Queen of the Moorlands'. Mailorder within the UK.

The Lincoln Whisky Shop
87 Bailgate
Lincoln LN1 3AR
Phone: +44 (0)1522 537834
www.lincolnwhiskyshop.co.uk
Mainly specialising in whisky with more than 400 different whiskies but also 500 spirits and liqueurs and some 100 wines. Mailorder only within UK.

Milroys of Soho
3 Greek Street
London W1D 4NX
Phone: +44 (0)20 7437 2385
www.milroys.co.uk
A classic whisky shop in Soho now owned by the retail wine merchant Jeroboams Group. A very good range with over 700 malts and a wide selection of whiskies from around the world. On-line ordering for shipping within the UK.

Arkwrights
114 The Dormers
Highworth
Wiltshire SN6 7PE
Phone: +44 (0)1793 765071
www.whiskyandwines.com
A good range of whiskies (over 700 in stock) as well as wine and other spirits. Regular tastings in the shop. On-line ordering with shipping all over the world except USA and Canada.

Cadenhead's Whisky Shop
26 Chiltern Street
London W1U 7QF
Phone: +44 (0)20 7935 6999
www.whiskytastingroom.com
Used to be in Covent Garden but moved and was expanded with a tasting room. One in a chain of shops owned by independent bottlers Cadenhead. Sells Cadenhead's product range and c. 200 other whiskies. Regular tastings and on-line ordering.

Constantine Stores
30 Fore Street
Constantine, Falmouth
Cornwall TR11 5AB
Phone: +44 (0)1326 340226
www.drinkfinder.co.uk
A full-range wine and spirits dealer with a good selection of whiskies from the whole world (around 800 different, of which 600 are single malts).Worldwide shipping except for USA and Canada.

The Vintage House
42 Old Compton Street
London W1D 4LR
Phone: +44 (0)20 7437 5112
www.sohowhisky.com
A huge range of 1400 kinds of malt whisky, many of them rare. Supplementing this is also a selection of fine wines. On-line ordering with shipping only within the UK.

Whisky On-line
Units 1-3 Concorde House, Charnley Road, Blackpool, Lancashire FY1 4PE
Phone: +44 (0)1253 620376
www.whisky-online.com
A good selection of whisky and also cognac, rum, port etc. On-line ordering with shipping all over the world.

FRANCE

La Maison du Whisky
20 rue d'Anjou
75008 Paris
Phone: +33 (0)1 42 65 03 16

6 carrefour d l'Odéon
75006 Paris
Phone: +33 (0)1 46 34 70 20

(2 shops outside France)

47 rue Jean Chatel
97400 Saint-Denis, La Réunion
Phone: +33 (0)2 62 21 31 19

The Pier at Robertson Quay
80 Mohamed Sultan Road, #01-10
Singapore 239013
Phone: +65 6733 0059
www.whisky.fr
France's largest whisky specialist with over 1200 whiskies in stock. Also a number of own-bottled single malts. La Maison du Whisky acts as a EU distributor for many whisky producers around the world. Four shops and on-line ordering. Ships to some 20 countries.

The Whisky Lodge
7 rue Ferrandière
69002 Lyon
Phone: +33 (0)4 78 42 48 22
Located in the heart of Lyon and run by Pierre Tissandier, son of the founder, this shop carries more than 1,200 different whiskies!

GERMANY

Celtic Whisk(e)y & Versand
Otto Steudel
Bulmannstrasse 26
90459 Nürnberg
Phone: +49 (0)911 45097430
www.whiskymania.de/celtic
A very impressive single malt range with well over 1000 different single

malts and a good selection from other parts of the world. On-line ordering with shipping also outside Germany.

SCOMA - Scotch Malt Whisky GmbH
Am Bullhamm 17
26441 Jever
Phone: +49 (0)4461 912237
www.scoma.de
Very large range of c 750 Scottish malts and many from other countries. Holds regular seminars and tastings. The excellent, monthly whisky newsletter SCOMA News is produced and can be downloaded as a pdf-file from the website. On-line ordering.

The Whisky Store
Am Grundwassersee 4
82402 Seeshaupt
Phone: +49 (0)8801-23 17
www.whisky.de
A very large range comprising c 700 kinds of whisky of which 550 are malts. Also sells whisky liqueurs, books and accessories. The website is a veritable goldmine of information about all things related to whisky. On-line ordering.

Cadenhead's Whisky Market
Luxemburger Strasse 257
50939 Köln
Phone: +49 (0)221-2831834
www.cadenheads.de
Good range of malt whiskies (c 350 different kinds) with emphasis on Cadenhead's own bottlings. Other products include wine, cognac and rum etc. Arranges recurring tastings and also has an on-line shop.

Cadenhead's Whisky Market
Mainzer Strasse 20
10247 Berlin-Friedrichshain
Phone: +49 (0)30-30831444
www.cadenhead-berlin.de
Excellent product range with more than 700 different kinds of whiskies with emphasis on Cadenhead's own bottlings as well as cognac and rum. Arranges recurrent tastings.

Malts and More
Hosegstieg 11
22880 Wedel
Phone: +49 (0)40-23620770
www.maltsandmore.de
Very large assortment with over 800 different single malts from Scotland as well as whiskies from many other countries. Also a nice selection of cognac, rum etc. On-line ordering.

Reifferscheid
Mainzer Strasse 186
53179 Bonn / Mehlem
Phone: +49 (0)228 9 53 80 70
www.whisky-bonn.de
A well-stocked shop often listed as one of the best in Germany. Aside from a large range of whiskies, wine, spirit, cigars and a delicatessen can be found. Regular tastings.

Whisky-Doris
Germanenstrasse 38
14612 Falkensee
Phone: +49 (0)3322-219784
www.whisky-doris.de

Large range of over 300 whiskies and also sells own special bottlings. Orders via email. Shipping also outside Germany.

Finlays Whisky Shop
Friedrichstrasse 3
65779 Kelkheim
Phone: +49 (0)6195 9699510
www.finlayswhiskyshop.de
Whisky specialists with a large range of over 1,400 whiskies. Finlays also work as the importer to Germany of Douglas laing, James MacArthur and Wilson & Morgan. On-line ordering.

Weinquelle Lühmann
Lübeckerstrasse 145
22087 Hamburg
Phone: +49 (0)40-25 63 91
www.weinquelle.com
An impressive selection of both wines and spirits with over 1000 different whiskies of which 850 are malt whiskies. Also an impressive range of rums. On-line ordering.

The Whisky-Corner
Reichertsfeld 2
92278 Illschwang
Phone: +49 (0)9666-951213
www.whisky-corner.de
A small shop but large on mail order. A very large assortment of over 1600 whiskies. Also sells blended and American whiskies. The website is very informative with features on, among others, whisky-making, tasting and independent bottlers. On-line ordering.

World Wide Spirits
Hauptstrasse 12
84576 Teising
Phone: +49 (0)8633 50 87 93
www.worldwidespirits.de
A nice range of c 500 whiskies with some rarities from the twenties. Also large selection of other spirits.

Whisk(e)y Shop Tara
Rindermarkt 16
80331 München
Phone: +49 (0)89-26 51 18
www.whiskyversand.de
Whisky specialists with a very broad range of, for example, 800 different single malts. On-line ordering.

WhiskyKoch
Weinbergstrasse 2
64285 Darmstadt
Phone: +49 (0)6151 99 27 105
www.whiskykoch.de
A combination of a whisky shop and restaurant. The shop has a nice selection of single malts as well as other Scottish products and the restaurant has specialised in whisky dinners and tastings.

Single Malt Collection
(Glen Fahrn Germany GmbH)
Hauptstraße 38
79801 Hohentengen a. H.
Phone: +49 (0)77 42 -857 222
www.singlemaltcollection.com
A very large range of single malts (c 600). Newsletter. On-line orders. Shipping also outside Germany.

Kierzek
Weitlingstrasse 17
10317 Berlin
Phone: +49 (0)30 525 11 08
www.kierzek-berlin.de
Over 400 different whiskies in stock. In the product range 50 kinds of rum and 450 wines from all over the world are found among other products. Mail order is available.

House of Whisky
Ackerbeeke 6
31683 Obernkirchen
Phone: +49 (0)5724-399420
www.houseofwhisky.de
Aside from over 1,200 different malts also sells a large range of other spirits (including over 100 kinds of rum). On-line ordering with shipping also outside Germany.

Whiskyworld
Ziegelfeld 6
94481 Grafenau / Haus i. Wald
Phone: +49 (0)8555-406 320
www.whiskyworld.de
A very good assortment of more than 1,000 malt whiskies. Also has a good range of wines, other spirits, cigars and books. On-line ordering.

World Wide Whisky (2 shops)
Eisenacher Strasse 64
10823 Berlin-Schöneberg
Phone: +49 (0)30-7845010

Hauptstrasse 58
10823 Berlin-Schöneberg
www.world-wide-whisky.de
Large range of 1,500 different whiskies. Arranges tastings and seminars. Has a large number of rarities. Orders via email.

HUNGARY

Whisky Net / Whisky Shop
Kovács Làszlò Street 21
2000 Szentendre

Veres Pálné utca 8.
1053 Budapest
Phone: +36 1 267-1588
www.whiskynet.hu
www.whiskyshop.hu
The largest selction of whisky in Hungary. Agents for Arran, Ben-riach, Glenfarclas, Gordon & Mac-Phail, Benromach, Douglas Laing, Springbank, Angus Dundee, Ian Macleod, Kilchoman among others. Also mailorder.

INDIA

The Vault
World Whiskies & Fine Spirits
Mumbai
Phone: +91 22-22028811/22
www.vaultfinespirits.com
India´s first curated fine spirits plat-form, opened in October 2013. An interesting concept where personal assistance in choosing a gift or planning an event is also part of the service. Expect many more brands to be added during 2014.

IRELAND

Celtic Whiskey Shop
27-28 Dawson Street
Dublin 2
Phone: +353 (0)1 675 9744
www.celticwhiskeyshop.com
More than 70 kinds of Irish whiskeys but also a good selection of Scotch, wines and other spirits. World wide shipping.

ITALY

Cadenhead's Whisky Bar
Via Poliziano, 3
20154 Milano
Phone: +39 (0)2 336 055 92
www.cadenhead.it
This is the tenth and newest addi-tion in the Cadenhead´s chain of shops. Concentrating mostly on the Cadenhead´s range but they also stock whiskies from other producers.

THE NETHERLANDS

Whiskyslijterij De Koning
Hinthamereinde 41
5211 PM 's Hertogenbosch
Phone: +31 (0)73-6143547
www.whiskykoning.nl
An enormous assortment with more than 1400 kinds of whisky including c 800 single malts. Arranges recurring tastings. On-line ordering. Shipping all over the world.

Van Wees - Whiskyworld.nl
Leusderweg 260
3817 KH Amersfoort
Phone: +31 (0)33-461 53 19
www.whiskyworld.nl
A very large range of 1000 whiskies including over 500 single malts. Also have their own range of bottlings (The Ultimate Whisky Company). On-line ordering.

Wijnhandel van Zuylen
Loosduinse Hoofdplein 201
2553 CP Loosduinen (Den Haag)
Phone: +31 (0)70-397 1400
www.whiskyvanzuylen.nl
Excellent range of whiskies (circa 1100) and wines. Email orders with shipping to some ten European countries.

Wijnwinkel-Slijterij
Ton Overmars
Hoofddorpplein 11
1059 CV Amsterdam
Phone: +31 (0)20-615 71 42
www.tonovermars.nl
A very large assortment of wines, spirits and beer which includes more than 400 single malts. Arranges recurring tastings. Orders via email.

Wijn & Whisky Schuur
Blankendalwei 4
8629 EH Scharnegoutem (bij Sneek)
Phone: +31 (0)515-520706
www.wijnwhiskyschuur.nl
Large assortment with 1000 diffe-rent whiskies and a good range of other spirits as well. Arranges recur-ring tastings. On-line ordering.

Versailles Dranken
Lange Hezelstraat 83
6511 Cl Nijmegen
Phone: +31 (0)24-3232008
www.versaillesdranken.nl
A very impressive range with more
than 1500 different whiskies, most
of them from Scotland but also a
surprisingly good selection (more
than 60) of Bourbon. Arranges recurring tastings. On-line ordering.

NEW ZEALAND

Whisky Galore
66 Victoria Street
Christchurch 8013
Phone: +64 (3) 377 6824
www.whiskygalore.co.nz
The best whisky shop in New
Zealand with 550 different whiskies,
approximately 350 which are single
malts. There is also online mail-order
with shipping all over the world
except USA and Canada.

POLAND

George Ballantine´s
Krucza str 47 A, Warsaw
Phone: +48 22 625 48 32

Pulawska str 22, Warsaw
Phone: +48 22 542 86 22

Marynarska str 15, Warsaw
Phone: +48 22 395 51 60

Francuska str 27, Warsaw
Phone: +48 22 810 32 22
www.sklep-ballantines.pl
The biggest assortment in Poland
with more than 360 different single
malts. Apart from whisky there is
a full range of spirits and wines
from all over the world. Recurrent
tastings and mailorder.

RUSSIA

Whisky World Shop
9, Tverskoy Boulevard
123104 Moscow
Phone: +7 495 787 9150
www.whiskyworld.ru
Huge assortment with more than
1,000 different single malts, mainly
from independent bottlers. The
range is supplemented with a
nice range of cognac, armagnac,
calvados, grappa and wines. Tastings
are also arranged.

SCOTLAND

Gordon & MacPhail
58 - 60 South Street, Elgin
Moray IV30 1JY
Phone: +44 (0)1343 545110
www.gordonandmacphail.com
This legendary shop opened already
in 1895 in Elgin. The owners are
perhaps the most well-known
among independent bottlers. The
shop stocks more than 800 bottlings
of whisky and more than 600 wines
and there is also a delicatessen
counter with high-quality products.
Tastings are arranged in the shop
and there are shipping services

within the UK and overseas. The
shop attracts visitors from all over
the world.

Royal Mile Whiskies (2 shops)
379 High Street, The Royal Mile
Edinburgh EH1 1PW
Phone: +44 (0)131 2253383

3 Bloomsbury Street
London WC1B 3QE
Phone: +44 (0)20 7436 4763
www.royalmilewhiskies.com
Royal Mile Whiskies is one of the
most well-known whisky retailers
in the UK. It was established in
Edinburgh in 1991. There is also
a shop in London since 2002
and a cigar shop close to the
Edinburgh shop. The whisky range
is outstanding with many difficult
to find elsewhere. They have a
comprehensive site regarding
information on regions, distilleries,
production, tasting etc. Royal Mile
Whiskies also arranges 'Whisky
Fringe' in Edinburgh, a two-day
whisky festival which takes place
annually in mid August. On-line
ordering with worldwide shipping.

The Whisky Shop
(See also England, The Whisky Shop)
Buchanan Galleries
220 Buchanan Street
Glasgow G1 2GF
Phone: +44 (0)141 331 0022

17 Bridge Street
Inverness IV1 1HD
Phone: +44 (0)1463 710525

11 Main Street
Callander FK17 8DU
Phone: +44 (0)1877 331936

93 High Street
Fort William PH33 6DG
Phone: +44 (0)1397 706164

52 George Street
Oban PA34 5SD
Phone: +44 (0)1631 570896

Unit 14
Gretna Gateway Outlet Village
Gretna DG16 5GG
Phone: +44 (0)1461338004

Unit RU58B, Ocean Terminal
Edinburgh EH6 6JJ
Phone: +44 (0)131 554 8211

Unit 23
Princes Mall
Edinburgh EH1 1BQ
Phone: +44 (0)131 558 7563

28 Victoria Street
Edinburgh EH1 2JW
Phone: +44 (0)131 225 4666
www.whiskyshop.com
The first shop opened in 1992 in
Edinburgh and this is now the
United Kingdom's largest specialist
retailer of whiskies with 22 outlets.
The two most recent to open up
were flagship stores in Piccadilly,
London and in Manchester. A large
product range with over 700 kinds,
including 400 malt whiskies and
140 miniature bottles, as well as
accessories and books. The own
range 'Glenkeir Treasures' is a

special assortment of selected malt
whiskies. The also run The W Club,
the leading whisky club in the UK
where the excellent Whiskeria
magazine is one of the member´s
benefits. On-line ordering and
shipping all over the world except
to the USA.

Loch Fyne Whiskies
Inveraray
Argyll PA32 8UD
Phone: +44 (0)1499 302 219
www.lfw.co.uk
A legendary shop! The range of
malt whiskies is large and they have
their own house blend, the prize-
awarded Loch Fyne, as well as their
'The Loch Fyne Whisky Liqueur'.
There is also a range of house malts
called 'The Inverarity'. On-line
ordering with worldwide shipping.

Single Malts Direct
36 Gordon Street
Huntly
Aberdeenshire AB54 8EQ
Phone: +44 (0) 845 606 6145
www.singlemaltsdirect.com
Owned by independent bottler
Duncan Taylor. In the assortment is
of course the whole Duncan Taylor
range but also a selection of their
own single malt bottlings called
Whiskies of Scotland. A total of
almost 700 different expressions.
On-line shop with shipping worldwide. The website has information
on whisky production and a glossary
of whisky terms.

The Whisky Shop Dufftown
1 Fife Street, Dufftown
Moray AB55 4AL
Phone: +44 (0)1340 821097
www.whiskyshopdufftown.co.uk
Whisky specialist in Dufftown in
the heart of Speyside, wellknown
to many of the Speyside festival
visitors. More than 500 single
malts as well as other whiskies.
Arranges tastings as well as special
events during the Festivals. On-line
ordering with worldwide shipping.

The Scotch Whisky Experience
354 Castlehill, Royal Mile
Edinburgh EH1 2NE
Phone: +44 (0)131 220 0441
www.scotchwhiskyexperience.co.uk
The Scotch Whisky Experience is a
must for whisky devotees visiting
Edinburgh. An interactive visitor
centre dedicated to the history of
Scotch whisky. This five-star visitor
attraction has an excellent whisky
shop with almost 300 different
whiskies in stock. Reccently, after
extensive refurbishment, a brand
new and interactive shop was
opened. Do not miss the award-
winning Amber Restaurant.

**Cadenhead's Campbeltown Whisky
shop** (Eaglesome)
30-32 Union Street
Campbeltown
Argyll PA28 6JA
Phone: +44 (0)1586 551710
www.wmcadenhead.com
One in a chain of shops owned by

independent bottlers Cadenhead. Sells Cadenhead's products and other whiskies with a good range of Springbank. On-line ordering.

Cadenhead´s Whisky Shop
172 Canongate, Royal Mile
Edinburgh EH8 8BN
Phone: +44 (0)131 556 5864
www.wmcadenhead.com
The oldest shop in the chain owned by Cadenhead. Sells Cadenhead's product range and a good selection of other whiskies and spirits. Recurrent tastings. On-line ordering.

The Good Spirits Co.
23 Bath Street,
Glasgow G2 1HW
Phone: +44 (0)141 258 8427
www.thegoodspiritsco.com
A newly opened specialist spirits store selling whisky, bourbon, rum, vodka, tequila, gin, cognac and armagnac, liqueurs and other spirits. They also stock quality champagne, fortified wines and cigars.

Whiski Shop
4 North Bank Street
Edinburgh EH1 2LPL
Phone: +44 (0)131 225 1532
www.whiskishop.com
www.whiskirooms.co.uk
A new concept located near Edinburgh Castle, combining a shop, a tasting room and a bistro. Also regular whisky tastings. Online mail order with worldwide delivery.

Robbie's Drams
3 Sandgate, Ayr
South Ayrshire KA7 1BG
Phone: +44 (0)1292 262 135
www.robbiesdrams.com
Over 600 whiskies available in store and over 900 available from their on-line shop. Specialists in single cask bottlings, closed distillery bottlings, rare malts, limited edition whisky and a nice range of their own bottlings. Worldwide shipping.

The Whisky Barrel
PO Box 23803, Edinburgh, EH6 7WW
Phone: +44 (0)845 2248 156
www.thewhiskybarrel.com
Online specialist whisky shop based in Edinburgh. They stock over 1,000 single malt and blended whiskies including Scotch, Japanese, Irish, Indian, Swedish and their own casks. Worldwide shipping.

The Scotch Malt Whisky Society
www.smws.com
A society with more than 20 000 members worldwide, specialised in own bottlings of single casks and release between 150 and 200 bottlings a year. Orders on-line for members only. Shipping only within UK.

Drinkmonger
100 Atholl Road
Pitlochry PH16 5BL
Phone: +44 (0)1796 470133

11 Bruntsfield Place
Edinburgh EH10 4HN
Phone: +44 (0)131 229 2205
www.drinkmonger.com
Two new shops opened in 2011 by

the well-known Royal Mile Whiskies. The idea is to have a 50:50 split between wine and specialist spirits with the addition of a cigar assortment. The whisky range is a good cross-section with some rarities and a focus on local distilleries.

A.D. Rattray´s Whisky Experience & Whisky Shop
32 Main Road
Kirkoswald
Ayrshire KA19 8HY
Phone: +44 (0) 1655 760242
www.adrattray.com
A combination of whisky shop, sample room and educational center owned by the independent bottler A D Rattray. Tasting menus with different themes are available.

Robert Graham Ltd (3 shops)
194 Rose Street
Edinburgh EH2 4AZ
Phone: +44 (0)131 226 1874

Finlay House
10-14 West Nile Street
Glasgow G1 2PP
Phone: +44 (0)141 248 7283

Robert Graham's Treasurer 1874
254 Canongate
Royal Mile
Edinburgh EH8 8AA
Phone: +44 (0)131 556 2791
www.whisky-cigars.co.uk
Established in 1874 this company specialises in Scotch whisky and cigars. They have a nice assortment of malt whiskies and their range of cigars is impressive. On-line ordering with shipping all over the world

Whisky Castle
Main Street
Tomintoul
Aberdeenshire AB37 9EX
Phone: +44 (0)1807 580 213
www.whiskycastle.co.uk
Whisky specialist situated in the heart of malt whisky country. With over 500 single malts, the specialisation is in independent bottlings. There is also a mail order shipping worldwide with the exception of USA.

SOUTH AFRICA

Aficionados Premium Spirits Online
M5 Freeway Park
Cape Town
Phone: +27 21 511 7337
www.aficionados.co.za
An online liquor retailer specialising in single malt whisky. They claim to offer the widest of range of whiskies available in South Africa and hold regular tastings around the country. Shipping only within South Africa.

SWITZERLAND

P. Ullrich AG
Schneidergasse 27
4051 Basel
Phone: +41 (0)61 338 90 91
Another two shops in Basel:
Laufenstrasse 16 & Unt. Rebgasse 18

and one in Talacker 30 in Zürich
www.ullrich.ch
A very large range of wines, spirits, beers, accessories and books. Over 800 kinds of whisky with almost 600 single malt. On-line ordering. Recently, they also founded a whisky club with regular tastings (www.whiskysinn.ch).

Eddie's Whiskies
Dorfgasse 27
8810 Horgen
Phone: +41 (0)43 244 63 00
www.eddies.ch
A whisky specialist with more than 700 different whiskies in stock with emphasis on single malts (more than 500 different). Also arranges tastings.

World of Whisky
Via dim Lej 6
7500 St. Moritz
Phone: +41 (0)81 852 33 77
www.world-of-whisky.ch
A legendary shop situated in the Hotel Waldhaus Am See which has an also legendary whisky bar, the Devil´s Place. The shop stocks almost 1,000 different whiskies and has a good range of other spirits such as rum, cognac and armagnac.

Scot & Scotch
Wohllebgasse 7
8001 Zürich
Phone: +41 44 211 90 60
www.scotandscotch.ch
A whisky specialist with a great selection including c 560 single malts. Mail orders, but no on-line ordering.

Angels Share Shop
Unterdorfstrasse 15
5036 Oberentfelden
Phone: +41 (0)62 724 83 74
www.angelsshare.ch
A combined restaurant and whisky shop. More than 400 different kinds of whisky as well as a good range of cigars. Scores extra points for short information and photos of all distilleries. On-line ordering.

USA

Binny´s Beverage Depot
5100 W. Dempster (Head Office)
Skokie, IL 60077
Phone:
Internet orders, 888-942-9463 (toll free)
Whiskey Hotline, 888-817-5898 (toll free)
www.binnys.com
A chain of no less than 29 stores in the Chicago area, covering everything within wine and spirits. Some of the stores also have a gourmet grocery, cheese shop and, for cigar lovers, a walk-in humidor. The whisk(e)y range is impressive with 700 single malts, 120 bourbons, 40 Irish whiskeys and more. Among other products almost 200 kinds of tequila should be mentioned. Online mail order service.

Statistics

The following pages have been made possible thanks to kind cooperation from four sources – The IWSR, Euromonitor International, The Scotch Whisky Industry Review and Scotch Whisky Association.

The IWSR

is the leading provider of data on wine, spirits and RTDs. The IWSR's database, essential to the industry, is used by all of the largest multinational wine and spirits companies, as well as many more local companies. The IWSR has a unique methodology which, by tapping into local country expertise, allows them to get closer to what is actually consumed and better understand how markets work. The IWSR conducts face-to-face interviews with 1,200 companies in 115 countries each year, with further input from 350 companies. The IWSR tracks overall consumption and trends at brand, quality and category level for wine, spirits and RTDs, and aims to provide data that is as accurate and detailed as possible. More information can be found on **www.iwsr.co.uk**

Euromonitor International

is the leading provider of global strategic intelligence on consumer markets. For more than 40 years, Euromonitor has published internationally respected market research reports, business reference books and online information systems, providing strategic business intelligence for the world's leading FMCG multinationals.
More information on **www.euromonitor.com**

The Scotch Whisky Industry Review 2013

is written and compiled by Alan S Gray, Sutherlands Edinburgh. It is now in its 35th consecutive year and provides a wealth of unique business critical information on the Scotch Whisky Industry. For more information visit **www.scotchwhiskyindustryreview.com**

Scotch Whisky Association (SWA)

is the trade association for the Scotch Whisky industry. Their main objective is to promote, protect and represent the interests of the whisky industry in Scotland and around the world. They also produce a plethora of statistical material covering production and sales of Scotch whisky. More information can be found on **www.scotch-whisky.org.uk**

Whisk(e)y forecast (volume) by region and sector 2012-2017

■ = positive volume growth   ■ = negative volume growth

SW=Scotch Whisky, IW=Irish Whiskey, UW=US Whiskey, CW=Canadian Whisky, OW=Other Whisky, TOT=Total.
The figures show CAGR% (Compound Annual Growth Rate) i. e. year-over-year growth rate.

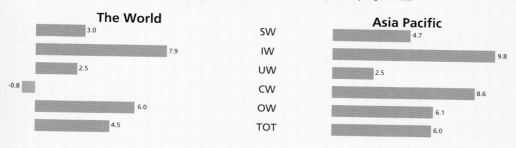

The World

SW	3.0
IW	7.9
UW	2.5
CW	-0.8
OW	6.0
TOT	4.5

Asia Pacific

SW	4.7
IW	9.8
UW	2.5
CW	8.6
OW	6.1
TOT	6.0

Europe

SW	0.6
IW	3.2
UW	3.9
CW	-1.5
OW	-2.3
TOT	1.1

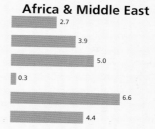

Africa & Middle East

SW	2.7
IW	3.9
UW	5.0
CW	0.3
OW	6.6
TOT	4.4

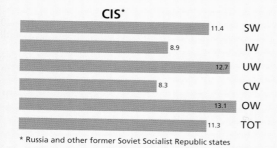

CIS*

SW	11.4
IW	8.9
UW	12.7
CW	8.3
OW	13.1
TOT	11.3

* Russia and other former Soviet Socialist Republic states

Duty Free

SW	4.7
IW	8.7
UW	8.5
CW	4.8
OW	5.8
TOT	5.5

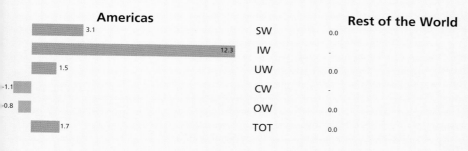

Americas

SW	3.1
IW	12.3
UW	1.5
CW	-1.1
OW	-0.8
TOT	1.7

Rest of the World

SW	0.0
IW	-
UW	0.0
CW	-
OW	0.0
TOT	0.0

Source: © The IWSR 2013

World Consumption of Blended Scotch

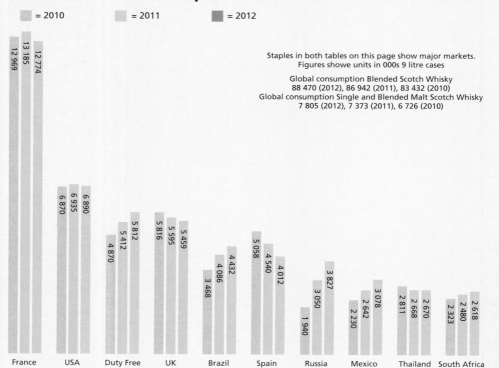

= 2010   = 2011   = 2012

Staples in both tables on this page show major markets.
Figures showe units in 000s 9 litre cases

Global consumption Blended Scotch Whisky
88 470 (2012), 86 942 (2011), 83 432 (2010)
Global consumption Single and Blended Malt Scotch Whisky
7 805 (2012), 7 373 (2011), 6 726 (2010)

France: 12 969 / 13 185 / 12 774
USA: 6 870 / 6 935 / 6 890
Duty Free: 4 870 / 5 412 / 5 812
UK: 5 816 / 5 595 / 5 459
Brazil: 3 468 / 4 086 / 4 432
Spain: 5 058 / 4 540 / 4 012
Russia: 1 940 / 3 050 / 3 827
Mexico: 2 230 / 2 642 / 3 078
Thailand: 2 811 / 2 668 / 2 670
South Africa: 2 323 / 2 480 / 2 618

World Consumption of Single Malt Scotch

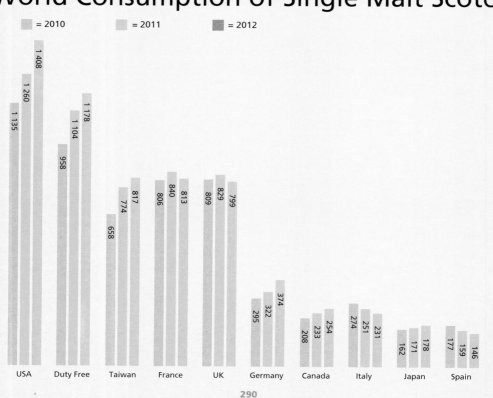

= 2010   = 2011   = 2012

USA: 1 135 / 1 260 / 1 408
Duty Free: 958 / 1 104 / 1 178
Taiwan: 658 / 774 / 817
France: 806 / 840 / 813
UK: 809 / 829 / 799
Germany: 295 / 322 / 374
Canada: 208 / 233 / 254
Italy: 274 / 251 / 231
Japan: 162 / 171 / 178
Spain: 177 / 159 / 146

The Top 30 Whiskies of the World

Sales figures for 2012 (units in million 9-litre cases)

McDowell's No. 1 (United Spirits), Indian whisky — 19,5
Johnnie Walker (Diageo), Scotch whisky — 18,9
Officer's Choice (Allied Blenders & Distillers), Indian whisky — 18,1
Bagpiper (United Spirits), Indian whisky — 14,1
Royal Stag (Pernod Ricard), Indian whisky — 12,8
Old Tavern (United Spirits), Indian whisky — 11,6
Original Choice (John Distilleries), Indian whisky — 10,9
Jack Daniel's (Brown-Forman), Tennessee whiskey — 10,7
Imperial Blue (Pernod Ricard), Indian whisky — 7,8
Hayward's (United Spirits), Indian whisky — 7,1
Jim Beam (Beam Inc.), Bourbon — 6,3
Ballantine's (Pernod Ricard), Scotch whisky — 6,1
Crown Royal (Diageo), Canadian whisky — 4,9
8PM (Radico Khaitan), Indian whisky — 4,9
Chivas Regal (Pernod Ricard), Scotch whisky — 4,8
J&B Rare (Diageo), Scotch whisky — 4,6
William Grant's (William Grant & Sons), Scotch whisky — 4,5
Director's Special (United Spirits), Indian whisky — 4,3
Jameson (Pernod Ricard), Irish whiskey — 4,0
Blenders Pride (Pernod Ricard), Indian whisky — 3,7
Gold Riband (United Spirits), Indian whisky — 3,5
The Famous Grouse (Edrington), Scotch whisky — 3,3
McDowell's Green Label (United Spirits), Indian whisky — 3,3
Dewar's (Bacardi), Scotch whisky — 3,0
Director's Special Black (United Spirits), Indian whisky — 2,9
Kakubin (Suntory), Japanese whisky — 2,8
William Lawson's (Bacardi), Scotch whisky — 2,6
Label 5 (La Martiniquaise), Scotch whisky — 2,5
William Peel (Bélvedère), Scotch whisky — 2,5
Bell's (Diageo), Scotch whisky — 2,5

Source: Drinks International, The Millionaires Club 2013

Global Exports of Scotch by Region

Volume (litres of pure alcohol)				Value (£ Sterling)			
Region	2012	2011	chg %	Region	2012	2011	chg %
Africa	21,255,357	19,057,777	12	Africa	238,667,193	224,098,833	7
Asia	72,996,101	76,666,463	- 5	Asia	929,418,877	911,872,078	2
Australasia	8,330,519	8,321,443	0	Australasia	87,045,600	78,471,748	11
C&S America	44,869,554	45,407,648	- 1	C&S America	505,376,527	489,279,849	3
Eastern Europe	3,400,605	3,956,298	- 14	Eastern Europe	39,314,962	48,982,325	- 20
Europe (other)	6,095,295	6,905,534	- 12	Europe (other)	86,313,046	77,164,062	12
European Union	117,951,239	132,303,170	- 11	European Union	1,326,040,679	1,448,326,333	- 8
Middle East	11,918,786	12,778,425	- 7	Middle East	147,366,007	151,318,182	- 3
North America	48,698,767	48,566,887	0	North America	913,253,679	796,247,171	15
Total	335,516,223	353,963,645	- 5	Total	4,225,760,581	4,225,760,581	1

Source: Scotch Whisky Association

Top 10 Scotch Malt Whisky brands - world market share %

Brand	Year	Share
Glenfiddich	2012	13,5
	2011	14,1
	2010	14,4
The Glenlivet	2012	11,5
	2011	10,6
	2010	10,2
The Macallan	2012	9,2
	2011	9,2
	2010	9,3
Glenmorangie	2012	5,7
	2011	5,2
	2010	4,9
The Singleton Dufftown, Glendullan, Glen Ord	2012	3,5
	2011	3,1
	2010	2,3
Glen Grant	2012	3,4
	2011	3,6
	2010	4,2
Aberlour	2012	3,0
	2011	2,9
	2010	3,1
The Balvenie	2012	2,9
	2011	2,7
	2010	2,7
Laphroaig	2012	2,8
	2011	2,8
	2010	2,8
Johnnie Walker Green Label	2012	2,5
	2011	3,9
	2010	3,7

Top 10 Scotch Blended Whisky brands - world market share %

Brand	Year	Share
Johnnie Walker	2012	20,2
	2011	19,2
	2010	18,4
Ballantine's	2012	6,6
	2011	7,0
	2010	7,2
Chivas Regal	2012	5,5
	2011	5,6
	2010	5,5
Grant's	2012	5,1
	2011	5,5
	2010	5,9
J&B	2012	4,5
	2011	5,0
	2010	5,5
Famous Grouse	2012	3,5
	2011	3,3
	2010	3,5
Dewar's	2012	3,4
	2011	3,6
	2010	3,9
William Peel	2012	3,0
	2011	3,0
	2010	2,9
William Lawson's	2012	2,9
	2011	2,4
	2010	1,9
Label 5	2012	2,6
	2011	2,7
	2010	2,5

Source: © The IWSR 201

Distillery Capacity

Litres of pure alcohol - Scottish, active distilleries only

Distillery	Litres	Distillery	Litres	Distillery	Litres
lenfiddich	13 000 000	Cragganmore	2 200 000	Glen Garioch	1 000 000
oseisle	12 500 000	Dalwhinnie	2 200 000	Tobermory	1 000 000
ilsa Bay	12 000 000	Jura	2 200 000	Oban	780 000
lenlivet	10 500 000	Speyburn	2 000 000	Arran	750 000
acallan	9 800 000	Knockdhu	1 900 000	Glengyle	750 000
aol Ila	6 500 000	Balblair	1 800 000	Glen Scotia	750 000
alvenie	6 400 000	Ben Nevis	1 800 000	Springbank	750 000
len Grant	6 200 000	Pulteney	1 800 000	Speyside	600 000
ufftown	6 000 000	Auchentoshan	1 750 000	Benromach	500 000
len Keith	6 000 000	Bruichladdich	1 500 000	Royal Lochnagar	500 000
lenmorangie	6 000 000	Glendronach	1 400 000	Glenturret	340 000
uchroisk	5 900 000	Glen Spey	1 400 000	Bladnoch	250 000
iltonduff	5 800 000	Knockando	1 400 000	Kilchoman	150 000
lenrothes	5 600 000	Ardbeg	1 300 000	Edradour	130 000
nkwood	5 600 000	Glencadam	1 300 000	Wolfburn	120 000
rdmore	5 400 000	Glenglassaugh	1 100 000	Daftmill	65 000
ailuaine	5 200 000	Glengoyne	1 100 000	Strathearn	30 000
lendullan	5 000 000	Scapa	1 100 000	Abhainn Dearg	20 000
len Ord	5 000 000				
omatin	5 000 000				
lynelish	4 800 000				
ininvie	4 800 000				
ongmorn	4 500 000				
annochmore	4 500 000				
eaninich	4 400 000				
ormore	4 400 000				
lenburgie	4 200 000				
lentauchers	4 200 000				
llt-a-Bhainne	4 000 000				
raeval	4 000 000				
raigellachie	4 000 000				
lenallachie	4 000 000				
och Lomond	4 000 000				
oyal Brackla	4 000 000				
amdhu	4 000 000				
amnavulin	4 000 000				
berlour	3 800 000				
ortlach	3 800 000				
almore	3 700 000				
berfeldy	3 500 000				
enrinnes	3 500 000				
ardhu	3 400 000				
lenfarclas	3 400 000				
acduff	3 340 000				
len Moray	3 300 000				
aphroaig	3 300 000				
omintoul	3 300 000				
ultmore	3 000 000				
eanston	3 000 000				
chgower	2 900 000				
ullibardine	2 900 000				
almenach	2 800 000				
enriach	2 800 000				
unnahabhain	2 700 000				
len Elgin	2 700 000				
lenlossie	2 700 000				
alisker	2 600 000				
air Athol	2 500 000				
lenkinchie	2 500 000				
ighland Park	2 500 000				
agavulin	2 450 000				
trathisla	2 400 000				
ettercairn	2 300 000				
trathmill	2 300 000				
owmore	2 000 000				

Summary of Malt Distillery Capacity by Category

Category	Litres of alcohol	% of Industry	Average capacity
Speyside (46)	207 700 000	62,1	4 515 000
Islands (7)	10 170 000	3,0	1 453 000
Highlands (32)	77 740 000	23,2	2 429 000
Islay (8)	19 900 000	6,0	2 488 000
Lowlands (5)	16 565 000	5,0	3 313 000
Campbeltown (3)	2 250 000	0,7	750 000
Total (101)	**334 325 000**	**100**	**3 310 000**

Summary of Malt Distillery Capacity by Owner

Owner (number of distilleries)	Litres of alcohol	% of Industry
Diageo (28)	105 230 000	31,5
Pernod Ricard (13)	58 900 000	17,7
William Grant (4)	36 200 000	10,8
Edrington Group (4)	18 240 000	5,5
Bacardi (John Dewar & Sons) (5)	17 840 000	5,3
Whyte and Mackay (4)	12 200 000	3,6
Pacific Spirits (Inver House) (5)	10 300 000	3,1
Beam Inc (2)	8 700 000	2,6
Moët Hennessy (Glenmorangie) (2)	7 300 000	2,2
C L Financial (Burn Stewart) (3)	6 700 000	2,0
Campari (Glen Grant) (1)	6 200 000	1,8
Benriach Distillery Co (3)	5 300 000	1,6
Ian Macleod Distillers (2)	5 100 000	1,5
Tomatin Distillery Co (1)	5 000 000	1,5
Suntory (Morrison Bowmore) (3)	4 750 000	1,4
Loch Lomond Distillers (2)	4 750 000	1,4
Angus Dundee (2)	4 600 000	1,4
J & G Grant (Glenfarclas) (1)	3 400 000	1,0
La Martiniquaise (Glen Moray) (1)	3 300 000	1,0
Picard (Tullibardine) (1)	2 900 000	0,9
Nikka (Ben Nevis Distillery) (1)	1 800 000	0,5
Rémy Cointreau (Bruichladdich) (1)	1 500 000	< 0,5
J & A Mitchell (2)	1 500 000	< 0,5
Isle of Arran Distillers (1)	750 000	< 0,5
Speyside Distillers Co (1)	600 000	< 0,5
Gordon & MacPhail (Benromach) (1)	500 000	< 0,5
Co-ordinated Developm. (Bladnoch) (1)	250 000	< 0,5
Kilchoman Distillery Co (1)	150 000	< 0,5
Signatory Vintage (Edradour) (1)	130 000	< 0,5
Wolfburn Distillery (1)	120 000	< 0,5
Francis Cuthbert (Daftmill) (1)	65 000	< 0,5
Strathearn Distillery (1)	30 000	< 0,5
Mark Thayburn (Abhainn Dearg) (1)	20 000	< 0,5

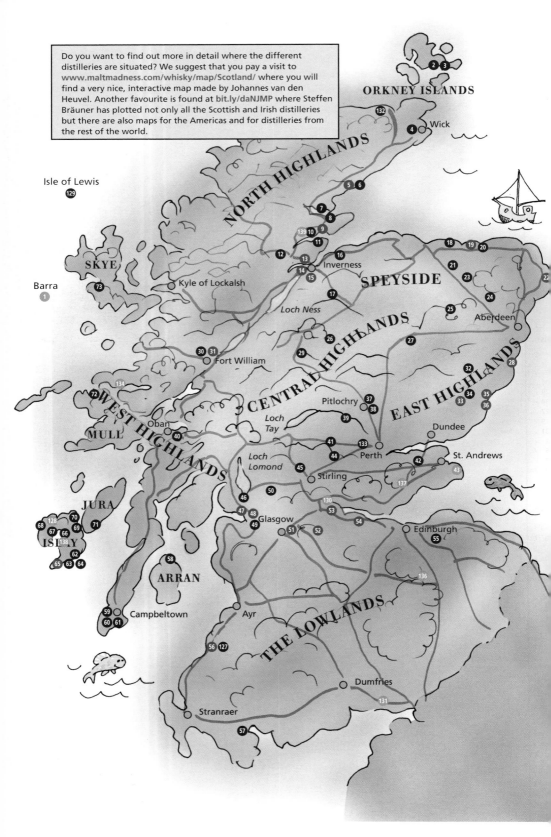

Do you want to find out more in detail where the different distilleries are situated? We suggest that you pay a visit to www.maltmadness.com/whisky/map/Scotland/ where you will find a very nice, interactive map made by Johannes van den Heuvel. Another favourite is found at bit.ly/daNJMP where Steffen Bräuner has plotted not only all the Scottish and Irish distilleries but there are also maps for the Americas and for distilleries from the rest of the world.

ORKNEY ISLANDS

Wick

NORTH HIGHLANDS

Isle of Lewis

SKYE

Barra

Kyle of Lockalsh

Inverness

SPEYSIDE

Loch Ness

Aberdeen

CENTRAL HIGHLANDS

Fort William

EAST HIGHLANDS

Pitlochry

Loch Tay

Dundee

Oban

MULL

WEST HIGHLANDS

Loch Lomond

Perth

St. Andrews

Stirling

JURA

Glasgow

Edinburgh

ISLAY

ARRAN

Campbeltown

Ayr

THE LOWLANDS

Dumfries

Stranraer

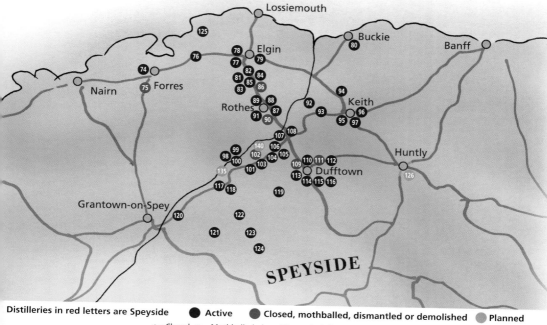

Lossiemouth

125

78 Elgin
76 77 79
82 84
74 81 85
75 Forres 83 86
Nairn

Buckie
80

Banff

94
Keith
89 88 92 96
Rothes 87 93 95 97
91 90

Huntly

107 108
140
99 106
98 102 105 110 111 112
100 104 109 126
135 103 113 Dufftown
101 114 115 116
117 118
119

Grantown-on-Spey
120

122

121 123

124

SPEYSIDE

Distilleries in red letters are Speyside ● **Active** ● **Closed, mothballed, dismantled or demolished** ● **Planned**

c = Closed, m = Mothballed, dm = Dismantled, d = Demolished

39 Aberfeldy	38 Edradour	100 Knockando	1 Barra	48 Littlemill (d)	95 Strathmill
106 Aberlour	130 Falkirk	21 Knockdhu	2 Highland Park	49 Auchentoshan	96 Glen Keith
129 Abhainn Dearg	32 Fettercairn	56 Ladyburn (dm)	3 Scapa	50 Glengoyne	97 Strathisla
134 Adelphi	138 Gartbreck	63 Lagavulin	4 Pulteney	51 Kinclaith (d)	98 Tamdhu
127 Ailsa Bay	13 Glen Albyn (d)	64 Laphroaig	5 Brora (c)	52 Glen Flagler (d)	99 Cardhu
119 Allt-a-Bhainne	105 Glenallachie	79 Linkwood	6 Clynelish	53 Rosebank (c)	100 Knockando
131 Annandale	76 Glenburgie	48 Littlemill (d)	7 Balblair	54 St Magdalene (dm)	101 Glenfarclas
25 Ardbeg	34 Glencadam	46 Loch Lomond	8 Glenmorangie	55 Glenkinchie	102 Imperial (d)
25 Ardmore	23 Glendronach	36 Lochside (d)	9 Ben Wyvis (c)	56 Ladyburn (dm)	103 Dailuaine
58 Arran	116 Glendullan	84 Longmorn	10 Teaninich	57 Bladnoch	104 Benrinnes
49 Auchentoshan	85 Glen Elgin	107 Macallan	11 Dalmore	58 Arran	105 Glenallachie
92 Auchroisk	35 Glenesk (dm)	20 Macduff	12 Glen Ord	59 Springbank	106 Aberlour
94 Aultmore	101 Glenfarclas	81 Mannochmore	13 Glen Albyn (d)	60 Glengyle	107 Macallan
7 Balblair	112 Glenfiddich	15 Millburn (dm)	14 Glen Mhor (d)	61 Glen Scotia	108 Craigellachie
135 Ballindalloch	52 Glen Flagler (d)	77 Miltonduff	15 Millburn (dm)	62 Ardbeg	109 Convalmore (dm)
120 Balmenach	24 Glen Garioch	115 Mortlach	16 Royal Brackla	63 Lagavulin	110 Dufftown
113 Balvenie	18 Glenglassaugh	33 North Port (d)	17 Tomatin	64 Laphroaig	111 Pittyvaich (d)
19 Banff (d)	50 Glengoyne	40 Oban	18 Glenglassaugh	65 Port Ellen (dm)	112 Glenfiddich
1 Barra	87 Glen Grant	111 Pittyvaich (d)	19 Banff (d)	66 Bowmore	113 Balvenie
30 Ben Nevis	60 Glengyle	128 Port Charlotte	20 Macduff	67 Bruichladdich	114 Kininvie
82 Benriach	96 Glen Keith	65 Port Ellen (dm)	21 Knockdhu	68 Kilchoman	115 Mortlach
104 Benrinnes	55 Glenkinchie	4 Pulteney	22 Glenugie (dm)	69 Caol Ila	116 Glendullan
74 Benromach	122 Glenlivet	53 Rosebank (c)	23 Glendronach	70 Bunnahabhain	117 Tormore
9 Ben Wyvis (c)	31 Glenlochy (d)	125 Roseisle	24 Glen Garioch	71 Jura	118 Cragganmore
57 Bladnoch	83 Glenlossie	16 Royal Brackla	25 Ardmore	72 Tobermory	119 Allt-a-Bhainne
37 Blair Athol	14 Glen Mhor (d)	27 Royal Lochnagar	27 Royal Lochnagar	73 Talisker	120 Balmenach
66 Bowmore	8 Glenmorangie	54 St Magdalene (dm)	28 Glenury Royal (d)	74 Benromach	121 Tomintoul
124 Braeval	78 Glen Moray	3 Scapa	29 Dalwhinnie	75 Dallas Dhu (c)	122 Glenlivet
5 Brora (c)	12 Glen Ord	88 Speyburn	30 Ben Nevis	76 Glenburgie	123 Tamnavulin
67 Bruichladdich	89 Glenrothes	26 Speyside	31 Glenlochy (d)	77 Miltonduff	124 Braeval
70 Bunnahabhain	61 Glen Scotia	59 Springbank	32 Fettercairn	78 Glen Moray	125 Roseisle
69 Caol Ila	91 Glenspey	133 Strathearn	33 North Port (d)	79 Linkwood	126 Duncan Taylor
90 Caperdonich (c)	93 Glentauchers	97 Strathisla	34 Glencadam	80 Inchgower	127 Ailsa Bay
99 Cardhu	41 Glenturret	95 Strathmill	35 Glenesk (dm)	81 Mannochmore	128 Port Charlotte
6 Clynelish	22 Glenugie (dm)	73 Talisker	36 Lochside (d)	82 Benriach	129 Abhainn Dearg
86 Coleburn (dm)	28 Glenury Royal (d)	98 Tamdhu	37 Blair Athol	83 Glenlossie	130 Falkirk
109 Convalmore (dm)	2 Highland Park	123 Tamnavulin	38 Edradour	84 Longmorn	131 Annandale
118 Cragganmore	102 Imperial (d)	10 Teaninich	39 Aberfeldy	85 Glen Elgin	132 Wolfburn
108 Craigellachie	140 "Imperial 2"	139 "Teaninich 2"	40 Oban	86 Coleburn (dm)	133 Strathearn
42 Daftmill	80 Inchgower	72 Tobermory	41 Glenturret	87 Glen Grant	134 Adelphi
103 Dailuaine	47 Inverleven (d)	17 Tomatin	42 Daftmill	88 Speyburn	135 Ballindalloch
75 Dallas Dhu (c)	137 John Fergus	121 Tomintoul	43 Kingsbarns	89 Glenrothes	136 Tweeddale
11 Dalmore	71 Jura	117 Tormore	44 Tullibardine	90 Caperdonich (c)	137 John Fergus
29 Dalwhinnie	68 Kilchoman	44 Tullibardine	45 Deanston	91 Glenspey	138 Gartbreck
45 Deanston	51 Kinclaith (d)	136 Tweeddale	46 Loch Lomond	92 Auchroisk	139 "Teaninich 2"
110 Dufftown	43 Kingsbarns	132 Wolfburn	47 Inverleven (d)	93 Glentauchers	140 "Imperial 2"
126 Duncan Taylor	114 Kininvie			94 Aultmore	

Index

Bold figures refer to the main entry in the distillery directory.

Index

Bold figures refer to the main entry in the distillery directory.

Index

Bold figures refer to the main entry in the distillery directory.